URBANIZATION AND LAND OWNERSHIP

IN THE ANCIENT NEAR EAST

■

VOLUME II
in a series sponsored by the
Institute for the Study of Long-term Economic Trends
and the International Scholars Conference on
Ancient Near Eastern Economies

A Colloquium Held at New York University, November 1996, and
The Oriental Institute, St. Petersburg, Russia, May 1997

EDITED BY

Michael Hudson and Baruch A. Levine

Peabody Museum of Archaeology and Ethnology
Harvard University
Cambridge MA 1999

COVER:
Cuneiform tablet recording the division of property at the New Canal among Egibi family heirs, noting plot sizes and agricultural use (see also pages 404-405). Babylon, 519 BC (Third Year of Darius). © The British Museum.

Table of Contents

3

PART IV
METHODOLOGY DISCUSSION AND SUMMARY

4

ACKNOWLEDGMENTS

We would like to thank the Robert Schalkenbach Foundation and the Henry George School of New York for funding both the November 1996 and May 1997 colloquia and their publication in this volume.

Also due our thanks are New York University for hosting the first set of meetings in New York City and the Oriental Institute in St. Petersburg, Russia, for hosting the second colloquium.

Thanks to the publication team at the Peabody Museum, Donna Dickerson and Amy Hirschfeld, for shepherding the work into print. As with our first volume, *Privatization in the Ancient Near East and Classical World*, Anne Robertson transcribed the oral discussion from audio tapes made at NYU and from audio tapes made by Christopher Kent from the St. Petersburg videotapes. Lynn Yost designed and typeset the book and prepared the illustrations for printing. This volume could not have been produced without their efforts.

Michael Hudson (ISLET)
Baruch Levine (NYU)

PREFACE

This volume is the second publication of the International Scholars Conference on Ancient Near Eastern Economies (ISCANEE), which is sponsored by the Institute for the Study of Long-term Economic Trends (ISLET). The first colloquium, *Privatization in the Ancient Near East and Classical Antiquity*, was published by the Peabody Museum of Archaeology and Ethnology (Bulletin 5) in 1996. With the present publication our group has begun to synthesize a new archaeological approach to studying long-term economic trends in their broadest social, institutional, ethnological, and intellectual context.

This colloquium was divided into two sets of meetings. The first six papers, dealing with the cosmological and archaeological dimensions of the most ancient Near Eastern cities, were delivered at New York University on November 14-15, 1996. The remaining seven Assyriological papers analyzing written texts were presented at the Oriental Institute of St. Petersburg on May 21-23, 1997. In addition to the papers published herein, oral presentations were made by Rita Wright (New York University) on the Indus Valley cities, Diana Craig Patch (Metropolitan Museum of Art, New York) on Egyptian cemeteries, Larry Stager (Harvard University) on the archaeology of ancient Israelite housing, and Johannes Renger (Freie Universität Berlin) on urban areas and foreign trade.

Present at the NYU meeting were representatives of the Henry George School, and in St. Petersburg, the Robert Schalkenbach Foundation president, Nicholas Tideman (Virginia Tech), and Fred Harrison (London) were present. Additional discussants were Larry Shiffman (New York University) and Sergei Koshurnikov (Oriental Institute, St. Petersburg). Other interested scholars attended each session.

The oral discussion of the papers by Muhammed Dandamayev, Carl Lamberg-Karlovsky, and Michael Hudson have combined the New York and St. Petersburg meetings, as these three papers were presented at both. The closing methodological discussion included only the St. Petersburg participants.

Introduction:
The New Economic Archaeology of Urbanization

Michael Hudson

It is now widely recognized that the study of civilization's economic institutions must incorporate cultural history. Nowhere is this more true than in the case of urban relations and land use. There has long been a tendency to view urban sites as developing automatically and almost inevitably as a result of growing population density and economies of scale resulting from the specialization of labor. This approach does not call for institutional explanations, much less the idea that other roads could have been followed other than that which has led to the modern world.

The members of this colloquium, by contrast, emphasize the degree to which historically unique ecological, ethnic, religious, and ideological dimensions shaped the differences between northern and southern Babylonian urban property relations and land tenure, that is, the milieu in which the formalities of real estate transfers are first found.

Every epoch's social institutions tend to build on what has gone before. Alexander Marshack shows how the social structures that shaped the way in which scattered groups convening at designated places (often ritual sites) developed already in Paleolithic times, long before the Neolithic and its agricultural revolution. These urban institutions governed temporary occupation of sites at particular times of the year to conduct exchanges of various forms, including marriages.

The occasional character of designating certain spots for such gatherings at specified calendrical intervals may help explain the symbolism so widespread in archaic cities throughout the world, with their four quarters and four to twelve gates. This spatial symbolism of the year's division into seasons and months — which is found in Egyptian urban symbolism, as shown by Prof. Goelet, and also in China (Wheatley 1971 [see p. 163 for full reference]) — appears to reflect the civic function of integrating early law with the natural regularities of the heavens. This "natural law" cosmology symbolized and indeed helped sanctify the worldly order emanating from urban centers.

Rather than reflecting a merely technological impulse, the most archaic urban sites appear to have played a ceremonial role in creating what could be called a cosmology of social life. In the Early Bronze Age,

Mesopotamia's temples and palaces elaborated exchange relations and their associated functions such as laws, weights and measures, contractual forms, and even proclamations of "forgiveness" of various offenses, fines, and personal debts of various forms so that the community and its families could maintain their economic viability and overall balance.

Cultural choice or historical inevitability?

If Bronze Age Mesopotamia did not separate the structuring of economic relations from myth and ritual, neither should modern assyriologists. Ignace Gelb has criticized the artificial academic division between cosmological studies and "onionology," that is, the analysis of economic records. The historian finds an interweaving of public and private, ethnological and legal planes, an intersecting of political control, economic power, and religious authority. The earliest transfers of land accordingly did not occur on a purely autonomous and self-referential plane. Only at the end of a long process did the practices put in place to govern the sale or forfeiture of urban and rural land and houses culminate in the idea of "market price" subject to due formalities.

The fact that the value of urban real estate in today's world far outstrips that of rural land (and even of industrial equipment and machinery) represents an ironic turn in the long sweep of economic evolution. The first urban areas appear to have been characterized above all by public gathering areas or temples that stood outside the market. Of course, it was natural for well-placed individuals to build townhouses or buy them from others in order to live in proximity to the public institutions through which commerce and other economic activities were organized.

This urban real estate became more readily alienable than rural subsistence land, whose transfer was long restricted to kin relations or neighbors (save for transfers to the ruler). To the extent that such land was alienable to outsiders, it usually was under economic duress. Such sales or forfeitures accordingly were made reversible for a certain period of time through redemption clauses. However, the cuneiform record shows townhouses, orchards, and improved lands being bought and sold freely from the second millennium onward.

The subject matter of this conference is how markets for land, orchards, and buildings evolved out of what went before, and how were prices for such transfers determined? When does the documentary record begin to show the uniformity in land prices that characterizes true markets?

It is easy to overlook how culture-bound modern real estate markets are. The day before our colloquium opened in St. Petersburg, for instance, President Boris Yeltsin unveiled Russia's proposed new income tax law, a week after issuing a decree permitting companies to obtain ownership of the land under their buildings. The decree was illegal. Only the Duma (Russia's parliament) is empowered to enact such a law, and it steadfastly refused to do so. This created a crisis with regard to who would control the land and receive its usufruct: the community (the state or locality) or private owners, starting with the best-placed public officials and their friends. Without a land law no legal context existed for real estate rights to be sold or otherwise transferred. No clear idea could be formed of the worth of urban enterprises or their fiscal role in the post-Communist economy.

This situation is strikingly similar to that of Bronze Age Mesopotamia in a number of ways. Most obvious for purposes of this colloquium is the absence of "modern" market relations. Also similar is the contrast between urban and rural land. Subsistence lands could not legally be sold or transferred in the ancient Near East, and they are likewise blocked from sale in Russia today. In both cases, however, there was a jockeying for position by outsiders (especially creditors) to gain some sort of rights to this land. In Russia today the outcome remains unclear — the same kind of grey area as seems to have existed in the Old Babylonian epoch. In both cases one finds land being transferred without a legal framework to govern such transfers.

Emerging from seven decades of communism, Russians have only sketchy ideas of how to estimate land values or the price at which to rent out urban sites. Indeed, the creation of a modern "western" real estate market does not appear to be inevitable, for as debates in Russia remind us, there are good age-old reasons for not creating laws that facilitate the ready transfer of land rights. When the China Hotel in Moscow recently was sold for a million rubles, it was an insider giveaway, as were other transfers of prime sites. An anthropologist might call this "gift exchange" on the part of President Yeltsin to his cronies. Most land transfers (can we really call them "sales"?) in recent years have been insider deals of this sort. (Indeed, one can view the past nine centuries of English history as the long consequence of William the Conqueror assigning land to his military officers.) Perhaps philologists and historians familiar with Bronze Age palace economies might classify such transfers as exemplifying the "redistributive" mode of exchange.

The more such political and ideological dynamics are recognized, the more the role played by technology shrinks. Technology opens up (and places limits on) economic potential but does not determine the extent to which a society will ground its urbanization in "market relations" rather than centralized planning or other administrative policies. There thus is little support among the colloquium's members for the idea that markets evolved automatically.

So we return to the basic irony of archaic urbanization and the emergence of real estate markets over a period that spanned thousands of years. The irony is that the most archaic urban areas evolved out of gathering sites, which were the prototypical public spaces — public in the sense of not being controlled by any individual, family, or clan (or even "the state"). Yet by the end of antiquity, urban real estate was well on its way to the modern situation in which it has become the largest privately owned economic asset.

These remarks are intended to provide a perspective for this colloquium's contribution to what may be called a new economic archaeology. One feature of our methodology is to take a broad, pan-disciplinary view to trace the symbiosis between the various strands of social, intellectual and religious thought that converged to shape the emergence of urbanization and absentee ownership of real estate in the ancient Near East.

One can only sell, forfeit, or otherwise transfer what is privately owned. To put matters the other way around, without being able to transfer one's land at will, there is no real "ownership" in the modern sense of the term. The public buildings and areas were the distinguishing feature of archaic cities, set apart from any single clan's control (save that of the ruler). How then are we to explain the alienation of urban houses and gardens occurring so much more readily in Sumerian and Babylonian towns than in the countryside for rural subsistence barley-land?

At what point does the documentary record enable us to find prices for urban land independent of prices for townhouses, that is, for the cost of structures? Do we have records of anyone buying a vegetable garden in order to build a townhouse? Is there any evidence of buyers tearing down existing structures to build newer, larger, and better ones? In today's world such shifts in land use represent the single most important economic dynamic of urbanization, as generations of real estate developers can attest.

Another relevant question to ask with regard to Babylonian real estate concerns the circumstances in which properties changed hands for less than the "full price." First of all, what determined "the price"? Did the clause refer to only partial cash payment being made? The discussants found this *not* to be the case. Did it mean that real estate changed hands under conditions of duress at a concessionary price (for instance, to foreclosing creditors)? The discussants found that this too was not the case.

The clause appears to mean simply that all the formalities had to be adhered to, above all, due notice being given so that the transfer could be duly witnessed to prevent subsequent disputes. The "full price" meant simply that no further payment was due.

The papers in this colloquium provide the context to trace how real estate transfers developed — practices whose strands in time would come together to create modern real estate markets.

The analytic dimensions of this colloquium

The contributions to this volume are divided into three categories. The first three papers deal with the emergence of early urban areas as ritual centers, integrating exchange and other economic phenomena into what might be called the social cosmology of organizing worldly life. Alexander Marshack traces the character of gathering places deep into the Ice Age when such sites were occupied on a seasonal basis (periodically in use, e.g., as in the spectacular French caves). His paper follows their evolution from Paleolithic Western Europe to the Near East at the start of the Neolithic. Ogden Goelet relates Egyptian urban iconographical symbolism to the archaeological and literary record. Michael Hudson traces how the characteristics of urbanization laid out by V. Gordon Childe in 1950 apply to southern Mesopotamia's temples as the region's defining urban feature.

The second dimension of this colloquium focuses on the physical archaeology of Near Eastern cities. Carl Lamberg-Karlovsky questions Childe's criterion of cities as being characterized by writing and literacy. It appears that many northern Mesopotamian cities are architecturally similar to those of the south (and even chronologically precedent), yet rejected writing and record-keeping. His paper discusses writing as an early centralized method of urban "control," and poses the question of whether cities were essentially centralized and coercive. Elizabeth Stone describes Mesopotamian cities as meeting places centered around the large public institutions. However, she points out that rather than being located physically in the center of cities (as would be the case in medieval Europe), Mesopotamia's temples and palaces were located near the edges of cities, at the wall separating them from their surrounding countryside. Giorgio Buccellati describes what his excavations at Urkesh can tell about the ethnological dimension of early urbanization.

The third set of papers examines what assyriologists have been able to extract from the cuneiform record concerning urban land use, land tenure, and the emergence of real estate as something privately owned and transferable. Marc Van De Mieroop provides an overview of Mesopotamian urbanization and early property transfers. Piotr Steinkeller shows how land-tenure practices varied geographically within the region. Nelli Kozyreva finds an ethnic dimension in Old Babylonian real estate transactions. Carlo Zaccagnini examines real estate records from northern Mesopotamia and Syria.

For the neo-Babylonian period, Muhammed Dandamayev summarizes land-use patterns in Sippar. Cornelia Wunsch describes the Egibi family archive spanning a number of generations and reconstructs the major sources of how the money was generated that ended up in control of the land. Baruch Levine distills what the biblical record has to say about urbanization in Judah and Israel. His analysis shows on the one hand how sketchy the biblical record is in comparison to the Mesopotamian core, and on the other hand how much may be inferred from the surviving texts when viewed in light of Mesopotamia's written records.

A summary discussion reviews the methodological problems involved in reconstructing the early emergence of real estate transactions, the formalities of pricing and paying for land, and the idea of market reference points for rental and land values.

* * *

A final few words are necessary to explain the terms "urbanization" and "land ownership" used in the title of this colloquium, which might otherwise appear anachronistic. Today, the term "urbanization" refers mainly to the ratio of a country's urban population relative to the total. This degree reflects the rural exodus that has occurred over the past century as the economy's focus has shifted from agriculture and husbandry to industry and the kinds of services found in cities — finance, communications, other private-sector service, and government employment.

This juxtaposition of urban to rural does not well suit the analysis of Bronze Age Mesopotamia. A symbiosis existed between cities and their surrounding lands. Most owners of townhouses held subsistence lands in the countryside, as such land provided the basis for citizenship (to use another rather anachronistic word).

The idea of cities as housing large aggregations as distinct from small villages or hamlets also is anachronistic, for the Sumerians and Egyptians used the same word to designate large and small cities alike. What was essential was not size, but structure. Indeed, "in the beginning" (prior to the Neolithic), this structure probably did not even involve year-round residence, but seasonal visitation for rituals and other social interaction. The characteristics of cities were those of gathering places and as such were influenced by the social purposes for such gatherings. These purposes were basically public and communal, such as attending the festivals that formed the basis for social cohesion in ancient times.

The essence of cities (before "the state" existed as such) was to act as the nexus of order, including legal judgment, which was long anchored in religion (at a time when religion itself dealt much more with worldly relations than is now the case). Cities were given their character largely by their city-temple and palace, at least in southern Mesopotamia (Babylonia), which forms the major focus of this colloquium.

The term "land ownership" (and hence, of real estate or real property) also requires some caveats to be borne in mind. First of all, there were different kinds of land: subsistence lands in the countryside (which were deemed inalienable on more than a temporary basis by their holders) and surplus-producing lands that were part of the market — orchards, vegetable gardens, and townhouses. These were alienable.

The idea of ownership necessarily involves the notion of alienability, mainly through direct sale or forfeiture to creditors. Rural land could be alienated temporarily but was supposed to be redeemed by its customary holders or else was restored to them by royal edict. Permanent sale of land was limited mainly to the cities.

The dynamics of balance between urban and rural land tenure were in a state of flux over time and also geographically between northern and southern Mesopotamia. Therefore, the concepts of "urbanization" and "land ownership" are not to be viewed as given or permanent, but as mutable and continually reinvented by the societies that form the subject matter for this colloquium.

Indeed, one might say that today's world is inverting many traditional urban-rural contrasts. In Mesopotamia the countryside was not economically disadvantaged but supplied the means of livelihood for the city-dwellers through their own direct ownership of rural land. This is why such land remained a prestige good throughout antiquity. The enclosure movement that accompanied the industrial revolution drove rural populations into the cities and helped these cities become economic centers. It was in these industrial areas that wealth was to be made, not in farming. But recent demographic statistics from Britain show rural living standards rising (by some measures) to exceed urban levels. In America it is now the large cities that are becoming anarchic. In these ways urban/rural relations continue to be in a state of flux.

PART I

URBAN AREAS AS COSMOLOGICAL AND RITUAL CENTERS

1

Space and Time in Preagricultural Europe and the Near East: The Evidence for Early Structural Complexity

Alexander Marshack
Peabody Museum of Archaeology and Ethnology*
Harvard University

Although this is a conference on urbanization, I have been asked to discuss a number of concepts related to the development of cultural complexity and seasonal or permanent gathering places derived from a study of two preagricultural, preurban hunting-gathering cultures. These concepts may help explain some of the processes involved in the rise of agriculture and the subsequent development of urbanization in the Near East, for they relate to the way in which archaic communities structured their modes of cultural complexity.

For the last thirty years I have been studying the symbol systems and cultures of the European Ice Age, 40,000-10,000 BC. Recently I compared these cultures and their symboling systems to the more or less contemporary preagricultural Paleolithic and Epipaleolithic symboling systems and cultures of the Near East. My objective was to inquire into the possible relevance of these early conceptual systems to the rise of agriculture — and, by logical extension, to the earliest urban forms.

The comparative data are new and for that reason still controversial. They reflect the complexity that developed in the conceptual ordering of time and space within the hunting-gathering cultures of the European and southwest Asian core area during the last Ice Age, *i.e.,* the late Upper Pleistocene and early Holocene. I believe that the beginning of agricul-

---

* The Near East research in this paper was funded by the American School of Prehistoric Research, Peabody Museum of Archaeology and Ethnology, Harvard University, with a grant from Jean Auel. O. Bar-Yosef and A. Belfer-Cohen

ture and urbanization in the Near East during the post-Ice Age Holocene represents a development that was derived in large measure from earlier modes of structuring economic and cultural activities and concepts in time and space.

The European Ice Age

The late Ice Age cultures of Europe began approximately 42-40,000 years ago when small groups of anatomically modern hunter-gatherers moved, apparently from the Near East, into a northern, mid-latitude, continental world. A relatively sparse Neanderthal population inhabited Europe at that time, utilizing a late Middle Paleolithic technology.

The European climate and the variable ecologies and species that the new populations found were markedly different from those in the Near East. There were essentially four seasons in much of Europe, involving severe winter frost, freezing of the rivers, and relatively long-distance seasonal migrations of the major herbivore herds. The dramatic spring thaw and floods often brought a regional return of the herds, migratory birds, and anadromous fish to the rivers. Within this mid-latitude seasonal rhythm, modes of subsistence and schedules varied within different regions. The late Pleistocene also was subject to short- and long-term periodic oscillations of climate. As a result, human groups often had to migrate and change exploitation strategies in order to adapt to new time and space processes and behavioral "calendars."

During the Ice Age the upper half of Europe was covered with a thick ice sheet. The hunting-gathering cultures were dispersed across the lower half. These cultures were almost entirely riverine, with human groups living and moving along a network of rivers that flowed westward to the Atlantic, south to the Mediterranean, and from the Russian plain to the Black Sea. The major Ice Age sites are usually found along these river networks, which were the walkways that structured the Ice Age cultures across a vast continental domain. Large riverine cultural centers or clus-

provided the Hayonim materials and the Israel Antiquities Authority gave permission to study artifacts in the Israel Museum and other collections. J. Tixier provide the bone from Ksar Akil. K. Wright, A. Garrard, the British Institute, and the American Center of Oriental Research made it possible to study the Jilat 7 artifact in Amman, and the Department of Antiquities in Amman provided permission to conduct research in Jordan. Particular appreciation is extended to O. Bar-Yosef, A. Belfer-Cohen, A. Garrard, and G. Rollefson for suggestions and corrections that aided in preparation of the text.

ters developed in France, in Moravia, and on the Russian plain, and a subsidiary riverine culture developed in Siberia on the Agara River.

An important and well-known concentration of sites occurred in southwest Europe along the dense network of rivers that flowed out of the limestone foothills of the Massif Centrale and the Pyrenean Mountains of France and the Cantabrian Mountains of Spain, all flowing westward towards the Atlantic. The limestone topography had created hundreds of caves and rock shelters in the valleys and along the rivers and small streams, and these became the loci for hundreds of sites that helped foster a unique Franco-Cantabrian development in symbolism and ritual.

Because oscillations in climate and weather periodically shifted between warmer, colder, drier, and moister periods, animal species changed their seasonal grazing grounds. Some disappeared, others returned when the climate changed, and some became extinct. The human populations had to move periodically and change their exploitation strategies and territories. Over time, concepts were developed that functioned across these climatic oscillations and variations (Gamble 1986; Jochim 1987; Soffer 1985, 1987). The Ice Age cultures acquired knowledge of their mid-latitude sky and the variability in seasonal processes, and they developed observational and conceptual time-and-space "calendars" that monitored and structured their territories. As these Ice Age populations increased, intergroup relations had to be maintained across increasingly large distances. Seasonal aggregations had to be ordered in time and space by use of a common, shared mid-latitude observational "calendar." That calendar would have mediated a tapestry of subsistence and cultural, ritual, interpersonal, and intergroup behaviors.

Les Eyzies on the Vézère River, the "capital" of Ice Age studies

Formal archeological study of these Ice Age cultures began in the second half of the 19th century at the small village of Les Eyzies-de-Tayac in southwest France. Les Eyzies sits on the shore of the Vézère River, a tributary of the larger Dordogne, which flows westward to the Atlantic and gives its name to that region of France (Map 1). To this day the "capital" of Ice Age studies, the village rests at the river edge below an abrupt, high limestone cliff and overhang. During the Ice Age, hunter-gatherers wintered under the overhang on a high shelf. Hallam Movius, Jr. of Harvard University for many years conducted excavation of an Ice Age shelter at one point on that shelf, the Abri Pataud (Fig. 1).

This shelter looks down on the village and river and across the river to the flood plain on which the herds of bison and horse, and at times

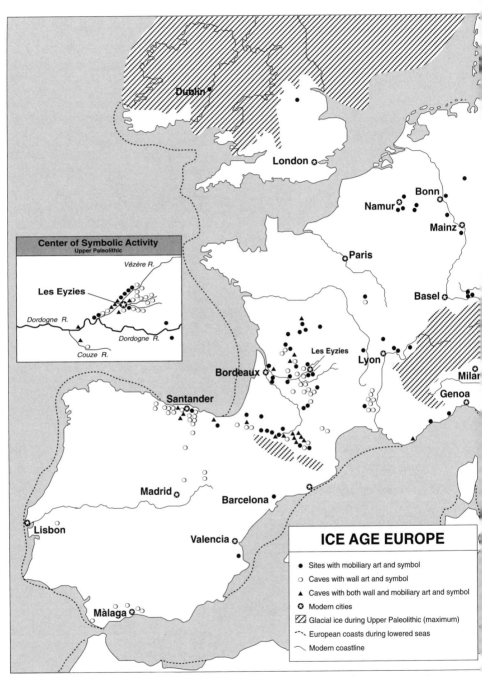

ICE AGE EUROPE

- ● Sites with mobiliary art and symbol
- ○ Caves with wall art and symbol
- ▲ Caves with both wall and mobiliary art and symbol
- ✪ Modern cities
- ▨ Glacial ice during Upper Paleolithic (maximum)
- ⌁ European coasts during lowered seas
- ⌢ Modern coastline

Center of Symbolic Activity
Upper Paleolithic

Vézère R.

Les Eyzies

Dordogne R.

Dordogne R.

Couze R.

Map 1. Location of shelters and caves with art along the network of major rivers in the Upper Paleolithic or "Ice Age" of Europe.

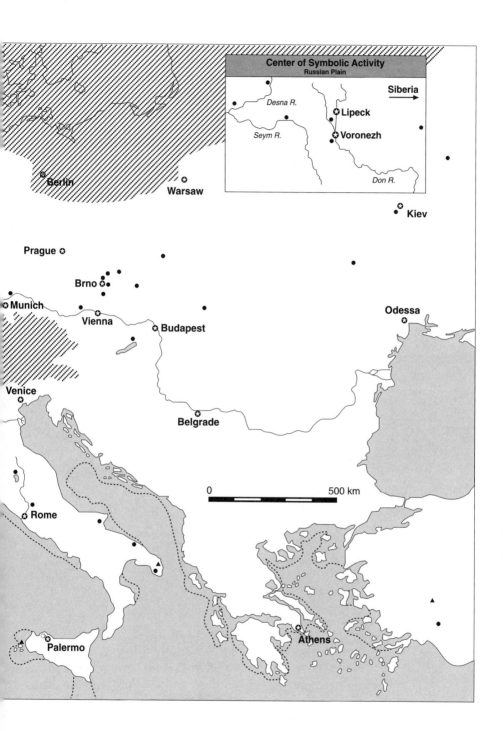

Center of Symbolic Activity
Russian Plain

Siberia

Desna R.
Lipeck
Seym R.
Voronezh
Don R.

Kiev

Berlin
Warsaw

Prague

Brno
Munich
Vienna
Budapest
Odessa

Venice

Belgrade

0   500 km

Rome

Palermo
Athens

Figure 1. The village of Les Eyzies. The houses below are at the river's edge on the valley floor, but other houses are on the cliff shelf under the overhang, where Ice Age hunters were sheltered.

mammoth and woolly rhino, once grazed and across which reindeer seasonally crossed in their seasonal migrations (Fig. 2). The Abri Pataud faces dead west, so that the sun set each evening beyond the flood plain and the low limestone hills that formed the western horizon. Every 29 or 30 days the sliver of the first lunar crescent would appear over these hills, following the setting sun down.

The Les Eyzies cliff shelf and overhang were used as a major shelter primarily in the "winter," when the cliff blocked the winds coming from the north and east. It also caught the winter afternoon sun until it set in the west. The Vézère River below froze each winter. Because of the site's location, the equinoctial autumn sun set dead west at the center of the low hills forming the horizon across the valley. At this position the setting sun marked the start of shortening of days and oncoming winter. Each evening thereafter the sun set progressively further south until, approximately three "moons" later at the winter solstice, it reached its low point on the horizon to the left. After reaching this point, the sun began its daily slow march northward till it reached the position that formerly had marked the autumn equinox, and now marked the spring equinox.

With the spring equinox, the thaw probably would have started with a breakup of the ice on the Vézère and the floods that followed. The

Figure 2. The valley of Les Eyzies with farms on both sides of the river as seen from the cliff shelf. The railroad bridge is built over the river on the ford that was once crossed by reindeer in their seasonal migration. The farmhouse across the valley, in the center, is dead West. The autumn and spring equinoctial suns, as seen from the cliff shelf, set behind the hills at this point.

reindeer herds that had wintered on the lowlands near the coast to the west arrived and crossed the river at the ford below the Abri Pataud, heading to their summer feeding grounds among the hills behind the cliff to the east. Reindeer probably were killed at the river crossing.

Some days after the breakup of the ice and the floods, hordes of Atlantic salmon would come upriver from the ocean to spawn in the Vézère and the many small tributary streams that flowed into it. Migratory summer birds arrived to nest and feed, while the bison and horse arrived from the coastal lowlands, grazing on the new grass as they passed along the river valley. The hunter-gatherers who were camped at the Abri Pataud would by now have left the shelf to begin their warm weather dispersal and their sequence of regional hunting, fishing, and gathering.

I note these processes because the Abri Pataud shelf was one point in an observational, seasonal "clock" or "calendar." From that shelf the sky, the river, the seasonal winds, and the periodic movement of animals, birds, and fish could be observed. Rock shelters such as the Abri Pataud were usually chosen to face some part of the sun's daylight transit, the animal realm, and a relevant portion of evening sky.

A. MARSHACK   25

Along these river networks are found winter and summer sites, specialized short-term exploitation sites, and sites at major river intersections and crossings that served as the places for seasonal meeting and aggregation. Within this tapestry of seasonal human movements, the limestone caves along the rivers in the Franco-Cantabrian region also became places for seasonal and territorial ritual and ceremony.

The village of Les Eyzies was the point at which formal archeological study of European "Prehistory" and the Ice Age cultures began. For more than a century thereafter, sites continued to be excavated in this riverine area. As a major center in the Franco-Cantabrian development of Ice Age cultures and of its archeological study, it can serve as an exploratory model.

As would be expected, the questions first asked by archaeologists of the Ice Age tools and art that began to be found were primarily descriptive and typological. There was awe at the sophistication of the excavated artifacts. The period was described as the "Reindeer Age" of the troglodytes or "cave dwellers," a mysterious distant prehistoric age that had included the extinct woolly rhino and mammoth. Hunting-gathering lifeways and concepts, and the possible relation of the tools and images to persistently changing regional climates and ecologies, were slowly uncovered, and these studies are still continuing. Bit by bit, the ancient cultures began to appear increasingly human, that is, extraordinarily complex and "time-factored" and *therefore* "modern."

Today, standing on the shelf and looking down on the valley, we see the simple pastoral scene shown in Fig. 2. But during the Ice Age the valley was the stage for a dynamic, processual complexity. The valley also has an interesting modern history. The railroad bridge that crosses the Vézère was located here because this was the low, white-water point on the river that reindeer herds had used for crossing during their migrations. It is also the ford at which salmon could be easily caught. While building the railroad bridge in 1868, land fill was needed. The talus at the foot of the Les Eyzies cliff was dug up and a cave was uncovered. Inside were three Ice Age skeletons, two males and one female. When alive, they probably had wintered on the shelf a few yards up the cliff, and had camped along the river. The cave was called Cro-Magnon, and so the makers of the Ice Age tools and the engraved images and seashell beads found in the burial — and the diverse Ice Age peoples that soon began to be uncovered across Europe — received the generic name of this cave: "Cro-Magnon," although they were not all of one type. Of particular interest, though seldom mentioned in the literature, the Cro-Magnon female had a large, symmetrical, oval hole in her skull, a hole of the size and shape that a hafted spear might make. The Cro-Magnons were therefore not only the makers of tools and art (a carved "Venus" figurine on a limestone block was found in the Abri Pataud excavation) but possibly also practitioners of personal violence and aggression.

I discussed the possibility of violence and aggression in a theoretical paper on the early human capacity that I presented more than a decade ago (Marshack 1985). But that possibility was seldom thereafter mentioned or cited in the literature, except for a recent footnote in a French journal that suggested that the hole in the skull probably had been made by a workers' pick-axe during the excavation at Cro-Magnon in 1868 (Delluc and Delluc 1989:397). Evidence for aggressive violence occurs in the recently discovered painted cave of Cosquer, where a prone human figure, presumably dead, is depicted as struck through by a barbed spear (Clottes and Courtin 1994:154-161 and Fig. 155). Other images of killing "humans" (or of human-like "spirits") also have been found in the caves. More recently, confirmation of interpersonal violence in the Ice Age was demonstrated when a flint point was found embedded in a human pelvis at a late Upper Paleolithic (Epigravettian) burial in San Teodoro Cave, Messina, Sicily (Bachechi et al. 1997). With these data it becomes clear that life, death, and "killing" in these Ice Age valleys was more complex than is apparent in the well-known voluminous evidence of subsistence and "art."

Slowly, the evidence for fully "modern" complexity began to be unraveled. Occasionally, with the tools, beads, and examples of "art," one found broken, fragmented pieces of bone that had been incised with an unusual, nondecorative type of marking. Not far from Les Eyzies at the rock shelter of the Abri Blanchard located on a stream flowing into the Vézère River, a broken bone retoucher was excavated in an early Aurignacian level, dated at c. 29,000-28,000 BC. The bone tool was broken back where it had been used to flake flint tools, but it was highly polished along the edges and the rear where it had been held. This worn, now nonfunctional tool had then been used as an available surface for incising an unusual design composed of sets of marks. In an area no larger than that of a large wrist watch, 69 marks had been accumulated in a serpentine manner, divided into small sets and subsets (Fig. 3a, b). The accumulation looked as though someone was keeping a record more than 20,000 years before the formal beginnings of writing and formal systems of arithmetic.

Serpentine or boustrophedon modes of sequencing are known in the early writing systems of Greece and even in the glyphic writing of the Maya. It is, apparently, a natural mode for linearly accumulating certain

Figure 3a. Blanchard bone plaque. Aurignacian period, c. 28,000 BC.

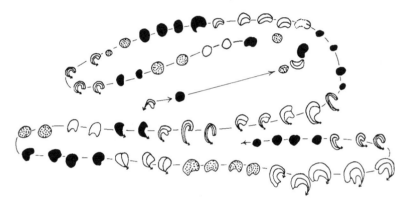

Figure 3b. Schematic rendition of the incised marks on the Blanchard bone plaque. The 69 marks are divided into approimately 24 subsets made by different points and types of stroke. The linear accumulation forms a serpentine image that models the waxing and waning of the moon. Aurignacian period, c. 28,000 BC.

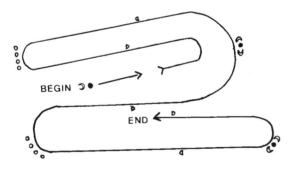

Figure 3c. Schematic rendition of the serpentine accumulation indicating the "turns" in the month that occur at right in the period of the crescents and invisibility and at left in the period of the full moon.

types of information. I therefore tried to determine what type or class of information might have been recorded during the early Ice Age in a linear, sequential, boustrophedon manner. I conducted numerous tests, finally testing the possibility that these Ice Age hunter-gatherers were recording the processes of time they lived by, perhaps lunar observations made over short periods. If, for instance, one began keeping a record in the "moon" or month of the first frost, it might be 2¼ months before the winter solstice appeared sometime in the "third" month. Or if one began recording in the "moon" or month of the winter solstice it could be 2¼ months before the thaw and the spring equinox. Small sets of "moons" or months could therefore have great importance.

The tests indicated that if the Blanchard serpentine was an observational rather than "arithmetic" record, then all the crescent moons and days of invisibility would fall at the right, all the half moons would fall in the middle of a row, and all the full moon periods would fall at left at the "turning" of the month (Fig. 3b). If one stood on the plateau above the rock shelter of the Abri Blanchard and watched the sky and kept such a record, then at the end of 2¼ months one might expect to see the distant arrival of reindeer herds in the valley of the Vézère and, after the thaw, the arrival of migrating salmon in the Vézère a few yards away.

© ALEXANDER MARSHACK

Figure 4. Large male salmon with hooked lower jaw carved in the limestone ceiling of the cave shelter of the Gorge d'Enfer, a few yards from the Vézère River, just outside the village of Les Eyzies.

JEAN VERTUT

Figure 5. Painted running horse in the cave of Lascaux, a cave in the low hills of the Vézère drainage. The horse is painted in its summer pelage. France, early Magdalenian period, c. 15,000 BC.

If we now return to the Abri Pataud and the valley of Les Eyzies, we find that within the regional cluster of rock shelters and caves along the Vézère and tributary streams one finds a surprising array of seasonal imagery. A ten-minute walk upstream from Les Eyzies, in the small rock-shelter cave of the Gorge d'Enfer, which opens to a small stream that flows into the Vézère, there is a three-foot-long male salmon that was carved into the limestone ceiling during the Gravettian period (Fig. 4). It has the hook or kype on its lower jaw that the male salmon acquires only in the period of spawning, after it has completed its migratory run upriver from the Atlantic. A short distance further upstream on the Vézère, at the riverside rock shelter of La Madeleine, which gave its name to the final Ice Age culture — the Magdalenian — we find an incised image of a decapitated sacrificed bear. The bear wakens from winter hibernation in the spring. Soon after the thaw there would be fishing for salmon in these waters.

Salmon and bear were among the first signs of spring. Ritual sacrifice of a bear may have occurred to welcome or ensure the spring rebirth of nature. Such bear rituals were still being performed in Pyrenean France in the late 19th century. At La Madeleine there are also images of the fish that would be caught here after the thaw (Marshack 1972, 1991b).

Figure 6. The winter pelage of the Przwalski horse, related to the horse of Ice Age in both form and coloring.

Still further upstream on the Vézère is the great middle Magdalenian sanctuary cave of Lascaux, with its images of a red deer stag baying in the autumn rut, bison in summer and winter pelage, and the well-known horse in its summer pelage and coloring (Fig. 5). There are images of the wild cattle that would have returned to these hills and valleys for grazing the new spring grass. Far to the south in France, in the cave of Niaux in the Pyrenean foothills, there are images of the winter horse in its heavy shaggy coat. The Ice Age horse in winter had a thick beard and a heavy coat (see Fig. 6), masking the summer pelage and tonal coloring found on the horse in Lascaux.

Facing the cave of Niaux across the valley is the cave shelter of La Vache, which contained a full set of seasonal images: a male reindeer with antlers following an antlered female at the end of the period of summer grazing in the Pyrenean foothills. There are also images of salmon, a bear, and a summer horse depicted in a scene of ritual sacrifice. There is also an image of a baying autumn bison, flowers in bloom, dying flowers in the autumn, etc. (Marshack 1970, 1972, 1991b, 1975).

Different Ice Age caves in France and Spain depict different species in their varying seasonal pelage and behaviors. Occasionally there are images of the lions that fed on these animals. Because of their location one assumes that the caves were often places for periodic regional rituals held at particular times and seasons, either in the expectation of a species' appearance or in a ritual acknowledgment of a successful appearance and hunting, or in the hope for a species' return in the following year. But animal images also could be used as symbols in a range of periodic and aperiodic rituals in the homesite as well as in the caves. If one takes the scatter of seasonal sites and the depictions of seasonal animals found at rock shelters and caves within the Franco-Cantabrian area, and adds to these the occasional examples of notation found at some sites, one obtains the sense of a networked region that was pragmatically, conceptually, and ritually mapped in time and space by widely dispersed human groups. These conceptual maps would have specified the places and times for specialized hunting as well as the periods for group dispersal and group aggregation. The cultural tapestry would have incorporated other rituals, some periodic and some aperiodic, such as those concerned with group membership and sexual maturation and differentiation and with events such as accidents, curing, pregnancy, birth, and death. The images encompass a broad range of periodic and aperiodic referents and rituals.

In areas of Europe where there were no caves, the homesites provide a comparable range of images. On the Russian plain there is evidence of a seasonal movement of human groups up and down the network of rivers that flow toward the Black Sea. There were summer and winter sites along these rivers, including riverside sites that were specialized for seasonal resource exploitation and for seasonal symbolic performance and production (Marshack 1979; Soffer 1985). Time and space were structured and mapped behaviorally and ritually, even where there were no sanctuary caves.

One of the first "calendrical" notations that I studied was incised on a section of mammoth ivory tusk found at the far eastern site of Gontzy on the Russian plain, located on the Udai River, a tributary of the Sula, which flowed into the Dnieper and then to the Black Sea (Marshack 1972, 1991b). The geographical span from the Franco-Cantabrian area to the eastern Russian plain encompasses almost the entire continent of Upper Paleolithic of Europe.

The ubiquity of Upper Paleolithic seasonal imagery is dramatically illustrated in the recently discovered Aurignacian cave of Chauvet located in central France on the Ardèche River, a tributary that flows eastward to the Rhône, which then flowed southward to the Mediterranean. The Rhône valley developed its own regional suBCultures. Chauvet is extraordinary because it contains highly sophisticated painting made during the

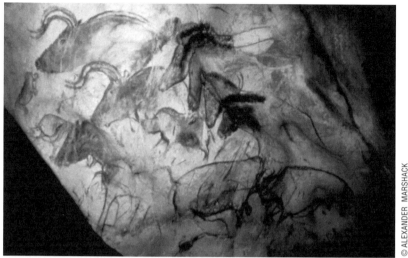

Figure 7. Painted horse heads in the recently discovered cave of Chauvet in their beard-less, summer form. Aurignacian period, c. 29,000 BC.

same early Aurignacian period, c. 29,000 BC, as the Abri Blanchard no-tation, incised on a different regional river that flowed westward to the Atlantic. The cave of Chauvet was visited and painted during the spring, summer, and autumn seasons, during an apparently cold climatic phase. There are paintings of the beardless summer horse (Fig. 7; one horse has the serpentine summer pelage marking found on the Lascaux horse in Fig. 5). There are images of hairless woolly rhinos in the "summer," of the wild cattle that seasonally roamed the Rhône Valley and its foothills, and images of the lions that fed on this seasonal bounty (Chauvet and Hillaire 1995; Marshack 1995a). The skull of a bear that may have hibernated in Chauvet during the winter, but was not in the cave during those seasons in which the hunter-gatherers entered, had been carefully placed on a stone pedestal.

Twenty thousand years later than Chauvet, near the end of the Mag-dalenian period and the Ice Age itself, c. 9500-9000 BC, a nonutilitarian fragment of bone was excavated in the Isère River, a riverside cave and rock shelter on a different tributary of the Rhône. The fragment had been cut from a tool that had broken during use. The fragment was then used to incise the most complex notation and composition to come from the European Ice Age (Marshack 1991c). It was clearly a highly evolved descendent of the serpentine notation found on the earlier Aurignacian plaque from the Abri Blanchard.

A. MARSHACK   33

The Late Pleistocene climate of Europe was warming and forests were moving slowly up the Rhône Valley. The animal species were changing. Mammoth and woolly rhino had disappeared, although the horse, bison, ibex, and lion were still present.

The terminal Ice Age hunter-gatherers staying at the Grotte du Taï had a view of half the sky, and from their hill, they could see across the river to the flood plain on which herds grazed and moved. They could observe the animals that seasonally crossed the river after the snows had melted, to graze on the new grass on the foothills behind the cave; and after the thaw they could fish in the river below.

The altered climate induced major changes in human behavior. Because of the warming and the presence of animals in this area through much of the year, the site of Taï was a sedentary or semi-sedentary site. In fact, sedentism had been increasing over time. The plaquette from the Grotte du Taï, roughly the same size as the earlier Blanchard plaquette, was more complex. It was incised with a series of long, horizontal containing lines composed of shorter sections appended to one another (Fig. 8). Each subsection was marked with its own set of marks. The direction of marking changed on each horizontal, so that the accumulation was marked and read in boustrophedon manner. When more room was needed at the end of a particular horizontal row, that row either descended at a right angle, was marked, and then ascended to the next row or, when more marks were needed at the other end of the plaque, they were incised below the horizontal (Marshack 1991c). This cumulative strategy created a continuous, serpentine sequence of differentiated sets and subsets that not only changed the direction of marking and reading for each row but allowed for sets to be added if needed at the end of each row.

Despite its complexity, the serpentine, boustrophedon mode was essentially the same as that found on the earlier Blanchard notation. Analysis indicated that each horizontal row recorded a five- or six-month period, with the "turns" in the notation occurring not at lunar phases, but at the solstices or the equinoxes. The main face of the plaque recorded a sequence spanning three and a half years.

The complexity of the notation indicated that one person at the Grotte du Taï, apparently a specialist, had watched the sky and monitored the subsistence and ritual "calendar." It may have been a shaman or an elder who kept and marked the plaque. Taking the body of Upper Paleolithic subsistence and the symbolic evidence, we have a cultural tapestry that was structured in time and space in many different ways and at different levels.

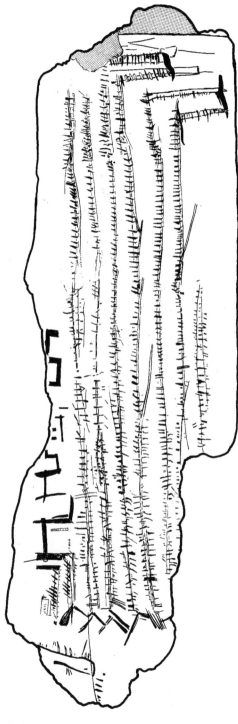

© ALEXANDER MARSHACK

Figure 8. Schematic rendition of the serpentine notation incised on a bone plaque from the Grotte du Taï, France. Terminal Magdalenian period, c. 9500 BC.

A. MARSHACK

Urbanization and Land Ownership in the Ancient Near East

WOOLLY MAMMOTH

RED DEER

WOODLAND BISON

ATLANTIC SALMON

WILD ASS

FALLOW DEER

RINGED SEAL

AUROCHS

NATIONAL GEOGRAPHIC SOCIETY
LLOYD K. TOWNSEND, ARTIST

Figure 9. The animal species hunted during the European Ice Age. All these animals had their own seasonal movements and behaviors. An Ice Age hunter and observer is keeping a record of the sequence of "moons" or months that mark the seasons (From Marshack 1975).

These sequences and processes in the cultural tapestry apparently were being monitored, evaluated, and maintained by specialists with knowledge of a widespread and ancient tradition. It was probably these specialists who evaluated and determined the times and places for aggregation and ritual, for the exchange of wives, resources, or artifacts. These intergroup relations could be maintained — across these networks of rivers and tributary streams — only if there was a common, shared "calendar," whether such a calendar was kept as a record or merely as an observational and mythologically embedded narrative sequence. One had to know when the herds would be present, when the fish would be running, when nuts and fruits would be available, in which phase of the moon of a particular season an aggregation could be sustained or a group ritual should be performed, and to decide whether it would be at riverside or in a regional cave. Inasmuch as almost *all* hunter-gatherers live by sequences of this type, the difference in the European Upper Pal-eolithic was that these continental cultures had developed abstract conceptual models to structure and maintain their cultural tapestries across large distances and networks of rivers and microecologies.

A drawing prepared by Lloyd Townsend of the National Geographic Society for a 1975 article on the Ice Age (Marshack 1975) schematically illustrates the processes I have described (Fig.9). Two hands are keeping an incised record in a surround of different species, each of which has its own seasonal ecology and behavior: the salmon of the rivers, the seal that followed salmon upriver into the estuaries and lowland waters, rutting deer and bison of autumn. These species were at different points in the realm at different times of the year and, as a result, they would be preferentially hunted in different seasons. Significantly, when the climate warmed and the forests began to move north into what had once been open grazing grounds, the large migratory herds disappeared and the Ice Age cultures collapsed. The caves ceased being used for periodic painting and rituals, and the great variability in homesite imagery across Ice Age Europe ended. A different and more abstract imagery developed as hunting-gathering groups increasingly congregated within the smaller, regionally bounded ecologies of the post-Ice Age Mesolithic (Marshack 1972, 1991b; 1969, 1976, 1977, 1983).

In investigating whether these modes of inquiry and concepts could be applied in the Near East, I was faced with a number of theoretical problems. There is no archeological evidence that other early hunting-gathering cultures developed or maintained the range and variety of symboling systems that had developed in Ice Age Europe or, for that matter, had developed complex systems of notation to cohere and maintain their cultures. The dispersed hunter-gatherers of the historic ethnographic period provide no evidence of having developed comparable traditions of record keeping.

The archaeological record, however, offers a number of insights. It is assumed that the European Aurignacian was developed by anatomically modern humans who moved northward into Europe during a temperate period. In Europe these migrants rapidly developed a bone industry and technology that was abetted by the presence of huge herbivore herds. As the human groups dispersed, they developed symboling systems that would cohere their culture across the great distances encompassed by the network of European rivers. But a question remained. Had they come into Europe carrying symboling traditions (cf. Marshack 1996), and did the symboling traditions they then developed disseminate into neighboring regions and back into the Near East? I had studied Upper Paleolithic symboling traditions that had dispersed as far east as the Angara River at

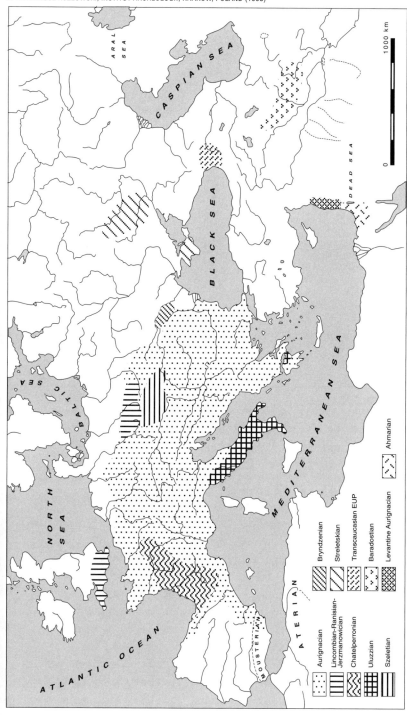

Map 2. Distribution of the major industrial variants of the earliest stages of the European Upper Paleolithic. (After Kozlowski and Kozlowski 1979.)

A. MARSHACK

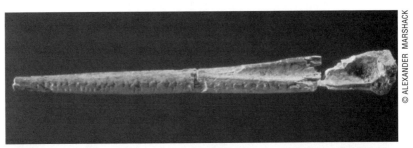

Figure 10 (top). A bone point from the Aurignacian site of Ksar Akil, Lebanon, c. 29,000 BC, incised with sets of marks made by different points, similar to incised sequences found in the Aurignacian and later periods of the European Upper Paleolithic.

Figure 11 (bottom). Bone points from the Aurignacian of Hayonim D, Israel, of the type found during this period in Europe.

Ma'lta in central Siberia, and I had found these traditions to have been derived, though regionally altered, from concepts that were present during this period in Europe. Post-Aurignacian Gravettian influences had extended across all of Europe. I also had tracked Magdalenian symboling traditions emanating from France as far east as Moravia in Central Europe and as far north as Poland. There was even some indication that Magdalenian symboling influences may have reached the Russian plain. Long-distance movements and a dispersal of cultural influences were clearly present during this period.

Could Upper Paleolithic influences, then, have extended southward, out of continental Europe? A schematic map of the early Aurignacian in Ice Age Europe indicates that it extended from Cantabrian Spain east-

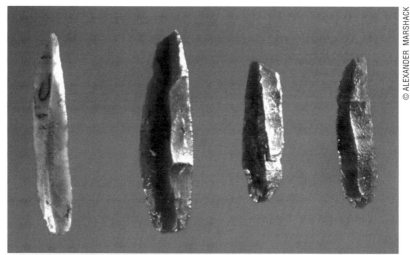

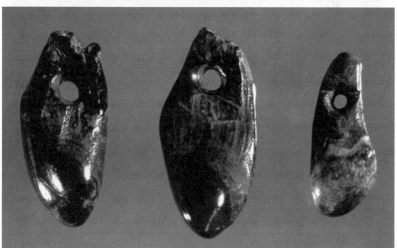

Figure 12 (top). Dufour points from the Aurignacian of Hayonim D, Israel, comparable to those found in the Aurignacian of Europe.

Figure 13 (bottom). Three animal tooth beads from the Aurginacian of Hayonim D, Israel, of the type found in the Aurignacian of Europe during this period, c. 29,000-28,000 BC.

ward across Europe and along the Mediterranean coast to Greece (Map 2). Of interest is the fact that an "Aurignacian" appears at the site Ksar Akil in Lebanon and in Israel at the Cave of Hayonim. At Ksar Akil there is even the suggestive example of a possible notation incised on a bone point. Both the bone point and the marking are made in the "European"

Figure 14. Hayonim terrace and valley as seen from the cave while undergoing excavation.

mode (Tixier 1974) (Fig. 10). Numerous Aurignacian bone and lithic tools and Aurignacian animal-tooth beads are found at Hayonim (Figs. 11-13). There also is evidence for a use of ocher and one image of a ritually "killed" and used horse incised on a pebble in an Aurignacian style (Belfer-Cohen and Bar-Yosef 1981; Marshack 1997). Could symboling concepts and technologies that were developed in Europe have entered the Levant with small hunting-gathering groups carrying the European Aurignacian culture? Could these traditions have been absorbed into indigenous Levantine cultures and populations? Could these "European" Upper Paleolithic traditions have then developed indigenous, Near Eastern regional modes?

Belfer-Cohen and Bar-Yosef have indicated that animal-tooth beads are also found in the much later Natufian, though they were made in a different manner. There is no evidence that the Aurignacian tradition influenced the later Natufian, but the Natufian use of bone suggests that an inquiry into the diverse early uses of bone needs ongoing investigation. Recent evidence, for instance, indicates that the animal tooth beads found at the Chatelperronian site of Arcy-sur-Cure in France were made by Neanderthals, without influence from or contact with the contemporary Aurignacians.

Early in my research in the Near East I examined motifs and images incised on stone from the Epipaleolithic sites of Öküzini and Karain in Anatolia, Turkey, dated c. 14,000 BC, that had strong similarities to traditions from this period in the late European Upper Paleolithic and in the Italian, or Mediterranean, Romanellian (Marshack 1995a,c; 1997). Had these European symboling traditions and modes disseminated to the Near East, or had they developed indigenously?

It was in the Epipaleolithic, Natufian period at the Cave of Hayonim in Israel that the most complex and intriguing data occurred. Hayonim is a large cave located among the inland hills of the western, temperate Mediterranean zone in Israel (Fig. 14). It fronts on a narrow valley and a wadi, the Nahal Meged, that is used today for occasional farming. Wild grasses still grow on the hillsides. The wadi is a tributary of the nearby Nahal Yassaf River which flows to the Mediterranean.

The cave and the narrow, small valley are totally different from the rich cluster of Upper Paleolithic rock shelters and caves found along the network of rivers that interlaced southwestern Upper Paleolithic Europe. The great variety of mid-latitude species and microecologies that were found along the rivers and hills of Ice Age Europe did not exist in the Levant, although native species of plants and animals did vary in the

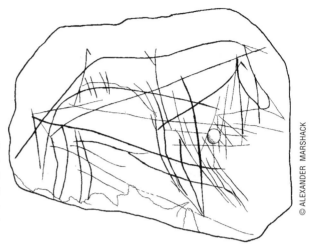

Figure 15. Limestone pebble with the engraving of a horse overmarked with darts and band motifs. Hayonim Cave, Aurignacian period.

© ALEXANDER MARSHACK

Levant, particularly when the climate went through periodic wet and dry, and cold and warm, cycles. Hayonim Cave had served as a shelter through many of these climatic cycles: in the Mousterian, in the Aurignacian, and in the later preagricultural Natufian.

Of particular interest was the fact that the Aurignacian hunter-gatherers who stayed at Hayonim produced bone points (Fig. 11), flint tools (Fig. 12), and animal-tooth beads (Fig. 13) similar to those found during this period in Ice Age Europe (Belfer-Cohen and Bar-Yosef 1981; Marshack 1997). They also produced symbols and images similar to those found in Ice Age Europe.

A limestone pebble, small enough to be held in the hand (12.4 cm long), had been used to abrade ocher powder or had been colored symbolically, perhaps because it was an idiosyncratic "exotic" that had a fossil shell protruding on both faces. The pebble subsequently was incised in different ways over a period of time. Engraved over the ocher is the simple outline of a running horse with a slit eye, made in what André Leroi-Gourhan (1967) had termed the early "Style I" for the west European Aurignacian and Upper Paleolithic (Fig. 15). The horse had been ritually "killed" with spears and darts coming from many directions, in a manner found both in the caves and on mobiliary artifacts during the European Upper Paleolithic. The horse was overmarked with multiple "band" or stream motifs, in a manner that animal images were often overmarked in the European Upper Paleolithic. Even the fossil intrusion had been surrounded with an incised pattern, suggesting that the stone itself, and the

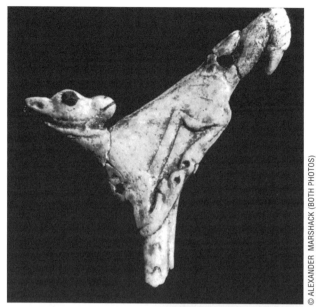

Figure 16 (above). A carved ibex kid with inset eyes on a broken Magdalenian reindeer antler spear-thrower from Bedeilhac, France. Middle Magdalenian.

Figure 17 (right). Bone sickle-handle from El Wad with a carved gazelle. Natufian period, c. 11,000 BC.

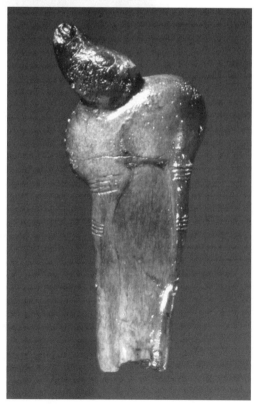

A. MARSHACK   45

fossil, may have been given symbolic value. On the rear face there was the crude image of a second horse.

This pebble had therefore been used symbolically in different ways over a period of time, perhaps by a ritual specialist. Such a ritual specialist also may have been involved in ordering and structuring the ritual "calendar" (cf. Marshack 1997). Significantly, the Aurignacian artifacts at Hayonim (Layer D) come from approximately the same period as the incised Aurignacian bone point found at Ksar Akil in Lebanon, c. 29,000 BP, and the developed Aurignacian in the west European Paleolithic. What then happened to the Aurignacian traditions and influences that entered the Near East? Did they disappear entirely, as the evidence would seem to suggest, or were aspects absorbed or adopted to influence later developments and traditions?

The next major occupation at Hayonim cave was the extremely important preagricultural Epipaleolithic or "Natufian," which developed from about 10,500-8,700 BC in the Mediterranean area of the Levant (Map 3). This was the late Pleistocene period in France that was undergoing major climatic change and provided us with the late Upper Paleolithic Grotte du Taï notation, suggesting an increase of sedentism for hunting-gathering groups. Major climatic changes were also occurring in the Levant, tending to increase sedentism and the seasonal gathering and storing of the wild cereals that grew on the hill flanks.

The earliest evidence for gathering wild cereals in this area occurs in the far earlier Kebaran culture at the site of Ohalo II, dated at c. 17,000 BC (Nadel 1990, 1991). As the late Pleistocene warmed in Europe, inducing new hunting-gathering adaptations and strategies, variable climatic cycles in the Near East had induced increases in sedentism and the gathering and storage of wild cereals. By the time of the Natufian we have evidence of compound, inset sickles being used to cut wild grasses.

An interesting comparison for this late period of the Pleistocene is evidenced by a spear thrower that comes from the Middle Magdalenian French cave site of Bedeilhac in the Pyrenean foothills (Fig. 16), and a sickle handle found in the Natufian cave site of El Wad, located on the coast not far from Hayonim (Fig. 17). The sickle has the carving of a gazelle, while the spear thrower has the carving of an ibex kid. One was a tool intended for cutting cereal in the right season, perhaps after the winter rains when grazing gazelle might be hunted more easily. The other was a hunting tool that could be used in the high valleys of the Pyrenean foothills to hunt in the springtime, when new grass had brought these animals and their young to the lower valleys and hills.

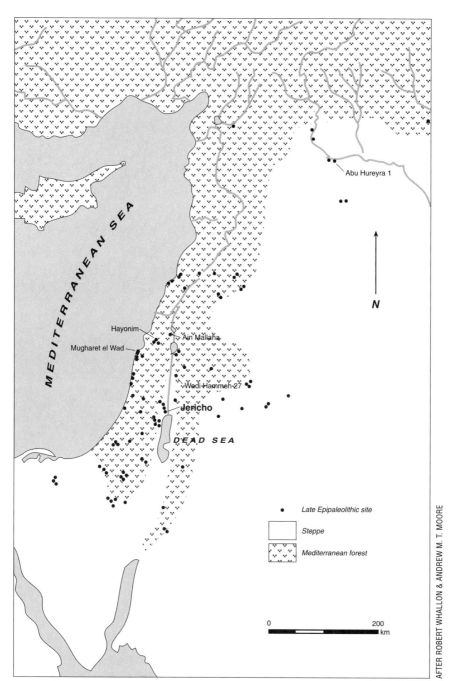

Map 3. Distribution of late Epipaleolithic sites (c. 12,000-10,000 BP) in the Levant. The sites are shown against the probable extent of the Mediterranean forest and steppe vegetation zones, c. 11,000 BP. (After Moore 1991. © International Monographs in Prehistory.)

A. MARSHACK

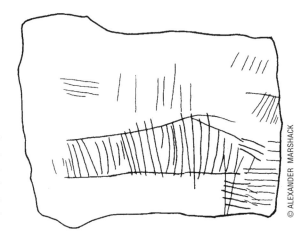

Figure 18. Limestone plaquette incised with a "ladder" motif and surrounding sets, excavated in an early Natufian layer on the Hayonim Terrace by F. Valla.

© ALEXANDER MARSHACK

The Cave of Hayonim provides an interesting and complex set of Natufian imagery for comparison with traditions found in Europe. Excavations on the terrace in front of the cave some years ago turned up a small (8.8 cm), nonfunctional, flat piece of stone that had been intentionally incised in a manner that could not be called either "decoration" or "art" (Fig. 18). Since it could not at that time be categorized, and since it represented no known Natufian "style," it was not published. However, the "style" or mode of marking by accumulating sets of marks on a containing line, or in a "ladder," was similar to modes of marking in Europe, in Anatolia (Marshack 1996, 1997), and in the earlier Geometric Kebaran of Israel at Urkan e-Rub II (Hovers 1990).

Analysis of the Hayonim terrace composition indicated that the central motif contained an apparent record for one observational lunar month, with a second month accumulated around it (Marshack 1997:74). Since the stone was portable, the marking could have been begun elsewhere and completed on the terrace. Though there was evidence for increasing sedentism during the Natufian, seasons and periods of mobile hunting occurred.

That the small plaquette represented a mode of "notation" was confirmed when similar accumulations began to be found inside the cave. One of the more important compositions was on a large limestone block of some forty or fifty pounds found within the cave in 1995 (Fig. 19). The block was too heavy to be carried, so that the composition had been accumulated inside the cave. The marking consists of tightly packed sets engraved by different points and to different rhythms and lengths. Like the plaquette on the terrace, it was incised within ladderlike containing lines. Once again, the composition could not be considered "art" or "decoration," but seemed to be a record or cumulative notation.

The possible presence of notation among the Hayonim compositions had earlier been suggested by Belfer-Cohen (Belfer-Cohen 1991). Analysis of the new block indicated that the notation represented a record for seven months (Fig. 20 a-d) (Marshack 1997), apparently maintained by a "specialist" — such as an elder or "shaman" — who monitored the changes in the seasons. Perhaps he evaluated the time of arrival and the amount of the winter rains, the differential appearance and growth of wild cereals, the preparation of the needed baskets and sickles, the subsequent harvest and storage, as well as the ritual calendar that depended on these estimates. He probably also estimated the time and size of intergroup relations and aggregation. The evidence for wild cereal storage at Hayonim is demonstrated by the presence of domesticated commensals such as mice, barn sparrows, and barn owls.[1] Different species of wild cereal mature at different times in different locations, depending on the time and quantity of the winter rains, and so the harvesting and gathering schedules had to be carefully estimated. In case of late arrival or failure, alternative strategies had to be planned.

As in the Ice Age of Europe, but in a different ecology and under different conditions, the hunting-gathering cultures in this area had adapted to a regional time-factored realm and had structured that realm pragmatically, culturally, and symbolically. In sedentary occupations involving wild cereal gathering, time and personnel had to be carefully scheduled, not only for the preparation of harvesting tools and baskets but also for alternative strategies and rituals that would take account of the periodic variations that occurred in the subsistence sequence.

Such variations would have increased in periods of climate and weather change. An increased storage of cereals represented one pragmatic answer to such variation, and an observational calendar kept by a specialist would have represented one means of monitoring and evaluating seasonal periodicities and their variation.

Climatic variations increased markedly during the Natufian, particularly with the sharp drop in temperatures brought on by Dryas III. Storage of cereals would have abetted survival and periodic aggregation and exchange among dispersed groups during such times. These processes would have invited sowing and carefully measured storage, processes that would have had to occur within a carefully monitored calendar frame.

One therefore must add to the material conditions and processes that have been suggested for the rise of agriculture and the subsequent

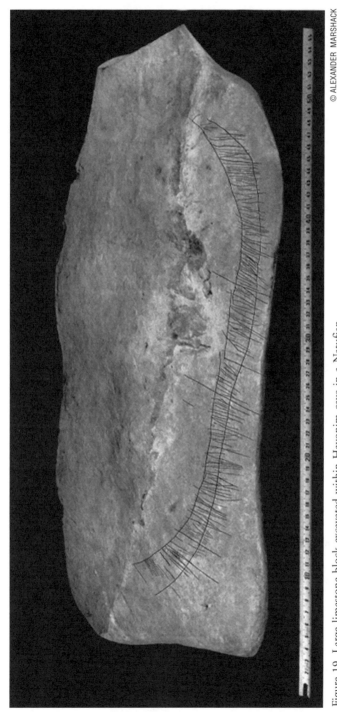

© ALEXANDER MARSHACK

Figure 19. Large limestone block excavated within Hayonim cave in a Natufian level, with a long notational sequence incised in the "ladder" mode. Excavated in 1994 by O. Bar-Yosef and A. Belfer-Cohen (Marshack 1997).

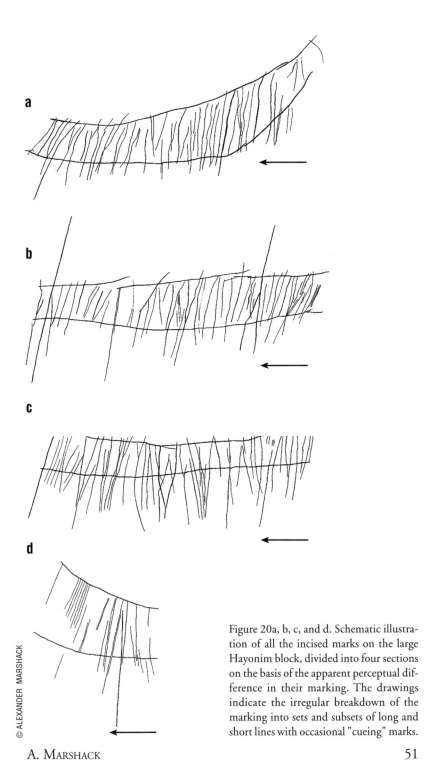

a

b

c

d

Figure 20a, b, c, and d. Schematic illustration of all the incised marks on the large Hayonim block, divided into four sections on the basis of the apparent perceptual difference in their marking. The drawings indicate the irregular breakdown of the marking into sets and subsets of long and short lines with occasional "cueing" marks.

A. MARSHACK

development of urbanization, the antecedent cultural and conceptual preparation that would have made adaptation to and use of these other manifests possible. When farming technologies finally moved northward, out of the Near East and into Europe, ancient traditions already were present among the Mesolithic hunting-gathering populations for structuring and time-factoring their mid-latitude four-season realm, often by a use of notation (cf. Marshack 1969; 1990:Fig. 23; 1972, 1991b). Agriculture and herding could be rather quickly adopted by these European hunter-gatherers, at first in part, then in its entirety. The Late Pleistocene, Upper Paleolithic Grotte du Taï notation evidenced a sophisticated level of hunter-gatherer time-factoring in the Rhône valley of France. But an almost contemporary notational accumulation occurs at the late Epigravettian site of Riparo Tagliente near Verona in northern Italy, dated c. 11,300-10,000 BC, the approximate period of the Öküzini notation in Anatolia and the Hayonim notation in Israel. The Riparo Tagliente notation is particularly interesting because a record-keeper from any of the European or Near Eastern sites with a tradition of sequencing a notation by sets and subsets would have understood the underlying mode found at Riparo Tagliente.

A limestone block, 27.6 cm long, was incised with a sequential accumulation of tiny sets and subsets ordered in a serpentine or boustrophedon manner (Fig. 21). Because of the scale of marking, comparable to the notational marking found at Taï, Öküzini, and Hayonim, it would have been impossible to read this notation by a counting or summing of sets. The maker could, however, easily determine at what point in the accumulation, or point in the year, a particular set or subset fell. A count of the accumulation was impossible, but shorter bouts of "counting" nevertheless would have been involved. The small subsets would have been counted when they were added to the notation, but subsequent readings would have been *positional* rather than arithmetic. These readings would have been made in conjunction with observation of the sky, the seasonal behavior of animals and plants, and the sequence of societal demands in the subsistence and ritual schedule, though these referents are not indicated or marked within the notation.

It is here argued that the level of notational abstraction, observation, and problem-solving present throughout the European Upper Paleolithic and Mesolithic was present also in the preagricultural Near East and Natufian. The short-lived Natufian ended when a change in climate and resulting demographic pressures increased the need for more careful planting, harvesting, and storage. The pragmatic and conceptual preparation

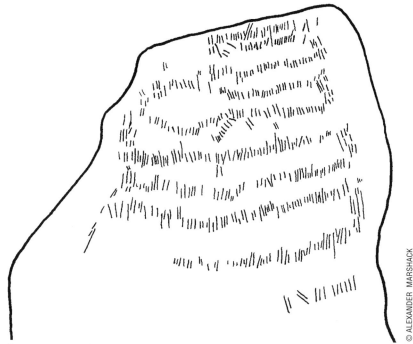

Figure 21. Incised notation on a limestone block from the late Epigravettian site of Riparo Tagliente, Italy, c. 11,300-10,000 BC, indicating the linear serpentine mode of accumulating sets and subsets.

for such change was already present. Agriculture, however, requires a more carefully structured calendar frame. It increasingly requires "time-factored" divisions of labor and skill, allotted times and places for specialized activities, and calendrically precise times for ritual, aggregation, and exchange.

To what degree and in what manner the time-factoring traditions developed in the preceding preagricultural cultures aided in the adaptations leading to agriculture, and then helped in structuring the more complex time-and-space complexities of urban societies, now needs to be carefully investigated. The well-known urban tapestries of temples, records, astronomies, and regional calendars, day-and-night hours, scheduled debts, and debt amnesties, and the increasing specialization of skills and the times and places for their use, all required a developing, increasingly precise, and carefully monitored calendar.

The evidence for a regional mode of record-keeping on stone at the early Pre-Pottery Neolithic (PPNA) farming village of Jerf el Ahmar in Syria (Stordeur and Jammous 1995, Stordeur *et al.* 1996) suggests one type of "time-factoring" and record-keeping that developed, c. ±9680-9790 BP (7680-7790 BC). The later use of clay tokens as a form of record-keeping, found at Jericho, 'Ain Ghazal, and other Neolithic sites around c. ±7200-6500 BC (9000-8500 BP), and the subsequent use of clay envelopes to hold them, represented another developing means of "time-factoring" economic and cultural information (Schmandt-Besserat 1988, 1991). A particularly interesting, but different example of such early Neolithic structuring occurs at the early PPNB site of Jilat 7, excavated from a level dated at c. 7500-7200 BC, and therefore perhaps slightly later than the incised pebbles found at Jerf el Ahmar in Syria but near the time of the appearance of clay tokens.

Jilat 7 is a seasonal winter/spring site located in the marginal subdesert region of Azraq, Jordan (Garrard et al. 1994). Domesticated cereals were found at the site, but it is not certain whether they were grown locally or transported from elsewhere in the region. Jilat 7 was apparently a temporary site located within a widespread conceptual map encompassing both mobile and more sedentary regional groups.

It is probable that within a region involving the seasonal movement by some groups and the beginning of more sedentary Neolithic settlements near well-watered locations by other groups, that there would have developed shared conceptual maps and models of the region and of neighboring groups indicating which aggregations were to be held at the proper time and in the proper place. The presence of beads from the Red Sea and the Mediterranean at Jilat 7, for instance, suggests a movement of trade goods coming from many directions: the acquisition of such materials would probably not have been random. A far more regular periodic dispersal and seasonal aggregation by members of a closely related farming and herding population is documented at the slightly later middle PPNB village of 'Ain Ghazal, located at a riverside some 60 to 70 kms north and west of Jilat 7.

At Jilat 7, a unique artifact was found, apparently documenting one aspect of shared calendrical knowledge that was available during this period. A small pebble (9.5 cm wide) made of a limestone not present at that site had been shaped to create a "square" tablet. One face had been carefully abraded to produce a flat plaque (the other face was untouched) and it had been scraped and rounded along the edges. The flat face was then incised with an unusual pattern that the excavators reported as a possible "calendar" (Garrard et al. 1994:92).

The pebble contains an unusual structure (Fig. 22a, b). Ten long strokes were incised from edge to edge, the stone was then turned 90° and four

Figure 22a. Intentionally shaped, polished, and incised limestone plaque from the Pre-Pottery Neolithic (PPNB) site of Jilat 7 in the subdesert region of Jordan, c. 7500-7200 BC uncalibrated.

Figure 22b. Schematic rendition of the structure, differences in the length and positioning of the incised marks and sets on the Jilat 7 pebble. Stroke number 15 apparently marks the stressed midpoint in the composition. Parts of three of the four strokes indicated at bottom left have their remnants present. A fifth may or may not have been present.

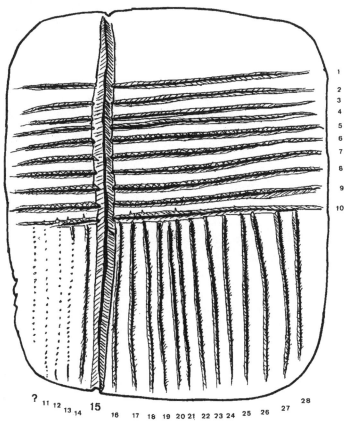

A. MARSHACK

small strokes were appended at left to the last stroke of the ten, and a very long fifteenth stroke was then incised over the original ten strokes. The fifteenth stroke seemed to be negating or summing the original ten. There followed thirteen small strokes, also appended to the last stroke of the original ten. The major visual element in this accumulation was the very long "15th" stroke extending vertically from one edge of the stone to the other.

In many early calendar structures, and in historic calendars derived from these early roots, the waxing period from birth of the first crescent to the period of the full moon represented the favorable portion of each month. The fifteenth day often was ritually observed as the culmination of the favorable waxing period; it represented the mythic period of full maturity. The following waning period from full moon to last crescent and invisibility was often considered to be unfavorable. This mythic structure for the month was observed throughout the year, but with variations: there were particular months that contained their own rituals and ceremonies, while the seasons had their own rituals and mythological nights and days of varying length. While the sequence of seasons could be read observationally, the structure of the lunar month, and its particular ritual and cultural/mythic significance at different times of the year, had to be learned and monitored.

In light of our knowledge of early lunar calendrics, it may be that the Jilat 7 pebble represented a generic model or template of the *cultural* month, perhaps used by a calendar keeper in conjunction with a seasonal calendar.[2] Such a lunar model could have been of use throughout the ritual year. The model or template could have been used by dispersed kinship groups to coordinate rituals and interchange. It also could have been used to mediate intergroup relations conducted over a large common calendrical cultural territory.

These analyses and suggestions for early modes of time-factoring indicate a long preparation preceding the explosive development of regional observational and record-keeping calendars and astronomies among the urban cultures that developed in the Near East and Egypt. The complex astrological/mythic observations and arithmetical computations that developed in these urban centers seem to represent late, regional developments of the traditions that were in use earlier (cf. Rochberg 1996).

Conclusion

If the scenario proposed in this paper is valid, earlier theories and models that attempted to explain the rise of agriculture in the essentially material and materialistic terms of regional resources, changes in climate and demography, technology, and modes of harvesting and storage, or in terms of the self-domestication of plants and cereals through periodic harvesting, may now also have to consider the long and incremental cognitive and conceptual preparation that made these other processes viable. There is no early agricultural civilization or culture that has not left evidence of a corollary development of an observational calendar and, often, evidence of some level of observational or record-keeping astronomy.

These cognitive and conceptual processes underlay and abetted the development of most archaic urban centers. This cognitive and conceptual calendrical preparation also appears to have played a role in the rapid dissemination of farming technologies and schedules in Europe. It is likely that comparable, though regionally different, cognitive and conceptual preparations were present in the development of regional agricultures around the world during the Holocene.

The development of urbanization among many of the world's agricultural societies derives from the human capacity to organize and maintain increasingly complex processes of production, relations, and concepts in time and space. The preagricultural hunting-gathering cultures of the late Pleistocene in Europe and the Near East, though they had adapted to different ecologies and climates, all developed "time-factored" concepts and technologies that, in the Near East, contributed to the inception and spread of agriculture in the Holocene that followed.

In both Europe and the Levant, the need to map and exploit periodically varying seasonal territories and ecologies and the need for seasonal aggregation among the dispersed, mobile hunting-gathering groups led to the development of common conceptual frames and, according to the archeological record, forms of "notation" or record-keeping. When the Pleistocene ended, these preparatory processes in the Near East abetted the rise and spread of agriculture and the subsequent development of settlements, early villages, then towns, and finally urban centers.

Wild seed gathering and forms of sedentism had begun in the Levant within the period of the proto-Magdalenian in France (c. 19,000 BP). In Europe forms of sedentism began to increase during the Magdalenian. In the Levant the increase in sedentism led to settlements with stone habitation structures and storage pits as early as the preagricultural Natufian at Jericho and Eynan/Mallaha. With the initiation of farming, true sedentary villages developed at locations near arable land and water. These settlements developed increasingly specialized, highly seasonal forms of production, aggregation, ritual, trade, and exchange. These early villages often also contained cult and ritual areas. By the time of the pre-pottery and early pottery Neolithic, particular settlements would become increasingly "urbanized."

When cultural calendar frames collapsed in these early formative periods for material reasons such as a change in climate or a significant depletion of resources, the cultures often disintegrated and populations were forced to develop new calendar frames to structure and maintain their new adaptations. Often aspects of old calendric lore were retained as a subset within these new, developing time-and-space tapestries.

The study of "urbanization" as an aspect of the human capacity for structuring processes, relations, and concepts in time and space and as the outcome of a long, often complex preparation with significant historical and regional variation is, of course, continuing.

Notes

Special thanks go to Lynn Yost for her update of the map art for this article.

1. Suggestions for year-round sedentary occupation at Hayonim also come from the frequency of juvenile gazelles found on Hayonim terrace (Davis 1983). Based on a study of the tooth cementum of gazelles killed and hunted during the Natufian at Hayonim, Lieberman (1991, 1993a, b) reports that the animals were killed during two periods of the year, between November and March (encompassing the period of the winter rains) and between April and October (encompassing the main period after the wild cereal harvests). Lieberman concludes that "the Natufians were either using Hayonim at least twice a year, or they may have permanently settled at the site." These findings, and those for domesticated commensals, tallies with the present analytical findings for notation on the Hayonim terrace and for long-term notations in the Hayonim cave interior.

2. The conceptual lunar model incised on the Jilat 7 pebble is similar to lunar structures or frames present among nomadic peoples of the Biblical period in this region. It is a conceptual model also present among Near Eastern derivative calendars that exist in modern times. This does not mean that all such lunar frames derive from the Jilat 7 model, but rather that the Jilat 7 structure may represent a widely shared early observational template used by different groups. Such a model or frame would be used differently at different times and seasons of the year by different groups speaking different languages or dialects, and it would have been used differently by groups at different levels of economic and social development. The Jilat 7 lunar model seems to represent one of the shared observational "equations" or templates of that region. It is a simple mythologized, observational frame. The observational, computational and astrological/mythic complexity that developed later among urban centers in the Near East and in Egypt, profusely documented in temple and palace records, probably has roots in such structures (cf. Parker 1950, 1957; Rochberg 1996). All Jilat 7 dates are C_{14} uncallibrated.

BIBLIOGRAPHY

Bachechi, L., P-F. Fabri, and F. Mallegni (1997), "An Arrow-caused Lesion in a Late Upper Palaeolithic Human Pelvis," *CA* 38(1):135-140.

Belfer-Cohen, A. (1991), "Art Items from Layer B, Hayonim Cave: A Case Study of Art in a Natufian Context," in *The Natufian Culture in the Levant*, ed. by O. Bar-Yosef and F. R. Valla (International Monographs in Prehistory, Ann Arbor):569-588.

Belfer-Cohen, A., and O. Bar-Yosef (1981), "The Aurignacian at Hayonim," *Paléorient* 7(2):19-42.

Chauvet, J.-M., and C. Hillaire (1995), *Chauvet Cave. The Discovery of the World's Oldest Paintings* (Thames & Hudson, London). US ed: *Dawn of Art. The Chauvet Cave: The Oldest Known Paintings in the World* (Abrams, New York).

Clottes, J., and J. Courtin (1994), *La Grotte Cosquer: Peintures et Gravures de la Caverne Engloutie* (Seuil, Paris).

Davis, S. J. M. (1983), "The Age Profile of Gazelles Predated by Ancient Man in Israel: Possible Evidence for a Shift from Seasonality to Sedentism in the Natufian," *Paléorient* 9:55-62.

Delluc, B., and G. Delluc (1989), "Le sang, la souffrance et la mort dans l'art Paléolithique," *L'Anthropologie* 93(2):389-406.

Gamble, C. G. (1986), *The Palaeolithic Settlement of Europe* (Cambridge University Press, Cambridge and New York).

Garrard, A., D. Baird, S. Colledge, L. Martin, and K. Wright (1994), "Prehistoric Environment and Settlement in the Azraq Basin: An Interim Report on the 1987 and 1988 Excavation Seasons," *Levant* 26:73.

Hovers, E. (1990), "Art in the Levantine Epi-Palaeolithic: An engraved Pebble from a Kebaran site in the Lower Jordan Valley," *CA* 31(3):317-322.

Jochim, M. (1987), "Late Pleistocene Refugia in Europe," in *The Pleistocene Old World: Regional Perspectives*, ed. by O. Soffer (Plenum Press, New York and London):317-331.

Kozlowski, J. K., and S. K. Kozlowski (1979), *Upper Palaeolithic and Mesolithic in Europe* (Polska Akademia Nauk, Wroclaw).

Leroi-Gourhan, A. (1967). *Treasures of Prehistoric Art* (Harry N. Abrams, New York):60.

Lieberman, D. (1993a), "The Rise and Fall of Seasonal Mobility Among Hunter-gatherers," *CA* 14(5):599-631.

— (1993b), "Variability in Hunter-Gatherer Seasonal Mobility in Southern Levant: From the Mousterian to the Natufian," in *Hunting and Animal Exploitation in the Later Palaeolithic and Mesolithic of Eurasia*, ed. by G. L. Peterkin, H. M. Bricker, P. Mellars:207-218.

Lieberman, D. E. (1991), "Seasonality and Gazelle Hunting at Hayonim Cave: New Evidence for 'Sedentism' During the Natufian," *Paléorient* 17(1):47-57.

Marshack, A. (1969), "New Techniques in the Analysis and Interpretation of Mesolithic Notation and Symbolic Art," in *Valcamonica Symposium, Actes du Symposium International d'Art Préhistorique*, 1968 (Capo di Ponte):479-494.

— (1970), "Le baton de commandement de Montgaudier (Charente): Réexamen au microscope et interprétation nouvelle," *L'Anthropologie* 74(5-6):321-352.

— (1972), *The Roots of Civilization* (McGraw Hill, New York).

— (1975), "Exploring the Mind of Ice Age Man," *National Geographic* 147(1):62-89.

— (1976), "Aspects of Style Versus Usage in the Analysis and Interpretation of Upper Paleolithic Images," in *Prétirage, Les Courants Stylistiques Dans l'Art Mobilier au Paléolithique Supérieur*, Colloque XIV, IX Congrés UISPP (Nice):118-146.

— (1977), "The Meander as a System: The Analysis and Recognition of Iconographic Units in Upper Paleolithic Compositions," in *Form in Indigenous Art: Schematization in the Art of Aboriginal Australia and Prehistoric Europe*, ed. by P. Ucko (Humanities Press, London; Duckworth, New Jersey):286-317.

— (1979), "Upper Paleolithic Symbol Systems of the Russian Plain: Cognitive and Comparative Analysis of Complex Ritual Marking," *CA* 20(2):271-311. Also discussion and reply to Boroneant and Frolov, *CA* 20(3):604-608.

— (1983), "European Upper Paleolithic-Mesolithic Symbolic Continuity: A Cognitive-comparative Study of Ritual Marking," in *Valcamonica Symposium III: Les Expressions Intellectuelles de l'Homme Préhistorique*. 1979. (Capo di Ponte):111-119.

— (1985) *Hierarchical Evolution of the Human Capacity: The Paleolithic Evidence*. Fifty-fourth James Arthur Lecture on "The Evolution of the Human Brain," 1984 (American Museum of Natural History, New York).

— (1990), "L'evolution et la transformation du décor du debut de l'Aurignacien au Magdalénien Final," in *L'Art des Objets au Paleolithique: Tome 2: Les voies de la recherche*, ed. by J.Clottes (Picard, Paris).

— (1991a), "A Reply to Davidson on Mania: Symbolic activity before the Upper Palaeolithic," *Rock Art Research* 8(1):47-58.

— (1991b), *The Roots of Civilization*. Second edition (Moyer Bell Ltd., Mt. Kisco, New York).

— (1991c), "The Taï Plaque and Calendrical Notation in the Upper Palaeolithic," *CAJ* 1(1):25-61.

— (1995a), "Images of The Ice Age," *Archaeology* 40(4):28-39.

— (1995b), Report in Otte, M., I. Yalçinkaya, *et al.* "The Epi-Palaeolithic of Öküzini cave (SW Anatolia) and its Mobiliary Art," *Antiquity* 69(266):931-944.

— (1995c), "Variabilité de catégorie dans l'imagerie symbolique d'Öküzini et de Karain (Turquie)," *L'Anthropologie* 100(4):586-594.

— (1996), "A Middle Paleolithic Symbolic Composition from the Golan Heights: The Earliest Known Depictive Image," *CA* 37(2):357-365.

— (1997), "Paleolithic Image-making and Symboling in Europe and the Middle East: A Comparative Study," in *Beyond Art: Pleistocene Image and Symbol*, ed. by M. W. Conkey, *et al.*, Memoires of the California Academy of Sciences (San Francisco):53-91

Moore, A. M. T. (1991), "Abu Hureyra and the Antecedents of Agriculture on the Middle Euphrates," in *The Natufian Culture in the Levant*, ed. by O. Bar-Yosef and F. R. Valla:277-314.

Nadel, D. (1990), "Ohalo II — A Preliminary Report. *Mitekufat Haeven*," *Journal of the Israel Prehistoric Society* 23:48-59.

— (1991), "Ohalo II — The Third Season," *Journal of The Israel Prehistoric Society* 24:158-163.

Parker, R. A. (1950), *The Calendars of Ancient Egypt*. "Studies in Ancient Oriental Civilization," 26 (The Oriental Institute of Chicago, University of Chicago Press, Chicago).

— (1957) "The Problem of the Month-names. A reply," *Revue d'Égyptologie*, 2:85-107.

Rochberg, F. (1996), "Astronomy and Calendars in Ancient Mesopotamia," in *Civilizations of the Ancient Near East*, ed. by Jack. M. Sasson, III:1925-1940. (Charles Scribner's Sons, New York).

Schmandt-Besserat, D. (1988), "From Accounting to Written Language: The Role of Abstract Counting in the Invention of Writing," in B. A. Rafoth and D. L. Rubin (eds.), *The Social Construction of Written Communication* (Ablex, Norwood, New Jersey):119-130.

— (1991), *Before Writing* (Austin: University of Texas Press).

Soffer, O. (1985), *The Upper Paleolithic of the Central Russian Plain* (Academic Press, Orlando).

—, ed. (1987), *The Pleistocene Old World: Regional Perspectives* (Plenum, New York).

Stordeur, D., and B. Jammous. (1995), "Pierre à rainure à décor animal trouvée dans l'horizon PPNA de Jerf el Ahmar (Syrie)," *Paléorient* 21(1):129-130.

Stordeur, D., B. Jammous, D. Hellmer, and G. Wilcox. (1996), "Jerf el-Ahmar: A New Mureybetian Site (PPNA) on the Middle Euphrates," *Neo-Lithics*, Newsletter of Soutwest Asian Lithics Research:1-2.

Tchernov, E. (1991), "Biological evidence for human sedentism in southwest Asia during the Natufian," in O. Bar-Yosef and F. R. Valla, eds., *The Natufian Culture in the Levant*:315-340.

Tixier, J. (1974), "Poinçon decoré du Paléolithique Superieur à Ksar'Aqil (Liban)," *Paléorient* 2(1):187-192.

2

"Town" and "Country" in Ancient Egypt

Ogden Goelet
New York University

It is unsettling to talk of "town and country" in Egypt when we con-sider the lopsided manner in which that ancient land has been preserved for us. We modern observers are compelled to view Egypt through a set of distorting lenses. Overwhelmingly our data is derived from mortuary and temple contexts in the dry desert environment that preserves evidence so well. Standing near an elite tomb on the desert plateau, we look down upon the Nile Valley, the countryside where the peasantry lived, those largely unknown men and women who supported the economy and yet, because that same river has erased their homes, have left so little of their lives behind. Thus, we see the Egyptian poor through the eyes of the rich and realize that, in a real practical sense, history is written not so much by the victorious as by the literate. We see Egypt, furthermore, predominantly through its South. Memphis, the real administrative capital of the land through much of Egypt's history, is only today beginning to emerge from the shadow of its more brilliant southern rival, Thebes (Fig. 1). In the Delta, the Hyksos capital of Avaris, modern Tel ed-Daba, is coming to light through the excavations of Manfried Bietak, one of the chief historians of Egyptian urbanism.[1] Yet, despite recent advances urban archaeology as a sub-discipline of Egyptology is still in its infancy.[2]

The puzzling nature of Egyptian urbanism — the so-called "town problem"

Many years ago, J. A. Wilson, one of the greatest Egyptologists of his time, could confidently state on the basis of the evidence available to him in 1955 that ancient Egypt was a "civilization without cities."[3] As my colleague D. O'Connor has pointed out, this statement has an element of truth to it, but only if one were to adopt a very limited definition of what constitutes a city.[4] This observation is particularly apt if one

Figure 1. A reconstructed view of Thebes, Egypt's ceremonial capital during the New Kingdom. The linked complex of divine temples — Karnak, Mut, and Luxor — appears at the bottom of the illustration. Across the river on the West bank are the mortuary temples that served the cults of the monarchs buried out of sight in the Valley of the Kings. The palace of Amenophis III with its enormous basin appears in

EDITIONS ERRANCE

the upper left. Communities both large and small have grown up around the quays and harbors attached to these institutions.

Source: S. Aufrère, J.-Cl. Golvin, and j.-Cl. Goyon, *L'Égypte restituée I. Sites et temples de Haute Égypte (1650 av J.-C. – 300 ap. J.-C.)* (Editions Errance, Paris 1991) 82-83.

O. GOELET

should propose a definition based on physical size and population as we do today.

The Egyptians had a wide number of terms for what might be broadly termed a natural or artificially established settlement, a short selection of which appear in the appendix to this article: first, some vocabulary for cities, towns, and villages — *niwt, dmi, wḥyt*; following these I have chosen some terms out of a vast terminology describing various forms of capital or residential cities, palaces, foundations, temples, pyramid cities, etc.: *ḫnw, ḥwt, ḥwt-ꜥꜣ, pr-ꜥꜣ, pr-nswt*, and many others; finally, I have added to this sampling a small number of words that are roughly equivalent to our broadly conceived antonym "country": *sḫt, šꜣ*, and *š*. Had I decided to include more of the Egyptian vocabulary for types of agricultural lands, the list of "country" terms would have grown to several pages in length. Similarly, the terminology for "town" could be considerably increased had I included the large number of words for various kinds of fortresses. In sum, what is presented here is only a sampling intended to convey a hint of the complexity and subtlety of the terminology involved — I make no claim to completeness by any means.

When Alan Gardiner set about to discuss the toponyms in his masterful publication of the Wilbour Papyrus, arguably one the most important economic documents of late Ramesside Egypt, he was faced with a baffling situation:

> . . . The vast majority of place-names in the Wilbour papyrus are unknown elsewhere, and my attempts to discover the corresponding localities by the usual methods have been singularly unsuccessful. One might have expected to find some of them mentioned in the important Cairo Inscription of Shoshenk I recently republished by P. Tresson, this referring to nearly thirty towns and villages in the Heracleopolite nome; in point of fact the inscription and the papyrus have not half a dozen place-names in common. Is this because the names of places were very ephemeral? The collection of Fayyum place-names made by Grenfell and Hunt in *Tebtunis II* has yielded nothing, and study of the modern atlas has proved equally unproductive. Must then the problem be abandoned as hopeless?[5]

When reading this passage, a solution immediately came to my mind, drawn from my interest in lexicography and from my sense of Egyptian law and administration. The Egyptians often classified the world by criteria that were radically different from ours. Their administrative documents appear to indicate that what ultimately concerned the Egyptians was not the size of the settlements involved, but whether or not these towns and village were relevant to the purposes of the document on which they appeared. Indeed, most translators have instinctively realized this and have rendered terms such as *niwt* or *dmi* variously as either "town" or "city," adjusting their translations to fit their concept of size of the place being described. The scribes who made the entries on the Wilbour papyrus had a different purpose at hand than the chancellery scribes who composed Sheshonq I's stela; in neither case was the size (or importance) of the local settlements probably a major consideration. Accordingly, my discussion of the Egyptian city from the Old Kingdom to the late New Kingdom will be focused on function rather than on size.

A somewhat analogous situation arises when one studies Egyptian official titles. Throughout Egyptian history, offices are normally grouped in official titularies according to their function. Offices connected with civil administration, for example, were set apart from those that might be considered religious titles. Yet, in the few administrative documents where we confront the reality of what these offices actually entailed, we find that a common title, such as *ḫnty-š*, often translated as "tenant farmer" or the like, will sometimes involve the performance of a ritual activity one day and an administrative function on the following day.[6]

The "town problem" and the faults of the lexicographers

I think that even the most devoted scholar of ancient Egyptian grammar would admit when pressed that the single greatest impediment towards understanding most Egyptian texts lies not in our imperfect comprehension of their grammar, but rather in our imperfect grasp of Egyptian vocabulary. By now it is a well-worn truism among Egyptologists that the Egyptians were intensely religious, yet had no word corresponding to our term "religion;" that they had a highly developed aesthetic sense, yet had no single word for "art;" that they ran a stable, complex, and highly bureaucratic society, yet had no equivalent to the term "the state." The common theme behind all these observations is that we frequently fail to realize that the Egyptians might have viewed the world entirely differently from the way we do. Even common terms in our language like "town," "city," and even "temple" might not have precise equivalents among the Egyptians, because concepts such as these are often heavily dependent upon social constructions.[7] Looking at Egypt's urban geography from a more functionally oriented viewpoint, it is more likely that a relationship to the Nile, not population size, may have had a greater impact on how the Egyptians categorized their urban settlements.

As far as function goes, the role of the city in Egyptian civilization goes to the heart of Egypt's style of government for most of its history. Ancient Egypt, as B. Trigger and others have pointed out,[8] can be best described as a "territorial state" rather than a "city-state," the pattern of urbanization we are familiar with in early Mesopotamia and Greece. In territorial states, there is a marked tendency towards urban centers with small populations, hierarchically arranged at the local, regional, and national levels. The ruling classes were apt to be concentrated at the great national capitals along with the upper ranks of the administrative elite. Unlike the pattern prevailing in the city-state, the main economic link between "town" and "country" would be the payment of taxes, rents, or other imposts. So great was the role of settlement function in Egyptian urbanization that provincial urban centers tended to be spaced at regular intervals of approximately 40 km, or a day's sail along the Nile.

There are some lexicographical principles that I believe have often been violated when looking at these and other words in Ancient Egyptian texts. First and foremost, there have been too many attempts to arrive at a "one size fits all" explanation of the terms involved. Such an assumption would violate one of the most important of all lexicographical principles, namely that common words seldom have one meaning, but instead acquire a fairly wide range of uses.[9] Another critical rule in lexicography is that words can readily alter their meanings with the passage of time and changing geographic location. In a shorter time span than the one between the beginning of the Eighteenth Dynasty and the end of the Twentieth Dynasty, much of the basic vocabulary on any given page of Shakespeare has changed to the extent that we today can only understand his works with extensive annotation. Among contemporary Egyptologists grammatical studies are increasingly focussed on "register," roughly speaking, the manner in which the language usage is governed by its social contexts. Grammar, to say nothing of vocabulary, can vary considerably between religious and administrative texts. The mutability of language is even more apparent when dealing with economic terms, which were altered to reflect changes in administrative and legal practices from dynasty to dynasty.

Some views of the Egyptian about cities and towns

Textual material is less prominent here than the pictorial evidence. This evidence, putting aside momentarily the question of land ownership,

Figure 2. A market scene from the Dynasty 5 joint tomb of the Royal Manicurists Niankhkhnum and Khnumhotep at Saqqara. Most markets in Egypt were like this, informally arranged. Although there is no indication that this scene was located at the local quay or riverside, New Kingdom equivalents often show boats nearby, tied up at the river bank.

Source: A. M. Moussa and H. Altenmüller, *Das Grab des Nianchchnum und Chnumhotep*. AV 21 (Von Zabern: Mainz am Rhein 1977) Abb. 10.

presents the image of the tomb owner as an agricultural administrator of his estate, sitting at the center of a system of redistribution. Particularly in the Old Kingdom, we almost never see any depictions of what we might consider town life, other than market scenes (Fig. 2).[10] We sense that an Egyptian noble's heart was truly at home in the countryside. When the word *nìwt* appears among the texts of an Old Kingdom official's tomb, it is almost always in connection with the places from which his funerary estate received their income.

Overwhelmingly, the New Kingdom noble, like his Old Kingdom counterpart, had his tomb decorated with paintings depicting life at his country villa, inspecting agricultural work in the fields, and his hunting and fishing *en famillie* in the vast riverine marshes along the Nile. Town scenes, if they occurred at all, depict a workshop or office which the official may have managed. In these representations the urban context is inferred, not explicit; the rest of the town is not shown. It is only in the repertory of tomb decoration at Amarna, a city intended to be a whole new way of life unto itself, that town scenes occur with any frequency.

A feature of Old Kingdom government reveals the fundamentally different role the Egyptians conceived for their cities within their society. R. Stadelmann has convincingly shown that during this period the royal residential city, the 𓏏𓏏 ⌂ *ḫnw*, was not permanently located, but instead moved about so that it almost always was situated near to where the ruling monarch's funerary monument was being constructed.[11] The writing of the term *ḫnw* with ☐ as a determinative during the Old Kingdom may thus be due to the intrinsically institutional and temporary nature of the Old Kingdom royal residential city. By the same token, the later appearance of ⊗, the "city determinative," in *ḫnw* beginning with the Middle Kingdom most likely reflects the fact that the royal residential city was at a fixed location from that moment on. The Old Kingdom association of the pyramid city with the capital city was so strong that in the case of one funerary establishment, *Mn-nfr-Ppii*, the pyramid city of Pepi I, its name later became identical with the Northern capital city, Memphis, itself.[12] This came to pass at a time when Pepi's name had become but a distant memory, while at the same time the area around his pyramid's valley temple had become a major debarcation point and consequently developed into one of the chief administrative centers for the Saqqara necropolis and its environs (compare similar situations at Giza, Fig. 3, and at Abu Ghurab, Fig. 4).

Literary and other evidence is more focused on the political dangers of the cities but, other than the potential of their inhabitants turning against the monarch, the urban areas do not appear to be intrinsically bad places. A model letter of the Middle Kingdom, in fact, apparently makes the opposite point, describing how a man is spending too much

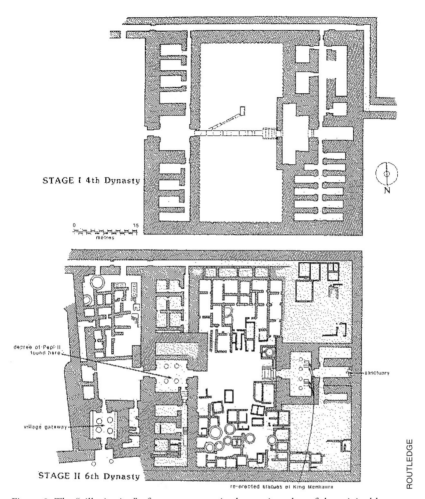

Figure 3. The "villagization" of a monument. At the top is a plan of the original layout for the Valley Temple of the Pyramid complex belonging to King Menkaure (Mycerinus) of Dynasty 4 at Giza. At the bottom is the same place towards the end of Dynasty 6 when the priests added to the building and adopted it for their living quarters. This is an illustration of tendency for the environs near the access areas of temples to develop into small towns with the passage of time.

Source: Kemp, B. J., *Ancient Egypt. Anatomy of a Civilization* (Routledge: London and New York 1989) Fig. 51 on p. 147.

of his time fishing and fowling, leaving his wife to mourn his lengthy absences.[13]

The occasional literary evidence of a negative attitude towards urban life is scanty and reminiscent of the feelings of the British aristocracy that all true values were drawn from land management and ownership. During the Ramesside Period, however, there is a scribal genre of texts praising the beauty and wealth of the capital cities of the land. Perhaps it is significant such literary praise of the city as a desirable dwelling place and a way of life derives primarily from the lower orders of society, namely the scribal class. This genre of text appears in the didactic literature that was created primarily as teaching material for young scribes learning their profession. The *topos* has been given the name "praise or longing for the city" by Miriam Lichtheim, who has noted its connection with propaganda for the pharaoh or a god. For scribes, city life probably offered more opportunities for success than work in the countryside. Also running counter to any distrust of urban life was a notion that although wealth was certainly ultimately land-based, it was equally true that long-term ownership was tenuous and land relatively inexpensive.[15]

The lexicography of nỉwt and dmỉ

Lexicography is that aspect of Egyptology where we probably encounter the best examples of the difficulties of attempting to understand one civilization according to the perceptions of another. In particular, our economic terminology seldom superimposes well on Egyptian culture. For example, it is often tempting to assume that the Egyptians may have made distinctions between "Church," "Crown," and "State," for administrative purposes at the very least. For instance, Gardiner mentioned " . . . obligations between temples, between temple and Crown" in his commentary on a Ramesside administrative document.[16] However, when we are confronted with the evidence from these economic papyri, the boundaries between such institutions seem rather blurred or nonexistent for all practical purposes.[17] Even though at times it may be tempting to adopt a counsel of despair and leave critical terms in transliteration alone, this is neither satisfying nor always practical.

As we have seen above, the two most common words in Egyptian for large-scale urban settlements appear to be *nỉwt* and *dmỉ*, both common words with wide scopes of meaning. A full treatment would be far beyond the scope of this communication and, if I say so myself, deadly dull. Consequently, I will sketch their usage through a few salient examples.

Since the words *nỉwt* and *dmỉ* are found together in a few passages, our immediate impulse would be to see in these examples the ancient Egyptian equivalents of our expressions "city and town" and "city and village" and their equivalents in nearly all European languages. In other

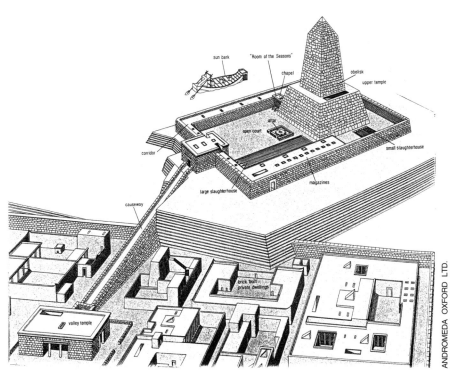

ANDROMEDA OXFORD LTD.

Figure 4. Reconstruction of the sun-sanctuary complex of King Niuserre of Dynasty 5 at Abu Ghurab. Over time a group of dwellings associated with those whose livelihood was connected with this institution has sprung up around the Valley Temple, originally standing at the end of the access canal and its boat basin.

Source: J. Baines and J. Málek, *Atlas of Ancient Egypt* (Facts on File: New York 1980) 154.

words, we would assume that the distinction between *niwt* and *dmi* would likewise be based in their size, as seems to have been the case with the Coptic descendants of these two terms.[18] Although the evidence does indicate that a *dmi* was on the whole a smaller "urban" entity than a *niwt*, this is a misleading distinction. Instead, I hope to show in the discussion to follow that it primarily was their *function* within Egyptian society that really differentiated them.

Let us first examine some of the ways in which the Egyptians used the word *niwt*. Since this is one of the most common terms in the Egyptian language, this discussion will only survey the problems associated with this word, which the Egyptians used in a very complex and constantly changing fashion. *Niwt* often appears in the earliest readable texts in conjunction with the word *ḥwt* a word meaning roughly "estate" or "foundation." Unfortunately space does not allow me to address here the thorny question of the difference between a *nıwt* and a *ḥwt*.[19] The administrative and legal inscriptions where these two words occur in parallel appear to express nuances of incorporation, endowment and exemption that elude us today. Both a *nıwt* and a *ḥwt* could be established by royal command, but a *nıwt* was more apt to exist in its own right, perhaps representing a settlement of great antiquity and often associated with a local temple. Overall, though, *nıwt* was the term with which the local officialdom as well as the priesthood were most often associated. Perhaps the best general translation I have yet seen offered for *nıwt* is the rather broad rendering suggested by Meeks in his *Année Lexicographique, i.e.,* "agglomeration," which conveys well the wide range of human (and divine) habitation types the term can express.[20]

The ideogram used in *nıwt* ⊗, Sign-list O 49 in Gardiner's *Grammar*, supposedly shows a circular, walled urban area with two main streets intersecting at right angles at the center. This presumably represents a simplified and idealized representation of the appearance of the earliest Egyptian cities in plan, and in fact, there may even be some archaeological evidence for cities based on this pattern.[21] In addition to this ideographic usage, the same sign is widely employed as a determinative to following a word to denote that it is toponym or a term for a settlement type. The *ḥwt*-sign ⌷ (Sign-list O 6) and ⬜ the *pr*-sign (Sign-list O 1) are frequently used in place names, both as formative elements as well as determinatives. The term *dmı*, however, exists only as a word with alphabetical elements and has no ideographic writing. The association of ⊗, the "*nıwt*-sign," as this hieroglyph is known among Egyptologists, with toponyms and the concept of settlement is so strong that during the First Intermediate Period and Middle Kingdom some place names have the group ⊗ *nıwt* appended rather than using the *nıwt*-sign alone. In the end run, the presence of the sign came to indicate little more than that the word was a "settled place" or "place name" as shown by its use as the determinative in ⬛ 𓈖 𓂝 ⊗ *Kmt*, the very word for "Egypt." In the case of another common word for Egypt, ⎯ 🝆 𓏤 ⊗ *T3-mry*, "the Beloved Land," two such determinatives occasionally appear during the Ramesside Period.[22] Strikingly enough, the "city sign" does not occur in foreign toponyms with the exception of temple towns in the colonized Nubian territories during the New Kingdom.

In lexicographical studies, the manner in which a word is modified can often be a deciding factor in determining meaning. This is particularly true of *niwt* and *dmi*, both of which have a number of distinctive genitival modifications associated with them. These features are not only distinctive, but critical for understanding their meaning, so my discussion will focus on this aspect of their usage.

The expressions *niwt.i*, "my city," and *sp3t.i*, "my nome," were the two most common geographical identifications that individuals make in biographical inscriptions. A standard passage in Old and Middle Kingdom biographical texts describes the transition from life to death in the following fashion: "I have come from my city (*niwt.i*), I have descended from my nome (*sp3t.i*) . . . " The close relationship between the two concepts "nome" and "city" persisted into later times. The phrase "in your city" eventually became little more than an equivalent of the English expressions "at home" or "in your home town."[23] Analogously, in provincial inscriptions the term *niwt* developed into little more than a synonym for "nome capital" and then, by extension, for the nome itself. In many instances, these small capital "cites" would hardly merit this description according to our criteria of size and population. Interestingly enough, one very rarely encounters equivalents of any of these expressions employing the term *dmi* in these contexts.

The use of *niwt* to mean "capital city" or the "royal residential town" developed out of the intimate association between the pyramid city and the royal residence during the Old Kingdom. At this time, one of the most important positions in the vizier's titulary was ⟨hieroglyphs⟩ *imy-r3 niwt*, "overseer of the (pyramid) city," eventually written simply ⟨hieroglyphs⟩, omitting the pyramid determinative. This usage took on a special significance in the case of Thebes, perhaps the best known of all Egyptian cites. By the Middle Kingdom it came to be called *niwt rst*, "the southern city," and *niwt*, "*The* City" *par excellance*, a usage that survived in NH, a Coptic name of Thebes.[24] In fact, so close was the association of Thebes with the term *niwt*, that it has been suggested that the heretic pharaoh Akhenaten may have even deliberately avoided the use of that word in connection with his new capital city at Akhet-Aten (modern Amarna).[25] In a like manner, but far less frequently, Memphis was referred to as "the Northern City."[26]

Another type of genitival modifier commonly found with *niwt*, but rarely with *dmi*, is an association with an important local deity. In its essence this usage is simply an extension of the association of the word *niwt* with the nome capitals. Accordingly, Thebes became the *niwt 'Imn,* "the city of Amun," or even *niwt 'Imn Mwt Ḫnsw,* "the city of Amun, Mut, and Khonsu,"[27] Dendera was named *niwt Ḥwt-ḥr,* "the city of Hathor," Heliopolis sometimes has the epithet *niwt 'Itm,* "the city of Atum," and so on, for many of the important religious centers of ancient Egypt.[28] In fact, several *niwt* acquired their distinction not because of their size, but due to the importance of their local temple. A similar type of phrase in which *niwt* has a primarily religious connotation is *niwt nt nḥḥ,* "the city of eternity," a common circumlocution for "necropolis."[29]

If this brief exposé of the word *niwt* shows how misleading it would be to render it simply as "city," there are even greater difficulties posed if one wished to associate the term *dmi* with "town" alone. In fact, one could even say that *dmi* provides a classic example of how easily we can be lead amiss by hastily drawing parallels with our linguistic usages. To begin with, unlike *niwt,* the term *dmi* has a rather clear etymology, since it most likely is derived from the verb *dmi,* "to touch, reach." Semantically a *dmi* would be a place at which one "touches," particularly when traveling by boat, always the chief mode of travel in ancient Egypt.[30] In many instances, then, the word *dmi* might be accurately rendered by the words "quay" or even "port," two meanings of this term that have long been recognized by scholars.[31] Having examined a large number of citations of *dmi* in the past few months, I would be prepared to assert that "quay" or "port" are far more often the correct translations than "town." Furthermore, I have noticed among these citations a great number of writings of *dmi* employing either ⵑ the "irrigated land-sign" (Gardiner Sign-list N 23) or the "river bank-sign" ⌐ (Gardiner Sign-list N 21) by themselves or as supplements to the *niwt*-sign. By contrast the term *niwt* is never found with these determinatives. This orthographic peculiarity alone should warn us that, from the ancient Egyptian point of view, a *dmi* was more than just a settlement type.

One of the most striking differences between *dmi* and *niwt* is the way in which the former term shows a predilection for genitival expressions, frequently appearing in front of the names of well-known cities, e.g., *dmi n Mn-nfr,* a place that we will discuss at greater length shortly. Once more, if we were to base our translation on analogies with English, French, or German phraseology, this would be the Egyptian equivalent of "the town of Memphis." However, on closer examination the translation of *dmi (n)* as "the town of . . ." appears suspiciously like an English expression badly dressed in Egyptian clothing. In the present example, we should bear in mind that Memphis was the administrative capital of the country and large enough to be called a city even by modern standards. This observation is borne out by the toponym list on the papyrus known as the Onomasticon of Amenemope,[32] where the term *dmi* leads off a list of place names including Memphis, Heliopolis, Pi-Ramesses, Hermopolis, and Elephantine, all surely "cities" according to our classification. The entry for Thebes that calls it *Niwt W3st nt 'Imn ḫnwt n dmi nb*, "Waset (Thebes), the City of Amun, mistress of every *dmi*," is particularly interesting, since it expresses a hierarchical principle ranking a *niwt* above a *dmi*, while at the same time indicating that *dmi* represented the primary "urban" component of the country. In addition, in this "*dmi*" once more shows its noticeable predilection for genitival or partitive expressions. Although the genitival extensions are also found with the term 𓏏 *w(3)ḥyt*, "village," as well, this is unremarkable, given that it is probably closely related to the word for "clan" and often associated with personal names.[34]

As I have noted above, genitival phrases appear in connection with *niwt*, but in quite a different manner than with *dmi*. *Niwt* only rarely appears as a compound before other toponyms such as city names, even though it is commonly employed before gods' names. This raises such questions as why the Egyptians could have an apparent equivalent of our expression "the city of New York" that consistently employed the word *dmi* but not *niwt*, and why even a temple could have a *dmi*.[35]

The attention paid here to the partitive modification of *niwt* and *dmi* is critical, particularly because *dmi* so frequently occurs in texts as *part* of a city or a temple. This aspect of the word can be readily connected with other themes often associated with a *dmi*, namely, boats and travel. Actually, this is hardly surprising, since nearly all long-distance travel and transport in Egypt was done on water. Nevertheless, a prime example of this association, a *locus classicus*, if you will, occurs in the *Tale of Sinuhe* when at one point in the hero's flight, he says:[36] "At dinner time I reached 'Cattle-Quay' *dmi n G3w (Ng3w ?)*. I crossed in a barge without a rudder, by the force of the westwind" (Sin. B 12-13). The transition between arrival at the *dmi*, here rendered by "quay," and crossing the river by boat could not be clearer. A major theme in Egyptian conceptions of the afterlife was travel into the next world by boat,[37] which gave rise to a metaphorical use of *dmi* as the place in which one "landed" safely in the beyond. A familiar passage from *The Dialogue of a Man with his Ba* has the *ba* describe the next world in the following terms: "Yonder is the place of rest, the heart's goal. The West is a landing place (*dmỉ pw ʾĪmnt*).³⁸ Similarly, boat metaphors abound in *The Tale of the Eloquent Peasant* because the peasant wishes to remind the corrupt officials persecuting him of the final, and presumably unsuccessful, boat journey they must inevitably take to the place of judgment in the next world:³⁹ "When falsehood walks it goes astray. It does not cross in the ferry . . . He who sails with it does not reach land; his boat does not moor at its landing place (*dmỉ*)" (Peas. B2, 98?).

The last passage is particularly instructive since it brings forth another important aspect of the *dmỉ* — its role as a port or dockyard where one could land wares. This feature of a *dmỉ* was especially significant, because within Egypt's redistributive economy the *dmỉ* thus became the natural site for markets both in urban areas and in the kuntryside. Much of what might be considered "private enterprise" was probably conducted at or near the local *dmỉ*, especially if that business involved distant property or institutions. An important group who undoubtedly were often found at the *dmỉ* were the *šwtyw*, perhaps best rendered as "traders" or "agents."⁴⁰ These low-status functionaries performed a complex role in the Egyptian economy which can only be sketched here. The *šwtyw* traveled on cargo boats about Egypt (and occasionally even abroad) engaging, among other things, in the exchange of surplus commodities on behalf of the temples. In all probability they worked for private people or on their own initiative as well. As can well be imagined, the *šwtyw* played a significant part in the development of the slowly developing "private sector." Also related to the function of the "port" (in its form either as *dmỉ* or *mr(y)t*) as both a landing stage and a place of business was an informal mail service wherein people would entrust boat captains or travelling messengers to drop off letters at stopping places along their routes.⁴¹

Lest one gains the impression from the citations above that instances where *dmỉ* is best rendered as "landing place" or "quay" are confined to literary sources, a particularly telling example appears in a passage from a private letter of the early Middle Kingdom in which a man complains:⁴² "Now the boat is moored at your landing place (*ỉmw grt mnỉ(w) r dmỉ.k*), but you only treat me badly in every way." The term clearly has the meaning twice in another business letter of the Middle Kingdom. First an official informs his boss of his arrival:⁴³ "It is a communication to the lord, l.p.h., to the effect that I arrived at the quay of Hutnebes (*dmỉ n Ḥwt-nb.s*), in the fourth month of *Šmw*, day 5, in the morning. I found that my lord had (already) sailed southwards." Shortly thereafter, he remarks:[44] "Thereupon I sent to you the director Henar by a *imw*-boat which I (had) found at the quay (*dmi*) of Hutnebes . . ." In both instances the expression *dmi n* is written ⌐⟨symbols⟩ and would make poor sense as "town of . . .". *Dmi* and the related words *mr(y)t* and *mnit* occur similarly in a number of other letters as the places where people arrive and depart or as the location for depositing or shipping various goods. A more thorough lexicographical study of these usages would add little to our knowledge of such sites and will not be discussed further here.

However, as I indicated above, there is a *dmi* that does merit additional attention, since it apparently was the location of a major deliberative council and, consequently, the site where important legal business was conducted in the Memphite region. I am referring here to *p3 Dmi*, "the Quay," the area in Memphis where so much of the action is set in the great legal inscription of Mose, an official of the reign of Ramesses II. Apparently significant legal cases would be heard there before the vizier and the "Great Council of the Quay," which was composed of the important men and women of the vicinity.[45] Most likely *p3 dmi* (*n*) *Mn-nfr* and *p3 Dmi* (*n*) *Ḥwt-k3-Ptḥ* known from several sources refer to the same place.[46] Presumably the location near the riverside had been adopted for this council's business, since it offered a convenient location for visiting officials, such as the vizier himself, and allowed for speedy dispatch of messengers and other agents.[47] Similarly, the *dmi* at the Delta capital at Pi-Ramesses also served as the place for legal activity or the announcement of royal proclamations, most notably the Hittite Treaty of Year 21 of Ramesses II.[48] The practice of choosing a convenient quayside location for conducting official business, as we shall see shortly below, had a parallel at the southern capital at Thebes where we encounter a place known as *Mrt*, "The Harbor," which was situated on the West bank so that the southern vizier could cross the river to meet conveniently with the local council.

Since access to water at the landing stage or the approach canal with its turning basin for boats was an indispensable part of any temple, it is hardly surprising that outside of the large urban areas a *dmi* was frequently located near a temple (Figs. 5 and 6). Even within cities, a major port was usually located near the local main temple as was the case at Karnak. One of the most massive of all construction projects during the New Kingdom was located at Malkata, the site of Amenophis III's Theban residential palace where an enormous pleasure lake was dug that also

Figure 5. A reconstruction of the East bank of the Nile at Thebes during the New Kingdom, showing the town built up around the Karnak Temple (at top) and the Luxor temple. In the upper left, a crowd of people (hard to see at this size)is shown gathered about the access canal and turning-basin basin harbor (*mrt*) on the occasion

of the Opet Festival. The Luxor temple below has a quay area (*dmi*) along its riverside edge instead. Agricultural lands begin immediately at the outskirts of the town.

Source: S. Aufrère, J.-Cl. Golvin, and j.-Cl. Goyon, *L'Égypte restituée I. Sites et temples de Haute Égypte (1650 av. J.-C. – 300 ap. J.-C.)* (Editions Errance, Paris 1991) 72-73.

O. GOELET

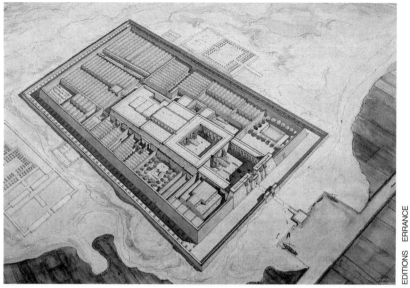

Figure 6. Reconstruction of the Ramesseum, the mortuary temple of Ramesses II ("the Great") at West Thebes. The lighter section of the complex is the temple itself. Within the enclosure walls of the temple is a vast complex of administrative buildings, and, significantly, many storerooms in which income in the form of grain and other produce were kept. At the front is the turning basin / harbor and ceremonial quay.

Source: S. Aufrère, J.-Cl. Golvin, and j.-Cl. Goyon, *L'Égypte restituée I. Sites et temples de Haute Égypte (1650 av. J.-C. – 300 ap. J.-C.)* (Editions Errance, Paris 1991) 72-73.

served as its port.[49] It is important to note at this point that although I have been discussing the term *dmỉ*, there were a few other less common words such as *mnỉw(t)*, "mooring place/post,"[50] and *mrt/mryt*, "quay, port,"[51] which signified essentially the same type of place and appear to have been used interchangeably.

Whichever term was employed, these riverside or canal-side areas near temples were the ideal places for kings to announce decrees on behalf of a god or foreign campaigns that would be conducted under the deity's aegis.[52] Since many of Egypt's temples were located in what could be considered the countryside by any standards, we can see that a *dmỉ* need not have had any real "urban" associations at its founding, yet often a permanent town or village eventually grew up around these temple quays or ports, and as mentioned above, they were the ideal locations for informal markets.[53] Excavations around the valley temples of Old King-

EDITIONS ERRANCE

Figure 7. A reconstruction of the walled village of Deir el-Medina, known as *P3-dmî*, "the *Dmî*," or *St-m3ᶜt*, "The Place of Truth." This village was atypical in that its inhabitants were government-supported workers who constructed the top-secret royal tombs; there was probably an unusually high literacy rate among these elite workers.

Source: S. Aufrère, J.-Cl. Golvin, and j.-Cl. Goyon, *L'Égypte restituée I. Sites et temples de Haute Égypte (1650 av. J.-C. – 300 ap. J.-C.)* (Editions Errance, Paris 1991) 72-73.

dom pyramid complexes have revealed settlements inside this type of riverine access building or directly adjacent.[54] A recent and most striking reconstruction of Niuserre's sun-sanctuary at Abu Gurab, shows how a small village of administrative buildings and private dwellings sprang up around the valley temple of that complex (Fig. 4).[55]

Having detailed the many instances where *dmî* primarily meant "quay" or "port," it is only fair to point out that there are also some very important instances where it does in fact mean "town" or "settlement." This usage, interestingly enough, is especially common in connection with foreign towns, which were frequently designated as *dmî*, although sometimes they were inland, far from the ocean or a river. Any New Kingdom royal inscription describing a military campaign abroad mentioned one or more such *dmî*, the most famous being Megiddo and Kadesh.

O. GOELET   85

This puzzling turn of phrase has been explained by D. Valbelle as instances when *dmi* refers to a type of walled fortress city or town.[56] Perhaps the presence of an enclosure wall is the reason why the distinctly land-locked and sequestered village of Deir el-Medina should have been called *p3 Dmi*, "the *Dmi*," by the royal necropolis workmen in their records (Fig. 7).[57] By the same token, these men seemed to have called the riverside quay on the West bank of Thebes *Mrt*, "*The* Port," perhaps in order to avoid confusion with their home village. In this case, since the word nearly always appears without the definite article, the word had become a place-name, pure and simple, reminiscent of La Havre.[58] Significantly, like *p3 dmi* at Memphis, this riverside area apparently was where both state and private legal business seems to have been conducted on the western side of Thebes. A somewhat ambiguous example of *p3 dmi* as either "quay" or "fortified city" occurs in an epithet occasionally applied to Ramesses II's great temple at Abu Simbel.[59]

Finally, we ought to discuss a few instances in which the word *dmi* appears in lists or in parallels with the terms *niwt* and *w(3)hyt*, "village," since such citations probably have contributed much to the perception that size is the differentiating principle underlying these words. The clearest example occurs in an inscription of Sheshonq I on behalf of the Arsaphes temple, which was to be supplied by various sites in the Herakleopolitan nome, namely (line 9) . . . *n3w niwwt dmiw whyw n Nni-nsw,* "the *niwt*s, the *dmi*s and the *why*ts of Herakleopolis."[60] Although the intent is clearly to move from the larger to the smaller units, there is nothing else in this quote which would require that *dmi* be translated as "town." As our discussion above has shown, "quay" would be an equally satisfying and logical rendering. Strikingly enough, in the main body of the text where the actual places supplying the animals are listed, the term *dmi* (sometimes written *dmit*) overwhelming predominates, preceding many of the toponyms. Often these toponyms, including the word *w(3)hyt*, are also accompanied by the definite article, an arrangement which strongly suggests that "quay" is the best rendering, *e.g., dmi t3 w(3)hyt Knit,* "the quay (of) the Village of Kenit." The other examples in which *niwt, dmi,* and *w(3)hyt* are grouped together merely list these words in that order.[61]

My discussion thus far is not intended just to make a few minor lexicographical distinctions. Once it becomes clear that *dmi* primarily meant "quay," and only secondarily "town," this observation leads to some important consequences for our view of Egyptian urbanism and the Egyptian economy as well. The term *dmi* and the closely related words *mryt* and *mnit* should be viewed functionally, not by size. These were the market and meeting places, usually located at the periphery of a city, where much of the land's business was conducted. Nevertheless, since a quay or a harbor would most likely be smaller than the village or city in which it was situated, there was some intuitive truth to the notion that a *dmỉ* would rank below a *nỉwt* in several respects.

The Nile as the main organizational principle in Egypt's economy

Since my talk is entitled "Town and Country," I will turn my attention now to the "country." Egyptian texts in which these two domains are contrasted are rather uncommon, the most striking example coming from a legal text in which a man divides his property into two categories:[62] *ḫt.i nbt m š3 m nỉwt n sn.ỉ 'Iḥy-snb,* "All my property (both) in the country and in the city (shall belong) to my brother, Iḥy-snb." Nevertheless, as I have stressed at several points in my lexicographical discussion above, I feel that from the countryside's point of view, more often than not it was the *dmỉ* rather than a *nỉwt* that represented the urban component of our modern conceptual pair "town and country." It was primarily the *dmỉ* with which the countryside normally interacted on an administrative and economic level, as the stela of Sheshonq I[63] and the Golenishef Onomasticon[64] so pointedly indicate. Strangely enough for an agricultural economy such as Egypt, the vocabulary comprising the various elements of the "country" in its broadest sense — , var. *sḫt,* *š3,* and sometimes simply *š* — was far less rich than its vocabulary for settlement types or even waterways. The unifying concept among these three terms for "country" is the word "field" in one form or the other. The determinatives and ideograms with which these terms were written convey that these areas were watery, even marshy, most likely conforming to our concept of a paddy. The limited number of general terms roughly corresponding to "country" is unsurprising because within the context of Egypt's overall landscape, the countryside, as the Nile Valley itself, was rather simple, consisting mainly of different types of agricultural lands crisscrossed by canals and waterways. What was not a field or a waterway tended to be a settlement on a mound or unused marshland. The degree of access to water, whether in the form of the inundation or irrigation, was generally the chief factor in determining the value of property. By contrast, the agricultural, legal, and economic classification of fields, was extensive and incredibly sophisticated.[65]

Merely to list the vocabulary connected with agricultural land would consume a considerable amount of time. Again, the intricacy of this terminology is hardly surprising. When it came to the practical matters of payments, endowments, taxation, etc., one should expect to find that, in an unmonetized economy like Egypt, the underlying realities were the grain and livestock being produced in the fields and the methods by which that produced was harvested, processed, then moved about within the agricultural system. In a territorial state such as ancient Egypt, most economic activity was of a highly regional nature, but when the more localized economy had to function within the national, redistributive economy, the temples and their vast network of subsidiary units came to the fore. As pointed out above, these institutions, which almost always were furnished with an access to the Nile or to a major canal, were the logical focal points for the interaction between "town" and "country." The local temple *dmi* or its equivalent naturally acquired a central role in Egypt's economic framework.

Some theoretical background for a new approach to the organization of Egypt

From the point of view of how the economy actually functioned, then, urbanism does not seem to be as important as the role of the temple. Even within the settled areas, the dock or quayside were the primary areas for economic activity. If anything, the town almost appears parasitic in this arrangement. With these concepts in mind, let us look at the administration of Egypt from the point of view of the temple, then the town, and finally at the countryside.

The elusive Egyptian state — the terminological problems. The reason we do so, again, lies in another terminological problem that I have already mentioned. The Egyptians had no one word that corresponds to our concept of "the state." An Egyptian king might rightly say *"L'État c'est moi,"* but, in doing so, he would be expressing a theoretical truth, not an operating principle.

Nswt "king" may appear in many titles, but, surprisingly, not many institutions use this term alone. The use of a king's specific name, however, is a very common practice in institutional names. No matter how it may have been expressed, the king's interaction with the economy was, on the whole, through various institutions that in modern terms would be called "the state" or "the palace." There are several institutions that could possibly fit this description — *pr-ꜥ3, pr-nswt, ẖnw* — all of which were not so much forms of settlement or habitation as they are adminis-

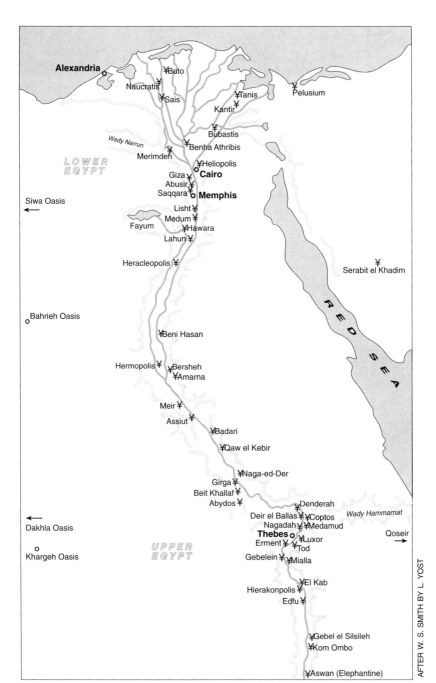

Map of the chief archaeological sites of ancient Egypt, with major classical and modern cities included. In Upper Egypt in particular, the main sites are fairly evenly dispersed, generally spaced about a half or full day's sail apart from each other.

Source: W. S. Smith, *The Art and Architecture of Ancient Egypt* (Penguin Books; Harmonsworth and Baltimore 1958) p. xxvi.

O. GOELET

89

trative units. Yet, as far as the question of which of these might best be the equivalent of "the state," none seems quite adequate. I shall not discuss the complex and elusive terminology of "state" in ancient Egypt further, except to say that in the actual administrative documents that we possess, the lines between these institutions always seem quite blurred.

The metaphors of the elusive Egyptian state and its structure. We can, however, continue with two interrelated observations: (1) the Egyptians were great administrators, and (2) at all times the Egyptians seem to have had a rather flexible organization of their state apparatus. Unfortunately, this latter fact is seldom apparent in tables of governmental organization one encounters, particularly in general histories of Egypt. These charts often suppose an underlying legalism, a constitutionalism, if you would, that was not present in actuality. Nevertheless, the lack of a firm method of organization and of operating within it is emphatically not a reflection of the Egyptians' mental laxity, but rather shows their practical flexibility in adopting viable ad hoc solutions. By contrast, it is virtually a truism in the history of governmental administrations that highly bureaucratized regimes become increasingly rigid, with a sclerosis eventually permeating the entire body politic.

Spalinger has done us the service of pointing out the essential stability of terminology and concerns among royal decrees of all periods.[66] It is important to remember, however, that although the vocabulary may have remained relatively consistent, the meanings of the words and the underlying procedures varied considerably over the course of time.

All discussions of government in ancient Egypt begin with the role of the king. The power of the temple in this government is the natural outgrowth of the principle that the king is the owner of all the land in Egypt. A common scene in New Kingdom temples shows the pharaoh offering a small figure of the goddess *Maat* to the gods, indicating he has been an effective custodian of the rightful order which the gods had entrusted him. On a metaphorical level, this ritual symbolizes what might be called the redistributive economy of *Maat*, which placed all Egyptians under an obligation to maintain the land in an equitable balance.

We can see a similar theoretical arrangement underlying the relationship between the gods, the king, his subjects, and the land. During the *Heb-Sed* ceremony, one of the high points of the entire festival was when the king ran between special boundary markers with the *imyt-pr* instrument in his hand. This ceremony, called "the donation of the field," symbolized the monarch's assumption of legal title over the Two Lands and was an important part of his ceremonial revitalization as well as his rule (Fig. 8). The great importance of this ritual race is shown by an inventory of a funerary temple of an obscure Fifth Dynasty ruler named Neferefre where many *imyt-pr* instruments were listed.

During the New Kingdom, a related ritual act in which the divine confirmation of royal ownership of Egypt was confirmed occurred when the King offered the symbol of *Maat* to the gods. By this gesture, the king returned the symbol of universal order to the deities who had entrusted him with its maintenance, and thereby, the right to all Egypt's land. A later genre of temple reliefs reminiscent of this presentation of *Maat* depicts the king presenting a symbolic field ⏛⏛⏛ *sḫt* to the gods, a more concrete expression of the ritual in the *Heb-Sed.*[67] The theoretical principle is essentially the same — the king must return parcels of land to the deities who had transferred the land to him. Of course, all the king's subjects realized that this image of the offered field also symbolized the redistributive nature of their economy, theoretically all performed on behalf of the monarch as the gods' chief administrator.

When all is said and done, such scenes express the king's ultimate dependence on the gods. In this respect it is important to note such scenes did not become an obligatory part of the decorative repertory of temples until the Third Intermediate Period, when the royal house was considerably weakened (Fig. 9). Nevertheless, we can trace the reasons behind the appearance of the "Presentation of the Field." As royal power declined in the late Ramesside period and the temples slowly became the effective administrators of Egypt, divine oracles were used increasingly to make legal and governmental decisions. A large percentage of such oracles involved disputes over property rights, most likely because the gods were now considered to be the ultimate owners of the land. The King was merely confirming in ritual what had become political fact — the preeminence of the temples in the economy and the governance of the land.

Legally, the centrality of the redistributive principle seems bolstered by the fact that there really does not seem to be much evidence for a concept of long-term private land ownership in Egypt at any time.[68] Even leases appear to be made on a short-term basis. A tenant or land-owner might have the rights of usufruct, to be sure, but this did not seem to guarantee the right of full alienation. It is interesting to note that the funding or sale of offices is frequently accompanied by the transfer of the right of usufruct and the relevant lands in connection with that function. To the modern observer, needless to say, the distinction between long-term usufruct and long-term land ownership seems to be rather vague.

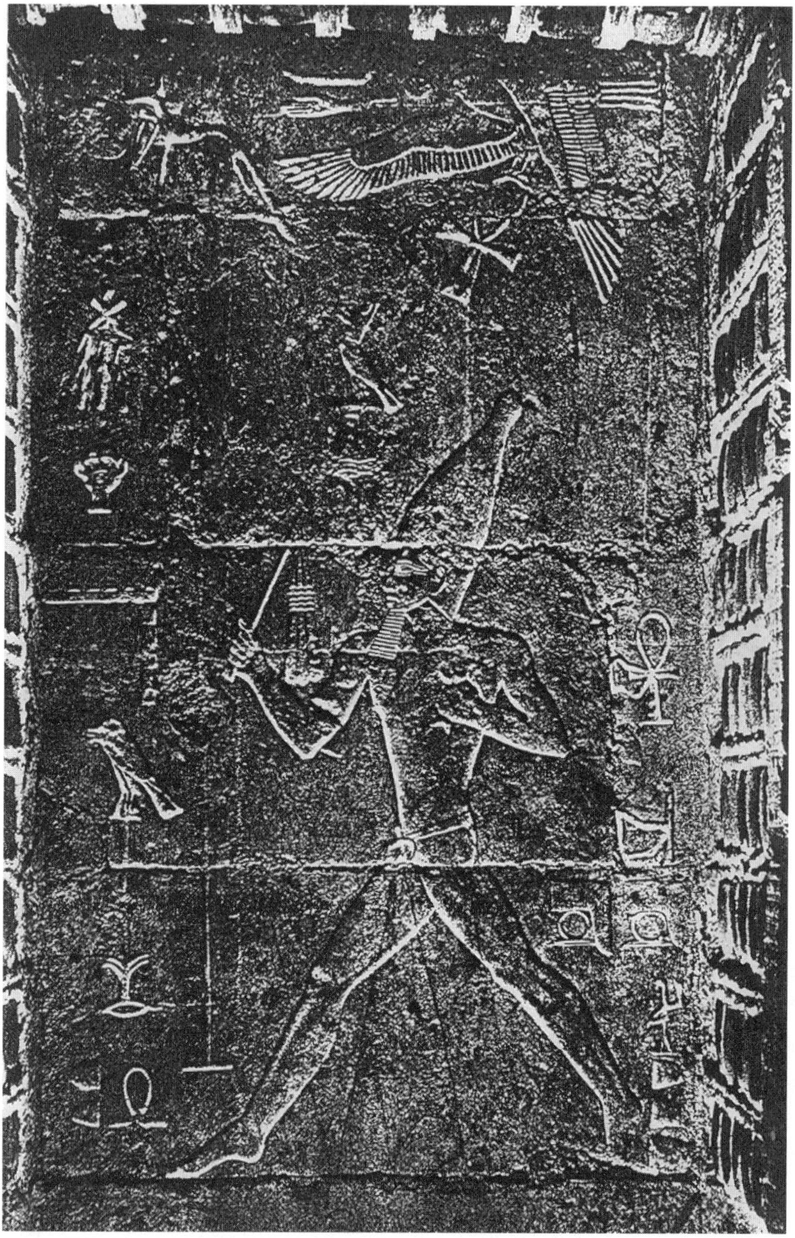

M. HIRMER / HIRMER VERLAG MÜNCHEN

Figure 8. King Djoser of Dynasty 3 performing the ritual race known as the "Donation of the Field." Some scholars have speculated that the unidentified object in his left hand contains the deed to all Egypt. By performing this ritual the monarch would assume theoretical possession of the all the land in the country.

Source: K. Lange and M. Hirmer, *Egypt. Architecture — Sculpture — Painting in Three Thousand Years*, 4th ed., revised and enlarged (Phaidon: London and New York 1968) Pl. 15.

Figure 9. Harnakht, the Great Chief of the Ma, presenting the *sḫt* (field) sign to the gods on a land-donation stela during the reign of King Sheshonq III of Dynasty 22 (Brooklyn Museum 67.118).

Source: K. A. Kitchen, "Two Donation Stelae in the Brooklyn Museum," *JARCE* 8 (1969-1970) Fig. 1.

The redistributive economy was made possible and actually structured in many of its aspects by the river. At the end point of each step of the redistribution system was the granary, be it a large administrative temple or a smaller granary of a high official in his private house. A passage in a Ramesside school miscellany links these elements together rather nicely (Pap. Lansing 8,8 to 9,1):[69] "(8,8) Behold, I am teaching you and making sound your body to enable you to hold the palette freely, to cause you to become (8,9) a trusty one of the king, to cause you to open treasuries and granaries, to cause you to receive (corn) from the ship at the entrance of the granary, (8,10) and to cause you to issue the divine offerings on festal days, attired in (fine) raiment with horses, whilst your bark is on (9,1) the Nile and you are provided with apparitors, moving freely and inspecting. A villa has been built in your city, and behold you hold (9,2) a powerful office, by the king's gift to you."

The Egyptian temple as the organizing institution within the ancient Egyptian economy

It is my conviction that the chief organizing principle of Egypt was the temple, not the city. Here I must emphasize the phrase organizing force, not ruling force. The temple was only occasionally the politically dominant power. In fairness, it should be noted that one reason for viewing the temple as the motivating principle of the Egyptian state is that virtually everything we know about Egyptian financial administration is ultimately connected with or handled through a temple. Of course, this imbalance of data is built into the way that evidence has been preserved in Egypt. Moreover, when kings undertook reorganizations of the nation's financial structure, they frequently used temples as the cornerstones of their projects. Significantly, during the Old Kingdom, a group of "New Cities" was created, it seems, chiefly for the benefit of the royal funerary temples. These new institutions appear to have been first created during the reign of Djedkare Isesi, the penultimate ruler of the Fifth Dynasty.[70] At that time the sun-sanctuaries we associate with this dynasty were no longer being built, a situation that almost certainly required a consequent reorganization of temple endowments throughout the land. The sun sanctuaries, not incidentally, may have actually been temples for the deified king as a sun-god.

At the same time, it seems that the structure of the priesthoods at these institutions were changing. Before the reign of Djedkare Isesi, the upper ranks of the priesthood would style themselves ḥm-nṯr + Pyr. Name "priest of the Pyramid City N," but this was now replaced by titles in the form of *ḥm-nṯr* + KN "priest of King N." The priests of the Old King-dom, it must be noted, were largely part-time temple employees who worked at their nominal institutions only when their phyle was on duty. In exchange for this work, they owned and worked lands held in usu-fruct, occasionally on behalf of several funerary establishments.

The people who worked these lands, in particular those who held the title *ḥnty-š*, perhaps roughly rendered as "one in front of the farming district" or "tenant farmer," in many ways were creatures of the institutions to which they were attached.[71] The *ḥnty-š* was an office that could imply either agricultural land-tenure or ritual functions, depending on what the needs were at a given moment. The Abusir papyri, records of a sun sanctuary and funerary temple founded by a king Neferirkare Kakai of the middle of the Fifth Dynasty, provide a remarkable example of the close association of these part-time temple employees with their deceased benefactor. In these documents, none of which date before the reign of Djedkare, a large proportion of the *ḥnty-š* (41%) were still named after Neferirkare Kakai, long after their patron king had died — and which occurred long before many of them had even been born. It would be interesting to know whether some of the same naming practices pre-vailed among the workers at Ramesside mortuary temple institutions, which were likewise created to maintain the cult of deceased monarchs.

A. Spalinger has pointed out that a constantly reoccurring theme in Egyptian royal decrees of all periods is the need to restrain rather sharply certain aspects of what we might consider the "state," "royal house," and their agents.[72] Out in the provinces especially, the *ḥnw* and the *pr-nswt* seem to be the chief manifestations of this encroaching royal power dur-ing the Old Kingdom, just as they continued to be during the New Kingdom. In the provinces the "state" frequently manifested itself in the form of traveling royal officials working for temples or the *pr-nswt*, liter-ally "king's house." Just as was the case in the decrees of the Old Kingdom more than a millennium previously, the form of encroachments most often proscribed in New Kingdom royal decrees is forcible appropriation of people, who are arbitrarily taken from the lands of one institution and forced to work on behalf of a different organization. I owe to my col-league Dr. Patch the important observation that the same state of affairs prevailed from the Predynastic Period well into the Old Kingdom. Later on, during the New Kingdom and the Ramesside Period, when vast tracks of fertile Nubian lands could readily be apportioned out for temple endow-ments, the chief problem facing these institutions was probably not a shortage of land, but rather a scarcity of the available farm labor. In this light, it is hardly surprising that the Egyptians extensively adopted the Near Eastern practice of deporting large numbers of people captured on campaigns as a means of ending such institutional competition for labor. Late Ramesside administrative documents like the Wilbour Papyrus attest to the high proportion of foreigners working Egyptian lands. These lands were primarily temple lands. One cannot look at the impressive size of temple holding in Papyrus Wilbour and Papayrus Harris I and not see a connection with the eventual decline of the power of the king.

Wright: If they had a need for labor and weren't using women in the fields, there must be some deep-seated ideology about divisions of labor and what women are permitted to do and what men are permitted to do. This is not a feminist question.

Goelet: As far as female agricultural labor goes, it is striking how seldom women (and children) are depicted performing any of the hard labor of plowing, sowing, etc. When engaged in field labor, they perform ancillary functions such as bringing water to the men in the fields and winnowing. This seems to be true not only in art, but in written records as well. Perhaps the Egyptians are presenting us with an idealized view of women's roles, but I doubt it. Another good example of this is the fact that virtually every noble lady of the New Kingdom at Thebes is said to be a songstress of Amun or of one of the other gods. These women are shown as participants in religious festivals shaking the sistrum, singing, and dancing. Yet out of the thousands of statues from the Karnak Temple, only two are of women. One of these has a presumably royal child sitting on her lap, so that she is there really because of that child and not so much by her own right. Thus, we might say that there is a strong decorum governing where and how women are represented. During the same time we have a woman with an extraordinarily important title of Divine Adoratrice, who incidentally was endowed with a considerable amount of land and exercised great political power by virtue of that fact. Nevertheless, one does not encounter this person with this ostensibly religious title appearing anywhere within the Temple of Karnak. Yet when it came to land ownership and similar economic and legal aspects of the land, it was a different matter. In Ramesside administrative documents, one occasionally finds women appearing in control of land. Women, furthermore, could own, dispose of, and alienate land as they pleased, within the normal constraints of the law. Even women not in the upper level of the elite had considerable independence. At Deir el-Medina the men who worked in the royal tombs often would be absent from the village for days on stretch, leaving their wives alone. This, incidentally, might have been one of the reasons for the enclosing walls about the village.

Stone: I want to go into your issue of the landing stage. One of the things we have in Mesopotamia is that they will describe it as the city (even though it may be just a village) and the quay. It is always with that "and." It may be a social distinction, because the closest thing you have to a guild is the guild of merchants. Many of them may be foreigners. So you may have this social distinction between those who deal in commerce and those who are residential. We may be dealing with a physical distinction or a social distinction. I don't think we know the difference at the moment. I was wondering whether there are any of these implications in the ways in which you were looking at landing stages.

Goelet: Not really. An important inscription by a Ramesside official by the name of Mes or Mose describes a long legal battle concerning the misappropriation of some fields in which he had an interest and which had been taken away from him by means of a finagled document. His case is conducted largely at Pa-Demi (the Demi) at Memphis, where the vizier holds his hearings. This was not so much a place in which either the low or elite class settled, it was just the place to which people gravitated, especially if they had to conduct business involving (as so often was the case) property that was at a considerable distance from where they were. The city of Memphis itself seems to have stretched out over a long area. And practically speaking, there was always a need for gathering places near the water. It is significant that the King sometimes proclaimed and began his military expeditions at Pa-Demi.

Buccellati: I was struck by the similarity with Mari on the middle Euphrates, which has a similar geographic location except for one thing that I will mention shortly. Mari's cemetery (Baghouz) is on the cliffs of the steppe. There are other cemeteries on the cliff. The arable area is very narrow. It is much like Egypt, except that instead of desert there is steppe, which allows for grazing of sheep and goats, but not cattle. This grazing developed more and more in the third millennium and provided a new source of income for the population of this narrow river strip. In my view this explains the Amorite expansion. One question about the terminology. Ms. Patch said that "Egypt" refers only to the river bank and the low desert. It seems very analogous to what I consider to be the case in Mesopotamia. In my view, the Mesopotamian term for itself is not Mesopotamia, but the four river banks, the four quarters of the world, meaning the areas that are arable. There is another term, used only at Mari, for the middle of the desert. I think it refers to a strip only about twenty or thirty kilometers wide. (That is the only area the government controlled; beyond that, it did not really have any control.) At Mari there is only the Euphrates — not four river banks, but only two. It therefore is called *ah purattim*, the bank of the Euphrates. (The modern Arabic word is *zor*.) Then there are the *basa'tum*, which are the two strips along the lower desert, and the *nawu*, which is the steppe where there is pasture land.

The *kasum* is the actual desert where there is no pasture. So I was wondering if there were equivalent words in Egyptian, and what they mean.

Goelet: The chief Egyptian term for Egypt was *T3wy* ("Tawy") "the Two Lands," referring to Upper and Lower Egypt. Beginning with the First Intermediate Period, they began developing another frequent term for their country, which eventually became a quasi-official term, appearing in such documents as the Treaty between the Hittite King and Ramesses II. This was *Kmt* ("Kemet") or "the Black Land," a term referring to the black soil near the river, *i.e.,* the Nile Valley itself and its low desert. It appears on the terminology sheets I have supplied written with the "irrigated land sign" that is also found in the first writing of the term *dmi* above. Evidently *Kmt* was normally written with the "city-sign." There were several words meaning "desert," the chief ones being *smit* ("semit") and *dšrt* ("deshret"), literally "the Red Land." In the Harpers' Songs there is a phrase "no man can linger in Egypt (*Kmt*)," meaning that no one can stay forever in the land of the living. Eventually one must come up here, to where the song is written, *i.e.,* the desert, the land of the dead, where people are buried. Thus there developed in these two contrasting words a distinction between the land of the living and the land of the dead that persisted into Coptic times.

Schiffman: What was the temple's physical position in Egypt's urban environment? Is there any sense in which the trdition of the temple in the city affects the manner in which the city might grow around it, and does your answer indicate anything about the temple's role in development *vis-a-vis* someplace where it's on the outskirts, bearing in mind also that ritual sanctification regulations might also be involved?

Goelet: There is a consensus among Egyptologists that one of the core meanings of *niwt* "city" is "temple city/town." Leaving aside for the moment the "chicken-and-egg" problem of whether the civil or the religious function predominated at the beginning, nearly all of the major cities in Egypt had temples as their central features. This was especially true in the Nubian territories that the Egyptians controlled. In addition, we can see confirmation of the process — temple first, then city — in the very name of Memphis on the vocabulary chart: *Mn-nfr-Ppii*. This place drew its name from the name of the mortuary or pyramid temple of the Old Kingdom monarch Pepi I. This town developed in the years long after that king's cult had become virtually defunct. Since the mortuary comples's valley temple was the major economic and administrative center in the neighborhood, and since its causeway offered the best nearby access to the desert plateau locally, a small town grew up around the valley temple where people working in the necropolis and other local officials lived. Whether or not this process of development was followed in all other urban settlements is dubious, but it was probably the case in a good deal of the major cities in Egypt. The question of sacred or sanctified land in Egypt ties into this phenomenon, but we have definitive answers to this in only a few places like Abydos.

Appendix: Selected Egyptian Vocabulary for Cities, Towns, and Other Settlements

The synoptic list below represents a selection, not a compendium of terms; it makes no claims as to completeness. The references given are drawn primarily from the major dictionaries and are likewise not comprehensive.

dmì [hieroglyphs] , [hieroglyphs] , [hieroglyphs] , [hieroglyphs] "landing-stage," "town," "(fortified) town;"[1] and note *dmì n 'Irnn3* [hieroglyphs] "the (fortified) town of Arinna"

nìwt [hieroglyph] , [hieroglyph] OK , [hieroglyph] MK ; "city, town, (capital) city (in Egypt)."[2] Used as a determinative: *3bdw* [hieroglyphs] "Abydos," *Kmt* [hieroglyphs] "Egypt;" but compare foreign cities: *Mktì* [hieroglyphs] "Megiddo," *Ht3* [hieroglyphs] "Hatti"

nìwt [hieroglyphs] , "(pyramid) city";[3] *Mn-nfr-Ppy* [hieroglyphs] , "(the pyramid city) Pepi-endures-and-is-beautiful;"[4] *Mn-nfr* [hieroglyphs] , "Memphis"[5]

w(3)hyt [hieroglyphs] , [hieroglyphs] , "village;"[6] *mrt* [hieroglyphs] , "port"[7]

Urban settlements and other establishments as "houses" or "estates"

hwt [hieroglyph] , "estate," "(established) estate"[8]

hwt-ntr [hieroglyphs] "temple" (lit. "the house/estate of the god");[9] *r3-pr* [hieroglyphs] , "temple, chapel"[10]

hwt-ꜥ3t [hieroglyphs] "the Great Estate," "temple"[11]

O. Goelet

Palaces and residential cities — the king's "house" or "city"

Mn-nfr   [hieroglyphs] "Memphis,"[12] also called *niwt mht* [hieroglyphs] "the Northern City"[13]

W3st   [hieroglyphs] "Thebes,"[14] also called *niwt rst* [hieroglyphs] "the Southern City," and *niwt* [hieroglyphs] "*the* City"[15]

pr-ʿ3   [hieroglyph] OK & MK , [hieroglyph] NK, "palace"[16] (lit. "the Great House/Estate"), later "Pharaoh"

pr-nswt   [hieroglyphs] , [hieroglyphs] , "palace," "royal estate"[17] (lit. "the House/Estate of the King")

hnw   [hieroglyphs] OK, [hieroglyphs] OK, [hieroglyphs] MK , "the Residence," (lit. "the Interior, the Home"), "the royal administrative city";[18] *'Iti-t3wy* "Itj-tawy," [hieroglyph] the Middle Kingdom residential city; later, a cryptic writing for *hnw*.[19]

ʿh   [hieroglyph] , [hieroglyphs] , "the (ceremonial) palace," "shrine";[20] *stp-s3* [hieroglyphs] OK , [hieroglyphs] MK "the (ceremonial) palace," "the palace counsel chamber"[21]

"Country" terminology

sht   [hieroglyphs] , [hieroglyphs] , [hieroglyphs] , "field," "paddy";[22] *shty* [hieroglyphs] "peasant"[23]

š3   [hieroglyphs] , [hieroglyphs] , "field," "meadow," "marsh"[24]

3ḥt   "field, arable land, mound, soil"[25]

i3t   , "mound," "tell," "*kôm*"[26]

š   , , "field," "plot," "pool,"[27] also a component of the common OK title *ḥnty-š*

"Town and country"

ḥt.i nbt m š3 m niwt n sn.i 'Iḥy-snb

"All my property (both) in the country and in the city (shall belong) to my brother, *'Iḥy-snb*"[28]

NOTES ON SELECTED EGYPTIAN VOCABULARY

[1]   *CDME* 313; *DLE* 4, 133; *Wb.* V 455, 5-10.
[2]   *CDME* 125; *DLE* 2, 6; *Wb.* I 346, 12-14.
[3]   *Wb.* II 211, 6.
[4]   *Wb.* II 63, 7.
[5]   *Wb.* II 63, 6.
[6]   *CDME* 66; *DLE* 1, 123; *Wb.* II 210, 6212, 4 (*nwt*).
[7]   *CDME* 112; *DLE* 1, 227; *Wb.* II 109, 12-110, 3.
[8]   *CDME* 165; *DLE* 2, 102-103; *Wb.* III 1, 4-2, 8.
[9]   *CDME* 166; *DLE* 2, 102; *Wb.* III 4, 11-5, 8.
[10]   *CDME* 146; *DLE* 2, 49; *Wb.* II 397, 7-8.
[11]   *CDME* 165; *DLE* 2, 102; *Wb.* III 3, 6-4, 6.
[12]   *CDME* 109; *Wb.* II 63, 7.
[13]   For this and the term in the previous note, see the discussion above, pp. 72 and 77.
[14]   *CDME* 54; *Wb.* I 259, 19-260, 2.
[15]   *Wb.* II 211, 7-8, and see the discussion above, p. 77.
[16]   *CDME* 89; *DLE* 1, 175-176; *Wb.* I 516, 2-517, 1.
[17]   *CDME* 88; *DLE* 1, 174; *Wb.* I 513, 3-5.
[18]   *CDME* 202; *DLE* 205; *Wb.* III 369, 16-370, 14.
[19]   *Wb.* III 369.

[20] *CDME* 46; *DLE* 1, 84-85; *Wb.* I 214, 10-21.

[21] *CDME* 254; *DLE* 3, 116; *Wb.* IV 340, 7-341, 11; but see also, O. Goelet, "The Term *stp-s3* in the Old Kingdom and its Later Development," *JARCE* 23 (1986):85-98.

[22] *CDME* 239; *DLE* 3, 82; *Wb.* IV 229, 8-231, 7.

[23] *CDME* 240; *DLE* 3, 82; *Wb.* IV 231, 15-232, 7.

[24] *CDME* 260; *DLE* 3, 130; *Wb.* IV 399, 7-400, 5.

[25] *CDME* 4; *DLE* 1, 8; *Wb.* I 12, 17-18.

[26] *CDME* 7; *DLE* 13 and 18; *Wb.* IV 26, 9-15.

[27] *CDME* 260; *DLE* 3, 129; *Wb.* IV 397, 1-398, 17.

[28] See the commentary above, p. 87.

NOTES

1. A recent summary of the excavations there can be found in M. Bietak, *Avaris. The Capital of the Hyksos. Recent Excavations at Tell el-Dab'a* (London 1996).

2. For a survey of the state of urban archaeology two decades ago, yet still largely valid today, see M. Bietak, "Urban Archaeology and the 'Town Problem' in Ancient Egypt," in K. R. Weeks, ed., *Egyptology and the Social Sciences* (Cairo 1979):97-144.

3. J. A. Wilson, "Buto and Hierkonpolis in the Geography of Egypt," *JNES* 14 (1955).

4. D. O'Connor, "The geography of settlement in ancient Egypt," in P. J. Ucko, *et al.*, eds., *Man, Settlement and Urbanism* (London 1972):683.

5. A. H. Gardiner, *The Wilbour Papyrus* II (Oxford 1948):36.

6. A. M. Roth, "The Distribution of the Old Kingdom Title ẖntj-š," *BSAK* 4 (1990) 183. In the Ramesside Period the common title rwḏw might similarly have had responsibilities that varied according to the task at hand, see J.-M. Kruchten, "L'évolution de la gestion domaniale sous le Nouvel Empire égyptien," in E. Lipinski, ed., *State and Temple Economy in the Ancient Near East* II. *OLA* 6 (Louvain 1979):522f..

7. G. P. F. van den Boorn, *The Instructions of the Vizier. Civil Administration in the Early New Kingdom* (London and New York 1988):107, henceforth cited here as G. P. F. van den Boorn, *Vizier.*

8. B. Trigger, *Early Civilizations. Ancient Egypt in Context* (Cairo 1993), esp. 1-14

9. O. Goelet, "*W3ḏ-wr* and Lexicographical Method," in U. Luft, ed., *The Intellectual Heritage of Egypt* (Kákosy Fs.). *Studia Aegyptiaca* 14 (Budapest 1992):214.

10. For a discussion of such scenes in Old Kingdom mastabas, see S. I. Hodjash and O. D. Berlev, "A Market-Scene in the Mastaba of *Ḏ3ḏ3-m-ʿnḫ* (*Tp-m-ʿnḫ*)," *AoF* 7 (1980):31-49. The captions accompanying these scenes never state where the activity is taking place, but the quay area of a town is more probable than other alternatives.

11. R. Stadelman, "La ville de pyramide à l'Ancien Empire égyptien," *RdÉ* 33 (1981):67-77; O. Goelet, "The Nature of the Term *pr-ʿ3* during the Old Kingdom," *BES* 10 (1989/90):77-90. This observation does not hold true for the New Kindom, see J. van Djik, "The Development of the Memphite Necropolis in the post-Amarna Period," in A.-P. Zivie, ed., *Memphis et ses nécropoles au Nouvel Empire. Nouvelles données, nouvelles questions* (Paris 1988):39-40.

12. C. M. Zivie, "Memphis," in *LÄ* IV (1982) 24-25.

13. W. C. Hayes, "A Much-Copied Letter of the Early Middle Kingdom," *JNES* 7 (1948) 1-10. This letter is part of the Middle Kingdom instructional book known as the Kemit, see E. Wente, *Letters from Ancient Egypt*. SBL Writings from the Ancient World 1 (Atlanta 1990):15-16, with references. Since some believe that these lines are spoken by a dancing girl, perhaps they are meant ironically.

14. M. Lichtheim, "The Praise of Cities in the Literature of the Egyptian New Kingdom," in S. M. Burstein and L. A. Okin, eds., *Panhellenica. Essays in Ancient History and Historiography in honor of Truesdell S. Brown* (Lawrence 1980):15-23.

15. On this point, see especially K. Baer, "The Low Price of Land in Ancient Egypt," *JARCE* 1 (1962):25-45.

16. A. H. Gardiner, "Ramesside Texts Relating to the Taxation and Transport of Corn," *JEA* 27 (1941):50.

17. This point has been made by several commentators, see E. W. Castle, *JESHO* 35 (1992) :270; J. J. Janssen, "Agrarian Administration in Egypt during the Twentieth Dynasty," *BiOr* 43 (1986):365; idem, "Prolegomena to the Study of Egypt's Economy during the New Kingdom," *SAK* 3 (1975):181-182. A remark in the last-named source stands out especially (181): " . . . it may be that the religious concept of pharaoh as the only high-priest in every sanctuary has had more practical consequences than usually realised."

18. See A. H. Gardiner, *Ancient Egyptian Onomastica* II, 1*, who notes that ⲧⲙⲉ, the Coptic equivalent of *dmỉ*, is used to translate the Greek word κώμη, "village." By virtue of its role as *nỉwt*, "*the* city," the Coptic toponym for Thebes is ⲚⲎ, *ibid.* 25*, but otherwise the word "city" is rendered by ⲡⲟⲗⲓⲥ.

19. See M. Atzler, "Einige Bemerkungen zu 🔲 und ⊗ im Alten Reich," *CdE* 47 (1972):17-44; G. P. F. van den Boorn, *Vizier,* 98-108.

20. See D. Meeks, *Année Lexicographique* I (Paris 1977) 77.2011; II (Paris 1978) 78.1997; III (Paris 1979): 79.1474, which suggest as the primary translations "agglomeration, cité, domaine." The term "agglomeration" recently appears also in connection with *dmỉ*, see A. Gasse, *Données nouvelles administratives et sacerdotales sur l'organisation du domaine d'Amon. BdÉ* 104, 1 (Cairo 1988):105 where the term *dmỉ* is defined as "le 'faubourg riverain' d'une agglo-mération."

21. For a different view, see J. van Lepp, "Is the Hieroglyphic Sign *nỉwt* a Village with Cross-Roads?" *GM* 158 (1997):91-100.

22. *Wb.* V:233ff.

23. H. Goedicke, "The Egyptian Idea of Passing from Life to Death," *Or* 24 (1955):227-229; *Wb.* II 210, 11.

24. A. H. Gardiner, *Ancient Egyptian Onomastica* II (Oxford 1947) 24*-25*; C. Cannuyer, "Akhet-Aton: anti-Thèbes ou sanctuaire du globe? À propos d'une particularité amarnaienne méconnue," *GM* 86 (1985):7-11.

25. W. J. Murnane and C. C. Van Siclen, *The Boundary Stelae of Akhenaten* (London and New York 1993):171 with n. 75; C. Cannuyer, *op. cit.*

26. A number of other places had nicknames meaning "the city." For example both Athribis and Tanis are called *niwt wrt* "Great City," see P. Vernus, *Athribis. BdÉ* 74 (Cairo 1974):425 and *idem*, "Un hymne à Amon, protecteur de Tanis, sur une tablette hiératique (Caire J.E. 87889)," *RdÉ* 31 (1979):108 (j).

27. A. Spalinger, "A new Reference to an Egyptian Campaign of Thuthmose III in Asia," *JNES* 37 (1978):37 (f).

28. *Wb.* II 211:9-13.

29. *Wb.* II 211:17.

30. A. H. Gardiner, *Ancient Egyptian Onomastica* II (Oxford 1947) 1* (313).

31. *Wb.* V 455, 10; B. Gunn, "[Review of] A. H. Gardiner, *Hieratic Papyri in the British Museum: Third Series*," *JEA* 22 (1936):104; R. O. Faulkner, *Concise Dictionary of Middle Egyptian* (Oxford 1962):313; G. Posener, *Littérature et Politique dans l'Égypte de la XIIe dynastie* (Paris 1956) 89, n. 2; W. K. Simpson, *Papyrus Reisner* II. *Accounts of the Dockyard Workshop at This in the Reign of Sesostris I* (Boston 1965):20; H. Goedicke, "The Route of Sinuhe's Flight," *JEA* 43 (1957):79; R. A. Caminos, *Chronicle of Prince Osorkon. AnOr* 37 (Rome 1958):29; E. Wente, *Late Ramesside Letters. SAOC* 33 (Chicago 1967):24.

32. A. H. Gardiner, *Ancient Egyptian Onomastica* II (Oxford 1947) 1* (313) with pl. X.

33. A. H. Gardiner, *op. cit.* II 24* (335f). It would also be possible to interpret *niwt* here as "*The* City," a common name for Thebes in New Kingdom times, see note 18 above.

34. *Wb.* I 258; R. O. Faulkner, *Concise Dictionary of Middle Egyptian* (Oxford 1962):66; L. H. Lesko, *A Dictionary of Late Egyptian* I (Berkeley 1982):123; A. H. Gardiner, *The Wilbour Papyrus* II:33; G. A. Gaballa, *The Memphite Tomb Chapel of Mose* (Warminster 1977):26 (7).

35. For the *dmi* of the Karnak temple, see the Knosso stela of Tuthmosis IV (*Urk.* IV 1545, 7), which mentions a *dmi n 'Ipt-swt*.

36 R. Koch, *Die Erzählung des Sinuhe*. *BiAe* 17 (Brussels 1990); translation M. Lichtheim, *Ancient Egyptian Literature* I (Berkeley 1975):224.

37. Even a brief exposition of this complex metaphor would take us too far afield from our present subject. For studies of important aspects of boat trips in the afterlife, see E. Hornung, *Die Nachtfahrt der Sonne. Eine altägyptische Beschreibung des Jenseits* (Zurich and Munich 1991); H. Willems, *The Coffin of Heqata (Cairo JdE 36418)*. *OLA* 70 (Leiden 1996):156-186; C. Jacq, *Le voyage dans l'autre monde selon l'Égypte ancienne, Épreuves et métamorphoses du mort d'après les Textes des Pyramides et les Textes des Sarcophages* (Le Rocher 1986).

38. Gardiner's translation, "The West is an abode," *Grammar*[3] 104, misses the point. As the preceeding part of the quote shows, the *Ba* wishes to draw a parallel between the words *st nfȝ*, "a place of rest" and *dmỉ*, see H. Goedicke, *The Report about the Dispute of a Man with his Ba. Papyrus Berlin 3024* (Baltimore and London 1970):115, and compare his remarks on the enigmatic phrase *dmỉ n msḥ*, "the shore/landing stage of a crocodile," *ibid.* 154.

A passage in which a *dmỉ* in the next world has similarly been rendered as "abode" occurs in *The Tale of the Eloquent Peasant*, B1:27, see M. Lichtheim, *Ancient Egyptian Literature* I (Berkeley 1975):171: "Don't raise your voice, peasant! Look you are bound for the abode (*dmỉ*) of the Lord of Silence." Of course, the alternate translation "quay" proposed here would also fit this context well.

39 M. Lichtheim, *Literature* I (1975):181.

40. The *šntyw* are a much-discussed aspect of ancient Egyptian economic history. For comprehensive studies of their role, see M. Römer, "Der Handel und die Kaufleute im Alten Ägypten," *SAK* 19 (1992):257-284; E. W. Castle, "Shipping and Trade in Ramesside Egypt," *JESHO* 35 (1992):250-253; W. F. Reineke, "Waren die *šntyw* wirklich Kaufleute?" *AoF* 6 (1979):5-14.

41. E. Wente, *Letters from Ancient Egypt*. SBL Writings from the Ancient World 1 (Atlanta 1990):10, henceforth quoted here as E. Wente, *Letters*.

42. Hekanakhte Letter I, vs. 1-2; translation of K. Baer, "An Eleventh Dynasty Farmer's Letters to his Family," *JAOS* 83 (1963):5; see T. G. H. James, *The Hekanakhte Papers and other Early Middle Kingdom Documents*. Metropolitan Museum of Art Egyptian Expedition Publications 14 (New York 1962):pl. 5. For some metaphorical or idiomatic interpretations of this passage, see H. Goedicke, *Studies in the Hekanakhte Papers* (Baltimore 1984):63.

43. P. Kahun VI.4, l-5 (my translation). F. Ll. Griffith, *The Petrie Papyri. Hieratic Papyri from Kahun and Gurob. Plates* (London 1898):pl. 30, henceforth

quoted here as F. Ll. Griffith, *Papyri from Kahun and Gurob*; E. Wente, *Letters* 80 (99).

44. P. Kahun VI.4, 12-13 (my translation). F. Ll. Griffith, *Papyri from Kahun and Gurob* Pl. 30.

45. On this council and *p3 dmỉ*, see G. A. Gaballa, *The Memphite Tomb-Chapel of Mose* (Warminster 1977):27 (11) and A. H. Gardiner, *The Inscription of Mes*. *UGAÄ* 4, 3 (Leipzig 1905):33-36. Gaballa believes that the word *dmỉ* developed an extended meaning, as *niwt* did, to mean "capital city" as well.

46. On the latter place, see G. P. F. van den Boorn, *Vizier* 99, n. 55.

47. For other citations of the *dmỉ* of Memphis in the early Ramesside period, Gaballa, *loc.cit.* lists *KRI* I 2, 11; 38, 4-5; 41, 13; 46, 5.

48. *KRI* II 226, 4, mentioning the *dmỉ* of Pi-Ramesses; for the *dmỉ* of Thebes, see *KRI* I 41, 4-5; 102, 13 and 15. There was also a *dmỉ* at the Middle Kingdom capital at Itj-tawy, see W. K. Simpson, "Studies in the Twelfth Egyptian Dynasty: I. The Residence at Itj-Towy," *JARCE* 2 (1963):53-54.

49. This port was known as *Maru-Amun*, see D. O'Connor, "Malqata," in *LÄ* III (1980):1173-1177.

50. For this and the related words, see *Wb.* II:72, 12-74, 14; R. O. Faulkner, *Concise Dictionary of Middle Egyptian* (Oxford 1962):107; A. H. Gardiner, *The Wilbour Papyrus* II:18; L. H. Lesko, *A Dictionary of Late Egyptian* I (Berkeley 1982):218.

51. *Wb.* II 109, 12-110, 3; R. O. Faulkner, *Concise Dictionary of Middle Egyptian* (Oxford 1962):112; L. H. Lesko, *A Dictionary of Late Egyptian* I (Berkeley 1982):227.

52. The *dmỉ* of the town or temple was used on two occasions by Sety I to make such a proclamation, see H. W. Fairman and B. Grdseloff, "The Texts of Hatshepsut and Sethos I inside Speos Artemidos," *JEA* 33 (1947):26 (3) with references. R. Caminos, *The Chronicle of Prince Osorkon*. *AnOr* 37 (Rome 1958) 29, however, believes that in the case of genitival modifications, the term *dmỉ* is better rendered as "town."

53. See above p. 81 and B. J. Kemp, *Ancient Egypt. Anatomy of a Civilization* (London and New York):253-255.

54. B. J. Kemp, *Ancient Egypt. Anatomy of a Civilization* (London and New York):144-149; M. Lehner, *The Complete Pyramids. Solving the Ancient Mysteries* (London and New York 1990) 232; G. Goyon, "Les ports des pyramides et le grand canal de Memphis," *RdE* 23 (1973):137-153.

55. J. Baines and J. Málek, *Atlas of Ancient Egypt* (New York 1980):154-155.

56. D. Valbelle, "Précisions apportées par l'iconographie à l'un des emplois du *dmì*," in P. Posener-Kriéger, ed., *Mélanges Gamal Eddin Mokhtar* II. *BdÉ* 97, 2 (Cairo 1985):315-319.

57. There, significantly, the word is normally written with an otiose *t*-ending. For a discussion of the term *dmì* in the context of Deir el-Medina, see D. Valbelle, *"Les ouvriers de la tombe." Deir el-Médineh à l'époque ramesside. BdÉ* 96 (Cairo 1985) 89; R. Ventura, *Living in a City of the Dead. OBO* 69 (Freiburg and Göttingen 1986):154f.

58. J. Černý, *A Community of Workmen at Thebes in the Ramesside Period.* BdÉ 50 (Cairo 1973):94, n. 8, makes the important point that the term *mrt* always appears without the article in the Deir el-Medina material. For two discussions of the location and significance of this place see, R. Ventura, *op.cit.* 79-82 and, differently, A. G. McDowell, *Jurisdiction in the Workmen's Community of Deir el-Medîna.* Egyptologische Uitgaven 5 (Leiden 1990): 223.

59. I. Hein, *Die ramessidische Bautätigkeit in Nubien. GOF* 22 (Wiesbaden 1991) 32.

60. P. Tresson, "L'inscription de Chechanq Ier au Musée du Caire: un frappant exemple d'impôt progressif en matière religieuse," in *Mélanges Maspero* I: *Orient Ancien. MIFAO* 66 (Cairo 1935-1938):821 and 839f.

61. For instance, line 11 of the Great Hymn to the Aten, see M. Sandman, *Texts from the Time of Akhenaten.* BiAe 8 (Brussels 1938):95, 13; Gardiner, *AEO* Plates, pl. 8a, with II 1*.

62. F. Ll. Griffith, *Papyri from Kahun and Gurob* pl. 12, 4; similarly, J. Černý, "The Stela of Merer in Cracow," *JEA* 47 (1961):7, 10: "I cut off all their fields and the mounds *m nìwt m sḫt* in town and in the country."

63. See p. 86 above.

64. See p. 79 above.

65. See, for example, A. H. Gardiner, *The Wilbour Papyrus* II:18-36.

66. A. Spalinger, "Some Revisions of Temple Endowments in the New Kingdom," *JARCE* 28 (1991):21-39.

67. H. Altenmüller, "Feld, Geben des F.," in *LÄ* II (1977):147-150.

68. See B. Menu, "Le régime juridique des terres en Égypte pharaonique. Moyen Empire et Nouvel Empire," *Revue historique de droit français et étranger* (Paris 1971):555-585.

69. R. Caminos, *Late Egyptian Miscellanies.* Brown Egyptological Studies I (Oxford 1954):400.

70. On these foundations, see W. Helck, "Felderverwaltung," in *LÄ* II (1977):152-153; H. Goedicke, *Königliche Dokumente aus dem Alten Reich. ÄA* 14 (Wiesbaden 1967):143-144. These "new cities" are attested as late as the Middle Kingdom in the biographical inscription of Khnumhotep II at Beni Hasan (l. 68), see p. Newberry, *Beni Hasan* I. *ASE* 1 (Oxford 1893):pl. 25.

71. A. M. Roth, "The Distribution of the Old Kingdom Title *ḥnty-š*," *BSAK* 4 (1990):177-186; O. Goelet, "The Nature of the Term *pr-ꜥꜣ* during the Old Kingdom," *BES* 10 (1989/90):77-90.

72. A. Spalinger, "Some Revisions of Temple Endowments in the New Kingdom," *JARCE* 28 (1991):21-39.

BIBLIOGRAPHY

Altenmüller, H. (1977), "Feld, Geben des F.," in *LÄ* II:147-150.

Atzler, M. (1972), "Einige Bemerkungen zu ⬚ und ⊗ im Alten Reich," *CdÉ* 47:17-44.

Aufrère, S., J.-Cl. Golvin, and J.-Cl. Goyon (1991), *L'Égypte restituée* I. *Sites et temples de Haute Égypte (1650 av. J.-C. - 300 ap. J.-C.)* (Paris).

Baer, K. (1963), "An Eleventh Dynasty Farmer's Letters to his Family," *JAOS* 83:1-19.

— (1962), "The Low Price of Land in Ancient Egypt," *JARCE* 1:25-45.

Baines, J., and J. Málek (1980), *Atlas of Ancient Egypt* (New York).

Bietak, M. (1996), *Avaris. The Capital of the Hyksos. Recent Excavations at Tell el-Dab'a* (London).

— (1979), "Urban Archaeology and the 'Town Problem' in Ancient Egypt," in K. R. Weeks, ed., *Egyptology and the Social Sciences* (Cairo):97-144.

van den Boorn, G. P. F. (1988), *The Duties of the Vizier. Civil Administration in the Early New Kingdom* (London and New York).

Caminos, R. A. (1958), *The Chronicle of Prince Osorkon. AnOr* 37 (Rome).

— (1954), *Late-Egyptian Miscellanies.* Brown Egyptological Studies I (Oxford).

Cannuyer, C. (1985), "Akhet-Aton: anti-Thèbes ou sanctuaire du globe? À propos d'une particularité amarnaienne méconnue," *GM* 86:7-11.

Castle, E. W. (1992), "Shipping and Trade in Ramesside Egypt," *JESHO* 35:239-277.

Černý, J. (1973), *A Community of Workmen at Thebes in the Ramesside Period. BdÉ* 50 (Cairo).

— (1961), "The Stela of Merer in Cracow," *JEA* 47:5-9.

Davies, N. M. (1958), *Picture Writing in Ancient Egypt* (London).

Erman, A., and H. Grapow, eds. (1928-1953), *Wörterbuch der ägyptischen Sprache*, 5 vols. (Leipzig and Berlin).

Fairman, H. W., and B. Grdseloff (1947), "Texts of Hatshepsut and Sethos I inside Speos Artemidos," *JEA* 33:12-33.

Faulkner, R. O. (1962), *Concise Dictionary of Middle Egyptian* (Oxford).

Gaballa, G. A. (1977), *The Memphite Tomb-Chapel of Mose* (Warminster).

Gardiner, A. H. (1947), *Ancient Egyptian Onomastica*, two vols., with plates (Oxford).

— (1957), *Egyptian Grammar*, 3rd ed., rev. (Oxford).

— (1905), *The Inscription of Mes. A Contribution to the Study of Egyptian Judicial Procedure. UGAÄ* 4, 3 (Leipzig).

— (1927), "Ramesside Texts Relating to the Taxation and Transport of Corn," *JEA* 27:19-73.

— (1948), *The Wilbour Papyrus*, four vols. (Oxford).

Gasse, A. (1988), *Données nouvelles administratives et sacerdotales sur l'organisation du domaine d'Amon*, two vols. *BdÉ* 104, 1-2 (Cairo).

Goedicke, H. (1955), "The Egyptian Idea of Passing from Life to Death," *Or* 24:225-239.

— (1967), *Königliche Dokumente aus dem Alten Reich. ÄA* 14 (Wiesbaden).

— (1970), *The Report about the Dispute of a Man with his Ba. Papyrus Berlin 3024* (Baltimore and London).

— (1957), "The Route of Sinuhe's Flight," *JEA* 43:77-85.

— (1984), *Studies in the Hekanakhte Papers* (Baltimore).

Goelet, O. (1989/90), "The Nature of the Term *pr-ꜥꜣ* during the Old Kingdom," *BES* 10:77-90.

— (1992), "*Wꜣḏ-wr* and Lexicographical Method," in U. Luft, ed., *The Intellectual Heritage of Egypt* (Kákosy Fs.). *Studia Aegyptiaca* 14 (Budapest) 205-214.

— (1986), "The Term *stp-sꜣ* in the Old Kingdom and its Later Development," *JARCE* 23 :85-98.

Goyon, G. (1971), "Les ports des pyramides et le grand canal de Memphis," *RdÉ* 23:137-153.

Griffith, F. Ll. (1898), *The Petrie Papyri. Hieratic Papyri from Kahun and Gurob*, two vols. (London).

Gunn, B. (1936), "[Review of] A.H. Gardiner, *Hieratic Papyri in the British Museum: Third Series*," *JEA* 22:103-108.

Gutgesell, M. (1982), "Die Struktur der pharaonischen Wirtschaft — eine Erwiderung," *GM* 56:95-109.

Hayes, W. C. (1948), "A Much-Copied Letter of the Early Middle Kingdom," *JNES* 7:1-10.

Hein, I. (1991), *Die ramessidische Bautätigkeit in Nubien. GOF* 22 (Wiesbaden).

Helck, W. (1977), "Felderverwaltung," in *LÄ* II:151-155.

Hodjash, S. I, and O. D. Berlev (1980), "A Market-Scene in the Mastaba of *D3d3-m-ʿnḫ* (*Tp-m-ʿnḫ*)," *AoF* 7:31-49.

Hornung, E. (1991), *Die Nachtfahrt der Sonne. Eine altägyptische Beschriebung des Jenseits* (Zurich and Munich).

Jacq, C. (1986), *Le voyage dans l'autre monde selon l'Égypte ancienne. Épreuves et métamorphoses du mort d'après les Textes des Pyramides et les Textes des Sarcophages* (Le Rocher).

James, T. G. H. (1962), *The Hekanakhte Papers and other Early Middle Kingdom Documents*. Metropolitan Museum of Art Egyptian Expedition Publications 14 (New York).

Janssen, J. J. (1986), "Agrarian Administration in Egypt During the Twentieth Dynasty," *BiOr* 43:351-366.

— (1975), "Prolegomena to the Study of Egypt's Economic History during the New Kingdom," *SAK* 3:127-185.

Kemp, B. J. (1989), *Ancient Egypt. Anatomy of a Civilization* (London and New York).

Kitchen, K. A. (1968-1988), *Ramesside Inscriptions*, seven vols. (Oxford).

— (1969-1970), "Two Donation Stelae in The Brooklyn Museum," *JARCE* 8:59-71.

Koch, R. (1990), *Die Erzählung des Sinuhe. BiAe* 17 (Brussels).

Kruchten, J-M. (1979), "L'évolution de la gestion domainale sous le Nouvel Empire égyptien," in E. Lipinski, ed., *State and Temple Economy in the Ancient Near East* II. OLA 6 (Louvain):517-525.

Lange, K., and M. Hirmer (1968), *Egypt. Architecture — Sculpture — Painting in Three Thousand Years*, 4th ed., revised and enlarged. (London and New York).

Lehner, M. (1990), *The Complete Pyramids. Solving the Ancient Mysteries* (London and New York).

Lesko, L. H. and B. S. Lesko, eds. (1982-1990), *A Dictionary of Late Egyptian*, five vols. (Berkeley).

Lichtheim, M. (1973-1980), *Ancient Egyptian Literature*, three vols. (Berkeley).

— (1980), "The Praise of Cities in the Literature of the Egyptian New Kingdom," in S.M. Burstein and L.A. Okin, eds., *Panhellenica. Essays in Ancient History and Historiography in Honor of Truesdell S. Brown* (Lawrence):15-23.

McDowell, A. G. (1990), *Jurisdiction in the Workmen's Community of Deir el-Medina. Egyptologische Uitgaven* 5 (Leiden).

Meeks, D. (1977-1979), *Année Lexicographique*, three vols. (Paris).

Menu, B. (1971), "Le régime juridique des terres en Égypte pharaonique. Moyen Empire et Nouvel Empire," *Revue historique de droit français et étranger* (Paris):555-585.

Moussa, A. M., and H. Altenmüller (1977), *Das Grab des Nianchchnum und Chnumhotep. AV* 21 (Mainz am Rhein).

Murnane, W. J., and C. C. Van Siclen (1993), *The Boundary Stelae of Akhenaten* (London and New York).

Newberry, P. (1893), *Beni Hasan* I. *ASE* 1 (Oxford).

O'Connor, D. (1972), "The geography of settlement in ancient Egypt," in P. J. Ucko, R. I. Tringham and G. W. Dimbleby, eds., *Man, Settlement and Urbanism* (London):681-698.

— (1980), "Malqata," in *LÄ* III:1173-1177.

Posener, G. (1956), *Littérature et politique dans l'Égypte de la XII* Dynastie* (Paris).

Reineke, W. F. (1979), "Waren die *šwtyw* wirklich Kaufleute?" *AFo* 9:5-14.

Römer, M. (1992), "Der Handel und die Kaufleute im Alten Ägypten," *SAK* 19:257-284.

Roth, A. M. (1990), "The Distribution of the Old Kingdom Title *ḫntj-š*," *BSAK* 4:177-186.

Sandman, M. (1938), *Texts from the Time of Akhenaten. BiAe* 8 (Brussels).

Sethe, K., and W. Helck (1914-1961), *Urkunden der 18. Dynastie* (Berlin and Leipzig).

Simpson, W. K. (1965), *Papyrus Reisner* II. *Accounts of the Dockyard Workshop at This in the Reign of Sesostris I* (Boston).

— (1963), "Studies in the Twelfth Egyptian Dynasty: I. The Residence at Itj-Towy," *JARCE* 2:53-54.

Spalinger, A. (1978), "A new Reference to an Egyptian Campaign of Thuthmose III in Asia," *JNES* 37:35-41.

— (1991), "Some Revisions of Temple Endowments in the New Kingdom," *JARCE* 28:21-39.

Stadelman, R. (1981), "La ville de pyramide à l'Ancien Empire égyptien," *RdÉ* 33:67-77

Tresson, P. (1935-1938), "L'inscription de Chechanq Ier, au Musée du Caire: un frappant exemple d'impôt progressif en matière religieuse," in *Melanges Maspero* I: *Orient Ancien. MIFAO* 66 (Cairo):817-840.

Trigger, B. (1993), *Early Civilizations. Ancient Egypt in Context* (Cairo).

Valbelle, D. (1985), *"Les ouvriers de la tombe." Deir el-Médineh à l'époque ramesside. BdÉ* 96 (Cairo).

— (1985), "Précisions apportées par l'iconographie à l'un des emplois du mot *dmì*," in P. Posener-Kriéger, ed., *Mélanges Gamal Eddin Mokhtar* II. *BdÉ* 97, 2 (Cairo):315-319.

Van Lepp, J. (1997), "Is the Hieroglyphic Sign *nìwt* a Village with Cross-Roads," *GM* 158:91-100.

Ventura, R. (1986), *Living in a City of the Dead. OBO* 69 (Freiburg and Göttingen).

Vernus, P. (1974), *Athribis. BdÉ* 74 (Cairo).

— (1979), "Un hymne à Amon, protecteur de Tanis, sur une tablette hiératique (Caire J.E. 87889)," *RdÉ* 31:101-199.

Wente, E. (1967), *Late Ramesside Letters. SAOC* 33 (Chicago)

— (1990), *Letters from Ancient Egypt.* SBL Writings from the Ancient World 1 (Atlanta).

Willems, H. (1996), *The Coffin of Heqata (Cairo JdE 36418). OLA* 70 (Leiden).

Wilson, J. A. (1955), "Buto and Hierkonpolis in the Geography of Egypt," *JNES* 14:209-236.

Zivie, C. M. (1982), "Memphis," in *LÄ* IV:24-41.

Zivie, A. P., ed. (1988), *Memphis et ses nécropoles au Nouvel Empire. Nouvelles données, nouvelles questions* (Paris).

3

From Sacred Enclave to Temple to City

Michael Hudson
Peabody Museum of Archaeology and Ethnology
Harvard University

The social sciences have long viewed the earliest cities as playing much the same role as they do in modern times: to serve as centers of government, and to undertake commerce and industry, reflecting the economies of scale resulting from their population growth.

Such speculations assume an almost automatic and inevitable urbanization stemming from material causes, a combination of increasing population density and new technologies ("the agricultural revolution"). To the extent that political and military dynamics are recognized, they are of a character more familiar in classical antiquity than in Neolithic Asia Minor and Early Bronze Age Mesopotamia where civilization's earliest cities have been excavated. This paper therefore addresses the genesis of cities not from the vantage point of how they ended up, but rather how they began as gathering places even before they became permanently occupied year-round sites.

To be sure, not all premodern cities developed in the same way. Each region had its particular characteristics. But from the vantage point of our own modern civilization, the great catalytic urbanization occurred in Mesopotamia. What gave its cities their distinctive character was their commercial and industrial role. (By "industrial" I mean the specialized handicraft industries organized primarily by the large public institutions.) I conclude that the unique way in which urban functions developed in southern Mesopotamia was influenced strongly by the region's ecological imperative to trade. There is no evidence for a comparable priority occurring in Mexico or Peru, China, the Indus Valley, or Egypt.

Since third-millennium Mesopotamia, urban density has been catalyzed by the defensive military need of inhabitants to gather in walled towns. Indeed, the word "town" derives from the German *Zaun* ("fence"), typically referring to the walled military camps planted across Europe by the Roman emperors in standardized designs. But civilization's first urban areas are not well characterized as such towns. Although Jericho appears to have been a walled center by about 9000 BC, its walls were not necessarily fortifications; they may well have been flood walls. In any event, when archaeologists next encounter urban sites, such as Çatal Hüyük in the sixth millennium BC, they find a cosmopolitan neutrality.

It appears that the earliest towns were sanctified from raids. Southern Mesopotamian fortifications, for instance, do not appear until relatively late, c. 2800 BC (Adams 1981). Centered on their city-temples, these public sites served as bridges for diverse groups to come together to transact arms-length commerce under an umbrella of common agreed-upon rules. I therefore suggest that if we are to take our clue from classical times, the model to be examined should be amphictyonic sites such as Delphi and Delos, where diverse groups seem to have mixed freely without fear of attack.

To perform this role of neutral bridges, such sites tended not to develop at the center of their communities (*i.e.*, "automatically" as a result of growing population density and scale), but at boundaries or natural crossroads *between* diverse communities. Assur, for instance, sat astride the Tigris intersecting central Mesopotamia's major east/west trade route, and many other entrepots likewise were situated near the sea or on major transport rivers. The landlocked town of Çatal Hüyük seems to have been the center of its own regionwide trading network (see Gelb 1986:165 for some qualifications).

Being host to a diversity of groups, such towns hardly would have been centers of political control over the land. This paper therefore focuses on the public character of the earliest cities in southern Mesopotamia as gathering places and ritual centers, and hence on the shaping role played by their temple precincts and, in time, the palace.

The earliest urban sites were sanctified, commercial, peaceful, and often multiethnic

The physical orientation and cosmological symbolism of archaic cities, their streets, gates, and the architectural character of their public structures reflect their role as sanctified commercial and ritual meeting places and temple areas long before centralized warmaking, political control, and taxation developed. As commercial entrepots they functioned as havens both in the sense of ports (German *Hafen*, as in what Karl Polanyi called "ports of trade") and as asylums, literally *havens* from the surrounding land (a theme which Baruch Levine will pick up in his contribution to the present volume).

The localization of specialized meeting areas for ritual and exchange may be found as early as the Ice Age, and later in sacred groves and seasonal gathering spots. These sites were occasional rather than year-round settlements. It therefore is appropriate to view them as social constructs independent of their scale, performing urban functions long before they came to grow substantially in size and attract year-round settled populations.

Temples and their precincts comprised the earliest city centers. Set corporately apart from the community at large to serve as self-supporting households of the city god and/or ruler, they were larger, more specialized, and more internally hierarchic than personal households. They also included many dependents whose families on the land were unable to care for them, *e.g.*, the blind and infirm, war widows and orphans, and others who could not function in normal family contexts. Placed in the institutional households that served as the ultimate sanctuaries, these individuals were put to work in handicraft workshops or other public professions (*e.g.*, the blind musicians) in an early form of welfare/workfare.

It appears that archaic populations felt that the best way to keep handicraft production and exchange in line with traditional social values was to organize such activity under the aegis of temples, or at least to establish a strong temple interface as a kind of "chamber of commerce." Public ritual and welfare functions already existed as the germ out of which this economic role would flower. As gathering places, temples became natural administrative vehicles for sponsoring trade. In retrospect it seems quite natural that the temple's ritual functions broadened in time to include the role of sponsoring markets. Populations attending sacred ceremonies engaged in trade and exchange, much as they did at the fairs of medieval Europe. Out of this commerce developed temple sponsorship of standardized weights and measures, contractual law, and the regularization and enforcement of trade obligations.

Much like the ancient cities of refuge (such as that to which Cain withdrew in Genesis 4 and that Numbers 35 and Joshua 20 describe as being established throughout Israel), temples served as sanctuaries for fugitives from the retaliatory fury of local feud justice. They also served as sanctuaries to store the savings of their communities — gold and silver, seeds, tools, and other sanctified assets deemed free from attack by neighboring communities that shared a common religious belief that such seizure would be sacrilegious.

If the earliest urban zones are to be viewed as *regimes*, the archaic concept of regime was not our modern idea. The word is semantically related to *regulate* and also reflects the idea of *regularity*, connoting the spirit of equity and evenhandedness that is called for in arms-length dealings and the adjudication of disputes. The underlying spirit is one of standardization. Weights and measures are regularized, as are contractual commercial dealings generally. Parties are treated equally and symmetrically rather than dominated, and relations are formalized so as to minimize dispute.

To implement their regulatory functions, temples (and later the palaces) developed specialized bodies of law, beginning with rulings and prices governing their own sphere of activities. At first they regulated the services that they performed directly — marriage and burial ceremonies, handicraft production via public guilds, and the prices and interest rates that merchants, public collectors, and other professionals could charge, especially in serving as intermediaries between public institutions and local and foreign communities. The resulting regime was essentially urban but was not necessarily one of political control or "the state."

Bronze Age public utilities were not yet organs of government

In viewing cities as evolving first and foremost out of ritual and related sanctified functions, I have no intention of reviving ideas from the 1920s and 1930s about the so-called temple-state. Temples did not even have the power to tax (although they charged user fees, sharecropping rent, and interest). In any event there was little private surplus to tax, a fact that obliged Bronze Age public institutions to be self-supporting and indeed, to act as entrepreneurs. Temples housed the workshops where most export textiles were woven (in contrast to the homespun for subsistence use). They were endowed with resources to support their community's dependent labor to weave textiles and undertake other export production. Toward this end, much of the community's land was set aside for use by the temples to support their nonagricultural labor force and official staff. Additional lands were held by the temples (and in time the palaces) on which to graze their herds, above all the sheep whose wool was woven by public dependents into the textiles exported for the raw materials not found in the Mesopotamian alluvium.

It was from this commercial production and export trade that southern Mesopotamia's pioneering economic innovations derived. It was the temples that organized trade and acted as embassies in founding foreign trade colonies, sponsoring these embassies as temple cults for merchants operating abroad. The temples thus provided an umbrella for commercial arrangements among disparate peoples, in large part precisely because their sacred status enabled them to serve as forums to settle debts and disputes between local residents and foreign merchants. In sum, temples were administrative nodes governing external contacts.

While social organization on the land remained kinship-based, that of the cities became part of a higher and more cosmopolitan social ordering. Neolithic urban sites, for instance, seem to have begun as publicly demarcated spaces cut out from the surrounding land to provide even-handed arms-length commercial contacts. This is something quite different from what occurred in classical antiquity. *Instead of Bronze Age Mesopotamian cities beginning as private agglomerations that in time developed more public characteristics, their evolution moved in just the reverse direction.* The trade and handicraft production formerly set aside in the public institutions were shifted into the personal households of chieftains, military headmen and other well-placed families as handicraft production typically was conducted from the aristocratic households based on the land. Meanwhile, the classical city became more a center of government than of industry. The modern type of state developed out of the communal sector as a whole rather than out of the temples as a corporately distinct public sector.

Eight characteristics of archaic Near Eastern urbanization

This paper makes eight points with regard to archaic urbanization.

(1) Cities were not an automatic by-product of population pressures sprawling inward from the land, but were a planned and structured response to the need to conduct external relations, above all trade. Southern Mesopotamia's city-temples organized commerce in ways intended to minimize conflicts or at least to resolve them in mutually agreed-on ways. Urban development thus may be attributed largely to heterogeneous groups coming together to engage in commerce and communal rituals.

(2) Early southern Mesopotamian cities took their character from their temples, which played a major role in this trade. Prior to the Bronze Age these temples served as ritual centers and gathering places, and their commercial functions evolved out of this role. The largest example in the fourth millennium was Uruk and its sacred Eanna district.

(3) Though textile weaving, pottery work, metalworking and other crafts began early, they were first systematically organized under public-

sector aegis in the temples rather than being left to individual families to develop for their own profit. Temples thus became the first corporate entrepreneurs. They organized craft workshops employing the community's dependent population, consisting not of a "class" (*e.g.* of wage-laborers) but of "unfortunates" (Babylonian *mushkenu*) — individuals who could not make a go of things in their traditional family context on the land. The blind and infirm and war widows and orphans were put to work at whatever tasks they might be able to perform, supplemented by other outsiders such as slaves and war captives. (See Gelb 1965 and 1972, and also Kramer and Maier 1989 for the Sumerian epic in which Enki specifies public-sector tasks for each type of misfit.)

(4) The evolving structure and organization of Near Eastern cities reflect shifts in the character of the public sector from sacred rituals to a growing commercial and handicraft role (via temples) to more worldly military concerns as the palace became increasingly important after 2800 BC.

(5) This secularization was followed by a privatization of real estate, starting with townhouses for the merchants and collectors who interfaced between the private/communal sector and the large public institutions. These houses occupied the city area that originally was the public space. The character of classical antiquity's cities was much further privatized as towns became economic areas whose commerce passed into the hands of individual households (the classical Greek *oikos*) rather than being centralized in the temples, palaces, or other public institutions.

(6) Only as cities became domiciles for the population at large (rather than public areas) did the state develop as modern writers define it. Whereas temples had been organized as autonomous corporate entities, military organization involved all society. Palace or aristocratic rule became predominantly military, posing for the first time the possibility of a truly general society-wide law. The land's oral common law adopted the forms that public law had innovated — inscription on stone or wood, publicly displayed.

(7) Archaeologists find that secularization, an increasingly military focus of social organization and the privatization of economic life went hand in hand with a trend toward smaller economic units. The scale of industry became smaller, as did that of cities.

(8) Geographically, the militarization of antiquity led to empire building. Whereas no Sumerian city was able to hold the "kingship of Sumer"

in the third millennium, things changed in classical Mediterranean antiquity. Imperial Athens and Sparta, followed by Rome, extended the scale of the political and urban unit beyond merely local scope. As recipients of tribute they built up grandiose public structures, as well as imperial bureaucracies.

Looking at the broad sweep of antiquity from the Early Bronze Age through the imperial Roman climax, one sees the function of capital cities shifting from amphictyonic or other ritual centers to political capitals. At the end of this process Rome emerged as a capital quite different from archaic towns. It was simultaneously a military, governing, and industrial center. This combination did not occur under the sponsorship of public temples, whose social functions became much more limited than had been the case in Bronze Age Mesopotamia. Nonetheless, capitals still sought to retain the cosmological idea of cities as centers of order such as had inspired the earliest temple-centered sites.

The idea of order was made more difficult by wealthy families asserting their economic interests at the expense of society at large. They in fact made public order impossible after the fourth century AD. Roman society polarized economically, cannibalizing its internal market and becoming deurbanized. Economic life reverted to self-sufficient agriculture, with complex organization surviving mainly on the monastic estates in the countryside.

Temple forerunners of cities — their public character and ritual permanence

The origin of urban forms reflects above all that of the temples that served as the focal point of the earliest gathering sites. The germs of this process are found already in the Ice Age. It therefore is appropriate to begin the discussion with the extent to which Ice Age, Neolithic, and Early Bronze Age ritual sites share the characteristics that urban historians subsequently have associated with cities.

It may seem unusual to begin the history of urbanization in the Ice Age, but this is a logical corollary of viewing cities as originating simultaneously in sacred cosmological functions — ordering their communities, supporting astronomical observers who helped administer the festival calendar, and sponsoring festivals of social cohesion — while also organizing external relations (trade and war) with the objective of preventing external trade and warfare from deranging the ordered proportions that governed domestic social life.

Organizational structures are more important than physical scale in tracing these proto-urban dynamics. I therefore begin by reviewing the Marxist anthropologist V. Gordon Childe's 1950 discussion of ten common features of urbanization, to show how these characteristics are found in ritual sites prior to the Bronze Age emergence of formal cities. Childe's criteria of urban development apply equally well to preurban sacred sites and their temples, because trade and exchange long retained ritual or "public" functions during the Neolithic and Bronze Age in the Near East. It was out of these public functions, above all the economic role of temples in this region, that the first cities emerged.

Anthropologists recognize seven primary urban sites. Following the three great Bronze Age civilizations in the third millennium BC — Mesopotamia, Egypt, and the Indus Valley — are the North China plain, the Maya and Central Mexican cities, the pre-Incan Andes, and Nigeria's coastal Yoruba territory. Tracing the urban forms for each of these seven regions back to their beginnings, Paul Wheatley (1971:9, 225) observes that

> We arrive not at a settlement that is dominated by commercial relations, a primordial market, or at one that is focused on a citadel, an archetypal fortress, but rather at a ceremonial complex. . . . The predominantly religious focus to the schedule of social activities associated with them leaves no room to doubt that we are dealing primarily with centers of ritual and ceremonial importance. . . . Beginning as little more than tribal shrines . . . these centers were elaborated into complexes of public ceremonial structures . . . including assemblages of such architectural items as pyramids, platform mounds, temples, palaces, terraces, staircases, courts, and stelae. Operationally they were instruments for the creation of political, social, economic, and sacred space, at the same time as they were symbols of cosmic, social and moral order.

The first urban sites were thus predominantly public areas, consisting above all of temples.

Functionally speaking, the localization of specialized ritual exchange centers is found already in the European Ice Age, between 30,000 and 10,000 BC, thousands of years before hunting-and-gathering bands settled down to cultivate the land on a year-round basis. By the Early Bronze Age for all practical purposes the temples (and in time the palaces) *were* the city.

Public officials and merchants built, bought, and sold townhouses primarily to interface with these public institutions — to trade their workshop wares abroad, to collect barley-rents and to sell their barley, and to interact in related ways with the temples and palaces. Thus, if urban areas were islands in predominantly agrarian societies, they were public-sector islands. Many preurban traditions remained to shape their urban cosmologies. It was these traditions that helped provide a forum for diverse groups to come together at these sites — civilization's earliest organized interactions among "outsiders."

In setting the materialistic "objective" tone for most modern discussions in his above-mentioned 1950 article, Childe described "the urban revolution" as having occurred c. 3500-3000 BC, contemporary with the origins of writing. Not concerning himself with the cosmological aspects of archaic cities, he focused on their overt physical characteristics and material economic conditions. Using this approach, he found towns to be more or less automatic results of the agricultural revolution that began around 9000 BC. The cultivation of crops and domestication of animals enabled enough surplus food, oil, and wool to be produced to support a permanent superstructure of handicraft, mercantile, and administrative occupations.

This labor was concentrated in urban complexes, especially in the temples and palaces that served as households of their local city-deities. Childe did not elaborate on the paramount role of temples in structuring the cosmological ordering of society — the order that formed the context for civilization's first urbanization — but upon examination, the ten characteristics he listed as constituting the urban revolution all describe temples so well that the temple focus of cities should have been readily apparent.

Childe found the most obvious characteristic of cities to be their size: "relatively large numbers of people in a restricted area." Their scale had to be large enough to support the second key urban feature: a specialized division of labor. This was associated with a third characteristic: social stratification, replete with hierarchies of authority, going hand in hand with the fourth characteristic: centralization of the economic surplus. This often was achieved by imposing taxes and tribute, and by a fifth urban feature: foreign trade, mainly in luxuries for the emerging stratum of wealthy landholders, merchants, officials, and warriors.

A sixth urban feature was the shift of political representation away from kinship ties to local territorial districts. Voting in the communal assemblies was done by neighborhood or ward (e.g., the Athenian *deme*), rather than by the clan membership that defined preurban communities.

A seventh urban characteristic was monumental public architecture. Writing (an eighth feature) was needed to coordinate record-keeping, production, and contracts, and promoted a ninth feature: development of the exact sciences, beginning with astronomy and mathematics, and flowering into physics and engineering. Childe held the tenth urban characteristic to be naturalistic art, especially portraiture to reflect the vanity of the emerging bourgeoisie.

Childe presented this list of urban characteristics as a relatively late phenomenon, more descriptive of the first millennium BC than the fourth or third millennium. His list says nothing explicitly about archaic cities being centered around temples, nor did he emphasize their multiethnic, often multilingual character.

What therefore remains to be done is to trace these urban characteristics further back in time. To incorporate them into a longer sweep of prehistory, we may best think of them as traditions of social intercourse rather than of cities as such. Most helpful is the idea of *civitas* denoting the social and civil structures that varied from one society to the next, rather than what the Romans called *urbs* (the root of English *urban*), connoting cities primarily in their physically extensive dimension.

Being a materialist (and indeed a technological determinist) and seeking universals, Childe viewed cities as developing automatically as a by-product of growing population density, specialization of labor, and the social stratification that came with a managerial class. From his perspective, cosmological considerations and the early catalytic role of temples seemed merely an incidental superstructure to this basic foundation. His approach led him not to remark on the degree to which his ten urban characteristics all are found in preurban ritual contexts. It therefore is relevant to review the temple antecedents that were the germs out of which increasingly secularized private-sector urban structures flowered.

Even before the development of towns (and indeed, before agriculture), public traditions must have provided a foundation for group behavior by establishing — and indeed, sanctifying — its rules. It therefore is appropriate to review how Childe's ten urban criteria reflect this public cosmology and its ritual functions.

(1) **Concentrations of people first occurred at ritual sites.** Only if we assume that the earliest gatherings of people must have been year-round does it follow that urban forms could not have developed prior to the agricultural revolution. Seasonal gathering sites existed already in Paleolithic times. The idea of sanctifying their ground must have survived to play a germinal role in patterning more permanent cities.

Preurban and Urban Traditions of Social Intercourse

Cities as Formal Urban Sites (after Childe 1950)	Public temples in third-millennium Mesopotamia and earlier
1. Concentrate people in a compact site.	Ritual ceremonies sanctify public space and incorporate its diverse occupants into an ordered community.
2. Specialization of labor.	The first formal professions were public workers organized into temple guilds and specialized cult-families.
3. Social stratification.	The word hierarchy has sacred connotations.
4. Centralized economic surplus.	Temples were civilization's first public storehouses and "containers," sanctifying food, seed, tools, and precious metals from outside seizure or domestic misappropriation.
5. Foreign trade.	Temples housed civilization's first handicraft workshops. In Mesopotamia they had the largest herds of sheep to provide wool for their dependent textile-making labor.
6. Territorial organization takes precedence over family lineages.	Sacred space set aside from ownership or control by any specific families. (Rulers did not speak of their parentage but described themselves as being nurtured or chosen by the gods, or "reborn" as members of sacred cults.)
7. Monumental public architecture.	The first stone architecture was public and ceremonial.
8. Writing and account-keeping.	These originally were public-sector functions.
9. Development of exact predictive sciences	Prediction began with calendar-making, omen-taking, and prognostication.
10. Naturalistic art, especially portraiture.	Subordination of realism to standardized traditions, often of a cosmological character. Cities as sacred and commercial gateways.

There is no indication that archaic rulers or the augurs who functioned as early city planners thought of urban entities primarily in terms of size. Bronze Age cities appeared to their contemporaries primarily as sacred temple and palace enclaves serving public functions. The Sumerian language used the word *uru* (Akkadian *alu*) to express the idea of village, town, and city without regard to size. For instance, in the time of Gilgamesh, c. 2600 BC, Uruk had fifty thousand inhabitants and spread over 400 hectares, extending a further 15 kilometers beyond the city walls. This made it the largest city prior to Republican Rome (Adams 1969, 1981:85). Yet Oppenheim (1965:115) points out that what seems to have been the key to it and other Mesopotamian cities was neither their size nor their walls, but the fact that they were situated on a water course. This was essential for to the trade in which every Mesopotamian city needed to engage.

Rulers were called *en* or *lugal* regardless of whether they ruled large cities or were chieftains of small tribal bands (Hallo 1957). Throughout the Bronze Age we find rulers of small towns communicating with more important rulers on the basis of equality, exchanging gifts seemingly without regard for the relative weight of their realms. Function rather than scale was thus the essential feature. (For instance, all of the Indus civilization's excavated settlements, from small villages to towns, exhibit a similar physical profile [Miller 1985; Morris 1979:14].)

(2) **Specialization of labor is documented most extensively in Mesopotamia's temple and palace workshops.** Families living on the land always have had to be relatively self-sufficient. Rural families throughout most of history have grown their own food, made their own clothes, and built their own homes and furnishings. Craft specialization has been carried to the furthest degree in cities.

When this specialization was first being formalized at the outset of the Bronze Age, the temples took the lead in organizing handicraft workshops. Gelb (1965, 1972) has shown how widespread has been the idea of setting aside a dependent specialized nonagricultural population in public institutions, especially to weave textiles. Ancient Mesopotamia (like India and Incan Peru) established public weaving workshops staffed with dependent labor, largely that of women and children.

The laws of Hammurapi (§274) c. 1750 BC list seal cutters, jewelers and metalsmiths, carpenters and house builders, leather workers, reed workers, washer/fullers, felt makers, and doctors as public professions. Throughout the Bronze Age most specialized professions seem to have been organized as public guilds.

Largely in response to the central production of exports in exchange for foreign raw materials, Mesopotamia's temples and palaces developed on a larger scale than did the households of chieftains and headmen in the less-centralized periphery, including the Mediterranean lands where such workshops were located mainly on private, landed estates (as they were in medieval Europe). Urban industry thus was characteristically a public phenomenon.

(3) **Social stratification began in the public temples and palaces.** Indeed, the word *hierarchy* derives from Greek *hiero* (sacred). Babylonian social stratification and wealth stemmed largely from economic status gained by interfacing as official or quasi-official *tamkarum* merchants, royal collectors, or other temple and palace administrators (Yoffee 1988, 1981). Profit-seeking activities spread from the large public institutions to the rest of society as ritual and administrative functions provided the major opportunities for seeking wealth in socially acceptable ways.

(4) **Concentration of the economic surplus was first achieved in the temple sector.** Temple workshops were set corporately apart from their communities and endowed with their own land, dependent labor, herds of animals, and stores of precious metals to support their handicraft activities and generate commercial surpluses. Many temple and palace lands were farmed by community members on a sharecropping basis, typically for a third of the crop or some other fixed proportion. Indeed, as history's first documented landlords, the temples earned the first known land-rent. Administrators were assigned such usufructs to provide food for their support and may have exchanged some of this barley-revenue for luxuries (Ellis 1976, Archi 1984). The resulting "redistributive" system of production and consumption preceded market trade and pricing by thousands of years. Also, as business corporations (in contrast to family partnerships), temples appear to have earned interest.

In short, *profit-accumulating enterprise was public long before being privatized.* This explains why the first economic accounting and the organization of large-scale handicraft industry appears first in public, often sacred, contexts. Temples systematized profit-seeking in ways that only gradually became acceptable for private individuals acting on their own. (Wealthy individuals were expected to use their resources openhandedly or consume them in conspicuous displays such as burials or marriage feasts.) Indeed, the temples' entrepreneurial functions emerged out of their sacred status "above" the community's families at large, most of which still functioned on a subsistence basis after taking into account their luxury spending.

The first organized surplus-yielding property thus was public rather than private (see Hudson and Levine 1996). Unlike the case with communal lands held by the population at large, temple and palace properties were not periodically redivided among community members. They were marked by boundary stones inscribed with cosmological symbolism of their permanent and irreversible alienation from their former communal-sector owners, *e.g.*, as on the stele of Manishtushu c. 2200 BC. (Gelb, Steinkeller, and Whiting 1989-1991 provide a survey.) No such markers have survived for individually allotted lands from this period, suggesting that any such markers were merely temporary, reflecting their land tenure.

(5) **Temple production played a central role in foreign trade.** In setting up trading posts or colonies to obtain foreign metal, stone, and even hardwood, merchants acted in association with their home-city temples to establish local branches as a kind of trade association (for example, the Assyrian trade colony of Kanesh in Asia Minor. See Leemans 1950, 1960; Oppenheim 1965; Larsen 1976; Archi 1984, as well as Hudson 1992). Mesopotamia's temple workshops seem to have consigned their luxury textiles and other goods to merchants, and many temple professions dealt with imported materials.

The Uruk Expansion c. 3500 BC appears to have been organized by the temples, planting colonies and trade missions westward across Syria to Asia Minor, southwest to Egypt, and eastward across the Iranian plateau (Algaze 1989). Likewise in archaic Greece, the Delphi temple played a major role in planning and allocating trade outposts and colonies. Organization of foreign trade via temple outposts lasted throughout classical antiquity even in free-enterprise zones such as Delos.

(6) **The urban shift away from family-oriented to territorial space began with temple cults.** Individuals were initiated into corporate groupings that replaced their biological families. Paternal authority and family structures were transposed onto the public plane in the form of temple and palace households, cults, and professional guilds.

Over a century ago the American anthropologist Lewis Henry Morgan's *Ancient Society* (1878) placed civilization's urban watershed in the sixth century BC. He focused on the reforms of Cleisthenes in Athens (509-507) and Servius in Rome (537) as replacing the clannish family contexts, based on rural landholding, with neighborhood political units. Toynbee (1973) followed with a similar analysis for Sparta's changes in the seventh century BC. Subsequent archaeologists have established that cities were organized on a district or "ward" basis thousands of years earlier. Already in Bronze Age Mesopotamia and Egypt, each local area took responsibility for maintaining its irrigation dikes and canals.

Assyriologists have noted that early Mesopotamian rulers downplayed their family identity by representing their lineage as deriving from the city-temple deities. Sargon of Akkad, often taken as a prototype for the myth of the birth of royal heroes (including Moses and Romulus) emphasized his "public family." In any event, archaic clan groupings seem to have been relatively open to newcomers. There is little Bronze Age evidence for closed aristocracies of the sort found in classical antiquity. Mesopotamia seems to have remained open and ethnically mixed for thousands of years, and the Sumerians probably incorporated strangers as freely as did medieval Irish *feins* and many modern tribal communities.

Clan lineages seem to have consolidated themselves (along with their property ownership) more readily in the periphery. Mycenaean chieftains built up unprecedented economic power by adopting the organizational and accounting techniques of Near Eastern enterprise. After 1200 BC warlord aristocracies parceled out Greek lands among their own closed ranks. When cities developed anew in the classical epoch, they once again administered themselves on the district basis described by Morgan.

(7) **Writing originated as a public-sector function.** Record-keeping served as a centralized control and scheduling device long before writing became a vehicle for personal self-expression, literature or abstract philosophy. The earliest notations and cylinder seals were developed to hold temple administrators accountable for their receipt and disbursement of rations and other resources. By the middle of the third millennium, written accounts were being used to schedule product flows. The other great inspiration for symbolic notation and counting was calendar-keeping, also a priestly task.

(8) **Monumental architecture likewise originated in the public sector.** The temple was the archaic skyscraper as well as the social and economic center of Bronze Age cities. Long before Near Eastern families adopted stone construction for their own homes, it symbolized the permanency of public institutions. The earliest stone architecture seems to have been used for public buildings, legal stelae, and boundary stones in Mesopotamia, as well as for tombs in Egypt and other regions (Raglan 1964:175-180). In Egypt and elsewhere, monumental stone architecture was used for funerary structures, which had a public character. The significance of their astronomical alignment and mathematical symbolism reflects the attempt to imbue public buildings with "natural order" (and

the spirits of the dead with "eternity" as reflected in the symmetrical motions of the heavens).

In sum, the use of stone and hardwood in public buildings reflected the eternal cosmos in an epoch when private residences were made of much less permanent mud bricks and reeds. And as noted above, the use of stone boundary markers rather than wooden or clay ones indicated that alienations of land to the public sector (usually to the palace) were irreversible, in contrast to communal land tenure.

With regard to the urban characteristics of monumental architecture, and also what Childe describes as naturalistic art, it may be relevant to note that sculptural aesthetics, public art, and urban cosmology dovetailed neatly with each other in a line that can be traced back to a common origin in temple architecture. Snodgrass (1980:179ff.) points out that the carving of statues presupposed a marble industry, which derived first and foremost from architectural demand, above all for building sanctuaries and temples. During the flowering of Greek city-states in 650-575 BC, he writes, "statues were still often produced by men whose professional training had been as masons or quarrymen." The Attic marble statues whose production flourished after 600 BC found their epitome in dedications to sanctuaries and grave monuments (*ibid.*, 145f.).

(9) **The formalization of arithmeticized, observational predictive sciences also was developed in a public context, often to aid in rituals.** Archaic counting apparently derived from calendar-making, as did astronomy and other predictive sciences, along with astrology and the taking of auguries. Such forecasting was used for public functions long before diffusing to the population at large.

Of a more practical calendrical nature were Mesopotamia's sexagesimal fractions and higher mathematics, developed in the third millennium. The 360-day administrative year helped provision the public labor force on a regular monthly basis. Large-number computation was used to schedule the rations and manpower needed to dig canals and similar engineering projects. The 360-day calendar also provided a modular format for the circular geometry to divide the ecliptic and zodiac, and hence to predict celestial cycles. In sum, Bronze Age mathematical, astronomical, and related knowledge was ritualistic as well as being used for public enterprise long before classical antiquity applied it to more secular tasks.

(10) **The first representational art is found in ritual contexts.** One cannot say that the phenomenon of "naturalistic" art is specifically urban. Long before settled agriculture supported year-round urbanization,

the remarkably naturalistic imagery of the European Ice Age had depicted the seasonal behavior and appearance of animals and fish, including the moulting of pelage, the growth and shedding of antlers, and the appearance of spring vegetation. Reviewing over twenty thousand years of Ice Age art and iconography, Marshack (1972, 1975) gives persuasive reasons for regarding much of that imagery as being referential in its seasonal contexts, probably because it was produced for seasonal ritual and mythic purposes.

What Childe seems to term naturalistic art is simply that which *lacks* the traditional dimension of symbolic cognitive meaning. But classical portraiture and statuary only gradually dispensed with the iconographic formalities traditionally used to indicate status. Although much Bronze Age statuary and portraiture appears naturalistic at first glance, the proportions of the head to the body and other ratios reflect a sexagesimal arithmetic in Mesopotamia and decimalized proportions in Egypt and Greece (Azarpay 1990). Even rulers whom one would expect to be pioneers of individualistic rendering, such as Gudea, were regressed into a set of standardized features (Winter 1989). Such symbolic and mathematized idealizations are the opposite of naturalism.

To sum up, all ten of Childe's urban characteristics turn out to be grounded in preurban ritual activities that long retained a public character, above all those associated with Bronze Age temples, their communal storage facilities, handicraft workshops, and sponsorship of the festivals that were the focal points of the archaic calendar. As a Marxist, Childe might have emphasized how cities, like every social organism, evolved in the wombs of their predecessors. Instead, he focused on cities simply as material consequences of a technological revolution, without tracing their genesis as sacred ritual sites.

No doubt if we could travel back in time to ask a Bronze Age Mesopotamian, Egyptian, or Canaanite about how to go about founding a town, or even to ask a classical Greek or Roman augur who knew the proper rites, we would hear little about Childe's materialist criteria for cities. There was no archaic or classical discussion of population pressure and democratic density, except to condemn it as a symptom of decay. There was no discussion of how the division of labor led to social stratification or to lower costs (and hence higher economic competitiveness), but only to higher-*quality* output (Lowry 1987:68ff.; Finley 1974). Nor did ancient writers discuss the urban character of writing and public architecture, science, engineering, and the secularization of art. As for the idea that cities tended automatically to grow larger and more complex over time, it took many centuries for classical Greece and Rome to achieve anywhere near the degree of specialization found earlier in Bronze Age Mesopotamia, and their industry was never as large-scale.

Even as cities became more secular in classical times, their administrative focus remained shaped to a large extent by sacred rituals. Town planners were augurs, more concerned with reading omens than with the more pragmatic aspects of city planning. In an epoch when medicine was ritualistic and doctors often were in the character of shamans, the idea of promoting health was to perform proper rituals at the city's foundation rather than to place cities on slopes for good drainage. (This is why it was considered auspicious to build Rome around the mosquito-ridden Forum.) Material considerations were incorporated to the extent that they could be reconciled with the guiding social cosmology.

Entrepot cities as enclaves from the laws of their lands rather than centers of law and power

The heterogeneous and multiethnic character of Near Eastern cities reflected their function as enclaves *from* the law of the land, *e.g.*, as free trade areas or cities of refuge. In this respect the most archaic urban sites were specialized islands — ritual centers, trading entrepots, and occasionally (but relatively late) imperial capitals and military outposts such as those of Sargon and his Akkadians. What is not found among early Near Eastern cities is the general-purpose *polis* of classical antiquity, whose citizen-landholders made laws covering their community at large and carried on industry through their own households rather than via corporately distinct public institutions.

Many millennia were required before a common body of law came to govern the city and the land, temples, and palaces in a single code. *Polis*-type cities and their law codes combining hitherto separate public and private, sacred and secular functions were relatively late. And when such cities arose, in classical times, they had become much more genetically closed than was the case in archaic towns.

Having summarized these various characteristics of the earliest urban sites, we are now in a position to turn to one of the most economically important types of archaic city: the trade entrepot. Beginning with Çatal Hüyük in Asia Minor c. 5500 BC, the earliest cities were multiethnic entrepots. They might range in size from a trading post (French *pôt*) to a full-fledged port city. Such commercial centers would have had to provide equal treatment for all parties, reinforced by the usual array of rituals.

In any event, such towns were different in principle from centers of political government or military power representing one territory's interests as distinct from those of other such groupings.

Near Eastern cities were centered around temples, which gave them a sacred status as well as serving as commercial administrators. Rather than being controlled by any one tribe, family, or locality (at least "in the beginning"), these temples were endowed by diverse parties as autonomous institutions to serve broad, community-wide interests. This public status explains why the earliest towns were militarily stable despite their lack of fortifications. Their cosmopolitan, often multiethnic character made their urban religion "higher" and more comprehensive than life on the land.

An important characteristic of entrepot cities was that they were founded at the external margin rather than in the center of their communities. The fact that they often were on watercourses or similar natural points of confluence reflects the fact that one of their major purposes was to deal with outsiders, above all, through trade.

Throughout the ancient world we find similar entrepot areas built up on offshore islands wherever these are conveniently at hand. Such islands had the advantage of having deeper harbors than were available onshore, but there also was a political reason to prefer them. Islands kept foreign mercantile contact out of local communities. This made them a path of least resistance as neutral commercial entrepots, facilitating arms-length contacts.

Egypt, for instance, restricted foreign contacts to the Delta region where the Nile emptied into the Mediterranean. The Etruscans confined their foreign commerce with the Phoenicians and Greeks in the eighth and seventh centuries BC to the island of Ischia/Pithekoussai, which became a base for the Corinthians and other merchants to deal with the Italian mainland. Cornwall's tin was exported via the Scilly Isles. The north Germans may have conducted the Baltic amber trade by way of the offshore (sacred?) island of Helgoland. Athens traded via its Piraeus port area.

Muhly (1973:227) notes the significance of island entrepots: "The early Greek commercial settlements in the west were made not on the mainland but on small offshore islands, such as Ischia, in the Baby of Naples, and Ortygia, just off Syracuse. The early Phoenician settlements in the west followed the same pattern, as shown by the settlements at Motya, off the western tip of Sicily, and at Gadir, in Cadiz Bay." Rhys Carpenter (1966:206f.) has attributed this to the fear felt by seaborne traders of "mainland native treachery," so as to be safe from land attacks. Perhaps the harbors also were secured from piracy.

Other such islands include the Scilly Isles off the coast of Cornwall, and the Bahrain islands, as well as Ru'ush eg-Gibal in the Gulf of Oman. Muhly adds (1973:399) that Fagerlie (1967) discusses the offshore islands of Øland and Gotland in northern Europe's amber trade. Homer's Odyssey has the Phaecians trade from an offshore island. (Note Hong Kong's role in today's world.)

This long historical tradition stands behind today's offshore enclaves. *They were stateless in the sense of lying outside the jurisdiction and control of any single territorial government.* They often were islands, figuratively if not literally, and many were situated at key transport junctions. (We find this same idea in the *karum* areas where trade was conducted, even in inland colonies such as karum Kanesh handling the Assyrian trade in Asia Minor. Larsen [1976] provides details.)

A characteristic of such sites was their exemption from control by any single regional or kinship-based grouping. Their inhabitants were treated equally (at least in principle), regardless of their private status. In the third and second millennia we find such cities marked by *kudurru* stones attesting to their exemption from tribute and quasi-taxes, something like Germany's medieval free cities.

The multiethnic character of southern Mesopotamian cities (and others as well) led them to formalize rituals of social integration to create a synthetic affinity. Urban cults were structured to resemble the family — a public family or corporate body with its own foundation story such as that of Abraham of Ur for the Jews, or heroic myths for Greek cities. Over these families stood the temples, "households of the gods," whose patron deities were manifestations of a common prototype and given local genealogies.

Commercial contacts led to cultural interchange and new cultural forms. Residents of gateway centers staged pageants to celebrate and cement their association. Olympia, Delphi, Nemia, and the Corinthian Isthmus staged pan-Hellenic games as friendly competitions to help integrate the Greeks (Raschke 1988). Such festivities have provided occasions for trade throughout much of history. Their public ceremonial character enabled them to provide an umbrella of peace over a market for commercial wares.

Cities of refuge

The first city that appears in the Bible (Genesis 4) is not a commercial port, administrative capital, or military outpost, but the city of refuge located "east of Eden . . . in the land of Nod," to which Adam's son Cain withdrew after he killed his brother Abel. This city evidently was already established and populated, but we are not told by whom.

Such cities of refuge are found not only in the Old Testament but also in Native American communities at the time of their first contact with white men, suggesting a nearly universal response to the problem of what to do with public offenders. Throughout history, exile has been a widespread punishment for manslaughter and other capital crimes, including treason. The exile is obliged to leave his native community on pain of death, liable to retaliation by the victim's family taking revenge. Sanctuaries for such fugitives must have been well peopled, for an early myth says that Romulus helped populate Rome by founding an asylum for them.

The Israelites are said to have created twelve cities of refuge, one for each tribal region. Genesis 9 stipulates that "Whoever sheds the blood of man, by man shall his blood be shed." Exodus 21 qualifies this by adding that as long as there was no deliberate murder with premeditated guile, "if he does not do it intentionally, but God lets it happen, he is to flee to a place I will designate." Numbers 35 reports that the Lord commanded Moses to "Speak to the Israelites and say to them: 'When you cross the Jordan into Canaan, select some towns to be your cities of refuge, to which a person who has killed someone accidentally may flee. They will be places of refuge from the avenger, so that a person accused of murder may not die before he stands trial before the assembly." Six towns were thus appointed, to be overseen by Levite priests. More details are provided by Joshua 20, a veritable manual for how to inaugurate a city or new society:

> The Lord said to Joshua: "Tell the Israelites to designate the cities of refuge, as I instructed you through Moses, so that anyone who kills a person accidentally and unintentionally may flee there and find protection from the blood-avenger.
>
> When he flees to one of these cities, he is to stand in the entrance of the city gate and state his case before the elders of that city. Then they are to admit him into their city and give him a place to live with them. If the blood-avenger pursues him, they must not surrender the one accused, because he killed his neighbor unintentionally and without malice aforethought. He is to stay in that city until he has stood trial before the assembly land until the death of the high priest who is serving at that time. Then he may go back to his own home in the town from which he fled."

Such cities are assumed to have been placed on hills, mountains or other prominent spots plainly marked, as described in Deuteronomy 19, but Levine (this volume) finds them to be temples in the city itself. In any event, each year public workers are reported to have been sent to repair the roads leading to them, and to maintain signposts guiding manslayers. Such cities were to be of ready access, situated "in the midst of the land" rather than in remote corners, so that they could be reached by a single day's journey. Presumably they were emptied in the general amnesties that find their roots at least as early as the Babylonian *misharum* Clean Slates and Egyptian *sed* festivals early in the second millennium.

Archaic cities as gateways

Entrepots throughout history have been multiethnic, attracting merchants and travelers from all over. The logic of their social relations has dictated that when disputes arise, they should be settled by administrative bodies or juries composed of all parties. To establish a standard of behavior (and of pricing, responsibility, and liability) these public areas developed their own rules, which seem to be the first to be written down. The most characteristic applications of early public law pertained to exchange and contact among alien-equals, and between the public professions and the communal/private sector. As noted above, such laws were distinct from the common law of the land, which took the form of oral traditions.

A variety of languages often is spoken in entrepots, just as they are in modern Hong Kong with its Chinese and English, Panama with its Spanish and English, and Lebanon with its Arabic and French. As historians of writing and the alphabet have described, Mesopotamian scribes developed phonetic symbols to transcribe the sounds of alien names and towns to render them from one language to another. This is what inspired the transition from word-signs to syllabic cuneiform in multilingual Sumer. The urban tradition of writing thus may be attributed to the multiethnic commercial character of archaic cities, and their need for record-keeping to seal contracts and treaties and to keep accounts.

Some parallels between archaic entrepots and modern offshore banking centers

A discussion of the origins of urbanization may provide some insight into the character of modern social problems by highlighting the long historical dynamic at work. Indeed, it may not be out of place here to point out that anti-states are well known in the modern world, above all in what the U.S. Federal Reserve Board classifies as eleven offshore banking centers. Five such enclaves are in the Caribbean: Panama, the Netherlands Antilles (Curacao), Bermuda, the Bahamas, and the British West Indies (Cayman Islands). Three enclaves — Hong Kong, Macao, and Singapore — were founded to conduct the China trade. The remaining three are Liberia, Lebanon, and Bahrain at the mouth of the Persian Gulf — the island that Bronze Age Sumerians called Dilmun when they used it to trade with the Indus Valley and the Iranian shore.

Nothing would seem more modern than these offshore banking centers. They are the brainchildren of lawyers and accountants in the 1960s seeking to weave loopholes into the social fabric — to provide curtains of secrecy ("privacy") to avoid or evade taxes, and to serve as havens for ill-gotten earnings as well as to facilitate legitimate commerce.

Whereas modern nation-states enact laws and impose taxes, such enclaves help individuals evade such regulations. And whereas nation-states have armies, these centers are the furthest thing from being military powers. They are antibodies to nationhood, yet more may be learned about Ice Age, Neolithic, and even Bronze Age public sites by looking at these modern enclaves than by examining classical city-states such as Athens and Rome.

A clue to the character of today's commercial enclaves and their Bronze Age forerunners is *their lack of political autonomy.* Instead of being politically independent, the modern offshore banking centers and free trade zones are small former colonies, *e.g.,* the Caribbean islands as well as Chinese entrepots. The Grand Cayman Island was a Jamaican dependency until 1959, when it chose to revert to its former status as a British crown colony so as to benefit from what remained of imperial commercial preferences. Liberia and Panama are U.S. dependencies lacking even their own currency system. (Both use the U.S. dollar.) Hong Kong did not gain title to its own land until Britain's leases expired in 1997. Panama is not scheduled to gain control of its canal until 1999. In sum, whereas political theorists define the first characteristic of modern states (and implicitly their capital cities) as being their ability to enact and enforce laws, offshore banking centers are of no political significance. In the sense of being sanctuaries from national taxes and law authorities, such enclaves are in some ways akin to the biblical cities of refuge. If they are not sanctuaries for lawbreakers personally, they at least provide havens for their bank accounts and corporate shells.

Like most archaic entrepot-cities, modern offshore banking centers are *situated at convenient points of commercial interface between regions,* typically on islands or key transport navels such as the Panamanian isthmus. They are separated as free ports politically, if not physically, from their surrounding political entities. They often are centers of travel and tourism ("business meetings"), and gambling. In antiquity they typically were centers for sacred festivals or games such as were held at Delphi, Nemia, the Corinthian Isthmus, or Olympus (whence our modern Olympic games originated in a sacred context).

Although Delphi and Olympus were landlocked (as was Çatal Hüyük), they were centrally located for their local regions. They served as religious and cultural centers, whose festivals and games could be conveniently attended by the Hellenic population at large. Even visitors who were citizens of mutually belligerent city-states enjoyed *sacred protection against attack*. Of course, today's enclaves no longer claim sacred status, except for the Vatican and its Institute for Religious Works promoting money-laundering functions (Yallop 1984:92ff.). Their commercial focus has become divorced from the religious setting associated with international commerce down through medieval Europe with its great fairs.

Such enclaves *rarely have armies of their own,* yet they are militarily safe. Thanks to their unique apolitical status, and indeed to their ultimate dependence on larger powers, their neighbors have little motive to attack them and every reason to use them as business channels and even for government transactions such as arms dealing, money laundering, and related activities not deemed proper behavior at home. The resulting commerce thrives free of regulations and taxes, conducted in militarily safe environments without the cost of having to support standing armies, and hence less need to levy taxes for this purpose or to monetize national war debts.

To create such enclaves has been an objective of mercantile capital through the ages. It patronizes the world's politically weakest areas as long as they do not do what real governments do: regulate their economies. This search for "neutral territory" expressed itself already in the Chalcolithic epoch, many millennia before private enterprise developed as we know it. The result of this impetus is that Neolithic towns such as Çatal Hüyük, Mesopotamian temple cities such as Nippur, island entrepots such as Dilmun, the Egyptian Delta area, Ischia/Pithekoussai, and the biblical cities of refuge share this important common denominator with today's offshore banking centers: *rather than being centers of local governing, legal, and military power, they were politically neutral sites established outside the jurisdictions of local governments.*

Whether the status of these urban sites was that of sanctified commercial entrepots or amphictyonic centers, they provided a forum for rituals of social cohesion to bolster their commerce. These rituals included the exchange of goods and women (intermarriage) — commerce and intercourse in their archaic sexual meaning as well as in the more modern sense.

I have cited above the archaic practice of conducting trade via island entrepots. The sacred island of Dilmun/Bahrain in the Persian Gulf represents history's longest lasting example of such an enclave. It served as an entrepot linking Sumer and Babylonia (whose records refer prominently to the "merchants of Dilmun") to the Indus civilization and the intervening Iranian shore. Its status as a sacred as well as commercial center may have been promoted by the fact that its waters were a source of pearls, prized as sacred symbols of the moon (being round, pale, and associated with deep water). It also seems to have served as a high-status burial ground for prosperous individuals or at least for parts of their bodies. (Lamberg-Karlovsky 1982 reports that there are more fingers and other limbs than full skeletons, as the Sumerians partook piecemeal in the island's sanctity. Some commentators believe that this may be simply the result of grave robberies through the centuries (see Moorey 1984). In any event these social and commercial virtues helped make Dilmun one of the most expensive pieces of Bronze Age real estate, not unlike modern Bahrain.

The commercial functions of such entrepôts were an outgrowth of their sacred status. For much the same reason that temples became the major handicraft production centers, their sacred status facilitated commercial development in ways that did not abuse Bronze Age sensibilities. By the same token, Bronze Age financial practices had ritualistic origins.

While structuring an economic context for large-scale enterprise within traditional social values and order, Bronze Age institutions provided leeway so as not to stifle commercial development with over-centralized control. This may be part of the reason why trade was conducted *outside* the city gates. The philosophy was to create "mixed economies" in which public and private sectors each had their proper role.

Delos: a classical prototype of modern Panama

This paper began by describing civilization's earliest cities as gateways and neutral zones. They were places where public institutions — first the temples and later the palaces — were endowed with resources to generate economic surpluses in profit-seeking ways not yet deemed proper for individual families. By the Hellenistic period in the second century BC, Delos exhibits the mirror image: a trading enclave enabling private individuals to escape from social rules, turning its temples into commercial embassies of the crassest sort.

During the millennium extending from about 700 BC to AD 300 the unchecked dynamics of commerce, usury, warfare, and slavery polarized Greece, Italy, and the Mediterranean region as a whole. From Persia to Italy, palace workshops and temple households gave way to smaller-scale and less formal family-based estates (*oikoi*) of warrior aristocracies. Most commercial wealth passed into private hands freed from the checks and balances of central overrides. This was particularly true after Alexander the Great's empire was parcelled out among his leading generals following his death in 323 BC. The ensuing Hellenistic regimes provided a free-for-all for wealthy families to do virtually as they wished.

Like most other Aegean islands, Delos was dominated by Athens until one of Alexander's generals, Ptolemy, gained control in 315 BC. Although poor in land and other natural resources and despite the fact that its port and harbor were not very good, Delos flourished as a commercial entrepot. Its temple of Apollo had long established the island as a deposit-banking enclave. Sacred oversight of deposits by Apollo's attendants was of critical importance in an epoch when no such thing as national deposit insurance existed.

Matters were catalyzed when Rome threw its support behind oligarchies throughout the Aegean and Greece, achieving suzerainty over the Mediterranean in 168 BC with the battle of Pydna. Until this time Delos had been overshadowed by the neighboring island of Rhodes. The latter was an ally of Rome, but its business standards were too high to facilitate the quick killings sought by Italian speculators, and in any case Rhodians had kept non-Greeks out of local banking and commerce. In 168 the Roman Senate undercut the island's power by making Delos a duty-free port.

This diverted much business away from Rhodes, and gained for Italian merchants and bankers a major foothold in the Aegean. The Delian temple and general economic administration were turned over to Rome's ally Athens, which evacuated many Delians and replaced them with Athenians, supplemented by an influx of Italian and Levantine adventurers. These newcomers used Delos as a locus for the Aegean grain trade and the maritime lending and insurance that grew out of it.

The island's commercial role was catalyzed in 146 BC when Rome destroyed Corinth and Carthage, and by the general breakdown of authority in the Aegean resulting from the fact that in destroying Rhodian naval power, Rome removed the single major check to piracy. Delos did not take its place in keeping Aegean commerce free from pirates. Indeed, it became their major market!

Matters were greatly aggravated after 142 BC when an ambitious military officer, Diodotus Tryphon, led a revolt to break Cilicia (in what is now southern Turkey) and neighboring Syria away from their Seleucid rulers. He organized the Cilicians into pirate fleets, and his freebooters managed to take over such government as there was in the region.

The pirates quickly monopolized the most lucrative trade of the period: that in slaves. As Strabo (XIV.5) described matters: "Prisoners were an easy catch, and the island of Delos provided a large and wealthy market not far away, which was capable of receiving and exporting ten thousand slaves a day. Hence the proverb: 'Merchant, sail in, unload, everything is sold.' . . . The pirates seeing the easy gains to be made, blossomed forth in large numbers, acting simultaneously as pirates and slave traders." They sold spoils and captives from Asia Minor, Syria, and Egypt to the burgeoning southern Italian market to work as slaves on the large agricultural plantations, in handicraft workshops, or simply as household servants.

The temple of Apollo, sun-god of justice, supporting rather than curtailing the activities of the influx of pirates, merchants, and usurers, provided a protective screen for the basest commercial speculations. The historian Mikhail Rostovtzeff (1941:542ff., 292) has described how "the free port of Delos [was] left completely in the hands of bankers, merchants and traders. . . . While in the early days of Delos the city was an annex to the temple, now the temple became a kind of appendix to the community, bankers with the corresponding amount of labor, mostly servile." Each of the island's ethnic and professional groupings formed its own cult association to represent its mercantile, shipping, and banking interests. From southern Italy, for instance, came the cults of Mercury and Maia, Apollo and Poseidon. A Phoenician cult was centered in a temple replete with porticoes to display its members' merchandise (Tarn 1952:261, citing Hatzfeld, *Les Trafiquants Italiens dans l'Orient hellenique*).

Yves Garlan (1988:183) refers to pirate-controlled Cilicia and its emporium on Delos as "counterstates," and Rostovtzeff (*loc. cit.*) calls them "a new phenomenon among the city-states of Greece." Tarn (1952:264ff.) calls Delos's relationship with the Cilician pirates an "unholy alliance . . . Delos became the greatest slave-market yet known, and as the eastern governments began to grow weaker their subjects were drained away; Bithynia is said to have been half depopulated." He concurs that Delos represented "a unique kind of form . . . the foreign business associations became 'settlers,' and in their totality constituted 'Delos,' seemingly without any city forms at all, but under an Athenian governor; that is, political precedents were subordinated to the requirements of trade." Thus, just as in today's world Panama and other offshore banking entrepots operate as the antitheses to nationhood, so in Rostovtzeff's description "the motley population of Delos had not the slightest inclination to become a city. They were perfectly happy to live the peculiar life of a free merchant community with no civic duties to fulfill and no liturgies [taxes] to bear."

The last thing the Delian merchant class wanted was a public authority to regulate its entrepot trade in captured cargoes, slaves or, for that matter, honest goods. "It is evident that the residents of Delos were not very much interested either in the temple or in the city," concludes Rostovtzeff (*loc. cit.*):

> Delos was for them not their home but their business residence. What they cared for most was not the city or the temple but the harbors, the famous sacred harbor, and especially the three adjoining so-called basins with their large and spacious storehouses. It is striking that while these storehouses are open to the sea there is almost no access to them from the city. This shows that very few goods stored in them ever went as far as even the marketplaces of the city. Many of them came to the harbor, spent time in the storehouses, and moved on, leaving considerable sums in the hands of the Delian brokers. In fact in the Athenian period the city of Delos was but an appendix to the harbor. So soon as the activity of the harbor stopped, the city became a heap of ruins and it was again the temple which towered over these in splendid isolation.

This characteristic of Delos's warehouses being only open outwards, not inland, finds a parallel in modern Panama's Canal Zone, whose warehouses likewise are bonded and set aside from the local economy (save for the National Guard's pilfering and shakedowns). Panama's imports from Asia are destined for other Western Hemisphere countries rather than for local consumption. Drug and arms shipments provide another analogue to Delian contraband. Finally, Panama's sizeable Oriental and European population working as brokers and bankers recalls the adventurers who made their way to Delos. Both that island and Panama became what are now called "dual economies": The Delian export trade involved the native population only minimally, much as is the case in Panama and other modern enclaves.

The anti-Roman leader Mithradates of Pontus received support from the Cilician pirates, and in turn gave his support to Delos. An uprising against Rome resulted in the massacre of Italian merchants and creditors throughout Asia Minor and Greece in 88 BC. Some 20,000 Romans and their retinues reportedly were killed on Delos and the neighboring islands. The pirates later turned on Delos and looted it. Rome retaliated, and the accession of Augustus a half-century later finally cleared the Mediterranean of piracy and restored peace. This dried up the sources of the Delian trade in slaves and pirate contraband.

As free-enterprise havens for their respective criminal undergrounds, both the Delian and Panamanian enclaves attracted the usual riffraff. What would be needed to complete the parallel between Panama and Delos would be a massacre of Americans in the Canal Zone comparable to that of Roman tax farmers and creditors in the first century BC. Even without so grizzly a climax, an obvious parallel remains: just as Rome finally closed down Delos, so the 1988-1989 American invasion to topple Noriega lay waste to Panama's economy. (However, whereas Rome proceeded to clean up Mediterranean piracy as a whole, the United States has not yet sought to close down criminal-enterprise zones in the Caribbean except for the Canal Zone.)

Summary: Near Eastern temples and their urbanizing functions

Bronze Age trade entrepots and temples were not governing centers to establish general laws and policies for their local landed communities. They had even less of the character of military centers. They did not have taxing authority beyond their local enclave limits. (That would have smacked of imperial tribute.) Indeed, the major Mesopotamian cities were freed from such tribute in the Middle and Late Bronze Age. This freedom was marked by *kudurrus* (Oppenheim 1977). Nippur, for instance, was "tax-free": Mesopotamian rulers exempted it from tribute. In this status as a "free city" we find a characteristic of modern commercial havens. No doubt this status was related to the fact that many of antiquity's trade enclaves were established literally as *islands of free enterprise.*

Such cosmopolitan islands were anything but "states" as usually described by political theorists. Indeed, today's ideas of public power are not much help in analyzing Bronze Age institutions. Conversely, by not viewing states as having a directly commercial role, modern political theorists miss the key characteristics of archaic urbanization and Bronze Age public institutions. Mesopotamian temples and palace were economic producers in an epoch when production had not yet passed into private hands.

While the temples had important worldly social functions, governing was not one of them. They were created to solve the most pressing economic problem of their time — to undertake the commercial enterprise aimed at securing foreign raw materials. Rather than being subject to the laws of any single territory, they had their own special laws, originally limited only to their territory and governing their public functions. They made economic policy to the extent that they established prices for food and other products, rented out sharecropping lands as history's first absentee landlords, extended credit at the first regularly attested interest rates, produced exports in their workshops, oversaw weights and measures, developed economic accounting, and stored seed, savings, money, and economic records. Yet in performing these functions, most Bronze Age cities and their temples fell short of the criteria of modern states as described by today's political theorists: the ability to make generally binding laws, declare war, and tax. The city-temples may best be thought of as *public utilities.* It was as such that they were accountable, whereas private partnerships were not. (Throughout antiquity the only business corporations that could be formed were for the purpose of undertaking public functions such as construction and tax farming.)

Inevitably, as towns developed into regional trade systems, their prosperity inspired local military rivalries while attracting the attention of alien raiders. Military and other secular forces played a growing role by the third millennium and sought to legitimize themselves by adapting the traditional repertory of cosmological symbolism, public architecture, and at least the outward forms of archaic ritual functions to their evolving circumstances.

Discussion

Wright: I really like your approach. In contrast to Childe, who just lists the elements of a city, you draw out a process of how a city develops. But there is something that bothers me. I know you are not saying that what happened in Mesopotamia happened everywhere, but there is a sense of inevitability in your argument. It is as if we could look into the future and see that the Cayman Islands eventually will become Washington D.C. or something like it.

Hudson: When you get a variety of differently organized societies interacting, nothing is inevitable. There are too many possible combinations. Sometimes when I look at antiquity, right down through the classical Greek and Italian cities, it almost seems as if every kind of structure that could be set up was tried. Even in today's world, each major region has its own distinguishing characteristics. That is what politics is all about. Antiquity could have gone a number of ways (and I suppose that some of us wish that it had). I am trying to separate the various diverse strands that came together in the particular way they did, that led to the modern world — first, regarding urban practices, and second, regarding urban real estate.

Wright: But you seem to require at each point to be able to identify one way of organizing the economy. This seems to deny the idea that you expressed in your paper in the Privatization volume, that several different types of economies could be happening simultaneously.

Hudson: I thought my point was exactly what you accuse me of *not* making. There were indeed several different types of economies going on. There was a symbiosis between urban areas and surrounding kinship-based lands — not a homogeneity between them, but a specialization of functions. Some were held in "neutral zones" as the path of least resistance. Precisely because of these differences, as well as different regional groupings, there had to be certain formally organized functions for these groups to come together under a public umbrella. This kind of umbrella worked best when it was sanctified by the temples.

Alex Marshack laid the groundwork for my approach by citing the kinds of ceremonies in which people would come together for marrying outside their own clan, for having relationships with other clans and other groups. In order to have these "exchange relationships," special mediating institutions had to be created. I characterized them as being neutral zones or areas. Today you could call them free enterprise zones or off-shore banking centers.

My point was simply that there is something "offshore" about the most archaic urban areas and religious centers *before* they became political centers. It is precisely because the participants in such gathering places are diverse that they tend to develop a carefully formalized character of equality, almost a schematized equality of the sort that is not needed when people are part of kinship relationships. Mutual outsiders deal with each other best when there is a formal "equality under the law." Hierarchic relationships, political control, and taxes make such relations less attractive and more coercive.

Stone: What you are saying sounds congruent with the views of Bob Adams, as I understand them. He stresses the different microenvironments within Mesopotamia and the need to bring populations together, as well as the importance of long-distance trade, although some people would debate that.

What I would like to emphasize, however, is that I don't find much difference in the conception of the city between the Protoliterate and Sargonic periods. I think one adds certain types of institutions, most notably the palace. But you start off with multiple types of economies, and then add another and another. That may be necessary in the case of the palace, for example, to stop others from fighting each other. But I don't see enormous differences from the Protoliterate through Sargonic periods, the Old Babylonian and probably even the Neo-Babylonian.

I also am increasingly unconvinced that the distinction between urban and rural, and kinship and nonkinship is all that valid. We tend to view things through the perspective of a particular temple archive or private archive, and then assume that these are two different sets of people. I think this happens simply because modern scholars individually tend to study the same type of archives, temple or private. Consequently, there comes to be a tacit assumption that the people documented in the temple archives as receiving rations from the state are different than the people who are living in the private houses and represented in those archives. I don't think this is the case. Just as you have cities with multiple economies, you have citizens participating in these multiple economies at the same time.

Hudson: I try to avoid using the word "state" for precisely that reason. I prefer the word public. The public sector coexists with the "private," but the community sets aside certain economic and social functions as being publically mediated. Many individuals play a dual role.

One of the important roles of the Mesopotamian temple was to mediate trade by overseeing weights and measures, creating the formalities of written agreements, and providing standards for contracts and rules for their enforcement. Standardization of exchange relations thus developed as a kind of public function. Sometimes *damgar* merchants are found receiving rations or donkeys from the temple, yet they probably lived in townhouses, as you observe.

Regarding the Mesopotamian workfare/welfare system, many of the women and children in the temple workshops were taken out of their family context on the land. The blind, crippled, infirm, or elderly might become part of the temple family. In the writings you find them described as a family of their own; that was their metaphor. The temple family included not only dependents, but also the *naditu* women, whose money was kept free. So you are quite right: there was a symbiotic relationship between these individuals, their families and the temple. But to have such a symbiotic relationship, you must have a specialization of public functions.

Dandamayev: What was the difference between those ceremonial cities you were talking about and ordinary villages?

Hudson: The special functions that occurred in the cities defined their role. Whereas ordinary village life was based on customary relationships of families within the same homogeneous area and its everyday activities, an important role of cities was to mediate among different groups, *e.g.*, for exchange and to organize ceremonies of broader group or regional cohesion. I think this explains why many cities were located at the boundaries of groups, not at their center. There was an external relation of the cities as mediators among diverse groups. One sees this most conspicuously in amphictyonic centers.

Dandamayev: Beginning from what time?

Hudson: I agree with Alex that the genesis of such practices is to be found deep in the Ice Age. Any group, no matter how small or primitive, has to deal with people outside of its own immediate members. So presumably "urban" areas are free zones where relationships with outsiders develop. I see this in Greece, and I cited Wheatley with regard to China. But I haven't seen it so much in Mesopotamia, which is why I am raising this theory with you to see if there is any basis for it in your experience.

Goelet: In Egypt the temple was more like a sort of military reserve unit, where you might have a small full-time staff. But there was not much of a professional priesthood until quite late. You had these phyles, and they were not part of a temple family. There are areas in most towns that do serve as offshore banking centers. Perhaps I should say onshore. Also in Egypt the connection between deities and towns is very strong. Whenever you see a god's name mentioned, it almost always is associated with a town.

Lamberg-Karlovsky: I am not sure I would agree with your equating the temple with the institution in which political power and centricity of organization actually took place. I think we can show already in the Samara period that there are architectural configurations that certainly do not seem to be temples, that aggregate differential wealth, that have the signifiers of decision-making aspects. Seals and sealing are already there. It is 2,000 years before your model, which views a single Mesopotamian entity, whereas there are several Mesopotamias, both ecologically and culturally.

Hudson: I agree that temples were not the centers of political power. That was the point that I was making when I described urban areas as neutral zones, even as sanctified neutral zones. They had a public function that is quite different from (and in my mind, prior to) a political function. If I understand what you are saying, aside from these areas that I am describing, there was power in the hands of private households. I agree.

Lamberg-Karlovsky: They may also have had the function of accumulating and redistributing wealth prior to the temple complex. The social, secular world was already complex and urban prior to the so-called Uruk explosion in which Mesopotamia, as Elizabeth said, has a common trajectory in the south. Before that, during the time in which the city is in fact being invented, the temple is much harder to find as either the economic, political, or archeological template that scholars credit it as being. I am trying to grasp what precedes the temple complexity and provides the foundation from which it developed.

Stone: Part of the problem is looking at the temple as separate from the family. The temple of Inanna could be seen as the temple of the "family mafia" (Lamberg-Karlovsky supplies this term). Family relationships underlie many of the institutions of the city.

Buccellati: It is my impression that the palace is more of a super mafia that overrides the others.

I have some difficulties with the picture that you present of the ceremonial importance of the cities. First, the model of the free-trade zone, or the modern free market, presupposes the city. It fits where there's a vacuum and draws on the opportunities that the urban world provides. Without the urban world there could not be a free market. But I think it is secondary or minor in terms of the structural understanding of what a city is.

Second, I think that the countryside is very urban. It depends totally on the city in terms of its function.

Third, I think you said that urban property was not subject to *andurarum* debts. But we have contracts in which houses are not subject to that, which implies that others are.

Finally, I think the political dimension is overriding. All the efforts of cities to defend their territory and wealth are essentially political.

Hudson: My impression is that townhouses were dealt with differently from rural lands. I think the issue is extremely important.

Within this context of whatever urban or rural activities were occurring for the production of an economic surplus, the gathering place or city provided a mediating function. This was organized in a way that created wealth, which made the urban areas, land, and housing increasingly different from rural subsistence land.

Levine: In my talk I am going to ask whether it is feasible to expect that we can understand this first moment in time, the very beginning of the process. My main interest is in religious institutions. I think they are the result of something that happens first, people coming together for whatever purposes. I am not doubting the primal nature of the religious urge or needs. They are there to start with, but institutionally speaking, it happens first that certain key conditions emerge. Because they have emerged for other, more practical reasons, you find that it also turns out to be a good setting for doing something about these urges, or for sanctifying, sanctioning, and demarcating these things.

So festivals happen when people are together, not vice versa. It is clear to me that the practical process occurs first. Then, these preexistent urges that are there — or the need to find some meaning in what is happening — utilize these preconditions. Then, cult centers arise. Once they arise, then of course you get a dynamic cycle going. People are attracted, and they also do business while they are there.

The question is, when is the first moment in this process? Can you get back to the ultimate beginning of this process of urbanization we are talking about. If we are going to do that, then religious institutionalism is on the very initial level, utilizing an opportunity that arose for a different reason. That is my response to Michael's presentation.

I have no objection to noticing, as an observable fact, that in the earliest communities you have some sort of sacred precinct present. I would expect that. When you are trying to get back to the origin of the process, I don't think it was there the first time they got together.

These people that Alex Marshack was talking about start calendars, and then when the time comes around there is a festival. These crystallize into all these institutionalizations of religion. I think the fallacy usually occurs in failing to distinguish between the primacy of the urge and need to symbolize what is happening, which is there very early on, from the beginning as part of their interior baggage. But it is not what really brings them together for the first time, even with respect to the family or the extended family. It seems to me that we should be looking for some practical need to get together, and then you celebrate that and utilize the occasion. It is a belated response.

Hudson: I worry that you are attributing to me too extreme a position. I agree with you that *after* people made arrangements to come together (for the practical reasons I had outlined), it was natural for them to trade, to want to "find meaning" in their social life, and in some cases indeed to develop your "religious feelings." But I suspect that "religion" in the earliest epoch meant putting structure into pragmatic, worldly life by *sanctifying* certain types of behavior or at least the idea of protecting (or constraining) certain types of behavior. Everything went together. And what we may call "religion" was simply providing rules.

At first, these rules had to be specially demarcated. There was not the idea of universal rules applying everywhere at all times. Trade, the exchange of women (or intermarriages among families, if you prefer to think of it that way) and simple conviviality must have required distinct sets of rules for particular occasions, so as not to "interfere" with other "normal" life (whatever that may have been). I suggest that this "specialness" played a major role in defining urban zones.

My construct is more logical and a priori than historical, I admit. Therefore, I can put it forward only as a tentative working hypothesis to be tested. The rules about which I am speaking became central to defining the unique structure of the earliest gathering places. If this idea is correct, then it would explain the cosmological symbolism that marks the earliest cities, at least in the examples I cited from Wheatley *et al.*

I infer that your criticism is that I may have drawn the contrast between civic and sacred, rural and urban too strongly. Perhaps so; but is the contrast helpful? That is the basic question I want to raise.

Renger: Take the case of the commercial relations of Gudea, the ruler of Lagash. Most of his contacts were with the west to obtain timber. I wondered what was happening at the other end. An interesting piece of evidence is a tablet from Ebla listing some of the property owned by the Royal House: 1,700 minas received from the cedar boxwood trade. This is the only reference to cedar and the other timbers in the Ebla texts. One has to conclude that the trade was coming through the Ebla territory. It was transported from the Mediterranean coast through Ebla. This is probably the toll that was paid to the House of Ebla by whoever transported it. I assume that if the rulers themselves were involved in the transportation of this that we would have more evidence from where this timber was shipped, but this is absolutely unique as far as I know.

Hudson: In any case, Ebla would not be my idea of a temple city. It is the kind of city you find more and more from the third millennium onward — a more "modern" type of urban area if you will. Once you find a city acting as a political center or an empire-builder, you have gone beyond the type of "neutral zone" that I am hypothesizing.

Renger: Well, as for the question of temples sanctifying the neutrality of the trading parties, I don't see any real hard evidence for that. What I remember is of course that in the gift exchange in the middle of the second millennium that Zaccagnini has described, we read the Amarna letters that guarantee the security of the traders and messengers bringing gifts from Mesopotamia to Egypt or vice versa. That depended on the local rulers. The Egyptian king could get the Palestinian kinglets to observe the peace of trade. The Hittites could make sure that the northern Assyrian kings would let the messengers pass on without touching the gold that was sent from Egypt. So it certainly does not look as if the temples had material authority to guarantee the security of trade in that period.

Hudson: I was postulating something earlier. I admit I was using a priori evidence and was inspired by Polanyi's idea of cities of refuge. My paper sought to formulate this idea as a hypothesis: if this *were* the origin of at least some cities (one type), then this is how they would logically have developed. I tried to fit the known archaeological evidence, realizing that I was talking about preliterate developments. So I think that my paper should be viewed as a question that I am putting to you: is it plausible? If so, are there facts that you know that would bear upon my hypothesis?

Zaccagnini: Of course, I was very much interested in Prof. Renger's comments, because they touch upon matters with which I have been dealing for a long time. My discovery of Polanyi goes back some 25 years, when I was preparing my book on the exchange of gifts in the Near East during the late second millennium (published in 1973). Ten years later I made use of the same methodological approach in the analysis of the gift exchange during the Old Babylonian period.

I have some questions. Speaking of "administered trade," Polanyi's concept does not refer to long-distance trade systems run by state (*i.e.*, palace or temple) organizations, but to mechanisms for price determination that are alternative to market supply and demand. Whether and to what extent Polanyi's paradigm can be profitably used in our present interpretations of ancient Near Eastern economies is of course another matter.

Prof. Renger just mentioned the inscriptions of Gudea. As a complement to this, I would like to draw attention to a well-known Sumerian literary text, the poem of "Enmerkar and the Lord of Aratta," on which I have recently commented, focusing on the contemporary yet conflicting presence of different exchange patterns — none of which can be identified with the standard "market" procedures — in the context of a typical long-distance trade scenario.

In my opinion, ancient Near Eastern institutional entities — palaces or temples — had little to do with "administered trade" (in Polanyian terms), although they certainly played a major role (especially in certain periods) in organizing, controlling, and benefiting long-distance trade commercial activities. Private individuals often seem to have acted independently of the state institutions, although we do have examples of joint ventures. Some years ago I examined the case of the Nuzi merchants. It is clear that the central administration had its professional traders, who had the status of palace dependants. At the same time, private individuals entrusted these merchants with their wealth, aiming to obtain individual commercial profit.

Another important question concerns who the ultimate beneficiaries of the imports of long distance trade were. The first and most reasonable answer is that they must belong to the social and economic elites of the ancient Near East. Yet if one thinks about the incredibly numerous occurrences of finished or worked products and of raw materials — metals in the first instance — that circulated outside the temple or palace economic spheres, we must fully acknowledge the presence of much wider scenarios, which included the participation of very different socioeconomic levels of population. By limiting myself to the case of Nuzi, the numerous transactions between private individuals in which real estate or movables (including people) were sold, pledged, or exchanged, it can be observed that the means of payment consisted of silver, gold, copper, tin, and bronze, in addition (or as a complement) to barley, livestock, textiles, etc. This means that eventually imports of foreign goods, which might have been used for jewelery, other luxuries, tools, or whatever other kind of artifacts, were also available to lower strata of local population and used in their everyday economic activities.

As far as the theory of "transaction costs" is concerned, I believe that the words of Douglass C. North can still be appreciated as an extension of Polanyi's concepts as applied to the ancient Near East. Is there any justification for assuming that what you call ports of trade like Ugarit, or other such cities, would insure a diminution or a minimization of transaction costs? How would you classify the four Italian *republiche marinare* — Pisa, Genoa, Venice, Amalfi?

Renger: With regard to Ugarit and the coastal cities of Syria-Palestine, I think of Tyre and Sidon in the Neo-Assyrian period. Sargon II of Assyria, Esarhaddon, and Assurbanipal dealt with them by trying to avoid their conquest. This shows that they were not considered similar to the other small states in the region. The Neo-Assyrian rulers realized that this was the best opening to the west to acquire goods and objects that they needed but could not acquire by sheer force such as expansionist imperial policies. I think that this might be the definition of ports of trade.

As for your mention of Douglass North and transaction costs, I am not sure that he really developed Polanyi's theory, because he did not like Polanyi's approach very much.

Zaccagnini: He tried to convert the social approach of Polanyi to a political significance.

Renger: But I think he had a harsh critique of Polanyi, so I am not so sure. Regarding your question about the beneficiaries of overland, long-distance trade, you spoke about precious metals. I think Oppenheim once described the way in which silver went into a larger stratum of society. If I read him correctly in his paper on overland trade given years ago at the International Economic History Congress at Leningrad — he didn't really explain it; it was more of an assumption — he said that kings would distribute these metals as gifts. He was labelling it as an osmotic process. I think we have now some proof of this. A few Mari letters to Zimri-Lim describe that his soldiers were distributed small amounts of silver. In one case there were about 1,000 men, and everyone got some sort of starlike plate or emblem of silver. This is one example.

The other letter describes a Mari contingent of troops coming into Babylon and parading in the gardens at night before Hammurapi, who then distributes silver rings and possibly some small emblems in different quantities according to the soldier's status and rank.

Hudson: Arthur Hocart (1927) and Lord Raglan (1936) made this same point.

Renger: I think that you have this example from Nuzi of trading agents of the king who were entrusted with small amounts of goods and staples by other individuals, to take them along and exchange them for something desired. Yes, why not. We have the same thing in the Cappadocian trade. They bring in tin and textiles and sundry items, small things like sandals or something like that.

Then you remarked that administrative trade means more than just being organized by government, vice versa and opposite to commercial transactions. Take the Piraeus situation. It was not open for commercial activity, but operated under the regulated conditions of the agora. These conditions were set by the city administration in Athens.

Zaccagnini: It is an alternative system for allocating food and services, differing sharply from the market system.

Renger: So I think that the question is about how administrative trade works versus a market competition that allows for supply and demand.

Lamberg-Karlovsky: I am interested in this aspect of differential transactions. I would like to know where this is coming from? Is the transaction cost a factor of distance, *i.e.*, of the cost of land transport? Where are you getting differential transaction costs? Is it an assumption or is it something that you can document?

Zaccagnini: It is a part of the theory of organization.

Lamberg-Karlovsky: It is quite a novel concept. In the southern Babylonian world, it is largely raw resources that are coming in, not finished products — the finished carnelian beads and Indus seals are exceptions. But these stand mostly as exceptions. The question of how the trade is organized from the periphery is quite interesting, because if you look at the Gulf, *i.e.*, metals are shipped from Oman to Mesopotamia, but if you look at virtually every site known in Oman, there is hardly a single artifact from the Mesopotamian world that is found in Oman. It contains a completely indigenous material culture with no evidence of Mesopotamian contact. I don't know what this pattern of asymmetry means, but there is clearly evidence of commerce coming into the Mesopotamian world, but it is difficult to find the Mesopotamian product in the outside world. The texts tell us that cereals and textiles were moving out. It is difficult to understand why it would be cereals. Why on the Iranian plateau would you need cereals? They are self-sufficient communities with adequate agricultural production. That would leave textiles almost entirely as the export item. The extent of asymmetry is interesting, but I don't know what it means.

Renger: I agree with you that the export of cereals doesn't make sense. I think that as long as you are shipping cereals by boat, it is feasible. But we have calculations from the Roman period that if you ship certain amounts of cereal by ox cart, after 50 or 100 kilometers it is eaten up by what you need to feed the oxen. We have that famous shortage of food in the north Assyrian inland around 350 AD. They were starving and yet seventy kilometers away there was plenty of barley. It simply was not feasible to transport that barley by land.

I don't think that they imported just an ordinary loin cloth, but they would look for something prestigious. That is what we know from the Anatolian trade. It was the prestigious type of textiles, as we have later from the Levant.

Hudson: From early Greek history I gather that temples played a major role in conveying commercial practices from the Levant to Greece in the 8th century BC. (I have given my reasons in Hudson 1992.) The Delphi temple certainly played a role in Greek commercial expansion and colonization. You also have the Assyrians evidently using temples as vehicles for their foreign trade expansion into Asia Minor. It was largely on these Near Eastern connections with the western periphery that I developed my idea of neutral zones.

Renger: Well, now that you bring up this point again, from the time I can pick up the documentary record regarding the foreign trade of Mesopotamian cities, I find trade and political control going together rather than being antithetical. After all, it was the palace rulers who administered such trade. Throughout the second millennium, rulers provided security for trade because they themselves were its major beneficiaries, often getting "first pick" of the imports. Administered trade and pricing is found especially by the Late Bronze Age palace economies (Renger 1984). By 1200 BC, much international trade consisted of prestige goods exchanged among rulers in something close to gift exchange.

Hudson: It certainly is true that once the area of conquest and empire-building developed, especially after the Akkadian period began around 2350 BC, the character of cities as I have described them changed over to the more modern character. With exploitative imperial relations, capitals indeed took on the character of administrative and political centers, although Nippur seems to have been a kind of amphictyonic religious center

We may see here the role of cities inverted from an archaic, "stateless," amphictyonic character to seats of dynastic war-kings in the empire-building epoch. This suggests a distinction between primary and secondary types of formation, without a straight-line development. If my hypothesis is valid, then one of the major questions concerning early urbanization is how the transition from such zones to military capitals and "states" occurred.

Renger: My point is that administered trade was conducted from the major political centers. And incidentally, only the elites were in a position to threaten trade, save for pirates and robbers along the route, in addition to being its major sponsors. Politically neutral "free trade" zones evidently had long ceased to exist in Mesopotamia, if they ever existed. The concept seems to be more modern and theoretical than can be confirmed in the archaic record.

Hudson: Perhaps a parallel development could have occurred. The economic historian is obliged to hypothesize a logical construct to explain how such trade may have occurred in the circumstances of its time.

When it comes to the documentary record, the differences between cities as "stateless zones" and their surrounding kinship-based areas would help explain why urban real estate is treated so differently from rural land in Bronze Age Mesopotamia.

In any event, a common characteristic shared by administered trade and exchange through "neutral zones" was their ability to serve as alternatives to price-setting markets.

I also would like to suggest that temple handicrafts may have been an outgrowth of public cult functions such as supporting the weak and infirm as a kind of Bronze Age workfare-welfare system.

Zaccagnini: The Mesopotamian traders were the elites of their communities. All gained by regulating trade.

BIBLIOGRAPHY

Adams, Robert Mc.C. (1969), "The Study of Ancient Mesopotamian Settlement Patterns and the Problem of Urban Origins," *Sumer* 25:111-23.

— (1981), *Heartland of Cities* (Chicago).

Algaze, Guiellermo (1989), "The Uruk Expansion: Cross-Cultural Exchange in Early Mesopotamian Civilization," *CA* 30:571-608.

Archi, Alphonse, ed. (1984), *Circulation of Goods in Non-Palatial Context in the Ancient Near East* (=Incunabula Graeca 82, Rome).

Azarpay, Guitty (1990), "A Canon of Proportions in the Art of the Ancient Near East," in Ann C. Gunter, ed., *Investigating Artistic Environments in the Ancient Near East* (Washington D.C.): 93-103.

Burkert, Walter (1984), *Die Orientalisierende Epoch in der griechischen Religion und Literature* (Heidelberg).

Carpenter, Rhys (1966), *Beyond the Pillars of Hercules*.

Childe, V. Gordon (1950), "The Urban Revolution," *Town Planning Review* 21:3-17.

Crawford, H. E. W. (1973), "Mesopotamia's invisible exports in the third millennium BC," *World Archaeology* 5:232-41.

Diakonoff, Igor M. (1982), "The Structure of Near Eastern Society before the Middle of the 2nd Millennium BC," *Oikumene* 3:7-100.

Ellis, Maria deJ. (1976) *Agriculture and the State in Ancient Mesopotamia: An Introduction to Problems of Land Tenure* (Babylonian Fund, University Museum, Philadelphia).

Ellis, Richard S. (1968), *Foundation Deposits in Ancient Mesopotamia* (New Haven).

Fagerlie, J. M. (1967), *Late Roman and Byzantine Solidi Found in Sweden and Denmark* (New York).

Finkelstein, J. J. (1981), "The Ox that Gored," *TAPS*, 71:Part 2.

Finley, Moses I. (1974), *The Ancient Economy* (Berkeley and Los Angeles).

Garlan, Yves (1988), *Slavery in Ancient Greece* (Ithaca).

Gelb, Ignace J. (1965), "The Ancient Mesopotamian Ration System," *JNES* 24:230-43.

— (1967), Approaches to the Study of Ancient Society," *JAOS* 87:1-8.

— (1971), "On the Alleged Temple and State Economies in Ancient Mesopotamia," in *Studi in Onore di Edoardo Volterra,* VI:137-54 (Milan).

— (1972), "The Arua Institution," *RA* 66:1-21.

— (1986), "Ebla and Lagash: Environmental Contrast," in Harvey Weiss, ed., *The Origins of Cities in Dry-farming Syria and Mesopotamia in the Third Millennium B.C.* (Guilford, Conn.):157-67.

Gelb, I. J., Steinkeller, Piotr and Whiting, R. M. Jr. (1989-91), *Earliest Land Tenure Systems in the Near East. Ancient kudurrus* (Chicago).

Gernet, Louis (1981), *The Anthropology of Ancient Greece* (Baltimore).

Hallo, William W. (1957), *Early Mesopotamian Royal Titles: A Philologic and Historical Analysis* (New Haven).

Hatzfeld, Jean (1919), *Les trafiquants italiens dans l'Orient hellenique* (Paris).

Haywood, Richard Mansfield (1967), *Ancient Rome* (New York).

Hocart, Arthur M. (1950), *Caste* (London)

— (1927), *Kingship* (London).

Holland, Louise Adams (1961), *Janus and the Bridge* (Rome).

Herzog, Ze'ev (1986), *Das Stadttor im Israel und in den Nachbarlaendern* (Mainz).

Hudson, Michael (1992), "Did the Phoenicians Introduce the Idea of Interest to Greece and Italy — And If So, When?" in Günter Kopcke and Isabelle Tokumaru, *Greece Between East and Weat: 10th-8th Centuries BC* (Mainz):128-143.

Hudson, Michael, and Baruch Levine, eds. (1996), *Privatization in the Ancient Near East.* Peabody Musem of Archaeology and Ethnology, Harvard University, Bulletin 5 (Cambridge, Massachusetts).

Humphries, Sarah (1978), *Anthropology and the Greeks.*

Jacobsen, Thorkild (1976), *The Treasures of Darkness* (New Haven).

Kraeling Carl H., and Adams, Robert M., eds. (1960), *City Invincible: A Symposium on Urbanization and Cultural Development in the Ancient Near East, Dec. 4-7, 1958* (Chicago).

Kramer, Samuel Noah and John Maier (1989), *Myths of Enki, the Crafty God* (Oxford).

Lamberg-Karlovsky, C. C. (1982), "Dilmun: Gateway to Immortality," *Journal of Near Eastern Studies* 41:45-50.

Lambert, Maurice (1960), "La naissance de la bureaucratie," *Revue Historique* 224:1-26.

Larsen, Mogens Trolle (1976), *The Old Assyrian City-State and its Colonies* (Copenhagen).

Leemans, W. F. (1950), *The Old-Babylonian Merchant: His Business and his Social Position* (Leiden).

— (1960), *Foreign Trade in the Old Babylonian Period* (Leiden).

Lethaby, W. R. (1892), *Architecture, Mysticism and Myth* (1974, orig. publ. London).

L'Orange, H. P. (1953), *Studies in the Iconography of Cosmic Kingship* (Oslo).

Lowry, S. Todd (1987), *The Archaeology of Economic Ideas* (Durham).

Marshack, Alexander (1972), *The Roots of Civilization* (New York).

— (1975), "Exploring the Mind of Ice Age Man," *National Geographic* 147(1):62-89.

Mellaart, James (1975), *The Neolithic of the Near East* (New York).

— (1987), "Common Sense vs. Oldfashioned Theory in the Interpretation of the Cultural Development of the Ancient Near East," in Linda Manzanilla, ed., *Studies in the Neolithic and Urban Revolutions. The V. Gordon Childe Colloquium, Mexico, 1986* (BAR International Series #349, Oxford):261-69.

Miller, Daniel (1985), "Ideology and the Harappan Civilization," *Journal of Anthropological Archaeology* 4:34-71.

Moorey, P. R. S. (1984), "Where did they bury the Kings of the IIIrd Dynasty of Ur," *Iraq* 46:1-18.

Morgan, Lewis Henry (1878), *Ancient Society* (New York).

Morris, A. E. J. (1979), *History of Urban Form: Before the Industrial Revolutions* (2nd ed.).

Muhly, James David (1973), *Copper and Tin: The Distribution of Mineral Resources and the Nature of the Metals Trade in the Bronze Age* (Hamden, Conn.).

Muller, Werner (1961), *Die heilige Stadt. Roma quadrata, himmlisches Jerusalem und die Mythe vom Weltnabel* (Stuttgart).

Murakawa, Kentaro (1957), "Demiurgos," *Historia* 6:385-415.

Murray, and Price, Simon (1990), *The Greek City* (Oxford).

Oppenheim, A. Leo (1949), "The Golden Garments of the Gods," JNES 8:172-193.

— (1965), Third International Conference of Economic History (Munich).

— (1977), *Ancient Mesopotamia* (Chicago).

Pfeiffer, John E. (1982), *The Creative Explosion: An Inquiry into the Origins of Art and Religion* (New York).

Polanyi, Karl, Conrad M. Arensberg and Harry W. Pearson, eds. (1957*), Trade and Market in the Early Empires: Economies in History and Theory* (New York).

Raglan, Lord (1936), *The Hero: A Study in Tradition, Myth, and Drama* (London).

— (1964), *The Temple and the House* (London).

Raschke, Wendy J. ed., (1988), *The Archaeology of the Olympics* (Madison, Wisc.).

Rostovtzeff, Michael (1941), *Social and Economic History of the Hellenistic World.*

Rykwert, Joseph (1988), *The Idea of a Town: The Anthropology of Urban Form in Rome, Italy and the Ancient World* (Cambridge, Mass.).

Snodgrass, Anthony (1980), *Archaic Greece: The Age of Experiment* (London).

Soffer, Olga (1985), *The Upper Paleolithic of the Central Russian Plain* (New York).

Stone, Elizabeth (1988), *Nippur Neighborhoods* (Chicago).

Struve, V. V. (1969), "The Problem of the Genesis, Development and Disintegration of the Slave Societies in the Ancient Orient" [1933], translated in I. M. Diakonoff, ed., *Ancient Mesopotamia* (Moscow):17-69.

Tarn, W. W. (1952), *Hellenistic Civilization* (New York).

Toynbee, Arnold (1973), *Constantine Porphyrogenitus and his World* (London).

Unwin, George (1918), *Finance and Trade under Edward III* (London).

— (1958), *Studies in Economic History: The Collected Papers of George Unwin* (London, 1927).

van Buren, Elizabeth Douglas (1931), *Foundation Figurines and Offerings* (Berlin).

— (1952), "The Building of a Temple-Tower," *RA* 46:65-74.

— (1952), "Foundation Rites for a New Temple," *Orientalia* 21:293-306.

Vernant, Jean -Pierre (1982), *The Origins of Greek Thought* (Ithaca).

— (1983), *Myth and Thought Among the Greeks* (London and Boston).

Versnel, H. S. (1970), *Triumphus: An Inquiry into the Origin, Development and Meaning of the Roman Triumph* (Leiden).

Wheatley, Paul (1971), *The Pivot of the Four Quarters: A Preliminary Enquiry into the Origins and Character of the Ancient Chinese City* (Edinburgh).

Winter, Irene (1989), "The Body of the Able Ruler: Toward an Understanding of the Statues of Gudea," in Herman Behrens, Darlene Loding and Martha T. Roth, eds., *Dumu-E2-Dub-ba-a: Studies in Honor of Ake W. Sjoberg* (Philadelphia: 573=83).

Yallop, David A. (1984), *In God's Name: An Investigation into the Murder of Pope John Paul I* (New York.)

Yoffee, Norman (1977), *The Economic Role of the Crown in the Old Babylonian Period* (Malibu).

— (1981) *Explaining Trade in Ancient Western Asia* (Malibu).

— (1988) "Aspects of Mesopotamian Land Sales," *American Anthropologist* 90(1):119-130.

Zaccagnini, Carlo (1973), *Lo scambio deidoni nel Vicino Oriente durante i secoli XV-XIII* (Rome).

— (1983), "Patterns of Mobility among Ancient Near Eastern Craftsmen," *JNES* 42:2-64.

— (1986), "The Dilmun Standard and its Relationship with Indian and Near Eastern Weight Systems," *Iraq* 48:19-23.

— (1987), "Aspects of ceremonial exchange in the Near East during the late second millennium BC," in Michael Rowlands, Mogens Larsen and Kristian Kristiansen, eds, *Center and Periphery in the Ancient World* (Cambridge).

PART II

THE ARCHAEOLOGY OF MESOPOTAMIAN CITIES

4

Households, Land Tenure, and Communication Systems in the 6th-4th Millennia of Greater Mesopotamia

C. C. Lamberg-Karlovsky
Peabody Museum of Archaeology and Ethnology
Harvard University

There are two sorts of wealth-getting . . . one is a part of household management, the other is retail trade.

— Aristotle, *Politics*

But what do we mean by an estate? Is it the same thing as a household, or is all property that one possesses outside the house also part of the estate?

— Xenophon, *Oeconomicus*

This paper points to the relatively widespread and continuous use of seals, sealings, and bullae in the contexts of private households beginning in the sixth millennium. These artifacts typically are taken, when combined with written texts, to be evidence for the appearance of a managerial bureaucracy, that is to say a state administration, which is said to emerge in the Uruk Period, c. 3400 BC, in southern Mesopotamia. That seals, sealings, and bullae were used in the sixth millennium as tools of communication, privileging certain individuals with access to areas and goods within the household context, *i.e.,* securing doors and sealing goods within ceramic containers, is less readily appreciated. The nature of these households, their relationship to land tenure and irrigation, as well as to household administration, in the use of these tools, will be examined in this paper.

Recently Piotr Steinkeller (1994), following I. J. Gelb's (1981) important definition of the "Kish Civilization," expanded upon the social and political distinctions that characterized southern and northern Babylonia. The differences between the north and south are as follows:

South	North
City-States	Territorial kingdoms
"Institutional households"	Dynastic/Patrilineages
Dominant female deities	Dominant male deities
Literacy c. 3000+	Literacy c. 2500+
Walled cities/temple precincts	Royal palaces
Irrigation agriculture	Dry-farming
Limited nomadism	Extensive nomadism

The distinctive nature of the social, political, economic, and ecological setting of northern and southern Babylonia were both qualitative and quantitative (see Steinkeller, in this volume). Thus, they were distinctions that made a difference! How far back can these differences be traced and how did they impact upon the developmental trajectories of southern and northern Babylonian civilization?

Over a decade ago Henry Wright (1984:41) remarked that specialized and hierarchically organized agencies of control did not arise abruptly in the Near East from a context of small egalitarian communities. Newly excavated sites in northern Mesopotamia and a reanalysis of evidence from the south offer little confidence in this view. Recently excavated evidence indicates that within basically egalitarian communities specialized devices of control — seals, sealings, and bullae — were "invented" and used for millennia before they were joined by that quintessential administrative tool, the inscribed tablet.

For decades archaeologists working in Mesopotamia have privileged such concepts as decision making, administrative heirarchies, and state formation suggesting that seals, sealings, bullae, and tablets are the central signifiers for each of the above (Wright 1984). Such a theoretical posture is seriously eroded by the recognition that three of the four signifiers exist millennia before administrative hierarchies and/or state formation. The archaeological evidence clearly supports the contention that within greater Mesopotamia, from the 6th to the end of the 4th millennium, the household was the primary unit of production and consumption. A household may be defined as a residential group that forms both a social as well as an economic unit of production and consumption. Members of the household consisted of kin and clients providing voluntary labor. Status was defined by the ability of one member of the household to exploit the labor of another — gender and age being the variables allowing for exploitation. Max Weber (1909) in his study of agrarian relations was perhaps the most prominent in a long line of scholars and historians who argued for the primacy of household organizations in the ancient Near East. Unfortunately, Weber's emphasis on the importance of the *oikos*, the household, was almost entirely forgotten due to the unduly influential and misdirected study of Father Anton Deimel (1931). His study of the temple archive of Bau, from the city-state of Lagash, argued that virtually all economic activity was in the hands of the temple. Based on this study, his student Anna Schneider (1920) popularized the view that within Mesopotamian city-states the "*templewirtschaft*," the temple economy, formed the focus of centralized power controlling both labor and land. The idea that initially the temple, and later the palace, held absolute sway over the political and economic organization of the community remains a belief with a powerful hold on the reconstruction of ancient Near Eastern society. This view emphasizes the role of powerful individuals, the importance of the centralized state, the absence (or insignificance) of private entrepreneurial behavior, and makes invisible not only the important role of households but the significance of small village communities. As a generalization, still adhered to by many that should know better, it offers a wholly distorted perspective on the social order of the ancient Near East.

A considerable theoretical bricolage continues to support a dominant ideological model, one which contends that family structures, the importance of kinship, and the role of households gives way to a bureaucratic meritocracy wherein ascribed status is replaced by individual achievement. Reifying evolutionary stages and positing structural polarities, *i.e.,* ascribed versus achieved, kinship (what anthropologists study) versus family (what sociologists study), extended versus nuclear, communal versus individual, *Gemeinschaft* versus *Gesellschaft*, from status to contract, from tribe to state, *et al.* are too frequently inappropriate or simply wrong. In fact, the types of function these attributes are said to fulfill are rarely stable and/or enduring. Over the past few decades a concept has emerged in discussing late-fourth-millennium Mesopotamia best referred to as the emergence of a "managerial revolution." This view contends that there was an evolutionary displacement of the family, of the household, and of kinship by managerial bureaucracies. Central to this view is the belief that with the emergence of a managerial bureaucracy, the concomitant social and settlement hierarchies become divorced from kinship patterns and household activities. Less explicitly stated, but implied, is the emergent importance of a bureaucratic meritocracy and the importance of individualism within the new social order. This conventional perspective argues for the increasing importance of a faceless bureaucracy replacing an earlier significance of kinship and the household — a perspective firmly embedded in Robert McC. Adams (1966) influential book, *The Evolution of Urban Society* (see particularly chapter 3: Kin and Class). Studies by Steinkeller (1987), Powell (1986), Zettler (1992), Diakonoff (1974), Gelb (1979), and Gelb, Steinkeller, and Whiting (1991), to mention but a few, all indicate that the household, the family, and the role of kinship continued to play a decisive role in the economic and political organization of Mesopotamia. Johannes Renger (1995) succinctly states: "The records, both written and archaeological, indicate that large institutional households decisively determined the social and economic reality in southern Mesopotamia, *i.e.,* Babylonia, at least since the latter part of the fourth and the beginning of the third millennium." Kinship was neither marginalized nor replaced by a meritocracy of individualism, rather, an increasing managerial bureaucracy emerged that was controlled by kin-related individuals (Zettler 1992, Stone 1987). Written records and archaeology provide evidence for the existence of large institutional households (*oikoi*) by the end of the fourth millennium. These institutional households were self-sustaining and autarchic economic units (Renger 1995). The household (*oikos*) constituted "the center of the productive economic activities we now handle through the market" (Lekachman 1959:3). It contained the communities' basic economic activities and was the focal unit of social organization. With reference to the larger village (polis), the household formed the building block for all larger social, economic, and political units. I shall argue in this paper that these large institutional households were already present millennia before the Uruk Period. Central to the argument is the presence, already in the sixth millennium, of bullae, seals, and sealings as well as a particular type of architectural template.

Typically, it is thought that it was during the Uruk Period (c. 3400 BC) of southern Mesopotamia that a communications revolution was first encountered. The tools of communication consisted of cylinder seals, sealings, bullae, and written texts (Adams 1996). These devices represent a technology that transmitted information and recorded it for future use and/or for the making of receipts and guarantees (Nissen, Damerow, and Englund 1993).

Carlo Zaccagnini (1981) has suggested that the earliest texts in Mesopotamia indicate the presence of what Karl Marx referred to as the Asiatic

Mode of Production, in which all-powerful elites obtain their ultimate source of power from the control of production, *i.e.*, the control of large scale waterworks, or the complete command over a powerful force, *i.e.*, an army. Zaccagnini has suggested that societies dominated by the Asiatic Mode of Production share the following characteristics:

1. A despot is the ultimate owner of all land.
2. Property is held in common at the village level.
3. The village is autonomous with respect to economic production and manufacture.
4. A large proportion of one's labor is taken by the ruler as tribute, or forced.
5. The city and country are not differentiated.

Within the Uruk Period in southern Mesopotamia, seals, sealings, bullae, and tablets provide a technology of social control; they were used for the monitoring of production, consumption, labor, property ownership, as well as for the securing of doors and transported merchandise (see the essays in Ferioli *et al.* 1994). These were the tools utilized by the elites for administering what Zaccagnini believes conformed to an Asiatic Mode of Production. Recent research, however, indicates that three of the four devices — seals, sealings, and bullae (and associated tokens) — have a far more ancient history and geographical distribution than previously suspected and, far from being elite devices, they appear to be utilized by ordinary households. Even during the Uruk Period, it is more than likely that the texts refer to individuals administering institutional households (Renger 1995) rather than to the "despots" of Zaccagnini's creation. The use of the seal and the bulla, from Anatolia to Iran, precedes their presence in southern Mesopotamia by several millennia. Joan Oates (1996:165) has recently written that:

> This prehistoric communication revolution began some 9000 years ago among the early agricultural communities of northern Mesopotamia and Syria. Like the invention of the computer, it involved the creation of an ingenious device which served both to transmit information and to record it for future reference. In Neolithic Mesopotamia this new device served also to identify property and to ensure its security, and in that sense to signal to us not only that society was becoming more differentiated (that is, that there were those with goods to protect or secure) but that man could no longer trust his fellow man. This prehistoric in-

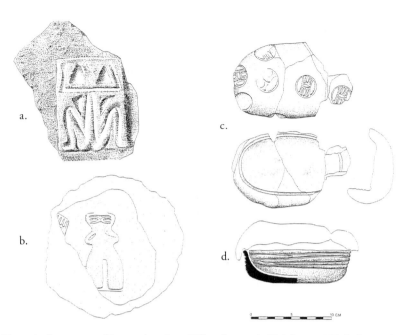

Figure 1. Samarran seal impressions from Tell es-Sawaan (a-b) (after von Wickede 1990) and Sabi Abyadh (c-d).

formation 'system,' the first such in human history, involved the use of simple seals carved with patterns that were impressed on plaster or clay. It was to form the basis of accounting procedures followed widely not only throughout the Near East but elsewhere in the ancient world, a 'system' of such simple efficiency that it remained an important administrative technique even after the development of writing.

The existence of geometric tokens within the Neolithic farming villages of the Near East and their presumed use as accounting devices is best articulated by Schmandt-Besserat (1992). In her view, the earliest stage of recording numeracy utilized the geometric token, followed by the use of the complex token and bulla, and still later, with an increasing complexity of communication needs, the cylinder seal was used for securing and identifying property, and finally, the seminal tool of bureaucratic administration, the inscribed tablet.

Recent excavations at Neolithic Sabi Abyadh, on the Balikh River in northern Syria, and a reanalysis of the excavations at Tal-i Bakun in southwestern Iran add a significant new chapter to the history of this "prehistoric

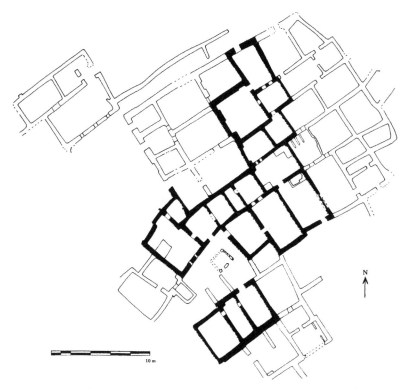

Figure 2. Tal-i Bakun A. Administrative quarter. The Northern Complex with buildings containing seals and sealings outlined in black (after Alizadeh 1994).

communication revolution." At the late-sixth-millennium site of Sabi Abyadh, within a Samarran cultural context (c. 5500 BC), approximately 300 clay sealings were recovered in association with geometric tokens (Fig. 1 c, d). The abundance of sealings and tokens, within household contexts, encouraged the excavators to write of stored "archives" in which "these objects were part of a widely accepted, standardized system of administration and recognition, involving well-developed concepts of ownership and the presence of the bureaucratic means to control it" (Akkermans and Verhoeven 1995:24). Seals and sealings from Samarran contexts were also recovered at Tell es-Sawaan (Fig. 1 a, b; von Wickede 1990).

From the first half of the sixth millennium, beginning with the Samarran sites of Sabi Abyadh and Tell es-Sawaan, there is a limited amount of evidence from a handful of sites that techniques of archiving, that is the use of seals, sealings, tokens, and bullae, were utilized within domestic contexts in village farming communities. At Arpachiyah in north-

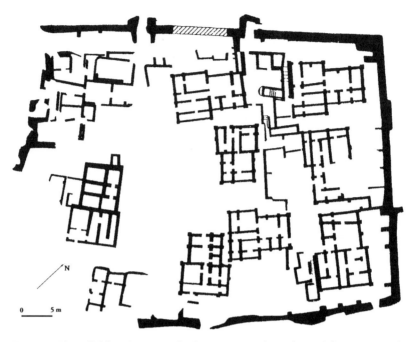

Figure 3. Plan of Tell es-Sawaan in the Samarran Period, Level IIIA (after Yasin 1970).

ern Iraq, a sealed clay bulla covering a knotted string for attachment to a container was recovered and is dated to c. 5500 BC (von Wickede 1990: Figs. 54-58); while at slightly later Tal-i Bakun a large number of seals and sealings were recovered from domestic houses (Fig. 2). Archaeologists have not recovered from any of the above sites, nor from other contemporary settlements, an architectural feature suggestive of centralized economic or political control, *i.e.,* elite signatures such as temples and/or palaces The only replicating architectural feature appears to be a substantial household that conforms to a single architectural template.

Beginning in the Samarran Period, as evidenced at Tell es-Sawaan, archaeologists uncovered seven ten- to twelve-room houses incorporating a fairly uniform interior T-shaped plan (see Fig. 3). These T-shaped buildings become the distinct architectural template for the domestic houses of the Samarran, Ubaid, and Uruk Periods. Thus, there is a remarkably long continuity in this architectural template — beginning as extended household units in the Samarran Period (5500+ BC) and ending up as what Renger (1995) calls "institutional households," his term for what others have referred to as "temples," in the Uruk Period (c. 3500 BC).

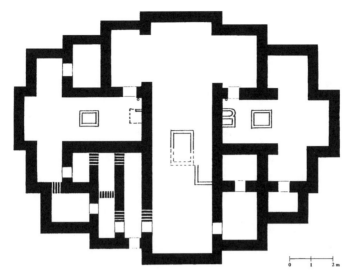

Figure 4. Kheit Qasim III. An Ubaid T-shaped building in the Hamrin (after Maisels 1990 and Forest 1984).

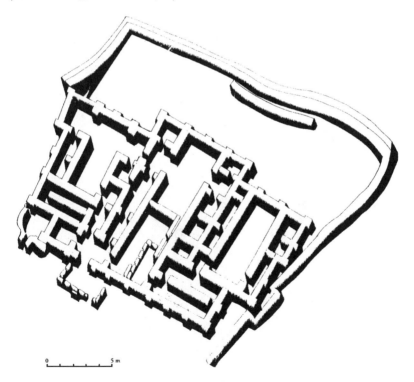

Figure 5. Building A, Level II at Tell Abada, an administrative structure of the Ubaid Period (after Jasim 1985).

C. C. LAMBERG-KARLOVSKY

Maisels (1990:163) writes:

I venture that here are encountered the early physical manifesta-
tion of the *oikos* [household], to be found in the Samarran/
Ubaidian line. But although *oikos* communities are confined to
this cultural lineage, which, of course, leads from the Ubaid
through the Uruk periods into the Early Dynastic of historical
Sumer, the number of sites on which *oikiai* occur are not few.

What P. J. Watson (1978:130-58) posited for the Samarran Period at
Tell es-Sawaan (Fig. 3), C. Forest (1994) and S. A. Jasim (1985), for the
Ubaid sites of Kheit Qasim III (Fig. 4) and Tell Abada (Fig. 5), and J. N.
Postgate and J. A. Moon (1984:73), for the Early Dynastic I at Abu
Salabikh all converge to support the continuous presence of a specific
type of extended household: the architectural signature of the T-shaped
buildings formed augmented and stratified households — that is to say
households that included dependent non-kin, clients serving a dominant
nuclear family. These *oikiai* were not simply extended co-residential groups
but economic entities, as recognized years ago by Diakonoff (1974) and
Gelb (1979). In this context it is relevant to point out that the very word
economy is derived from two Greek words *oikos*, the household, and *no-
mos*, referring to the law. At this juncture it is important to point out that
over 30 years ago Robert McC. Adams (1966:108) already recognized
that the much misunderstood "*tempelwirtschaft*" (temple economy) of
the southern Mesopotamian world was in reality a self-sustained institutional household:

Hence the Bau [a temple in the city-state of Lagash] administration should not be construed as a political structure superimposed
on a pattern of atomistically conducted agricultural operations
merely to facilitate the passive collection of taxes or tribute. It
was, in fact, an oikos in the classic Weberian sense, an authori-
tarian superhousehold in which a remarkably differentiated labor
force of clients undertook to provide their lords with goods and
services.

One might add that by "lords" is simply meant the head of the household, not a titulary title (see below). In the third millennium the texts
clearly indicate that this individual was the senior male within an extended family. Unfortunately, there remain far too many authors who
continue to beat an artificial horse by caricaturing the southern Mesopotamian social landscape as dominated by a monolithic, all-embracing,

universal "temple economy." The wobbly legs of this dead beast are readily exposed by the data recovered from archaeology and the texts, which support a more complex, diversified, and competing world of institutional households.

Mitchell Rothman (1994) in his careful analysis of late-fourth-millennium seals and sealings from the Ubaid Period at Tepe Gawra concludes that they were recovered from "private" houses and functioned to control domestic craft activities (Fig. 6). This conclusion is similar to that reached in the more recent excavations of the "Ubaid colony" at Degirmentepe where sealings were found throughout the settlement in "domestic" houses (Esin 1994). Similarly, Pierre Amiet (1994) in his study of fourth-millennium glyptic at Susa notes the essentially "private" context from which the seals and sealings were recovered. Thus, a consistent line of evidence, from different time periods and cultures, indicates that from the first half of the sixth millennium until the Uruk Period, seals, sealings, and bullae were recovered on a number of excavated sites from Sabi Abyadh in northern Syria to Tepe Yahya in southeastern Iran (a convenient review of the evidence is available in Schmandt-Besserat 1992 and in the important volume of Ferioli *et al.* 1994.) It is of special significance to note that:

1. On every site from which early glyptic evidence was recovered, the individual noted the "domestic" and/or "private" context from which the seals, sealings, and bullae were recovered. Thus, the beginnings of archiving and the "prehistoric communications revolution" took place within what Marshall Sahlins (1972) calls the "domestic mode of production," within the kin units of extended family, lineages, etc. and not within the later contexts of the temples and palaces.

2. In the Uruk Period the southern Babylonians (the Sumerians?) add to the long established tradition of using seals, sealings, and bullae their invention of the inscribed tablet. Seals, sealings, and bullae were earlier utilized in domestic contexts but with the invention of the written tablet the above items and the inscribed tablet form the fundamental units for recording within an institutional context: the temple (Nissen 1988:95-110). This evidence suggests that from long enduring, relatively small, egalitarian communities (using seals, sealings, and bullae for administering their household needs) "specialized and hierarchical organized agencies of control" arose relatively rapidly within the Uruk Period. Clearly, the Uruk evidence points to a dramatic shift toward

an increasing institutional control over a bureaucracy responsible for the monitoring of labor, production, consumption, etc.
The invention of a technology, writing, with the relatively rapid
development of large-scale temple institutions reinforced the development of a social technology of control using tablets, seals,
and sealings.

3. The function of seals, sealings, and bullae was transformed
when written tablets were added to the use of the above. With
the introduction of the written tablet, the use of seals and sealings was transported from an earlier use in domestic contexts to
an institutional function. In the Uruk context, and for the next
several millennia, seals, sealings, bullae, and written texts functioned as administrative devices for managerial control. These
were the tools of an administrative bureaucracy devoted to controlling production, consumption, land consolidation,
inheritance, debt, marriage, etc. Thus, the origins and earliest
use of seals, sealings, and bullae bore little relationship to their
later function — as is frequently the case, the origins of a technology do not reflect their final disposition.

In the narrowest sense, technology is represented by the objects people
make, from hand-axes to written tablets and nuclear installations. Anthropologists may call them "artifacts" while engineers may refer to them
as "hardware"; irrespective of their name they need to be invented, designed, and manufactured. In the Uruk Period the use of seals, sealings,
and bullae, previously items that functioned in the domestic mode of
production, were added to the invention of the inscribed tablet to form
the bases of administrative paraphernalia that permitted bureaucrats to
monitor and control an emerging centralization of the economy. The
processes that brought about the development of this technology required
a larger system of hardware, namely, the development of bureaucratic
institutions directed by dynastic kings, as well as a wholly new scale of
labor control, settlement size, procurement of raw materials, etc.; and
last, but far from least, new "software" in the form of human knowledge
and new skills: scribes, accountants, et al. (Grübler 1996:22).

The social world of Uruk communities was utterly unlike its predecessors yet certain artifacts they employed can be traced to a remote
antiquity. In an important paper Reinhard Bernbeck (1995:9) has shown
that in the Hassunan and Samarran societies of the early sixth millennium there were distinctly different modes of production while the

settlement systems, house forms, grave goods, technological base, and, we might add, the presence of seals and sealings — were the same. He writes that " they [Hassuna and Samarra] indicate a basically egalitarian system in both cases. It will be shown below that the main differences are situated in the economic sphere, *i.e.,* in forms of cooperation, in means of labor, and in the social relations of production." Thus, in considering aspects of house construction, kiln size, and the manufacture of ceramics the author shows that work in Hassunan society was generally more repetitive and less complex than in Samarran society.

Land tenure has a special focus in this conference, and of particular importance are the different ecological conditions that confronted the Samarran and Hassunan societies. Insufficient rainfall made irrigation a precondition for survival for all known Samarran villages. Hassunan villages, on the other hand, are located in regions of sufficient rainfall for dry-farming. The preparation of irrigated land requires a major labor investment but has the reward of removing the risk and vagaries of annual rainfall, and offers, on average, a higher yield of harvested grain per hectare than that derived from rainfed farming. With the development of an irrigation technology, land is no longer a natural factor in the production of a harvest; under irrigation, land has to be transformed to become cultivable soil. Households had to invest their labor in the preparation of land and the construction of canals which, in turn, made land a more valuable means of production than the quasi-unlimited lands available in the context of dry-farming. Thus, where irrigation technology is practiced, one might expect that individual households would strive to keep their lands intact by increasing the rigidity of control and ownership of the land through mechanisms of inheritance, marriage rules, etc.

Hassunan and Samarran societies appear to be organized along communal and relatively egalitarian lines. There is simply no evidence from burials, architecture, or settlement pattern to support the presence of centralized political systems, *i.e.,* temples, palaces, rank-size settlement, or in the accumulation of differential wealth, social hierarchy, etc. This is not to say that there were not significant differences between Hassuna and Samarran society. Compared to the Hassunan communities, those of the Samarran practiced irrigation (Oates and Oates 1976), had larger houses/compounds (Bernbeck 1995), and were fortified (Mami, Songor A, Tell es-Sawaan). In every Hassunan community in which extensive areas were excavated (Umm Dabaghiyah, Hassuna, and Yarim Tepe), large "communal" storage facilities were uncovered while at the Samarran sites of Tell es-Sawaan, Chogha Mami, and Sabi Abyadh, small "annexes" attached to individual households served their storage requirements. The presence of communal storage facilities in Hassunan villages and individual household storage in Samarran communities suggests that a greater social distance characterized the households of the Samarran settlements.

There is little doubt that fundamental differences characterize the relatively contemporaneous Samarran and Hassunan communities. The importance of irrigation in Samarran society (and the consequent importance of land ownership, water control, canal construction and maintenance, etc.), their larger households, the evidence for fortification systems, differences in the organization of labor as documented by Bernbeck (1995) and the differences in storage facilities attest to the nature of these distinctions. On the other hand, there is no evidence for differences in settlement size, political centralization, differential access to wealth, or hierarchies of economic and/or political power in either the Hassunan or Samarran cultures. Both societies can be described as having a "domestic mode of production" (Sahlins 1972). The differences in Hassunan and Samarran society may suggest the beginnings of a dissolution in the domestic mode of production — the transformation of a society structured more along hetarchical lines, as in the Hassunan, compared to one increasingly oriented toward hierarchical systems (Samarran). Within the Samarran culture this transformation may be due, at least in part, to a greater attachment to the land (ownership by individual household?) necessitated by the labor-intensive requirements of irrigation agriculture. Initially, both Hassunan and Samarran societies appear to be hetarchically structured, that is to say their social organization was not dictated by an hierarchical system of centralized control but by the interactions of many agents following local rules of self-organization. Within hetarchical structures there is no single "highest level" or "monitors" of the type that characterize social hierarchies (Hofstadter 1980:134). The Samarran evidence, compared to the Hassunan, suggests a greater movement toward the development of hierarchy, at least in the control of labor (Bernbeck 1995). Hetarchical societies are different from hierarchical ones in a number of ways, not least in that the former structure their adaptation "from the bottom up" while the later do so from the "top down." The significant social difference characterizing the Hassuna and Samarra (c. 5500 BC) from the later Uruk cultures (c. 3500 BC) is that in the former decision making and its social organization was structured "from the bottom up" while in the later if flowed from the "top down." This transformation, from hetarchical to hierarchical social organization, unfolded within the context of a changing scale in both the size and the function of individual households. When change did occur, in the Uruk Period, it was explosive and enduring. It was not a sequence of gradual changes within egalitarian societies that brought about the "urban revolution," as suggested by Henry Wright (1984), it was an eruptive revolutionary transformation that could well have occurred in less than a hundred years. Years ago, Joseph Schumpeter (1939:102) suggested that cultural and technological changes occurred in waves of innovation that appeared "more like a series of explosions than a gentle, though incessant, transformation." Around 3500 BC the invention of the written tablet, the innovative development of the cylinder seal (derived from the earlier stamp seal first used by the Hassuna/Samarra cultures) and a tenfold increase in settlement area necessitating the extensive deployment of irrigation and land consolidation, a process referred to by Adams (1981) as "hyper-urbanization," provided the principal elements for fueling fundamental social changes. As Nissen (1988:67) has pointed out, these social changes were contemporaneous, perhaps, at least in part, resulting from favorable climatic changes, which stemmed the floods that inundated large tracts of land and made possible large areas for new permanent settlement.

Tools of any kind require a specific context in order to function. Just as tools come about as a result of invention and innovation, so also do the social institutions in which the tools find their context. It is impossible to separate the tools — the texts, seals, and sealings — from the social institution in which they operated: the institutional household, what Weber (1936) referred to as the oikos (see below). The uses to which a new technology is put is as inherently unpredictable as are the unforeseen consequences in the functioning of a newly developed social institution. No one at 5500 BC could foresee the future history of seals and sealings and certainly no one saw in them the germ of an inscribed tablet.

The transformation of a social order based upon hetarchical principles to one structured along increasingly hierarchical lines characterized the generalized development of the Hassuna to the Ubaid. A nascent hierarchy of Ubaid settlements is complemented by differential house sizes and a modest degree of increasing wealth in the hands of individual households. Thus, at Tell Abada different house sizes (from 70m^2 to 240m^2) are known while a single prominent building, of exceptional dimension and construction, suggests that one household achieved a prominent position (see Fig. 5). Within that household archaeologists recovered seals, sealings, and something the author refers to as "proto-tablets." The beginnings of the loss of social coherence that characterizes household production, the first hints of which appear in Samarran times, become more pronounced in the Ubaid; specific large household units, of the type uncovered at Tell Abada, were now able to secure a nascent power base within the community. Were individual households responsible for the construction of the earliest public buildings (temples) in the late Ubaid Period? By what process were individual households transformed into, or come to dominate, the earliest public institutions (temples)? Despite the limited emergence of socioeconomic differences in the Ubaid Period, there are hardly any differences in the quantity or quality of goods found in burials, exotic goods found in the community, or craft specialists attached to an identifiable institution. Gil Stein (1996:28f) puts it this way:

> The available evidence strongly suggests that while craft specialization clearly existed during the fifth millennium BC, production took place in numerous independent workshops, and not through the centralized elite control over attached specialists (p. 28). . . . the basis of wealth in Ubaid Mesopotamia appears to have been the ritually based mobilization of surplus cereals in an irrigation-based economy. Although craft specialization appears to have been widespread in Ubaid society, the location of workshops and the nature of the goods produced conform to the expectations for independent, rather than attached specialization. . . . The production of prestige goods by attached specialists does not really begin until the following Uruk period (p. 29).

The Ubaid Period has been characterized as a series of small, ideologically linked chiefdoms (Wright 1984:68). I frankly doubt that the word "chiefdom" is appropriate within the Ubaid setting. Nevertheless, there is a greater degree of economic differentiation, ceremonial elaboration, and regional centralization (numerous small 1 hectare villages and a few 10+ hectare towns) within the Ubaid settlements when compared to the communities of the preceding periods. Temples of the Ubaid Period are known from a number of sites in southern and northern Mesopotamia (Roaf 1995:427). Yet their precise function remains conjectural. However, given the fact that the later Ubaid temples at Eridu maintained the architectural signature of the earlier T-shaped household structures, it is not unreasonable to suggest that the temple was itself an extension of the household, deriving its legitimacy, increasing authority, and wealth through the construction of a religious ideology.

In recent years there has been a return to a concern for the Mesopotamian world of the neighborhood (Stone 1987), the family (Gelb

1979, Postgate 1992), and private economic activity (Silver 1983, Powell 1986, Lamberg-Karlovsky 1996). In fact, temples, as Zettler (1992) has shown for the Ur III Period, were originally households writ large, managed by individual families over the course of generations. In this view households form the very foundation for the rise of complex society in the Near East. One may envision that the secular households, beginning in the Samarran with a speeding of the pulse in the Ubaid, became increasingly competitive and bifurcated into institutional entities representative of both secular and religious authority. By the first half of the third millennium, secular households gave rise to nascent dynasties of hereditary lords while other households turned to the increasing bureaucratization of the sacred. In turn, each of the above institutional households attempted to take their slice of tax from the remaining households not identified with either of the above.

It is important to recognize that throughout the vast majority of Near Eastern antiquity the private household remained the primary focus of economic activity. A concentration upon the temple and the palace distorts the social order of the greater Mesopotamian world. The individual household contributed its own labor and/or service in return for commodities obtained by barter from other households, or alternatively, produced a substantial amount of its own food and goods from its own lands and craft production. The balance of power was a jousting match between the sacred, the secular, and the independent households that dotted the landscape. At different times and for different reasons one or the other attained political dominance.

By the end of the third millennium, the secular institution of kingship managed to absorb into its own management the institutional offices within the temples. Precisely what the factors were that allowed for the increasing inequality between households that resulted in the emergence of the powerful institutions of palace and temple remain unclear. Kuijt (1996) has recently advanced the notion that ritual behavior and religious ideology were fundamental in maintaining egalitarian societies in the early Neolithic. Perhaps so. In Mesopotamia, on the other hand, it would appear that ritual and religious ideology were the very agents responsible for social stratification, allowing for an increasing inequality between households and fostering the institutionalization of both temple and palace household estates. It is difficult to imagine the transformation from hetarchical households to bureaucratic states in the absence of what Max Weber considered an essential handmaiden of change: conflict. Yet, nowhere in the archaeological or textual record do we see evidence for the conflicts, tensions, or warfare that must have accompanied the emergence of powerful centralized bureaucracies that characterized the Uruk Period (3500 BC).

Mario Liverani (1984) has distinguished between village-level life and the great state organizations of Mesopotamia. He proposes two modes of production, of organizing economic productivity: the Palace and the Family [household]. Typically, scholars have emphasized what Leo Oppenheim (1964) called "The Great Organizations," the temple and the palace, and all but ignored the family and the household. In too many portraits of the ancient Near East, society becomes a caricature in which the temple/palace is depicted as the singular force in economic, political, and religious activity. Liverani's more balanced view proposes two modes of production, which he calls the Palace and the Family. The former was politically dominant, but the latter was economically more productive. The economic power of the Palace was consistently undermined by (1) the giving of land allotments instead of rations, and (2) accepting the son as a successor to the work of the father, eventually making it difficult to dislodge the family from the land. Liverani's ideas are of importance in pointing out the constant tensions that characterized the relations of the palace and the family household, relations that in almost all periods were motivating factors that brought about important social change.

We return with some final comments pertaining to the "prehistoric communication revolution." We have seen that seals, sealings, and tokens are found in numerous Hassunan, Samarran, and Ubaid settlements, as well as on sites like Tal-i Bakun and Tepe Yahya in Iran and distant Degirmentepe in Anatolia. These devices were utilized over the course of several millennia by different cultures and by individual households whose economic organization suggests a "domestic mode of production" and where decision-making argues for hetarchical structures rather than hierarchical systems of control. One artifact, one of crucial significance, is added to this communication revolution; the inscribed tablet. It was an Uruk invention that took place in southern Mesopotamia. For millennia seals, sealings, and bullae were in use in areas outside of southern Mesopotamia, but for almost half a millennia before writing was adopted in northern Mesopotamia, the inscribed tablet remained restricted to its southern Mesopotamian homeland. The introduction of writing into Iran, northern Syria, and Anatolia during the Uruk Expansion (at which time the largely Sumerian population of southern Mesopotamia colonized the above regions) was an event that endured for several centuries. Following the collapse of the Uruk colonies, communities continued to manage their household property and personnel with the help of seals and sealings, as they had done for a millennia, but rejected the use of the inscribed tablet, whose existence and function they were certainly aware of.

A similar situation prevailed in the slightly later Proto-Elamite expansion throughout the Iranian Plateau. The Proto-Elamites introduced the inscribed tablet on sites distant from the Proto-Elamite heartland, *i.e.,* at Tepe Yahya, Sialk, Hissar, and Shahr-i Sokhta. Following the collapse of the Proto-Elamite communities, the indigenous settlements continued using seals and sealings but discontinued the use of the inscribed tablet. In southern Mesopotamia the written tablet functioned within social institutions that were centrally controlled with respect to labor, production, and consumption. Cultures lacking a centralized bureaucracy had little use for an invention dedicated to administering a bureaucratic hierarchy. In rejecting the use of the inscribed tablet, they simply rejected an artifact that had neither function nor utility in their own society.

In southern Mesopotamia the institution responsible for the management of this bureaucracy was the temple/palace and, not surprisingly, it is exclusively in those contexts that writing is found throughout the first half of the third millennium. Within the Uruk city-states of southern Mesopotamia, the function of seals, sealings, and bullae was transformed. These objects no longer functioned as a communication device within and between individual households, as in the Samarran and Ubaid settlements. Within the Uruk Period, the written tablet was added to these devices and the entire complex was utilized, for the first time, within an institutional context, the temple/palace. An earlier technology of seals and sealing was transformed and writing invented to provide a social technology of administrative control. On the one hand, the invention of this social technology played a leading role in the transformation of society while, on the other hand, the transformation of society toward a greater complexity precisely required inventions that would enhance a bureaucratic control over information and communication. This view privileges a single technology, writing, within the context of a newly formulated institution, the temple/palace. Both the technology and the institution were necessary, and eventually became sufficient, to sustain the early years of the "urban revolution."

The invention and sustained presence of writing in southern Mesopotamia and its absence in the north of Mesopotamia (until introduced by Akkadian conquest) is yet another difference between northern and southern Mesopotamia. When writing was introduced into the north it assumed the same function it had in the south — an authoritative instrument of control wielded by the palace administration.

C. C. LAMBERG-KARLOVSKY

The Uruk temple was the seat of authority, the center of a developing bureaucracy, and the locus for the invention of writing. Uruk temples were centers of control wherein ritual functioned as a mechanism of social regulation, bestowing power upon a select number while affording others opportunities for social mobility. With the invention of writing, used in combination with the earlier cluster of seals, sealings, and bullae, a nexus of technological innovations offered an unparalleled versatility in administrative control. The extraordinary technological invention of writing seems assuredly linked, if not central and systemically related to, the more extensive cultural transformations that characterize the Uruk Period. The development of a social institution, the temple, that formalized both belief and behavior in conjunction with a cluster of tools, principally the newly invented tablet, associated with the earlier innovation of seals and sealings, go hand-in-hand in what I believe was a rapid and dramatic transformation of what we call the "urban revolution." Writing played a crucial role, perhaps *the* crucial role, in fostering the rapid growth of craft specialization within the context of temple and state institutions. The interrelationship of writing and its institutional context the temple/palace is well recognized by Robert McC. Adams (1996:39) who writes in his recent book:

> Writing also made an important contribution to the amassing and allocation of scarce raw materials by the great palace and temple organizations that may have forced the initial construction of cities and certainly dominated them. . . . there is a nexus of functional interdependencies closely linking writing to the florescence of the crafts and urban societies nourishing the demand for their products.

Writing was perhaps the single most important token in the process of urbanization. Its invention created a tool that when combined with earlier devices, seals, sealings, and bullae, was linked to yet more extensive cultural transformations. Writing was a wholly new solution to an old problem — social organization and control. After using seals, sealings, and bullae for thousands of years, the invention of the tablet appears to be an overnight occurrence, an unforeseen event that transformed society and accelerated its rate of change in unpredictable directions. No one could foresee that the earliest tablets, entirely devoted to economic accounting, contained within them the transformative power of unforeseen refinements and applications that, unpredictably, led to the manipulation of a "mouse" on a video monitor and algorithms with dramatic and unpredictable consequences in altering our own social (now global) order.

Summary

I began this essay by outlining the specific differences that recent authors believe distinguish southern Mesopotamia from northern Mesopotamia. We noted that beginning with the Samarran Period and continuing throughout the Ubaid and Uruk Periods, both northern and southern Mesopotamia contained a similar template of architecture, the T-shaped building, and that within these structures were found the earliest seals, sealings, and the occasional bullae. It is my belief that these dwellings represent an augmented, segmentary household, an economic *oikos* as discussed by Weber, dominated by a single family but containing clients that were non-kin. The archaeological record supports the notion that by the middle of the fifth millennium there were large institutional households (*oikoi*) that were spread throughout Mesopotamia, extending from central Anatolia (Degirmentepe) to southern Iran (Tal-i Bakun). By the end of the fifth millennium, each of these institutional households was a self-sustaining, autarchic, economic entity. There is sufficient evidence, from the excavation of a number of these households, as evident at Sabi Abyad, that access to spatial areas and to specific goods contained within jars, matting, etc., was controlled by the use of stamp/cylinder seals and sealings.

The use of seals and sealings was introduced from the Near East into Egypt in Naqada II/III times, basically contemporaneous with their use in the Levant in the last centuries of the fourth millennium. In both regions seals and sealings functioned within a household context. The use of these tools (seals, sealings, bullae, tokens, *et al.*) indicates that a managerial system, within an institutional household context, existed millennia before the Uruk Period, when the above tools were joined by the written tablet to suggest, in conjunction with settlement pattern analysis, the emergence of a bureaucratic state. Why did the institutional household "take-off" in the Uruk Period? Why was it that in southern Mesopotamia the *oikos* was transformed in scale into a central institution that increasingly swallowed up its competitors? Recently Renger (1995:278) has offered a partial answer: "land consolidation in the hands of the members of the ruling elite or of the institutional households . . . this land consolidation is the cause of the gradual disappearance of the village community system." Thus, in southern Mesopotamia households involved in the consolidation of land attained a greater competitive edge over households with less land. Land consolidation, in turn, undermined the communal ownership that Renger believes characterized the earlier "village community." I frankly doubt that communal ownership of land ever fully characterized a stage of "village community;" already in the

Samarran Period one can detect the presence of the T-shaped building, the signature of the self-sufficient *oikos*. The hypothetical construct of communal property owned by all members of an equally hypothetical construct called an egalitarian society comes to us from Condorcet in the eighteenth century by way of Marx and Engels in the nineteenth century.

In the twentieth century the presence of this "stage," in the cultural evolution of village life, has yet to be convincingly demonstrated in the archaeological record and, perhaps more importantly, within the ethnographic literature. One may readily ask what brought about the land consolidation that Renger believes characterized southern Mesopotamia? Why was land consolidation an essential feature of southern Mesopotamia? I would argue that what came to distinguish the *oikos* of southern Mesopotamia (beginning in the Uruk Period) from that of adjacent regions had a great deal to do with environment and ecology. Quite simply put, southern Mesopotamia was virtually alone in requiring extensive irrigation technology to sustain the increased agricultural production needed for its expanding populations, which in the Uruk Period were rapidly creating large-scale urban environments (for southern Mesopotamian environment and irrigation, see Potts [1996] and Oates and Oates [1976] for expanding settlements and urbanization, see Adams [1981]).

Renger (1995:272) has recently implicated irrigation as a factor responsible for transforming the "village community system" into "large institutional households." In his words:

> When irrigation management became the concern of the "state" or its institutions, a conflict arose between central powers and local or village communities. As a result, control over arable land shifted gradually to the institutions of the territorial entities that organized, built, and maintained the irrigation system. Between 2800-2400 BC, the remnants of the village community system were gradually absorbed by these large institutional households. ... Between circa 3300 and 2400 BC, the number of small rural settlements gradually declined while urban settlements increased in size.

Renger implicates irrigation as, at least partially, responsible for the shift from the "village community" to the "institutional household." It is apparent from the above discussion, that the household already played a major role in the Samarran Period (5500+ BC), throughout the Ubaid Period, and in the Uruk Period, when Renger sees the emergence of the "institutional household" (c. 3300 BC). By the Uruk and Jemdet Nasr periods, these "institutional households" could produce large-scale harvests and control considerable land; a single administrative document from Uruk records at least 720,000 liters of emmer harvested from over 600 hectares (Renger 1995:273).

Differences in the size and in the scale of the household operation, from the Samarran to the Uruk Period, is what is of significance. The idea of a gradual evolutionary trajectory leading from the "village community," in which the village holds land communally, to the emergence of individual "institutional households," each controlling their own land, is a hypothetical construct without evidence or merit. There is archaeological evidence, as discussed above, for the presence of large-scale households prior to the Uruk Period. Certainly the extensive household of Ubaid date at Tell Abada (see Fig. 5) could have been involved in land consolidation requiring increased irrigation and a multiplying number of clients to sustain the augmented household. Such an extensive household would have necessitated administrative and managerial needs and with sustained growth the needs for regulating labor, land use, production, and consumption *et al.* would give the household and the community that invented the inscribed tablet an adaptive advantage over competing institutional households. The ecological conditions in southern Mesopotamia required irrigation to be employed if settlement size and population numbers were to expand, which is precisely what happened. Ecological determinants, within a fragile environment, worked in conjunction with land consolidation, irrigation technology, managerial bureaucracies, and increasing literacy and numeracy to enhance the competitive edge of specific institutional households in southern Mesopotamia. Each of the above attributes, operating as both cause and effect, resulted in a spiraling indeterminacy that brought about increasing settlement size, social complexity, and we may assume conflict. By the third millennium an age of great households fostered a piety of great assemblies. The great households legitimized their authority by religious ideology and devoted themselves to the worship of a patron divinity. Thorkild Jacobsen (1957:119), in his classic paper on political development in Mesopotamia suggested that *lúgal* (later meaning king) originally denoted the head of a great household, great because he (the texts indicate it was a male) commanded the "great house," the *é-gal*, *ekallum*, which consisted of both kin and retainers. Smaller households, the *oikos*, lacked a *lúgal* and were referred to as *é*, or *bîtum*. While the earliest written texts, c. 3400 BC, attest to the significance of the institutional household (Renger 1995), almost four millennia later, within the context of kingship, colonialism, and the Roman Empire, the Mishnah reaffirms the centrality of the household within another region of the Near East: Israel. In summarizing the view of the Mishnah, a law code dated to around 200 AD, Jacob Neusner (1990:53) writes:

> The singularity of the household was not in its physical let alone genealogical traits, but in its definition as a distinct unit of economic production. What made a household into a household was its economic definition as a whole and complete unit of production, and the householder was the one that controlled that unit of production; that economic fact made all the difference, and not that all the householder's members were related (that was not the fact at all). . . . What made the household into a social unit was the economic fact that among its constituents, all of them worked within the same economic unit and also worked in a setting distinct from other equivalently autonomous economic units.

The household, as the building block of the neighborhood, the village, and the city, has an exceptionally long history in the Near East. Modern ethnoarchaeological studies attest to its enduring significance today (Kramer 1982; Watson 1979). The evolution of the household forms the foundation for an understanding of the social order and its evolution in the Near East. Throughout most of the Near Eastern Bronze Age in Anatolia, the Iranian Plateau, and the Levant, the domestic household remained the principal institution of ownership, production, and consumption. Throughout the third and second millennia, the powerful institutional households of temple and palace were largely confined to greater Mesopotamia. While the organization of labor, the procurement of raw resources, and the management of "state" are relatively well known for greater Mesopotamia, resulting largely from over a century of studying the texts, the same cannot be said for regions beyond Mesopotamia, where illiteracy continued to prevail well beyond the Iron Age. Beyond the realms of Mesopotamia, the study of the household and the domestic mode of production has hardly begun. Beyond the world of Mesopotamia, a contextual analysis of the full compliment of material remains recovered from a single household simply does not exist! Without such an analysis the building block of the social world of the ancient Near East, namely the nature, variation, and functioning of the household will continue to elude us.

Recent archaeological research in northern Mesopotamia continues to expand our understanding of 4th-Millennium developments. The precocious evolution of the city of Uruk in southern Mesopotamia during the late Uruk Period, characterized by the invention of writing, the development of monumental architecture, and an apparent rapidity of urbanization, can now be compared to a comparable but chronologically *earlier* evidence from northern Mesopotamia! Tell Brak is presenting us with a better dated and a better stratified sequence of Uruk Period materials than is available from any southern Mesopotamia site (Oates and Oates 1997). Of special importance is the recovery of bevelled rim bowls, a single numerical tablet, and numerous geometric tokens from a level 16 house, well dated to the Middle Uruk Period, c. 3500 BC. This household also contained substantial ceramics, with elaborate pottery marks, wooden objects, ivory, several Eye-Idols, and a bead of rolled gold-sheet. It remains uncertain whether this is a domestic or an institutional household, however, its relatively rich association of materials suggests the latter. It is at this time, during the Middle Uruk Period, that Brak attains its maximum size, said to be "certainly over 100 hectares." In discussing the materials of the Middle Uruk period at Brak, Joan Oates (1997:291) suggests that this is "unique evidence not only that the widespread accounting system attested more widely in Late Uruk times had its origins some centuries *before* but that these developments are well-represented on *indigenous northern sites*" (emphasis mine).

There is an increasing body of data to suggest that north Mesopotamia was not merely a derivative of the urban, literate world of southern Mesopotamia. The evidence from Brak, combined with that of Hamoukar, Tell al Hawa, contemporary Nineveh, and the Tabqa dam sites excavated in the 1970s offers more than a substantial hint of an earlier, seemingly independent, and indigenous north Mesopotamian urban complexity, one that came into contact with a more centralized, literate southern Mesopotamian Late Uruk world. This evidence, in conjunction with the earlier Hassuna and Ubaid cultural complexity of northern Mesopotamia, requires a revision in our perception of southern Mesopotamia as the progenitor of urban complexity throughout northern Mesopotamia. There is emerging a need to reconsider the simplistic view that an expanding southern Mesopotamian urban core undertook an expansive "colonization" of a remote and underdeveloped northern periphery. The possibility exists, remote though it may seem at the moment, to stand the centrality of southern Mesopotamia, as the civilizing agent of the north, on its head!

Discussion

Buccellati: I would like to play the devil's advocate. I wonder whether the distinction you make between north and south based on ecology may be a problem with the sources. In the alluvial south, silt covers up small sites. Possibly one reason why we have more small sites in the north is that they have been better preserved. In the south it is not necessarily that they were not there, just that they were not as well preserved.

The second point is linked with that. You said that domestic production is associated with seals and sealings, and therefore predates or is an antecedent of writing as an institution. Could it also be that in the north we have this 500-year gap because, in effect, we have found fewer major buildings that have been excavated.

The second point that I think is interesting about writing's impact is that there is a scribal class. It was not the politicians or war-leaders who invented writing, yet they retained control. They were able to harness the power of the tool so that the scribes, wealthy or important as they may have been, never became the political rulers. They never gained control and power. You said that at Tell el Abadah that seals and sealings were found together.

Lamberg-Karlovsky: Sealings in many different contexts were the dominant find. I don't have any problem with any of your comments. Certainly in the south the alluviation may have buried some of those earlier sites. We know from Adams' survey that there are a couple of sites that have painted pottery that may be "Samaran-like." The sites may be there. And archives also may exist in that 500-year gap in the north. All I am doing is describing the general situation as we know it today. New information may topple the whole story, but at the present moment I think the evidence is overwhelmingly in favor of saying that scribes were the software. They were programmed by the political elite. It took a long time before they were permitted or supported to write poetry. First, they had to write just the economic accounts.

Goelet: I think you have come close to saying that writing produced wealth. Where do you see this new money coming in as a result of the appearance of writing? Or are you saying that writing produces demand?

Lamberg-Karlovsky: I am saying that writing was both cause and effect. Causally, it effected the accumulation of power for a growing number of individuals who controlled that tool. It was both causal in accumulating power, and its effect was to increase that power.

I don't think that many of us today understand the full consequences of the computer revolution and how it is transforming us. We certainly don't know where it is going to go. I think in 3400 BC those boys and girls had no idea that what they were going to be dealing with, in the end, was computers. It was an unforeseen consequence. Writing was and is a tool of power, and one that was monopolized for a period of time. To a certain extent it still is in the form of censorship. It remains a tool of enormous power.

Goelet: In Middle Kingdom Egypt we also have the phenomenon of a large scribal group created virtually out of nothing. An enormous explosion of scribes occurred roughly between Sesostris II and III.

Levine: Can you tell when the tablets became authoritative items of reference?

Lamberg-Karlovsky: I would say that from the time we first see them, in the Professions List (in Uruk context), there is already a hierarchical listing of the professions: Who is answerable to whom? It is already there. The interesting aspect is that there is no earlier evolutionary evidence prior to those texts, but there already is a hierarchy that is transmitted on the tablet.

Buccellati: I think the significance of the Professions List was its very existence. It is not part of an oral tradition. It is a conceptualization of their world which can exist only in writing. Nobody goes around saying this sort of thing. It only exists in the written word. The writing acquires a personality of its own which did not exist in the pre-literate conceptualization of the world.

Levine: When you want to know, you look at the tablet. It is what the tablet says.

Lamberg-Karlovsky: Yes. I think the list of professions starts with the king.

Stone: I don't think that is entirely true later on, because you have legal texts in which the tablet seems to be only a list of witnesses. If you don't have witnesses, you can't do anything. So you can't produce a tablet saying "I own this house." You can only produce a tablet that says, "These are the people who can say that I own this house." There also are texts that say that the witnesses cannot be found. Whereas the text is much more authoritative for us, for them it was the witnesses.

Lamberg-Karlovsky: I think it is best said in the books written or edited by Jack Goody on writing: in a world in which most people are illiterate, writing has a magical and mysterious quality. The tablet itself contains power, it is a signifier of power.

Schiffman: I know you said that you were not going to deal with temple versus palace, but for those of us more interested in the continuation, there is an open question. Do you have even a two minute comment on where your evidence leads?

Lamberg-Karlovsky: I think that in the Ubaid Period a large household that previously had some political decision-making authority incorporates also an aspect of the nonsecular. That household becomes not a temple, but itself a sacred place. Somewhere in the Ubaid there is a building at Eridu that looks like it could function as both a corporate household and a temple. A household shrine is put into a previous household — a powerful household. The individual who was before a patriarch is now also a religious leader. I think such a process characterized the Ubaid Period, and I think it is so smooth a transition from secular to sacred that you can hardly distinguish it within the archaeological record.

Stager: If you postulate this early household as the basic unit of your economy, and then develop the same model at different scales (so that you eventually end up with a very strong, paramount householder who later is called a king), do you get any intermediate level of intersecting households early on? In other words, is there some differentiation in scale among the households, or are many individuals controlling more or less the same amount of power and land? How would you recognize a small king in this early prehistoric world?

Levine: Regarding irrigation, the best-known historical model in terms of documentation comes from the Nabatean culture. The Nabatean king controlled irrigation absolutely. Everyone had to make a payment to him. It might be interesting to see what constitutes an economy that relies totally on irrigation. The primacy of the state leads to this question.

Renger: Two questions have arisen: the village community and the temple city. These are two separate issues. The way the discussion has developed over the last two decades is away from what Gelb, Jacobsen and Falkenstein said. Gelb's ideas are built on the objection to the temple-city concept of Falkenstein. And his arguments are built on a series of developments or evolutions concerning the existence of the village communities of the Old Babylonian Period.

As far as the question of the village community is concerned, of course it is in a certain way a construct. But the village community also has left some traces in the written record. For instance, in the early third millennium in the so-called *kudurrus*, quite a number of instances deal with collective ownership. People relinquish their rights on the land they own or hold. I think that this could be constructed or seen as the leftover of collective use of land which was slowly turned over to central institutions.

The so-called temple city is more a problem of terminology. When we talk about temples, we tend to think about the Uruk IV and V temples. There are some archaeologists who have doubts about calling these buildings temples. I don't know how this question comes out, but the point is that when I say institutional households, you say that this means temples. I don't mean that. I use the term institutional household so as to avoid the words temple and palace, because I have difficulty in establishing the existence of a palace. So when I say institutional household, it means an *oikos* household of whatever scale.

Priam is not an institutional household. This is the household of a big manorial lord of the kind that Max Weber referred to as an *oikos*. He is going one step further: the *oikos* of a manorial lord is identical with a political entity (to avoid the word state). If we look at Troy, we cannot really prove it is a palace. If you look at what Machteld Mellink excavated, then we have the palace or manorial mansion and the surrounding plain on which she found peasant houses. This is a type of early *oikos*. I cannot imagine that the examples you show here are individual *oikoi* of a certain time. I don't know how they developed into that scale. Whether they expropriated the village community is another question.

Lamberg-Karlovsky: Let me say this about the village communities. Forty or fifty years ago the chronology of the Mesopotamian world, beginning with the end of the Uruk Period c. 3000 BC, was about the same as it is today. What has changed is both the nature and chronology of the period of village life. Fifty years ago village life was thought to have begun around 5000 BC. Today that time scale has nearly doubled. Today the archaeologists talk about village farming life extending beyond 9000 BC. Village life had an exceptional duration prior to the invention of the city in southern Mesopotamia c. 3500 BC. Unfortunately, we are still stuck in thinking about the village community in much the same way as V. Gordon Childe did decades ago. Villages are typically taken to be self-sufficient, communal in organization, basically egalitarian, and relatively changeless. Such a characterization might be acceptable for 8500 BC but is it true for 5000

BC? I think not. I think that already by 6500 BC, that is, within the Pre-Pottery Neolithic B, there is considerable diversity in wealth, and within the social, political, and economic organization of the village community.

At this time Ain Ghazal in Jordan is already 10 hectares, a substantial town. There are other settlements at this time that suggest a considerable settlement site hierarchy. These large sites fail to sustain themselves and we have little understanding of the causes that effected the first collapse of what we might term a "town process" that preceded the urban process by several thousand years. Within these early villages and towns, the structure of the households, their production and consumption patterns, as well as the lines of authority that structured their relations are all but unknown to us. It is a fundamental period of change that we have not yet begun to address.

Levine: Does change keep changing? If things are always changing, are there lulls, not to speak of regressions? Or failures? Can you project the rate of change? Something pops up singularly, and then you don't see the likes of it again for a long time after. Do we assume continuity, memory, the road past? Are people reinventing several millennia later? Are they aware of the past?

I find all that all kinds of people assume that what they see was always there. They are not aware of lapses or intervals. On the other hand, I know people who think that because they didn't see it, it was never there. Are we assuming cognizance? We seem to be assuming a certain cognizance of the earlier on the part of the later resurgence. Was there something material, physical, retrievable that made people think? For instance, I know that when you talk about lapses of several centuries, such as the late Bronze Ages, some people make assumptions that there was uninterrupted continuity. We know there was not.

Renger: Look at the history of western Africa. Until World War II — by and large — they did not use the plow, and so for millennia they remained on that hoe type of agriculture despite the fact that Eastern Africa, exposed to the influence of Near Eastern agricultural technology, had a plow. In Somalia and Ethiopia they had it. When the development agencies (UN, UNESCO, etc.) came in after the Second World War they were still hoeing their fields. So obviously there are areas of stagnation.

Lamberg-Karlovsky: It is difficult to say whether it is really stagnation. Clearly, it would appear that people chose not to write. There were areas adjacent to those that were literate that continued not to write. A good example of this is regions of the Iranian Plateau and northern Babylonia that resisted writing for centuries, if not millennia. There was a time when the above regions were in contact with literate people — the Uruk expansion, or the Elamites. It seems almost at times as if it was an obstinate choice *not* to adopt writing. I don't know why. All I can say is that there were peoples in contact with those who were literate who chose not to adopt writing. We privilege writing as being something very beneficial. We have a value attached to it. But obviously other cultures didn't, because they didn't adopt it. You could point to certain technologies — steel, carbon alloy steel production, was present in the Luristan culture c. 1200 BC. They knew how to make carbonized steel, and it lasted for about two and half generations, then they stopped. Why they decided to stop making steel completely eludes me.

Stager: Maybe we expect too much in this leap from the household to the king, because of the later examples in which the differentiation is so much greater and the scale is so different. In some places it seems that the concept actually was quite similar: the king was just *pater familias* in a household writ large.

You have some examples later from the West in which the term *bayit* or *bitum* means "house," "household," and "dynasty." The hierarchy of households range from the domestic ones of *pater familias* to the royal estates of the king to the divine realm where the deity is head of the cosmic household. The Assyrians used the term *bit-Humri*, the household/dynasty of Omri to refer to the northern kingdom of Israel in 8th-century-BCE records. More recently a 9th-century-BCE victory stele erected by the Aramaeans at Dan refers to the southern kingdom of Judah as *bet*-David, or the household of David, as though the king were father of the whole state. So this kind of homologous nesting of households can go all the way up the hierarchy of overarching domains from *pater familias* at the domestic level, to the king at the state level, to the deity at the cosmic level. I don't really know what to call this hierarchy of patrimonial authority.

Lamberg-Karlovsky: Patrimonial state would be fine.

BIBLIOGRAPHY

Adams, R. McC. (1966), *The Evolution of Urban Society* (Aldine. Chicago).

— (1981), *Heartland of Cities* (University of Chicago Press. Chicago).

— (1996), *Paths of Fire* (Princeton University Press, Princeton).

Akkermans, P. P. M. G. and M. Verhoeven (1995), "An Image of Complexity: The Burnt Village at Late Neolithic Sabi Abyadh, Syria," *American Journal of Archaeology* 99:21-58.

— and K. Duistermaat (1997), "Of Storage and Nomads: The Sealings from Late Neolithic Sabi Abyad, Syria," *Paleorient* 22/2:17-44.

Alizadeh, A. (1994), "Administrative Technology and Socio-economic Complexity at the Prehistoric Site of Tall-i Bakun, Iran," in Ferioli, P., *Archives Before Writing* (Scriptorum, Rome):35-55.

Amiet, Pierre (1994), "Sceaux et administration à l'époque d'Uruk á Suse" in Ferioli, P., et al., *Archives Before Writing* (Scriptorum, Rome):87-95.

Bernbeck, Reinhard (1995), "Lasting Alliances and Emerging Competition: Economic Developments in Early Mesopotamia," *JAA* 14:1-25.

Deimel, Anton (1931), Sumerische Templewirtschsft den Zeit Urukagina und Seiner Vorgänger (Rome).

Diakonoff, I. (1974), "Structure of Society and State in Early Dynastic Sumer," *Monographs of the Ancient Near East* 1(3) (Malibu).

Esin, Ufuk (1994), "The Functional Evidence of Seals and Sealings at Degirmentepe' in Ferioli, P., *Archives Before Writing* (Scriptorum. Rome):59-93.

Ferioli, P., E, Fiandra, G. Fissore, and M. Frangipane (1994), *Archives Before Writing* (Scriptorum, Rome).

Forest, C. (1984), "Kheit Qasim III: The Obeid Settlement," *Sumer* 40:119-121.

Forest, J. D. (1984), "Kheit Qasim III, An Obeid Settlement," *Sumer* 39:40-85.

Gelb, I. J. (1979), "Household and Family in Early Mesopotamia," in *State and Temple Economy in the Ancient Near East*, ed. by Edward Lipinski (Department of Oriëntalistiek, Louvain) I:1-97.

— (1981), "Ebla and the Kish Civilization," in Luigi Cagni, *La Lingua di Ebla* (Istituto Universario Orientale, Series Minor XIV, Napoli):9-73.

Gelb, I., P. Steinkeller, and R. M. Whiting (1991), *Earliest Land Tenure Systems in the Near East* (Oriental Institute Publications 104, Chicago).

Goody, Jack (1990), *The Oriental, The Ancient and the Primitive: Systems of Marriage and the Family in the Pre-industrial Societies of Eurasia* (Cambridge University Press, Cambridge).

— (1996), *The East in the West* (Cambridge University Press, Cambridge).

Grübler, Arnulf (1996), "Time for a Change: On the Patterns of Diffusion of innovation," *Daedalus* 125; No. 3:19-42.

Hofstadter, D. R. (1980), *Gödel, Escher, Bach: An Eternal Golden Band* (Vintage Books, New York).

Jacobsen, T. (1957), "Early Political Development in Mesopotamia," *ZA* 18:91-140.

Jasim, S. A. (1985), "The Ubaid Period in Iraq. Recent Excavations in the Hamrin Basin," BAR International Series 267(i) (Oxford).

Kramer, Carol (1982), *Village Ethnoarchaeology: Rural Iran in Archaeological Perspective* (Academic Press, New York).

Kuijt, Ian, ed. (1996), "Househol Ritual and Community Cohesion in the Levantine Neolithic," in *Social Configurations of the Near Eastern Early Neolithic: Community Identity, Heterarchical Organization and Ritual* (Cambridge University Press).

Lamberg-Karlovsky, C. C. (1996), "The Archaeological Evidence for International Commerce: Public and/or Private Enterprise in Mesopotamia," in *Privatization in the Ancient Near East and Classical World*, Michael Hudson and Baruch Levine (eds.) Peabody Museum Bulletin 5, Harvard University, Cambridge, Mass.

Lekachman, Robert (1959), *History of Economic Ideas* (Harper, New York).

Liverani, Mario (1984), "Land Tenure and Inheritance in the Ancient Near East: The Interaction Between 'Palace' and 'Family' Sectors," in *Land Tenure and Social Transformations in the Middle East*, ed. by Tarif Khalidi (America University, Beirut):33-44.

Maisels, Charles K. (1990), *The Emergence of Civilization* (Routledge, London).

Neusner, Jacob (1990), *The Economics of the Mishnah* (University of Chicago Press, Chicago).

Nissen, Hans (1988), *The Early History of the Ancient Near East 9000-2000 BC* (University of Chicago Press, Chicago).

C. C. LAMBERG-KARLOVSKY

Nissen, H., P. Damerow, and R. Englund (1993), *Archaic Bookkeeping: Early Writing and Techniques of Economic Administration in the Ancient Near East* (University of Chicago Press, Chicago).

Oates, J. (1996), "A Prehistoric Communication Revolution," *CAJ* 6:165-73.

Oates, David and Joan Oates (1976), "Early Irrigation Agriculture in Mesopotamia," in *Problems in Economic and Social Archaeology*, ed. by G. Sieveking, I. H. Longworth and K. E. Wilson (Duckworth, London):109-135.

— (1997) "An Open Gate: Cities of the Fourth Millennium BC (Tell Brak 1997)," CAJ 7, No. 2 cf.287-297.

Oppenheim, A. Leo (1964), *Ancient Mesopotamia: Portrait of a Dead Civilization* (Chicago).

Postgate, J. N. (1992), Early Mesopotamian Society and Economy at the Dawn of History (London and New York).

Postgate, J. N. and J. A. Moon (1984), "Excavations at Abu Salabikh. A Sumerian City," in *National Geographic Reports* 17 (1976):721-43.

Potts, D. (1996), *Mesopotamian Civilization. The Material Foundation* (Cornell University Press, Ithaca).

Powell, Marvin (1986), "Economy of the Extended Family According to Sumerian Sources," *Oikumene* 5:9-13.

Renger, Johannes M. (1995), "Institutional, Communal, and Individual Ownership or Possession of Arable land in Ancient Mesopotamia from the End of the Fourth to the End of the First Millennium BC." Symposium on Ancient Law, Economics and Society, edited by James Lindgren, Laurent Mayali, and Geoffrey P. Miller. *Chicago-Kent Law Review* 71; No. 1, Part 2:269-319.

Roaf, M. (1995), "Palaces and temples in Ancient Mesopotamia," in *Civilizations of the Ancient Near East*, ed. by Jack Sasson (Simon and Schuster, New York):423-441.

Rothman, M. S. (1994), "Sealings Use and Changes in Administrative Oversight and Structure at Tepe Gawra during the Fourth Millennium," in Ferioli, P., *Archives Before Writing* (Scriptorum, Rome):19-121.

Sahlins, Marshall (1972), *Stone Age Economics* (Aldine. Chicago).

Schmandt-Besserat, D. (1992), *Before Writing* (University of Texas Press, Austin).

Schneider, Anna (1920), *Die Anfänge der Kulturwirtschaft: Die Sumerische Tempelstadt* (Baedeker, Essen).

Schumpeter, J. (1939), *The Theory of Economic Development* (Harvard University Press, Cambridge).

Silver, Morris (1983), *Economic Structures of the Ancient Near East* (Barnes and Noble, New York).

Stein, Gil (1996), "Producers, Patrons, and Prestige: Craft Specialists and Emergent Elites in Mesopotamia from 5500- 3100 BC," in *Craft Specialization and Social Evolution: In Memory of V. Gordon Childe*, ed. by Bernard Wailes (University of Pennsylvania, Philadelphia):25-39 .

Steinkeller, Piotr (1987), "The Foresters of Umma," *Labor in the Ancient Near East*, ed. by Marvin Powell (American Oriental Society, New Haven):73-115.

— (1994), "Early Political Development in Mesopotamia and the Origins of the Akadian Empire," in *Akkad: The World's First Empire*, ed. by M. Liverani (Padua).

Stone, Elizabeth (1987), *Nippur Neighborhoods* (Oriental Institute, Chicago).

Watson, P. J. (1978), "Architectural Differentiation in Some Near Eastern Communities, Prehistoric and Modern," in *Social Archaeology*, ed. by C. L. Redman, M. Beeman, F. Curtin, F. Langhorne, W. Versaggi, and J. Wanser (Academic Press, New York).

— (1979), *Archaeological Ethnography in Western Iran*. Viking Fund Publications in Anthropology 57 (University of Arizona Press, Tucson).

Weber, Max (1936), *The Agrarian Sociology of Ancient Civilizations* (NLB, London).

von Wickede, A. (1990), *Prähistorische Stempelglyptic in Vorderasien* (Profil Verlag, Munich).

Wright, H. (1984), "Prestate Political Formation," in *On the Evolution of Complex Society in Honour of Harry Hoijer*, ed. by T. Earle (UCLA Department of Anthropology, Malibu, California 1982):41-77 .

Yasin, W. (1970), "Excavation at Tell es-Sawaan, 1969. Report on the Sixth Season's Excavations," *Sumer* 26:3-20.

Zaccagnini, Carlo (1981), "Modo di produzione asiatico e vicino Oriente antico: Appunti per una discussione," *Dialoghi di Archeologia* 3:3-65.

Zettler, Richard (1992), *The Ur III Temple of Inanna at Nippur* (D. Reimer, Berlin).

C. C. LAMBERG-KARLOVSKY

5

The Constraints on State and Urban Form in Ancient Mesopotamia

Elizabeth C. Stone
State University of New York, Stony Brook

In spite of Julian Steward's (1958) introduction of the key concepts of multilinear evolution and the culture core, from the mid-1960s until quite recently, archaeologists studying the development and structure of early complex society adopted the much more restrictive models proposed by Service (1975) and Fried (1967). In the spirit of nineteenth-century theorists, they saw all complex societies as alike, the end product of a similar process of development. For them, a complex society's key feature was the development of hierarchy based on the ability of an hereditary few to exploit the labor of the many through the monopoly over the means of production — arable land — and the means of coercion.

During the last decade, a more multifaceted approach to complex society has begun to appear. One recent concept is that of Peer Polity Interaction, focusing on the dynamic interaction between neighboring states or complex chiefdoms (Renfrew and Cherry 1986). Southall's (1956) concept of the segmentary state has been reinvigorated and conceptually broadened by separating ritual suzereignty from direct political sovereignty (Southall 1988). Eisenstadt and his colleagues (Eisenstadt, Abitbol, and Chazan 1988) — in a book that has not had the impact it deserved, due, I assume, to the obliqueness of the writing — have made a distinction between congruent and noncongruent states in Africa, focusing attention on the relationship between the political and social orders. Crumley and her colleagues (Crumley 1979, 1994, Marquardt and Crumley 1987, Brumfiel 1995) have introduced the idea of heterarchy to a literature on complex societies that had been obsessed by the concept of hierarchy.

Finally, and most relevant to the present discussion, Trigger (1993) has provided a more detailed exposition on his earlier (1985) distinction between city states and territorial states. He contrasts early territorial states such as ancient Egypt and Inca Peru with city states such as the Maya, the Yoruba, and ancient Mesopotamia. He describes territorial states as made up of a network of quite small administrative centers inhabited almost exclusively by the ruling class, administrators, elite craftsmen, and retainers. The bulk of the population are excluded from these centers, being dispersed broadly over the countryside. Trigger argues that the economies in such states exhibit a similar dichotomy. The economic benefits of those complex societies take the form mainly of exotic goods brought in by long-distance traders and the products of skilled artisans. These goods are exclusively reserved for the elites. These elites are of course supported by an agricultural surplus, which territorial states simply appropriated.

In contrast, city-state societies consist of networks of adjacent but independent states sharing a common culture, belief system, and status symbols, but which actively compete over territory, trade routes, and resources. Dominated by a large, populous, usually walled city, these states are typified by a small geographic area. Unlike the centers of territorial states, many farmers find their homes in these cities, along with the elites, administrators, and craftspeople.

The economies of city states also differ from those of territorial states. According to Trigger (1993) the movement of agricultural surpluses into the center in city states is not due simply to appropriation but rather to a complex system of exchange. Under these circumstances, exotic materials and the products of urban-based workshops are made available to all members of the society.

Trigger's definition of the differences between these two types of complex society is masterful, but I think his argument falls down when he tries to address causality. He initially expected to find clear ecological differences between city states and territorial states. When this idea failed, he resorted to suggesting that perhaps territorial states grew up in areas with lower population density relative to arable land. He never indicated why this might be important and admitted at the end of his argument that the data were consistent regarding this suggestion (1993:13). In avoiding the issue of causality, he has plenty of company. None of the litany of theorists mentioned above have explained *why* the patterns they are describing might have come about. The exception was Steward (1958) with his idea of the culture core, but he never developed this to its full potential.

Without understanding the causes underlying the structural differences that have been observed in complex societies, we will never be able to distinguish the significant variables from those that are unimportant, nor will we come to an understanding of how some societies transform themselves from city states to territorial states or vice versa.

In this paper I argue that there are, indeed, key differences in the environments in which we find city states and territorial states. However, these are not defined by basic divisions between irrigation societies versus non-irrigation societies, for instance. Instead these distinctions focus on the two key resources for agricultural production: land and labor. This model argues that territorial states are found in areas where arable land is both permanent and bounded, providing a clear opportunity for elites to maintain the necessary labor force through their control over access to arable land. City states, by contrast, are found in areas where productive land is both temporary and mutable, forcing the elites to find means other than direct coercion in order to maintain the necessary agricultural labor force.

To illustrate these differences, we can take Egypt and Inca Peru as examples of territorial states, and Babylonia, the Maya, and the Yoruba as examples of city states. Egypt has long been known as the "gift of the Nile." Without the river it would join the rest of the Sahara as one of the most uninhabitable parts of the globe. But with it, thanks in part to the regularity and timing of its inundation, Egypt long served as the bread-basket of the entire Mediterranean world (Butzer 1976). The annual flooding of the Nile Valley not only provided the water needed to prepare the land for sowing the new crop, but also washed away any accumulated salts while providing a new, nutrient-rich layer of silt. Thus the area covered by the inundation is prime agricultural land, the regularity of that inundation makes that land permanent and the escarpment at the edge of the flood plain provides a clear boundary between the desert and the sown. Moreover, even in the early days of the Egyptian state, the surrounding desert was not suitable for pastoralism or any other viable economic endeavor, providing no alternative way of life for the population of ancient Egypt.

Although superficially very different, the mountainous area occupied by the Inca Empire shares many of these same characteristics. There, the permanence of the land is the result of an extensive investment in agricultural terraces — which are specifically designed to maximize the concentration of nutrients in these narrow strips of arable land — and the boundedness of the land is due to height and ruggedness of the terrain, resulting in a series of "economic islands" (Moseley 1992:43). Although the high puña could be used by pastoralists and hunters, it is only in the northern part that it can support any such groups on a permanent basis (Moseley 1992:28f), so, as was the case in Egypt, these highlands could not provide a permanent refuge area for disaffected members of the Inca state.

The classic city-state societies of Mesoamerica and West Africa are located in very different geographic areas. Both the Maya and the Yoruba occupy tropical forest areas that can only be cultivated by employing swidden agriculture. Here, the bulk of agricultural production comes from fields that are cleared and cultivated for relatively short periods before being permitted to revert to either bush or forest again. Under these circumstances it is impossible for any central authority to maintain a monopoly over arable land because that land keeps changing. Moreover, bringing new land under cultivation does not require any central direction. The only requirement for opening new land is the ability to mobilize labor, whether this is achieved by an extended family or by a large state organization. The presence of extensive uncultivated forests in the area provides a potential alternate lifestyles for any who are disaffected with the central authority. Hunting in the forests near the Maya and Yoruba cities was very important, and to the north of Yorubaland were areas dominated by cattle herders.

At first blush, the geography of southern Mesopotamia may seem similar to Egypt and dissimilar to the tropical forest areas of the Maya and Yoruba. After all both Egypt and Mesopotamia are located in extremely desertic areas that are only made habitable by the presence of large watercourses flowing though them. But here the similarity ends. Whereas Egypt only had one river—confined in a narrow floodplain for most of its length, Mesopotamia had two great rivers, which bifurcated into multiple branches as they flowed through the broad, flat Babylonian plain.

Like the Maya and the Yoruba, cultivable land in southern Mesopotamia required labor for its creation—in this case through the construction of irrigation canals. Moreover, the land so created was not permanent, since the combined scourges of salinization and siltation led to the collapse of these systems after a few decades (Poyck 1952, Jacobsen 1982, Powell 1985). Although large scale canal building required the organizational skills of state society, smaller scale systems can and have been constructed by small groups since the valley was first settled (Fernea 1970). Like tropical forest areas, the uncultivated wasteland was capable of supporting alternative lifestyles — pastoralism in the desert and fishing and hunting in the marshes.

The model

These differences in ecology had a profound impact on the social, political, and economic structure of territorial states and city states. The fact that control over land represented control over the labor force needed to work it in territorial states, allowed the development of a hierarchical political system in which positions of authority were carefully controlled and were assigned on the basis of inheritance. The result was a highly centralized political system based on a powerful ruler supported by an hereditary aristocracy. The rest of the population was essentially disenfranchised. As social mobility was virtually unknown, a clear and permanent divide was maintained between the elites and the bulk of the population.

The peasants were tied to the state by their need for arable land, in exchange for which they were obliged to yield up any surplus production. Moreover, the elites were able to maintain exclusive rights over the state's productive potential. All exotic goods and products of elite craftspeople stayed in their hands. Under these circumstances, the peasantry continued to live an essentially Neolithic life, making their own tools and ceramics, and building their own houses. The only difference was that the state could appropriate their labor for major construction projects and could tax their agricultural surpluses.

Where several of these polities were located in adjacent regions, the takeover of one by another was relatively easy. Once the neighboring elites had been co-opted into the expanding state (whether accompanied by military threats or actual battle), the land they controlled would have accompanied them. The inclusion of local elites in the new ruling class would effectively remove potential sources of opposition from within then new state (see Eisenstadt, Abitbol, and Chazan 1988).

City states, by contrast, could not use coercion in order to maintain their labor force. If they tried, there was always the possibility that people would vote with their feet and leave state society altogether. Under these circumstances, any political system had to involve the population as a whole in decision making, at least at the most basic level. Popular assemblies and advisory councils thus typify city states; they are much less common in territorial states. However they are constructed, these assemblies provided representation for the basic building blocks of city states — affiliated groups consisting of both elites and nonelites. Here the nonelites made up the key commodity, labor, while the elites served as their representatives within the larger society.

E. STONE   207

Decision-making in city-state societies was the result of consensus-building between the various elites. The large institutions, the agriculturally based population, the merchants, and the artisans all competed with one another for political ascendancy and forged a larger consensus through the organs of popular government.

Even though these elites held real political power in city states, unlike those in territorial states, they could not become entrenched. Instead, social mobility tended to be high, as different families rose and fell in status over time. The high cost of elite status — reflecting the need to maintain the loyalty of one's followers, coupled with a partitive system of inheritance — further weakened the population's economic base from generation to generation. In due course, new elites would rise to the top, often based on wealth accumulated as a result of the high levels of entrepreneurial activity typical of city states. The net effect was that the major divisions within city states were not vertically based on class as in territorial states, but rather horizontally based on affiliations between elites and their nonelites.

These bonds weakened when elites began to segregate themselves from the bulk of the population, spurring an outward migration of the urban population. At first these disaffected groups would establish more or less independent settlements on the fringes of the city state. But when these peripheral groups became sufficiently numerous, they could begin to threaten the stability of the city's internal political structure. This would explain the volatile political history so typical of city states.

The combination of competition and consensus necessary for the successful maintenance of this political system is not without its drawbacks — the most serious problem being tendency towards factionalism. It is in this context that we must see the role of kingship. In city states the ruler had to be above the political fray in a position to arbitrate if the system's competitive character got out of hand. In such instances the ruler served both as the single uniting symbol of the otherwise fractured city and as the ultimate arbitrator.

Rulers of city-states also differ from those of territorial states in that their power often is limited at least partly because they have no hereditary aristocracy through whom they can rule. Kings of ancient city states were noteworthy in their separation from the rest of the population. This might be effected through divinity, but unlike the divine kings of territorial states, in city states their divinity served to restrict their freedom of action. These kings were surrounded by taboos and were expected to perform a large number of elaborate rituals.

Such rulers also were separated from the rest of the population by being outsiders. As kings could not be seen to be biased toward one group or another, it was seen as a benefit that rulers had few if any direct allies within the city state. Just as Florence and Athens called upon foreigners to come and rule them when factionalism became a problem, the ancient city states relied on outsiders to serve as their figureheads in many instances. Since these rulers did not have a natural constituency, their palace retinue often consisted largely of slaves.

In the economic realm, city states placed a heavy emphasis on entrepreneurial activity. Merchants and artisans represented a significant independent segment of society. While they participated in the larger political system, they also were responsible for the economic success of the city-state system. Although the major institutions and elites clearly had greater access to imported materials and the products of urban workshops, they did not have exclusive rights. All members of city-state societies had access to these goods. Indeed, in city states the surplus production of the agricultural sector did not fall into the hands of the central administration through direct appropriation as much as through the exchange of rural products for urban ones. Finally, without a relative degree of economic freedom, the economic fluidity needed to make possible the high levels of social mobility in city states could not have been achieved.

The downside of the city-state system lay in the impossibility of extending this political system over large distances. The city state worked because the key political players all lived in the same city and therefore had the possibility of settling their differences through face-to-face interaction. City states never occurred in isolation and the different polities that made up their overall system shared a combination of competition and alliance-building typical of political relations within the cities. The physical separation that existed between city states, however, meant that their differences were more often settled by active warfare than by discussion.

The problems began when one city state succeeded in conquering its neighbor or neighbors. Unlike territorial states, where the hierarchical system of political organization easily could be extended to any freshly absorbed territories, this was not the case with city states. When the latter were joined together into larger imperial units — which happened with some frequency — two quite different types of political organization were in place. The process of consensus building continued within the basic units of society — that is, the old city states — but this existed side by side with the imposition of imperial rule by the conquering state. Because of the conflict between the philosophies behind these two systems, the city states never became fully reconciled to their absorption in the larger unit. This eventually lead to the collapse of the system back into city states.

Ancient Mesopotamia

So far, this discussion has been largely theoretical. Mesopotamia has been just one of the city-state societies under discussion. Indeed, the understanding of the structure of city states in general has been drawn more from the better-known Yoruba than from Mesopotamia. Under these circumstances, the burning question is the degree to which such a model fits current understandings of how ancient Mesopotamia was organized.

A quick glance at the literature on the structure of society in southern Mesopotamia indicates the coexistence of two quite different models. Modern scholars reading the same texts and looking at the same archaeological data have come up with radically different views on the essence of Mesopotamian society. One view — adumbrated by Assyriologists such as Gelb (1965, 1967, 1976) and Diakanoff (1971, 1972, 1974a, 1974b), and pursued by archaeologists like Zagarell (1986), Pollock (1983, 1989) and Wright (1984) — sees Mesopotamian society as highly stratified, providing few opportunities for social mobility. The major view held by others — mostly scholars more at home in both assyriology and archaeology, such as Postgate (1992), Steinkeller (1987b), and myself (Stone 1987; in press) — is of ancient Mesopotamia as having been much less stratified and having numerous potential avenues for social mobility.

Much of the difficulty here lies in the inherent opaqueness of the written documents. Most texts provide information on the concerns of the bureaucrats working for the central institutions. These groups always organize their subjects in a rigid, hierarchical way, irrespective of the actual characteristics of the society concerned (Steinkeller 1987b). Those aspects of Mesopotamian society that would provide critical information on the issues of concern here are particularly poorly documented in the textual record. The role played by the assembly in Mesopotamian politics is fraught with uncertainty. Jacobsen (1943, 1957) has argued that it was the key decision-maker in the early Mesopotamian cities, but most scholars suggest that it was limited to judicial matters in later years, for it is its judicial decisions that are found recorded on cuneiform tablets. Postgate (1992:269-270), by contrast, suggests that it was through the assembly that the will of the gods was determined in such critical decisions as the appointing of a new ruler.

Textual information is largely silent also with regard to the role played by residential neighborhoods. Above, I have argued that a key difference between heterarchical city states and hierarchical territorial states is that in the former, elites and commoners built political bonds through co-residence in residential districts, whereas in territorial states they are physically separated. There exist textual references to such residential neighborhoods, but they are very rare; indeed, it is not even clear how we should relate these units (*babtu*) to the archaeological remains of domestic architecture (Stone 1987, 1997).

Another important but poorly understood issue is the organization of manufacturing — again an area where our written sources are surprisingly mute. Ancient Mesopotamian artisans were highly skilled, but the written record reveals remarkably little about how production was organized. The degree to which a central authority is able to control and limit the importation, production, and distribution of high-quality goods tends to reflect a society's degree of hierarchy. Lack of such information makes it enormously difficult to understand basic aspects of ancient Mesopotamian society.

The virtual absence in the cuneiform texts of references to assemblies, neighborhoods, and manufacturing does not necessarily mean that they were unimportant or minor aspects of Mesopotamian society. The Mesopotamian textual record is full of lacunae caused both by sampling problems and, more importantly, by the process of selection made by the ancient scribes as to what needed to be recorded and what did not. It is here that the archaeological record can be brought to bear. Although it too is incomplete, at least its lacunae are caused by natural forces like decay which, unlike the ancient scribes, do not discriminate among classes of society or institutions.

But, the archaeological record can only be brought to bear to solve these basic disagreements if a link can be made between archaeologically recoverable data and the basic structures of society as a whole. Fortunately, geographers have long argued that social relations are mapped physically in the remains of human settlements — not only over the landscape as a whole, but also within actual settlements (Johnston 1980; Rapoport 1977). The difficulty for us is that their work has focused on the physical organization of modern cities, which are different in every way from their ancient counterparts. It is therefore up to us to develop an understanding of the ways in which the physical organization of ancient settlements mirrored underlying social and economic organization. This can be achieved by comparing the organization of cities in territorial states (*e.g.*, Cuzco) with those of city states (*e.g.*, Yoruba cities).

This process yields the following expectations: cities characteristic of hierarchical territorial states are characterized by a unified but not very large urban space, in which the major institutions — religious, political, economic, etc. are physically concentrated. The population of these centers are dominated by elites, bureaucrats, and highly skilled craftspeople — especially those who produce goods for elite consumption, with only their servants and slaves constituting any nonelite segment. Finally, it is within these cities that both wealth and high-quality luxury goods are concentrated. Beyond these settlements lie the scattered farmsteads and villages of the bulk of the population, whose material culture remains are little different from their Neolithic ancestors, since they have virtually no access to the goods produced by the urban-based artisans.

By contrast, the urban centers of less hierarchical city-state societies are large and populous, but broken into many different sectors. Most obvious are the physical divisions between the major political, religious, and economic institutions, but the residential sector is also subdivided into numerous face-to-face communities or neighborhoods. Unlike cities in territorial states, these neighborhoods are not made up entirely of elites, nor are there some elite and some nonelite areas. Instead each residential district is similar to the others in providing housing for all social classes. The presence of large numbers of nonelites in these cities — many of whom are farmers — allows for a more even distribution of manufactured goods, with no segments of society denied access to these goods. Finally, since the key resource in these societies is labor rather than land ownership, even quite small settlements have their own elites and populations with access to manufactured goods.

With these concepts in mind, let us turn to the archaeological record for Mesopotamia. If its city planning conforms to the model of urban organization typical of the less hierarchical city states, then it is likely that the interpretations of the textual sources preferred by Postgate, Steinkeller and myself is more likely to be correct. If, on the other hand, the archaeological data show a clear pattern of wealth concentration, of separation between elites and nonelites in terms of residence, and of close physical proximity of the key institutions, then the interpretation argued by Gelb, Diakonoff, and others is probably more accurate.

The first issue is whether Mesopotamian cities were spatially unified or segregated. Compared with other Middle Eastern tell sites, the remains of Mesopotamian urban centers are noteworthy for their multi-mounded aspect. Recent survey work at Mashkan-shapir (Stone 1990, 1994; Stone and Zimansky 1994, 1995) has revealed a total of five major and more minor canals running within that city. Given that major watercourses are known to have divided other ancient cities such as Nippur (where the ancient Euphrates is even noted on the Kassite map of the city [Roaf 1990:81]), Ur (Woolley and Mallowan 1976: 10, Pl. 115, 116), Kish (Moorey 1978:48; Gibson 1972), and Babylon (Roaf 1990:192), to name a few — it seems likely that the divisions between all or most of the mounds of Mesopotamian cities were caused by watercourses. Indeed, aerial photographs of Larsa (Huot, Rougeulle, and Suire 1989) indicate the presence of major linear features within the city. These have been interpreted as roads by the excavators, but to this author they more closely resemble canals, similar to those found at Mashkan-shapir. Indeed, an examination of a SPOT satellite image of the area around Larsa indicates that at least one of these features left visible traces as it continues beyond the city walls. The argument that these traces at Larsa are canals is further strengthened, to my mind, by the massive gates that guarded their passage through the city walls and the much smaller gates that are present nearby. This pattern suggests that at Larsa, as at Mashkan-shapir and indeed much of modern southern Iraq, the roads followed the watercourses, requiring both water and land traffic to be controlled on entry into the city.

These intramural canals and rivers would have served as major dividing forces within the city. Herodotus (I.186) claims that it was only in his time that a bridge was built over the Euphrates as it flowed through Babylon; before that the inhabitants had to rely on ferries to move from one part of the city to the other. At Mashkan-shapir (Stone and Zimansky 1995) one canal has an identifiable crossing point, but it is not clear whether this represents a pair of quays or the supports for a bridge. Whichever was the case, the division of these cities by canals and rivers meant that traffic between the various districts was seriously impeded.

If this were not enough, there is also evidence that intramural walls also were used to segregate particular districts. At Abu Salabikh the West Mound (Postgate 1983) was divided into a number of residential districts by walls, and a similar wall has been found at Khafajah separating the residential district by the Temple Oval from the rest of the city (Delougaz, Hill, and Lloyd 1967:Plate 14). Walls also were used to delimit institutional zones, as in Ur's Temenos Wall, which the excavator believed had its origin as early as the late third millennium (Woolley 1974:55-60). At Mashkan-shapir, internal walls have been identified, which segregated both the cemetery and the probable administrative center from the rest of the city (Stone and Zimansky 1995).

These data suggest that Mesopotamian cities were indeed extremely segregated spaces, broken into numerous residential and institutional zones by both water and active construction. Unfortunately, given the huge size of Mesopotamian urban sites, the ways in which communication was effected between the different parts of these cities is not yet understood.

Nevertheless, it was within these spaces that the major structuring institutions of the cities were to be found, the most important of which was the temple. Most cities had one major temple — usually raised up on a platform or ziggurat. These temples formed the visual focus of the city — its skyline if you will — but they were not, in general, located in the heart of the city. The asymmetrical location of the main temple is perhaps best seen at Mashkan-shapir, where it is located at the very edge of the city (Stone and Zimansky 1995). Moreover, this location cannot be ascribed to chance — the result of unplanned growth of the city in one direction rather than another. Mashkan-shapir grew from a small town or village of less than 5 ha. into a major city as the result of the deliberate construction of its city wall by Sin-iddinam. Thus Mashkan-shapir is the closest thing to a planned city that we have for Mesopotamia, and yet the temple is located on one edge of the city. The major temples at Ur (Woolley and Mallowan 1976:Pl. 116), Nippur (Gibson 1978; Roaf 1990:81), Khafajah (Delougaz 1940:Pl. II), Ischali (Hill, Jacobsen and Delougaz 1990:2, 4), and Tell Agrab (Delougaz and Lloyd 1942:Pl. 25) are also located well to one edge of their respective cities. Indeed, the asymmetrical position of buildings like the early temples at Tell 'Uqair (Lloyd and Safar 1943) and Tell 'Ubaid (Hall and Woolley 1927) suggest that the underlying ideology behind their location goes back to the dawn of Mesopotamian civilization. Perhaps the somewhat more central location of temples at Larsa and Uruk is more the result of the town growing out around them than an indication of their original placement.

Temples are not the only major institutions to have been located at one edge of Mesopotamian cities. Palaces and administrative centers are also noteworthy for their asymmetrical location, and for their distance from the main temple. The early palaces at Kish (Moorey 1978:Map C), Eridu (Safar, Mustafa, and Lloyd 1981:31), the later Sin-kashid palace at Uruk (Roaf 1990:60), and Zimrilim's palace at Mari (Parrot 1958:Pl. I) are all located well to one side of these ancient cities. Postgate (1992:137) has argued that this location is the result of a lack of available space in the center of the city rather than of deliberate intent, but here again the location of the administrative district at Mashkan-shapir (Stone and Zimansky 1995) at the edge of this planned city, suggests that the position of these palaces may not be as accidental as may at first appear.

So far the evidence presented has indicated that the main religious and administrative institutions of Mesopotamian cities were separated from the rest of the city by their location toward the edge of these urban centers. Larsa is an exception to this pattern. Both its palace and temple are located close to the middle of the city, in close proximity to one another. The mound topography might suggest that a canal divided the two buildings, and both buildings are located toward the western side of the site, but nevertheless the data indicate that Nur-Adad's palace differs in its location from other Mesopotamian palaces (Huot, Rougeulle, and Suire 1989). A single exception does not, however, negate the veracity of the larger picture. Although there are too few known palaces for the non-centric location of these institutions to be indisputable, that is not the case for the major temples. Here the data are overwhelming that the most important economic power in these cities and their symbolic and visual focus was generally to be found at the periphery of the built-up area.

The other major structuring features of Mesopotamian cities — manufacturing and marketing areas — are less easy to identify archaeologically. We have a general understanding of the locations of "smokestack" industries based on where their by products are concentrated on the surface. At Mashkan-shapir (Stone and Zimansky 1995), Abu Salabikh (Postgate 1990:103-4), al-Hiba (Carter 1989-90) and Larsa (Huot, Rougeulle, and Suire 1989), these seem to be concentrated in one area toward the edge of the site (the leeward part at Mashkan-shapir), but this is not consistent at other sites. It also appears that at Ur, ceramic manufacturing — or at least the production of terracottas — was concentrated in an area outside the city itself, at Diqdiqqa (Woolley and Mallowan 1976:86).

This pattern should not be taken to indicate that all manufacturing was necessarily concentrated only in one area. But the only data that can be brought to bear come from the survey at Mashkan-shapir (Stone and Zimansky 1995). Its manufacturing area has clear evidence for a concentration of ceramic production around a small canal designed, presumably, to provide the needed water. We also found large numbers of cuboid and other small grinding and polishing stones in this general area, stones that may have been used to make stone bowls. These data would tend to suggest that in addition to "smokestack" industries concentrated in the southeastern portion of the site, it housed a broader range of manufacturing activities. However, we also encountered the remains of ceramic industries — in the form of the traces of kilns and kiln wasters — in other parts of the site, especially to the north.

The only other evidence from Mashkan-shapir are the ten concentrations of cuprous slag and copper fragments that were found at the site. These are found in all parts of the site, but a majority are located along the major east-west road that ran through the middle of the site, tying together areas that were otherwise separated by watercourses. These concentrations are scattered along this street, so there cannot have been one copper/bronze production area. These remains probably reflect a combination of what we would now consider manufacturing and marketing. It seems likely that the work of the smiths involved the repair of metal objects, the recycling of broken fragments into new objects, and—certainly in some cases according to our evidence—the small-scale smelting of copper. Under these circumstances, the primary motivation behind their location would have to be ensuring access by their customers.

One of the least understood aspects of ancient Mesopotamian cities is how goods were distributed. The Mashkan-shapir street with the copper-workshops strung out along it might indicate that such major arteries served also as the place where artisans of all kinds plied their trade — perhaps in much the same way as the British "High Street" or the American "Main Street." But if so, there is little trace of such places in the textual record — except perhaps in the tendency for artisans to live next to other artisans but not necessarily those of the same craft. The written record would suggest that commercial activities were concentrated in squares located near city gates — areas yet to be excavated. It should be noted, however, that the Mashkan-shapir street almost certainly ran between two of the main gates of the city — so these two sources of information may not really be in conflict.

There is one other area where the texts would place exchange activities and that is the karum, the quay or harbor of the city. It was here that the merchants lived, but there is some debate as to whether this area was actually within the city or outside it. The written sources frequently refer to the "city and the karum," which may either indicate a physical separation, or the social and administrative distinctions between the merchants and the rest of the population that are so evident in the textual record. No karum has been excavated in Mesopotamia proper, but intramural harbors have been identified at both Ur (Woolley and Mallowan 1976:10) and Mashkan-shapir (Stone and Zimansky 1995) and probably existed in other cities as well. But no significant excavations have yet taken place in the vicinity of these harbors to tell us whether they represent the karums of these cities, or if these should be sought beyond the city walls.

The data outlined above suggest that Mesopotamian cities had their major religious, administrative, productive, and exchange foci located in different areas, but generally towards the periphery of the site. The bulk of these cities were residential, and it is the structure of these residential districts that may be the most eloquent regarding the degree of hierarchy enjoyed by this society. Excavated remains of residential districts cover virtually all periods of Mesopotamian history. Although some details of the plans of these structures change over time, one aspect is constant: every excavated domestic area of sufficient size has shown evidence of larger, well-appointed houses with small, poor houses nestled between them. This pattern suggests that elites and nonelites were not separated by residence one from the other.

The lack of differentiated elite and nonelite residential areas is made especially clear by the Old Babylonian remains from Nippur and Ur. At Nippur (Stone 1987), two residential districts were excavated on Tablet Hill, separated by only 30 meters one from the other. Both have patterns of large and small houses within them, and in terms of overall material culture there is little to choose between them. However, the associated textual sources suggest that one area, TA, was occupied primarily by small farmowners, while there is little evidence for real property ownership on the part of the residents of TB.

At Ur, three different residential districts were excavated (Woolley and Mallowan 1976). One, EM, was located near the religious center and was occupied by those tied to the temple (Charpin 1986). A second, AH lies across the main canal from the temple precinct and has a more entrepreneurial character (Van De Mieroop 1992). The last is much smaller, located next to the city wall but again divided from the other two by another canal. All three areas have both large and small houses, a similar material culture, and intramural graves, which included both well-appointed burials with rich grave goods and very simple inhumations (Luby 1990). Together these data suggest that neither wealth nor class served to distinguish one residential district from another. Rather, occupation, relationship to one of the urban institutions, or some other principle of affiliation served to characterize these neighborhoods. Thus in TA the very wealthy landholders living in House K lived together with the much poorer family in House I (Stone 1987), and this pattern of the rich and poor members of the same occupational group living together seems to be mirrored in all other habitation areas for which we have sufficient data.

These data indicate that the pattern of residence based on vertical divisions between affiliated groups rather than horizontal divisions between classes noted for other less hierarchical city-state societies is well substantiated for Mesopotamia. In those other societies, this pattern was associated with broad-scale access to manufactured goods by the population as a whole. We have already noted the close similarities in the material culture inventories from different excavated residential districts within a single city, and this pattern is confirmed by the survey data from Mashkan-shapir where both copper/bronze (an imported, manufactured material), and cylinder seals (the Mesopotamian badge of office) — were more or less evenly distributed over the entire site (Stone and Zimansky 1995). But we can, I think, go further than this. By the second millennium BC, there is virtually no evidence for the use of stone tools.[1] Everyone seems to have had access to metal tools, even if only the wealthy could afford the luxury of bronze vessels and elaborate jewelry. This is in sharp contradistinction to contemporary Egypt, where only the elites used metal implements.

This issue of the overall distribution of wealth is seen most clearly when we look at the rare small sites that have been excavated in southern Mesopotamia. Only two of these have been subject to extensive excavations — the 1 ha. second millennium sites of Tell Harmal (Baqir 1946, 1959) and Haradum (Kempinski-Lecompte 1992). These are both noteworthy in that they are walled and have administrative and religious foci in spite of their small sizes. That is, they are structured as cities in miniature, rather than as villages that are functionally differentiated from the larger cities. It is true that their temples and administrative centers (or mayor's houses) are not peripherally located as was the case in the urban centers, but then these sites are about the same size as typical residential neighborhoods within cities and would represent a single face-to-face community rather than a community made up of a series of competitive and consensus-building interest groups. Like the residential districts excavated in the larger cities, these settlements too had large, well-appointed houses abutting smaller, poorer structures. But what is noteworthy is how similar they are in terms of activities and material culture to their larger counterparts.

Both Haradum and Tell Harmel were literate. Not only were texts associated with the administrative centers, but — as was the case in the larger cities of that time — virtually every house had its stores of contracts, letters, and the like. A comparison of the material culture inventory of Haradum (and Tell Harmel to the extent that is accessible) with that of the major cities of the day — Nippur, Ur, Sippar, Isin, Mashkan-shapir — shows no significant differences. They all have decorative terracottas — including terracotta statuary decorating the temples at Isin, Mashkan-shapir, Haradum, and Tell Harmal — metal tools and implements, cylinder seals, etc. Thus, if Tell Harmal and Haradum are typical of small Mesopotamian sites — and now that there are two of them that seems more likely — the vast differences between the elite dominated cities and the rest of society seen in territorial states like Egypt and Peru simply did not exist in Mesopotamia. Instead, the goods and services that are the product of civilization were available to rich and poor, and to the population of both the big cities and the larger rural hinterlands.

Conclusions

The data presented above indicate significant similarities between the archaeological record of ancient Mesopotamian cities and the evidence from the urban centers of other city-state societies — even in the second millennium when periods of political unification were hardly unknown. The linkage of the spatial data with the underlying social and political forces associated with city states and territorial states, allows archaeological data to be used to contribute to debates on the nature of Mesopotamian society, which have heretofore taken place among assyriologists. If the model presented at the outset of this paper is correct — and there is considerable data to support it — the organization of Mesopotamian cities suggests that this earliest of civilizations was not built upon principles of hierarchy as has been suggested by some, but rather on the development of consensus between differently constituted interest groups. This is especially satisfying both as an affirmation of the suggestion made by Adams as early as 1966 that a major causative factor in state formation was the need to reconcile differences between competing interest groups, and as an example of the importance of cities as "meeting places" argued by Michael Hudson.

Discussion

Hudson: If I were going to buy a house, would I want to buy a house that was at the center of this city or would I want to buy a house at the periphery?

Stone: I think it depends who you are, what you are doing, where you are situated in the society, and with whom you have connections. There is no evidence from Ur that there is any difference whatsoever between living next to the temple in area EM or next to the city wall. The houses are the same size. They have the same types of artifacts. They have tablets. They have the same range of burial goods. There is absolutely no statistical difference between them.

Hudson: So there is no plan of site prices for real estate?

Stone: The trouble with real estate is that you really have to know what condition the real estate is in. The only thing in terms of prices is from what I was working on from Nippur. When things got so bad in southern Mesopotamia that sites like Ur were abandoned, prices of real estate in Nippur plummeted. They did so everywhere.

One of the positive things about the texts from Nippur is that they come from Penn tunnels mostly. They probably come from everywhere, to the extent that we know where they came from. Penn did a pretty good job of riddling all parts of the site with tunnels, so we are not just dealing with limited samples. There is nothing to back up a statement that real estate prices are different from one area to another.

Buccellati: I wonder about the supposed difference between a territorial state and a city state, because a city-state is also territorial.

Stone: I might agree. I am using that term because Trigger has used it. I would probably draw the distinction between a nation state and a city-state.

Buccellati: The reason for the bond among the people was territorial, because we don't have any evidence there was any sense of national identity.

I personally make the distinction between city-state and extended territorial state or macro-regional state, which could apply to Trigger's territorial state. Mari is, in a sense, a territorial state because it has a boundary in the steppe. The steppe is boundless, but Mari is bounded by it because there are no other kingdoms within it. So it is really a macro-regional state.

One point on which I think I disagree is that you said that one reverts to city-state status. That doesn't seem to me to be the case particularly after the middle of the second millennium. The middle of the second millennium is a major break where there is a major division between north and south. In a sense you really do have Babylon and Assyria (and whatever contractions there are), but essentially there is a major cut along the middle of the region. This is one of the reasons why Mari never came back. There was no room for that kind of state. So it seems to me that after 1500 BC there are no more city states in the technical sense. Not only were there no kingdoms that were cities, but there was also no longer the spirit.

Stone: But you have the Isin domination. You have the interregna, that may be relatively brief in the Sealands and things like that. I obviously was concentrating on Mesopotamia in the third and second millennia, but one of the things I wanted to stress at the beginning is that I see this as an initial explanation for how the state develops and for its character. I also think that the further north you go, especially in Mesopotamia, there are more possibilities for the transformation of one type into another, especially of the city-state into whatever the term should be.

Notes

1. This statement is always rather difficult to demonstrate since most Mesopotamian sites have underlying fourth millennium levels where stone tools were common — leading to such stone tools being found in later levels. Moreover, it is not clear that all excavators included stone tools in their object inventories. However, at Mashkan-shapir, in spite of a substantial Uruk substrate, we found only 39 stone tools on the surface of the site in contrast to more than 2 kg of copper/bronze on the surface of the site.

BIBLIOGRAPHY

Adams, Robert McC. (1966), *Evolution of Urban Society* (Aldine Publishing Co., Chicago).

Baqir, Taha (1946), "Tell Harmal: a preliminary report," *Sumer* 2:22-30.

— (1959), *Tell Harmal* (Directorate General of Antiquities, Baghdad).

Brumfiel, Elizabeth M. (1995), "Heterarchy and the Analysis of Complex Societies: Comments," in *Heterarchy and the Analysis of Complex Societies*, Robert M. Ehrenreich, Carole L. Crumley and Janet E. Levy (eds.). *Anthropological Papers of the American Anthropological Association* 6 (American Anthropological Association, Arlington):125-131.

Butzer, Karl (1976), *Early Hydraulic Civilization in Egypt: A Study in Cultural Ecology* (University of Chicago Press, Chicago).

Carter, Elizabeth (1989-90), "Surface Survey of Lagash, al-Hiba, 1984," *Sumer* 46:60-63.

Charpin, Dominique (1986), *Le clerge d'Ur* (C.N.R.S., Paris).

Crumley, Carole (1979), "Three locational models: An epistomological assessment of anthropology and archaeology," in M. Schiffer (ed.), *Advances in archaeological method and theory*, 2 (Academic Press, New York):141-172.

— (1994), "Historical ecology: a multidimensional ecological orientation," in C. Crumley (ed.), *Historical Ecology* (School of American Research Press, Santa Fe):1-16.

Delougaz, Pinhas (1940), *The Temple Oval at Khafajah* (Oriental Institute Publications LIII. Chicago: University of Chicago Press).

Delougaz, Pinhas, Harold D. Hill, and Seton Lloyd (1967), *Private Houses and Graves in the Diyala Region* (Oriental Institute Publications 88, University of Chicago Press, Chicago).

Delougaz, Pinhas and Seton Lloyd (1942), "Pre-Sargonid Temples in the Diyala Region," Oriental Institute Publications 58. (University of Chicago Press, Chicago).

Diakanoff, Igor M. (1971), "On the structure of Old Babylonian society," in Horst Klengel (ed.), *Beiträge zur Sozialen Struktur des altenVorderasien*. (Akademie verlag, Berlin):15-31.

— (1972), "Socioeconomic classes in Babylonia and the Babylonian concept of social stratification," in D. O. Edzard (ed.), *Gesellschaftklassen im alten Zweistromland und in denangrenzenden Gebeiten*. (Verlag de Bayerischen Akademie der Wissenschaften, Munich):41-52.

— (1974a), "Slaves, helots and serfs in early antiquity," *Acta Antiqua* 22:45-78.

— (1974b), *Structure of Society and the State in Early Dynastic Sumer* (Undena Press, Malibu).

Eisenstadt, S. N., Michel Abitbol and Naomi Chazan, eds. (1988), *The early state in African perspective* (E. J. Brill, Leiden).

Fernea, Robert A. (1970), *Shayck and effendi: changing patterns of authority among the el-Shabana of southern Iraq* (Harvard University Press, Cambridge).

Fried, Morton (1967), *The evolution of political society: an essay in political anthropology* (Random House, New York).

Gelb, Ignace J. (1965), "The ancient Mesopotamian ration system," *JNES* 24:230-243.

— (1967), "Approaches to the study of ancient society," *JAOS* 87:1-8.

— (1976), "Quantitative evaluation of slavery and serfdom," *JCS* 25:195-207.

Gibson, McGuire (1972), *The city and area of Kish* (Field Research Projects, Coconut Grove).

— (1978), "Nippur 1975, A Summary Report," *Sumer* 34:114-121.

Hall, H. R. and Woolley, C. L. (1927), *Ur Excavations I: Al Ubaid* (Trustees of the Two Museums, London and Philadelphia).

Hill, Harold D., Thorkild Jacobsen and Pinhas Delougaz (1990), Old Babylonian Public Buildings in the Diyala Region, *Oriental Institute Publications* 98. (Oriental Institute Press, Chicago).

Huot, Jean-Louis, A. Rougeulle and J. Suire (1989), "La Structure urbaine de Larsa. Unde approche provisoire," in J-L. Huot (ed.) Larsa: Travaux de 1985 (Éditions Recherche sur las Civilisations, Paris):19-52.

Jacobsen, Thorkild (1943), "Primitive democracy in ancient Mesopotamia," *JNES* 7: 36-47.

— (1957), "Early political development in Mesopotamia," *ZA* 52: 91-140.

— (1982), *Salinity and irrigation agriculture in antiquity: Diyala Basin archaeological projects report on essential results, 1957-8* (Undena Publications, Malibu).

Johnston, R. J. (1980), *City and Society: An Outline for Urban Geography* (Hutchinson, London).

Kempinski-Lecomte, Christine (1992), *Haradum I: Une ville nouvelle sur le Moyen-Euphrate (XVIIIe-XVIIe siäcles av. J-C)* (Éditions Recherche sur les Civilisations, Paris).

Lloyd, Seton and Fuad Safar (1943), "Tell Uqair: Excavations by the Iraq Government Directorate of Antiquities in 1940 and 1941," *JNES* 2:131-158.

Luby, Edward M. (1990) *Social variation in ancient Mesopotamia: an architectural and mortuary analysis of Ur in the early second millennium BC* (State University of New York at Stony Brook: Unpublished PhD. Dissertation).

Marquardt, William H. and Carole L. Crumley (1987), "Theoretical issues in the analysis of spatial patterning," in *Regional dynamics: Burgundian Landscapes in Historical Perspective*, C. Crumley and W. Marquardt (eds.) (Academic Press, San Diego):1-18.

Moorey, Roger (1978), *Kish Excavations 1923-1933* (Clarendon Press, Oxford).

Moseley, Michael (1992), *The Incas and their Ancestors* (Thames and Hudson, London).

Parrot, André (1958), *Mission archéologique de Mari II: Le palais* (Librairie Orientaliste Paul Guethner, Paris).

Pollock, Susan (1983), "Style and Information: An Analysis of Susiana Ceramics," *JAA* 2:235-390.

— (1989), "Power Politics in the Susa A Period," in E. F. Henrickson and I. Thuesen (eds.), *Upon this Foundation* (Museum Tusculanum Press, Copenhagen):281-292.

Postgate, Nicholas (1983), "The West Mound Surface Clarance," *Abu Salabikh Excavations, I* (British School of Archaeology in Iraq, London).

— (1990), "Excavations at Abu Salabikh, 1988-89," *Iraq* 52:95-106.

— (1992) *Early Mesopotamia: Society and Economy at the Dawn of History* (Routledge, London).

Powell, Marvin (1985), "Salt, Seed and Yields in Sumerian Agriculture. A Critique of the Theory of Progressive Salinization," *ZA* 75:7-38.

Poyck, A. P. G. (1952), *Farm studies in Iraq* (H. Veeman & Zonen N. V. fur Mededelingen van de Landbourhogeschool, Wageningen).

Rapoport, Amos (1977), *Human Aspects of Urban Form* (Pergamon Press, Oxford).

Renfrew, Colin and John F. Cherry (1986), *Peer Polity Interaction and Socio-Political Change* (Cambridge University Press, New York).

Roaf, Michael (1990), *Cultural Atlas of Mesopotamia and the Ancient Near East* (Facts on File, New York).

Safar, Fuad, Mohammad Ali Mustafa and Seton Lloyd (1981), *Eridu* (State Organization of Antiquities and Heritage, Baghdad).

Service, Elman R. (1975), *Origins of the State and Civilization* (W. W. Norton, New York).

Southall, Aiden W. (1956), *Alur society: a study in processes and types of domination* (Heffer, Cambridge).

— (1988), "Segmentary states in Africa and Asia," *Comparative Studies in Society and History* 30:52-82.

Steinkeller, Piotr (1987a), "The Administrative and Economic Organization of the Ur III state: the Core and the Periphery," in Robert Biggs and McGuire Gibson (eds.), *The Organization of Power: Aspects of Bureaucracy in the Ancient Near East* (Oriental Institute Press, Chicago):19-41.

— (1987b), "The Foresters of Umma: Toward a Definition of Ur III Labor," in M. Powell (ed.) (1993), *Labor in the Ancient Near East* (American Oriental Society, New Haven).

— (1993) "Early political development in Mesopotamia and the origins of the Sargonic Empire," in M. Liverani (ed.), *Akkad — The First World Empire: Structure, Ideology, Traditions* (Sargon, Padua):107-129.

Steward, Julian (1958), *Theory of Culture Change* (University of Illinois Press, Urbana).

Stone, Elizabeth C. (1987), "Nippur neighborhoods," *Studies in ancient Oriental civilization* (Oriental Institute Press, Chicago):44.

— (1990), "The Tell Abu Duwari Project, Iraq, 1977," *Journal of Field Archaeology* 17:141-162.

— (1994), "The anatomy of a Mesopotamian city: the Mashkan-shapir project," in *Bulletin of the Canadian Society for Mesopotamian Studies* 27: 15-24.

— (1995), "The development of cities in ancient Mesopotamia," in J. Sasson (ed.), *Civilizations of the ancient Near East I* (Scribner's, New York):235-248.

— (1997), "Houses, Households and Neighborhoods in the Old Babylonian Period: The Role of Extended Families," in K. R. Veenhof (ed.), *Houses and Households in Ancient Mesopotamia* (Nederlands Historisch-archaeologisch Instituut te Istanbul, Istanbul):229-235.

— in press. "City-states and their centers: The Mesopotamian example," in D. Nichols and T. Charleton (eds.), *The Archaeology of City States: Cross-Cultural Approaches* (Smithsonian Press, Washington).

Stone, Elizabeth C. and Paul Zimansky (1994), "The Tell Abu Duwari Project, 1988-1990," *JFA* 21, 437-455.

— (1995), "The Tapestry of Power in a Mesopotamian City," *Scientific American* 272:92-97.

Trigger, Bruce (1985), "The evolution of pre-industrial cities: A multilinear perspective," in F. Geus and F. Thill (eds.), *Méllanges offerts . . . Jean Vercoutter* (Éditions Recherche sur les Civilisations, Paris):343-353.

— (1993), *Early Civilizations: Ancient Egypt in Context* (The American University in Cairo Press, Cairo).

Van De Mieroop, Marc (1992), "Society and Enterprise in Old Babylonian Ur," *Berliner Beiträge zum Vorderen Orient* 12 (Dietrich Reimer Verlag, Berlin).

Woolley, Sir Leonard (1974), *Ur Excavations VI: The Buildings of the Third Dynasty* (London and Philadelphia, The Trustees of the Two Museums).

Woolley, Sir Leonard and Sir Max Mallowan (1976), *Ur Excavations VII: the Old Babylonian Period* (British Museum Publications, London).

Wright, Henry T. (1984), "Prestate political formations," in Timothy Earle (ed.), *On the Evolution of Complex Societies* (Undena, Malibu)

Zagarell, Allen (1986), "Trade, Women, Class, and Society in Ancient Western Asia," *CA 27*:415-430.

6

Urkesh and the Question of Early Hurrian Urbanism

Giorgio Buccellati
University of California, Los Angeles

In answering the call to consider the interplay between economy and early urbanization, I wish to address three questions: (1) how the exercise of power, *i.e.*, *political development*, was an essential condition of that interplay; (2) how distinctive *geographical environments* provided diverse production and marketing landscapes; and (3) how *ethnic factors* may be identified that helped shape the configuration of both the market and the city. The exposition is essentially programmatic, and the argumentation in the nature of a proposal rather than of a demonstration, so the evidence provided will remain indicative. As indicated in the title of my paper, I will pay special attention to the northern portion of Syro-Mesopotamia and will refer to results from my own fieldwork in the area, in particular at the ancient city of which we have been excavating the remains, *Urkesh*, modern Tell Mozan, because the freshness of the discovery has given me new impetus to locate in a proper context the historical meaning of our finds.

Let me mention briefly a question of methodology. As a contribution to our hosts' interest in "long-term" trends, I will try to show how growth in complexity went hand in hand with a *progressive symbolic distancing from the immediacy of natural sequences*. I will use this concept to define urbanization, industrialization, and ethnic consolidation. Let me use a well-known example. Hunters or gatherers collect their food supply in relatively ready form; farmers, on the other hand, have made a symbolic connection between two moments that are not immediately co-present in nature, sowing and harvesting; not only that, but they have also learned how to induce the chain of events that leads ultimately to harvesting. In other words, farmers have learned how to symbolically bridge the hidden steps of a natural sequence and have also learned how to impose their own sequence so that it replaces the one found in nature. Writing extends the symbolic reach even further, because it allows the dissection of a natural sequence and its rearrangement along different lines of analysis which were never possible before. A list of workmen's rations is, conceptually, much more than a linear sequence of items. It allows symbolic sorting based on the written embodiment rather than on the concrete persons and goods involved — for instance, sorting and totalling by location, foremen, goods received, etc. I will look for similar categories in addressing our three questions of the political dimension of urbanization, of industrialization, and of ethnic consolidation.

The political impact of urbanization on economic development

Early urbanization as identical with state formation: the city-state as state-city. The concept of "urbanization," as seen in its earliest developmental stages when cities first came into being, describes a very complex process, which includes social, political, technical, and ideological aspects, as well as the economic ones on which we are focussing today. From a socio-political point of view, it may be viewed as a demographic coalescing of such proportions that face-to-face recognition among its individuals was no longer possible. And yet it was, at the same time, a coalescing that resulted in tightly knit organisms controlled by a clear-sighted leadership, which gave a sense of finality to this organism and shaped its structure in such a way that it acquired a suprapersonal, or public, identity of its own. In this sense, early urbanization is identical with state formation; the structures that held together the human group were in the first place structures of power, which provided purpose and constraint. Obviously, a host of other factors played a major role in allowing the city to come into existence and to flourish, such as the territorial contiguity within large permanent settlements or the new communication techniques brought about by writing. But it was political leadership that served as the determinant component. If, then, early cities were all, indeed, city-states and state-cities, it follows that a question about economic aspects of urbanization involves a question about the impact that politics had on economic processes and institutions. The city as an instrument of power channeled resources in certain specific directions; concretely, things were procured, produced, and transported in response not only to market demands, but also to political decisions, which were in the hands of the urban elite. In other words, how did the exercise of power channel and control, to its own advantage, the production and distribution of goods?

We will look first at the role of the palace, then at the phenomenon of industrialization.

The palace as the pinnacle of power and wealth. From all we know about Mesopotamian institutional development, the palace was at all times, almost without exception, at the pinnacle of the structure of power.

There is little doubt that the palace represented the *greatest concentration of unencumbered wealth* in any given city. What I mean by "unencumbered wealth" is that all entitlements, however permanent in practice, were in fact subject to direct royal decisions. In contrast, the revenues of the temple were encumbered for uses that could not be subject to the personal decision of the temple administrators. This should not be taken to mean that the temple admninistrators could not use the funds as they saw fit for either the temple's or their own personal gain; it only means that the range of initiative was limited to their specific locality (city and temple), so that they would not, for instance, open or annex other temples. State revenues, on the other hand, gave the king a greater range of choices. There were of course *de facto* entitlements — such as public works or defense — but specific allocations were the king's choice. There is no indication that a distinction was made between personal and public aspects of royal finances, so that the income from state revenues corresponded effectively to the personal income of the king. On the one hand, the palace concentrated in itself the wealth of both the state and the private family of the king; on the other, there was only one palace in any given city, since no other concentration of wealth could match the sources of income of the king. It appears then that the king was without question and in all cases the one who had by far the greatest economic leverage of all, whether individuals or institutions.

Such a privileged status for personal economic growth was not challenged because its recognition was essential to the very sense of self-identity of the city as a body politic. For it was the king's power that ensured the internal cohesiveness of the new public entity, the city-state or state-city. *Coercive force* was clearly a major tool in the hands of the king: the king was, inter alia, the military chief who would use war as a mechanism for expanding his power base and widening his revenue support. He was also the beneficiary of all forms of taxation, to the point that fines for the breach of *private* contracts were payable not only to the offended party, but to the king! Such regulatory functions were as essential to the continued existence of the city as they are profitable to the individual whose leadership was accepted as indispensable, without ever any real challenge to his role and consequent privilege.

But power was not only exercised through coercive force. There were also *integrative mechanisms,* which the palace employed to foster the sense of identity of the group. We may too easily dismiss the value of such mechanisms by considering them as mere rhetorical expressions of self-serving propaganda. They were that, of course. But the care with which they were proposed to their target audience, across boundaries of time and space, indicates that they catered to the expectation of the subjects as well as to the vainglory of the king. I am thinking of ideological models that were presented to the social group and were accepted by it, for instance the king as shepherd, as father, as beloved of the gods. I am especially thinking of the recurrent royal *topos* of economic prosperity, which each king boasts to have brought about in his reign. Whether or not the boast corresponded to reality, the very existence of the cliché implies that the king was in some ways bound by his subjects' expectations.

Coercive force and integrative mechanisms must certainly have been present in preurban times, though it would be difficult to find specific evidence to that effect: we may assume, in other words, that it was in similar ways that preurban leadership would also foster loyalty and solidarity within the group — through adjudication, defense organization, ideological uplifting, and facilitation in the access to resources. But there were certainly major differences. For one thing, the urban leader, as distinct from his preurban counterpart, was known personally to a very small proportion of his subjects. Even more importantly, the benefits of the new urban system accrued in an increasingly more lopsided manner to the personal advantage of the ruler and his family. And the well-being of the social group as a whole was predicated more and more on profoundly regulatory interventions on the part of the king. In other words, power made cohesiveness possible for larger and larger aggregates of human beings, but this cohesiveness was translated in real benefits for an ever smaller percentage of individuals. What this really meant may best be assessed by considering the perceptual impact of industrialization.

Industrialization as the economic correlative of urbanization and state formation. Industrialization, in its most basic sense, may be understood as the segmentation of the procurement, production, and marketing processes in such a way that the individuals involved in each of the segments, or even subsegments, are not in control of the overall process; in fact, they are often not even in full control of their particular segment. This means that single individuals in this economic chain can easily be replaced. As a result, they cannot alter on their own the particular mechanisms to which they are assigned, nor can they effectively command the best profits for their own personal gain.

Understood in this sense, industrialization goes hand in hand with urbanization as a political process. We have seen how urbanization first happened when a social mass, not otherwise bound by such natural bonds as face-to-face recognition, congealed in such a way as to allow a new suprapersonal bond to form. In this sense, then, *urbanization* is the establishment of a public "persona" that in effect bonds and controls persons through impersonal means. *State formation* is the political dimension of the same process, and *industrialization* the economic dimension. All three aspects are closely bound with each other and cannot properly be understood apart from each other.

As an example of this concept of "industrialization," I will refer to a set of data that I published a few years ago in connection with our excavations in the early 80s at the protoliterate site of Qraya, near Terqa, in Eastern Syria. I have subsequently done experimental work on this topic with a colleague who is an expert in the technology of salt, Beatrice Hopkinson. The experimental aspect of this research is still unpublished, and I will describe it here briefly to the extent that it helps one to understand industrialization as I have just described it.

The problem with Qraya is that it is a site with many of the specific characteristics of early urban sites of the classic Uruk Period, but is clearly not a city, nor is it near any other major urban center. The first question then is: why is a site, which looks urban but is not, in fact, a city, located in a region with no traces of urbanization?

The second question relates to a type of vessel that is characteristic of this urban-like assemblage, the bevelled-rim bowls. As in most sites of this period, in Qraya, too, there were hundreds of complete exemplars and thousands of sherds, in relatively limited excavation areas; mass produced, mass used, and mass discarded, they are as indicative as anything of an industrial type of function. So, again, what is the meaning of industrial activities in the middle of nowhere?

The solution proposed to account for both problems is that Qraya was a specialized site established for the exploitation of salt deposits for the food preservation needs of the northern cities in the Khabur area. The experiment we did at Qraya went through the following steps.

(1) Salt was brought from the salt playas of Bouara to Qraya, which is the closest point on the Euphrates. It is important to note that (a) small proto-literate encampments have been found in the steppe between Qraya

and Bouara and that (b) salt purification requires a vast amount of running water, for which of course the Euphrates was a perfect source.

(2) Salt was then placed in large vats for a preliiminary sedimentation process, and it must be noted that such vats are prominent in the Qraya ceramic assemblage.

(3) The resulting brine was then placed in another vessel characteristic of the Qraya (and Uruk) assemblage, namely spouted jars. Different types of impurities would settle either above or below the spout, so that the brine in the middle of the jar would loose all impurities.

(4) The clear brine was then poured in platters, (again, very prominent in the assemblage), which were placed on fireplaces with ceramic grills. Such fireplaces and grills are prominent in the stratigraphic record of Qraya, and, significantly, there is considerable water runoff (without trace of organic components) right next to the grills.

(5) When the brine reached a certain temperature, it would suddenly condense into very pure crystals, which were scooped with pottery ladels into the bevelled-rim bowls, placed on the grills around the platters, where the salt would dry very uniformly on account of the porosity of the ceramics and the conical shape of the bowls. Salt cakes could be extracted by breaking the bevelled-rim bowls, hitting if necessary their base (which accounts for the unusual quantity of longitudinal breaks, and the equally unusual pattern of discard).

At Qraya the resulting product was most likely put to immediate use by salting fish from the Euphrates to be shipped north. But otherwise the salt cakes were shipped in their original containers, a procedure that seemed uneconomical (given the weight of these bowls) until a very plausible reason emerged as I observed what would happen to salt stored (in this case in our expedition house in Mozan) in containers other than the porous bevelled-rim bowls. Even today, some five years after our experiment, the salt stored in bevelled-rim bowls is still usable, while that stored in other ceramic vessels is hopelessly contaminated by the disintegration of the vessel.

Salt procurement as I have described it, is of particular significance because it shows a type of industrialization (in the sense described earlier) that is remarkably advanced and very closely dependent on urbanization as a sociopolitical phenomenon. Goods were not simply received through transshipment across intermediate markets; there was, rather, a single, unified market, which recognized the need for a particular resource, identified a place of procurement without any preexistent indigenous population (and obviously without any preemptive operation), set up with

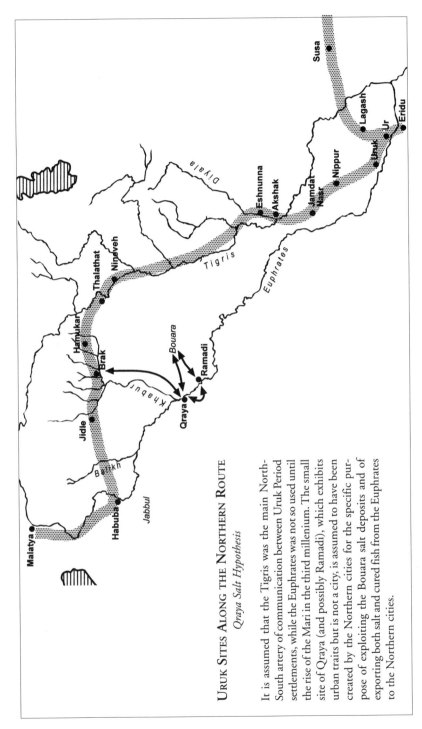

URUK SITES ALONG THE NORTHERN ROUTE
Qraya Salt Hypothesis

It is assumed that the Tigris was the main North-South artery of communication between Uruk Period settlements, while the Euphrates was not so used until the rise of the Mari in the third millenium. The small site of Qraya (and possibly Ramadi), which exhibits urban traits but is not a city, is assumed to have been created by the Northern cities for the specific purpose of exploiting the Bouara salt deposits and of exporting both salt and cured fish from the Euphrates to the Northern cities.

its own know-how and its own labor force (a fairly complex production chain), and delivered the finished goods to its own markets through a specialized shipping system of its own.

This process can best be understood within, first, the specific geographic setting of Northern Syro-Mesopotamia; and, second, the impact of ethnic awareness on the definition of economic domains. To these two topics we will turn now, in sequence.

The rural hinterland: production and marketing landscapes

Sociopolitical and economic significance of the hinterland. While I believe it is valid to say that the early city-state *was* a state-city, we need to qualify this correlation as soon as we look at the simple fact that every city required, from the very beginning, a rural hinterland. If so, the concept of city applies properly to the built-up environment, which is properly distinct from the non-built-up environment of the surrounding landscape. This perception is reflected in the ancient semantic dychotomy between "city" and "country," *uru* vs. *kur* in Sumerian and *Élum* vs. *Étum* in Akkadian. The "state" is the "country," and as such it is larger than the "city."

Yet, if it is legitimate to say that the "country" environment is not built-up, it would be incorrect to consider it undeveloped. The rural hinterland is highly developed in a variety of ways. There is of course the agricultural aspect of cultivation. But more than that, there is a close cultural dependence on the city and institutions on the part of the hinterland's population. This is what I have called a "para-urban" type of relationship, which can be described concretely in terms of such diverse factors as the enforcement of the law, the enactment of cultic rituals, the availability of technology, the supply of specialized resources, the coordination of public works, and the imposition of taxation or of conscription, none of which is available in a nonurban setting. In this sense, then, the hinterland is indeed part of the "city" even if it is discrete from it architecturally and demographically.

The economic impact of the hinterland is of course of fundamental importance. The agricultural base it provides is the most obvious aspect of the close correlation between hinterland and city. But there are other aspects as well. I would like to mention here the one pertaining to demographics. The rural classes were dependent on the city for all the various cultural needs that I have just enumerated (law, cult, technology, supplies, public works); but the fruition of these needs was filtered through the very distance that intervened between the peasants and the decisional centers in the city proper. Such distance might not be great in terms of the physical horizon, but it was extremely real in perceptual terms. So we witness here another example of what I have described above with regard to industrialization: the application of distancing mechanisms. The creation of the city was co-terminous with the creation of the rural, paraurban classes. Preurban settlements could not obviously be classified as rural hinterland, regardless of the outward similarity in their size and internal differentaition. What distinguishes the paraurban hinterland is precisely its dependence on the urban center, a dependence that implies both control and distance. And such ability to impose long-distance controls lies at the heart of urbanization: the longer the chain of command, the less it can be questioned. The overarching coordination of the system as a whole, its articulation in discrete segments that work towards a shared goal, this is the product of the urban mental template, and it results in the same kind of symbolic distancing from a natural sequence that we noticed in industrialization. The economic impact of urbanization on the rural hinterland can thus be defined as a form of industrialization of the farming cycles.

Towards a structural classification of hinterland types. In the urban situation of southern Mesopotamia there is a close perceptual link between the rural or paraurban landscape and the built-up or urban environment. Such a perceptual link is emphatically proclaimed by an element of this built-up environment, which is uniquely characteristic of that urban landscape, the ziggurat. The temple tower rises as a single architectural element above the city skyline, *i.e.*, there is, for the most part, only one such construction in any given city. And this high point of the urban conglomerate is visible for miles around, almost to the edges of the hinterland. In this respect, the temple tower is the unifying element that defines the "country" around the "city," as if a pivot on which hinges the perceptual integrity of the population, both urban and paraurban.

But such a well-defined horizon becomes less applicable as one moves away from the irrigated area of the great "river banks." In the irrigable alluvium, the landscape is essentially conditioned by cultural geography. Elsewhere, instead, the hinterland has a configuration of its own that conditions and limits the possibilities of cultural intervention. While, in the South, territorial expansion came from the progressive appropriation of major existing urban centers by other urban centers, in the Center and the North the territorial size of the hinterland was much more extensive to begin with. Territorially, Mari was the largest state of the entire Syro-Mesopotamian area, because its peasant classes (the Amorites) had already incorporated the vast rangelands of the steppe in the third millennium. But even in the dry-farming area, the territorial expanse of the hinterland was much larger than in the South. The consequence was a greater distance in the exercise of the capillary controls that urban state administration required. In other words, the "paraurban" condition in the South meant that the rural classes were all in close perceptual proximity of their urban point of reference, while in the Center and the North "paraurban" would have meant, for many, simply the knowledge that a city existed, without necessarily a visual, perceptual verification of its physical reality. This would have posed a different set of problems in terms of the integration of hinterland and urban center. I think that ethnicity was a factor in solving these problems. But before we consider the question of Hurrian ethnicity, two points must be raised about the geography of the Khabur region.

Geography vs. politics (Mozan/Urkesh and Brak/Nagar). While much more is known to date about Tell Brak, ancient Nagar, than about Tell Mozan/Urkesh, enough has already emerged to suggest that the differences between the two sites are greater than their similarities. This seems unexpected at first, since they both lie well within the same general geograhical area, *i.e.*, the dry-farming area of the Khabur plains. The only difference in this respect is that Nagar's location in the southern part of the plains places it on the edge of the zone of useful rainfall, meaning that in drier winters the rainfall might be insufficient to produce an adequate harvest; Urkesh, on the other hand, is in a favored zone, where climatic differences may account for degrees of productivity, but never for a lack of it. There are otherwise no natural barriers between Urkesh and Nagar, no mountain ranges, no major rivers.

And yet there are considerable differences in material culture between the two sites, particularly in the architecture, in the glyptic and, it would appear, in ethnic affiliation, if we are right in thinking that Urkesh was Hurrian, and Nagar was not. We will return to this in a moment. But there is also another line of argument that points to the existence of a boundary between Urkesh and Nagar. The latter is mentioned prominently in Ebla, and has provided direct evidence of Akkadian occupation. Urkesh, on the contrary, is never mentioned either in Ebla or (with only one possible exception) in the Akkadian royal inscriptions, even though the archaeological evidence from the excavations shows that it was a major city at least from ED III onward. It appears as though Urkesh belonged essentially to a different world, which did not interact directly with Ebla, and was either not attractive enough for an Akkadian invasion or sufficiently powerful to resist it.

Royal Building AK at Tell Mozan (ancient Urkesh) in front of the tell slope, with the slopes of the Tur-Abdin leading to the Hurrian hinterland of the Anatolian platueau in the background. This could be the political and economic center that controlled the Hurrian highlands.

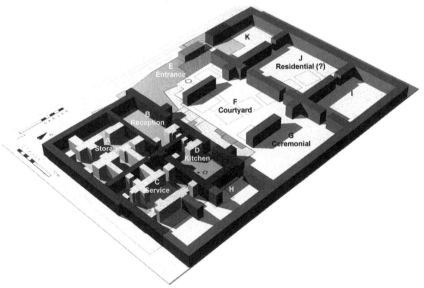

Royal Building AK (Royal Palace of Urkesh?). Seal impressions found in this building identified the city and the provided information on the royal court of Urkesh.

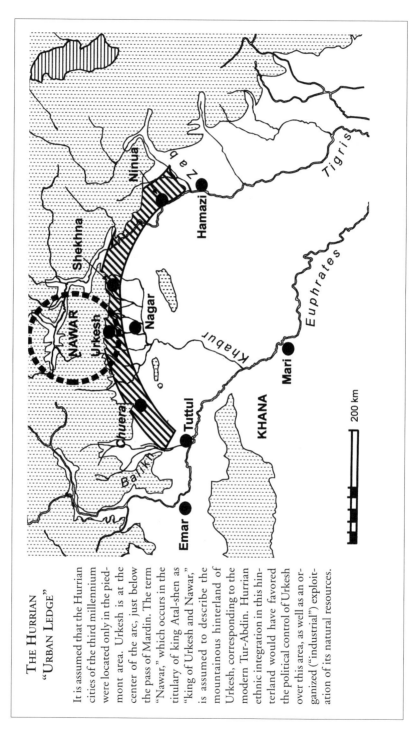

THE HURRIAN
"URBAN LEDGE"

It is assumed that the Hurrian cities of the third millennium were located only in the piedmont area. Urkesh is at the center of the arc, just below the pass of Mardin. The term "Nawar," which occurs in the titulary of king Atal-shen as "king of Urkesh and Nawar," is assumed to describe the mountainous hinterland of Urkesh, corresponding to the modern Tur-Abdin. Hurrian ethnic integration in this hinterland would have favored the political control of Urkesh over this area, as well as an organized ("industrial") exploitation of its natural resources.

The presence of such an unexpected boundary between Urkesh and Nagar may be explained partly through their orientation towards the highlands, which displays at first a deceptive symmetry. Nagar controls the major route to what is today southern Iraq, across the Sinjar, and Urkesh, the major route to the Anatolian plateau, across the Tur-Abdin and particularly the Mardin pass. This symmetry, which seems at first to point towards a parallelism between the two cities, offers instead a clue to their distinction. The Sinjar offers no special natural resources, and thus the proper hinterland of Nagar is the Khabur Plain. The Tur-Abdin, on the other hand, is rich in resources (copper, timber, stones), and it is an essential component of the hinterland of Urkesh.

The highlands' urban ledge (Urkesh, Nawar, and Subartu). It may be, in fact, that the highlands represented the primary and most distinctive hinterland of Urkesh, as with the steppe for Mari. There is, in this perspective, something of an urban ledge along the southern border of the highland, where places like Chuera (of which we know the ancient name, Harbu, only for later periods), Mozan/Urkesh, and Leilan/Shehna were major centers, each with a similar, if different, hinterland in the highlands to their immediate North. In the third millennium, urbanization proper had not yet taken place in the highlands, and it appears that, instead, the highlanders moved to the piedmont area to establish their first cities. When we call these Hurrian cities, we presume that the trend towards urbanization originated in the highlands and resulted in the establishment of urban centers whose distinctiveness depended on their hinterland. But the term Hurrian is attested later and entails a rather broad concept, to which I will return in a moment. First I wish to focus on the term Nawar, which is closely associated with Urkesh. It occurs in the royal titulary of Atal-Ïen, who calls himself "king of Urkesh and Nawar." Nawar is generally assumed to be the same as Nagar, *i.e.*, as referring to the site of Tell Brak. If so, Atal-Ïen would have ruled over the entire Khabur Plains and would have incorporated in his title the names of the two major cities of that territory. For reasons that I cannot explain here, I believe that Nawar is *not* the same as Nagar, hence that it does not refer to the site of Tell Brak, but rather that it refers to the immediate hinterland of Urkesh, in particular the highlands of the Tur Abdin in the region of the modern city of Mardin. This is in line with a pattern that is common in the royal titulary of the central and northern regions of Syro-Mesopotamia, though not in the South. In other words, I consider Urkesh/Nawar to be parallel to Mari/Khana or Aleppo/Yamkhad. This dichotomy between city and region (where the concept of region certainly included ethnic factors as well) was not found in the South because the hinterland regions of cities like Ur or Kish did not differ in any substantial way from each other, so that the names Ur or Kish referred to both the urban center and its hinterland.

The economic significance of the hinterland has to do with the way in which the urban center can harness the resources available and bring their exploitation to levels that would be unimaginable without the organization provided by the urban center. The city arises from the hinterland at the same time that it defines it. The hinterland provides the production and marketing landscape within which the urban economy can most directly unfold. In the South, such landscape was exclusively agricultural. In the Middle Euphrates (with essentially only the urban center of Mari and then, briefly, Terqa), the hinterland consisted of two alternative landscapes, the agricultural corridor along the river banks, and the steppe rangeland used for a new industrial approach to animal husbandry. The landscape of the Hurrian hinterland, the urban ledge of Tur-Abdin, benefitted from excellent conditions for farming and animal husbandry, but added to them the control of major natural resources in the highlands. To properly understand the economic significance that the control of this hinterland provided to cities like Urkesh, we need to investigate what mechanisms made it possible for the urban center to retain control over such diverse and widespread hinterlands. One such mechanism may have been the underlying ethnic affinity that bound urban and rural classes together.

Ethnic awareness and economic regions

Definition of ethnic group. An underlying problem in the use of the concept of ethnicity is the loose way in which the term is understood and applied to historical analysis. As one of Oppenheim's epigrams in *Ancient Mesopotamia* (1964) aptly indicates, the formula "Regnum a gente in gentem transfertur" is often applied as a rather elementary explanatory mechanism of historical development: the Akkadians versus the Sumerians, the Amorite invasions, the split between Babylonians and Assyrians, etc. There has been no serious attempt to define what, if anything, these terms stand for. And one has the uncomfortable impression that any "people" for which a gentilic adjective is applicable qualifies as ethnic. In other words, we assume that there were Sumerians, Amorites, Babylonians or, for that matter, Hurrians simply because we have, in English (!), an adjective that refers to a people. Consequently, we speak normally of Amorite kingdoms, Babylonian art, Assyrian religion as if these were well-defined ethnic phenomena, and while in fact they stand for rather vague regional, chronological, and political configurations.

It is however possible, I believe, to specify explicit and rigorous criteria that allow us to define when the concept of ethnicity is properly applicable and are useful in providing a valid historical categorization of the facts as we know them. The question of a "Hurrian" culture, and in particular of Hurrian art, is a celebrated example, and a renewed discussion is timely in view of our findings at Mozan/Urkesh. Accordingly, I will first propose an explicit definition of the concept, then try to show its applicability to Urkesh and the Hurrians, in order to conclude by showing the link between economic development and the kind of broad group solidarity that ethnic awareness provides.

What is, then, an ethnic group? I use the term for what I consider to be a concrete social reality in the history of ancient Syro-Mesopotamia. As such, it was operative in terms of its internal power of aggregation, and, externally, in terms of how it affected other sociopolitical entities. There is also evidence for group consciousness; in other words, members of the group exhibited awareness of their belonging to it. I suggest that the key elements that help define an ethnic group are as follows. It is (1) sufficiently large to preclude the possibility of face-to-face association, and (2) sufficiently consistent through time to span several generations while retaining its internal aggregation. It has (3) a marked sense of identity, generally expressed through a proper name referring to the group. The members share (4) a number of cultural traits, ranging from material culture to ideology and religion, from customs and lifeways to language. These traits are (5) ascribed (they are acquired at birth, or through a birthlike process of assimilation), but they are (6) nonorganizational, i.e., they do not, in and of themselves, motivate the group into a special kind of coordinate action, and they are mostly (7) symbolic in nature.

When using archaeological and textual sources, as in our case, I identify a group as "ethnic" when such a distributional patterning can be found recurrently over a large area and long period of time. The textual component is of critical importance, since nothing can otherwise really be proven (though it might be implied) about self-awareness, about linguistic cohesiveness, and about self-identity resting on a common name.

In the light of this definition, a number of other concepts may then be more specifically understood and kept distinct from that of ethnicity. Thus, for instance, the tribe can be defined as an organizational subset of an ethnic group, *i.e.*, a full ethnic group or a portion thereof that is also held together through some form of actual or potential organizational mechanism (political, religious, etc.).

Application to Urkesh and the Hurrians. The earliest attestation for Hurrian as a language comes from late-third-millennium Urkesh. Admittedly, the documentation is still limited. We have only, from the late third millennium, (1) the well-known foundation inscription of king Tish-Atal, which is inscribed on a stone tablet and on the bronze plaque that is found below the paws of two distinct lion figures, serving as foundation deposits for a temple built by the king in Urkesh, and (2) the numerous inscriptions of king Tupkish on royal seals found during our excavations. Nothing of the sort has been found in Brak/Nagar, where archaeological exposure has been much more extensive than at Mozan/Urkesh and where the only official inscription records the presence of the Akkadian king Naram-Sin.

To attribute special significance to the Hurrian documentation from Urkesh, however limited in size, is, I believe, justified. A scribal tradition does not arise in a vacuum, particularly when it is used to convey an official message, whether on a foundation document or on several royal seals. This does not mean that we are necessarily bound to find, in Mozan/Urkesh, a Hurrian archive. Playing the devil's advocate, I am fully prepared to accept the possibility that (1) normal administrative procedures were carried out in Sumero-Akkadian, that (2) real archives, administrative, political, or literary, may not be in store for us since the palace shows no trace of destruction, and that (3) remnants of a Hurrian scribal tradition may therefore continue to be limited to occasional finds of political texts such as foundation inscriptions and seals. (A more realistic hope is that we may find impressions of the royal seals used personally by the king and the queen, since the numerous ones we have found so far, important though they may be, were used by their administrators.) But, for all of this, even the limited evidence we already have is very eloquent. Think of it: there is, in neither Ebla nor third-millennium Mari, any equivalent of Urkesh evidence, however limited, *i.e.*, no trace of a political text written entirely in the local language. Also significant is the Hurrian title *endan*, which is the only non-Sumero-Akkadian title known in all of Syro-Mesopotamia for the third millennium.

Particularly significant with regard to the issue of ethnic identity is the nature of this early Hurrian scribal tradition, namely that the documents stemming from it are political texts. This implies two important

Seal of Innin-Shadu (top), an Akkadian name with both local and Southern elements.

Seal of queen Uqnitum's nurse, Zamena (second from top), a Hurrian name, who is in charge of the children and principle wife of the king. The Star and human-headed bull could be symbols for the crown prince.

Seal of queen Uqnitum's female cook (name obliterated, third from top), possibly the head cook, preparing lamb and butter.

Seal of the thronebearer of Tupkish, the king (left). The word for king is the Sumerian logogram *lugal*.

Seal of "Tu[pk]ish [king of Ur]kesh" (the name of the king, Tupkish, is Hurrian). From other impressions we know that he used the Hurrian word for "king," even though this particular seal does not preserve the line with the title.

"Uqnitum, queen." The name of the queen in Akkadian. The queen's title is given with the Sumerian logogram NIN.

Queen's seal, "Uqnitum, the wife of Tupkish." Several other seals of the queen bear the title "wife of Tupkish," or simply "the wife." This stresses the importance of the "dynastic program," whereby the primary royal wife claims that title for herself and succession for her son.

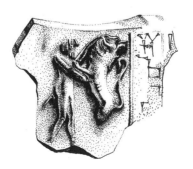

Crown prince's seal, "[. . .] son of the king." The title gives the Hurrian word for "king." Unfortunately, the name of the prince is missing. It would be especially interesting to know if the crown prince had a Hurrian or an Akkadian name.

presuppositions: on the one hand, a royal will to affirm the distictiveness of its ethnic background, through the use of titles and texts that are wholly rooted in Hurrian; and, on the other, the scribal skills required for rendering complete Hurrian texts in the cuneiform script.

In addition, there is the important evidence of onomastics, for which, too, the earliest evidence comes from Urkesh. With the onomastics there is, generally, the double problem that (1) one cannot simply equate the linguistic analysis of the names with the ethnic affiliation of the name bearers, and that (2) the spread of names may be the result of factors quite different from ethnic expansion. In our case, it seems beyond dispute that Hurrian name-giving is solidly attested at least as of the last quarter of the third millennium; that there is a high degree of onomastic dispersion (the diversification of social classes for which the names are attested); and that its point of highest concentration is precisely in our region.

Another significant trait that helps us to define in some preliminary way a special Hurrian identity has to do with religious factors. Most of what we know about Hurrian myth and cult comes from texts preserved in a Hittite environment almost a thousand years after our period. But there begin to emerge interesting correlations between these texts and the finds from our excavations that suggest some direct line of continuity. Here I will illustrate two such possible points. The first pertains to myth. A seal impression from our excavations depicts a divine figure who is astride a mountain range; no such *topos* seems to be known from Akkadian glyptic, and it is tempting to interpret this as a representation of Kumarbi, who is often described in the later myths as walking in the mountains.

The second point about religion has to do with cult. A highly detailed representation on the seal of the cook of the queen of Urkesh shows a man with a knife leading a goat to be slaughtered on a butcher's block on which lies a jar turned on its side; a second scene on the same seal shows a woman who is churning butter. A very suggestive link has been proposed (in a forthcoming article) by a Research Associate of the Mozan/Urkesh project, Dr. Alex Martin, between this scene and a Hurrian ritual preserved in a much later Hittite context: the text mirrors, with uncanny accuracy, the details depicted on our seal. The parallels are too minute and too close to be accidental, so that it seems legitimate to assume that the ritual was distinctive enough to be singled out as particularly characteristic of a Hurrian milieu. (Which is all the more interesting considering the obvious Biblical counter-parallel of the injunction against boiling a kid's meat in its mother's milk! Deut. 14:21; Ex 23:19.)

While I cannot enter into details here, it will be sufficient to mention that there is, to match this linguistic and cultural evidence, a correlative cluster of material culture traits, in particular with regard to architectural and ceramic traditions, such as the nature of construction with stone foundations and lower courses or the so-called metallic ware. This helps us define an archaeological area that essentially overlaps the highland's region and the urban ledge, *i.e.*, what may be referred to, geographically, as the region of Subartu. This homogeneity of material culture goes back, in part, to late prehistoric periods, and it was only interrupted by the strong Uruk type presence from the South at the end of the fourth millennium. This Sumerian presence was significant enough to bring urbanization to the area (possibly in the wake of a natural disaster at the end of the Khalaf period, as I have proposed in a publication of our excavations at Tell Ziyada), but it did not develop into any system of long-lasting political control, so that already in the early part of the third millennium they were readily replaced by a renewed strong indigenous tradition, which may precisely be identified with the new Hurrian urbanization.

Economic impact of ethnicity. We must now ask: what is the relevance of ethnicity for an understanding of economic development and patterns of land use in the early periods of urbanization? The answer is suggested by the considerations I have advanced earlier about the nature of the urban hinterland. If we look at the political dimension of urbanization, it appears that the cohesiveness of a large human group was an essential precondition for the development of industrial types of production and marketing. The early city provided exactly that, not just in the built-up environment of the city as an architectural entity, but in its hinterland as well. The earliest cities, in the South, defined the extent of their hinterland almost in terms of a radius of visibility from the top of their temple tower. Territorial contiguity, understood perceptually in direct reference to the built environment, served as a strong bond of solidarity for the human group. The "servants of the king" are at the same time the "sons of the city."

But in the central and Northern parts of Syro-Mesopotamia environmental factors caused the hinterland to be much vaster than in the South, from the beginning. Even though settled, the Hurrian highlands remained sparsely populated over a relatively vast geographical area. And this was probably a good reason why ethnic awareness came to play an important role, perhaps as important as with the Amorites in the region of Khana. It is interesting to note in this connection the contrast between

Southern terms, like "Babylonians," which derive from cities, and Northern terms, like Amorites or Hurrians, which do not (there is no city called Amurru or Hurri). In other words, Amorite and Hurrian serve as referents of proper ethnic realities, while Akkadian and Babylonian serve as referents of political organisms. Alternatively, Amorites and Hurrians were ethnic groups, while the Babylonians were not. Ethnicity, then, helped ensure the bond of solidarity within vast hinterlands that had not yet been integrated by urban political means. I think it may be argued, in fact, that ethnicity was not properly a factor before urbanization created the notion of a hinterland. Of course, villages or nomadic human groups would have shared common cultural factors, and to that extent there would have been a prehistoric place for ethnic awareness. But, in practical terms, ethnicity would have become an operative factor of political development only when it was seen to serve the integrative purposes of the early states, *i.e.*, when urbanization first began. Accordingly, as we begin to gain a deeper understanding of historical development in the center and the North, we will have to pay greater, and more careful, attention to this important factor.

We may assume that the major *economic* impact would be the fact that ethnic solidarity favors the implementation of a what may be called in effect a *common market*. An integrated economic region would certainly have been a goal of the political leadership, since *it* would be the first to reap economic benefits from such a situation. Not that ethnic cohesiveness would in and of itself guarantee a commonality of interests and an integration of markets. But in the presence of powerful central controls, such cohesiveness would be made to serve a common economic good, which of course coincided with the personal advantage of the ruling class. Avoiding the need of costly transshipments, affected as they were by merchants' markups and intermediate tariffs, an integrated market would place the procurement and disposition of resources from the Hurrian hinterland, especially metal, under the single control of the king of Urkesh.

The myth of Silver

Let me bring my paper to a conclusion by referring briefly to a Hurrian myth about Urkesh. It serves as a poetic retelling of the themes I have been developing. The myth is about Silver, the metal, deified.

First act: The young god, Silver, lives with his mother away from the city, hence presumably in the mountains where silver, the metal, is actually mined. He does not know who his father is, and the boys with whom he plays make fun of him as if an orphan. Resentful, he strikes them and runs home weeping. He is in such a bad mood that, even as he asks his mother about his father, he starts hitting her as well. Interpreted, this means (in my euhemeristic reading of things!) that there is little harmony in the mountains, with strife among the smaller settlements, even when something precious, like silver, is available. There is a generic sense of dependence from a higher level of integration, but it remains unknown (the *topos* of the unknown father).

Second act: The mother reveals to Silver the secret of who is father is: "Oh Silver! The city you inquire about, I will describe to you. Your father is Kumarbi, the Father of the city Urkesh. He resides in Urkesh, where he rightfully resolves the lawsuits of all the lands. Your brother is Teshup: he is king in heaven and is king in the land. Your sister is Sauska, and she is queen in Nineveh. You must not fear any of them. Only one deity you must fear, Kumarbi, who stirs up the enemy land and the wild animals." For which again I propose the following exegesis: recognizing the authority of the city down in the plains brings both peace (through justice) and ethnic awareness (through recognition of one's father).

Third act: Silver takes off for Urkesh to look for his father, but does not find him, because, just when the boy went seeking his father in the city, the father has taken off in turn for the mountains — as if in a reciprocal interaction between city and hinterland! "Silver listened to his mother's words. He set out for Urkesh. He arrived in Urkesh, but he did not find Kumarbi in his house. He, Kumarbi, had gone to roam the lands. He wanders about up in the mountains." Here this portion of our text breaks off, but here is also where, it seems, we encounter Kumarbi on one of our seal impressions, as he roams through the mountainous hinterland of Urkesh.

PART III

LAND TENURE AND REAL ESTATE

Thoughts on Urban Real Estate in Ancient Mesopotamia

Marc Van De Mieroop
Columbia University

The urban character of Mesopotamian civilization is well known: the quantity and size of the cities in the region is unparalleled in antiquity. These cities had many and varied functions. What allows us to designate settlements as cities is the fact that they acted as political, cultural, and economic centers for a geographical area substantially surpassing their own borders. They derived their urban status from their service to a hinterland, the size of which varied enormously. Cities rank at the top of a hierarchy in which each settlement is assigned a position based on the number of lower-ranked communities it serves, with nonurban centers ranking lower. That cities could also act as places of residence is perhaps of secondary importance. Intuitively, we equate cities with dense habitation, but that criterion alone is not an accurate measure that allows us to distinguish cities from nonurban settlements, such as villages, hamlets, and suburbs. The absolute number of inhabitants that defines a city cannot be established and, especially for antiquity, would be totally arbitrary. Do 1,000, 10,000, or 50,000 inhabitants make a city? We cannot say. Hence a functional definition of a city as a central place, providing services for its surroundings, is a more accurate designator, although also here we are faced with an arbitrary choice of a cutoff point of the number and regularity of services involved.

In practice we equate Mesopotamian cities with the *tells* we see today all over the countryside of Iraq and Northern Syria. With few exceptions, all the *tells* that have been excavated have been called cities by their investigators: since we tend to focus on substantial-sized mounds in archaeological research, this is probably accurate. I am not so sure, however, that all of these *tells* served as places of residence, and I must acknowledge straight away that much of my argument is based on an absence of data.

It seems to me that some of the northern Mesopotamian cities in the early second millennium, such as Shubat-Enlil (Tell Leilan) and Qattara (Tell Rimah), did not contain more than a few residences within their city walls, and the walled areas were reserved for official buildings, such as palaces, temples, and administrative buildings. The majority of people seem to have lived outside the walls. I readily admit that this impression is based on the fact that archaeologists even today prefer to excavate monumental architecture, rather than domestic dwellings and that we may be totally misled by what is published so far. And thus I would again like to repeat my plea that archaeologists investigate the domestic areas of Mesopotamian cities more.

In this contribution I would like to discuss some aspects of the urban residences as we know them through texts and archaeological sources. I will concentrate my remarks on the early part of Mesopotamian history, very roughly from 3000 to 1500 BC and on Babylonia, where we find the best textual information, sadly, mostly out of archaeological context. I will discuss who owned houses, who bought and sold these houses or parts thereof and why, what exactly was sold, how a sale was concluded, and what determined the price. My remarks will be primarily a collection of data, with little interpretation. It will become clear that the evidence available to us is too inconclusive to establish patterns, especially regarding the alienation of real estate.

First I have to point out some aspects of our written documentation. We have no registers of house-owners, no title deeds, but we find a class of documents that record the transfer of a house through sale or inheritance. The sale documents record, in their fullest format, that a piece of real estate of a particular type and size, and bordered by the property of others, was sold by one party to another usually for an amount of silver. An oath that this transfer would not be contested in the future was sworn in front of witnesses, and the tablet was dated. Such a contract was kept by the new owner of the house, who was given existing earlier sale documents from the archive of the seller (Charpin 1986a). The transmission of documents regarding real estate property can be become very complex. For instance, when a unit was divided into pieces and only part of it was sold, the seller could not release the document that proved his ownership. Thus a special note had to be drawn up to ascertain that fact (Janssen et al. 1994). Such records may have become more important in late Babylonian times, as the evidence from Sippar-Amnānum is extremely extensive. The obsession with them is attested by the fact that Ur-Utu, or his servants, ran into the house on fire in order to save them (Janssen

1996). What remained of primary importance is that the owner could document the legitimacy of his or her claim to the property. There is some indication that house-sale documents were kept in a public archive, such as a chapel in the AH site at Ur (Van De Mieroop 1992:140) or the palace in Eshnunna (Whiting 1977:69), but I do not think that these were copies of records kept at the buyer's home, or that we have evidence of a public registry office. These records might have been kept in the public office in lieu of the home for safe keeping. In any case, the buyer became the holder of the sale document, not the seller.

Inheritance divisions indicate how a number of brothers divided amongst themselves their father's property, including the house. The size of the areas of the dwelling given to each brother is carefully recorded, and each one probably obtained a copy of the record, or at least a statement of what was his own share. Ownership by either means needed thus only to be demonstrated with a document when a piece of property was acquired from someone else: a transfer needed to have taken place before a document was drawn up, and the apparent reason for the document was to protect the new owner against future lawsuits. Hence, through these texts we are aware of the ownership only of houses that had been transferred from one person to another.

We can study who owned houses through various types of sources. Most informative are the cases where we find private archives within the archaeological context of a scientifically excavated house. We can assume that they represent the records of one or more occupants of that house; especially when sale documents are included, can we assume that these occupants owned their house. Obviously, it is not always certain that this is the case: they may have been given the house as a residence by someone else, or by a temple or palace. Unfortunately, only a small number of houses with archives have been excavated in Southern Mesopotamia from 3000 to 1500 BC and none before the Isin-Larsa/Old Babylonian period.[1] I can only think of three sites where we have this information: Ur, Nippur, and Sippar-Amnānum.

The archives from the residential areas at Ur have recently been extensively analyzed in a number of books (Charpin 1986b, Diakonoff 1990, Van De Mieroop 1992). They provide the most extensive information on the occupants of houses. We can determine that people with different professional activities resided in the various areas of town excavated, all seemingly owning their residences. In the so-called AH site, a substantial number of residents were involved with private financial transactions, and the management of different sectors of the economy in which silver was needed. They collected rents and taxes for the public institutions, financed trade expeditions, organized the provisioning of the palace with certain food products such as bread, and issued loans for numerous purposes. It cannot be proven with certainty that they owned their residences, but this seems likely since several documents of new acquisitions or inheritance divisions including urban real estate were found (see Van De Mieroop 1992: appendix B).

On the eastern city wall at Ur in the so-called CLW site a considerable number of real estate transactions were found. Unfortunately the archaeological context is too poorly known to determine exactly what houses were involved. In the period from 1817 to 1813 BC, a man called Adad-gugal expanded the 60 square meters of roofed area, which he had received as his inheritance share, by at least 126 square meters, acquired from his neighbors. He ended up thus with a residence of at least 186 square meters, which is comparatively large as I will discuss later. The published archaeological information does not allow us to determine where that house was, however. The inhabitants of the CLW site were seemingly entrepreneurs like those of the AH site and they owned their houses.

Those of the last area with domestic architecture excavated at Ur were differently engaged. The inhabitants of the area south of the Ekishnugal temple complex devoted to Ur's main deities, Nanna and Ningal, were mainly working for that temple. They were active as cult personnel and administrators, provided scribal education for their colleagues' sons, and even in their unusual onomasticon showed their close connection to the temple they served. That they owned their houses is clear from the real estate transactions found there. For instance, the house No. 5 Quiet Street, belonged from at least 1894 to one Ekigalla, whose name "temple, great place" suggests that he was a temple dependent. At some time unknown to us, the house was sold to Ku-Ningal, the temple archivist, who in 1814 exchanged it for the neighboring house, No. 7 Quiet Street. It is thus clear that in his person he could buy and sell his residence, and that the temple did not own the houses in this area.

For the city of Nippur we have a fortuitous situation: we can place the sale documents of one house exactly in their archaeological context, with such a degree of accuracy that we can identify single rooms sold at a particular moment in time (Stone 1981; 1987:64-7; slightly different in Charpin 1989:99-104). These texts belong to one of two residential areas excavated, TA and TB, each containing several houses, which have been studied in detail. Unfortunately, the publication of texts of these houses has focused on the sale documents (Charpin 1990:9), and we cannot say much about the inhabitants' professional activities with certainty. Elizabeth Stone did draw a clear distinction between the professional status of the inhabitants of the two house sites, however. Those of the so-called TA site she described as people who made a living by managing privately held real estate and temple prebends, while those of the TB site were landless bureaucrats, in her opinion. Moreover, she concluded that the inhabitants of the TA site owned their houses, which show a great deal of variation in design, size, and quality, while those of the TB site were housed by the institution that employed them. The houses in the latter site are said to be of similar size and plan to each other and well constructed, "following formalized plans prepared by architects employed by the dominant institution and made few concessions to the individual needs of the families which resided in them." (Stone 1987:126). If this conclusion is correct we would have here evidence of people housed by their employing institutions and not owning their residences. Still, a desire to become a real estate owner seems to have existed, as one inhabitant of the TB site, Atta, is identified by Stone as "a first-generation property owner" (1987:97).

The third Old Babylonian site where we know of a private archive within its domestic archaeological context is Sippar-Amnānum (modern Tell ed-Der) in northern Babylonia. There was excavated the house of a lamentation priest of the goddess Annunītum, one Ur-Utu, which contained some 2,000 tablets and fragments. These include private loan contracts, sales and rentals, and administrative texts such as ration lists for military and religious personnel. A substantial number of letters were found, as well as religious texts (prayers, omens) and school texts. The archive covers a period of 250 years, ending in the year 1629, when the building was burned down in a serious conflagration, and the area was abandoned for 200 years (Gasche 1989:42, 105-7; Janssen *et al.* 1994). Because of this disaster the archive is extremely well preserved, despite efforts by the owner or his servants to save important documents (Janssen 1996). Unfortunately, only few of these texts are fully published so far (Van Lerberghe and Voet 1991, with list of other publications on p. xii), but the team of epigraphists has recently issued a number of articles where they reconstruct the history of the house in detail. In contrast to the situation at Nippur, the house was never architecturally divided into inheritance shares, nor was any piece of it sold. Ur-Utu's father, Inanna-mansum, bought the site on which it was located, removed all previous constructions, including the tombs, and built a new residence for himself. He lived there for some twelve years, with two of his sons and his daughter, and when he died the brothers contested the division of the property. Only after seven years was Ur-Utu able to confirm his claim to almost half of the house, to enjoy it for six years longer, when it was destroyed (Janssen *et al.* 1994). The reconstruction of this history is extremely detailed because the records of ownership were so carefully kept. They do make clear that high temple priests, such as Inanna-mansum and Ur-Utu, owned their houses privately.

So far, the private archives found in secure archaeological contexts that allows us to determine the ownership of a residence with relative certainty, remain thus few. In a number of other Old Babylonian sites — Isin, Sippar, and Haradum — archives have been found in house remains, but the tablets and/or archaeological remains have not been published to date.[2] In addition to those ideal situations in which archaeology and texts may be analyzed together, we also have a much larger group of texts in which the ownership of urban real estate is demonstrated in sale documents. When the principal characters in these texts are known from other types of contracts, we can often say something about their professional activities. But such texts are typically illicitly excavated and without archaeological context, greatly limiting our knowledge about these individuals.

To investigate the professions of buyers and sellers of houses in the third-millennium texts from Babylonia, one can consult the tables published by Gelb, Steinkeller, and Whiting (1991:18-20). They include priests, temple and palace officials, and a variety of artisans from masons to potters. In the Ur III texts we find a number of merchants as buyers, some of whom may appear elsewhere as money lenders (*e.g.,* Ur-Šulpa'e in Steinkeller 1989:text 18). Unfortunately, most of these private transactions have not been studied yet in their archival context, so we cannot say much about the main characters in these sales. We seem to be able to conclude, however, that palace and temple dependents could own their residences.

Yet, houses could also be given, and taken away, by the king. In one of the legal texts of the Ur III period, the en-priest of Nanshe, Ur-Gula, asserts that "the king has given the house to me." Afterwards it had belonged to his servant, Huwawa, but was then "taken" by the royal messenger. Perhaps the messenger had confiscated the house, although this is not explicitly stated. After his claim, the house was returned to Ur-Gula (Falkenstein 1956:text 178a). In the lists of properties confiscated by Ur III kings, recently studied by Maekawa (1996), houses do not seem to appear, however, while fields and orchards were seized. The victims were high palace dependents, and the absence of houses from the property taken may actually be interpreted either as an indication that they did not own their houses and that they automatically lost their residences when they fell out of favor, or as an indication that their houses were considered to be sacrosanct property. We do have, however, a unique text that lists properties seized by the palace for nonrepayment of debts (Waetzoldt and Sigrist 1993). These properties included houses, furniture and tools, and slaves; wives and daughters were also distrained. And there is a highly unusual text that may indicate the assignment of residences by the palace to individuals. MVN 15:215 lists ten plots, roofed areas and courtyards, eight followed by a personal name, two by a designation of a workshop. The total surfaces are added together at the end. If this record derives from the palace administration, which seems likely (Waetzoldt 1996:146), it may indicate that some of its dependents were assigned house-space for private or professional reasons. These bits of evidence make likely Zettler's suggestion that a house was one of the "perks" of high office for select officials of the Ur III state (Zettler 1996: 96). Thus, I think that we can conclude that in the Ur III period most people owned their residences, but that the palace could assign residences to some of its dependents.

From the Old Babylonian period we have several archives whose archaeological context is lost but which nevertheless provide good information about the type of people who owned urban real estate. I will discuss just a few of them. From the northern Babylonian city of Dilbat, we have a substantial archive from the family of Iddin-Lagamal stretching over four generations. It does then represent the archive of the most recent generation, and the sale documents within it were kept to demonstrate the legality of the family's current ownership. We see that the family not only acquired a great amount of urban real estate, especially under Iddin-Lagamal and Nahilum, but also fields in the countryside. It seems that much of the family's income derived from its agricultural land. We may have evidence here, then, of a family of rural estate owners, who had a substantial residence within the city (Jones 1967:148-64; Klengel 1976).

Another man who had landholdings in the countryside and is known to have acquired urban real estate is Balmunamhe from Larsa. His primary income seems to have derived from his agricultural estates, including cereal fields and orchards. A village near Larsa was in fact named after him. He also owned flocks of sheep and goats and may have managed palace herds. With his wealth he was able to acquire a substantial amount of real estate in the city: we know of his acquisitions of 2,520 m² for a total amount of 3,090 grams of silver over some fifteen years (Van De Mieroop 1987:15), and there is little doubt that he owned his house.

To recapitulate, houses were owned by a wide variety of people throughout the early history of Babylonia: palace and temple dependents, and seemingly independent businessmen and artisans from various walks of life. As owners they were able to sell their property. Despite the variety of people attested in our texts, we have to keep in mind that we are still looking at a select class of the urban citizenry, those who had written documents in their possession. Especially when we try to reconstruct house ownership on the basis of personal archives, we must realize that only a small number of urban residents had economic activities that were sufficiently complex to merit documentation. Many residents of the areas we know archaeologically did not have tablets in their houses. When property was transferred from one person to another, a contract does seem to have been needed, and there is no reason to think that such a necessity was limited to a select group of citizens. Still, it is possible that some inhabitants of Babylonian cities did not have documentary evidence for the ownership of the house in which they dwelt. Finally, we can wonder about those numerous manual laborers who were employed by temples and palaces, especially in the third millennium. Were the millers of Early Dynastic Lagash, for instance, housed by their employer, or did they have their own houses? It is clear that these workers had nuclear families, spouses and children, and that they returned home after work. They cooked, as their rations were unprepared foods, and had a family life. The ration lists actually seem to indicate that they could either reside in a private residence or in lodgings provided by the palace. For instance, HSS 3:26 lists women who live in the palace, *é-gal-la ì-se*$_{12}$, as opposed to those who live with another individual, PN-*da e-da-se*$_{12}$ (Selz 1993:text 25, *e.g.*, col. 3:5-7; col. 4:13-4).

The reasons for the sale of a house or a part thereof are never stated in the documents at our disposal. We can thus only speculate. In cases where one brother sells his inheritance share to another, we may assume that it was considered better to keep property undivided to prevent its dissipation. Thus in Nippur we see how a house divided among four brothers soon is only owned by two of them (Stone 1981:25). Other people were interested in expanding existing houses, which is clear when the documents state that they acquired a plot neighboring their own. House exchanges also occurred and suggest that people, reasonably, tried to have adjoining properties. The term "house sale" is actually inaccurate: the surfaces sold are often too small to encompass a whole house and must have been rooms or even parts of rooms. Therefore the exact measurements had to be provided in the documents. Diakonoff has stated that whole dwellings were never sold in Old Babylonian times, at least not in the kingdom of Larsa. He sought the reason for this restriction in the fact that family members had been buried underneath the floor, a well-known practice in ancient Mesopotamia (1985:55, n. 2). The problem, however, with this logical constraint on sales is that such burials are to be found almost everywhere in the houses, not only in "domestic chapels" as Woolley suggested (1976:33). So, how could one have sold anything, unless the burials we have found derive from various owners who each used a different room? Nor does the respect for the dead seem to have lasted long. Woolley himself describes how old interments were unceremoniously cast aside when a new occupant of the vault arrived (1976: 34). Moreover, in the case of the house of Ur-Utu at Sippar-Amnānum, it seems that the original acquisition of the house-plot by his father was followed by a clearing of the surface, removing all existing tombs (Janssen *et al.* 1994:116). We do know of some exchanges of what seem to have been entire houses, so people may also have sold their undivided property, including tombs underneath the floor. At Emar in Syria, some contracts do stipulate that the tombs were sold with the houses (Durand 1989), which leads us to wonder what happened to them in Babylonia. If people were indeed able and willing to sell their entire residence, we have to wonder about the social repercussions of this act. Did the sale have consequences such as the loss of citizenship? Or are the attestations of such complete sales misleading, and were the sellers involved resident elsewhere in town? These are questions we unfortunately are not able to answer.

The fact that entire houses are rarely, if ever, sold has led to misconceptions about the sizes of houses in Mesopotamia. We can determine now with certainty that people were able to acquire very substantial residences for themselves by amassing numerous lots in successive transactions, although the individual lots acquired were mostly small. Gelb asserted twenty years ago that the houses in Babylonia were much smaller than archaeologists used to think, because the areas documented in discrete sale contracts were extremely limited in size: an average of 48 m^2 in third-millennium texts, and even less in the Old Babylonian period (1976:197-8). We can demonstrate now that he was mistaken.

A survey of the lots of real estate attested in sale documents, shows that they were indeed extremely small, at least for southern Babylonia. In Fara period texts they vary in size from 42 to 72 m^2, in pre-Sargonic texts from Lagash, from 18 to 63 m², and in Sargonic texts, from 24 to 66 m². In Ur III texts, however, the lots recorded are actually much larger. The smallest is 36 m², but 7 out of 15 occurrences are of areas over 100 m². Attested are 108 m² (twice), 132 m², 176.4 m², 216 m², and 366 m². The largest area attested is 840 m² of an empty lot (all data are taken from Gelb, Steinkeller and Whiting 1991:plates 116-165). The unique Ur III text, YOS 4:300, lists a number of lots that were seemingly bought, varying in size from 36 m² to 108 m² (Waetzoldt 1996:146). For the Old Babylonian period, several groups of texts show that areas sold were again small. In the texts from Ur the smallest lot sold measures 2.45 m² (UET 5:153); the type of property is unknown since the text is broken. Of roofed areas sold we find a variation from 3.36 m² (TSifr 9) to 144 m² (UET 5:151), but the latter house was probably located outside the city and thus an anomaly. For abandoned houses the variation is from 6 m² (TSifr 8) to 93.3 m² (TSifr 7) (Van De Mieroop 1992:200-01). In contemporary Kutalla (Tell Sifr) we find similarly small areas, the smallest being 6 m² (TSifr 61), the largest 120 m² (TSifr 65) (Charpin 1980:165-6). The extreme smallness of some areas sold is mind-boggling: an area of 2.45 m² is only approximately 1.5 by 1.5 meters! In the calculation of that area the measurement is exact to the centimeter: the text records 3 ⁵/₆ gín 15 še. In the calculation by Charpin (1980:167) the še is ¹/₆₀ of a gín. The latter is .6 m², a še is thus 10 cm², hence about 3 x 3 cms. Powell, on the other hand claims that the še in area measure is ¹/₁₈₀ of a gín, *i.e.,* 3.33 cm² (1987-90:478-9). That seems entirely unlikely to me, as a small hole in the mudbrick wall would amount to more than a še. Even if a še is 10 cm², the accuracy of measurement is amazing.

In northern Babylonia the data from two sites show substantial differences. The house lots found in the texts from Dilbat are similar in size to those found in the south: from 9 m² to 78 m² for roofed areas and from 12 m² to 155 m² for unimproved lots (*é-bur-bal*) (Koshurnikov 1996:257-8). In Old Babylonian Sippar the areas recorded in sales can become much larger. They vary from 4.5 m² (Dekiere 1994-5:text 5) to 648 m² (*ibid.*, text 200) for roofed areas, and from 12 m² (*ibid.*, texts 34 and 268) to 540 m² (*ibid.*, text 181) for open areas (*é-ki-gál*). The latter plot is sold together with 198 m² roofed area, which amounts to a large house. A number of substantial house plots were sold: two of 432 m² (texts 159 and 167), and quite a few of more than 100 m² in size. It is interesting that a high percentage of the plots sold are exactly 36 m², 1 sar, or a multiple thereof: I count 59 lots whose sizes are recorded, of those 15 are 1 sar, 4 are 2 sar, 1 is 3 sar; 5 are 4 sar, 1 is 5 sar, 1 is 6 sar, 2 are 12 sar, 1 is 15 sar, and 1 is 18 sar, *i.e.*, 28 in total. A similar situation is visible at Kutalla as demonstrated by the list provided by Charpin (1980:165-6). This indicates that the *sar* was an important standard measure used by builders and that even after houses had undergone alterations, many of the rooms still reflected this basic unit. Houses were thus not built in an haphazard manner, but involved some amount of planning.

But sale documents rarely, or never, indicate the total area of the house involved, and the figures listed above do not tell us what that would have been. For such information we can turn to texts that seem to document the size of entire residences when these are surveyed for division, most often at the time of inheritance. From the Ur III period we have an account from Girsu of the property of Allamu, which was divided among four persons and the "staff of the chair of Allamu." Only two of the individuals mentioned seem to have been sons of his. The residential property involved includes a house of 792 m^2 in Ur, one of 288 m^2 in Ursagpa'e, and one of 360 m^2 in Sugan (Maekawa 1996:151-2). These are substantial places. The houses confiscated for debt are much smaller, but still considerable in size: they vary from 108 m^2 to 180 m^2 (Waetzoldt and Sigrist 1993:277; Waetzoldt 1996:145).

From the Old Babylonian period we have a group of inheritance-division texts that allow us to reconstruct the size of the deceased father's house. There are too many of them to be mentioned individually, so again I will select some texts from a few sites. In the texts from Ur we see a great variety. Some houses are indeed small: one 24 m^2 house is divided between two brothers, the eldest receiving 13.2 m^2, including 10 percent extra for his preferential share (TSifr 5). Another family has a small house of 29.7 m^2 in the city, yet large orchards in the countryside, which may indicate a landowning family with a *pied-à-terre* in town (YOS 5:148). Large residences did exist, however: the largest documented had 207.6 m^2 of roofed area, with a well-house (é-tul) of 18 m^2 (UET 5:117).[3] From Sippar, whose abundant documentation I have not been able to survey in detail, we find a share of one of seven brothers, which amounts to 72 m^2 of roofed area near the Shamash gate, 22.2 m^2 near the Nemelum gate, and 54 m^2 elsewhere. If all seven brothers received the same amount, the father's combined real estate property amounted to 1,037.4 m^2 (VS 8:52-3).

That people could have large houses is also visible from archives of individuals and families where strings of acquisitions of real estate are recorded. Often these took place over many years, and we cannot always be certain that no plots were sold off at the same time. But, it can sometimes be demonstrated that lots were consciously joined together. Charpin (n.d.) has re-analyzed the archives of Eštar-ili and his son Iddin-Amurrum from Larsa and has shown that the father acquired a total of 276.2 m^2 over a 20-year period, and the son 201 m^2 over 11 years.[4] When the sons of Iddin-Amurrum divided his house (TCL XI:174), the roofed area alone amounted to only 276 m^2, while the two previous generations had acquired a total of 344.85 m^2 of roofed area over the years. This seems to indicate that over the years some property had been sold, complicating calculations of this type.

In Ur, we find the archive of Adad-gugal of the CLW site, whose urban real estate holdings can be reconstructed as follows. He started out with his inheritance, which he received in the year 1817:1 2/3 sar (60 m^2) roofed area in the city and 1 sar 15 gín (45 m^2) roofed area in the harbor. It seems that he and his brother had decided to leave the urban house intact in the hands of Adad-gugal, while they split the harbor property in half (UET 5:108). Soon afterwards Adad-gugal expanded his property (Table 1).

In this short period of time, he is thus able to expand his property by more than 126 m^2 for a total of more than 186 m^2. These calculations do not account, naturally, for any information that may have been lost.

Perhaps the most extensive policy of acquisition of urban real estate is attested in the texts from Kutalla. These show the activities of Ṣilli-Eštar and his brother Awil-ili, who bought, over a period of 18 years, areas amounting to about 850 m^2, many of them contiguous. Early on they concentrated on roofed area, but afterwards their acquisitions were exclusively of buildings in disrepair (Charpin 1980:79-118; 1983). Charpin originally thought these men were real estate speculators who bought and sold houses, because he considered the areas involved too great for a private residence. But now he believes that these could have been acquisitions for their personal use (n.d.). Again, we cannot assume that those well-known buyers of real estate never sold any of it, but still the reason for these acquisitions seems to have been personal use rather than speculation in property.

The figures from inheritance divisions and successive real estate acquisitions indicate that the "houses" recorded in the sale documents are not entire dwellings, but only rooms, something Diakonoff stated already in 1973. When Gelb proclaimed, based on figures in sale contracts, that an average house was only "roughly 6 by 6 yards" (1976:198), he was mistaken. Many houses were larger. This conclusion is not only borne out by the texts, but also by the archaeological data.

Table 1
Urban real estate acquisitions by Adad-gugal of Ur

Text UET 5	Date	Roofed Area	Seller	Neighbors
144	VII//1815	[ ]	Uri-hegal	Adad-gugal, Ili-idinnam
152	II/20/1814	1 sar 10 gín	Sin-idinnam	Ipquša, Ali-ūta, Adad-gugal
145	VIII//1814	1 sar	Sin-paṭer	Ilum-gamil, Sin-paṭer
146	V//1813	1 ¹/₃ sar	Sin-paṭer	Sin-iqīšam, Adad-gugal

What convinced Charpin that large residences could have existed in Babylonian cities was the archaeological record from Larsa. Aerial photographs of that site had indicated to the archaeologists that a number of large buildings were situated in the eastern sector (Huot *et al.* 1989). Upon excavation of some of them, it was determined that these were residences of substantial size: 534 m², 483 m², and 117.45 m². Moreover, they were located at a good distance from one another, as in a wealthy neighborhood, instead of the cramped layout of inner cities we find elsewhere in Mesopotamia (Calvet 1994, 1996). Extensive traces of looting in modern times suggests strongly that these were the houses in which the private archives of the Old Babylonian entrepreneurs from Larsa had been gathered, now sadly without archaeological context (Charpin 1996:224). They are thus indeed "the palaces of rich merchants" (Charpin n.d.).

The archaeological record obviously has great potential to show what people's houses looked like. Moreover, it does not limit itself to the houses of people who kept written records. Unfortunately, even today too few residential areas have been excavated, and the data on houses often remain unanalyzed.[5] Before comparisons between archaeological remains and written documents are possible, we have to determine what measure to take. The Babylonians measured only the inside of the rooms! This is clearly demonstrated by Stone's analysis of houses at Nippur (1981) and is very logical. How could one have measured the thickness of the walls, which were shared by neighboring houses, or how could one have pulled a measuring chain within the house through the inside walls? Thus, when archaeologists measure house sizes, they cannot use groundplans derived from the excavations, merely taking the outside walls as guidance, but they must calculate the inside areas of each room. The difference between the two measurements is enormous. If we take, for instance, the famous plan of No. 3 Gay street at Ur (Woolley 1976:plate 22) and measure the house in its entirety *extra muros*, we obtain a measurement of 144 m². However, the combined interior measurements of all rooms only amounts to 96 m², 66 percent of that area. Calculations based on other published plans have yielded comparable results. Even on an ancient house plan, found on a tablet from Tello of the Old Akkadian period, we find the same ratio (Heinrich and Seidl 1967:28). The editors of the tablet have converted the measurements on the plan to the metric scale, and I will use their calculations here. The entire building measures 164.5 m², while the inside space is 89 m², only 54 percent. Thus the available floor space is what was measured by the Mesopotamians in their records, and what we need to calculate when trying to compare texts to archaeology.[6]

Moreover, Stone has argued that a distinction was made between the roofed floorspace (é-dù-a) and the courtyard. In the Old Babylonian texts from Nippur studied by her, only roofed floor space was taken into account. Thus, when four brothers divided House I of the TA site, they only took into account the roofed rooms, not the courtyard (Stone 1981:20-5). The latter, measuring some 4.5 m², is not mentioned in the text at all. Ethnographic evidence from contemporary Iraq, where only roofed areas are calculated in establishing the value of a house, confirm this idea (Stone 1981:33). Thus again, when we try to compare archaeological to textual data, we should regard the courtyard as something separate from the rest of the house. Unfortunately, it is not easy to determine whether a courtyard was located in the house, and if so, where. Margueron argues that we have been too much influenced by the contemporary situation in the Middle East, where houses almost always have a courtyard, in our reconstruction of ancient houses. In his opinion, unroofed areas were not so common in antiquity (1980; 1996). Ground plans of houses in the archaeological record reveal two basic types: those with rooms in linear alignment and those with rooms organized around a central space. In the first type, courtyards seem unlikely; in the second, the central space may or may not have been roofed. This uncertainty prevents us from relating texts to archaeological remains, except in highly fortuitous cases.[7] Because of the textual information adduced above, we can now regard some of the large excavated buildings as private residences rather than as administrative buildings or the like. For instance, the so-called Khan in the AH site at Ur (No. 11 Paternoster Row), already measuring 253.5 m² of roofed floor space, although incompletely excavated (Van De Mieroop 1992:156), could have been a private house.

When using measurements of houses in archaeological reports and studies, we must be careful to find out what exactly is included before we relate them to information found in texts.[8] The variation in house sizes in the archaeological record is great. In Old Babylonian Ur, we see in the EM site houses of 12 m² (1 Gay St.) to 90 m² (2 Quiet St.); in the AH site from 9.7 m² (2 Store St.) to 253.5 m² (11 Paternoster Row). We do not know the function of many of the excavated structures: No. 2 Store Street may have been a shop, while No. 11 Paternoster Row may have been a hostel, as Woolley suggested (1976:139, 150). Without detailed recording and study of the finds in all excavated rooms, we will never be able to determine what the uses of these buildings were. We can calculate the average house sizes in various areas and compare them, as in Ur, where those in the Mausoleum site average 74.4 m², those of the northern half of the AH site 72 m², those of the EM site 54 m², and those of the southern half of the AH site 40 m² (Van De Mieroop 1992:224-5). This may give us some idea about the wealth of the inhabitants of these neighborhoods, if we make the unproven assumption that the size of the house reflects the wealth of its inhabitants. The study of residences in the archaeological record is thus still remarkably lacking hard data, something that could be easily addressed in future excavations. So far we can say that house sizes seem to have varied enormously, from the tiny hovels at Ur to the merchants' palaces at Larsa. More research is desperately needed.

What exactly happened at the time of sale of a house is hard for us to reconstruct, but there are some indications of the protocols involved. Among the people present at the sale of a house were a number of officials, whose duty it was to see that all went according to the rules (Steinkeller 1989:97-103; Gelb, Steinkeller, and Whiting 1991:237-9). Their exact titles changed from period to period, but the officials involved seem always have performed the same role: they made the intention of selling publicly known, and they made certain that the measurements of surface and payment were accurate. In texts from the Fara period are found the "master house surveyor" (um-mi-a lú-é-éš-gar), and the "street herald" (nigir-sila) or "chief herald" (gal-nigir), who often received a payment for their services. In Pre-Sargonic texts from Lagash we find the "town herald" (nigir-uru) performing these functions, while in the Ur III period a "weigher of silver" (kù-lal) is often attested. The latter was a goldsmith or smith, who had to make certain that payment was correct (Steinkeller 1989:92-7).

The peg (Akkadian *sikkatum*) was an important tool in a house sale. Its function can be interpreted in two ways: either it was used to announce the sale or it functioned as a measuring instrument. Early Dynastic house sales sometimes contain the phrase that the herald has "driven the peg into the wall, and poured oil" (Edzard 1968:53, 70). Moreover, some house-sale documents of the Early Dynastic, Old Akkadian, and Ur III periods, as well as documents of field and even slave sales, are cones rather than tablets. They are pierced along their axes, which suggests that they were attached to wooden poles, and it has been convincingly argued that they were driven into the wall of the sold property (most recently Steinkeller 1989:238-41). We do know that the publication of the intent to sell real estate was very important. This is most elaborately related in the Middle Assyrian Laws (Tablet B § 6, Roth 1995:177f.) which demand that in the month prior to a sale, an announcement had to be made three times in the city Assur and three times in the city where the property to be sold was located, before permission to sell could be granted. It was critical that no claim upon the property existed. The fact that the sale was effected would also have been announced by the inscription upon the peg (CAD S:250-1).

On the other hand, the peg could also have been used to attach the measuring rope (Buccellati 1996:135). In either case, this object was a symbol of a sale and can be associated with the pegs in foundation deposits that survive throughout Mesopotamian history (Ellis 1968:46-93). There existed an Old Babylonian title, *rabi sikkatim*, "great one of the peg," whose holder clearly had some function in house sales. In Kutalla Qišti-Erra and his son Ili-ippalsam held this title in succession, and they witnessed 17 of the 32 house-sale documents found there. The title, somewhat mysteriously, was interchangeable with that of mayor (Akkadian *rabiānum*, Charpin 1980:191-3), a much more encompassing office, but perhaps in smaller towns the mayor was also in charge of ensuring that house sales went according to the rules. In Old Babylonian Ur, Nerebtum, and Eshnunna, the same function was in the hands of an official entitled ka.ki in Sumerian, *kakikkum* in Akkadian (CAD K:43-4). He was responsible for the proper execution of the real estate transactions; this is demonstrated by a legal text from Ur, which states after a list of witnesses (including two with the title ka.ki), "these are the witnesses in whose presence the ka.ki appeared, and at the command of the judge(s), Attā, son of Būṣaya gave (case variant: confirmed) the right to hold and possess 18 m² of roofed area to Ea-gamil and his brother Apil-kittim" (UET 5:252, Charpin 1986b:72-4). The numerous house-sale documents from Eshnunna, still unpublished, were all prepared by the ka.ki, whose seal was seemingly rolled all over the tablet before it was written. These texts also contain the phrase: "the ka.ki measured (the house)" (ka.ki in-gíd) or "the ka.ki sealed (the tablet)"[9] (Whiting 1977). In any case the ka.ki was a supervisor of house sales in these cities.

I would also suggest that, in the Early Dynastic period at least, the price of a house was established by pouring grain onto the floors of the rooms. This is suggested by a passage in the so-called Reforms of UruKAgina of Lagash, which state: "When the house of an important man borders on that of a royal subject (šub-lugal), and the important man states, 'I want to buy it.' Whether he lets him buy it, stating, 'Pay me the amount that I want. My house is a container, fill it with barley,' or whether he does not let him buy it, the important man will not strike him." (Sollberger 1956:52, C col. XI lines 1-18). This passage indicates, in my opinion, that at some time in early Mesopotamian history the value of a house was determined by the size of the interiors of the rooms, which were filled up to a certain height by barley poured into them. Again this shows that only the interiors of rooms were of importance to Mesopotamians and that living surface alone was measured. Admittedly, prices are rarely indicated in grain in the texts at our disposal, but there are examples of the practice in the pre-Sargonic and Sargonic periods (*e.g.*, DP 31, BIN 8:38). Moreover, certain texts of these periods list a price in silver but then indicate as well what its equivalent value in grain would have been. For instance, in one case a house of 24 m^2 is sold for 10 shekels silver, stated to be the equivalent of 13^1/$_6$ UL of barley, about 1,878 liters (Hallo 1973:236-8). This seems to indicate a transitional phase between calculating prices in grain and in silver. Once silver became the dominant means of payment, this system was seemingly abandoned. Obviously, the thickness of the layer of the grain determines the price of the house, and how that was computed is the final question I will discuss here.

This paper has dealt extensively with the sale of urban real estate, and an important question I have avoided so far revolves on the issue of prices. How was the price of a piece of property established, and can we today find out what the determining elements in that process were? If we can identify the price-setting mechanisms, we can perhaps find out whether there was something like a real estate market in early Babylonian history. We can establish long lists of house areas and their prices from the sale documents available to us and try to distinguish a pattern. The following example (Table 2), from Old Babylonian Sippar, will show how enormous the variation seems to be (all texts are taken from Dekiere 1994-5).[10]

Table 2
House prices at Sippar

Text	House type	Size (m²)	Price (grams of silver)	Grams of silver per m²
121	é-dù-a	54	440	8.15
129	é-ki-gál	72	44	0.6
158	é-dù-a	44.4	10.6	0.24
164	é-kislah	54	24	0.44
165	é-dù-a	84	664	7.9
181	é-dù-a	198		
	é-ki-gál	540	352	0.47
182	é	10	8	0.8
190	é-ki-bal	18	40	2.2
215	é-kislah	162	144	0.88
308	é-bur-bal	72	32	0.44
321	é-ki-gál	36	36	1
337	é-ki-gál	36	16	0.44
356	é	39	88	2.2
388	é-ki-gál	138	49.3	0.35
408	é-ki-gál	36	16	0.44
412	é-dù-a	36	32	0.88
415	é-dù-a	18	100	5.55
416	ki-gál	90	20	0.22
418	é-ki-gál	42	18.6	0.44
434	é-ki-gál	42	60	1.43
436	é-dù-a	36	40	1.11
437	é-dù-a	36	6.6	0.18
474	é-dù-a	36	84	1.16
494	é-ki-gál	54[11]	54.6	1.01

There are several criteria that we can assume to have determined the price per m² of a piece of real estate, based upon contemporary practices: type of property, its condition, its location, and the general economic conditions in the city where the sale took place.

The type of property and its condition are only indicated in the most summary terms in the sale documents: the exact wording used varied from city to city, at least in the Old Babylonian period where we have the most abundant documentation. Thus the Sippar texts listed in Table 2 distinguish between "roofed area" (é-dù-a), "open area," *i.e.*, an unbuilt lot and perhaps a courtyard (é-ki-gál and é-kislah), and "unimproved land" (é-bur-bal, é-ki-bal). Some of the same terms are found in the Dilbat texts (Koshurnikov 1996). Those are not very informative distinctions, and sometimes the contract does not even bother to use them, providing only the generic term "house" (é). In the southern cities of Larsa, Kutalla, and Ur we often find the indication that the property is "in ruin" (é-[ki-]šub-ba: Charpin 1980:165-6; Van De Mieroop 1987:12; UET 5:157, etc.), or that it is a "storage house" ([é-]gá-nun: Charpin 1980:165; Matouš 1950:21).[12] There are some rare other specifications (Edzard 1972-5:221). All in all it is a very meager set of terms to describe the type of property being sold. Looking at the prices per m², we can state in general terms that the roofed areas seem more expensive than the others, but far from always. In the Sippar record, é-dù-a does fetch some of the highest prices (8.15 and 7.9 grams of silver per m²), but also some of the lowest (0.18 grams of silver per m²). In Kutalla, where many of the recorded lots are abandoned buildings (é-ki-šub-ba), the prices of roofed areas vary from 2 grams to 1.22 grams per m², those of abandoned buildings from 0.88 grams to 0.33 grams per m² (Charpin 1980:165f.). We can thus state that the type of property sold did affect the price, but surely did not determine it entirely.[13]

Location could also be an important factor in establishing the value of a house, but here again we see a lack of specificity in our sources. Although it is sometimes indicated that the property is situated on a square or a street or next to a temple, these indications are quite rare and are meaningless to us. When the names of the neighbors are provided, it is done in order to identify the lot clearly, and it does not provide to us any indication of whether or not this is a good location. A distinction is sometimes made between property in the city itself and in the surrounding villages, and the latter may be cheaper. In the Kutalla texts, for instance, the three abandoned lots that are the cheapest on record, 0.22 grams of silver per m², are located in the village Ashashir (Charpin 1980:82f.). In the Sippar texts, undeveloped lots in villages (Dekiere 1994-5:texts 337, 388, 416) are seemingly cheaper than those in the city Sippar-Amnānum (Dekiere 1994-5:texts 129, 412, 434, 474), but similar in price to those of Sippar-Yahrurum (Dekiere 1994-5:texts 408, 418) or cheaper (Dekiere 1994-5:text 321). Thus general guidelines can hardly be established.

Finally, it is possible that the prices of real estate were influenced by the economic and political conditions prevalent at the time of the sale. To evaluate this possibility, we have to be able to tie in the dates of our contracts with political events as known from other sources, and we need sufficient numbers of texts to establish a pattern in the changes of prices.

Table 3
House prices in Nippur (grams of silver per m²)

Text	Date	Price (grams of silver per m²)	
PBS 8:6	1895-74	2.45	
SAOC 44:16	1895-74	0.97	(includes é-dù-a and kislah)
PBS 8:103	1868-61	5.2	(includes é-dù-a and kislah)
PBS 8:22	1837	2.4	
SAOC 44:37	1833-31	5	(includes é-dù-a and kislah)
TIM 4:11	1830-28	18.3	(includes 2 doors)
ARN 26	1800	1.8	(includes 1 door)
PBS 8:110	1794	4.4	
SAOC 44:17	1784	2.13	(includes door and bolt)
BE 6/2:6	1782	2.27	(includes 2 doors)
BE 6/2:12	1758	5.9	(includes 1 door)
BE 6/2:18	1752	0.83	
PBS 8:142	1748	7	(includes 1 door)
BE 6/2:33	1739	4.6	
BE 6/2:34	1739	4.6	
BE 6/2:35	1739	3.6	
BE 6/2:38	1738	0.5	
TIM 4:22	1738	1.2	
SAOC 44:43	1738	1.6	
OECT 8:1	1738	1	(includes door and bolt)
TIM 4:9	1738	2.18	
Bab. 7:p. 71	1738	1.16	
SAOC 44:46	1733	1.5	
SAOC 44:47	1732	0.7	

ADAPTED FROM STONE 1977:274

Stone (1977) has argued that we can do this successfully at the site of Nippur in the Old Babylonian period. She recognizes general economic upheaval in the period after 1739, when Samsu-iluna of Babylon forcibly reconquered southern Babylonia, which had rebelled against its rule. The consequences of that reconquest were severe. We see a gradual collapse of the urban system spreading from the very south northwards, until it reached Nippur in 1720, possibly due to a diversion of irrigation water for military purposes (Gasche 1989). Samsu-iluna's campaign seems to have caused a severe economic crisis in Nippur, with a general fall in prices due to panic selling by small landowners. Stone claims that urban real estate prices were affected as well and that these plunged in the year

1738. She provides a table of prices to demonstrate this (1977:274), which I have reproduced here (Table 3) with some corrections and additions.[14]

There is indeed a drop in prices visible in 1738, but I would be cautious about stating that it reflects a general trend: there are only 24 prices preserved, 16 before the crisis, 8 after. This is a very small sample. Moreover, 9 of the 16 pre-crisis prices are not just for roofed area, but include a courtyard, or doors and locks. The price of the latter fixtures cannot be established separately and is included in the price of the real estate, which obviously raises the amount of silver per m². So we are confronted with a number of uncertainties that limit our ability to connect price fluctuations to political conditions. Yet, I am not as skeptical about Stone's results as others have been (Bobrova and Koshurnikov 1989) and can imagine that political events seriously influenced economic conditions.

An attempt to establish a similar relationship between prices and political life with the material from Ur failed to show any conclusive indication of such an economic shift, however, as the table (Table 4) of the prices of roofed area over the years will show.[15]

The price changes in this table cannot be related to any major political events, as far as I can see. The prices started out relatively high in the days of the Abisare of Larsa, but then seem to have plunged 30 years later under Nur-Adad. The low prices continued into what seem to be the peaceful reigns of Warad-Sin and Rim-Sin, two kings who devoted a lot of attention to the city of Ur according to their building inscriptions. The penultimate text on the list shows, however, how a political act can have an effect on the price: in YOS 8:139 an area is sold "after the royal command," thus probably after the *mīšarum*-edict of that year (Kraus 1984:35). This was a sale forced upon the seller, and he was seemingly allowed to charge a nominal price only.

But the last text on the list shows, once again, how incomprehensible the reasons for price fluctuations are. In YOS 12:42, dated to the first year of Samsu-iluna, a small area of only 6 m² is sold from one brother to another for 1.820 kilograms of silver! This is an extremely high amount, and surely the buyer must be paying it for reasons that are entirely beyond the information provided in the text. Another example is found in the list of Sippar texts provided above. In texts 436 and 437, two equal-sized lots of roofed area in the village of Dunnum are sold, 48 days apart. They are most likely adjoining, and each belonged to one son of Sin-nāṣir. Both are bought by the same man, Ibbi-Ninšubur, son of Warad-Sin. The first lot fetched a price 60 times that of the second! Why this is so remains totally unclear to us. We cannot ask of our documentation infor-

Table 4
House prices in Ur (grams of silver per m²)

Text	Date	Price (grams of silver per m²)
UET 5:131	1903	22.22
UET 5:134	1896	20.2
UET 5:132	1895	18
UET 5:136	1865	1.3
UET 5:139	1823	4.4
UET 5:141	1821	2.66
UET 5:142	1821	3.3
TSifr 93	1821	6.9
UET 5:143	1818	5.9
UET 5:152	1814	2.8
TSifr 9	1813	6.7
UET 5:147	1812	10.66
UET 5:148	1812	6.1
UET 5:149	1811	4.8
UET 5:150	1807	4
YOS 8:139	1798	0.5
YOS 12:42	1749	303

mation that it was not meant to provide. To the people involved in these transactions, all that counted was that a record of full payment of the price was available, to be kept by the new owner so that he could prove his right to the property. How the price was set was of no importance. We may conjecture that the political and economic climate, the relationship of the contracting parties, the condition of the building, and its location had something to do with pricing, but our documentation will not reveal it to us.

I will state in conclusion that I do not believe that there was any real estate market in the modern sense of the word in ancient Babylonia. Indeed, people owned their houses and could sell parts thereof, or perhaps even entire dwellings. But the sales were usually to relatives, mostly male siblings, or to neighbors who wanted to expand their own property. It seems rare that someone moved into a neighborhood and bought himself a house, as we do today. Thus, special conditions always played a role that affected the price offered, and they were probably more important than the ups and downs of a real estate market. Political and economic conditions could perhaps force people to sell some property to raise funds, but these were special situations. Long-term price fluctuations cannot with certainty be observed or related to political or economic changes. My view is determined primarily by the overall view I hold on the ancient Mesopotamian economy, but it seems to accommodate the evidence available better than if we assume the existence of a fully developed market economy.

DISCUSSION

Levine: There are typologies in the Achaemenid period, and after that in the Hellenistic and Talmudic periods, that go all the way back to pre-Sargonic times — descriptions of real estate parcels, distinctions between courtyards that are covered or fenced in, and so forth. Many Aramaic terms derive from Akkadian antecedents, which in turn are sometimes translations from the Sumerian. Such continuity and stability of descriptive purchase and sale formulae is amazing over a period of at least two thousand years. And it still continues into Islamic documents. We have virtually verbatim translations of the same formulas. This shows what a prodigious achievement was made some 4,000 years ago.

The demotic and Byzantine Greek documents show a remarkable similarity. This implies the transmission and adaptation of an entire legal tradition, in a number of different languages spanning different religions, ethnicities, and geographic regions.

Having said this, it seems to me that there is an awful lot going on that is being assumed under a sale or purchase. My first question is what kind of a sale are we dealing with? Is it a sale or is it a lease? Is it an irreversible and irretrievable sale for full price? What is the reason for the sale? Does the person desperately need cash?

What is the economic incentive for selling off part of a house, thereby diminishing one's own family's living quarters? Is the sale forced as a result of debt? Why would a person sell a parcel to someone in his family for so much more than to an outsider? Is this a method of transferring wealth from one part of the family to another or to the next generation? In this case the sales document won't tell you what the house is worth, because so much is loaded onto this legal vehicle. It is concealing another transaction through the sale of the house, using the transaction for purposes ulterior to surface appearances.

Van De Mieroop: I cannot think of any evidence where we see a tradition of debt owed by one neighbor to another, which finally leads to the property's sale to pay off the debt. The problem is that our texts would never say, "This is someone I knew for a long time, etc."

I do not find any legal restrictions on house sales in our documentation.

Lamberg-Karlovsky: I built a number of mud-brick houses in the Near East in the context of our excavations. Why does one house cost more than the one right next door? You pay depending upon what kind of beams and plaster you build it with, what kind of door, what kind of reeds and how they are matted. The cost of adjacent houses can vary greatly as a result of the cost of construction and their embellishments. Even today you can rent half a room. You pay for whether it is going to be built with reed mats or mud bricks, whether it has a dome and whether or not it has a window. We rented a number of partial buildings. The texts don't give us the variables that probably caused these differences.

Van De Mieroop: The vocabulary in the texts on which I am working is extremely limited.

Stager: In the Levant we have examples of what are called house-cluster compounds. There are multiple houses around a large courtyard. Perhaps multigenerational groups lived in them. Do you have evidence of anything like that?

Van De Mieroop: It is a difficult question. There is an idea that there are certain areas where extended families lived in Old Babylonian Ur, but I think the evidence is slim. We have alleys that could be cut off or enclosed, and these may have been associated with family lines. I cannot find any clear evidence of extended families living along lines of property or common areas.

Hudson: You mentioned the size of buildings. I understand the measurement typically is neither from inside nor outside the wall, but rather from its center, the midpoint of the bricks of both walls. You wouldn't have to drill a hole in the bricks to measure this if the bricks were of a standardized size throughout the region. I understand that in Mesopotamia the bricks were indeed standardized in size.

Van De Mieroop: I have done these calculations. In the few places we find them it is just within the walls, and the thickness is not considered. The layers of plaster and so on are not considered. There is some mention made of separation walls, and there are contracts that talk about responsibility for maintaining the walls.

Tideman: The difficulties that Marc mentioned about all kinds of missing information and different combinations of information in different cases are things economists have to deal with quite a bit. I would look forward to the possibility of turning a graduate loose on the kind of data and see if he could make sense out of the systematic components of this mass of data.

Van De Mieroop: My limited knowledge of statistics tells me that the material may be much too limited. If we had lists for single years, or for five years, with some twenty texts per year, that would suffice as a starting point. Even where there are thousands of texts available, as for Sippar, there are very few texts giving the kind of information you want.

Renger: Why should they measure? If I buy a house, and it is described as neighboring x and y, this is sufficient. If you rent a house, so far as I know, the rent doesn't specify the area rented. It just says the house of x or y is rented for a year or whatever. It doesn't state the size.

Lamberg-Karlovsky: The difference in price might be because of size, but we don't know.

Renger There could be also other reasons. I don't know how much house rents fluctuate.

I have another question. If a person sells an entire house, what does he gain or lose? Does he lose citizenship, the right to stay and live in the city and to have the privileges of a person living in the city? We know from the first millennium that citizens of certain big cities such as Sippur and Nippur were privileged in terms of not having to pay taxes or dues or whatever, or render services to the king or his palace. If you sold your house, you lost your special privilege.

This also connects with the story of Elizabeth Stone, because if there was a crisis, where did these people go? Who would accept them as new citizens? It doesn't seem to make sense. We have one instance of a kind of collective exile, as Finkelstein described. People were leaving Warka in the south in the late Samsuiluna period. A whole group of temple people were removed and can be found in northern Babylonian Kish. This probably is an organized resettlement. I don't think they just decided suddenly to go to Kish, for there was neither social nor spatial mobility in that society.

Lamberg-Karlovsky: On the basis of the archeological evidence, there had to have been mobility. There are shifts over time, new villages are founded, and villages also are abandoned.

Renger: These are organized moves.

Lamberg-Karlovsky: How do you know that?

Renger: Hammurapi tells us. After his conquest of the south, he reorganized the irrigation system, because he had abandoned the western Euphrates branch as a strategy to dry out Larsa. Then he says, "I resettled these people." Rim-Sin in an earlier period said he had new canals dug in the south to settle people and open new grain fields," for which he includes new settlers.

I think a person was not free on his own just to decide that he didn't like to live somewhere any more. He could not decide that the pastures were not green enough there, and so he decided to move north or south. People were part of a social system and somehow were embedded in a palatial system, and were not free to move around.

Van De Mieroop: I have written about the issue of urban privileges. I think that they are found relatively late in Mesopotamian history, in the late second and early first millennium as part of a policy. You have to get citizens in these old urban centers to collaborate with the Assyrian king.

With regard to mobility, there are people who have property both in town and in the villages. How this comes about is an important question.

Harrison: You state that your limited data do not allow generalization, but you made one when you said that there is no real estate market. Yet all the things that you describe are characteristic of a real estate market. Perhaps you may be distracted by the concept of what a market ideally is. It doesn't really have to be limited to cash transactions arrived at impersonally. Manhattan has large slices of properties where people occupy apartments for reasons other than just cash. Real estate location may connote status or access to power networks. Around universities, prices are below normal market levels. If, after the next nuclear war, Martian archaeologists were to descend on Manhattan and only find leases from New York University, they might say that this is not a market in Manhattan because of the restriction of access to those properties, whose price is not decided in a so-called free market. Yet we know that there is a property market in Manhattan.

All I can say about the precision with which space was measured is that it obviously must have been regarded as important and valuable in these urban locations. This is a characteristic of a market. Unless we can agree on what we mean by market, we will fail to reach a consensus on other issues.

Van De Mieroop: If you speak of a market where prices fluctuate according to supply and demand pressures — the modern concept of market economy — I think that certainly is not present in the evidence I find. If a market is just a general term indicating that things are being sold, then perhaps this is indeed a market. New York's real estate market fluctuates because of economic conditions and political circumstances, but most of all because of supply and demand. I do not think that is a relevant consideration in Mesopotamia. I have not found any evidence for anyone saying that they felt cramped in Nippur and therefore wanted to get into the city because that is where everybody lives, and therefore was willing to pay a high price.

As for the exactness of spatial measurement, I think the space is measured exactly because it is not an entire house.

Renger: So if you have a house of 800 square meters, it is only part of something?

Van De Mieroop: This is so rare.

Wunsch: How do you define a property? You can define it by naming the neighbors, but they may change. So you must make sure that you cannot appropriate part of a neighbor's house. I think the measures also served as a means to make sure of how much you have got. And in time, people came to buy land according to a certain area per shekel. Someone will buy a house of a fixed measure, and then they measure and find out if it is bigger or smaller. Some contracts state that the house is bought "as is," and others say that it is to be measured and then the balance will be paid. My question is why they indicate an amount of money per square unit, and not only the measures and the price. That is Neo-Babylonian. The only thing I can imagine is to reflect a certain standard.

Van De Mieroop: Do you see a great variation in these prices?

Wunsch: Not so much, although there is some. But it is remarkable that there are standards at all, at least that we can deduce from what little evidence we have.

Koshurnikov: There may have been a reasonable price, but not a market price. By "market," some people understand different things, and they tend to see markets in terms of modern times.

For particular periods, there was a kind of business in dealing with real estate. The figures show that the Iddin-Lagamal family in Dilbat acquired much more space than they had at the end, and they traded their own house in the time of Hammurapi. I understand that we need to look into local material and understand every transaction, but at the same time we can say that there was some reasonable price for a given situation.

We also have examples from Dilbat where people move from one location to another. There is a sale of a person who bears the name of Marduk and his father's name has the theophorous Esagila. This points to Babylon. He sold his real estate and the witnesses are named, people from Dilbat. They don't mention the location where the real estate is sold. We also have a resale in Dilbat in which the price was lower.

We have to look at the documents, not just tables. We can keep a kind of dynamic picture of the situation, because I cannot believe that ancient people were not reasonable in the sale of their property.

NOTES

1. At Shurrupak, several private archives from the mid-third millennium were seemingly found in private houses, but most of these texts cannot be traced (see Martin 1988:85-103 for a detailed survey). The archive of a man named Gamgam was found in a secure archaeological context, but Martin is inconsistent about its exact origin. On p. 102 she places it in trench II i, while in Table 16 on p. 88 she states its origin as square FE.

2. At Isin several houses containing more than 200 tablets of private economic character were excavated in an area designated as Nordabschnitt II (Hrouda 1977:23, 25; 1981:34-9). These texts are only very summarily catalogued (Hrouda 1977:88; 1981:95-6). In Sippar, two Old Babylonian houses with about 100 tablets were found (Postgate and Watson 1979:154). Neither the texts nor the houses have been published. In the Northern site of Haradum several archives have been found in houses, but the texts are only referred to in a general article (Joannès 1985).

3. The size of the share of the third brother, Nigga-Nanna, is not preserved, but since he is not the eldest brother, I assume that it is the same size as that of Urubku ($72 m^2$). The eldest brother, Ea-bani, actually receives only 63.6 m^2, but is compensated for his loss with a well-house of 18 m^2 and something else now illegible (lines 18-9).

4. I am grateful to Dominique Charpin for having given me a copy of his manuscript and have made a few changes to his calculations. I have also combined both the areas of roofed building and of open space here.

5. Although this seems to be a very popular topic for Master's theses or their equivalent, the resulting analyses are not published to my knowledge. An excellent example of such a work is the Magisterarbeit by Beate Schröder, *Die Gliederung des altbabylonischen Wohnhauses nach den privaten Rechtsurkunden und dem archäologischen Befund,* submitted to the Freie Universität Berlin in 1996. Unfortunately, I obtained access to this work only after it was feasible to integrate its observations in this paper.

6. The house-lot bought by Inanna-mansum, Ur-Utu's father, at Sippar-Amnanum, may be an exception where the entire area of the site was recorded in the original sale document (Janssen *et al.* 1994), as the existing house was to be torn down by the new owner. There are, however, some problems with the correlations between textual and archaeological data that have not yet been convincingly solved, in my opinion.

7. I am convinced that Stone was successful in doing so for a house in Nippur (1981). Charpin has attempted a similar correlation for Nos. 5 and 7 Quiet St. of the EM site at Ur (1986b:52-5), where he must assume the absence of an open courtyard. I have very tentatively suggested a coincidence be-

tween texts and house remains for No. 2 Church Lane in the AH site at Ur (1992:144-5).

8. For instance, in her study of residential architecture of the Late Early Dynastic Diyala region, Henrickson seems to provide calculations of house areas based on exterior measurements. This makes the use of her histograms difficult (1981:fig. 11).

9. Strangely, the single Akkadian version of the expression ka.ki in.gíd is ka.ki iknuk. Either two different activities are recorded, or the Sumerian verb in.gíd somehow means "he sealed."

10. Only those texts where all the information needed is available are included in this chart.

11. Included in this price and in the one of 474 is a small amount identified in Sumerian as si.bi. This was an additional payment, possibly made by the buyer to guarantee that the sale would be completed before the actual sale-price is paid (Wilcke 1971).

12. Correct é-nun(-na) in his discussion to gá-nun(-na).

13. Koshurnikov 1996 seems to suggest that the condition of the property was the crucial factor in determining the price of a house lot, and that deviations from the usual "price range" can always be explained due to special circumstances. Those special circumstances elude us most of the time, however, and can be highly varied in nature.

14. I have provided the standard Assyriological abbreviations for text references. Some new texts were added, all published by Stone in SAOC 44 (1987), which is also where all 3N-T texts listed by her were published. I cannot find all the evidence needed to calculate the price per m² in some of the texts in Stone's table (TIM 4:18, ARN 153, PBS 8:44), and have omitted them from my list.

15. I have selected those texts where only é-dù-a is sold and where both the price and the area are certain.

BIBLIOGRAPHY

Bobrova, Larisa and Koshurnikov, Sergei (1989), "On Some New Works in the Social History of the Old Babylonian Period," *Altorientalische Forschungen* 16:51-60.

Buccellati, Giorgio (1996), "The Role of Socio-Political Factors in the Emergence of "Public" and "Private" Domains in Early Mesopotamia," *Privatization in the Ancient Near East and Classical World* (Michael Hudson and Baruch Levine, eds.), Cambridge, MA:129-47.

Calvet, Y. (1994), "Les grandes residences paléo-babyloniennes de Larsa," *Cinquante-deux reflections sur le proche-orient ancien offertes en hommage à Léon De Meyer* (H. Gasche *et al.*, eds.), Peeters, Louvain: 215-28.

— (1996), "Maisons privées paléo-babyloniennes à Larsa: remarques d'architecture," in Veenhof, ed.:197-209.

Charpin, Dominique (1980), *Archives familiales et propriété privée en Babylonie ancienne. Étude des documents de «Tell Sifr»* (Geneva).

— (1983) "Une famille de marchands babyloniens à l'époque d'Hammurabi," *Journal des Savants* 1983:3-17.

— (1986a), "Transmission des titres de propriété et constitution des archives privées en Babylonie ancienne," in K. Veenhof (ed.), *Cuneiform Archives and Libraries* (Istanbul):121-40.

— (1986b), *Le clergè d'Ur au siècle d'Hammurabi* (Geneva-Paris).

— (1989), "Un quartier de Nippur et le problème des écoles à l'époque paléo-babylonienne," *Revue d'assyriologie* 83:97-112.

— (1990), "Un quartier de Nippur et le problème des écoles à l'époque paléo-babylonienne (suite)," *Revue d'assyriologie* 84:1-16.

— (1996), "Maisons et maisonnées en Babylonie ancienne de Sippar à Ur. Remarques sur les grandes demeures des notables paléo-babyloniens," in Veenhof (ed.):221-8.

— (n.d.), "La politique immobilière des marchands de Larsa à l'époque paléo-babylonienne," in J.-L. Huot (ed.), *Larsa, travaux de 1987 et 1989* (in press) (Paris).

Dekiere, Luc (1994-5), *Old Babylonian Real Estate Documents*, parts 1-4 (Ghent).

Diakonoff, I. M. (1973), "Problems of the Babylonian City in the Second Millennium BC," *Drevni i Vostok. Goroda i Torgovlia* 1:221-5.

— (1985), "Extended Families in Old Babylonian Ur," *Zeitschrift für Assyriologie* 75:47-65.

— (1990), *People of Ur* (Moscow).

Durand, J. M. (1989), "Tombes familiales et culte des Ancêtres à Emâr," *NABU* 1989/112.

Edzard, D. O. (1968), *Sumerische Rechtsurkunden des III. Jahrtausends aus der Zeit vor der III. Dynastie von Ur* (Munich).

— (1972-5), "Haus. A. Philologisch," *Reallexikon der Assyriologie* 4, Berlin-New York:220-4.

Ellis, Richard S. (1968), *Foundation Deposits in Ancient Mesopotamia* (New Haven-London).

Falkenstein, Adam (1956), *Die neusumerischen Gerichtsurkunden* II (Munich).

Gasche, H. (1989), *La Babylonie au 17ᵉ siècle avant notre ère* (Ghent).

Gelb, I. J. (1976), "Quantitative Evaluation of Slavery and Serfdom," in B. Eichler, *et al.*, (eds.), *Kramer Anniversary Volume* (*AOAT* 25) (Neukirchen): 195-208.

Gelb, I. J., Steinkeller, P., and Whiting, R. (1991), *Earliest Land Tenure Systems in the Near East* (Chicago).

Hallo, William W. (1973) "The Date of the Fara Period," *Orientalia* 42:228-38.

Heinrich, E. and Seidl, U. (1967), "Grundrisszeichnungen aus dem Alten Orient," *Mitteilungen der Deutschen Orient-Gesellschaft zu Berlin* 98:24-45.

Henrickson, Elizabeth F. (1981), "Non-religious residential settlement patterning in the late Early Dynastic of the Diyala region," *Mesopotamia* 21: 43-133.

Hrouda, B. (1977), *Isin-Išān Baḥrīyāt I. Die Ergebnisse der Ausgrabungen 1973-1974* (Munich).

— (1981), *Isin-Išān Baḥrīyāt II. Die Ergebnisse der Ausgrabungen 1975-1978* (Munich).

Huot, Jean-Louis *et al.* (1989), "La structure urbaine de Larsa. Une approche provisoire," in J-L. Huot (ed.), *Larsa. Travaux de 1985* (Paris):19-52.

Janssen, C. (1996), "When the house is on fire and the children are gone," in Veenhof, ed. 1996:237-46.

Janssen, C., Gasche, H., Tanret, M. (1994), "Du chantier à la tablette. Ur-Utu et l'histoire de sa maison à Sippar-Amnānum," *Cinquante-deux reflections sur le proche-orient ancien offertes en hommage à Léon De Meyer* (H. Gasche *et al.*, eds.) (Peeters, Louvain):91-124.

Joannès, Francis (1985), "Haradum et le pays de Suhum," *Archéologie* 205:56-9.

Jones, Tom B. (1967), *Paths to the Ancient Past* (New York).

Klengel, Horst (1976), "Untersuchungen zu den sozialen Verhältnissen im altbabylonischen Dilbat," *Altorientalische Forschungen* 4:63-110.

Koshurnikov, S. (1996) "Prices and types of constructed city lots in the Old Babylonian Period," in Veenhof (ed.):257-60.

Kraus, F. R. (1984), *Königliche Verfügungen in altbabylonischer Zeit* (Leiden).

Maekawa, Kazuya (1996), "Confiscation of Private Properties in the Ur III Period: A Study of é-dul-la and níg-GA," *Acta Sumerologica* 18:103-68.

Margueron, Jean (1980) "Remarques sur l'organisation de l'espace architectural en Mésopotamie," in M. T. Barrelet, ed., *L'archéologie de l'Iraq du début de l'époque néolithique à 333 avant notre ère* (Paris):157-69.

— (1996), "La maison orientale," in Veenhof (ed.):17-38.

Martin, Harriet P. (1988), *Fara: A Reconstruction of the Ancient Mesopotamian City of Shuruppak* (Birmingham).

Matouš, Lubor (1950), "Les contrats de vente d'immeubles provenant de Larsa," *Archiv Orientalni* 18/4:11-67.

Postgate, J. N. and Watson, P. J. (1979) "Excavations in Iraq," *Iraq* 41:141-81.

Powell, M.A. (1987-90) "Masse und Gewichte," *Reallexikon der Assyriologie* 7 (Berlin-New York):457-517.

Roth, Martha T. (1995), *Law Collections from Mesopotamia and Asia Minor* (Atlanta).

Selz, Gebhard J. (1993), *Altsumerische Verwaltungstexte aus Lagaš* Teil 2.1 (FAOS 15.2) (Stuttgart).

Sollberger, Edmond (1956), *Corpus des inscriptions "royales" présargoniques de Lagas* (Geneva).

Steinkeller, Piotr (1989), *Sale Documents of the Ur-III-Period* (Stuttgart).

Stone, Elizabeth C. (1977), "Economic Crisis and Social Upheaval in Old Babylonian Nippur," in L. D. Levine and T. C. Young, Jr. (eds.), *Mountains and Lowlands* (Malibu):267-89.

— (1981), "Texts, Architecture and Ethnographic Analogy: Patterns of Residence in Old Babylonian Nippur," *Iraq* 43:19-33.

— (1987), *Nippur Neighborhoods* (Chicago).

Van De Mieroop, Marc (1987), "The Archive of Balamunamḫe," *Archiv für Orientforschung* 34:1-29.

— (1992), *Society and Enterprise in Old Babylonian Ur* (Berlin).

Van Lerberghe, K. and Voet, G. (1991), *Sippar-Amnānum. The Ur-Utu Archive I* (Ghent).

Veenhof, Klaas R., ed. (1996), *Houses and Households in Ancient Mesopotamia* (Istanbul).

Waetzoldt, H. (1996), "Privathäuser: ihre Grösse, Einrichtung und die Zahl der Bewohner," in Veenhof, ed. 1996:145-52.

Waetzoldt, Hartmut and Sigrist, Marcel (1993), "Haftung mit Privatvermögen bei Nicht-Erfüllung von Dienstverplichtungen," in M. Cohen, D. Snell, and D. Weisberg (eds.), *The Tablet and the Scroll: Near Eastern Studies in Honor of William W. Hallo* (Bethesda):271-80.

Whiting, Robert H. (1977), "Sealing Practices on House and Land Sale Documents at Eshnunna in the Isin-Larsa Period," in McGuire Gibson and Robert D. Biggs (eds.), *Seals and Sealings in the Ancient Near East* (Malibu): 67-74.

Wilcke, Claus (1971), "Zu den spät-alt babylonischen Kaufverträgen aus Nordbabylonien," *Die Welt des Orients* 8:254-85.

Woolley, Leonard (1976), *Ur Excavations VII. The Old Babylonian Period*, London.

Zettler, Richard L. (1996), "Written Documents as Excavated Artifacts and the Holistic Interpretation of the Mesopotamian Archaeological Record," in J. S. Cooper and G. M. Schwartz (eds.), *The Study of the Ancient Near East in the 21st Century* (Winona Lake):81-101.

8

Land-Tenure Conditions in Third-Millennium Babylonia: The Problem of Regional Variation

Piotr Steinkeller
Harvard University

(with the collaboration of Glenn R. Magid,
Harvard University)*

The objective of this paper is to address the question of regional differences that can be discerned in the socioeconomic and political makeup of third-millennium-BC Babylonia. My particular focus will be land-tenure conditions. This problem is not entirely new to the members of this group. Some aspects of it were dealt with by Dietz O. Edzard in his contribution to the 1994 meeting, which has since appeared under the title "Private Land Ownership and its Relation to 'God' and the 'State' in Sumer and Akkad."[1] My paper is meant to continue and to amplify this discussion.

I will begin with some preliminaries. First, I would like to offer a brief description of the political and socioeconomic conditions in Babylonia during the third millennium BC. For reasons of time, this sketch will be essentially confined to Pre-Sargonic times. For the developments of the Sargonic and Ur III periods, I refer you to a recent article by Johannes Renger, entitled "Institutional, Communal, and Individual Ownership or Possession of Arable Land in Ancient Mesopotamia from

* This paper has benefited from the scholarly advice and editorial assistance of Glenn R. Magid, who has also contributed the Appendix (pp. 322-324). I gratefully acknowledge this contribution. Thanks are due also to Jerrold S. Cooper, Mario Liverani, and Elizabeth C. Stone for reading the original manuscript and offering numerous suggestions. It goes without saying that they bear no responsibility for the views expressed here.

the End of the Fourth to the End of the First Millennium BC."[2] Without any question, this exceedingly important work is by far the best and most authoritative study of land-tenure conditions in Mesopotamia to date. In my opinion, it should be required reading for anyone seriously interested in the socioeconomic history of antiquity.

A few words about the geographical terminology used in this paper: "Babylonia" means southern Mesopotamia, a section of the alluvium extending from the south of Baghdad as far as the Persian Gulf. "Southern Babylonia" equals "Sumer," while "northern Babylonia" corresponds to "Akkad." The border between the two ran just north of Nippur and was marked roughly by the site of Abu Salabikh.

The conditions obtaining in southern Babylonia

The key feature of the organization of southern Babylonia was the institution of the city-state.[3] In its classic form, the city-state formed a clearly demarcated unit, comprising a major city, the state's capital, and the surrounding countryside, with its towns and villages. The city-states bordered contiguously on one another, and there was little, if any, neutral space between them.

An exceedingly important fact about the southern organization is that it constituted a closed, highly balanced political system, which assumed the existence of permanent, divinely sanctioned borders between individual city-states. City-states may even have been loosely united into a sort of religious confederacy, some analogy for which may be provided by the Delphic league.[4]

In terms of its socioeconomic organization, the southern city-state can best be described as a pyramid of temple-based communities, each such community being administratively and economically tied to a different temple estate or temple household. Temple estates, which comprised virtually all the economic resources available in a given city-state, in particular, its holdings in arable land, were considered the outright property of the local pantheon. As envisaged by the ancient Sumerians, the relationship between the members of the community and the divine owner of the estate was a reciprocal one: the community managed the estate on behalf of the deity, received divine protection in exchange, and partook in the proceeds of the estate, agricultural and otherwise. According to their position within the community, its higher-ranking members received larger or smaller subsistence fields and, for the duration of their obligation to the estate, they were provided with food and clothing allotments. Individuals belonging to the lower strata of the community worked for the estate full-time and were alimented all year round. Each estate had a hierarchically organized managerial body.

Together, the temple communities of a given city-state formed one gigantic super-community, which was nominally subordinated to the divine master of the city-state. At the apex of this super-community stood the ruler of the city-state, who bore the title ensik.[5] The ensik functioned as an earthly representative or vicar of the deity, his role being comparable to that of the steward of an estate belonging to an absentee owner. In theory, the ensik was divinely selected, but in practice, of course, his office was hereditary. It is important to stress that the ensik held virtually absolute power over the resources of all the temple estates, which he, together with his family, managed through the medium of individual temple organizations. In practical terms, therefore, the entire surplus of the city-state remained at the exclusive disposal of the ruling family.

In all probability, this particular form of socioeconomic organization had its roots in "true" or pristine communal groupings, which operated at the village level. It would not be unreasonable to assume that village or rural communities were characteristic of the socioeconomic landscape of southern Babylonia during the earlier phase of its prehistory — the Ubaid through the middle Uruk period. However, such communities seem to have disappeared by the late Uruk period, since, already at that time, temple communities, and even proto-city-states, were clearly in existence.[6]

In this connection it is significant that, already in the Pre-Sargonic period, no trace of communal ownership in land (land held by village communities) can be detected in southern Babylonia. Neither do we find any indication there of the existence of large extended families or clans. There is some evidence of the survival of what may be identified as territorial clans or groupings (Sumerian im-ru-a),[7] which were comparable to Egyptian nomes. However, those groupings appear to have had no independent economic significance.

At this point, it is useful to explain in greater detail what "temple estate" or "temple household" actually means. It must be said at the outset that the appellative "temple" is misleading, since the economic institution in question had little to do with temples and the cult more generally. (I will return to this problem later on; see also the Appendix, by Glenn R. Magid, at the end of this paper).

As I would define it, the "temple estate" was an integrating organizational scheme that brought together economic resources and social groups distributed among different ecological zones. It is clear that already in the

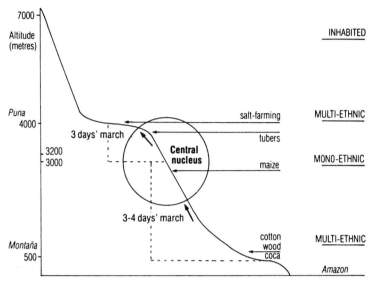

Figure 1. Territory of the Chupaychu: 2,500 to 3,000 domestic units in 1562 (after Godelier 1986:89).

Pre-Sargonic period rural populations of southern city-states were fully incorporated into the state economy. This was true, as well, of individuals residing in and exploiting the most marginal ecological niches. Examples of such persons include the sea-fishermen, the fowlers, the salt collectors, and the harvesters of thickets or copses, which grew along the rivers and canals.[8] The means by which this integration was achieved was the institution of the "temple estate."

To make clearer what I have in mind, let me present, by way of illustration, a description of the so-called "vertical" economy of Andean societies under Inka domination,[9] which, in my opinion, offers an instructive parallel to the southern Babylonian situation.

In the Andean economy, each community was divided into three or more groups, which were distributed among different ecological zones. To take the community of Chupaychu as an example (see Fig. 1),[10] at 3,200 meters was the center or mother village of Chupaychu, where the ceremonial, political, and religious sites of the community were located and where the nucleus of the population lived and grew maize and tubers. In Puna, at 4,000 meters, small groups extracted salt and were engaged in the large-scale breeding of llamas and alpacas. In the Montana, a zone situated several hundred meters above the Amazon, some other families cultivated cotton and were engaged additionally in the collection of timber and coca leaves. In this arrangement, members of each group, though permanently domiciled in the ecological zone they were exploiting, retained all rights to fields belonging to the central village. In this way, each society formed a string of ecological and economic islands scattered around a center.

I would argue that the southern Babylonian city-states showed a similar type of organization, in which segments of a community, permanently domiciled among various ecological zones, at the same time retained full rights to fields and other resources belonging to the mother community.[11] This is precisely the situation one encounters in the city-state of Girsu/Lagash in the Pre-Sargonic period (and later, in Ur III times). There, the "marginal" professional groups like sea-fishermen, salt-collectors, and foresters, though residing deep in the countryside, were regularly granted subsistence fields and other forms of alimentation by the temple estates with which they were institutionally associated.[12] Because of this, the economy of Girsu/Lagash and other southern city-states could be described — to paraphrase Murra's terminology — as "horizontal" or, perhaps more aptly, as "cross-ecological." (See Fig. 2.)

In this connection, yet another characteristic feature of the southern "temple community" needs to be highlighted. Although, as noted earlier, the "temple community" was organized hierarchically, it was not a hierarchy of individuals, but of nuclear or small extended families. In other words, the "temple community" formed a pyramid of individual families or households.[13]

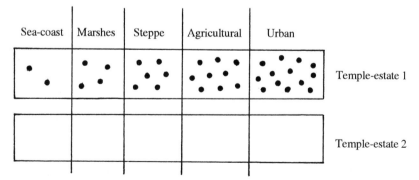

Sea-coast	Marshes	Steppe	Agricultural	Urban	
					Temple-estate 1
					Temple-estate 2

Figure 2. The southern Babylonian temple-estate as a cross-ecological integrating mechanism (dots represent individual families).

This point has important implications for understanding early Babylonian labor. If the temple community was a sum of individual households, it follows that most of the economic activity or productive work in a given city-state was carried out on the family level. Put differently, the economy of the city-state was by-and-large family based.

Let me illustrate this with a concrete example. If one finds, in a tablet from Girsu/Lagash, a list of ten carpenters under a single supervisor, the reality behind this record is not a team of individual workers permanently confined to a specific institutional work-space and totally dependent for their subsistence on their employer, but an aggregate of ten families, working in individual home-based workshops. By-and-large those families of carpenters worked independently from one another, and their work was merely coordinated by the supervisor in question. After fulfilling their prescribed work quota, they worked for themselves and retained whatever profit they realized.[14]

It needs to be stressed, however, that the temple community, as I have described it, constituted only one dimension of southern society; there existed another, more elusive, system of social organization. Cutting across the pyramid of the temple community was an independent social network, which brought individual families together to form a distinctive set of groupings, such as city-wards and village communities (here, of course, I mean "secondary village communities," local self-governing arrangements of adaptive nature that in no way were a continuation or survival of the hypothetical pristine communal system). It appears that those groupings, which have left little reflection in the surviving written record, were based primarily on the principle of shared space or territory, rather than on common descent (see Fig. 3).

As for the southern system of land tenure, I have already noted that the ownership of arable land was an exclusive prerogative of the gods. Accordingly, there was no individual ownership in arable land, and, consequently, holdings could not be alienated. All of these points find ample documentation both in economic and historical sources.[15] Here I should point out that these restrictions applied only to arable land, since orchard land was treated quite differently. The latter type of holding could be individually owned and alienated.[16] As for the reasons for this different treatment, I will discuss this problem in detail later on.

Although nominally owned by the gods, all of the arable land in a given city-state was effectively controlled by the secular organs of that state, that is, the office of the ensik and the managerial organizations of temple estates. A major portion of these holdings was cultivated directly

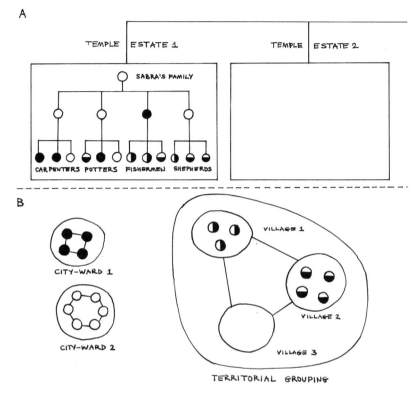

Figure 3. The two modes of social organization: the same seventeen families as part of the temple-estate (A) and as members of self-governing bodies (B).

by the agricultural bureau of a given estate. The remainder was subdivided as subsistence land among the higher strata of the temple community.[17] The size of the subsistence field (šuku) depended on the individual's ranking within the estate's organization. The ensik and members of his family were entitled to truly enormous areas of šuku. For example, the ensik of Girsu/Lagash named Lugalanda held 591 iku of land (1 iku = 0.3528 ha; 591 iku = 208.5 ha),[18] while the holdings of Shagshag, the wife of his successor, amounted to 918 iku (= 323.9 ha).[19] The individuals at the bottom of the ladder, such as craftsmen, shepherds, and fishermen, received as little as 2 iku (0.7 ha) of land per person.

I wish briefly to digress at this point to comment on the inherent difficulty of using the terms "private property" and "individual ownership" in the context of land-tenure systems operating in ancient and, more generally, traditional societies. My comments have no claims to originality, for the facts they describe are taken for granted by social historians. But because these facts are not commonly known to the students of the ancient Near East, it is useful to spell them out.

That an individual, separate from a social group, could be sole and exclusive owner of immovable property is a very recent notion. As stated by Carl Brinkmann:

> The vesting of land tenure in an individual as distinct from a social group, whether of contemporaries or of successive generations is thus a very modern concept incapable of complete fulfillment even in a capitalist economy. But so also is land tenure as an individual right exclusive of other concurrent rights. What must seem a contradiction in terms to the property notion of Roman or of modern civil law — namely, that there may be two or more property rights in the same thing — is evidently the most general rule in the institutions governing the tenure of land.[20]

This means that in traditional societies more than one property right is always attached to a given piece of real estate. Moreover, those rights usually form a hierarchy.[21] Thus, it is possible to visualize a land-tenure system in which the ultimate owner of all arable land is the king, and in which, simultaneously, land is freely sold among individuals. Theoretically, a buyer retained an exclusive right to his purchases vis-à-vis other individuals, but this right was inferior to that of the king, who, under certain conditions, could confiscate the holdings in question, thereby reverting them to the crown. In fact, such a system is documented in the ancient Near East.[22]

For all these reasons, it is impossible to speak of private or individual ownership of land — in the sense in which these terms function in developed Roman or modern law — when referring to the situations existing in ancient times. What we find instead are different forms of possession (German *Bezitzung*, French *droit d'usage*). In this way, apparent instances of the alienation of arable land — for example, those documented in the sources from northern Babylonia during the Sargonic and Old Babylonian periods — involved the transfer of possession rights only. Because of this, one could even argue that, in absolute terms, no material distinction existed between such land and that acquired by single individuals (or better, nuclear families) through the mechanism of the šuku institution, which regulated the distribution of arable land on the principle of alimentation.

The main outlines of the system obtaining in southern Babylonia in Pre-Sargonic times were already drawn, quite accurately in my view, by Anton Deimel.[23] This picture was later refined by Adam Falkenstein.[24] In order to indicate the emblematic role of gods and temples in this system, and partly for lack of a better designation, Deimel introduced the term "temple economy" to describe it. This choice of words proved very unfortunate, for it obscured Deimel's true intent and led to all sorts of misunderstanding.[25] Unfortunately, the word "temple" conjures, especially for those who are not intimately familiar with third-millennium economic records, the notion of a theocratic state, run by hordes of priests. In actuality, nothing could be farther from the truth. There was nothing inherently "religious" or "priestly" about the organization of temple estates. Their managerial organizations, headed by the sangas and sabras, were purely secular bodies. To be sure, there was an undeniably religious aspect to the offices of the sanga and the sabra, but this was equally true of everyone else in the temple community, since everyone partook of the same subservient, yet, at the same time, intimate, relationship with the divine owner of the temple estate. This peculiar meshing of the secular and the religious, in which it is impossible to draw a clear line between one and the other, is in fact the most distinguishing feature of the southern system.

It must be emphasized again that in that system individual temple estates did not operate as independent bodies, free to make their own economic decisions, especially with regard to how their surpluses should be utilized. That power rested in the hands of the ensik, who, via the managerial organizations of individual estates, effectively controlled and disposed, at will, all the resources of the city-state. Although the official ideology of the city-state made it impossible for the ensik to "own" arable land — a privilege reserved for the gods — in practical terms he had virtually unlimited access to landed holdings through the institution of subsistence land. As I noted earlier, the ensik and his family held huge areas of sᵛuku, which, for all practical purposes, functioned as individual property. The only difference between the sᵛuku and what in common parlance is called "individual" or "private" property is that it could not be alienated (although it could be deeded to an heir or even transferred to another person in lieu of monetary compensation).[26]

In real terms, therefore, the ensik of Lagash held as much economic and political power as the more autocratic rulers of contemporary northern Babylonia, or *almost* as much. This qualification is necessary, since ideology *does* matter. There can be no doubt that the official ideology of the city-state, which was imbued with a communal spirit and professed that all members of the state should have their share in it, must have had at least some restraining influence over how much of the common wealth the ensik could appropriate for his and his family's private use.

Finally, I must mention, at least in passing, the question of the developments that occurred at Girsu/Lagash during the reign of UruKAgina.[27] It is well known that, before UruKAgina's reign, the ensik controlled the economy of Girsu/Lagash via the temple estate called é-mí, "the estate or the household of the Woman." However, during the reign of UruKAgina this estate was renamed é-Ba-ú, "the estate of the goddess Bau." This turn of events has been interpreted by some scholars to signify that, before UruKAgina, the estate in question was under the private ownership of the ensik's family. However, with the reign of UruKAgina, it became a bona fide temple estate and was duly assigned to the goddess Bau. This interpretation sought support in the so-called "Reforms of UruKAgina,"[28] whose alleged intent was to correct the abuses perpetrated by the ensik and his family against the temple estates and against the priestly class more generally. Seen in this light, UruKAgina emerges as a partisan of the priestly faction, who encroached on the ensik's secular office and reversed the balance of political and economic power at Lagash in favor of the temples and their organizations. This line of reasoning has even led to speculation that the very system of the "temple economy" was invented by UruKAgina.[29]

Of course, the truth was quite different. A careful reading of the "Reforms" shows that this document is free of any anti-ensik bias. The abusers implicated in it are equally the ensik *and* the chief officers of temple estates. UruKAgina's intent clearly was to present himself as a defender of the traditional values of the temple community, who strove to restore that community to its pristine, ideal form and return it to its rightful divine owners. A likely outsider,[30] UruKAgina apparently sought to legitimize his rule, through a direct appeal to the populace of Lagash, by promising to correct the injustices that had been inflicted on the temple community by the perverted ways of its ruling circles. However, this was nothing more than a clever ploy, since, once safely in power, UruKAgina abused the system even more than his predecessors had. This is demonstrated by the fact that, during his reign, the "estate of the Woman," in spite of its official restoration to the goddess Bau, not only continued to be exploited directly by the ensik and his family, but was also expanded to twice the size that it had been before.

The conditions obtaining in northern Babylonia

As I have argued elsewhere,[31] compared with the political and socioeco-nomic system of southern Babylonia, that of northern Babylonia (during the contemporaneous period) showed various significant differences. In fact, I cannot take credit (or blame) for this observation, since closely similar conclusions had been reached, several decades ago, by Adam Falkenstein[32] and Dietz O. Edzard.[33]

First of all, there is no evidence that northern Babylonia ever sup-ported a system of city-states, even remotely comparable to that of southern Babylonia. All indications are that northern Babylonia formed a single territorial state, which was controlled, during most of the Early Dynastic period, by the city of Kish. Second, and even more importantly, there is no evidence for the existence in the north, throughout the entire third millennium, of temple estates. Here, of course, I mean temple estates like the ones in the south, since there is no question that temples per se, that is, architectural loci of divine cults, were very much in evidence all over northern Babylonia.

On the basis of the Pre-Sargonic records that come from northern Babylonia (which unfortunately are few), and extrapolating from data available for the same region in the Sargonic period, one concludes that northern Babylonia had what can essentially be described as a palace economy, that is, that its economic life was dominated by the royal pal-ace. The primary possessor of arable land was the king, although there also existed land in individual "ownership," as well as land belonging to large extended families. Irrespective of their possessor, those holdings usu-ally took the form of large, extensively cultivated estates, thus resembling the situation in southern Babylonia. However, unlike in the south, in the north one also detects the presence, though limited, of small- and me-dium-sized individual holdings. And, significantly, in the north arable land could be "alienated," which of course was not true of the south.

It is instructive to compare these data with those pertaining to the kingdom of Ebla in northern Syria. There, one observes a socioeconomic system that is in complete variance with that of southern Babylonia, al-though it shows a significant affinity with that of northern Babylonia.[34] At Ebla, political and economic power rested, to the apparent exclusion of all other social groups, in the hands of the royal family and the aristoc-racy. Control of economic resources and of the means of production by the king and the aristocracy, usually related to the royal family, appears to have been nearly total.[35] The palace organization was preeminent in all areas of economic activity. The primary possessors of land were the king and his family, who were free to dispose of it at will. There survive numerous records of land-grants that were made by the king and the members of his family, involving truly enormous acreages. Such donations often included whole villages with their resident populations.[36]

But the strongest contrast with southern Babylonia is perhaps presented by the fact that not even a trace of temple estates, so characteristic in the south, can be detected at Ebla. Here it should be noted that there are also no indications of land remaining in the possession of rural communities.

This picture of the organization of Ebla has been a matter of general agreement for some time now. I refer here to the work of Alfonso Archi[37] and Giovanna Biga,[38] as well as my own discussion of this problem.[39] Recently, however, important new evidence, which further strengthens these conclusions, has become available. This evidence comes primarily from a dossier of five tablets that was discovered in the southern wing of Palace G at Ebla, separate from the main archive.[40] These and several other Ebla documents, five of which are summarized below,[41] offer the best illustration to date of the degree to which the control of Ebla's economic resources was concentrated in the hands of the royal family. According to text no. 1, for example, the royal family "owned," by conservative estimate, 17,601 ha of land. The same text also credits them with very extensive herds of cattle and sheep, numbering 11,401 head of cattle and 118,715 sheep. Their property included, additionally, 1,500 minas of gold, 4,300 minas of silver, and some 15,710,400 liters of barley.

The conditions evident at Ebla in Pre-Sargonic times were not unlike those in the same region during the second millennium BC, at places such as Alalakh, Ugarit, and Emar. In fact, it appears that in both cases one deals with basically the same socioeconomic system, which should perhaps be identified as the northern Syrian model.

Here it should be pointed out that a similar socioeconomic organization is found at Pre-Sargonic Mari.[42] And, as is strongly suggested by recently published tablets from Tell Beydar in the Khabur triangle,[43] which are contemporaneous with the Ebla and Mari sources, a related, if not identical, system obtained at that time in the Khabur region.

As I have suggested earlier,[44] the political and socioeconomic makeup of northern Babylonia during Pre-Sargonic times appears to have been closely analogous to that of contemporary Ebla and Mari. In fact, " . . . in terms of its political and economic institutions, the pre-Sargonic north showed much closer links with northern Syria than with southern

Babylonia. Moreover, it would appear that the traditions of northern Babylonia and those of Syria shared a common origin."[45]

This concludes my historical sketch. The data thus presented permit the following general observations about the economic foundations of Babylonia.

In both southern and northern Babylonia, the characteristic feature of the economy was the preponderance of large estates employing extensive agricultural methods. In the south, such estates remained in the nominal ownership of the gods; in the north, their respective possessors were the king, wealthy "private" individuals (usually connected with the royal family), and, at least in the Pre-Sargonic period, large extended families. In southern Babylonia, there is virtually no evidence for the existence of small- and medium-sized holdings of arable land, individually "owned" and cultivated by nuclear families. Such holdings seem to have existed, on at least some scale, in northern Babylonia, although their economic importance was much lesser than that of large estates. It is also evident that, in northern Babylonia, arable land could, at least under certain conditions, be "alienated," which was normally not the case in the south.

Similarities and contrasts

Two questions therefore arise: first, why was the extensive, large-scale mode of cultivation dominant both in southern and northern Babylonia? Secondly, why do the two systems differ in other respects?

I will begin with the issue of similarities. In my view, the question of why large-scale, extensive forms of land utilization were dominant throughout Babylonia has a fairly straightforward answer. It would seem that a combination of factors was at work, some purely economic and others ecological in nature.

Economic determinants. Among the economic factors or determinants one needs to consider in this connection, the most important is the economics of plow cultivation, as it is practiced in the semi-arid conditions of the Mediterranean and Western Asia. For this issue, I rely primarily on the work of Paul Halstead[46] and Jack Goody.[47]

Let me begin with some basic facts about agricultural methods.

(a) Manual cultivation, with intensive husbandry methods, produces relatively high yields, but it is small-scale and requires high labor inputs and thus produces little if any surplus over and above the subsistence needs of the workforce. Plow-cultivation, by contrast, is large-scale, demands low inputs of human labor, and has the potential to produce large yields.

(b) However, the cost of purchasing and maintaining a team of oxen exceeds the financial capacity of an individual nuclear family. Here, additionally, it must remembered that, in ancient Babylonia, a very special kind of plow was employed, namely, the seeding plow, a huge device whose operation required a team of four oxen or donkeys, in addition to a specialized team of plowmen.

(c) According to modern data, ownership of a pair of oxen is economically feasible only where a family's holdings exceed 3-4 ha. Halstead believes that 5 ha is the lowest acreage possible.[48] In third-millennium BC Babylonia, this would correspond roughly to 18 iku or 1 bùr of land. (Note: 1 iku = 0.3528 ha; 1 bùr = 6.35 ha.)

However, even assuming that a nuclear family owned enough land to justify the use of a plow and had the resources necessary to maintain oxen, it would hardly have been able to take full advantage of the plow's potential. This is because the maximum harvesting capacities of a family labor force barely matches the normal cultivation potential of a pair of oxen.[49] Thus, efficient plow agriculture requires that extra labor be procured at the harvest time.

Thus it is evident that, within in the ecological parameters of the Mediterranean and Western Asia, there is a direct relationship between plow cultivation and the capacity to produce agricultural surpluses. Put simply, without recourse to plow cultivation, no surplus is realistically attainable.[50] But the use of a plow is not economically unrestricted, for it is feasible only above the nuclear family level: the resources of a single family are insufficient to cover the costs either of oxen or of additional labor that is required for the harvest.

Constraints imposed by the ecology of the alluvium. There are various ecological constraints that must be considered. It is quite evident that the ecosystem of the Mesopotamian alluvium favors, even dictates, large-scale extensive cultivation. First, economically viable cereal production in the alluvium is not possible unless the principle of fallow is religiously applied (most commonly, one half of the total acreage available is left uncultivated yearly). And, of course, the most effective use of fallow is on large tracts of land.

Moreover, as is generally known, in the Mesopotamian alluvium cereal cultivation is impossible without artificial irrigation. Only minimal artificial irrigation can be done on the individual-family level. Under such conditions, irrigation works are indispensable for securing an agricultural surplus, but even a small-scale irrigation system exceeds the labor capacity of a single family. To create such a system, and even more importantly, to maintain it, suprafamily organizational arrangements — be they voluntary or coercive — are required.

Then, as well, there are the peculiarities of the Euphrates and the Tigris regimes, chiefly the fact that the beds of both rivers (especially that of the Euphrates) are subject to frequent shifts and dislocations. As a result, the morphology (or, in other words, topography) of the canal system is exceedingly unstable and experiences significant changes from one flood season to another. Under these conditions, the idea of a small or midsize field as a permanent physical entity (meaning, field x, which extends from point a to point b and remains in the same location year after year) does not realistically exist. This is especially true of the southern portion of the alluvium. In the northern alluvium the situation is somewhat different, as I will show later in this paper.

The three factors just described, namely, the fallow requirement, the need for extensive irrigation works, and the shifting nature of the alluvium's hydrological system preclude (or, at the very least, significantly hinder) the existence of small- and medium-sized landed holdings in the form of permanently fixed fields. This, in turn, makes impossible the existence of small, individually owned farms.[51]

That said, I will now describe how the system worked in reality. Typically in southern Babylonia during the third millennium BC, an individual family held a tract of arable land as their subsistence field, which most commonly measured 6 iku or 2.1 ha of land. Although this plot was administratively part of a specific, topographically bound agricultural district (*Flur*), it lacked, beyond that point, any fixed physical coordinates. What that meant, in practical terms, is that each year the family in question would be assigned a topographically different six iku of land.[52]

It must be stressed, however, that these observations only apply to arable land. As I noted earlier, orchard land and similarly, house lots were subject to a completely different set of rules. Throughout the third and second millennium BC, both in southern and northern Babylonia, orchard land and house lots could be privately owned and freely alienated.

There is a simple explanation for this difference, I believe. The reason, I would suggest, is that orchard land and, even more so, house lots are permanently fixed in space. Furthermore, the cultivation of orchards (specifically, date-palm groves with vegetables and spice plants grown in furrows) has different requirements than that of arable land. This form of cultivation calls for intensive husbandry methods; it is small-scale and thus can be done on the nuclear family level; it does not require extensive irrigation works; it is carried on throughout the year — in short, the opposite of what cereal cultivation involves. It seems that under the ecological conditions of the Mesopotamian alluvium, date-palm and vegetable production is optimally carried out on the individual family level; in fact, this is how orchards were exploited in southern Babylonia during the third millennium BC. This was even true of the orchards belonging to temple estates.

These conclusions should and must be qualified: there is no question that, due to the volatility of the alluvium's hydrological system, orchards, too, were prone to physical dislocations, although certainly not to the same degree as was arable land. And this is probably the main reason why, when they are sold, orchards are often described not in terms of their acreage but of the numbers of date-palms growing in them.[53]

For the reasons above, it follows that the alluvium is naturally predisposed toward land-tenure systems that concentrate arable land in large, extensively cultivated and centrally managed estates. As our data show, in ancient times the power in charge of such estates could be any authority influential enough to exercise the necessary level of control, be it the temple, the palace, a rich private individual, or even a large extended familial grouping. Clearly, without such high concentrations of landed, animal, and human resources, ancient Babylonians would not have been able to produce agricultural surpluses and, therefore, to create an urban civilization.

Why was there regional variation? I now pass to the question of differences between the southern and northern systems of land tenure, which is the main focus of this investigation. This variation primarily affects the manner of ownership. Although both systems emphasized large, extensively cultivated estates, in the south such estates remained under the nominal ownership of temples, whereas, in the north, their respective owners were the royal family, as well as rich private individuals and large extended families. Another obvious contrast is the presence in the north of small- and medium-sized individual farms. Such holdings were virtually nonexistent in the south.

I submit that this variation is explained primarily by the ecology of the Mesopotamian plain. Additionally, factors of history, culture, and perhaps even religion seem to have played a role. Let us examine these factors in some detail.

The ecology. It is generally recognized that northern Babylonia constitutes a distinctive ecosystem. Compared with the southern portion of the alluvium, the northern one shows considerably more channelization; there, the Euphrates "flows through a relatively narrow plain where changes that would be normal for a slowly flowing river with almost no gradient had little latitude to develop."[54] In the south, by contrast, the river branches into parallel arms, and flows over a broad plain. Owing to substantial silting, the bed of the Euphrates is raised above the level of the plain, which makes possible the arrangement on the slopes of its levees of blocks of elongated fields. Such an arrangement is more difficult in the north, where the Euphrates flows on or just below the level of the plain.[55] Thus, from the standpoint of geomorphology, the northern alluvium represents what may be described as a "valley zone," by contrast with the "delta zone" of the southern alluvium.[56] This geomorphological variation generated two very different modes of irrigation: "furrow irrigation" in the "delta," and "basin irrigation" in the "valley," a further consequence of which was the different shape of fields in each of the two zones.[57]

Importantly, the northern alluvium also contains more areas which, while unfit for cultivation, are perfectly suitable for pastoralism.

With this, yet another point of great consequence is closely connected. As the findings of surface surveys have demonstrated, the northern alluvium had a significantly different settlement pattern. The sites there are fewer, more linear in distribution, and less dense, "suggesting" — in the words of Juris Zarins — "a distinctly different utilization of the plain."[58] To quote Zarins again, "the distinctive ecology of Akkad favored — as it does now — a dimorphic approach to society. In that way the pastoral populations and settled farmers and urban dwellers together formed a unique settlement pattern in the northern alluvium."[59]

Rather than rely mainly on farming, as was the case in the southern portion of the alluvium, in historical times northern Babylonia consistently showed a balanced mixture of farming and pastoralism. As far back as prehistoric times, this region always had a strong pastoral element, which interacted with the settled population. For example, from the Ur III period we have evidence of extensive pastoralism in northern Babylonia, on a scale that was unknown in the south.[60] On the other hand, cereal agriculture was much less developed there than in the south.

Owing to the higher degree of channelization, the geomorphology of the northern alluvium is more stable and thus experiences less seasonal variation. As a result, its topography appears to be more constant than that of the southern portion of the alluvium. This, in turn, permits the existence of a fairly permanent map of individual fields.

In fact, it has been noted by at least one scholar that the physical makeup of fields in northern Babylonia was in several respects "distinctive and different" from those in the south.[61] In the south, narrow elongated strips prevailed — this shape being functionally related to the needs of "furrow irrigation" and of plowing with the huge seeding plow. In the north, by contrast, one finds much smaller fields. Moreover, in most cases, northern Babylonian fields show an "irregular shape, broadly trapezoidal, with opposite sides frequently of different lengths, and especially with a pretty variable relationship between length and breadth, *which means that indications of the cardinal points are genuine* [italics added] rather than stereotypically assigned to long and short sides."[62] Liverani's conclusion about the cardinal points being genuine is particularly germane to our discussion, since this fact can only signify that the fields in question represented permanent topographical features.

Equally pertinent to us is that, in trying to account for the different field shapes in the southern and northern portions of the alluvium, Liverani excludes any ethnic explanation of this variation (as reflecting a contrast between Sumerian and Akkadian customs).[63] He suggests, instead, a combination of ecological and social causes:

> It seems evident that the elongated strips received 'furrow irrigation,' while the square fields received 'basin irrigation'; that the former system prevailed in the delta and the latter in the valley; that the southern landscape required major public coordination, while the northern could be more easily managed by small communities or individual families.[64]
>
> . . . the arrangement of a 'southern' landscape, with its blocks of elongated strips, perpendicular to the irrigation canals, requires a notable degree of coordination, and is best suitable for the planned colonization of an entire area by a large agency (temple or palace). The northern landscape, on the contrary, can be arranged also by means of repeated individual decisions. So the prevalence of elongated strips in the south goes along with the prevalence of temple properties in the same area, versus the prevalence of family properties in the north.[65]
>
> [The smaller size of fields in northern Babylonia is] "the result of family-based ownership and organization of the land as opposed to the planned administration of a temple organization.[66]

To conclude this part of my discussion, it may lastly be considered that small- and medium-sized farms were more economically viable in the north, since the northern population subsisted on a mixture of agriculture and pastoralism, rather than almost exclusively on agriculture, as was the case in the southern alluvium.

History, culture, and religion

Factors of history, culture, and religion, which seem to have played at least some role in shaping the south-north dichotomy, were discussed at considerable length by Renger in the article cited earlier,[67] and my comments are meant only to augment his discussion. To be sure, the issue of ethnicity in third-millennium-BC Babylonia is a dangerous territory to tread, especially in light of the awful record of the treatment of this problem in the (none too distant) Assyriological past. Nevertheless, I believe it is equally irresponsible — not to say naive — to avoid dealing with this issue altogether. Since it is indisputable that the origins of southern (Sumerian) and northern (Akkadian) societies were separate, logic dictates the a priori assumption that, at least in the initial stages of coexistence, the two societies were significantly different. There was certainly no conflict between them, at least none along ethnic or racial lines. If there was a conflict, it was a creative one, by which two radically different societies and cultures cross-fertilized one another and eventually produced a completely new paradigm.

The data on hand — though far from complete — are sufficient to show that the early southern and northern Babylonian societies followed markedly different and, to a large extent, separate lines of historical development. In the south, one finds essentially a sedentary population of agriculturalists with a strong communal identity, which very likely was formed as early as the beginnings of the fourth millennium BC (*i.e.*, in the Ubaid period). It may be speculated that the social matrix of that early population was the village or rural community. Through the process of clustering, rural settlements merged together, forming progressively larger and larger territorial units: first, groups of villages joined together by a single irrigation system; next, territorial clans or nomes; and finally, city-states. This process was accompanied by concurrent developments in ideology, which, on the one hand, made the temple the focal point of the entire society, and on the other, clustered local pantheons together to form progressively more and more extensive groupings of divine families, in reflection of transformations taking place at the political level.[68] An obvious corollary of this development was the notion of a city-state as an aggregate of agro-industrial complexes owned by an extended divine family.

Northern Babylonia, by contrast, seems to have always supported a dimorphic society: a mixture of sedentary agriculturalists and semi-nomadic pastoralists. It is quite certain that the roots of northern society belonged to a seminomadic reality, which was characterized by the presence of a tribal organization, as well as by a sheikh-like leader as the dominant political figure. As Renger describes the development of north-ern institutions:

> ... even after having settled more or less permanently in the alluvial plain and having turned into an agricultural society, the Semites seem to have retained these patterns of organization. Thus, the sheikh became king. His position as a landholder most likely derived from his position as head of a clan whose collective landholdings he controlled. Further land consolidation, in the course of which the village community system gradually lost its strength, bolstered the king's position as the dominant landholder in the north.[69]

It goes without saying that the different cultural and — especially — religious traditions of the early Sumerian and Semitic populations also must have contributed to this dichotomy. An important characteristic of the Sumerian religious system was that its gods were territorially bound. In that system, each major deity needed his or her own domain; in fact, to be a god in Sumer meant to control a specific patch of earth. The Semitic gods, by contrast, were not bound to any single place, which is typical of a nomadic population with a migratory way of life. To quote Renger again:

> Thus, the local manifestation of the deities worshipped by a Semitic population is less important, resulting in less imposing structures like temples and their economic institutions.[70]

Conclusion

I would like to point out that much of the regional variation I described in this presentation survived well into the second millennium BC, and perhaps even much later. To be sure, the southern and northern systems of economic and political organization largely merged together and be-came — for all practical purposes — a single entity. This happened through a process of conversion that was already well under way during the third millennium BC. This conversion affected other aspects of life as well, so that one can speak, by the middle of the second millennium, of such phenomena as Sumero-Babylonian culture and religion and even the Sumero-Akkadian language. Still, some of the differences endured. The dominance of temple estates in the south, by contrast with their com-parative insignificance in the north, continued during Old Babylonian times and survived, at places such as Uruk, until the end of the Neo-Babylonian period. Even more significantly, as late as the Old Babylonian period, individual ownership of arable land was rare and of little economic importance in southern Babylonia.

Discussion

Lamberg-Karlovsky: I don't understand why private property in the north has to emerge from a seminomadic or nomadic community when we have quite large settled communities there from at least 7000 BC on. I think you make a greater degree of complexity for southern versus northern agriculture than might be warranted.

Steinkeller: To respond to your remarks, I wish to clarify a couple of points. As defined in my paper, "north" is specifically *northern Babylonia*, while the evidence you are referring to comes from *northern Mesopotamia*, which introduces an additional level of complexity — the reliance of that region on rain-fed farming. Also, in no way am I suggesting that, in northern Babylonia, individual property in land developed in an exclusively seminomadic environment. All I am saying is that pastoralism played a much greater role in the north than in the south and that some of the northern (Akkadian) institutions may have had their roots in a semi-nomadic (tribal) social reality — as contrasted with the southern society, whose origins were agrarian and communal.

Further, I am not denying that small-scale individual farming is possible throughout the Mesopotamian alluvium. Surely, it is possible — as demonstrated by the modern ethnographic data for Iraq, but it results in a subsistence economy only. In order to produce agricultural surpluses that could finance cities, temples, ziggurats — in other words, to create an urban civilization — the ancient Mesopotamians had — because of the peculiarities of their natural environment — to employ extensive agricultural methods, which called for large concentrations of land and other resources. Again, let me stress that individual farming, supported by small irrigation systems, is not impossible in the alluvium. It can exist — as it did in some parts of Iraq until recently. But such farming is confined to the bare subsistence level, being thus incapable of advancing the society to the level of urban civilization.

Renger: It is now a well-known fact that there were different land-tenure systems in northern Babylonia and in the south, starting in the third millennium when we have documentation from both. Before the third millennium we don't really have much evidence except for a few *kudurru* stones. But really dense evidence appears only around the beginning of the second millennium.

In northern Babylonia we have sales documents that tell of small plots of land being alienated and small plots of land rented by individuals. In the south there are more than 300 documents referring to the alienation of real estate that deal with improved and unimproved houses or house lots, orchards, that is, urban real estate, and — in a very few cases, which you can count on the fingers of your two hands — fields. But when we look closely at them, we find something rather curious about them. The fields are situated in outlying areas and usually are small and in odd locations. If you look at some of the inheritance documentation from some of the very rich families from Larsa, there are only one or two cases where fields among the paternal estate are given away. Otherwise there are lumps of gold, 10 or 20 slaves, orchards and houses, and whatever. If you look at a particular family archive where you can follow up for over three generations from Rimsin to Samsuiluna, you find a political shift within the duration of this archive. There is not a single field, but only houses, orchards, and so on mentioned in this archive. This is something that I have mentioned earlier. Just as a reminder, the Mesopotamians made a clear distinction between houses and orchards, intramural versus extramural real estate.

I think you (Piotr) are right to try to explain the difference between land-tenure systems in the north and in the south. So now the question is how to explain the impact of economic and ecological factors. You, Karl, refer to seminomads, and Hassuna, and places farther to the north. But we don't find any settlements in northern Babylonia. They are in the alluvial plain between Sippar and Nippur. We really shouldn't use this area.

You explain that the south needs large plots of land because of the irrigation system, because of the fallow regime, and I agree with you. But I am still puzzled, because whatever the irrigation system might be, what did they do with the fallow regime? If you do some leeching or draining or whatever, you only can do it in large plots. If you have single plots that belong to one person and are delineated by dikes and ditches, then I have no explanation for the problem. I see a problem because this cannot be alleviated by any redistribution.

Steinkeller: A partial answer to your question probably is that, as I was stressing in my paper, large concentrations of agricultural land predominated not only in the south, but also in the north. I assume that such northern estates were fallowed in exactly the same way as it was done in the south. On the other hand, the conditions in the northern section of the alluvium may have been sufficiently different to permit — in the case of small individual holdings — the use of a less stringent regime of fallow. But I agree with you that it is a problem, for which I cannot offer a fully satisfactory explanation.

Notes

1. Edzard 1996.

2. Renger 1995.

3. See Falkenstein 1974; Steinkeller 1992, 1993.

4. See Jacobsen 1957:106-109. The existence of such a religious organization can be demonstrated as early as the Uruk III period. See Steinkeller in preparation.

5. For this office, see most recently Steinkeller in press.

6. This is shown by the surviving examples of archaic "city-seals" (Matthews 1993:33-50; Steinkeller in preparation), as well as by the evidence of Uruk III economic sources, which prove the existence, at places such as Uruk, Jemdet Nasr (ancient NI+RU), Tell ᶜUqair (ancient Urum), and possibly Larsa, of the administrative and economic organization closely similar to that of southern Babylonia in Pre-Sargonic times (Englund 1996:17).

   N.B.: The fact that Jemdet Nasr and Tell ᶜUqair — both of which are situated in *northern* Babylonia — apparently conformed in archaic times to the *southern* mode of organization probably reflects the early Sumerian presence in this region (as part of the so-called "Uruk expansion") prior to the advent of proto-Akkadians. See Steinkeller 1993:111.

7. Important evidence for the existence of such groupings is provided by the description of the construction of the Eninnu, Nigirsu's main temple at Girsu/Lagash, at the time of Gudea (c. 2100 BC). For that building project, the city-state's entire population was mobilized (at least symbolically). At the ritual "ground-breaking" ceremony, the workforce (or more likely their representatives) presented themselves divided into three territorial clans (im-ru-a), of Ningirsu, Inanna, and Nanshe respectively, each carrying its totemic standard (Gudea Cylinder A = Edzard 1997:78 xiv 7-27). This tripartite composition probably reflected the original division of Girsu/Lagash into three discrete political units or proto-city-states: the northwest territory around Girsu = the domain of Ningirsu; the central territory around Lagash = the domain of Inanna; and the southeastern territory around Nimin (Nina) and Sirara = the domain of Nanshe (cf. Selz 1990). It appears quite certain that in Gudea's time, this tripartite subdivision of Girsu/Lagash was no longer a political or administrative reality and that it survived only on a ritual level. But the im-ru-a, denoting either a small grouping of villages or an extended rural family, was still a living phenomenon at Shuruppak in the Early Dynastic IIIa period (c. 2400) (Visicato 1995:16-17, text no. 185, 25f.), and perhaps even as late as the Ur III period (Falkenstein 1956:329f., text no. 201). That the im-ru-a was a territorial unit finds support in the lexical equation im-ru = *pù-a-tu* (Ebla Vocabulary 1338), where

the Semitic word is evidently *pāṭu, pattu,* "district" (see Steinkeller apud Visicato 1995:17). If the word im-ru-a is to be analyzed as a variant spelling of (or a term related to) im-dru-a (Akk. *pitiqtu*), "earthen wall" (as marking borders of fields), we would find here further indication of its territorial sense. For the concept of "territorial clan," see Sahlins 1968:52-53 and Keesing 1975:31.

8. See Steinkeller 1987a:74ff.

9. The term "vertical economy" was coined by the anthropologist John V. Murra (1972; 1980), who also used the term "vertical integration" to describe the underlying mechanism.

10. Murra 1972; Godelier 1986:88ff.

11. This point will be fully discussed and documented in my monograph "Population Density and Settlement Patterns in Southern Babylonia under the Ur III Dynasty: The Case of the Province of Umma" (in preparation).

12. Steinkeller 1987a:74-88.

13. This agrees with the assumption that, as forcefully and convincingly argued by J. David Schloen (1995), ancient Near Eastern societies — including the Babylonian one — are best explained by the Weberian model of patrimonial domination. In Weber's model, all economic and human resources are integrated into a single socioeconomic system subordinated to one ruling body. In spite of its apparent monolithic nature, such a system is actually a pyramid of individual households linked together by a network of mutual rights and obligations. When viewed from this perspective, the society is "a complex and decentralized hierarchy of households nested one within another and held together by dyadic 'vertical' ties between the many different masters and servants who are found at each level of the hierarchy" (Schloen 1995:150).

14. Steinkeller 1996.

15. A systematic discussion of this problem will be offered by Glenn R. Magid in his Ph.D. thesis, "Fields, Kings, and Gods: An Archival Study of Land Tenure and Sumerian Statehood at Early Dynastic Lagash" (in progress). See provisionally his Appendix below and Magid 1996.

16. See Steinkeller 1989:127-128; Gelb, Steinkeller and Whiting 1991; Renger 1995.

17. See, in general, Falkenstein 1974:14; Steinkeller 1987a:100f.

18. Allotte de la Fuÿe 1908-20:text no. 574 i 5-v 4.

19. Selz 1989:190-191, text no. 31 ii 4-5.

20. Brinkmann 1933:74. See also Godelier 1986:85: "Thus, nowhere — not even in the most developed of capitalist societies — does there exist individual property in land which the individual may himself wholly use and abuse. Everywhere there exists some kind of limitation upon his right, which is founded upon the prior existence of a communal right, a State, nation, crown and so on. . . . When, in the course of history, there have been individuals who have possessed a prior right to the whole of a territory and to all of a society's resources, as was the case of the Pharaohs of Egypt or with the Inca, they never possessed it as an individual title, but because they were 'gods' and personified to a higher degree the 'sovereignty' of the State and the power of a dominant caste/class over all the other groups and castes/classes of the society. In these examples, a superior individual's 'property' is both the form and the effect of the concentration of landed property in the hands of a class and/or the State." And see also Adams 1982:1: " . . . the idea of property, no less in land than in anything else, is itself only to be understood as a historically conditioned social construct. Access to and control over property has always been conditioned by successive accretions of rights and obligations that may survive or be altered only slowly according to the at least autonomous dynamics of all conceptual systems. Some of these accretions originate in local custom or in prevailing patterns of kin loyalty, with shadings of moral or legal authority introduced by the rich diversity of oppositions and alliances that go on within any generalized set of norms. Others set the interests of the individual or his family off against those of all or part of a community, while still others involve individuals, families or communities with the supervening powers of the state. But behind this misleadingly unifying facade of codes and constitutions, the whole corpus of such accretions cannot constitute a harmonious, balanced system of legal precepts together with their applications. That would seem to be a fairly neutral historical generalization . . ."

21. Schloen 1995:64-66, 102-103, and 242: " . . . the 'ownership' of land in the ancient Near East did not entail exclusive possession but involved a customary hierarchy of rights of use and disposition."

22. For example, at Ugarit (see Schloen 1995, esp. pp. 143ff.). There are strong reasons to believe that a variation of this system operated in Middle Babylonian Emar. On the basis of the fact that, at Emar, the most commonly documented "sellers" of immovables are jointly the god NIN.URTA and the city of Emar (usually referred to as the "elders of Emar"), some scholars have concluded that these elders held more land than the king (Fleming 1992:65-66), and that there was "economic preeminence of city officials over the Crown" (Beckman 1997:106). This even led to a suggestion that the kingship of Emar was of "limited" nature (Fleming 1992 and Beckman 1997). But it appears that in reality the holdings of NIN.URTA and the city of Emar remained under the ultimate control of the king of Emar (or

perhaps even under that of the king of Carchemish, Emar's political superior). This is demonstrated, in my opinion, by the cases in which the property sold by NIN.URTA and the city of Emar had earlier been confiscated from its previous owner "because he committed a grave transgression against his lord" (Fleming 1992:65, n. 43; Beckman 1996:30; Beckman 1997:105f.). I believe that, in these examples, the unnamed "lord" (*bēlu*) can only be the king of Emar (or that of Carchemish). Accordingly, it appears that the system of property rights at Emar was as follows: apart from the land managed directly by the king (which is documented independently), there existed a fund of "communal" land, classified as the property of NIN.URTA and the city of Emar. The latter land was, at least in theory, owned and managed by the city organization, which had the right to convert it into manifestly individual property. Its ultimate owner, however, was the crown, which very likely was also the actual beneficiary of any proceeds that "sales" of such land would generate.

23. Deimel 1931.

24. Falkenstein 1974. This is not the place to discuss *alternative* reconstructions of the socioeconomic organization of early Sumer (*e.g.*, that of Igor M. Diakonoff). A systematic critical assessment of all the existing theories will be given by Glenn R. Magid in his Ph.D. thesis (see above n. 15).

25. A parade example here is Benjamin R. Foster's article "A New Look at the Sumerian Temple State" (1981), which, as lacking the grasp of either the evidence or the issues involved, has only compounded the confusion. For reasons unclear, this piece has had quite a resonance in the field and is still cited as gospel by some unwary nonphilologists. See *e.g.*, Rita Dolce (1993:509, n. 2), who believes that "the debate which raged around the various studies on the subject of the temple organizations in Mesopotamian economy, [was] taken up in a critical manner and, to a great extent, resolved by B. R. Foster" — a sadly inaccurate description of the facts.

26. Such was the case at least in the Sargonic and Ur III periods. See Steinkeller and Postgate 1992:98-100.

27. For this issue, see Maekawa 1973-74; Nissen 1988:147f.; Selz 1995:53ff.

28. The most up-to-date text edition is Steible 1982:288-324, Ukg. 4-5, Ukg. 6. For the historical and legal significance this document, see, most recently Maekawa 1973-74; Edzard 1974; Nissen 1982, 1988:147f.; Selz 1992:204ff.; 1995:29ff. An extensive study will be offered by Glenn R. Magid in his Ph.D. thesis (see above n. 15).

29. See Nissen 1982; 1988:147-148.

30. See Selz 1992:204f.; Postgate 1992:268. Marvin A. Powell (1996) questions whether UruKAgina was an usurper, suggesting (without offering any

hard evidence) that he was a member of the ruling family of Girsu/Lagash. But even if that was the case (which I doubt), UruKAgina, coming from a collateral line of the family, would still have been a political outsider who needed to legitimize his accession to the throne.

31. Steinkeller 1993:117-123. See also Gelb, Steinkeller, and Whiting 1991:13-26.

32. Falkenstein 1974:14f., 18f.

33. Edzard 1967:76f.

34. Steinkeller 1993:123-126.

35. Cf. Biga's conclusion (1995:297): "It is clear that economic power, and therefore political power at Ebla, rested in the hands of the royal family and very few other families of land owners. Together, they possessed the greater part of the tillable land around Ebla as well as enormous herds of cattle, thus also controlling the textile industry on which Ebla's commercial activity was based."

36. Steinkeller 1993:125f.

37. Archi 1992; 1993a.

38. Biga 1995.

39. Steinkeller 1993:123-126.

40. Archi 1993b.

41. Texts from Ebla:

Text 1

(Archi 1993b:8-18, text no. 2)

Type of property	Owner/beneficiary
a) land	
422,000 GÁNA.KI[a]	Idanekimu (prince)
6,600 GÁNA.KI	Dubigalu
70,300 GÁNA.KI	Bumau
b) cattle and sheep[b]	
9941 cattle (= 389 minas of silver)	EN (the king)
760 calves of the steppe (= 25.2 minas of gold)	EN
64,515 sheep	EN
54,200 sheep	EN received (ŠU.DU$_8$)
700 cattle	Bumau

c) barley (income from land)

464,000 gubar[c] of barley	Idanekimu (prince)
100,000 gubar of barley	EN
221,520 gubar of barley	3 UGULA KÁ LÚ Si-si[ki]

d) silver

1,000 minas	BA-Ashtar
800 minas, interest bearing loan	the town of Kamlulu
800 minas, interest bearing loan	Uti (son of vizier Ibrium)
1,700 minas, proceeds from cedar and boxwood (trade)	Ibbi-zikir (vizier)

e) gold

1,500 minas	NÍG.SÁM ba-rúm

---

[a] If GÁNA.KI (also GÁNA.KEŠDA) equals 1/10 iku [1 iku = 0.3528 ha], then 422,000 GÁNA.KI represents 14,888 ha = 15 km².

[b] The combined totals of the cattle and sheep are 11,401 and 118,715 respectively. N.B. another Ebla tablet (75.1700), which appears to list the total movable property of the palace, records 8,770 cattle and 138,620 sheep.

[c] 1 gubar is probably 20 liters.

TEXT 2

(Archi 1993b:4-8 text no. 1)

An inventory of the property controlled by the ruler of Ebla (EN) and the vizier Ibizikir, expended on behalf of three princes.

71,000 GÁNA.KI units of land;
1,410 cattle;
1,000 calves;
92,700 sheep;
161,460 gubar measures of barley.

TEXT 3

(Dietrich 1993:94)

An inventory of the property donated by Irkab-Damu, EN of Ebla, to Tisha-Lim, an Eblaite princess, queen of Emar. Cf. Fronzaroli 1984:2-4, text no. 1, 14-18, text no. 2.

49,000 gubar measures of barley (income from land), in 7 GNs;
6,800 GÁNA.KEŠDA units of land in 27 GNs;
90 oxen;
13 mares;
4 young mules;
12 . . . ;
26 wagons;
4 carpenters?;
3 leather-workers?;
14 (other) craftsmen?

Text 4

(Edzard 1981:67, text no. 27a)

An inventory of the land held by Tisha-Lim.

2,600 GÁNA.KI units of grain-producing (ŠE.BA) land in 3? GNs;
9,000 GÁNA.KEŠDA units of land in 5 GNs.

Text 5

(Archi 1993c)

An inventory of the property of Tisha-Lim.

64 minas of silver, 40 shekels of gold, 57,000 gubar of barley, 180 cattle	3rd year (or: 3 years) - not (yet) received = outstanding;
16,800 sheep	since the 11th month - not (yet) received = outstanding;
119 garments, 217 female slaves, 64 male slaves, 40 mules, 30 mares	(on hand);

Account (ŠID) of Tisha-Lim; 6th month.

42. Steinkeller 1993:126f.

43. Ismail *et al.* 1996.

44. Steinkeller 1993:126f.

45. *Ibid.*:127.

46. Halstead 1995.

47. Goody 1976:106-110.

48. Halstead 1995:16.

49. Halstead 1995:16.

50. Cf. Halstead's observations: " . . . it is tempting to speculate, on theoretical grounds, that extensive yard-agriculture played a major role in financing the surplus necessary to support many Near Eastern civilizations" (1995:18-19); " . . . the ox-drawn plough permits large-scale surplus production and so enables the support of non-producers, such as an elite and its retainers; extensive plough agriculture is also 'wasteful' of land (compared to intensive manual cultivation) and so promotes land shortage, which in turn makes possible uneven access to land" (*ibid.*:18). And cf. also Goody's remarks: "The increase in productivity that the plough allows has two implications for stratification: it enables a ruling group to develop a much greater standard of living out of the agricultural production (to which, of course, it makes some contribution by way of investment in machinery and protection from interference), but it also means that the producers themselves are ranked on the basis of their command of the means of production, that is, their differential access to land and equipment" (1976:108).

51. Here it is not irrelevant that, under the land-tenure conditions existing in the alluvium of southern Iraq as recently as the 1950s, the economic position of small landowners was inferior to that of tenant sharecroppers on large holdings, the latter enjoying higher income and subsistence levels (Poyck 1962; Fernea 1970:48-54). Fernea's explanation of this seeming paradox (1970:108) is instructive, for he might equally well have been referring to the ancient conditions of land utilization: " . . . Poyck's data clearly demonstrate that the largest estates in the Middle Euphrates region are more productive than small farms. They are more productive in terms of quantity and value of crops per unit area of farm land, but also, and more surprisingly, appear to provide a higher income for the tenant-cultivator, despite the high rents the sharecropper must pay to the landlord. Why? The answer is clearly that *the small, independent landholding tenure system is maladapted to traditional methods of cultivation still followed in this region* [italics added]. Extensive cultivation requires a flexible relationship between land and people, a situation in which land may be used for a time and aban-

doned, as its fertility declines, to the natural process of recovery . . . Unquestionably, under traditional methods of cultivation, the 'best' condition of land tenure found at the time of this study, that is, the one most likely to preserve a high level of soil fertility for the longest period of time, was the one concentrating a large area of land under the ownership and direction of one man. On such estates the necessary prerequisite of extensive cultivation could best be met: flexible land use with rigorous adherence to the fallowing pattern. The traditional tribal system of land tenure and use was also well suited to traditional methods of extensive cultivation; indeed the two aspects of agriculture must have evolved together in this region. What is perhaps most unusual about this eco-agricultural pattern in general is that it is is *both* extensive and depends upon irrigation" (1970:53-54).

52. This assumes that the šuku holders cultivated their plots *themselves*. However, there is no compelling evidence that this was the case. A more likely possibility — dictated equally by economic and practical considerations — is that šuku plots were cultivated and harvested *en masse* by the granting institution, by means of its own teams of plowmen (the so-called GÁNA-níg-en-na/GÁNA-gud organization) and of conscripted harvesters, with the yield then distributed among šuku holders, based on their designated lot size and the average yield per iku from the overall cultivated area. See in detail Magid's Ph.D. thesis.

53. See Steinkeller 1989:126f.

54. Nissen 1988:145.

55. Liverani 1997:221f.

56. Nissen 1988:144f.; Sanlaville 1989; Zarins 1990:55f.; Liverani 1997:221-222. Cf. also Stone 1997:20: "There were subtle differences in the external environment between the north and south alluvium. The greater instability of watercourses was in the wide, flat southern sector, which also had — and has — the largest concentration of marshlands. Farther north, where the third-millennium-BC population was more Semitic and less Sumerian, the valley was quite narrow (narrower even than today), the watercourses more permanent, and the vast, unbroken desert — suitable only for seasonal grazing — at closer proximity."

57. Liverani 1997:222.

58. Zarins 1990:55.

59. Zarins 1990:55. Cf. also Zarins 1989:41-45.

60. This evidence comes from the Drehem sources concerning the royal herds of sheep and cattle. Such herds, which appear to have been administered *directly* by the central government (*i.e.*, without the involvement of the

local provincial administration), are documented primarily for northern Babylonian and peripheral locales. See Steinkeller 1987b:29-30 and n. 37.

61. Liverani 1990:173. See also Liverani 1996, 1997.

62. Liverani 1990:173.

63. Liverani 1997:220-221.

64. Liverani 1997:222.

65. Liverani 1997:221.

66. Liverani 1990:173.

67. Renger 1995:283-284.

68. Such a historical development took place in the city-state of Girsu/Lagash, which came into being from the merger of three — originally politically independent — territories, whose respective "owners" were the deities Ningirsu, Inanna, and Nanshe. See above n. 7.

69. Renger 1995:283.

70. Renger 1995:283.

APPENDIX:

TEMPLE HOUSEHOLDS AND LAND IN PRE-SARGONIC GIRSU

Glenn R. Magid
Harvard University

Almost 1,800 tablets from ED IIIb Girsu span roughly three decades in the economic life of a major temple "household" or "estate." For the reasons Dr. Steinkeller adduces above, this terminology is problematic. The é-mí/é-Ba'u documentation is as concerned with the care and feeding of the gods as it is with that of their worldly patrons. It seems that the archive's exclusive purpose was to record and facilitate an exceedingly complex and regular flow of goods and services among persons and institutions within and (in the case of mercantile activity) beyond the limits of the state.

The cult as such is amply represented in the cuneiform materials. Given the circumstantial nature of our evidence, it appears that expenditures for cultic purposes were relatively modest, except for ceremonial instances of conspicuous consumption. The economic significance of the cult was entirely superseded by the mundane concerns of day-to-day urban administration. As the Girsu tablets make clear, affairs of state were coordinated by an essentially "secular" and hierarchical officialdom. Hence, the source of these tablets would more appropriately be designated by a neutral term such as "institution," "household," or "estate," devoid of theocratic religious connotations.

If only by default, the Girsu archive must be central to any model of Sumerian land tenure. No archive of comparable size or scope has been discovered for the Early Dynastic and Pre-Sargonic periods, although the scattered data on land use and land rights that tablets from various sites in southern Mesopotamia have yielded provide adequate grounds for sketching a general impression of the land-tenure system. Several important studies have been devoted to this issue (see the main text and its bibliography). It is not my purpose here to revisit the subject of Dr. Steinkeller's paper. Land distribution in the northern versus the southern part of the alluvium reflects fundamentally different principles. At the root of this divergence were a broad array of competing ecological, social, and historical factors.

All hypotheses about Sumerian land tenure subscribe to the general applicability of documentary evidence, whether they approach Deimel's temple-state model, the royal-versus-communal-sector model of Russian scholars, or a compromise between them. It goes without saying that myriad circumstances in antiquity — differential access to land and labor, for example — prompted local variations in resource deployment, and such differences were reflected in contrasting economic records. Archival texts from southern Mesopotamia evince a degree of variation in a range consistent with their chronological and geographical distribution, while supporting the broad characterization of a distinctively southern type of economic integration.

The classic models of this type were developed on the basis of the Girsu tablets, which remain the richest source of information for a localized diachronic investigation into land-tenure practices. Their systematic analysis from the perspective of land tenure is therefore essential. The temple-state hypothesis, stripped of its theocratic baggage, best fits the evidence at hand, but it is far from a fully articulated model. I would like to discuss a few of the many remaining interpretive challenges posed by this archive.

The following preliminary remarks derive from a survey of documents pertaining to extramural property:

(1) Information on land per se, in particular the names of *Fluren* in the area of Girsu, may be found in several hundred tablets. Nearly 200 documents treat various aspects of the cultivation cycle. A subset of roughly 150 texts designate land by means of different circumlocutions (šuku X, ú-rum X), as the "property" of specific persons or institutions (X). These tablets span the years Enentarzi 4 (Selz 1989:209, text no. 42) to Urukagina 4 (*e.g.*, Allotte de la Fuÿe 1908-20:texts nos. 588-590), and list nearly 100 field names, although the number shrinks by about 10 percent when likely variants are eliminated. Peak numbers of field names are found in years Lugalanda 4 (22) and UruKAgina lugal 1 (38), with remaining years attesting between 3 and 16. Besides a possible but speculative correlation between UruKAgina's expansion of é-Ba'u and the (perhaps) unusually large number of fields open to cultivation in his first lugal year, no obvious correlation would account for the variability observed. More likely, these figures are simply an artifact of extant documentation. If so, we are at a loss to identify patterns of growth or decline in the household economy on the basis of these data.

(2) Šuku-ensik and ú-rum Baranamtara/Ba'u are mutually exclusive markers. It remains unclear whether the totality of the ensik's sustenance parcels are subsumed under the first of these rubrics, or whether plots

thus marked are the contribution of the queen's household to a šuku-ensik fund, perhaps maintained by all the households. More generally, the relationship between šuku parcels given out to officials, the ruler's šuku, and níg-en-na land remains obscure. The last term usually, but not always, qualifies šuku-ensik parcels; sometimes, but not always, qualifies the šuku plots received by officials. There is no discernible pattern of distribution. Should we assume that the concept is an explicit or implied superordinate category in all land tablets and that it denotes all landed holdings, including everything qualified as sustenance (šuku) and rental (apin-lá) land?

(3) The relationship between the ensik/lugal and é-mí/é-Ba'u is obscure. Direct intervention by the city-ruler in household affairs is most palpably manifest at the outset of UruKAgina's reign. Are we justified in correlating UruKAgina's takeover (and secondarily his "Reforms") with the fact that the term šuku-ensik is last found in that king's first lugal year?

(4) Evidence for other major households (not including é-Ningirsu and the children's households, for which see Maekawa 1973-74) is scant. The documents under consideration yield no references to fields in connection with potential household names (é-. . .). Such names, e.g., é-Dumuzi(-abzu), é-Nanshe, and é-Nin-tu appear elsewhere in the archive, but their independent status as economic units comparable with é-mí/é-Ba'u cannot be verified. Such households must have existed, but their shallow imprint on our documents raises the question of whether the Girsu archive should be regarded as a state, a city, or simply a household repository, and whether by extension é-mí/é-Ba'u can reasonably be considered the state's administrative center. Tantalizing data to consider in this connection are those field names formed on the model GÁNA DN (DN = devine name). Abba, Enlil, Inanna, Nanshe, and Ningirsu are thus represented in texts dating to UruKAgina and Lugalanda. Could these names signify association with the gods' households, by analogy with GÁNA-Ba'u (attested only under UruKAgina)?

This list can be expanded indefinitely. Given advances in the field of Sumerology over the last few decades, especially in the area of social and economic history, the time is ripe for a systematic reevaluation of the Girsu archive and the long languishing temple-state controversy. I hope that my dissertation in progress may contribute to this project.

BIBLIOGRAPHY

Adams, Robert McC. (1982), "Property Rights and Functional Tenure in Mesopotamian Rural Communities," in *Societies and Languages of the Ancient Near East: Studies in Honour of I. M. Diakonoff*, ed. by J. N. Postgate et al. (Warminster):1-14.

Allotte de la Fuÿe, François-Maurice (1908-20), *Documents présargoniques* (Paris).

Archi, Alfonso (1992), "The City of Ebla and the Organization of its Rural Economy," *Altorientalische Forschungen* 19:24-28.

— (1993a), "Fifteen Years of Studies on Ebla: A Summary," OLZ 88:461-71.

— (1993b), *Five Tablets from the Southern Wing of Palace G - Ebla*. Syro-Mesopotamian Studies 5/2 (Malibu).

— (1993c), "Une autre document de Tiša-Lim, reine d'Imâr," *MARI, Annales de Reserches Interdisciplinaires* 7:341-342.

Beckman, Gary (1996), *Texts from the Vicinity of Emar in the Collection of Jonathan Rosen*. History of the Ancient Near East, Monographs 2 (Padova).

— (1997), "Real Property Rights at Emar," in *Crossing Boundaries and Linking Horizons: Studies in Honor of Michael C. Astour*, ed. by Gordon D. Young et al. (Bethesda):95-120.

Biga, Giovanna (1995), Review of A. Archi, *Five Tablets . . .* , in *Journal of the American Oriental Society* 115:297-98.

Brinkmann, Carl (1933), "Land Tenure," in *Encyclopedia of the Social Sciences*, vol. 9, ed. by Edwin R. A. Seligman (New York):73-76.

Deimel, Anton (1931), *Sumerische Tempelwirtschaft zur Zeit Urukaginas und seiner Vorgänger*. Analecta Orientalia 2 (Rome).

Dietrich, Manfred (1993), "'Besitz der Tisha-Lim': Zuwendungen des Königs von Ebla an die Königin von Emar," *Ugarit Forschungen* 25:93-98.

Dolce, Rita (1993), Review of F. R. Kraus, *The Role of Temples from the Third Dynasty of Ur to the First Dynasty of Babylon*, in *Orientalische Literaturzeitung* 88:509-513.

Edzard, Dietz O. (1967), "The Early Dynastic Period," in *The Near East: The Early Civilizations* [original German 1965], ed. by Jean Bottéro et al. (tr. R. F. Tannenbaum; New York):52-90.

— (1974), "'Soziale Reformen' im Zweistromland bis ca. 1600 v. Chr.: Realität oder literarischer Topos?," *Acta Antiqua Academiae Scientiarum Hungaricae* 22:145-156.

— (1981), *Verwaltungstexte verschiedenen Inhalts.* Archivi Reali di Ebla 2 (Rome).

— (1996), "Private Land Ownership and its Relation to 'God' and the 'State' in Sumer and Akkad," in *Privatization in the Ancient Near East and Classical World*, ed. by M. Hudson and B. A. Levine. Peabody Museum Bulletin 5 (Cambridge, MA):109-128.

— (1997), *Gudea and His Dynasty.* The Royal Inscriptions of Mesopotamia, Early Periods 3/1 (Toronto).

Englund, Robert K. (1996), *Proto-Cuneiform Texts from Diverse Collections.* Materialen zu den frühen Schriftzeugnissen des Vorderen Orients 4 (Berlin).

Falkenstein, Adam (1956), *Die neusumerischen Gerichtsurkunden, Zweiter Teil*, Bayerische Akademie der Wissenschaften, Philosophisch-Historische Klasse, Abhandlungen, NeueFolge Heft 40 (Munich).

— (1974), *The Sumerian Temple City* [original French 1954]. Monographs in History: Ancient Near East 1/1 (tr. Maria deJ. Ellis; Los Angeles).

Fernea, Robert A. (1970), *Shaykh and Effendi: Changing Patterns of Authority Among the El Shabana of Southern Iraq.* Harvard Middle Eastern Studies 14 (Cambridge MA).

Fleming, Daniel E. (1992), "A Limited Kingship: Late Bronze Emar in Ancient Syria," *Ugarit Forschungen* 24:59-71.

Foster, Benjamin R. (1981), "A New Look at the Sumerian Temple State," *Journal of the Economic and Social History of the Orient* 24:225-41.

Fronzaroli, Pelio (1984), "Disposizioni reali per Tiṯaw-Liᵓm (TM.75.G.2396, TM.75.G.1986+)," *Studi Eblaiti* 7:1-22.

Gelb, Ignace J., Piotr Steinkeller, and Robert M. Whiting (1991), *Earliest Land Tenure Systems in the Near East: The Ancient Kudurrus.* Oriental Institute Publications 104 (Chicago).

Godelier, Maurice (1986), "Territory and Property in Some Pre-Capitalist Societies," in Maurice Godelier, *The Mental and the Material* [original French 1984] (tr. Martin Thom; Thetford):71-121.

Goody, Jack (1976), *Production and Reproduction: A Comparative Study of the Domestic Domain.* Cambridge Papers in Social Anthropology 17 (Cambridge).

Halstead, Paul (1995), "Plough and Power: The Economic and Social Significance of Cultivation with the Ox-Drawn Ard in the Mediterranean," *Bulletin on Sumerian Agriculture* 8:11-22.

Ismail, Farouk et al. (1996), *Administrative Documents from Tell Beydar (Seasons 1993-1995)*. Subartu II (Turnhout).

Jacobsen, Thorkild (1957), "Early Political Development in Mesopotamia," *Zeitschrift für Assyriologie* 52:91-140.

Keesing, Roger M. (1975), *Kin Groups and Social Structure* (New York).

Liverani, Mario (1990), "The Shape of Neo-Sumerian Fields," *Bulletin on Sumerian Agriculture* 5:147-186.

—— (1996), "Reconstructing the Rural Landscape of the Ancient Near East," *Journal of the Social and Economic History of the Orient* 39:1-49.

—— (1997), "Lower Mesopotamian Fields: South vs. North," in *Ana šadî Labnāni lū allik: Beiträge zu altorientalischen und mittelmeerischen Kulturen, Festschrift für Wolfgang Röllig*, ed. by Beate Pongratz-Leisten et al. Alter Orient und AltesTestament 247 (Neukirchen-Vluyn):219-227.

Maekawa, Kazuya (1973-74), "The Development of the É-MÍ in Lagash During Early Dynastic III," *Mesopotamia* 8-9:77-144.

Magid, Glenn R. (1996), *Fields, Kings, and Gods: An Archival Study of Land Tenure and Sumerian Statehood at Early Dynastic Lagash*. Harvard University PhD dissertation prospectus.

Matthews, Roger J. (1993), *Cities, Seals and Writing: Archaic Seal Impressions from Jemdet Nasr and Ur*. Materialen zu den frühen Schriftzeugnissen des Vorderen Orients 2 (Berlin).

Murra, John V. (1972), "El 'control vertical' de un máximo de pisos ecológicos en la economía de las sociedades andinas," in Inigo Ortiz de Zúñiga, *Visita de la provincia de León de Huánuco* [1562], vol. 2, ed. by John V. Murra (Huánuco):429-476. Reprinted in John V. Murra, *Formaciones económicas y politicas del mundo andino* (Lima 1975): 59-115.

—— (1980), *The Economic Organization of the Inka State*. Research in Economic Anthropology, Supplement 1 (Greenwich, CT).

Nissen, Hans J. (1982), "Die 'Tempelstadt': Regierungsform der frühdynastischen Zeit in Babylonien?," in *Gesellschaft und Kultur des Alten Orients*, ed. by Horst Klengel. Schriften zur Geschichte und Kultur des Alten Orients 15 (Berlin):195-200.

—— (1988), *The Early History of the Ancient Near East* [original German 1983] (tr. Elizabeth Lutzeier, with Kenneth J. Northcott; Chicago).

Postgate, J. N. (1992), *Early Mesopotamia: Society and Economy at the Dawn of History* (London).

Powell, Marvin A. (1996), "The Sin of Lugalzagesi," *Wiener Zeitschrift für die Kunde des Morgenlandes* 86:307-314.

Poyck, A. P. G. (1962), *Farm Studies in Iraq* (Wageningen).

Renger, Johannes M. (1995), "Institutional, Communal, and Individual Ownership or Possession of Arable Land in Ancient Mesopotamia from the End of the Fourth to the End of the First Millennium BC," in *Symposium on Ancient Law, Economics, and Society*, Part II, ed. by J. Lindgren et al., *Chicago-Kent Law Review* 71 no. 1:269-319.

Sahlins, Marshall D. (1968), *Tribesmen* (Englewood Cliffs).

Sanlaville, Paul (1989), "Considérations sur l'évolution de la basse Mésopotamie au cours des derniers millénaires," *Paléorient* 15/2:5-27.

Schloen, J. David (1995), *The Patrimonial Household in the Kingdom of Ugarit: A Weberian Analysis of Ancient Near Eastern Society*. Harvard University PhD dissertation.

Selz, Gebhard J. (1989), *Die altsumerischen Wirtschaftsurkunden der Ermitage zu Leningrad*. Freiburger Altorientalische Studien 15/1 (Stuttgart).

— (1990), "Studies in Early Syncretism: The Development of the Pantheon of Lagash — Examples for Inner-Sumerian Syncretism," *Sumerological Studies* 12:111-142.

— (1992), "Enlil und Nippur nach präsargonischen Quellen," in *Nippur at the Centennial: Papers Read at the 35ᵉ Recontre Assyriologique Internationale, Philadelphia, 1988*, ed. by Maria deJ. Ellis. Occasional Publications of the Samuel Noah Kramer Fund 14 (Philadelphia):189-225.

— (1995), *Untersuchungen zur Götterwelt des altsumerischen Stadtstaates von Lagaš.*. Occasional Publications of the Samuel Noah Kramer Fund 13 (Philadelphia).

Steible, Horst (1982), *Die altsumerischen Bau- und Weihinschriften, Teil I. Inschriften aus 'Lagash.'* Freiburger Altorientalische Studien 5 (Wiesbaden).

Steinkeller, Piotr (1987a), "The Foresters of Umma: Toward a Definition of Ur III Labor," in *Labor in the Ancient Near East*, ed. by Marvin A. Powell. American Oriental Series 68 (New Haven):73-116.

— (1987b), "The Administrative and Economic Organization of the Ur III State: The Core and the Periphery," in *The Organization of Power: Aspects of Bureaucracy in the Ancient Near East*, ed. by McGuire Gibson and Robert D. Biggs. Studies in Ancient Oriental Civilization 46 (Chicago):19-41.

— (1989), *Sale Documents of the Ur III Period*. Freiburger Altorientalische Studien 17 (Stuttgart).

— (1992), "Mesopotamia in the Third Millennium BC," in *The Anchor Bible Dictionary*, vol. 4, ed. by David N. Freedman (New York):724-732.

— (1993), "Early Political Development in Mesopotamia and the Origins of the Sargonic Empire," in *Akkad, the First World Empire: Structure, Ideology, Traditions,* ed. by Mario Liverani. History of the Ancient Near East, Studies 5 (Padua):107-129.

— (1996), "The Organization of Crafts in Third Millennium Babylonia: The Case of Potters," *Altorientalische Forschungen* 23:1-22.

— (in press), "On Rulers, Priests, and Sacred Marriage: Tracing the Evolution of Early Sumerian Kingship," in *Proceedings of the Second Colloquium on the Ancient Near East: Priests and Officials in the Ancient Near East,* ed. by Kazuko Watanabe and Daisuke Yoshida (Heidelberg).

— (in preparation), "Archaic City Seals and the Question of Early Babylonian Unity," to appear in *Thorkild Jacobsen Memorial Volume,* ed. by Tzvi Abusch.

Steinkeller, Piotr, and J. N. Postgate (1992) *Third-Millennium Legal and Administrative Texts in the Iraq Museum, Baghdad.* Mesopotamian Civilizations 4 (Winona Lake).

Stone, Elizabeth (1997), "City-States and Their Centers: The Mesopotamian Example," in *The Archaeology of City-States: Cross-Cultural Approaches,* ed. by Deborah L. Nichols and Thomas H. Charlton (Washington):15-26.

Visicato, Giuseppe (1995), *The Bureaucracy of Šuruppak.* Abhandlungen zur Literatur Alt-Syrien-Palästinas und Mesopotamiens 10 (Münster).

Zarins, Juris (1989), "Jebel Bishri and the Amorite Homeland: The PPNB Phase," in *To the Euphrates and Beyond: Archaeological Studies in Honour of Maurits N. van Loon,* ed. by O. M. C. Haex *et al.* (Rotterdam):29-51.

— (1990), "Early Pastoral Nomadism and the Settlement of Lower Mesopotamia," *Bulletin of the American Schools of Oriental Research* 280:31-65.

9

Economic Aspects of Land Ownership and Land Use in Northern Mesopotamia and Syria from the Late Third Millennium to the Neo-Assyrian Period

Carlo Zaccagnini
Naples

This paper deals with land use and ownership in northern Mesopotamia and inner Syria, based on selected analysis of the written evidence provided by palace, temple, and private archives, from the second half of the third millennium to the late seventh century BC (*i.e.,* the end of the Assyrian empire).[1] I do not claim to present a detailed and exhaustive treatment of all available sources but will focus on selected documentation retrieved at Ebla, Mari, Nuzi, Emar, and the Neo-Assyrian capital cities.

Despite the considerable chronological gap that separates the earliest from the latest documentation, the geoclimatic environments as well as the socioeconomic backgrounds of these different documentary corpuses are not too dissimilar and in fact disclose encouraging (and as yet largely unexplored) research opportunities.

My working agenda will be limited to an evaluation of real estate assets, which were the object of grants, deeds of sale, leases and mortgages, by taking into consideration especially the size of the plots of land and their expected yield rates. A combined analysis of both sets of data can provide important clues for appreciating the significance of these transactions with respect to the basic subsistence requirements of the ancient Near Eastern family groups. On the other hand, it gives us the opportunity to enlarge the ongoing discussion about the socioeconomic backgrounds and the procedural mechanisms that contributed to determine the "market" evaluation of landed property. However, this latter issue will not be dealt with in this paper, as it deserves a detailed treatment of its own.

The feasibility and the opportunity of investigating the evidence provided by very different and chronologically distant sets of data is fostered by the similarity of some basic features displayed by the documentation that shall be the object of the present discussion.

Let us first consider the characteristics of the rural landscape of Assyria, the Nuzi area, and the Euphrates valley at the site of Emar. According to the available statistics,[2] the region around modern Mosul and Kirkuk is comprised within the 200- and 400-mm isohyets, which, in a broad sense, represent the borderline of dry-farming. More precisely, the average yearly rainfall in the area of Kirkuk (= ancient Arraphe, some ten miles southeast of Yorghan-tepe [= Nuzi]) is approximately 380 mm, whereas the adjacent countryside southwest of the city, which corresponds to an ample sector of the ancient Arraphean/Nuzian farmland, is located between the 300- and 200-mm isohyets.

The countryside of the Assyrian heartland, corresponding to the region of Nineveh/Mosul, receives the same amount of rainfall (*i.e.*, c. 380 mm) as does the area of Nimrud/Kalkhu, whereas the region of Assur is comprised within the 200- and 300-mm isohyets.

The site of Emar, whose grassland is partially located on the bank of the Euphrates, enjoys no more than 200 mm of yearly rainfall. The Ebla region (inner Syria) is located between the 300- and 400-mm isohyets,[3] whereas coastal Syria receives more than 400 mm rainfall.

Thus it is quite evident that the Nuzi and Assyrian farmlands could practise dry-farming agriculture. However, as we learn from the abundant documentation provided by the Nuzi archives, crop-raising depending on rainfall was supported and implemented by a fairly extensive network of canals and minor river streams deriving from the Tigris and its tributary rivers (*e.g.*, the Little Zab). On the contrary, the Emar farmland almost exclusively depended on the Euphrates' waters: the proximity to the river of a considerable number of land parcels — whose transfer is recorded in the Emar archives — confirms the above observation. However it should be noted that the absence of any explicit reference to the river as one of the actual borders of many fields, and the present uncertainty concerning a number of topographical features that are recorded in the description of the fields' location,[4] forbid us, for the time being, to speculate about the real extent of the dependence of Emar's agriculture on the water resources obtained from the Euphrates. At any rate, we may safely assume that the northern Mesopotamian and Syrian agricultural set-ups have little if anything to share with the irrigated agriculture of the third- to first-millennium in southern Mesopotamia.

Strictly related to the geoclimatic features of Upper Mesopotamia and inner (and coastal) Syria are the scattered pieces of information concerning the yield rates of the fields. To my knowledge, the only consistent evidence concerns the Nuzi farmland: the topic of the Nuzi grain yields has been dealt with in some detail,[5] and I shall come back to it later on. On the contrary, nothing is known about the grain yields in the Neo-Assyrian period[6] — a tentative albeit highly hypothetical suggestion has been proposed by Postgate in his comment on some Middle Assyrian texts published 15 years ago.[7] The situation at Emar is obscure too. We do not have any information or indirect hint about the yield rates — a comparison with a handful of data recently made available from the rich Mari archives is of little help, as will be seen presently. In addition to this, a few data are available for third- and second-millennium Syria (Ebla and Ugarit), but their tentative interpretation is still in a very preliminary stage.

In order to obtain a concrete appreciation of the data provided by the sources, our first step is to reconstruct the seed-to-crop ratios; in addition to this, it is essential to convert the ancient measures of capacity and surface into modern terms, *i.e.,* liters and hectares. Due to the persisting great uncertainty that characterizes the reconstruction of ancient Near Eastern metrology,[8] the figures that follow are far from certain and only aim at proposing an acceptable framework for future discussion.

The irrigated Nuzi fields, or the fields bordering on watercourses with possible access to irrigation facilities and whose rates of yield ranged from c. 10 to 8 homers of barley per 1 homer of land, would produce some 670 to 540 liters per hectare.[9] Medium or lower yields, especially referring to nonirrigated fields, ranged from c. 7 to 4 homers of barley per 1 homer of land, corresponding to some 470 to 270 liters/ha. Inferior yields, from less than 4 to c. 1.5 homers, would correspond to some 240 to 100 liters/ha.

The Ebla evidence concerning barley yields has been provisionally worked out, especially by L. Milano[10] and by A. Archi.[11] Before entering into some details, it should be stressed that various uncertainties still affect the "decyphering" of this Eblaic textual material: on the one hand, the few accounts that record total amounts of tilled land and quantities of grain (barley in the first place, plus other items like sheep and cattle) do not allow us to infer an automatic relationship between the two sets of data, in terms of (yearly) cereal yields. On the other hand, the matter of the Eblaic surface and capacity measures, with respect to more or less contemporary Mesopotamian values, is still debated: the gána (.kešda).ki has been alternatively reckoned at $^1/_{10}$ or $^1/_6$ of 1 iku, *i.e.,* c. 360 or 600 m^2; the tentative value of the gubar has been set at 20 liters. As a consequence of this, it is no surprise that the various attempts at reconstructing the unitary barley yields of the Ebla farmland are quite divergent.

Some ten years ago, Milano[12] suggested a possible average of 1-to-4 seed-to-crop ratio, corresponding to some 240 liters/ha. Although his interpretation of the texts that supported his hypothesis was later modified,[13] his working hypothesis has not been altered.[14] Based on the evidence of a tablet retrieved in 1982 outside the area of the Ebla central archive (TM.82.G.266), Archi worked out quite different reckonings of the possible yield rates at Ebla.[15] Without entering into unnecessary detail, it can be said that by combining the figures recorded in TM.82.G.266: Obv. I 1-2 (422,000 gána.ki-measures of field) with those of Obv. I 5-II 3 (464,000 gubar-measures of barley, plus 10,060 gubar-measures of the otherwise unknown sig$_{15}$-cereal),[16] we get a rate of 370 liters/ha (with a gána.ki reckoned at $^1/_6$ iku) or of 624 liters/ha (with a gána.ki reckoned at $^1/_{10}$ iku). Commenting on this set of data, Archi has suggested quite different figures, on the assumption that the ancient production of barley could have been 10 quintals/ha, "which, however, could only be achieved in favorable years," or — more probably — 5.5 quintals/ha.[17] I fail to understand the basis of Archi's reckonings, which, in any case, yield figures too high in the general framework of ancient Syrian dry-farming.[18]

Before the publication of TM.82.G.266, a different approach to the subject matter of Ebla grain yields had been undertaken by J. Renger. On the basis of a detailed evaluation of the Syrian geoclimatic environment in relation to the probable size of the Eblaic population, its nourishment necessities, and the consequent required extension of the tilled land, he suggested a barley yield rate of c. 600 kg/ha, corresponding to some 840 liters/ha.[19] The notable divergences between the above figures bespeak the preliminary stage of the overall reconstruction of the Eblaic agricultural set-up — one can hope that additional information will be made available, although it should be acknowledged that the greatest majority of the Ebla epigraphic corpus is by now sufficiently well known. At any rate, and for the time being, the above noted divergences advise against suggesting median values among extreme figures.

A few texts from Mari provide interesting yet problematic data concerning the possible barley yield rates. Common to these texts is the listing of various land surfaces located in different territories of the Mari kingdom, coupled with amounts of barley. From ARM XXIII 426, we learn of yields amounting to 370, 581, and 235 liters per hectare.[20] In light of comparative evidence, these figures make good sense and appear to be quite realistic. On the other hand, apparently similar accounts like *e.g.*, those of ARM XXIII 591, and ARM XXIV 2 and 3[21] are puzzling, since they show much higher yield (??) rates ranging from c. 1,600 to 2,500 liters/ha (ARM XXIII 591), from c. 2,500 to 5,900 liters/ha (ARM XXIV 2), and from c. 2,800 to 8,000 liters/ha (ARM XXIV 3). Again, while waiting for welcomed new pieces of textual evidence, it seems preferable to refrain from commenting on these data.

The Ugarit yield rates, as reconstructed by M. Liverani on the basis of the text PRU V 13,[22] range from 5:1 to 3:1: in this case too, figures are well comparable with the average data stemming from the Northern Mesopotamian and inner Syrian regions. By assuming similar sowing rates, the barley produce of the Ugaritic farmland would range from c. 335 to 200 liters/ha.

I will now turn to the central subject matter of my paper, namely a tentative assessment of the economic significance of the several hundred deeds of transfer (sales in the first place, and leases, mortgages, exchanges, etc.) recorded in Mesopotamian and Syrian documents, with specific reference to the crucial issue of the relationship between the indispensable alimentary necessities of the nuclear family groups — which basically depended on the yearly barley produce of their own parcels of land — and the dimensions of their real estate properties.[23] Another strictly related issue is the overall evaluation of the socioeconomic significance of the purchase prices attested in the real estate deeds of transfer. As anticipated above, this matter will be dealt with elsewhere.

As concerns Nuzi, I will use the synthetic collection of data that I assembled in 1979[24] as a basis and shall take into account the pertinent observations of R. McC. Adams in his review of my book.[25] As far as I can judge, subsequent publications of additional Nuzi texts, stemming from private archives,[26] have not substantially altered the overall scenario that I sketched 19 years ago. An outstanding feature displayed by the Nuzi texts related to field transactions is the small surface of the plots of land: out of some 500 occurrences, which I listed in my book, c. 77 percent concerns parcels of land ranging from a handful of square metres (!) to 3 ha. Fields measuring from 1 to 3 ha represent 40 percent of the total; fields whose dimensions range from 3 to 10 ha are 20 percent; larger fields, measuring from 10 up to 40 ha are only 3 percent. These statistics derive from a comprehensive analysis of texts of various kinds (sales, mortgages, exchanges, etc.) but also hold true with specific refererence to outright sales, which, according to the well-known Nuzi practice, are patterned according to the legal format of personal adoptions (*tuppi mārūti*). The above-sketched survey is even more significant if related to the relationship between irrigated versus nonirrigated plots of land.

Out of some 140 real estate transfers,[27] the number of parcels whose surface measures 3 or more ha is quite low (c. 30 percent); in most cases they are nonirrigated fields. Irrigated fields, or fields adjoining to watercourses, whose yearly rates of yield ranged from c. 10 to 8 homers of barley per 1 homer of surface (*i.e.,* c. 670 to 540 liters/ha), are remarkably small: out of 26 instances, only 4 plots measure 2 homers, while 4 others measure from 3 to 6.2 homers.

All in all, we are led to the conclusion — already briefly anticipated by Adams — that the great majority of family landed property that was the object of the Nuzi deeds of sale could not represent the exclusive source for the maintenance of the single peasant family units. Assuming a minimal yearly need of c. 600-700 liters of barley for a peasant family unit consisting of a married couple with two children, a suckling baby, and possibly an aged father/mother (-in-law),[28] and in consideration of the 2-year rotation system of ancient Mesopotamian crop raising (1 year cultivation and 1 year fallow), one would need at least some 8 to 4 ha of irrigated land, or some 10 ha of dry-farmed land, for the basic maintenance of a family unit living in the modern area of Kirkuk. The data at hand show that this was not the case; therefore one would be tempted to suggest that the land parcels that were alienated (or in any case transferred) to third parties did not represent the entire real estate patrimony of the sellers but only a share of it. Although this possibility should not be ruled out a priori, I strongly suspect that the evidence provided by the Nuzi *tuppi mārūti* reflects a socioeconomic stage of the local peasantry marked by a progressive worsening of the self-sufficiency of small independent landowners, whose physical maintenance had to be ensured by other incomes in addition to those deriving from the exploitation of their own farmland.

As concerns Ebla, only tentative working hypotheses can be put forth, as the meagre and controversial textual evidence does not warrant any sound conclusions. It has been noted that the most recurrent size of subsistence plots of land, which were allotted by the central administration to some officials, is the round figure of 200 gána.ki (round multiples are also attested, albeit sporadically),[29] According to the different values reckoned for this surface measure (*i.e.,* $^1/_{10}$ or $^1/_6$ of one iku), 200 gána.ki would correspond to c. 7 or 12 ha respectively. On the basis of the above hypothesized barley rates of yield, we would get, in either case, some 4,400 liters/ha of yearly barley production; assuming a customary 50 percent fallow (and disregarding the amounts of cereal to be used as fodder for draft animals and to be stocked as seed for the following year), we should conclude that a parcel of land of 200 gána.ki could produce some 2,200 liters per year — a figure that, incidentally, perfectly fits Renger's estimate of the subsistence requirements of ancient Near Eastern families.

The relevant Neo-Assyrian evidence — which covers a time span of at least 170 years (from the early eighth century to the last days of the empire) — poses several problems. Aside from the long-standing debate about the absolute value of surface and capacity measures,[30] nothing is really known about the barley yield rates of the Assyrian farmland under state, temple, or private control and exploitation during the first half of the first millennium. Postgate's assumption[31] that "1 homer of land yielded about 600 kg of barley [*i.e.,* c. 720/840 liters]" is a mere guess; also considering his caution in proposing a parallel ("perhaps unjustified, and certainly an unjustifiable assumption"[32]) between the tentatively reconstructed Middle Assyrian and the totally unknown Neo-Assyrian yields.

In the absence of any bit of information about the yield rates of Assyrian rain-fed fields,[33] we can only hypothesize that the average Neo-Assyrian barley crops ranged from no more than c. 600 down to c. 200 liters/ha.[34] Based on these figures, we can provisionally agree with Postgate's hypothesis according to which the yearly maintenance of an Assyrian family group required some 5 homers (= hectares) of farmland, "half in cultivation each year," in areas of irrigated agriculture and as much as twice that in regions of rain-fed land.[35] As possible textual support for this assumption, Postgate draws attention to the isolated occurrence of Esarhaddon's land grant in favor of the chief haruspex Marduk-šumu-usur: the allotted plot of land, precisely measuring 10 homers, was located in the district of Halahhu (in the area north of Nineveh and Horsabad) — the document can be dated to 667 BC.[36] Be that as it may, we can provisionally conceive that the physical survival of an Assyrian peasant family needed c. 5 (irrigated) to 10 (rain-fed) hectares of farmland.

A comprehensive perusal of the fields' surfaces recorded in Assyrian deeds of sale — from the early eighth to the last decades of the seventh century — shows an astonishing range of variations in the sizes of the conveyed plots of land.[37] Large estates, possibly consisting of different adjoining parcels, could reach 50 and even more hectares, whereas, on the contrary, we have evidence of sales of fields measuring less than 1 hectare. On a first and very preliminary approximation, one would be tempted to suggest that the Neo-Assyrian evidence reflects two basically different patterns of land-ownership: large estates, on the one hand, possibly belonging to more or less closely related family groups and, on the other, a consistent number of minor estates whose dimensions were smaller than 10 hectares and even less. Comparison with the dimensions of the parcels of land that were the object of deeds of lease favors the hypothesis that in many cases we are dealing with individual holdings that were "marginal or submarginal from the viewpoint of a family's minimal subsistence needs."[38]

Even more intriguing is the situation at Emar. In addition to the fact that we do not have any clue concerning the local barley yield rates, in irrigated and nonirrigated farmlands, considerable uncertainty exists about the absolute values of the length and surface measures that are used in the Emar texts in order to record the fields' dimensions. If we assume that the basic surface measure in use at Emar — i.e., the iku — corresponded to a square of 1 × 1 linear iku (=120 cubits, that is c. 60 m), one square iku would measure c. 3,600 m², that is slightly more than ⅓ hectare. A general scrutiny of the pertinent textual evidence shows that fields of 1 square iku occur with a remarkable frequency — greater but also smaller field surfaces are recorded too. Further note that the transacted plots of land appear to be located in different areas. It is certainly no surprise that a considerable number of land parcels adjoins the Euphrates. This fact would induce us to surmise that they benefited from irrigation facilities, also if — as noted by Liverani — the Emar terminology describing the "fronts" of the fields "seems to imply that the fields were not directly irrigated from the river."[39] Be that as it may, in the absence of any data concerning yield-rates and tentatively relying on the comparative evidence referring to the irrigated Nuzi farmland, we can hypothesize that the minimal subsistence requirement for an Emar family, at the end of the Late Bronze Age, was ensured by a field of 6 square iku, yielding some 600 barley liters/ha. However, only a limited number of cases conform to such a pattern, thus suggesting that the overall situation experienced by the Emar peasantry closely resembled those that have been previously commented on.

As a provisional conclusion to the above brief remarks, it can be argued that in peripheral areas outside the Mesopotamian alluvium, the overall pattern of private land ownership from the late third to the mid-first millennium displays an apparently similar structure. Its main tract is a disproportion between a relatively small number of large patrimonies owned by individual latifundists and a vast number of small plots of family land. In the former case the agricultural activities carried out for the absentee landlords were performed by a subordinate workforce, i.e., local peasantry residing on the spot. In many cases (the Nuzi and Neo-Assyrian evidence are quite instructive), there is clear evidence that these people were the former owners of the land, which they had to sell in order to settle economic difficulties. In the latter case, the peasants' plots of land were directly exploited by the single family groups.

As noted before, and on a very general level, one hardly can avoid the impression that the great majority of privately owned fields, of which mention is made in hundreds of deeds of transfer from various regions and periods, could not represent the exclusive source of maintenance of an average ancient Near Eastern family unit. The relatively small dimensions of most plots of land, coupled with their average modest barley yield rates, lead to the conclusion that the indispensable nutritional requirements of northern Mesopotamian and Syrian "free" peasantry had to be ensured by additional incomes, at least during the historical phases documented by the various sets of textual evidence commented on so far. Also taking into account the possible retrieval of further documentation that could perhaps partially modify the current historical reconstruction of this ancient Near Eastern scenario, we should conclude that the various archives providing evidence for more or less consistent episodes of real estate sales unambiguously reflect a basic trend — a generalized disintegration of family rural properties that were conveyed to single individuals building up vast and even huge land patrimonies.

On the other hand, one can safely assume that the absence of documentary evidence recording real estate transfers (and related transactions, mortgages in the first place) simply bespeaks a "normal" situation, whereby family land was automatically transmitted within the family units, according to customary inheritance practices based on lineage criteria that normally did not require ad hoc written stipulations.[40]

I revert to the issue of the small dimensions of the "subsistence" fields owned by peasant families. Given that the available information stems from a vast number of deeds of transfer, it is appropriate to wonder whether, and to what extent, the parcels of land conveyed from a multitude of peasants to some rich landowners represented the entire real estate patrimonies of the sellers, or only part of them. An apparently good test for attempting to solve the dilemma is to compare the surfaces of the fields recorded in the various deeds of transfer with those that occur in contemporary wills, which can offer useful pieces of information about the real dimensions of (some) family real estate patrimonies.

A preliminary and by no means exhaustive perusal of the wealthy Nuzi evidence is indeed interesting yet not entirely conclusive. In most cases the testaments[41] do not provide any itemized description of the bequeathed real estate properties but synthetically state that "all my fields, houses, etc." are transmitted to one sole or more heirs.[42] Nevertheless, whatever the dimensions of the landed properties recorded in the Nuzi wills might have been, one gets the impression that in most cases we are confronted with patrimonies belonging to fairly rich people and that the average dimensions of these immovable properties do not correspond with those of the common peasant family units. In this regard it is perhaps worthy of note that in those isolated cases in which an itemized description of the bequeathed properties is explicitly recorded, the land surfaces assigned to single heirs appear to be centered on the round figure of 10 hectares.[43] As was tentatively argued before, this represents the minimal basis for the yearly maintenance of a Nuzi family group. If we assume that not all deeds of sale necessarily concern the entirety of the individual family real estate properties — and this certainly is the case for the minute portions of land that frequently are attested in such deeds — we hardly can avoid the impression of a general and progressive impoverishment of the rural strata. Quite often they had to resort to interest-bearing barley loans (*hubullu*), in many cases secured by personal or real estate guarantees (*tidennūtu*). Eventually — or in a short time — they had to sell off their real estate properties, or at least part of them (*mārūtu*).[44]

As a revealing counterpart to this seemingly generalized pattern of a limited and basically non-self-sufficient structure of peasant land ownership, we have clear evidence of large real estate patrimonies owned by a relatively small number of wealthy landlords. We find members of the king's family, court dignitaries, and individual private entrepreneurs as title holders of vast estates, often located in different, even remote, areas of the single state territorial administrations. Despite minor local differences, the evidence stemming from the Nuzi, Middle-, and Neo-Assyrian archives (and, to a lesser extent the Ebla, Ugarit, and Emar corpuses) reveals the various procedures and the final issues of this sector of private land ownership.

On a basic level one can point out two different (and at times complementary) mechanisms through which large estates were built up — royal grants and purchase strategies. The latter were carried out through appropriate procedures eventually leading to land dispossessions from previously indebted rural family groups. Both mechanisms are well attested in second- and first-millennium documentation and need not be further commented on here in detail.[45] In any case, an astonishing divergence can be prima facie perceived between the two sectors of private land ownership. Just to give a few random examples, I can point out the case of Tehip-tilla, the well-known Nuzi businessman. The total amount of his transacted real estate holdings adds up to slightly more than 1,000 ha, but Maidman[46] has reasonably argued for an entire patrimony close to some 2,000 ha. Also at Nuzi, and on a much more limited scale, the sister of Šilwa-teššup — son of the king — receives, as part of her dowry, 180 ha of cultivated land;[47] in 670 BC, Atar-il, eunuch of the crown prince of Babylon, buys an entire village — an estate of 500 ha of land.[48]

Scores of other similar examples could be adduced here. They would confirm the contemporary presence of the two well-defined and dramatically divergent patterns of real estate property in the peripheral areas outside the Mesopotamian irrigated plain, especially from the mid-second to mid-first millennium. The evidence from late third and early second millennium Syria (Ebla and Alalah VII) seems to entirely conform to the above sketched patterns. However, further detailed analyses of the present and future available documentation are required before attempting a more refined sketch of this crucial subject matter.

DISCUSSION

Hudson: Are you saying that there was no land market in which the yield of rural land is correlated with its price?

Zaccagnini: My basic and final contention is that — at least in the period stretching from the mid-second millennium to the end of the Assyrian empire — we do not have any definite evidence supporting the existence of a true land market in which prices were primarily determined by the mechanisms of demand and supply. This is not to deny that despite the puzzling oscillations of land prices on the one hand, and the generalized phenomenon of low prices attested in land transactions on the other, the economic evaluation of land was, at least in principle, correlated with the size, location, and fertility of the plots. However, other factors did play an important, and contrasting, role. Perhaps I shall have the opportunity to come back to this point later on in the discussion.

Let us take the case of Nuzi. According to my reckonings of the different yield rates, the purchase price of a field — as recorded in the so-called "real estate adoptions" (*tuppi mārūti*) — very seldom exceeded the equivalent of two crops and was often set at a one-to-one ratio. This scenario is largely confirmed by the evidence provided by loans secured by mortgages (*tuppi tidennūti*) of definite or indefinite duration, in which plots of land are handed over to the creditor, who will cash the yearly yields in compensation of the accruing of interest. There we observe that in most cases, one single crop is enough to refund the creditor of the whole capital he has lent.

Hudson: I am referring to whether you find a relationship between price and the size of the land's yield. If there is little relationship, I think we could agree that there is no land market in the modern economic sense of the term.

Zaccagnini: As I mentioned before, there is an undeniable relation between the economic evaluation of farmland and its expected yield. But moving on from there, we find a number of features that do not conform to this basic pattern. Just to take an example, both the Nuzi and Neo-Assyrian documents provide consistent evidence of extremely high prices paid for the purchase of minute parcels of grassland, whose dimensions do not even reach one hectare, whereas larger plots are transacted at much lower prices. One could speculate that the former ones benefited from particular irrigation facilities (though this certainly is not the case at Nuzi) or some other special characteristic, but eventually this kind of reasoning turns into a circular argument.

Renger: One thing you mentioned really astonishes me. You quoted an example with a 4-to-1 yield-to-seed ratio. This is near to what we find in the really bad years in central Europe in the 15th century. We have in Attica a ratio of 7 to 1, and of course in Mesopotamia under completely different circumstances we have 16, 20, or even 24 to 1.

Zaccagnini: As concerns Nuzi, the data that I have collected and commented on — also in comparison with other ancient and modern Near Eastern (and medieval European) sets of evidence — are entirely coherent with the overall framework of a predominant dry-farming set-up.

Renger: But when you told me about areas within the 400-m isohyet, it is good agricultural land and gets lots of rain at the right time. What I want to pursue is the relation between annual yield and the equivalent value given for a field. I calculated this for the Old Babylonian period in Mesopotamia, but I forget the exact figures right now. I think it is between 3 to 7 times the annual yield. You are talking about just one annual yield as the equivalent for a field given in Nuzi. The *tuppi mārūti* already could have a prehistory in the sense that the person giving up his field already is indebted to the person buying the field. In that case the apparent price does not reflect the loan money that already has been transferred, to say nothing of the interest that may have accrued. My point is that the one-to-one ratio is only part of the story. If you add the debt the seller has incurred, you may come up with a different ratio.

Zaccagnini: We have some bits of evidence that show the sequential connection between a loan (*hubullu*) that was not repaid and a subsequent new loan contract secured by a personal or real estate guarantee (*tidennutu*), which could eventually end with a definite sale contracted according to the legal format of an adoption (*mārūtu*). However, independently of the prehistory of each deed of land sale, which could obviously affect the final price paid by the purchaser, the patent overall situation of past and present economic difficulties, which eventually determines these sales, casts significant light on the recurrent phenomenon of low prices in ancient Near Eastern land transactions (including those of Egypt).

Levine: I think we are coming back to the same question: what factors account for these sales? What we would call a market sale is significant if we have information showing that the piece of land is worth so many crop years. It is another story, of course, if the land sale is really to satisfy some debt. We have a very encumbered economic situation. It is not like I won the lottery and had a lot of money and wanted to go out and buy some land.

For real estate today, we have estimates of how many years income equal the sales price. So if I am going to pay $300,000, I want it to pay for itself in eight years or whatever. Theoretically, yield is the key to almost everything. But there are so many gaps — and mitigating factors — in our documentation that it is hard to get an objective market fix.

I don't know whether the question really should be whether or not there is a market. The question is that in estimating the value, you need to have some kind of clear commercial standard of reference. What significance is there to say that this piece of land was sold for what it would yield in just one year? There must be a host of other factors that account for why the land was sold. These factors may have nothing to do with pure economic valuation.

I think this is one of the major problems that has been emerging from these discussions. The colloquium so far has been circling around this issue of our perspective, terminology, and definitions, and the evidence. But you are working with the direct evidence, which seems to tell us an astonishing thing that appears to make little business sense.

Are we talking about sale or purchase? Is the orientation of the document that of the purchaser or the seller? Who is making the statement in our documents? Why would somebody sell something as necessary as land for that kind of price? What are we not seeing here?

Harrison: In Britain over the last five years, hundreds of houses have been sold below their current market value. They were repossessed by financial institutions. Tell me what the difference is between that phenomenon in our modern market economy and what you are now describing. Your point is entirely legitimate, but it is not inconsistent with the concept of a market.

Zaccagnini: I accept your observation but do not agree with you about the feasibility of offering the same explanation for the recent episodes of low sale prices of houses experienced in Britain over the last five years, and the overall picture of low — and even more important, apparently "irrational" — prices that are recorded in ancient Near Eastern real estate sales. For reasons that I have already alluded to, the concept of a market — according to our modern viewpoint — does not seem to be at work, or perhaps only within a limited extent, in the sphere of real estate transactions. The sheer fact that we observe a short-term episode, or a long-term phenomenon of low prices in houses, estates, and land conveyances (respectively in modern Britain and in second/first-millennium northern Mesopotamia and Syria) does not rule out the possibility that substantially different economic and extra-economic mechanisms are at work, albeit yielding comparable final issues.

I will limit myself to Nuzi. There you find a few people who purchase great amounts of small, medium, and large plots of land and become owners of huge estates, scattered all over the country. They are absentee landlords: the agricultural activities were carried out by the resident farmers, former owners of the land and later on reduced to the state of tenants, after selling their family properties under the urge of personal economic difficulties. Similar cases are attested some 800 years later, at the end of the Assyrian empire.

Regardless of the fact that at Nuzi real estate transfers are concluded by resorting to the legal format of personal adoptions, what you have in either case are outright deeds of sale. However, in a broader perspective, and taking into account the socioeconomic setting of these land conveyances, we can perhaps attain further insights beyond the simple facts.

Harrison: It has been suggested that the seemingly anomalous range of prices contradicts the concept of a market, but I think you will find this to be the case throughout the entire historical record. Very small pieces are sold for large prices, and so on. Yet today in Britain, small pieces of farmland are sold for far more than larger pieces. That is consistent with your record in Nuzi.

The sale of land for an extremely high price to one's cousin is a bit of a puzzle and does not seem consistent with the idea of market relations. But relating it back to the idea of small tracts going for high prices, the fact is that if you want to sell a piece of land, who really wants it? The answer is, the person who lives closest to you. He may be over a barrel, for he can't get contiguous land anywhere else. If he wants to buy it he may have to pay three times more than someone on the other side of town. It is simply a case of there being what is called a seller's market.

Lamberg-Karlovsky: One of the problems here is that we really don't have a good idea of what the availability of land is. These are not large populations; the area is fairly underpopulated. What is happening to all that land? Who owns it, and what happens to it in the context of the land that is not owned?

When you are using England, you are using a land mass in which all the property is owned and there is a fairly dense population. But we are dealing with an epoch in which the population density relative to the availability of land is not known. There probably is an enormous amount of land that is ambiguous or not owned.

Harrison: Here in Russia, much land has little value because there are millions of acres up in Siberia. Why would someone in a village in Mesopotamia pay a higher price if there is so much free or unclaimed land? It has got to have been that the free land was either inaccessible or there wasn't any available. You would not rationally pay for land if you could get it for free.

Dandamayev: They paid a very high price in Neo-Babylonian times, according to my estimates.

Tideman: As someone who looks at anomalous data from time to time, when I see things as disparate as this it occurs to me that somebody might be lying. Could you comment on the possibility that even if the document has witnesses, maybe something else is going on. Maybe they are saving taxes or doing something else. Is there some personal motive that could be advanced by mistaking the actual price in the document.

Zaccagnini: Could there be any reason for reporting a lie? No, I can't think of any.

Stager: With regard to this business of selling to your cousin or other relative, in Biblical material there is the concept of the *go'el*. You sell to your relative in the hope that in better days you may get your property back. Is there any such institution that you can think of outside of that realm where this principle might be operative?

Zaccagnini: As far as I know, in the Syro-Mesopotamian cuneiform documentation there is no strictly comparable evidence of the *go'el* institution. Nevertheless, the traditional concept that family real estate property — at least in principle — should not be alienated is clearly attested. Suffice it to recall here the well-known case of Nuzi land sales, which take the form of an adoption, whereby the purchaser gets title to what he buys as an "inheritance share," bequeathed by his (fictitious) adoptant father (= the seller).

On the other hand, the recently published Emar archives provide highly interesting and as yet unparalleled evidence of real estate sales stipulated between members of one family group — brothers, in the first place.

Quite often the texts specify that the buyer has purchased a field (or a house, a garden, or whatever other portion of immovable property) "as an alien" (*kî/kîma nakiri*). The obvious implication of this formulaic device is that the transaction is not subject to the customary principles that rule the matter of transfers of family land, whatever these might have been in the 13th-century-BC city of Emar.

Renger: Some court procedures in Nuzi tell us that two generations after fields were acquired by Tehiptilla and others — by means of sale-adoption and under pressure — they had to be returned to the original owner or holder of the field in question.

Zaccagnini: Whatever piece of textual evidence you may allude to, I believe that the socioeconomic background and the legal/procedural mechanisms of Late Bronze Age private land alienations in Upper Mesopotamia and Syria are sufficiently clear and should no longer represent a matter of controversial disussion.

NOTES

1. This paper is a result of the research project "Political institutions and economic structures in the ancient world" that I have directed at the University of Bologna, and later on at the Istituto Universitario Orientale of Naples, with the financial support of the Italian Ministry of Universities.

2. E. Wirth, *Agrargeographie des Irak* (Hamburg 1962), Abb. 7, before p. 13; E. Guest, *Flora of Iraq*, I (Baghdad 1966), fig. 5, facing p. 12 and fig. 6, pp. 14-15.

3. Cf. A. de Maigret, "Il fattore idrologico nell'economia di Ebla," *OA* 20 (1981):1-36. Cf. E. Wirth, *Syrien. Eine Geographische Landeskunde* (Darmstadt 1971), Karten 3-4.

4. See provisionally N. Bellotto, "The Emar Fields," in *Proceedings of the XLIV R.A.I.* (Venice 1997), in press.

5. C. Zaccagnini, "The Yield of the Fields at Nuzi," *OA* 14 (1975):181-225; further comments in *id.*, "The Price of the Fields at Nuzi," *JESHO* 22 (1979):1-31; see further *id.*, "Again on the Yield of the Fields at Nuzi," *BSA* 5 (1990):201-217. For a different opinion see G. Dosch, *Zur Struktur der Gesellschaft des Königreichs Arraphe* (Heidelberg 1993), esp. 139-144; most recently G. G. W. Müller, *Studien zur Siedlungsgeographie und Bevölkerung des Osttigrisgebietes* (Heidelberg 1994), esp. 228-234.

6. Cf. the short remarks of J. N. Postgate, "The Ownership and Exploitation of Land in Assyria in the first Millennium BC," in *Mélanges A. Finet* (Leuven 1989):141-152, esp. 151 with n. 112 [= "Grundeigentum und Nutzung von Land in Assyria," in *Jahrbuch für Wirtschaftsgeschichte*, Sonderband 1987 (Berlin 1988):89-110].

7. J. N. Postgate, review of H. Freydank, *Mittelassyrische Rechtsurkunden und Verwaltungstexte* II (Berlin 1982), *Orientalia* 59 (1990):83-85, esp. 84f.

8. See *e.g.*, the lengthy article of M. Powell, "Masse und Gewichte," in *RlA* 7, (Berlin-New York, 1987-1990):457-517.

9. The lower figures that I indicated in *OA* 14 (1975), esp. 194, were based on an *imēru* surface measure reckoned at 18,000 m²; this view has been later modified in my "Notes on the Nuzi Surface Measures," *UF* 11 (1979):849-856. Based on a comparative analysis of the data referring to third-millennium archives of Gasur (the later Nuzi), I was led to conclude that the surface of one *imēru* was c. 11,000 m², *i.e.*, slightly above 1 hectare. This view has been provisionally, and tentatively, accepted by scholars concerned with the Middle and Neo-Assyrian evidence (J. N. Postgate, in the first place).

10. L. Milano, "Barley for Rations and Barley for Sowing (ARET II 51 and Related Matters)," *ASJ* 9 (1987):177-201, esp. 189-192; later on, the author has partially modified his view: "Ebla: gestion des terres et gestion des ressources alimentaires," in *Amurru* 1 (Paris 1996):137-171, esp. 140f, with previous bibliography.

11. A. Archi, *Five Tablets from the Southern Wing of Palace G-Ebla* (= Syro-Mesopotamian Studies, 5/2) (Malibu 1993):8-18 (text no. 2); cf. G. Biga's review in *JAOS* 115 (1995):297f; cf. most recently P. Steinkeller's contribution in this volume.

12. Milano, *ASJ* 9 (1987):192.

13. Milano, *Amurru* 1:137-141.

14. *Ibid.*, pp. 140-141, n. 49.

15. Archi, *Five Tablets*, esp. 12-14.

16. Both entries concern landed property and cereal incomes, presumably deriving from the same land, that are attributed to the prince Idanekimu.

17. Archi, *Five Tablets*, 13-14.

18. Further note that 1 liter of barley — *i.e.*, in round approximation, 1 sìla — is no more than 0.8 kg and possibly even less.

19. J. Renger, "Überlegungen zur räumlichen Ausdehnung des Staates von Ebla an Hand der agrarischen und viehwirtschaftlichen Gegebenheiten," in L. Cagni (ed.), *Ebla 1975-1985* (Napoli 1987):293-311. According to Renger (*ibid.*:304f, n. 4), 1 liter of barley corresponds to 0.6 kg.

20. For the sake of simplicity I have accepted the recurrent reckoning of 1 sìla at 1 liter: figures listed above are slightly different from those reckoned by B. Lafont, *ARM* XXIII:321.

21. Not to speak of *ARM* XXIII 69, most recently commented on by M. Luciani: *NABU* 1997/25:24-25.

22. M. Liverani, "Economia delle fattorie palatine ugaritiche," *Dialoghi di archeologia*, NS 1/2 (1979):57-72, esp. 59f; later on republished in C. Zaccagnini (ed.), *Production and Consumption in the Ancient Near East* (Budapest 1989):127-168, esp. 130-132.

23. The average size of ancient Near Eastern family groups was plausibly six units (*i.e.*, an adult married couple, an old man/woman and three children): cf. Renger, *Überlegungen* (n. 19):304, with quote of previous literature.

24. C. Zaccagnini, *The Rural Landscape of of the Land of Arraphe* (Roma 1979):164-201 (Appendix II).

25. R. McC. Adams, RSO 54 (1980): 381-388, esp. 385-386.

26. See in the first place the Chicago texts *JEN* VII published by M. P. Maidman, *Joint Expedition with the Iraq Museum at Nuzi, VII. Miscellaneous Texts* (= Studies on the Civilization and Culture of Nuzi and the Hurrians [SCCNH] 3) (Winona Lake, IN 1989) (catalogue and cuneiform copies): cf., among other reviews, C. Zaccagnini: *AfO* 38-39 (1991-92):174-179 and J. Fincke: *WO* 23 (1992):165-167; M. P. Maidman, *Two Hundred Nuzi Texts from the Oriental Institute of the University of Chicago* I (= *SCCNH* 6) (Bethesda, MD 1994) (transliteration, translation and commentary of 100 of the former 200 tablets). See further the 529 texts housed at the Harvard Semitic Museum, which have been catalogued and published according to Lacheman's cuneiform copies and partially commented on by M. A. Morrison and D. I. Owen in *SCCNH* 2 (Winona Lake, IN 1987):357-702; *SCCNH* 4 (Winona Lake, IN 1993); *SCCNH* 5 (Winona Lake, IN 1995):87-357.

27. Cf. Zaccagnini, *OA* 14 (1975):205-207; *JESHO* 22 (1979):4-6; cf. *BSA* 5 (1990):205-206.

28. The amount of barley has been tentatively reckoned on the basis of the Nuzi rations for slave male and female adults, and for childs and maids (cf. briefly G. Wilhelm, Das Archiv des *Šilwa-Teššup*, 2 (Wiesbaden 1980):22. Considerably higher figures (*i.e.*, 2,160 liters per year, for a 5-person family) have been elaborated by Renger, *Überlegungen* 304-305, on the basis of the ancient Mesopotamian ration system, as reconstructed by I. J. Gelb, *JNES* 24 (1965):230-243. It is quite evident that we are faced with enormous discrepancies, which are hardly to be reconciled: as far as I can judge, additional comparative evidence with other systems of grain alimentary rations (*e.g.*, those which were distributed to the Roman citizens in the early imperial period) does not help.

29. Milano, *ASJ* 9 (1987):191; *id.*, in *Amurru* 1:139.

30. For which cf. also J. N. Postgate, *Fifty Neo-Assyrian Legal Documents* (Warminster 1976):67-72.

31. In *Mélanges A. Finet*:151.

32. *Ibid.*:151, n. 112.

33. It seems appropriate to recall here the well-known boast of Ashurbanipal, who reported that "Adad sent down his rains for me; Ea released his ground water for me. Barley grew 5 cubits [= c. 2.5 m] in its furrow, the ear reached $5/6$ cubit in length [= c. 25 cm]. The grassland consistently produced heavy

harvests, luxuriant crops": A. C. Piepkorn, *Historical Prism Inscriptions of Ashurbanipal* I (Chicago 1933):28-31: I 27-31.

34. In this regard I refer to Postgate's tentative reckonings, based on the Middle Assyrian text VS 21, n. 23: Obv. 1-20 (*Orientalia* 59 [1990]:84-85).

35. Postgate, *Mélanges A. Finet*:151.

36. S. Parpola, *Letters from Assyrian and Babylonian Scholars* (=SAA X) (Helsinki 1993) no. 173: cf. Postgate, in *Mélanges A. Finet*:151, with n. 113. Just out of curiosity, I quote here the evidence of a fragmentary Nimrud letter written some 30-40 years earlier: in it, an Assyrian official announces the highly favourable results achieved in the last harvest of crown-land and underscores the overall propitious copper:barley exchange rates throughout the country: the district of Halahhu is explicitly mentioned as a paramount example of the optimal "market" trend (I have recently dealt with this letter in "Price and Price Formation in the Ancient Near East. A Methodological Approach", in *Prix et formation des prix dans les Économies antiques* [Saint-Bertrand-de-Comminges 1997]:374-375, and expressed doubts on the reliability of the figures recorded therein).

37. A preliminary tabulation of data, which only includes those instances in which both field surfaces and sale prices are recorded or preserved, was quite recently arranged by F. M. Fales, "Prices in Neo-Assyrian Sources," *SAAB* 10 (1996 [=1997]):11-53. I was unable to consult the extensive work of K. Radner, *Die neuassyrischen Privaturkunden* (Helsinki 1997), which appeared when this article was already in print.

38. This view was expressed by R. McC. Adams, *RSO* 54 (1980):386, with reference to the dimensions of the Nuzi fields, as attested in real estate transactions.

39. "Reconstructing the Rural Landscape of the Ancient Near East," *JESHO* 39 (1996):1-41, esp. 32f.

40. Land bequests to family members, especially occurring from the mid-second millennium, are the patent issue of a notable change in the traditional inheritance mechanisms, which were previously patterned according to the customary laws of family and kinship structures. More precisely, what comes to the fore is a non-infrequent deviation from the automatic privileged rights of succession in favor of the first (male) borne.

41. Cf. R. Beich, *Nuzu Last Wills and Testaments*, Ph.D. diss., Brandeis University 1963; J. S. Paradise, *Nuzi Inheritance Practices*, Ph.D. diss., University of Pennsylvania 1972.

42. An almost identical formulation is exhibited by the Emar wills.

43. See *e.g., HSS* XIX 2: 2-11; 12: 7-10.

44. See briefly, among others, C. Zaccagnini, "Osservazioni sui contratti di 'anticresi' a Nuzi," *OA* 15 (1976):191-207; *id.*, "Land Tenure and Transfer of Land at Nuzi (XV-XIV Century BC)," in T. Khalidi (ed.), *Land Tenure and Social Transformation in the Middle East* (Beirut 1984):79-94; *id.*, "Proprietà fondiaria e dipendenza rurale nella Mesopotamia settentrionale (XV-XIV secolo a.C.)," *Studi Storici* 25 (1984):697-723.

45. See *e.g.,* C. Zaccagnini, "Asiatic Mode of Production and Ancient Near East. Notes Toward a Discussion," in *id.* (ed.), *Production and Consumption*, 56-98 ("Transfers of villages"); M. P. Maidman, *A Socio-Economic Analysis of a Nuzi Family Archive*, Ph.D. diss., University of Pennsylvania 1976; L. Kataja and R. Whiting, *Grants. Decrees and Gifts of the Neo-Assyrian Period* (= SAA XII) (Helsinki 1995):esp. 1-45 ("Royal Grants of Land or Tax Exemption to Individuals or Temples"); F. M. Fales, "The Assyrian Village of Bit Abu-Ila'a," in C. Zaccagnini (ed.), *Production and Consumption*:169-200.

46. Maidman, *A Socio-Economic Analysis*, 205-206.

47. *HSS* XIII 417; cf. *HSS* IX 24.

48. T. Kwasman and S. Parpola, *Legal Transactions of the Royal Court of Nineveh*, Part I (= SAA VI), (Helsinki 1991), no. 287.

10

Sellers and Buyers of Urban Real Estate in Southern Mesopotamia at the Beginning of the Second Millennium BC

Nelli V. Kozyreva
Oriental Institute, St. Petersburg

In studying the sale of urban real estate and other landed property in ancient Mesopotamia, the central questions concern the identity of the sellers and buyers and the position they occupied in the city's hierarchy. What was their social status? What were their ethnic roots?

At the end of the third millennium BC, most Mesopotamian cities were exposed to severe shock resulting from the disintegration of the Ur III kingdom. After an extended chain of military and natural catastrophies, many cities were partly or completely destroyed and their population scattered. Eridu, Kish, Shuruppak, and some other cities never recovered. Other towns gradually were rebuilt, and indeed their urban areas were considerably extended. In the first half of the second millennium the built-up urban areas of some cities reached the largest size they would achieve for the entire period extending from the mid-third millennium BC down through Hellenistic times. Archaeological data show that the residential districts of Eshnunna, for instance, extended far beyond the city walls (Postgate 1992:76), while Ur spread to an area covering 60 ha. (Van De Mieroop 1992:7), considerably more than its size before or after the Old Babylonian period.

The Amorite dynasties who came to power throughout most of Mesopotamia at this time played an important role in restoring the devastated cities and attracting back a large part of their populations. Royal inscriptions announce that many Amorite rulers built new palaces and restored city temples that had been destroyed. They are said to have gathered the urban inhabitants who had been scattered by the warfare and returned them to their former dwellings.

Apart from returning the indigenous population to the cities, these kings also brought their fellow Amorite tribesmen into urban life. The List of Amorites published by I. Gelb (1968), for instance, states that thirty representatives of noble Amorite families were allowed to settle in Eshnunna. The names of the suburbs of Sippar in this period (Sippar Amnanum, Sippar-Jahrurum) confirm this trend.

A distinctive feature of the Old Babylonian textual record is the sharp increase in the number of private documents, whereas the Ur III record consists almost entirely of administrative documents. About eight hundred contracts documenting the sale of real estate (fields, orchards, and houses) are known from the Old Babylonian period (Renger 1994:186), not taking into account the divisions of family property and various other types of legal records relating to real estate. Most of these records concern urban real estate, that is, houses and plots within the city areas of southern Mesopotamia.

There are two ways to identify the parties to such transactions: prosopography and the seal impressions that appear on most private documents.

A study of the proper names that appear in the Old Babylonian real estate documents shows no correlation between the names of Sumerians, Akkadians, and (as we can call them) "strangers" within the proportion of the different ethnic groups who inhabited the cities. The analysis of proper names made for Sippar by Rivkah Harris (1972) and the similar analysis by Elizabeth Stone (1987:63) for Nippur show that most of the new urban dwellers gave their children traditional local names, presumably to ease their assimilation into the native population. This explains why the proportion of proper names that are alien or not customary for these cities decreased sharply during the second or third generations of the newcomers.

This obliges us to be careful in using proper names to determine the social and ethnic affiliation of the parties to real estate transactions. Nonetheless, a study of proper names shows that in many cases the vendors and buyers of urban real estate came from the local areas, and in some cases we even can trace direct family connections between sellers and buyers.

Even better is the extensive information that appears on seal inscriptions on private documents. Seal impressions were made by the direct parties to the transactions, witnesses, and other individuals who had an interest in the real estate being transferred. About half of the surviving documents have such seal impressions.

I have analyzed some 1,200 seal inscriptions from this period and find that more than half represent an inscription on which the seal's owner calls himself by his father's name and also calls himself the slave of some god. The owners of seals with such inscriptions represent probably the most active group of the city population.

The names of the gods mentioned in these inscriptions may be ranked in order of the frequency with which they appear on real estate documents. These gods evidently were the most honored group among this population. The list thus represents a kind of artificial pantheon for this group of city inhabitants. If we compare this list with the traditional lists of the main Mesopotamian gods and with the official city pantheons known to us, we find some essential differences between them.

First among the gods honored by the owners of seals is Amurru. His name appears in some 30 percent (nearly a third) of the cases. Second on this list is the goddess Ninsiana (12 percent, that is, about an eighth of the cases). Third place belongs to the god Sin, one of Mesopotamia's two major astral gods. However, he is never mentioned alone. His name is always coupled with that of some other god, usually with Amurru. The name of Sin is mentioned alone only in 3 percent of the cases. Shamash, the second major astral god, appears yet more rarely.

Ranking the gods according to the frequency of their mention in seal inscriptions, we obtain the following list:

Amurru
Ninsiana
Sin (paired with another god, usually Amurru)
Adad/Ishkur
Ninshubur
Nergal
Enki
Nabu
Sin
Shamash

Over thirty other gods are mentioned in seal inscriptions, but the relatively rare occurrence of their names suggests that they were probably the family gods of the seal owners.

My analysis of seal inscriptions thus shows that for most of southern Mesopotamia's urban population intensively engaged in private activity — and particularly in urban real estate transactions — the family god was the West Semitic deity Amurru.

It seems logical to conclude that a considerable proportion of urban real estate buyers were the people who had moved into the cities rather recently, *i.e.*, newcomers or their descendants. But as noted earlier, in many cases the seller of urban real estate also came from the same surroundings. We thus may infer that a considerable number of transactions involving urban real estate were concluded within a limited, restricted circle of the city population. For many of these people, their family god was Amurru, the main god of the Amorites, who most recently had migrated into the urban areas of southern Mesopotamia.

In some cases the new inhabitants probably were presented with large plots of urban land by the kings. Some evidence for this comes from Eshnunna and Larsa. Later, the process of redistributing urban plots took place inside these family groups. The newcomers seemingly tried to attract their relatives and tribesmen to the city life, selling them small urban plots.

This activity can be traced in private contracts, whose volume increases sharply in this period. The principal aim for many of these transactions (judging by the tiny sizes of the real estate being bought) was an attempt to achieve a certain place in the urban hierarchy, or at least to assume the legal status of city dweller so as to become a full and equal member of the city community. One of the fundamental conditions of assuming such rights was probably the owning of urban real estate.

Analysing the names of the contractual parties and their seal inscriptions permits us to draw the following conclusions:

1. Transactions concerning urban real estate took place almost exclusively within a narrow circle of families or neighborhoods.

2. Most of the people involved in this process were representatives of the new city population.

3. Urban real estate transactions appear hardly to have touched the indigenous population and their traditional economic structures.

In conclusion, I find that the sale of urban real estate in southern Mesopotamia in the Old Babylonian period presents a phenomenon that is not only economic but also social. This process reflected the political and demographic changes that took place in this region in the first half of the second millennium. This assumption bears out what Karl Polanyi stressed: economic processes and behavior in preindustrial economies were embedded in social relationships and were influenced by socially determined behavior (Renger 1994:204).

Hudson: There must have been some mechanism for determining sales prices for urban property, unless they were determined in a random and arbitrary manner.

Kozyreva: It is difficult to answer that. I don't think anyone knows. Prices of course were dependent on economic factors, but they seem to have no commercial features and no features of profit. My supposition is that the prices of urban plots, such as fields and orchards, were connected in some way with what could be got from the plot of the same area. I cannot cite evidence for this idea.

Renger: I think your paper was an important contribution in that we always wonder who was permitted to live in a city. We know from the European middle ages that you couldn't just move into a city, buy a house, and settle down. There were severe restrictions, because being a member of a town community gave you some exclusive rights, such as freedom from taxes or whatever. The question in ancient Mesopotamia is who was permitted to live in a city, because it had to do with social statutes.

Leo Oppenheim had a hypothesis derived from the sales contracts of urban real estate in Sippar, in the north. When a *naditu* sold her house or an urban plot, she retained an *ezibtu*, a leftover of very small size. His idea was that this small piece of urban land was her retainer so that she could remain a citizen. As long as she had this, she had the right to remain a citizen of Sippar. Whether this hypothesis is true or not, it is an interesting idea. What you told us is that you have newcomers from the new wave of Semitic tribal elements. They move into the cities and take up residence there apparently by force. I think this is something interesting to follow up.

Kozyreva: In my opinion just the members of the city community were the most free and privileged part of the population. And it was the result of their position as members of the temple personnel of city gods. This was the right that gave them the possibility to live in the city, to use all the privileges and to have a claim on city ground. The newcomers tried to become members of that community by becoming temple personnel. I think they found their place in the city hierarchy by becoming the personnel of the junior gods of the city pantheon.

Levine: This question points up a problem. From my perspective it is somewhat loaded. You are already assuming a market. You are assuming that prices could be set on some basis. You have estimated or expected crop yields, how much the taxes on them are, and so forth. In the case of agricultural and horticultural production you have a series of fairly regulated ways of estimating how much a field was worth. But urban land has many factors that intervene in what we would call "the market."

Take for example the institutional connections. Our apartment in NYU is worth two and a half times what we would pay on the open market, because it is tax free as long as I am a member of the university. It is subsidized. Multiply that by ten times and you get a picture of one of these ancient Mesopotamian towns. There are so many institutional privilege factors that it would make it very difficult to answer the questions that Michael has posed about finding some systematic or rational pattern to real estate prices.

Is there a way of knowing what these plots are worth? Do they become more valuable over time? Do people ever buy or sell these plots in a distinctly speculative manner? That question would have to be modified. How different it is when you think about the modern city, where there are more factors that enter into assessing the value of a piece of real estate. If you intend to buy a house, you get an assessment because you are going to get a mortgage from a bank. The bank has a list of fairly objective criteria to determine what a building is worth. In modern times you have a complex of factors that tell you what a piece of property is worth. This probably is a universal methodological problem.

Kozyreva: We must resolve this problem from the vantage point of ancient economies rather than to try to explain them from the modern economic point of view. Preindustrial economies are very different from modern economies. Unfortunately we often try to find in preindustrial economies the features we know in our own lives from our modern economy problems.

Lamberg-Karlovsky: This distinction is obviously a basic theme of this colloquium. I think that most of us believe that the ancient economy is somewhat different, as opposed to those who want to see the ancient economy as analogous to ours, in the same way as there are biological homologies that should not be confused with analogies.

Renger: To continue with regard to two things that Baruch said. My first comment regards real estate, or the sale or alienation of real estate at least in some cities of southern Mesopotamia, Ur and Kutalla. It seems to be regulated, or even restricted. This we may deduce from the fact that records of sale for urban real estate mention an official, a *kakikkum* in Ur and other places, who is always among those witnessing the sale of urban real estate, and in Kutalla we have a *rabi sikkatim*, the "big one of the stick" (or peg), besides the *rabianum*, the head of the city administration. I think this would also probably reflect then on the question of what prices are charged, because there is a restriction on who and how urban real estate can be alienated.

I remember two examples. In a 20th-century Laotian peasant community, we observe that rental fees reflect not only fertility of the soil, but also kinship relations. The closer the kinship relation, the higher the rent. The farther you are removed from the landlords or whatever, the lower the rent. In 18th-century Italian villages you have fields that are sold, and again the price becomes higher the closer you are related to the seller, and lower the more distant you are. Someone from the city, not at all related to a seller in a town, would get a lower price. This shows the completely different motivations, attitudes, and aspects in prices governing these contracts.

Stager: I was wondering whether you detect a preference for kin or relations in this circle of purchasers. In other words, if you had to alienate your property, you allowed the first redemption for the closer kin. Is that relevant?

Kozyreva: I think that the circle of vendors and buyers of urban real estate was very much restricted because the indigenous population of the city probably had no need of such transactions. In most parts this process occurred among the newcomers only. It was rather difficult, I think, for the stranger to become an equal city dweller. If a family had such an opportunity, it tried to attract its relatives and tribesmen to the city dwelling also. The opportunity to sell urban real estate existed, but was very much restricted. The transactions of such kind had to be witnessed by special officials. The price of different kinds of urban real estate was strictly determined by the law (Michalowski and Walker 1989). The price of one measure (1 sar) of a house plot, for instance, was 1 shekel of silver.

Van De Mieroop: It seems to me that evidence that you use in your paper is rather contradictory. You say on the one hand that the Amorites abandoned their names very soon to take up traditional Sumerian and Babylonian names. On the other hand, you suggest that the god Amurru is the most popular god in the seal inscriptions, so that they did not abandon their devotion to him on their seal patterns, but they were willing to abandon their name patterns.

Kozyreva: I think we can overcome this contradiction by remembering the difference between the official cult and popular religions in Ancient Mesopotamia. It was very important for the newcomers to take their own position in the city hierarchy and to turn over this position to their children who had to become equal city dwellers. And that is why they named their children after the main city god. In their family life they probably tried to keep their Amorite roots and honored their family gods. The seal inscription reflected just this side of their life.

Van De Mieroop: Dandamayev has written that in the Neo-Babylonian period you believe there was no racial hatred. But isn't the fact that people are so anxious to abandon their own names an indication of the opposite?

Dandamayev: They did not abandon their religion, but living in another ethnic background, they could readily adapt themselves to local life. Of course, in the second and third generations people of various ethnic backgrounds gradually adopted local customs, local religion, and so on.

Levine: In every age you have the problem of the onomasticon. You have theophoric names and the problem of how significant they are. I've been studying them in different connections. We don't know in every case why people want to hold onto some sense of origin, or at least the name. I also have discovered a discrepancy in the invocation in the name of the national god, particularly in the Ammonite onomastic of the seventh century BCE. You don't find the name of the national god *milkom* mentioned in personal names more than two or three times. Forty-six of a hundred and some names are *el* names. The rest are all kinds of different names. And yet when you are invoking god in some prayer or worship or blessing, you do use the name of the national god. It seems to me that there are so many different factors that account for the selection of names that it is hard to say. There are too many motivations we not privy to.

My general impression is that there are different agendas. There is a basic difference between a prayer cult inscription referring to dynastic gods and national gods and so forth, where there is much more reason to honor the god. I don't think it is necessarily a contradiction. It is a question of what context they are used in.

BIBLIOGRAPHY

Gelb, Ignace J. (1968), "An Old Babylonian List of Amorites," *JAOS* 88:39-46.

Harris, Rivkah (1972), "Notes on the Nomenclaure of Old Babylonian Sippar," *JCS* 24:102-104.

Michalowski, P., and C. B. J. Walker (1989), "A New Sumerian 'Law Code,'" in *Studies in Honor of Ake W. Sjöberg* (Philadelphia):389-395.

Postgate, (1992), *Early Mesopotamian Society and Economy at the Dawn of History* (London and New York).

Renger, Johannes (1994), "On Economic Structures in Ancient Mesopotamia," *Orientalia* 18:157-208.

Stone, Elizabeth (1987), *Nippur Neighborhoods* (Chicago).

Van De Mieroop, Marc (1992), *Society and Enterprise in Old Babylonian Ur* (Berlin).

11

Land Use in the Sippar Region
During the Neo-Babylonian and Achaemenid Periods

Muhammed A. Dandamayev
Oriental Institute, St. Petersburg

The city was the most important and perhaps the most stable institution of the Mesopotamian social structure. Although cuneiform texts frequently mention pastoral regions as the opposite of the city, the inhabitants of Mesopotamia (and apparently also other parts of the Ancient Near East) did not distinguish between city and village. The Akkadian designation of the city was *ālu* (always written URU), a term that denoted almost any dwelling place, a village as well as a city.

What was of decisive importance was the city's political and cultural role, not its size or population. An alu signified any permanent settlement consisting of houses built of bricks, as long as it constituted a certain administrative unity.[1] In Neo-Babylonian and Achaemenid times, small cities in Babylonia were from 9.6 to 22.5 hectares and large cities from 22.6 to 60 hectares. Some 32 percent of the inhabited area was occupied by small cities (see Brinkman 1969:347).

In antiquity the city dominated the countryside, but the urban population itself was chiefly engaged in agriculture. Indeed, fields, orchards, and pastures were located within the city as well as outside. Land beyond the city walls was considered a continuation of the urban territory and was under the jurisdiction of the city's authorities. Rural areas adjoined the city extending in all directions for up to 5 or 6 km, and their land was tilled mainly by people who lived within the city walls. The cities thus were agricultural as well as handicraft centers.

According to Curtius Rufus (5.1, 25-27), Babylon encompassed 365 stadia (obviously a calendrical number). Domestic structures extended over only 80 stadia (1 stadium = c. 185 meters), while the remaining area was sown or covered by gardens. Cuneiform texts mention fields "located in the middle of the city." Thus, a document drafted in 618 BC records the sale of a field (*eqlu*) located "in the inner part (*qerbu*) of Babylon (BE 8 7:2). Another document, drafted in Babylon c. 592 BC, states that a field situated "in the middle of the city"[2] of Uruk was given as a dowry for a bride.

Usually the city consisted of temples, the royal palace or the residence of the governor, and houses of citizens located inside the walls. Each city had several gates. Cities on the coasts of rivers had harbor ports where various transactions were made.

From the earliest periods, legally equal citizens typically met in popular assemblies at the main temple of Babylonian cities. These communities of citizens probably were made up originally of owners of landed property, *i.e.*, fields and gardens (Oppenheim 1977:113). But as Oppenheim has noted (1985:579, n. 4), the social and administrative structure of Mesopotamian cities remains unknown to us to a considerable degree. We do not even know the population of individual cities. As to rural regions, situated far away from cities and inhabited by various groups of dependent population, the structure of self-government did not spread to them.

The Babylonian temples were centers of social as well as religious life. A city's main temple was located on a high terrace and was considered the house of its principal deity. Its administrative apparatus consisted of civil servants who performed no sacral functions, which were carried out by professional priests.

During Neo-Babylonian times, the development of technology, crafts, and market relations led to the more intensive building of cities as administrative, hand-work, and cultural centers. It was above all during the reign of Nebuchadnezzar II that the city of Babylon as it is known to us was built up intensively. A rectangle of about 404 hectares, comprising more than a quarter-million inhabitants, the city had eight gates to streets, some as wide as five meters or more. Most houses had two stories. Those of the poor were about 30 square meters, while the wealthy had houses up to 1,600 square meters (Reuther 1926:96-105, 120ff.).

The substantial growth of Babylon's population required imports of food and other commodities, which were supplied by businessmen. One was Iddina-Marduk, son of Iqishaja, descendant of Nur-Sin, whose transactions are recorded in about four hundred documents drafted during the period from 557 to 517 BC. His agents bought large amounts of garlic, barley, and dates from suburbs of Babylon and other rural areas, transferring these products to Babylon by canals, where they were sold. He also traded in livestock and wool (Wunsch 1993: I:19-61).

During the period under consideration, two towns can be designated as temple cities: Uruk and Sippar. Of the two cities named Sippar that are attested to in economic and legal documents, Sippar of the goddess Anunitu (the site of Tell ed-Dêr) did not play much of a role at that time (see Joannès 1988:74, 77), and from which we have only a limited number of Neo-Babylonian documents; and Sippar of Shamash (the site Abu-Habba), designated as Great Sippar,[3] and from which come the Ebabbara archives. (According to VS 6 87, drafted in Sippar in 541, a slave woman by the name Bissa borrowed ten (?) empty vats and was obligated to return them in "Great Sippar.")

Extensive documentary evidence is provided by the archives of the Eanna temple in Uruk, dedicated to the goddess Ishtar, and Ebabbara in Sippar, temple of the sun god Shamash. Unfortunately, our information about private households in these cities is very limited, although most information from other cities comes from private archives. This presents many difficulties in our attempt to create a comprehensive picture of the Neo-Babylonian city, and perhaps the perceived difference between temple cities and the others reflects the character of our sources. Nevertheless, in contrast to other Neo-Babylonian temples (including even Esagila in Babylon, temple of Marduk, the supreme state deity), Eanna and Ebabbara possessed exceptionally large proportions of land and other property.

Both sanctuaries were economic centers for their respective cities and their rural regions. For instance, Uruk's Eanna temple possessed hundreds of slaves and also engaged in business operations and domestic and international trade. This temple also owned great herds of cattle and sheep and a large number of fowl. Specifically, its 12,923 *kur* (c. 16,000 hectares) of land (Jursa 1995:194) supported from 5,000 to 7,000 head of cattle and 100,000 to 150,000 head of sheep and goats (San Nicolò 1948:285).

In this article I shall try to trace the main outlines of economic activities in Neo-Babylonian cities based mainly on documents from Sippar, but also using evidence from other towns. At present, more than 5,000 economic, administrative, and legal documents from the end of the seventh century through c. 475 BC have been published from Sippar. The overwhelming majority come from the Ebabbara archives.

Sippar was one of the ancient centers of Babylonian culture and preserved this role during the first millennium BC. In particular, a Neo-Babylonian library was discovered at Sippar's Ebabbara temple. The tablets were found in good condition, still arranged in a small room on clay shelves. According to a preliminary estimate, about 2,000 tablets were stored there, including hymns, myths, omens, and astronomical, mathematical, and historical texts, as well as copies of earlier royal inscriptions (see al-Jadir 1987:18 ff.).

The Ebabbara temple comprised three sanctuaries: one of Shamash, Sippar's titulary god; the shrine of his wife Aya; and the chapel of Bunene, his vizier. Topographical texts contain the measurements of their cellae, including a gateway of Shamash's cella at 15 meters high (George 1992: 215-219).

The structure of the Ebabbara administration differed from that of other Babylonian temples, whose chief administrators bore the title *šatammu*. The Ebabbara was headed by the Priest (*šangû*) of Sippar, the most important administrative official of the temple. Despite his title, he did not carry any specific cultic functions. At the same time he seems to have been the governor of Sippar (cf. MacGinnis 1995:114-116). In this position he presided over the royal tribunal and decided various private litigations (see Cyr. 328; Camb. 412, etc.).

Second place in the Ebabbara administration belonged to the *qīpu*, whose primary function was to represent the interests of the king in the temple. He received important instructions from the king and was in command of the soldiers settled in Sippar. He was also in charge of the temple workers sent to carry out *corvée* service for the king (see MacGinnis 1995:117f.).

In Sippar, as well as in other privileged Neo-Babylonian cities, important issues of a local nature were solved by the elders (*šibūtu*) and citizens (*mār-banê*) — mainly property litigations between individuals (Camb. 412; CT 55 113; Cyr. 271, 328, etc.) and other judicial decisions regarding property matters (CT 2 2; Cyr. 281, etc.).

The role of the Ebabbara temple in the economy of Sippar and its region was great. First of all, it had a large working staff. Its agricultural staff consisted of temple farmers and gardeners. Lists have been preserved that contain the names of about 120 able-bodied temple farmers (*ikkarus*). There were also about 60 gardeners and orchard keepers. The temple could cultivate only about one-third of its land with its own farmers; and therefore had to lease two-thirds of it to tenants (*errēšus*). They did not belong to the temple personnel but worked for a specific amount of the harvest.

The exploitation of the lands belonging to Ebabbara was to a considerable extent dependent upon an institution headed by officials who bore the titles *rab/bēl sūti*. They were rent collectors, who leased large tracts of land for which the amount of rent was established at the drawing up of the contract. The temple also supplied rent farmers with *ikkarus*, implements, and livestock.

The first rent collector in Sippar was appointed by king Nabonidus himself and acted in his post during the years 557-539. Nabonidus leased him practically all of the date palm groves belonging to Ebabbara for 10,000 *kur* (18,000 hl or 1,350,000 kg) of dates a year to be paid to the temple. As seen from other texts, this amount constituted approximately the whole annual income of Ebabbara in dates. As to the grain fields, under Nabonidus they remained in the hands of the temple farmers and tenants. During his reign, they delivered 5,000 *kur* (9,000 hl or 558,000 kg) of barley a year to the temple. Later, under the Achaemenid kings, grain fields were also at the disposal of rent collectors (see Jursa 1995:85ff.).

Barley was the most widely cultivated grain. Many documents, however, state that land was leased to convert the grain fields into date palm groves. Thus, an intensive use of land was typical of the Ebabbara temple, which possessed approximately 330-430 *kur* (412.5-537.5 hectares) of date palm plantations, and about 1,000 *kur* (1,250 hectares) of grain fields, part of which lay fallow (see Jursa 1995:192f.).

One of the storehouses of Ebabbara was located in the harbor of Sippar where barley and dates were brought via the Euphrates and, at least one more storeroom was located in the center of the city.[4] In the same center, some livestock sheds and fowl runs also were located (see Jursa 1995:4, with references).

Letters from Ebabbara archives contain orders to issue barley, dates, and vegetable oil from temple granaries as rations to temple slaves and wages to artisans and officials. A considerable number of texts record the issue of cattle, sheep, ducks, and fish for offerings to gods.

In addition to farmers and gardeners, the temple personnel consisted of weavers, bleachers, porters, ironsmiths, coppersmiths, carpenters, jewelers, leatherworkers, architects, beer brewers, bakers, shepherds, bird feeders, etc. Ebabbara had on its permanent staff at least 125 skilled craftsmen (see MacGinnis 1995:160). Taking into account all available data, the temple personnel consisted of approximately 1,000 individuals. In addition, the temple also used other skilled artisans, even hiring them from other cities, including Babylon. One single text mentions 123 hired laborers who worked for the Ebabbara temple (CT 56 665). Besides, some artisans worked within specified periods of time for an income (prebend), which was paid only to persons who had the right to enter the inner sanctuary of the temple and perform duties mainly relating to the cult (butchers, bakers, beer brewers, etc.).

Such temple shares could be rented out. Let us consider a few texts. In 487 BC a holder of a temple prebend hired Bel-remanni, son of Mushebshi-Marduk, descendant of Priest of Shamash, to perform his duties of the brewer's prebend at Ebabbara for the days 23rd and 26th of the month Shabaṭu. In return for the right to receive a share of the temple income, Bel-remanni was to provide — punctually — bread and beer for the Ebabbara temple offerings and, in addition, pay one *kur* of barley a year (VS 5 109). In another document (VS 4 200), the same Bel-remanni was to pay 22 shekels of silver for the performance of the brewer's prebend in "the house of Shamash in Sippar" (*i.e.*, in Ebabbara), which belonged to a certain Shapik-zeri. This Bel-remanni is referred to in many documents over the course of forty-five years, 532-487 (BRM I 70; Cyr. 260; VS 3 9,99,135 a, etc.). He frequently appears as a debtor borrowing loans in kind and money (see, *e.g.*, VS 3 89,99,208, etc.). During some period of his life he served as a scribe of the Ebabbara temple (see, *e.g.*, BRM I 70). According to CT 56 196, drafted in 527, he was issued five shekels of silver by Ebabbara officials in order to buy dates from Telmun (Bahrain) for the temple sacrifices. In Cyr. 260 in 532 a certain Nidintu owed 5 *kur* 1 *pān* 3 *sūt* (c. 954 liters) of barley to Bel-remanni as rental payment to Ebabbara. The document was written by Bel-remanni himself (see also Camb. 288). As seen from VS 4 145, Bel-remanni and his brother Shamash-naṣir delivered to a certain Remut-Shamash, 12.5 shekels of silver as rent for a boat. The payment was made upon order of the Priest of Sippar. According to VS 6 121, a certain Mushezib-Marduk was obligated to pay Bel-remanni 3 *sūt* (18 liters) of good wine from the district of Suhu (a region on the middle Euphrates), apparently as his share from a mutual business venture (cf. Dandamayev 1995:34ff.).

Temple prebends were not restricted to cult requirements. According to Cyr. 304, the income derived from the trade of the boatman was given for rent to a certain Ṭabija, son of Bel-na'id.

The Ebabbara temple had a limited number of craftsmen among its slaves. The document Camb. 398 records the obligation of an Ebabbara slave who was a weaver to deliver some garments to the temple. But most temple slaves were unskilled laborers used as porters, guards, etc. The decisive role in temple crafts and trades was played by free persons who worked for wages or the right to receive a share of the temple's income as prebends.

Many documents throw light on the activities of a weaver by the name Nabu-naṣir-apli who worked together with his slaves for the Ebabbara temple for at least for 21 years (from 552 through 531) for wages in money and in kind (see Dandamayev 1984:290ff.; add to the documents cited there: CT 57 168 and 344). Another weaver frequently mentioned in Ebabbara texts is Nabu-bel-shumati. In 551 he was paid 5 shekels of silver and 1 *kur* of barley (CT 57 164) by the temple. A weaver of the same name is referred to 55 years earlier in VS 6 16, drafted in Sippar in 606. According to this text, he was paid 14 minas 51$^{1}/4$ shekels of silver for making various wool garments of apparel for the goddess Shala. In all probability, this amount was intended not only for Nabu-bel-shumati alone, but also for some of the weavers who worked with him. Also known are other weavers who were citizens of Sippar and worked for Ebabbara (see, *e.g.*, CT 55 408; CT 56 104, 629, 668, etc.).

Three apprenticeship contracts have been preserved from Sippar. Two of them come from the Ebabbara archives. According to one of them, a temple slave was sent to learn the craft of sack-making (Nbn. 172). A second document states that an Ebabbara slave was sent for two years as an apprentice to a hunter to learn his profession (Bongenaar and Jursa 1993:31ff.).

The apprenticeship contract Cyr. 313 comes from a private archive. As it states, a certain Nabu-shum-iddin, son of Ardija, and his wife Ina-Esagil-belet have given their slave Nidintu to Liblut, son of Ushshaja, for six years to learn the bleacher's trade. According to the conditions of the document, the slave's masters intended to present him to the Ebabbara temple after he had completed his training.

Artisans made contracts with customers for a fixed fee. Although few such texts survive from Sippar — a fact that can be explained by the paucity of private documents known from there — the character of such contracts can be demonstrated by texts from other cities. In several documents from Babylon, Itti-Marduk-balatu of the Egibi business house appears as the customer. A shoemaker made four pairs of leather shoes for him (Nbn. 566). The same customer issued 23 *kur* of dates to a beer brewer to make 25 vats of first-quality beer (Nbn. 600). He also paid one *mina* of silver for tanning hides (Cyr. 148). TCL 12 101 states that Itti-Marduk-balatu ordered a necklace from a jeweler made of 303 stones "of beautiful appearance."

Similar contracts are known also from the archive of the Murashû business house in Nippur, which come from the second half of the fifth century. For instance, a member of this family ordered a ring with a gem mounted in gold with a guarantee for 20 years against the gem's falling out (BE 9 41).

We do not have any documentary evidence that the Babylonian craftsmen sold their goods at market, although indirect data attest to this.

Such transactions probably were not made in written form. According to a labor contract drafted in Sippar in 480, a certain Uluaja, son of Nabu-ittannu, placed his younger brother to work on digging a canal for 9 shekels of silver a month and for his food (Joannès, *Textes Économiques* 89).

The merchants (*tamkārus*) can also be mentioned among the various professional groups of Sippar. Some of them were employed by the Ebabbara temple but most of them were independent traders engaged in domestic and international commerce. For instance, a certain Shamash-iqisha is referred to in many documents drafted in Sippar during Nabonidus' reign, selling oxen and sheep to be used for Ebabbara offerings (CT 55 68, 692, 699). Another merchant sold Ebabbara two full-grown sheep and three lambs for 20.5 shekels of silver (CT 55 608). According to CT 55 823, the chief merchant in Sippar presented one piece of linen fabric for the god Shamash.

Commercial partnerships of two or more persons conducting business and dividing profits and losses were of great importance in trade. For instance, Nabu-eṭir, a citizen of Sippar, invested one *mina* of silver for a business venture with two other individuals who were equal partners. "From the venture they will pay Nabu-eṭir 10 shekels of good silver per year" (the translation is quoted from MacGinnis 1994:119, No. 2).

Camb. 412 is a record of court proceedings concerning two *minas* of silver belonging to the business capital of two persons, which was invested during the period between the years 559 to 530. The decision in the case was made in 522 by the Priest of Sippar and "elders of the city."

Activities of some other private citizens of Sippar can be demonstrated in the following examples. Marduk-sum-uṣur, son of Iddin-Marduk, descendant of Ea-epesh-ili, can be traced in documents for a period of 32 years (539-507). In 539 he took a loan of 30 shekels of silver from a certain Shulaja. The money was borrowed not in Sippar, but in Bīt-shar-Bābili, a suburb of Babylon (CT 55 117). In 523 in Sippar he issued a loan of barley (the amount is destroyed) to one of his contracting parties (CT 55 120). The next year he is listed among the witnesses of a document that records the obligation of a certain Tattannu to deliver 20 ducks to the Ebabbara temple. This Tattannu acts here as a guarantor for a temple bird-keeper who failed to produce the ducks in his charge during an inspection (Camb. 407/408). In 522, before Marduk-shum-uṣur and some other citizens, an artisan was issued 2 *minas* 40 shekels of gold to manufacture a vessel for Ebabbara (Graziani 1991:No. 11). In 518 he paid a part of his debt of about two minas of silver, which he owed to a woman and her daughter (CT 55 95). Finally, in 517 he is listed among the witnesses of a promissory note (Dar. 417).

His son Iqishaja is also known from documents drafted between the years 515 and 497. In 515 he borrowed 50 shekels of silver from a citizen of Sippar with the obligation to pay off within three months (Stevenson 1902:No. 34). In 511(?) he again appears as a debtor of five shekels of silver (CT 55 93). CT 55 104, drafted in Babylon in 504, states that he took a loan of ten shekels of silver from a certain Adad-attan, and a third party was the guarantor for the debtor. In 506 he is listed among witnesses of a promissory note (Dar. 433). To judge from a document drafted in Babylon in 503, this Iqishaja rented a prebend that belonged to a certain Nabu-zeri-iddin of the same Ea-epesh-ili family and paid the son of the holder of the prebend for it (MacGinnis 1991/92:No. 11).

In one text he is responsible for the vindication of a guaranty given at the sale of a slave woman bought by a certain Kabtaja, the wife of Ardija, son of Nabu-mushetiq-udde, from Rindu, daughter of Remut. Later Rindu sold this slave to Iqishaja himself (CT 4, pl. 47, No. 1). Finally, in CT 55 192 he took some bronze objects fabricated by the above-mentioned Ardija from one talent (30 kg) of bronze issued by the Priest of Sippar. Thus, to judge from this text, Ardija was an artisan who worked for Ebabbara and Iqishaja and was perhaps a temple functionary.

Iqishaja-Marduk, son of Gimil-Shamash of the same Ea-epesh-ili family, is attested in Sippar texts in 514-489. He and an Ebabbara official were present when a sheep was given to the temple as a tithe (CT 55 745). According to Dar. 365, 12(?) shekels of silver constituted the rest of the price of a house he had purchased. In Dar. 433 he granted a loan of 5(?) *kur* of dates to one of his contacting parties. He is also listed among witnesses of a document recording the right to irrigate some Ebabbara land leased to two rent collectors (Jursa 1995:No. 53; see also CT 2 2).

The population of Sippar, as well as of other cities of the country, included a number of free resident foreigners. For instance, in 503 a piece of linen was lost in Ebabbara and the loss was reported to the officials of the temple. Then a piece of Egyptian linen was found among the things of one of the temple personnel, and the officials asked him where he had obtained this fabric. He replied that he had bought it from an Egyptian who lived in the city and witnesses corroborated this statement (CT 2 2).

The bulk of the population owned only relatively small plots of land ranging from a half to two or three hectares. It was profitable to engage in gardening or horticulture (mainly the cultivation of date palms). As van Driel points out, "the expansion of the orchard at the expense of the arable area of the field seems to be a general feature of the period" (van Driel 1988:132). In addition to temples and the king, some businessmen and other wealthy individuals were also large landowners. There is a document of exchange of grain fields between the king Nebuchadnezzar II and a private man by the name Haltiku, son of Ahheshaja. The fields were located along the coast of the Euphrates in the Sippar region, and each of these fields were of 120 *kur*, that is, 162 hectares. The document was drafted in Babylon in 599 (Bruschweiler 1989:153ff.).

Although the greater part of the lands in the rural environs of Sippar belonged to Ebabbara, private land ownership apparently also continued there, as the above-mentioned document on the exchange of fields attests. But small plots of land are not usually mentioned in any texts, since their owners cultivated these plots themselves together with their families, without the help of other persons.

The important question is whether the craftsmen lived on their trades or from their land. It seems that such artisans as the above-mentioned weaver Nabu-naṣir-apli had enough income from Ebabbara to live on, but nearly all free people possessed lands either in cities or in their countryside.

Some craftsmen appear as tenants on the land, including temple land. Camb. 57 states that in 538 the Ebabbara temple leased out fields to a carpenter, as well as to five farmers (*ikkarus*) and a number of individuals designated only by their personal names. The amount of the rent constituted 292 *kur* 3 *pān* (52,668 liters) of dates, of which 11 *kur* (1,980 liters) were paid by a carpenter, Nergal-remanni by name. He is mentioned also among Ebabbara tenants in some more texts dated from 542 to 518. For instance, in CT 57 2 (line 11), he paid 25 *kur* of dates (see also CT 57 204:4; 886:9; Dar. 136:11; cf. also Jursa 1995:150, with references to BM 74524 and 61077).

A linen weaver, Gimillu by name, is referred to as a tenant of an Ebabbara date palm grove in 487 (BM 74524:11; see Jursa 1995:218f.). Apparently, the same Gimillu appears in a number of other texts from Sippar. In Nbn. 1072 he was issued 24 *minas* (c. 12 kg) of wool for dyeing (the year is destroyed). In 529 he was again issued 23 *minas* of wool in order to make some garments for Ebabbara gods (Camb. 90; cf. also Camb. 256). This information can be supplemented by documents from other cities. GCCI II 378 from the Eanna archives in Uruk mentions a smith as a tenant of a field.

Evetts, Ev.-M. 23 from Babylon records that a royal carpenter by the name Marduk-ahhe-uṣur, son of Marduk-ibni, bought a field of 4 *pān*

(10,800 square meters) and one more field with date palm trees on it, including also the right to irrigate it from a canal. As seen from the text, these fields had been taken by him as security for three *minas* of silver 13 years before the drawing up of the document about their sale. In 560 Marduk-ahhe-uṣur paid 3 minas 41$^{1}/_4$ shekels of silver, including 5$^{1}/_4$ shekels as an additional payment (cf. Sack 1972:76, where the text is collated).

Needless to say, state and temple officials were owners of land. For instance, Dar. 194 (line 4) records the sale of a field bordering on a date palm grove which belonged to the governor of Kish.

Many scribes were permanently engaged in royal or temple service as their main source of income. Temple scribes, for instance, were paid from one to three *kur* of barley or dates a month (see YOS 6 32, 96; YOS 7 110, etc.), but also owned real estate. Sometimes they rented temple fields and engaged in trade and money-lending operations. According to a document drafted in Borsippa in 552, a royal scribe sold his grain field and a date palm grove for 1 *mina* and 1 shekel of silver. The text states that this amount of money was intended to be used to pay off the debt of this scribe to Ezida, the temple of the god Nabu in Borsippa. The contract was written by the debtor himself (BE 8 44).

Nabu-eresh, son of Tabnea, descendant of Ahu-bani, is known as a scribe for private contracts in Babylon during the reign of Nabonidus (Nbn. 336, 501, 605, etc.). He started his scribal career being a rather well-to-do man, but failures pursued him constantly and apparently brought him to ruin. He owned at least one field and ten slaves but eventually lost all his property.

Abundant documentary evidence has been preserved on the real estate of some Babylonian business houses, including the Egibi family (see Krecher 1970:24ff.). Its head, Nabu-ahhe-iddin, bought fields, orchards, and date palm groves located in the area of Babylon, which bordered on his own lands (Nbn. 178, 193, 203, 418, 477, 1111). He usually leased his fields and houses (Nbn. 47, 309, 353, 623, etc.). His son Itti-Marduk-balaṭu lived in Babylon in a "big house" (Nbn. 1047). He bought and sold houses, fields, slaves, and so on, in Babylon, Borsippa, Kish, Uruk, and some other cities (Camb. 217, 226, 375; Cyr. 172, 264, etc.). Several documents regarding his commercial transactions were drafted in Ecbatana, the capital of Media, and in various towns of Elam and Persia (Cyr. 15, 29, 60, etc.).

Nergal-ushezib, another member of the Egibi family, was a scribe in Babylon during the years 517-502 (Dar. 166, 488) and also leased fields and date palm groves of the Egibi business firm to other persons (Dar. 154, 402-404, etc.) or sold them (Dar. 465-467, etc.). Marduk-naṣir-apli of the Egibi house exchanged a field of two *kur* (one *kur* = 13,500 square meters), located in the district of Dilbat, for a field of six *kur* near Babylon which bordered on his own land. As the difference in the price for the field in Dilbat area, he paid four *minas* of silver (Dar. 265). This real estate was rented out (Dar. 172-175, 350, etc.). Together with his brothers he owned a field near Babylon, with a Persian dignitary, Bagasaru, who was paid his rent in garlic, dates, barley, wheat, etc. (Dar. 527, 534, etc.). In one case his rent amounted to 170 *kur* of barley (Dar. 296).

The powerful Egibi family was one of the business houses that were selling, buying, and exchanging houses, fields, and other property. Such businessmen also received money on deposit, gave and received promissory notes, paid the debts of their clients, and invested capital in commercial companies. But these business houses did not use the money entrusted to them on deposit as a means of credit but worked with their own resources. Thus, some activities of Babylonian businessmen bore the character of professional banking operations, but they did not function with the aid of other people's money. When they used money belonging to other individuals, it was done in the form of loans.

Long before the Neo-Babylonian period, land had become private property and was freely sold, given, or mortgaged and then could be alienated through foreclosure. This was one of the ways by which temples and private individuals gained land. Temple land could not be alienated, but private persons could resell land obtained through foreclosure, and thus such lands were not removed from the market.

Some people apparently borrowed money to buy real estate with the purpose of making a profit. For instance, according to TCL 13 193, Marduk-naṣir-apli of the Egibi family borrowed forty-four minas of silver from a royal official for the period of three months under the security of eight slaves, as well as land planted with date palms and under cereal cultivation in a suburb of Babylon. If the loan was not paid off within the specified period of time, all eight slaves and the land were to become the property of the creditor. It seems logical to conclude from this document that Marduk-naṣir-apli was in an urgent need for money to buy more fields, houses, slaves, or whatever. The document concerning the division of the property of the house of Egibi mentions more than 100 slaves, 16 houses and other buildings in Babylon and Borsippa, 12 minas of silver; but fields, cows, oxen, asses, horses, and other property were left for the time being in common ownership (Dar. 379). Some of the houses belonging to the Egibi family were rented out, and thus they were acquired in order to draw revenue (for references, see Krecher 1970:75 f.).

It seems that there are no real estate sales among the published documents from Sippar. However, as seen from many Neo-Babylonian contracts, the land was freely sold, mortgaged, given, and so on. From Uruk, which, like Sippar, was a temple city, we have estate sale documents. For instance, in 611 a field of 250 x 250 cubits (15,625 m²) located near Uruk was sold for 1 *mina* 20 shekels (BIN I 130). A date palm grove of 7.5 *kur* (c. ten hectares) near Uruk was sold in 603 for 32 *minas* of silver (Joannès, *Textes Économiques*, No. 78).[5]

The area of Babylon

Let us consider some documents concerning the sale of grain fields and orchards in various parts of Babylonia. A document from 535 records the sale of a grain field and a date palm grove of 1 *kur* 4 *pān* 3 *sūt* 3 *qa* (25,875 m²). Of them, 2 *pān* 3 *qa* (5,625 m²) of the field planted with trees cost 1 *mina* 15 shekels of silver and 1 *kur* 2 *pān* 3 *sūt* (20,250 m²) of cultivated and newly developed field was sold for 45 shekels. As seen from the text, all in all, 4 *kur* 3 *pān* 5 *sūt* 3 *qa* (64,575 m²) of land was sold for 5 *minas* 49 shekels (Cyr. 160/161; Wunsch 1993:No. 292). In 583, 1 *kur* 1 *pān* 3 *sūt* (17,550 m²) of a field with nine date palms on it was sold for 1 *mina* 2 shekels of silver (Nbk. 135). VS 5 7/8 drafted in 586 records 2 *minas* of silver as the price of a field of 1 *kur* 2 *pān* (18,900 m²). In VS 5 105 from 490, 1 *kur* 1 *pān* (16,200 m²) of a field and of an orchard of date palms cost 2 *minas* 2 shekels of silver. A field of 1 *kur* 5 *sūt* (15,750 m²) planted with date palm trees was sold in 519 for 6 *minas* 29 shekels (Dalley, Edinburgh, No. 75).[6]

• **Borsippa area.** In 452 a portion of a field and of an orchard of 1 *pān* (2,700 m²) was sold for 1 *mina* 1 shekel of silver. As seen from the text, this estate was alienated because of a debt to the temple Ezida in Borsippa charged against the father of the owner of the field (BE 8 44). 3 *pān* 2 *sūt* (9,000 m²) of a field on which "date palms stood" was sold in 545 for 6 *minas* 30 shekels of silver (TCL 12 30). A field of 3 *sūt* (1,350 m²) with some date palms on it was sold in 541 for 30¹/₂ shekels of silver (NBC 8395, see Joannès 1989:350). In 502 a grain field of 1 *pān* 3 *sūt* (4,050 m²) planted with date palm trees was bought for 2 *minas* 50 shekels (VS 5 92).[7]

• **Dilbat's region.** In 490 1 *kur* 1 *pān* (16,200 m²) of a grain field was sold for 2 *minas* of silver (VS 6 157).

• **Nippur area.** In 514 a field and an orchard of 2 *sūt* (900 m^2) were sold for 28$^1/_2$ shekels of silver (BRM I 73; see also BE 8 58).

• **Ur area.** UET 4 14 (523 BC) records the sale of a date grove of 210$^1/_2$ x 120$^1/_2$ cubits for 3 *minas* 10 shekels. UET 4 17 (497 BC) states that a field and a date grove measuring 150, 127, 60, 60 cubits respectively cost 20$^1/_2$ shekels of silver (see also UET 4 12, 13, 18-21).

A few more documents throw light on real estate prices. Dar. 3218[8] states that a field was alienated "at the rate of six akalu per shekel of silver" (line 12). The document was drafted in Babylon in 510 and records the sale of 6 *kur* (81,000 m^2) of grain land and of an orchard set with date palms for 32 *minas* (c. 16 kg) of silver. According to VS 5 4 (Babylon, 628), a field was sold "at the rate of six *akalu* and a third of an *akalu* (per shekel)." As Powell notes, this document states, that "4 *kur* of land (7,200 *akalu*) are being sold at the rate of one shekel of silver per 6$^1/_3$ *akalu*. The price is given as 19 *minas* (= 1140 shekels)."[9] Finally, to judge from the above-mentioned Evetts, Ev.-M. 23, a grain field was sold "at the rate of six *akalu* and two-thirds of an *akalu* per shekel." Thus, according to these texts, c. 41.664 m^2 cost one shekel of silver, which means that one hectare of land cost approximately four *minas* of silver. In other words, in these cases the price for a hectare of land was the equivalent of the wages of an adult hired laborer for 20 years (cf. below). This is an extremely high price. But, as we have seen above, a hectare of land could cost 2 *minas* of silver or even less. The minimal price of one hectare of field was usually about one *mina* of silver, *i.e.*, the equivalent of five years' wages of a hired laborer. It is obvious that the price on land depended on its quality, location, and other factors, which we often can only guess (cf. the list of land prices in van Driel 1988:152-158).

Stolper (1994:337f.) has noted that only six documents recording sales of arable land and orchards are known among legal texts dated between Xerxes and Alexander the Great (485-330). In his opinion, this scarcity can be explained at least partly by the assumption that real estate sale documents were kept separately from promissory notes and other such routine texts, as they "established primary title to ownership of the land . . . and they should therefore have been permanently archived." In relation to this, the following considerations might also be important. First of all, documentary evidence for the late Achaemenid period is scant. Besides (and this is more important), in traditional societies real estate constituted the last resources on which its owners lived and therefore was sold only in extreme circumstances.

This is not the place to discuss the comparative prices of various commodities, but without going into detail, a few remarks can be made here.

The average annual rate payments for houses usually fluctuated from 5 to 20 shekels. But in 559 a house in Sippar was rented for 1³/₄ shekels of silver a year (Evetts, Ner. 29). In 493, a house of 288.75 m² located in Sippar was sold for 2 *minas* 18 shekels (VS 5 103). A house of 22.5 x 21.5 cubits (c. 193.5 m²) was sold in Uruk for 1 mina 36 shekels (YOS 17 322; for more details see Joannès, *Textes Économiques*, 289 f.).

It goes without saying that house prices and rents were determined not only by their dimensions and locations, but also by other circumstances that usually remain unknown to us. For instance, there is a case of an exceptionally high rent for a short period of time. The house was situated "on the ramp of Bēl" in Babylon and rented to Enlil-šum-iddin, a member of the Murašu house, who came to the capital from Nippur and stayed there "until the departure of the king" (the time of the departure is not specified). All the rental, which constituted one *mina* thirty shekels of silver was paid in advance, in February, 423 BC (BE 10 1 = TuM 2-3 29). The reason this house was so valuable during the period of the king's stay in Babylon is more or less obvious. Apparently, Enlil-šum-iddin wanted to demonstrate his loyalty to Darius II, who had just ascended the throne after a serious struggle for power.

Agricultural prices depended on the season of the year. One *kur* of barley or dates normally cost about one shekel of silver, and a *kur* of sesame, 7.5-9 shekels. One talent (30 kg) of salt cost 1 shekel. The price of one *mina* (c. 500 grams) of wool was c. 0.25 shekel; 5 *minas* of linen as material, 1 shekel; one garment, 2 shekels; one coat, 8 shekels; 5 pairs of shoes were sold for 1 shekel. An ox or cow cost between 7 and 37 shekels, and was rented for about 10 shekels a year. Prices on asses varied from 28 to 52 shekels. The normal price for a sheep was 2 shekels (for references, see Dandamayev 1988:54f.; see also Dubberstein 1939:20ff.).

The living standard in Babylonia during the period under consideration was relatively high. The wage of an adult worker was in average 12 shekels a year, or about 6 liters of barley or dates a day (see Dandamayev 1988:54f.). In the Neo-Babylonian period prices were gradually rising, and they rose by the end of the Achaemenid period approximately one and one-half times. But wages also grew.

The following are data about the living standard during the seventh through the fourth centuries. According to Nbn. 113, drafted in Sippar in 553, a certain Na'id-Marduk, son of Shamash-balassu-iqbi, upon divorce was obligated to pay his wife and son as alimony 4 *qa* of food, 3 *qa* of beer (*i.e.*, about two liters of food and 1.5 liters of beer apiece) daily, as well as 15 *minas* (c. 7.5 kg) of wool, one *pān* (c. 36 liters) of sesame, one *pān* of salt, and 4 *sūt* of cress seeds a year. This obligation was accepted before the Priest of Sippar. Also drafted before the same official was CT 55 133. This poorly preserved text also states the alimony for a divorced wife which consisted of [. . .] food, 4 *qa* of good beer a day, 2 *sūt* (12 liters) of salt, etc., per year. In Cyr. 339 a woman manumitted her slave on the condition that he supply her one *sūt* (c. 6 liters) of food and the same amount of good beer daily, a certain amount of cress seeds and salt monthly, and, finally, one talent of wool for clothing and three sheep annually. The document was drawn up in the presence of the Priest of Sippar.

A craftsman (*ummānu*) received 4 *sūt* of flour a month as his food portion (Cyr. 106), *i.e.*, about 0.8 liters a day. A door-keeper of a court of law was issued 4 *pān* of barley for six months (GCCI II 65), *i.e.*, again about 0.8 liters daily. Fifty workers (*ṣābē*) received 123 *kur* of barley and dates for a one-year period (Nbn. 469), *i.e.*, about 1.26 liters per man a day. Another person was issued 1 *pān* 4 *sūt* (60 liters) of barley and the same amount of dates as his monthly rations (Cyr. 296). Thus, the average daily quota of food rations for a free adult worker fluctuated between one and two liters of grain but was usually about one liter. The same amount of food was also issued to slaves (see Dandamayev 1984:239ff.).

Landless people could rent another's land along with the necessary implements and draught animals or could become hired laborers. Parties of hired workmen not infrequently numbered serveral hundred persons. They would not agree to work for low pay and refused to work when they were not paid on time or when their food supplies were interrupted (for details, see Dandamayeve 1984:302ff.).

Self-sale became an exceptionally rare phenomenon, possible only under catastrophic circumstances. The practice of pledging one's own person disappeared, and impoverishment and enslavement of free persons was by no means large-scale in nature. Precisely for this reason, in contrast to all the preceding periods in the history of Mesopotamia, debt slavery played an insignificant role and did not constitute a serious menace for the society. Therefore the limitation of debt slavery to the specific length of time established by the Code of Hammurapi was no longer in effect (see Dandamanyev 1984:175ff.). For the same reason, during the Neo-Babylonian and Achaemenid periods, neither *misarum* nor *andurarum* acts were in effect, by which the Babylonian kings of the second millennium BC, *inter alia*, restored rural lands to their original owners, proclaimed liberation of debt slaves, and released debts. It is also quite obvious that in contrast to earlier periods, there were no sanctions against alienating rural lands.

As is well known, Karl Polanyi contended that a market economy did not exist in the ancient Near East. This model was adopted by A. Leo Oppenheim and then by economic historians and assyriologists under his influence who assumed that the ancient Near East economies were nonmarket in character. But the above presented documentary evidence on the free alienation of land, on the great role played by free hired labor, as well as a great abundance of information on intensive market relations in the Babylonian economy of the first millennium BC, attest that the economic structure of this period differed from that of the second millennium. Practically speaking, it would seem that any fundamental differences between the market economies in Babylonia during the period under consideration and in the classical world cannot be established. Therefore, Polanyi's model of a self-sustaining economy cannot be applied to Later Babylonia.

DISCUSSION

Hudson: You have described the extent to which temples as public institutions were self-supporting. In modern times, of course, they wouldn't be. They would levy tithes or other requests for contributions to get their support. Taxation has become one of the major defining characteristics of the modern state. I would like to know when real estate taxes or fees developed and to what extent they shaped the land market.

Dandamayev: As to taxes on land, in Achaemenid times we don't have any actual documentation, as far as I know, although Herodotus says that land was assessed according to its quality and monetary taxes were levied. The great Assyriologist Leo Oppenheim wrote that next to nothing is known about taxes in Babylonia.

Hudson: Did taxes influence the relations between the city and the country? And did they lower land's price?

Dandamayev: Physically, there was countryside, but socially, as far as I can judge, there was no countryside. There was no difference. If a field or an orchard was located in a city, its price was relatively higher. This can be shown from documents.

Stone: You have given us a lot of numbers. I was interested in the amount of the rations, because I think that it is always difficult for us to assess rations. You can take all different kinds of economic resources and turn them into what they call a wheat equivalent. Then you can assess total incomes. Basic subsistence is about 256 wheat equivalents per year per person. If you take one liter per year, that comes to about 300 liters of wheat equivalent per year per person. If you go up that goes much higher. He also provides numbers on the average per capita income for Iraq in 1954, which was about 580.

What that tells us is that when you have people getting 6 liters a day, that is a lot. We use the term ration, but I wonder whether we shouldn't be using the term salary, because it is regular, and it certainly is not designed simply to support and feed just one individual, but probably a household, family, or a larger group. The term "ration" is so loaded that we always have trouble with it. I think when we look at the numbers they tend to be much higher.

Dandamayev: Babylonia was a rich country, although Egypt was richer. These 6 liters of barley or dates is a fact that is attested in many documents, but it was paid in silver. It was a normal price. Sometimes they also receive 1 liter a day of food portion. But perhaps 6 liters a day is not too much if the recipient had a wife and/or children to support.

Buccellati: On the one hand we see the difference between rations and wages, and on the other hand the difference between field and orchard. They are technical terms that do not have much to do with consumption levels, but rather with remuneration. The ration therefore is different from the wage. Often, workers just get something, but we don't quite know what. So I wonder if the difference between wage and ration depends on *when* they are paid. The ration would be distributed daily, and the wage would be paid monthly or whatever. In that case the 6 liters would be a wage.

Lamberg-Karlovsky: In speaking of land, you said that the people had property of 0.5 to 3 hectares. That is not a terribly large farm. Were there any individuals who owned large farms?

Dandamayev: Yes, of course, 100 hectares of land or more.

Lamberg-Karlovsky: Not attached to either the temple or the palace?

Dandamayev: It was private property bought and sold.

Lamberg-Karlovsky: So there are sizable estates, and yet land is quite expensive — 4 mina for a hectare. A number of years ago Diakonoff said that in the third millennium land was cheap. Do you recall that?

Dandamayev: When the population was not large and there was much land, perhaps so. I don't know, but for this period we have documentary evidence that still needs to be researched. A hectare of land cost 1 mina of silver or more, sometimes even up to 4 minas.

Wunsch: I would like to say one thing concerning the term "temple cities" referring to Uruk and Sippar. You have pointed out that this idea reflects the bias of our sources. Our evidence is dominated by the temple archives from these cities. We might term Babylon a temple city as well if we had the evidence from its Esagila. On the other hand, there is the evidence of some private houses in Uruk where we find private archives of people whom we find mentioned in the temple records. This shows that those people mentioned in temple records are some sort of functionaries of the temple, making the same sort of business transactions that we find in Babylon private archives. So there may not have been much difference between business life in Babylon and Uruk. It is just that we have recovered quite different parts of the evidence. That is why our picture is so different.

Dandamayev: That is right, but perhaps only partly. The Eanna economy really seems to have been different from the Esagila economy. We do have some documents from the Esagila archive that show that it had other sources of income. Uruk's temple had extensive lands. There was private activity, but there are so far published private documents, I guess about 100.

Renger: A comparison of the Old Babylonian period to the Neo-Babylonian period shows lots of differences. For one thing, there are some very advanced types of legal instruments that are even more modern than in Roman law, for example, the law of representation. If you let yourself be represented in business dealings by someone, his word stands for your word. You don't have that liability in Roman law.

There is a highly developed use of debt notes. The holder can use them to settle his own debts. Of course, this has nothing to do with modern ways of using promissory notes as a kind of monetary instrument, because such IOUs can be circulated only among a small circle of friends well known to one another. So we should not overemphasize this practice.

Regarding your last comments about the wages of workers, you give some figures that I think are quite interesting. You talk about a range of 0.8 liters per day up to and 1½ liter of grain for daily wages for an artisan. This is the bare minimum for subsistence. Less than 1 liter of barley per day is half of what an ordinary worker got in the third millennium. Rations of 1½ or 1¼ liter are even less than what was received a thousand years earlier. Whether the recipients could live from it or had other sources of income or means to feed themselves is another story. But it shows that this kind of remuneration remains stable over more than a thousand years. There is no inflation or growth in wages paid. If you look at the collection of law prescriptions of Hammurapi, you have a kind of a tariff for craftsmen of about 8 liters of barley a day — quite a difference! It needs to be kept in mind when comparing Old and Neo-Babylonian economic situations.

Wunsch: The rate at which a slave is paid or given provisions should also be compared to what craftsmen get. Such figures should be checked and placed in the context of the whole transactions. When slaves are rented out, or when they run away, usually the one for whom the slave works is obliged to pay 1 sila and sometimes more, that is, more than 1 liter per day for this slave.

Hudson: But what the slave is worth as an employee is not necessarily what he is remunerated. The difference represents what economists would call the employer's profit.

Zaccagnini: The amount of barley mentioned corresponds to one sila. This is the minimum daily barley ration, and usually is issued to women rather than to male workers. I would not say that this is the salary (*idu*) for a more or less specialized worker, which is precisely what is mentioned in the laws of Eshnunna, in those of Hammurapi, and is also recorded in some Mesopotamian lexical texts. These say that the daily wages (*idu*) amounted to one *sutu* of barley (c. 8 liters, according to the Mesopotamian metrology, or c. 6.7 liters at Nuzi), which is the equivalent of one mina of copper. This standard amount corresponds to the sum that was charged to defaultant (indentured) workers, or to people who bore responsibility for them, as daily hire for a substitute.

A daily one-liter barley ration hardly represents the minimum alimentary supply to ensure the worker's survival. At any rate, the relationship between wages and rations is a subject matter still fully open to debate.

Dandamayev: Babylonian traditions were very conservative, perhaps unnecessarily so. Regarding the laws about which Prof. Renger spoke, we certainly must differentiate between wages and rations. Rations for a worker amounted to from 1 liter of barley a day, irrespective of whether or not he was free, an artisan, or a slave. But the wage level was established at 6 liters of barely or dates. In most cases it was paid in silver, but this is rather theoretical. We have many documents about this. Sometimes workers require exceptionally high wages of 1 mina a year. Wages could fluctuate from 3 shekels to 1 mina of silver a year. So we don't have to believe all these traditional notions. In any case, in the Neo-Babylonian period there is a substantial difference between theoretical and practical cases.

About inflation, prices did rise. We can trace it for 200 years of Achaemenid rule in Mesopotamia. Prices went up about 1½ times. But wages also rose, so the situation was not one of stagnation.

Hudson: I don't want to lose sight of the first point. We know what went into the Middle Babylonian period and we know what came out in the Neo-Babylonian period. It would be interesting to know how we got there. If the Neo-Babylonian period was *not* a market economy, was it catalytic to the emergence of the real estate market?

Renger: One point that has been discussed for a long time is the conception of the Egibi and Murashu as business enterprises. We now know from the Murashu archive that this is not a banking house. There was no banking. The Murashu conducted their activities vis-a-vis the royal Achaemenid administration and family. They had large land holdings, which they administered for a fee. You mentioned Kessler's texts from Uruk, and also that individual families operated in the context of (and for) the big institutions in Warka for the Eanna temple, and in other places for the king. And Dr. Wunsch has shown that the Egibi followed the same set of practices. This raises the question of what influence and power this apparently independent class of rich merchants had on the king. They apparently conducted their own business as entrepreneurial businessmen.

You cannot have an independent group of businessmen, rich and powerful in terms of accumulated treasures, gold, silver, and staples, and at the same time have a strong royal power and administration. There must be some conflict of interest. Either you solve this problem by institutionalizing the power these persons have, or an open conflict results.

In Athens the public assembly decides which way to go. In Rome the senatorial class runs the state as a family business. But Babylonia still has powerful kings such as Nabonidus and Nebuchadnezzar, and later the Achaemenids. They run the business, they run the state, and they do it very effectively. When Nebuchadnezzar came to power, big cities such as Uruk, Sippar, and Babylon were run in the same way as in the period when no king was really powerful. The king then appointed a person he trusted to sit beside each official known by several terms (*e.g.*, *sha reh sharri*). Down through the Achaemenid period they sat as controllers beside the local administrators, looking to see that the silver owed to the king actually was collected rather than put in the Eanna temple or somewhere else. I think we have to conceive of the whole social and economic setup in this period with this awareness in the back of our mind of who had the power.

Dandamayev: Yes, we have in the Neo-Babylonian period a powerful king, but there is no state economy as in earlier periods. As to Nebuchadnezzar, he could condemn somebody to death for reasons of state and confiscate his land, but this is exceptional. I do not believe that Babylonian kings intervened in any private activity. The private business houses tried to establish contacts with palace administration and the king himself, but still they were autonomous. There was no state economy to feed and clothe most people. There was nothing of that kind during the Achaemenid period in Mesopotamia as far as I know.

Levine: What about the population? It seems to me that employers would try to get workers to work for less. John L. Lewis once said that you don't have to worry about prices, the bosses will take care of that and try to get the highest price. You only have to worry about wages. In this contrast between earlier and later times, was it because there were more workers available in Neo-Babylonian period that you could get labors for less?

Dandamayev: Of course there was competition among free people, and we know that temples had a choice as to whom they would rent. Sometimes they rejected the conditions of a would-be renter and tenant, and rented their land to someone else under different conditions. Such competition also exists among workers. The impression one gets from reading Neo-Babylonian temple letters and other documents is that there were not always sufficient workers available. Slaves were an insufficient supply of labor, as they were not very efficient workers. Businessmen had to hire people who worked efficiently for their wages and who performed high quality work. To be sure, in some cases this work could be performed with the help of slaves and other types of dependent labor.

Levine: Are you saying that standard of living was lower for workers in Neo-Babylonian times?

Dandamayev: It actually was much higher. In contrast to normal times in earlier periods, there was no famine, and normally the standard of living was much higher.

Wunsch: I am not convinced about that. I think we have to take into account the fact that there were several different kinds of workers. There was an enormous amount of construction work underway during the period of Nebuchadnezzar and Nabonidus. Who did it all? The normal assumption is that it was performed by forced labor such as war captives, as well as landless hired workers. They had to be fed because they had no land in the city. This was the market that the business families supplied when they undertook their commodity trade from the rural area around Babylon to the city. They got rich on this trade, but the workers probably just got subsistence and little more.

We cannot compare these middle class families whose archives we have with workers on a construction site for instance or with those workers in agriculture, because most agricultural workers were not paid in money but in kind by the date orchards. These were rented out on a sharecropping basis. The same probably is still the case for farm land. So the number of hired workers does not seem too high for the overall picture of society. It is restricted to artisans, and to those employments that are restricted to certain seasons in the year, such as harvest time.

Steinkeller: How would describe land-tenure conditions in the Neo-Babylonian period? Who are the main owners of land according to your interpretation? What were the main categories of owners?

Dandamayev: Anybody could own land, but the main category consisted of citizens and all kinds of people — craftsmen, businessmen, and any ordinary type of individual. There was no obstacle to land ownership. Anyone who could afford it could buy land.

Steinkeller: Who were the biggest landowners?

Dandamayev: The Egibi family, for example. We know about such people because their various interests are recorded in texts. We know of one man mentioned only once in our cuneiform documentation, but who had a field of 162 hectares.

Steinkeller: What about the king's lands?

Dandamayev: We have on record that they were rented out.

Steinkeller: What about *kudurrus*?

Dandamayev: They are not found in the period under consideration. As far as we can judge, royal land had to be leased out to sharecroppers, because otherwise it would have been impossible to cultivate.

Steinkeller: What was the source of the king's income — rents from these estates?

Dandamayev: I think there was a distinction between state income and the income of the royal family. The income from the king's land was the king's own personal income. He also received taxes, but that was state income. It is difficult to make a clear distinction between the royal family's private income and state income, but nevertheless it existed. The income from the king's land was used not for state purposes, but for private use of the royal family. Perhaps there was no strict demarcation, and the king perhaps could use the state income when he needed it. But royal land seems not to have contributed anything to state income.

Notes

1. See CAD A/I:379; Oppenheim 1977:115; Orlin 1975:34; Hallo 1971:59; Cardascia 1951:2, n. 6). Cuneiform texts are cited by the abbreviations of the Assyrian Dictionary of the Oriental Institute of the University of Chicago (CAD).

2. TCL 12 32:6: AŠ MURUB$_4$ URU

3. Line 6:Sip-par[ki] GAL[i]; (see Zadok 1985:271).

4. Ina qabalti āli

5. From Uruk see also: AnOr 8 8, 23; AnOr 9 7; BIN I 127; BIN II 131; TCL 12 33.

6. From the area of Babylon see also: BE 8 7; BRL 4, p.69; Dar. 321, 466; Evetts, Ev.-M. 14; Sack 1972, No. 13; TCL 12 19; VS 5 20; Weissbach, Mis. (WVDOG 4), pl. 15, No. 2.

7. From Borsippa area see also Böhl, Leiden Coll., pp.118 ff., No, 886.

8. See also its duplicate TCL 13 190.

9. Powell 1984:37, n. 18. Cf. Powell 1990:483 where it is stated that 1 *akalu* = c. 6.9444 m².

BIBLIOGRAPHY

Bongenaar, A. C. V. M., and M. Jursa (1993), "Ein babylonischer Mäusefänger," *WZKM* 63:31-38.

Brinkman, J. A. (1969), "Ur: The Kassite Period and the Period of the Assyrian Kings," *Orientalia* 38:310-348.

Bruschweiler, F. (1989), "Un échange de terrains entre Nabuchodonozor II et un inconnu dans la région de Sippar," *RA* 89:153-162.

Cardascia, G. (1951), *Les Archives des Murašû* (Paris).

Dandamayev, M. A. (1984), *Slavery in Babylonia* (DeKalb).

— (1988), "Wages and Prices in Babylonia in the 6th and 5th Centuries BC," *Altorientalische Forschungen* 15:53-58.

— (1995), "The Ebabbar Temple and Iranian Magi," *Altorientalische Forschungen* 22:34-36.

van Driel, G. (1988), "Neo-Babylonian Agriculture," *Bulletin on Sumerian Agriculture*, vol. IV:121-159

Dubberstein, W. H. (1939), "Comparative Prices in Later Babylonia (640-400 BC)," *AJSL* 56:20-43.

George, A. R. (1992), *Babylonian Topographical Texts* (Orientalia Lovaniensia Analecta 40, Leuven).

Graziani, S. (1991), *Testi editi ed inediti datati al regno di Bardiya* (Istituto Universitario Orientale. Supplemento n. 67 agli Annali - Vol. 51, fasc. 2, Naples).

Hallo, W. W. (1971), "Antediluvian Cities." *JCS* 23:57-67.

al-Jadir, W. (1987), "Une bibliothèque et les tablettes." *Archéologia* 224:18-27.

Joannès, F. (1988), "Sippar à l'époque récente." *RA* 82:74-77.

— (1989), *Archives de Borsippa. La famille Ea-ilûta-bâni* (Geneva).

— (1982), *Textes Économiques de la Babylonie recente* (Paris).

Jursa, M. (1995), *Die Landwirtschaft in Sippar in neubabylonischer Zeit* (AfO, Beiheft 25, Vienna).

Krecher, J. (1970), *Das Geschäftshaus Egibi in Babylon in neubabylonischer und achämenidischer Zeit* (Diss. of Münster University).

MacGinnis, J. (1991/92), "Neo-Babylonian Prebend Texts from the British Museum," *AfO* 38/39:74-100.

— (1994), "Harrānu Texts from the British Museum. *Iraq* 56:117-121.

— (1995), *Letter Order from Sippar and the Administration of the Ebabbara in the Late-Babylonian Period* (Poznan).

Oppenheim, A. L. (1977), *Ancient Mesopotamia* (Chicago).

— (1985), "The Babylonian Evidence of Achaemenian Rule in Babylonia." *The Cambridge History of Iran*, Vol. 2:529-587 (Cambridge).

Orlin, L. L. (1975), "Ancient Near Eastern Cities: Form, Function and Idea." L. L. Orlin (ed.), *JANUS. Essays in Ancient and Modern Studies*. The University of Michigan (Ann Arbor):25-54.

Powell, M. A. (1984), "Late Babylonian Surface Mensuration," *AfO* 31:32-66.

— (1990), "Masse und Gewichte," *RlA*, 7:457-517.

Reuther, O. (1926), *Die Innenstadt von Babylon* (Merkes). *WVDOG* 47.

Sack, R. H. (1972), *Amèl-Marduk 562-560 BC* (Alter Orient und Altes Testament 4. Neukirchen-Vluyn).

San Nicolò, M. (1948), "Materialien zur Viehwirtschaft in den neubabylonischen Tempeln. I," *Orientalia* 17:273-293.

Stevenson, J. H. (1902), *Assyrian and Babylonian Contracts with Aramaic Reference Notes* (New York).

Stigers, H. G. (1976), "Neo-and Late Babylonian Business Documents from the John Frederick Lewis Collection," *JCS* 28:3-59.

Stolper, M. W. (1994), "On Some Aspects of Continuity Between Achaemenid and Hellenistic Babylonian Legal Texts." Sancisi-Weerdenburg *et al.* (eds.), *Achaemenid History* VIII:329-350 (Leiden).

Wunsch, C. (1993), *Die Urkunden des babylonischen Geschäftsmannes Iddin-Marduk* (Cuneiform Monographs 3 a. b. Groningen).

Zadok, R. (1985), *Geographical Names According to New-and Late-Babylonian Texts* (Beihefte zum Tübinger Atlas des Vorderen Orients 8, Wiesbaden).

12

The Egibi Family's Real Estate
in Babylon (6th Century BC)*

Cornelia Wunsch
Heidelberg-Perth

General conclusions about economics and society, and specifically about urban and rural relations for each period under discussion, can be reached only by studying the available archaeological and textual information. This process must not be restricted solely to the collection of facts in and of themselves but must include an evaluation and interpretation of the data in their proper context. It therefore is necessary to discuss the archival background of the texts, including the inherent limitations of the information that can be obtained from them.

Our knowledge of the Neo-Babylonian period is based mainly on economic and legal records from temple archives (especially Eanna of Uruk and Ebabbar of Sippar) and private archives of a few well-to-do Babylonian families, while evidence from the royal administration is still lacking. The incomplete picture provided by these sources is further biased by the fact that much of what we know about private business is owed to (and overshadowed by) a single archive, that of the Egibi family of Babylon.[1] This paper therefore aims to discuss data from this important archive. Although the family's economic activities must serve as a representative exemple for a whole group of contempory entrepreneurs, they also are exceptional with respect to their degree of economic success and available evidence for it.

* Unpublished tablets from the British Museum are quoted and published with the permission of the Trustees of the British Museum. I am especially indebted to C. B. F. Walker, who has made available to me the information he has collected about the tablets from the Babylon collection. The present study has been supported by a Postdoctorate Grant from Deutsche Forschungsgemeinschaft.

Chart 1

Genealogical Tree (Abbreviated)

Men, *Women*, Spouse (∞)

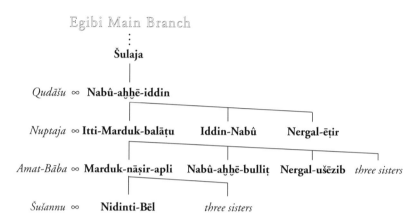

Egibi Main Branch

Šulaja

Qudāšu ∞ Nabû-aḫḫē-iddin

Nuptaja ∞ Itti-Marduk-balāṭu   Iddin-Nabû   Nergal-ēṭir

Amat-Bāba ∞ Marduk-nāṣir-apli   Nabû-aḫḫē-bulliṭ   Nergal-ušēzib   *three sisters*

Šušannu ∞   Nidinti-Bēl   *three sisters*

The Egibi archive

The Egibi archive from Babylon originally may have contained two and a half to three thousand tablets covering more than one hundred years from the reign of Nebuchadnezzar II to the beginning of Xerxes' rulership (sixth and early fifth centuries BC). The texts show members of five generations of this family branch actively involved in business transactions.

The surviving tablets of this archive came to light in the early 1870s through clandestine excavations by native peoples in the Babylon area; the tablets ended up being sold to antiquities dealers in Baghdad. Most of the tablets were acquired by George Smith for the British Museum.[2] When they arrived in London in several lots between 1876 and 1881, mixed with tablets from other proveniences, they were registered according to their date of arrival. A fraction of the archive ended up in other collections.

Thanks to the publication of these British Museum texts by J. N. Straßmaier in the 1880s and '90s, assyriologists have been able to study them. But this pioneering work could not be completed during his lifetime and is still far from being finished. This published corpus lacks much of the evidence from the fourth and most of the fifth generation. Many undated texts remain unpublished, as do fragments whose dates are miss-

CHART 2

EGIBI FAMILY CHRONOLOGICAL FRAMEWORK

Egibi generation	Regnal Years of King		Julian calendar
(1) Šulaja	20 - 21	Nabopolassar	606 - 605
	0 - 23	Nebuchadnezzar	604 - 582
(2) Nabû-aḫḫē-iddin	15 - 43	Nebuchadnezzar	590 - 562
	0 - 2	Evil-Merodach	561 - 560
	0 - 4	Neriglissar	559 - 556
	0 - 13	Nabonidus	555 - 543
(3) Itti-Marduk-balāṭu	5 - 17	Nabonidus	551 - 539
	0 - 9	Cyrus	538 - 530
	0 - 8	Cambyses	529 - 522
	0	Darius	521
(4) Marduk-nāṣir-apli	1 - 35	Darius	521 - 487
(5) Nidinti-Bēl	32 - 36	Darius	490 - 486
	0 - 4	Xerxes	485 - 482

ing or whose state of preservation makes deciphering difficult. The present writer had the privilege of searching through the British Museum's uncatalogued Babylon collection and found a large number of fragments that could be related to already published Egibi texts. Information from this material has been included in the present paper.

The main points concerning agriculture and land tenure as reflected in the published Egibi texts recently have been summarized by van Driel,[3] to whom this paper is indebted. The new texts and fragments do not radically change the picture he obtained, but they provide a broader basis for judgement, many more details, and hence call for the correction of some minor points. Nevertheless an exhaustive study of the Egibis' land and house-sale contracts with their retroacta, rent contracts, and related notes of obligation is still needed[4] and the provisional character of our results at present must be stressed, as well as the need for more serious work on this important archive.

Real estate documentation

The size and location of the Egibi's landed property can be deduced from various kinds of records. Land-sale contracts usually indicate at least the rough location, the names of neighbors, surface measure, quality, and price of the property. Often they contain exact measurements of the boundaries and the price according to different agricultural use. But this information is only available if the tablet is in a perfect state. Sales contracts inform us about purchases made by the family (because the relevant documents and retroacta were kept in the family archive), but we have only accidental evidence concerning resales. None of the contracts preserved names a family member as vendor, probably because sellers had no reason to keep such records and consequently did not receive a copy. Evidently the previous sales contract (or a copy of it) had to be handed over to the new owner, in order to prove the vendor's entitlement to sell the property. We therefore lack most of the records referring to fields and gardens that must have temporally belonged to the family. This makes it difficult to deduce the extent to which estates were bought and resold in order to obtain larger or more suitable parcels, or the degree to which the Egibis may have been involved in land speculation. It is only through exchange records, debt notes, or receipts concerning balances owed on the purchase price, or accounts settled among family members with regard to their inheritance shares in properties that were sold, that sales made by the Egibis can be traced.

In addition to sales contracts, some other categories of texts refer to real estate transactions: receipts or debt notes concerning part of the price owed, records about the measurements of fields or house plots, and the resulting compensation payments in cases where the area turned out to be larger or smaller than calculated, subsequent witnesses to the contract (in order to preclude litigation on their part), or litigation before judges, and dowry proposals involving real estate or inheritance divisions.

Rent contracts and debt notes pertaining to commodities to be delivered by the tenants of rental properties are the main sources of information about land use and income. Many more documents are available from the fourth generation than from earlier times, as rent contracts usually covered only three to five years, and outdated documents no longer were kept in the archive. Unfortunately, these texts do not state explicitly the local details. This makes it difficult to link them to estates known from other sources. The same applies for house rental contracts. Furthermore, debt notes typically deal with only one product — usually dates or barley — and do not indicate how large an area is involved. It therefore is uncertain whether the amount given represents all the lessor's share in the field's yield or only part of it.

No evidence indicates that Šulaja, the representative of the first generation of our Egibi branch, inherited or owned arable land. The early records suggest that he was engaged in commodity trade, especially in the rural areas near Babylon in long-standing partnerships with other traders. Only one rental contract shows his involvement in agricultural affairs other than trade. He appears as a tenant of land owned by the king, for an unlimited period, to cultivate dates and share the income. But the state of the text and the lack of related records provide no further details.

Šulaja's son Nabû-aḫḫē-iddin carried on his father's business and rose economically and socially. Like his father, he was engaged in *ḫarrānu* partnerships with other traders.[5] The stipulations in these contracts make it clear that the business was highly profitable. One partner supplied the financial backing, while the other oversaw the field work, *i.e.,* lending the silver to farmers, collecting the payments due in commodities at the time of harvest in the countryside (usually at the canal), negotiating with officials about taxes and transport fees, renting boats for shipment, and storing and selling the products (although textual evidence is lacking for this last step).

Each partner shared in the profits (termed *utru* "excess"). This equity stipulation distinguishes these contracts from normal interest-bearing loans at the usual annual 20 percent interest rate, secured by pledges. The money-providing partner in such *ḫarrānu* undertakings could only expect to make a good deal if the anticipated profit rate equalled or exceeded 40 percent (as his half share provided just the net 20 percent return at this profit rate).

In the early stages we do not find Nabû-aḫḫē-iddin acting as a senior partner. Apart from members of the Egibi family, at least a dozen other people are documented as being involved in the same kind of business, and the Egibis certainly were not the only ones to become rich in this way.

Nabû-aḫḫē-iddin was trained as a scribe. While acting as a court scribe during the reign of Nebuchadnezzar II, he established business contacts with Neriglissar that evidently paid off when Neriglissar gained power.[6] Nabû-aḫḫē-iddin's first land purchase in the Babylon area dates from this time.[7] The transaction deserves attention not only because of the remarkable size of the parcel, but because of the circumstances that caused the vendors to sell and the sources of the purchase money. The surviving records also provide details concerning its structure, use, and revenue, as well as its use and disposition during three generations within the family. It therefore serves as a good example for land tenure and will be discussed more extensively below.

Few details are known about Nabû-aḫḫē-iddin's involvement in politics or the extent of his business relations with high-ranking individuals. But his position did not rely entirely on his patron Neriglissar, for he was able to consolidate his influence under the reign of Nabonidus as well, when he started acting as a royal judge. Growing wealth and power are reflected in a large number of land and house-sale contracts dating from this period.

Apart from overall growth, the process of dividing, exchanging, and reassembling plots and shares in commonly held properties begins in the following generation. But only transactions involving the eldest sons are well documented, as the family business and its archive was handed down to the firstborn.

After Nabû-aḫḫē-iddin's death at the beginning of the 13th year of Nabonidus (543 BC), his eldest son took charge of the family business on behalf of the heirs. For at least seven years the inheritance seems to have remained undivided. Unfortunately, no contract enables us to estimate the actual size of Nabû-aḫḫē-iddin's legacy and to compare it with the evidence obtained from the surviving tablets.[8] From several indications, however, we may deduce that the inheritance division took place after the second year of Cyrus's reign, although the fields might have been excluded and managed together for some years.

Only after the death of Itti-Marduk-balāṭu does evidence show a measuring and subsequent physical division of a large plot of land between Itti-Marduk-balāṭu's heirs on the one side and his brother on the other (discussed below). In the next generation the eldest brother likewise acted as head of the Egibi family business, for almost fourteen years before the inheritance was divided. This time, the respective document is extant, but deals only with houses, slaves, and property in ḫarrānu partnerships, while gardens and fields were still held jointly. It thus is still not possible to assess the total value of the landed property, but the surviving evidence of land purchased by the Egibi family is presented in Chart 3.[9]

The location of fields and gardens

Most of the fields and gardens mentioned in sales and rental contracts lie in the region around Babylon. Their location is usually specified with respect to rivers and canals, the city gates, and their neighbors. The rough character of this description, however, does not allow a mapping of the area. The New Canal outside the Enlil Gate, the Borsippa Canal and the Šamaš Gate, the Banītu Canal with the Zababa Gate, and the Euphrates in connection with the districts Šuppatu and Litamu near the Uraš Gate are mentioned in the records. Until recently, all of it has been located in the south and southeast of Babylon. A recent study by A. R. George on the topography of Babylon, however, has relocated the Enlil Gate in the northwest on the west bank of the Euphrates.[10] Therefore, the idea that the Egibis' interest in land acquisition was directed and concentrated only in the southern region cannot be upheld. Nevertheless, they preferred certain areas for their trade and land purchases. Exchange contracts, for instance, indicate a tendency to give away single lots, especially outside the Babylon region, for adjacent ones in areas where the family already held properties.

Prices for fields and gardens

Comparision of the Egibi archive's data[11] on prices in relation to the quality and agricultural use of land does not indicate any obvious sign for a fluctuation in prices from 575 to 510 BC. This finding is corroborated by a scattering of reliable and comparable data from other archives. Date orchards with fruit-bearing trees inside the city walls fetch the highest prices, followed by those just outside the city. One shekel of silver (about one month's wage of a hired worker) buys three to ten GAR (22.5 to 75 square meters). Gardens with only (or partially) young trees, or scattered date palms, are cheaper (up to 20 GAR per shekel). But it is difficult to compare and fully evaluate the data, for prices would have depended on the density of the palm trees, a figure that we hear of only occasionally when the actual number of trees per area is given.

The graph provided by Müller (1995-96:175) for prices in Babylon in the 6th century BC likewise does not show evidence for a significant increase in garden prices.[12] Yet it denotes a rapid increase in barley prices from about 530 BC on, while date prices remain stable for two more decades (p. 165). He endorses van Driel's finding that date palm cultivation was intensified during the 6th century BC in order to meet the expanding city's demand.[13] This view can now be supported by new evidence from the Egibi archive.

Arable land costs less than gardens. A shekel buys 30 to 100 GAR, depending on the proportion of fallow or low-quality land. Prices for particular plots of course also depend on circumstanes that cannot be found in sales contracts: access to irrigation water and waterways, soil quality, other geographic considerations, and also the particular circumstances that prompted the sale.

The circumstances of the acquisition

Archival evidence reveals some of the reasons why landed property was sold.[14] One example in which special circumstances apply already has been mentioned: a sale by order of the king and judges (5R 67, 1; see

Chart 3

Egibi Family Real Estate

Transaction	Year	Size	Price		Quality *	Location
NAI						
Speleers 276	0 Ngl	1 kur	5 m		zaqpu	Qalūnu, Kutha
5R 67,1	0 Ngl	24 kur	22 m	20 š	zaqpu, mērešu, taptû	Nāru eššu (new canal), Enlil Gate, Babylon (1)
BM 41511	3 Nbn	0.2.3.3.9 kur	4 m	10⅔ š	zaqpu	Bāb nār (canal entrance) Barsip, Babylon
Nbn 116	3 Nbn	5.1.3.5 kur	20 m	37 š	zaqpu, mērešu, kišubbû	Nār (canal) Banītu, Zababa Gate, Babylon (2)
BM 32163	4+x Nbn	1 kur		?	zaqpu, tālāni	Nār Banītu, Babylon (2) **
Nbn 178	4 Nbn	0.1 kur	1 m	22½ š	zaqpu	Nār Barsip, Babylon
Nbn 193	5 Nbn	0.0.2 kur		33 š	zaqpu	Bāb nār Barsip, Šamaš Gate, Babylon
Nbn 203	5 Nbn	0.0.2.5.6 kur		48 š	zaqpu	Bāb nār Barsip, Babylon
private	8 Nbn	2.1.4 kur		?	pî šulpu	Ḫanšu (50-field) šaŠa-Nabû-šu
BM 33056	[9] Nbn	1.2.3 kur		?	?	Uraš Gate, Babylon
Nbn 418	10 Nbn	0.0.2.2 kur		x+8½ š	?	Ḫarru (irrigation ditch) ša Ḫazuzu
Nbn 437	10 Nbn	0.1 kur	1 m	3 š	zaqpu	Bitqa (irrigation ditch) ša Ile"i-Bēl, Zababa Gate, Babylon (3)
BM 32492	10 Nbn	0.0.4.0.9 kur		?	zaqpu	Bitqa-ša Ile"i-Bēl, Zababa Gate, Babylon
Nbn 440+	10 Nbn	1 kur		15 š	mērešu, taptû	Uraš Gate, Babylon
Nbn 477	10 Nbn	0.1.5.4 kur	1 m	11 š	zaqpu, tālāni	Uraš Gate, Babylon
TCL 160	?	?		?	zaqpu, pî šulpu	Bāb nār Barsip, Babylon (4)
BM 34015	?	?		?	?	Uraš Gate, Babylon **
BM 35028	?	?		?	?	[Uraš Gate, Babylon] **

below). More often, vendors were forced to sell in order to settle debts. Sometimes these debts had been accumulated for two generations, collateralized by real estate that finally had to be sold. But only rarely do we find that the creditor himself has bought the property. If he were interested in doing so, he would arrange to make the purchase via a third party acting as intermediary.

Sometimes the property was held jointly by several heirs or business partners. In such cases the property's revenue simply was divided among the entitled parties rather than the property being physically subdivided. One or more (or all) of the heirs might sell a property. When only one co-owner sold, the buyer would either initiate a formal division of the property, or would participate in the joint venture's income in proportion to his ownership share.

The shifting composition of the property's heirs, as well as the names of their neighbors, suggests in several cases that plots typically were owned by one family for at least three generations, during which time they un-

Transaction	Year	Size	Price	Quality *	Location
NAI and/or IMB					
Nbn 372	9 Nbn	1.1 kur	x+20 š	?	Ḫarru ša Ḫazuzu
BM 32197	?	?	?	?	[Ḫarru ša Ḫazuzu] **
IMB					
Nbn 687	12 Nbn	0.1.4.0.8 kur	3 m 42½ š	zaqpu	Zababa Gate, between walls, Babylon
BM 47925	?	?	?	?	? **
Cyr 161‖1	3 Cyr	1.4.3.3 kur	2 m 3 š	zaqpu, mērešu, taptû	Šuppatu, Babylon
Cyr 161‖2	3 Cyr	1.1.4 kur	37¼ š	mērešu, kalû, gābibi	Šuppatu, Babylon
Cyr 161‖3	3 Cyr	?	43⅓ š	zaqpu	Šuppatu, Babylon
Cyr 161‖4	3 Cyr	?	43⅓ š	zaqpu	Šuppatu, Babylon
Cyr 161‖5	3 Cyr	[0.3.2 kur]	1 m	zaqpu, mērešu	Šuppatu, Babylon
Cyr 161‖6	3 Cyr	?	(35 š)	[...], kišubbû	Nār Madānu, Uraš Gate, Babylon
OrAn 14	7 Cyr	0.0.4.1 kur	42 š	zaqpu	Bitqa-ša Ile"i-Bēl, Zababa Gate, Babylon (5) **
(Camb 217)	7? Cyr	3 kur	x+2 m	zaqpu	Bāb nār Kutê labīri (6)
Camb 286	2 Camb	1 kur	?	mērešu, taptû	?
Camb 226	3 Camb	?	4 m 30 š	?	Giššu Gate
Camb 375	7 Camb	0.3.4 kur	?	?	Bāru eššu
BM 31931	x Cyr/Camb	?	x m 58⅔ š	pî šulpu	Šuppatu, Babylon **
MNA					
Dar 26	1 Dar	2 kur	9 m 30 š	zaqpu, kišubbû	Litamu, Uraš Gate, Babylon **
Dar 102+	3 Dar	1.0.5 kur	9 m 39⅓ š	zaqpu	Bāb nār Kutê labīri, Ištar Gate, Babylon **
Dar 152	4 Dar	3 kur	10 m 35 š	zaqpu, mērešu, taptû	Litamu, Uraš Gate, Babylon
Dar 202	6 Dar	?	?	?	Litamu, Uraš Gate, Babylon **
Dar 227	7 Dar	1.0.2 kur	4 m 2⅔ š	zaqpu, mērešu	Litamu, Uraš Gate, Babylon
BRM I 73	8 Dar	0.0.2 kur	28½ š	zaqpu	Litamu, Uraš Gate, Babylon
Dar 321	12 Dar	6 kur	32 m	zaqpu	Nāru eššu, Dūru-ša-kāri rabî
BM 31913	22 Dar	?	26 š	zaqpu, kalû, gābibi	Šaḫrīnu
BM 32016	x Dar	?	?	?	(Nār Banītu, Zababa Gate, Babylon) (7)

* see Chart 4 for terms
** Adjacent to a field already owned by the family
(1) Half share with Nergal-ušallim// Ile"i-Marduk
(2) Half share with Nergal-bānûnu// Rab-banê
(3) Half share with Rīmūt//Eppeš-ilī, second half later bought by IMB
(4) Half share with Bēlšunu//Sîn-imittu
(5) Former half share of Nbn 437
(6) 0.2.3 kur later sold to son-in-law
(7) MNA's wife buys back a share in the field Nbn 116

‖ = several plots
// = filiation

NAME ABBREVIATIONS
Camb = Cambyses
Cyr = Cyrus
Dar = Darius
IMB = Itti-Marduk-balāṭu
MNA = Marduk-nāṣir-apli
NAI = Nabû-aḫḫē-iddin
Nbk = Nebuchnezzar
Nbn = Nabonidus
Ngl = Neriglissar

WEIGHT
1 shekel (š) (about 8 grams)
1 mina (m) (about 500 grams)

SURFACE
1 kur (54,000 square cubits, about 13,500 square meters)
5 PI = 1 kur
30 bán = 1 kur
360 silà = 1 kur
3600 GAR = 1 kur

CAPACITY
1 kur (180 liters), same subdivision as surface measures.

C. WUNSCH

CHART 4

FIELD AND ORCHARD PRICES

Record	Year	King	Area per shekel	Location
Date orchard, fruit-bearing trees (*zaqpu, iṣṣi bilti*)				
5R 67, 1	0	Ngl	6.66 GAR	New Canal
Nbn 437+	10	Nbn	6 GAR	Bitqa-ša-Ile"i-Bēl
Nbn 687	12	Nbn	2.73 GAR	Zababa Gate, betw. city walls
Cyr 161‖1	3	Cyr	10 GAR	Šuppatu
Dar 26	1	Dar	5.45 GAR	Litamu
Dar 102	3	Dar	3.75 GAR	Old Kutha Canal
Dar 152+	4	Dar	3.6 GAR	Litamu
Dar 227	7	Dar	3.75 GAR	Litamu
Date orchard, unspecified or mixed-age trees (*zaqpu*)				
BM 32640	30	Nbk	6 GAR	New Canal
Speleers 276	0	Ngl	6 GAR	
Nbn 116	3	Nbn	6 GAR	Banītu Canal
BM 41511	3	Nbn	3.75 GAR	Borsippa Canal
Nbn 178	4	Nbn	3.75 GAR	Borsippa Canal
Nbn 193	5	Nbn	3.75 GAR	Borsippa Canal
Nbn 203	5	Nbn	3.75 GAR	Borsippa Canal
Nbn 477	10	Nbn	10 GAR	Uraš Gate
Cyr 161‖6	16 Nbn-3	Cyr	c. 15 GAR	Madānu Canal
OrAn 14	7	Cyr	6.5 GAR	Bitqa-ša-Ile"i-Bēl
BRM I 73	8	Dar	4.3 GAR	Litamu
Dar 321	12	Dar	6 GAR	New Canal, Dūru-ša-kāri-rabî
Dar 466	18	Dar	2.68 GAR	Uraš Gate
Date orchard, young trees (*tālānu*)				
5R 67, 1	0	Ngl	20 GAR	New Canal
Grain field (*mērešu, pî šulpi*)				
Dar 227	7	Dar	25.7 GAR	Litamu
Grain field (*mērešu*) *and freshly broken land* (*taptû*)				
BM 32640	30	Nbk	45 GAR	New Canal
5R 67, 1	0	Ngl	60 GAR	New Canal
Nbn 440+	10	Nbn	60 GAR	Uraš Gate
Cyr 161‖1	3	Cyr	100 GAR	Šuppatu
Dar 152+	4	Dar	30 GAR	Litamu
Grain field (*mērešu*) *and/or unused* (*kišubbû*) *or low-quality land* (*kalû, gābibi*)				
Nbn 116	3	Nbn	60 GAR	Banītu Canal
Cyr 161‖2	3	Cyr	c. 65 GAR	Šuppatu
Dar 26	1	Dar	60 GAR	Litamu
Unidentified quality				
BM 33056	9	Nbn	more than 20 GAR	Uraš Gate
Cyr 161‖3/4	3	Cyr	15 GAR	Šuppatu
Cyr 161‖5	3	Cyr	c. 20 GAR	Šuppatu
BM 31346‖1	x	Cyr/Camb	11.25 GAR	[Šuppatu]
BM 31346‖2	x	Cyr/Camb	45 GAR	[Šuppatu]

‖ = several plots

derwent several inheritance divisions. In such cases the main reason for selling the property probably was not so much financial as practical. When shares got too subdivided, this made the administration of income and expenditures too complicated. Sale was preferable simply to enable each party to consolidate his or her own resources.

Purchase patterns with regard to financing seem to have changed from the Egibi family's second and third generation to the fourth. In the second generation, Nabû-aḫḫē-iddin bought real estate either as sole buyer or together with business partners as an investment outlet for his profits earned originally in commerce.[15] Many of the properties that he and his son Itti-Marduk-balāṭu purchased had been the objects of lawsuits or had been pledged by their owners as collateral for loans or other debts. But in the fourth generation, Marduk-naṣir-apli is found buying fields without making full cash payment.

To the Babylonians, legal real estate sale requires the price to be paid in full. Every sales contract therefore contains a quittance clause for the entire purchase price as part of its forumla. Sales for less than full payment can be traced only if separate debt notes are preserved specifying the balance remaining due as part of the purchase price. But in all our cases the balance was owed to the vendor himself, not to a third party. The money was not actually borrowed from (or turned over by) the vendor; rather, the unpaid debt was a result of a (temporary) absence of cash on the part of the buyer. The partial balance remaining on the purchase price (or part of it) was paid several months or even years after the sale took place.

There is increasing evidence that the Egibi family's homes and fields, as well as slaves, were pledged and even forfeited for nonpayment. These signs suggest a shift in the family's business strategies and attitude regarding landed property. Obviously part of their real estate was employed in the normal course of business.

The field at the New Canal

According to sales contract 5R 67, 1 (= BM 41399 from 8/11/0 Neriglissar, 559 BC) Nabû-aḫḫē-iddin purchased a 24 kur estate (about 324 000 square meters, 2300 x 140 m) located on both sides of the New Canal (nāru eššu) opposite the Enlil Gate outside the walls of Babylon.[16] It is the largest plot of land ever attested as having been bought by a member of the Egibi family. The contract was drafted in the presence of high ranking witnesses: the governor (šakin ṭēmi) of Babylon and a team of eight royal judges and four scribes. All of them impressed their seals on the margins of the tablet, an indication of the transaction's importance.

Normally the presence of judges was not necessary for a land-sale contract to be valid. Only in cases of litigation or other problems were judges involved to certify the property's title. However, the transfer of landed property seemed to have required some act of publicity, referred to in the set phrases by *šīma nabû* "to announce the purchase (price)," although we do not know precisely in which way. Land-sale contracts (apart from documents issued by judges in the process or as a result of a lawsuit) appear to have been the only type of private legal documents from the period in question to be sealed, although not all of them are. Only a few scribes seem to have specialized in drafting sale records and were licenced to use seals. Their function therefore might be described as that of notaries.[17]

In our above example, four brothers appear as sellers of the field (obviously inherited from their father), while Nabû-aḫḫē-iddin acts as the sole buyer. However, the purchase price — 22 minas and 20 shekels — was not handed over to the vendors, but was given to the Esagil Temple as a compensatory payment to satisfy its claims against the four brothers for oxen owed to the temple. Van Driel (1985-86:63f.) points out that the sale was forced. He suspectes the reason concerned backlogs due for the delivery of oxen to the Marduk Temple.

Several hitherto unknown documents from the British Museum shed new light on this affair. The four brothers who sold the field to Nabû-aḫḫē-iddin handed over to him the previous purchase contract called *ummi eqli* "mother of the field" to attest to the legitimacy of the transfer. It was a regular practice to hand over such records (or copies of them) to the buyer; the vendor often was obliged to do so under the terms of the contract. In many archives such retroacta have been found and identified.

In this particular case the identification of the *ummi eqli* was difficult, as the previous purchase was not arranged by the father of the four brothers, but through a third person acting as a front man. We learn this fact, along with the name of the intermediary, only through another tablet (BM 32184), drafted two years after Nabû-aḫḫē-iddin had bought the field. The tablet's poor state of preservation prevents its full content and purpose from being determined with certainty, but it mentions the circumstances surrounding the previous sale and hence represents the key to identifying the *ummi eqli* and provides additional information about the parties involved.

It shows that the father of the four brothers, Marduk-ēṭir, son of Marduk-zēra-ibni from the Ēṭiru family, was governor (*šakin ṭēmi*) of Babylon in the 30th year of Nebuchadnezzar II, at which time he arranged for the field to be bought. He seems to have been in trouble after Neriglissar became king, as an unfortunately damaged part of BM 32184 reads: *ina qībāti šarri* [. . .] *Marduk-ēṭir ina šakin ṭēmūti mārē Bā*[*bili* ...] *ana mārē Bābili turru iqabbi* "by order of the king . . . M. from(?) the government of the people of Babylon . . . to the people of Babylon he promised to give back." This suggests that the land sale was ordered by Neriglissar, and it does not come as a surprise to find Nabû-aḫḫē-iddin profiting from his good business connections with this king.

A comparison of the two sale contracts — 5R 67, 1 and its *ummi eqli* BM 32640 — reveals that the *šakin ṭēmi*'s representative paid 19 minas and 8 shekels in total, while Nabû-aḫḫē-iddin paid 22 minas 20 shekels. This was nonetheless a lower price per square measure of date orchard and arable land, for in the intervening fifteen years the field had undergone intensive cultivation, which considerably increased the proportion of date orchard. At first it measured only 4 PI[18] (one thirtieth of the total surface), but according to 5R 67, 1 it consisted of 10 PI with fully grown trees and more than 9 PI with young trees. This means that nearly one sixth was cultivated with date palms. Therefore the field's value had increased more than the slight rise of the purchase price indicates, and Nabû-aḫḫē-iddin made a very good deal.

Some 41 years later, when Nabû-aḫḫē-iddin's son and grandsons divided up their shares in this field, the respective plots were measured and mapped (BM 30627, see below). By this time the area cultivated with date palms represented more than one fourth of the total surface, stretched along both sides of the canal. It seems that at this point, date palm cultivation had reached the limit set by the irrigation facilities. This is indicated by a stipulation in a rental contract (BM 31401) in which one of the tenants is permitted to cultivate an area in addition to his lot, but must water this land with buckets (*i.e.,* it could not be irrigated directly).

The aforementioned record BM 32184 contains some further important information. It states that Nabû-aḫḫē-iddin had bought the field and established a half-share with Nergal-ušallim, the son of Šuma-iddin from the Ile"i-Marduk family. The key words *aḫi zitti*, "half share," call to mind the appropriate clauses in *ḫarrānu* records, in which usually two businessmen agree to undertake certain business affairs together and to share the profits and losses. No such record is known about a partnership with Nergal-ušallim, but it must be pointed out that Nabû-aḫḫē-iddin bought several other properties together with three persons who had worked as his *ḫarrānu* partners.[19] Except for these cases he always acted as the sole buyer. We therefore may assume that Nabû-aḫḫē-iddin assigned

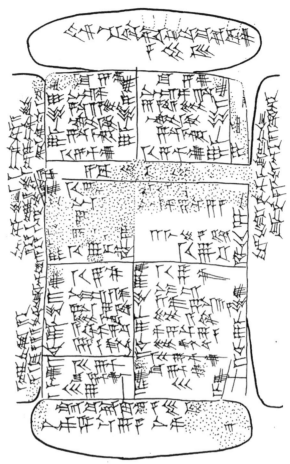

Illustration of a cuneiform tablet recording the division of property at the New Canal among Egibi family heirs (BM 30627, obverse), c. 11 x 7 cm. (See cover photo.)

a half share to Nergal-ušallim in the aforementioned property because the money paid for it had originated from their joint business. In this context the purchase of gardens and arable land should be understood as representing a secure and profitable investment of their commercial profits. One certainly can conclude that Nabû-aḫḫē-iddin at this point in his career did not yet possess the means to buy the whole lot for himself. Until today, the evidence from 5R 67, 1 (the sales contract) suggested that he purchased and owned 24 kur, a remarkably large estate as compared to the size of the other lots he bought. It now turns out that only half of it should be considered for calculations of the size of the Egibis' landed property.

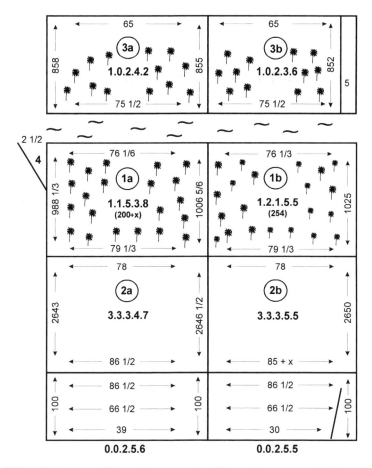

BM 30627 (schematic). Length measures in cubits, surface measures (bold type) in kur, and number of palm trees in parentheses.

The property was held in common after its purchase and rented out by Nabû-aḫḫē-iddin and his partner (or the latter's heirs) to a series of tenants until it was finally divided among members of both families after Nabû-aḫḫē-iddin's death.[20] It is difficult to estimate the actual yield of this field or to establish a relation between its purchase price and the revenue.[21] Some surviving debt notes concern the volume of dates from orchards at the New Canal owed by the tenants to Nabû-aḫḫē-iddin and his partner, but they only refer to rent charged on the date palms. We have no evidence about the grain field or the crop underneath the trees. Liv 12 (from the third season after the purchase) specifies 165 kur of dates and by-products owed by two persons, one of whom is Nergal-ušallim's slave. A debt note has been preserved from the 9th year of Nabonidus, in which four persons owe 171 kur, one of them a slave of Nabû-aḫḫē-iddin. These figures seem plausible[22] and the records are likely to refer to our field, although perhaps Nabû-aḫḫē-iddin and his partner owned or rented and sublet additional lots in the same area. A revenue of about 150 kur (27,000 liters) represents a value of 2 minas 30 shekels of silver, given the "ideal" exchange rate of one kur per shekel that seems applicable until the end of Nabonidus's reign.[23] This figure compares well with the interest of 2 minas 24 shekels that could be obtained from 12 minas of silver (the price portion Nabû-aḫḫē-iddin paid for the land cultivated with date palms) at the usual annual interest rate of 20 percent.

Another unpublished document (BM 31959), drafted during the first years of Darius's reign,[24] reveals the property situation after Nabû-aḫḫē-iddin's death. According to this document he had transferred his field at the New Canal to his wife Qudāšu and granted her lifetime usufruct. In addition, his three sons were designated as remaindermen after her death and were to inherit "according to their shares," i.e., the oldest son was to receive a double portion. We therefore may expect Qudāšu to have received the field's yield after her husband's death. In fact, her ownership of the field is attested by three records. In two debt notes, Cyr 123 and Camb 118 (from the 3rd year of Cyrus and the 2nd year of Cambyses, 536 and 528 BC respectively) tenants owe her dates as rent for the field at the New Canal. The tenant mentioned in Camb 118 also appears in the rent contract BM 31401. This fragmentary text seems to contain an additional stipulation to a previous contract. Obviously the tenant is assigned a lot that cannot be reached by normal irrigation, but must be watered with buckets.[25] The crop is to be shared with Qudāšu.[26]

After Qudāšu's death, her sons — Itti-Marduk-balāṭu, Nergal-ēṭir, and Iddin-Nabû — took over the field in the 7th year of Cambyses (523 BC). BM 31959 speaks of the brothers having divided the field; Iddin-Nabû immediately transferred his quarter to his brother in order to settle debts. Later on Nergal-ēṭir used his share as a pledge (Camb 372). Nevertheless, the field was not physically divided but was held in common and the yield was distributed according to their shares until the 3rd year of Darius (519 B.C.). Only after the death of Nabû-aḫḫē-ddin's eldest son, Itti-Marduk-balāṭu, did his heirs initiate a formal division of the property.

Two records refer to this division and provide information about the field's size and shape, soil quality, and agricultural use including the number of date palms, the names of the field's neighbors, and the manner of partition. Dar 80 (with duplicate BM 32216) is the division contract, and BM 30627 the corresponding field plan[27] (see illustrations on pp. 404-405).[28] Both tablets were drafted by the same scribe in front of the same witnesses in a settlement at the New Canal, that is in the region where the field is located and the measuring took place. Both records are slightly damaged, but some of the gaps can be filled by data from the other text.

The obverse of BM 30627 depicts a rectangle that is divided vertically into two sections. Horizontally they are subdivided into four parts each, the first border being specified as *nāru ešu*, the New canal. The lengths of all sides (in cubits) are indicated in each part as well as the corresponding Babylonian surface measure and the agricultural use. This sketch does not represent a field plan to scale, but is an abstraction, for the lot actually is almost 30 times longer than it is wide.[29] The owners of the neighboring plots are named in the margins. The reverse of the tablet summarizes the size of the shares and assigns the left half to Nergal-ēṭir, the right half to Marduk-nāṣir-apli and his brothers. Evidently the long field has been divided vertically at a right angle to the canal in order to provide both sides with access to the irrigation facilities. This achieved a balanced proportion of date orchards to arable land for both shares and therefore assured that the same surface area represented an equal value.

The length and surface measures, as well as the names of the neighbors, correspond with the data that can be read in the badly damaged division contract Dar 80 and help to reconstruct the missing parts. The map reveals some interesting details of the field layout that are rarely expressed so explicity in other sources. On the south bank of the canal we find an area of date orchard that contains about 500 trees on 38,520 square meters[30] (*i.e.,* one tree per about 77 square meters or 130 trees per hectare in modern metrology). The area north of the canal is described as consisting of two thirds palm orchard, obviously streched out along its bank. Further away from the canal we find an area suitable for barley cultivation, starting at a distance of 500 meters south of the canal and having a length of over 1.37 kilometers. Its bottom end is trapezoidal and leads to a basin or drainage canal.

Seven years after the division took place, Nergal-ēṭir died, and we find his widow and daughters in the contract Dar 265 exchanging his lot with Marduk-nāṣir-apli and his brothers for a smaller field in Dilbat and a compensation payment that was used to settle Nergal-ēṭir's debts. After all this, Nabû-aḫḫē-iddin's original share was reunited in the hands of his grandsons but probably was divided again some years later.

Discussion

Hudson: You mentioned earlier that you found that when something had to give, it was control of the land rather than the debt burden, in contrast to the *andurarum* and *misharum* Clean Slates of the Old Babylonian period. In other words, debt created an inexorable relationship that altered land-tenure relations.

Wunsch: I was referring to cases where the land was not alienable (royal fiefs, for instance) and was connected with services to be performed by its holder. M. W. Stolper analyzed the underlying patterns reflected in the Murasû archive. Although such land holdings could not be sold, they could be used as a pledge in exchange for a loan. At first they only served as a security for the debt. But if the debtor fell behind with interest payments, the land was converted into an antichretic pledge; that is to say, the creditor was entitled to take possession of the pledged land and enjoy its usufruct in lieu of interest payments on the outstanding debt. He thus became the virtual owner and was entitled to rent it out.

This shift in the control of the land through debt did not necessarily change the land's use or occupancy. The most appropriate tenant was the debtor himself. He ended up working the field, performing the duties that were linked with it while trying to repay the capital amount of his debt. This was of course more difficult under such conditions, as a substantial part of the crop had to be paid as rent to the creditor-lessor. Indebtedness therefore created a long-term dependency that provided the creditor with access to land and its usufruct even though no actual transfer of title took place.

Harrison: Was the New Canal part of the landscape, or was it built artificially, and if so, who built it and was responsible for maintaining it?

Wunsch: It definitely was not part of the original landscape. It was the task of the king to have such canals dug and maintained. This was an organized palace responsibility. The users of the irrigation waters had to pay for their use.

Renger: The revenue was paid to the royal administration, at least in the Achaemenid period under Persian domination.

Harrison: How did they establish the amount to be paid? Did it depend on the land's location near or far from the water? Was there something recognized as being a favorable location?

Wunsch: Probably, and we would know more about it if we had the royal administration archives. But all we have got are clauses in rent documents stating that the canal fee (*gugallūtu*) is paid or not paid. We have no idea about the specific proportion of the harvest that is to be paid to the canal authorities. Neither its amount nor the size or location of the property is mentioned in these texts. They only record the amount of dates or barley still to be delivered as rent by the tenant to the lessor. The appearance of such a clause in a contract between lessor and tenant however suggests that the officials actually dealt with the tenant when they came to collect the fee. But it was not considered to be part of the rent.

We also know that the Egibis had an obligation to supply corvée labor to work on the canal system and to perform other construction work. It is not clear just what the basis was for having to provide such workers. Was it because of their own land holdings, or because they were managing other land, for instance temple estates? We know that temples had to provide labor for canal maintenance and construction. We can assume the same for large private land owners.

The canal inspector (*gugallu*) was responsible for organizing maintenance work at the local level, while the owner had to keep intact the intake of water from the canal system into his own field.

Dandamayev: You said that there are no documents in which members of the Egibi family appear as sellers of land. You explain this by the fact that when a landholder sold his land, he turned over all earlier sales documents relating to this land to the new buyer. But some other explanation is possible in this particular case. Why should members of the Egibi family sell any land? They may sell slaves, but why would they sell any land? After all, land was the most valuable property, and everybody tried to acquire it. Nobody would have wanted to sell. Therefore, selling would be expected only in cases of extreme need or by old owners who had no children. I am not sure that the Egibis were forced to sell land.

Wunsch: They were certainly not forced, as they had alternatives. But there might have been cases when their neighbors wished to buy a plot and offered a good deal. The Egibis have sold a certain piece of land as a favor to someone whom they could expect to be helpful for their business. It was probably not very effective to manage scattered fields in faraway areas anyway. Indeed we have one record that points out that the Egibis sold properties, but it is not a sales contract. The record (Liv. 33) states that two brothers sold one field plot each in which the other one had a half share. As they had not yet divided the inheritance of their father, neither of them would have had full title to any field. The purpose of this record was to oblige both of them to have the plots measured in order to make sure that they were of equal size and value. Should one of them be larger or smaller, the other brother would have to be compensated. I think we can deduce from these traces that the Egibis indeed sold plots of land.

I agree that land was the most valuable asset and that people tried to avoid selling their land. It was, after all, their livelihood. The reason why the Egibis were willing to sell land voluntarily was precisely the fact you cite, that they were incredibly rich. They had lots of such little bits of properties, and they obviously sold some of them for the sake of other business operations. In this case they did not treat land as a vital source of their subsistence, but as an asset to be used in the most economic manner.

Dandamayev: You mentioned that the governor of Babylon was ordered by the king to sell his land. This document is difficult to interpret, for it is destroyed in a crucial place. I can understand that he could remove his officials, but I doubt that he could order somebody to sell his land if it was that person's own property. This would be against traditional custom, a violation of the rights of citizens. So your interpretation is difficult for me to accept.

Wunsch: We do not know exactly the contents of the king's order, but it resulted in the sons of the governor selling the field. It should be noted that it was not the king who took the money. The purchase price went to the Esagila, the Marduk temple. The king simply might have acted in his capacity as supreme judge. I infer that we must assume that the governor somehow was involved in the administration of the Marduk temple, perhaps with the temple's cattle as oxen are mentioned. Perhaps he simply profited from his position and put something aside. Or, he still owed something to the temple. I don't find it strange that his sons inherit his debts and have to (or decide to) sell.

Renger: There was no constitutional provision regarding property. This is not a free country or even a civic society. This is a despotic king who is the supreme ruler of his country and can do with his subjects as he wants, within certain limits. If there was something he thought had to be straightened out, then he could order it.

Stager: It depends on the customary law and tradition. A king may be the ruler, but that doesn't mean he can pluck away everything he wants in a noncustomary manner. Of course, the situation will vary from society to society. Now if your society has no customs against this sort of thing, then the king could do it.

Renger: This is not a case in which the king takes the land for himself. There were some claims from the temple that were served by royal order to return the proceeds.

Levine: The king is an enforcer.

Hudson: From the vantage point of the economic historian, one of the most interesting things in your paper is the last document you mention, which is about a property that seems to have been bought in conjunction with a loan. Moses Finely mentioned that he had looked through all of the literature of Greece and Rome and had not found a single instance of anyone borrowing money to make money, of any productive loan. Do you believe that you have found something in the Neo-Babylonian period that would represent borrowing money to make money via land ownership?

Wunsch: First of all, it is difficult to trace such cases, as the transfer of property requires the price to be paid in full for the transaction to be valid. Therefore, every sales contract contains a quittance clause that states that the full amount of money has been paid. Our only chance to detect loans linked with purchases are additional debt notes that specify the money as part of the purchase price or interest payments.

Such cases occur, but normally it is a small fraction of the price only (for instance, to be paid when the vendor brings family members as additional witnesses to the contract or hands over a previous record to the new owner). In such cases the buyer simply withholds part of the price to reenforce an obligation. No actual loan is involved. Sometimes, the payment is delayed by some days.

But there is one case (Dar 152 and relating records) in which about three quarters of the price of a field are owed by the Egibis to the vendor. Part of it has to be paid within one month, the balance within three months. From an additional record (Dar 217) we learn however, that it had not yet been paid in full after two years. There is no mention of interest payments, and we cannot exclude that there was some commercial connection.

However, according to a lawsuit (Nbn 356), a couple bought a house and a quarter of the price was a loan. After the death of the husband, the wife tried to keep up with interest payments but eventually failed and the house had to be sold. One of the stipulations made by the judges was that the creditor's claim had to be paid out of the purchase price with first priority. This example at least illustrates that purchase at credit was actually practiced, although we cannot term it a productive loan.

Hudson: In terms of quantity this may not be important, but structurally speaking, it seems very important.

Renger: On the other hand, in terms of these business ventures in which someone provided commodities to another person to trade, we do not find people making deposits with others as bankers who turn around and use it to finance trading ventures. So what Cornelia said (and you pointed out from classical antiquity, Michael) — the fact that there was no credit being used or created for investment — also applies to Mesopotamia in this period. This document seems to be a very exceptional case. I don't remember any other like it.

Wunsch: I guess it goes together with a tendency we can observe in that generation of the Egibis. They are freer to pledge their own property. Obviously they undertook numerous ventures that required them to pledge their property as security to back their commitment. There even was a foreclosure, and the pledged property actually was sold. At first glance you would not expect this in so rich a family. What it seems to indicate is that the Egibi were using their land more as an asset in the modern way, rather than with the attitude of someone who had to earn a living from that property.

Hudson: Do you have examples of people buying an urban property and changing its land use from one type of activity, such as gardening, to one yielding a higher rent, such as building a residential town house?

Wunsch: We find cases of people buying urban property, tearing down whatever is on it, and building something new. We see the Egibis buying houses and renting them out, often for very high rents.

Hudson: Is there such a thing as what modern economists call "rent of location," with some sites being more valuable than others because of their proximity to the gates or markets, or to the palace and temples?

Wunsch: The problem is that the houses are not well described in the rent contracts, which hardly ever enable us to identify them with the properties known from our purchase contracts. We therefore cannot establish any link between the size of the properties and their rental income. Even in house sale contracts the information on location is far from being satisfactory. Usually only the town district and the names of neighbors are given, but rarely a street name. There is no chance of creating a land-value map. Of course, when the house of a high official of even the palace of the crown prince is mentioned as adjacent property, we can presume that the property is prestigious and valuable.

The important point is that landowning by itself did not make high profits. Land prices did not increase in the way that they would in modern European or American cities. For agricultural properties, prices did not increase significantly either, unless their owner invested money to plant date palms or improve the infrastructure, for instance. When background information on landowners is available, they seem to have derived their wealth not from urban real estate (for there does not seen to have been speculative activity in this period), but rather from their position in the temple or royal administration, or from commerce such as buying commodities in the countryside and delivering them to Babylon.

NOTES

Babylonian dates are cited in the following form: day/month/regnal year, King's name. Filiations are referred to by the person's name/father's name/ancestor's name or person's name//ancestor's name.

1. For general information on the archive, Weingort (1939) and Ungnad (1941-44), concentrate on the family relations and establish the genealogical tree. Krecher (1970) catalogues the published records where members of the main family branch are involved and provides abstracts (*regestae*) of these documents together with an index of subjects and valuable cross-references. Van Driel (1985-86) gives an outline of the family business during the first and second generations. Roth (1991) and Wunsch (1995-96) deal with dowries comprising real estate and the property left to and by the women who married into and out of the Egibi family.

2. For details, see Reade (1986) and Evers (1993).

3. van Driel (1985-86, 1988 [152-55 presents a table on "Land in the Egibi archive"], 1990 [esp. concerning agricultural terminology]). Previous studies by Beljavskij (1968) and Martirosjan (1977) on land tenure according to the Egibi archive hardly reached an audience outside Russia.

4. My forthcoming *Studien zum Egibi-Archiv. 1. Die Felder und Gärten* deals with the family's fields and gardens and will contain text editions (including copies of unpublished texts) of the material in question. For the present, unpublished texts are quoted by their BM number for identification.

5. Lanz (1976) provides a detailed study of such *ḫarrānu* undertakings during the Neo-Babylonian period and deals with the affairs of members of the Egibi family on pp. 148-165.

6. For a recent treatment and details of the "Neriglissar connection," see van Driel (1985-86:57-59), summarizing: "Commercial relations, neighborliness and politics are closely connected."

7. The first purchase attested at all took place only three months before in the Kutha area: Speleers *Recueil* no. 276 (cuneiform text, abbreviation listed in CAD and AHw under Speleers or Recueil).

8. We have to assume that the existing tablets refer to the one half share of Itti-Marduk-balāṭu, the eldest son who took over his father's business and archive, whereas sale documents referring to the shares that later have been assigned to the younger brothers must have been handed over to them and left the archive. The same happened in the next generation and another set of documents is probably missing for this reason. There is evidence for Itti-Marduk-balāṭu and Marduk-nāṣir-apli trying to buy back shares from their brothers or other relatives, but it remains uncertain for various reasons to what extent we have knowledge of Nabû-aḫḫē-iddin's activities in land purchase.

9. Such references are omitted in debt notes, etc., that merely mention a "field in . . . " without any details.

10. George (1985-86: 9; 1992:24 with map).

11. Chart 4 arranges the prices according to land quality and the date of the contract. Some texts are mentioned in more than one section when they indicate different prices for different sorts of land. The sign || followed by a number refers to contracts about several plots (numbered in sequence) that may contain in themselves various types of land. For a recent discussion of the meaning of the terms describing the fields according to quality and agricultural use, see van Driel (1990:220).

12. The data have been treated with statistical methods in order to emphasize trends, but unfortunately there is no table to indicate where the data themselves derive from. Most likely the majority of the sources from the period in question are extracted from the same texts dealt with in the present paper. They therefore are not suitable as additional support for my observations.

13. Van Driel (1990:144-146); for new evidence from Sippar see Jursa (1995:122f.).

14. Speleers *Recueil* Nr. 276: Two heirs were indebted to a third person, the debt dates back to their grandfather's time; Nbn 116: purchase by a front man; BM 32163+: the field had been pledged to the vendor's daughter-in-law (as security for her dowry silver) before being sold to NAI and his partner; Nbn 178: sold by three heirs; BM 33056+: three heirs, indebted to a third person, a lawsuit with a relative had to be settled before the sale could be completed; Nbn 418: several heirs and various lawsuits (Nbn 372, 477, BM 34015, BM 35028 and BM 32197 refer to several sales by members of the same family); Nbn 687: the vendor was first indebted to IMB and the field served as pledge, debt title and pledge were then transferred to a royal official before finally IMB bought the field and paid the vendor's creditor; Cyr 161: sale by three heirs, the lessor was indebted to IMB's parents-in-law and two more creditors; OrAn 14: two heirs of a former business partner of NAI sold to IMB in order to settle debts owed to a third person; Camb 217: The vendor was originally indebted to IMB, part of the purchase price was not paid immediately but owed to the vendor at a 20 percent interest rate; Camb 375: exchange contract; BM 31939: vendor indebted to IMB; Dar 26: sale within the familiy (vendor is MNA's father-in-law); Dar 102+: a receipt reveals that the price was paid in total only eight years after the purchase, the dissolving of a *ḫarrānu* undertaking is mentioned as well. Dar 152: bought at credit (two thirds of the purchase price out of which 5 m were to be paid within one month, 2 m 10 š with three months, nevertheless, years later 2 m are still owed to the vendor); Dar 202: only a quittance of a fraction of the purchase price is extant; Dar 227: 1 m out of a total purchase price of 4 m is owed to the vendor on an interest-free basis; BRM

I 73: sold by three heirs; BM 31913: total purchase price paid in full only after 9 months; BM 32016: sale within the family.

15. For references, see note 20.

16. According to George (1985-86:9; 1992:24), this gate lay to the northwest. The canals and water courses near it must be relocated accordingly, as pointed out by van Driel (1990:218).

17. A study on this subject by H. D. Baker and the present writer is to be published in a forthcoming volume of *Iraq*.

18. This figure has been calculated on the basis of a total of [23].2.3 kur (confirmed by BM 32184:15) and the relation of 6 GAR per shekel for date orchard and 45 GAR per shekel for arable land, both figures given in BM 32640.

19. Nbn 116 and related documents: more than 5 kur, commonly owned with Nergal-bānûnu//Rab-banê; BM 32163+: 1 kur with Nergal-bānûnu//Rab-banê; Nbn 437:1 PI with Rīmūt//Eppeš-ilī; TCL 13, 160: field of unknown size together with Bēlšunu//Sîn-imittu.

20. We have have only indirect proof that after Nabû-aḫḫē-iddin's death the field was properly divided. Another 16 years later, according to the field plan BM 30627, the shares of Nabû-aḫḫē-iddin's heirs measured about 12 kur; the neighbour at one of the long sides is a member of the Ile"i-Marduk familiy and very likely a descendent of Nergal-ušallim.

21. The ratio between the shares of lessor and tenant is not relevant in this context, and therefore will be left aside.

22. A recent discussion of the available information for date crops in Neo-Babylonian times can be found in Jursa (1995:148-50). On the basis of data from the Sippar temple archive, he concludes that 30 to 40 kur of dates per kur of surface were expected to be paid as *imittu* rent (comparable with our case). This was an average figure, with extremes being as high as 70 kur and as low as 7 kur. Given a surface measure of 2 kur of fruit-bearing trees and 2 more kur of young trees by the year 0 Ngl (*i.e.,* probably starting to yield crops by the time when our debt notes were drafted), the amounts of 165 kur and 171 kur are within the expected range.

23. See Müller (1995-96:165). However, this figure normally refers to the price paid by traders to farmers, or the equivalents of commodities in silver mentioned in debt notes. The actual income might therefore be higher.

24. Duplicate: BM 41551. Although the year in these tablets is not preserved, prosopographical evidence suggests that the record is to be dated between the 1st and 3rd years of Darius (521-519 BC).

25. *ina dāli dalû*. CAD D p. 56, s.v. dalû suggests this term means the drawing of water from wells rather than canals.

26. The clause *šá ú-še-la* Q. *it-ti* PN *ta-ak-kal* "whatever he causes to grow, Q. will consume it with PN" does not specify the proportion, but it probably implies equal shares.

27. By a lucky chance we are able to link such a field plan to an archive and to the actual contract for which it has been established. By contrast, none of the mostly fragmentary field plans published by Nemet-Nejat (1982) contains comparable details, and all of them lack archival background information. Part of the maps, termed "field plan" by the author, actually refer to houses (as pointed out by Liverani (1996:35)). For the identification of a house plan and its corresponding sales contract, see Joannès (1990).

28. The tablet will be fully published and studied in the present writer's forthcoming volume (see note 4).

29. Liverani (1996:35-37) has calculated the average length-width relation of fields on the basis of field plans and property descriptions in Neo-Babylonian contracts. For date palm orchards, he quotes an average ratio of 7:1 (with examples from the Egibi and Sîn-ilī archives showing a 20:1 ratio). He points out that orchards generally have a more elongated shape than grain fields "as a result of more specific irrigation needs and practices."

    However, these figures do not say too much. If we take our field as an example, the ratio at the time of purchase was 15:1, after the first division between the business partners, it was 30:1. After the division documented by BM 30627, it was as much as 60:1. When MNA bought back the share of his uncle, it reached 30:1 again. This shows the degree to which the ratio is determined by the stage of the ongoing process of division and reuniting of shares.

    Our evidence is very accidental. When we take only the date-orchard stripe alongside the canal into consideration, the ratios would be roughly 3.5:1, 7:1, and 15:1. As the distance between the trees was about 8.5 to 9 meters in each direction (see next note), a single plot at its 60:1 stage was only 5 trees (or 40 meters) wide. The length of a garden plot is determined by the irrigation facilities. Therefore the only useful figure that might emerge at the end is that of the minimum size of a plot, when further division was prohibited by practical reasons.

30. This figure corresponds with the data from Sippar provided by Jursa (1995:150, n. 302: 6.5 to 10 meters distance between trees).

BIBLIOGRAPHY

Beljavskij, A. (1968), "Zemlevladenie doma Ègibi," *Geografičeskoe obščestvo SSR, Doklady otdelenii i komisii* 5:160-181.

van Driel, G. (1985-86), "The Rise of the House of Egibi: Nabû-aḫḫē-iddina," *JEOL* 29:50-67.

— (1988), "Neo-Babylonian Agriculture," *Bulletin on Sumerian Agriculture* 4 (Cambridge):121-159 [pp. 152-155: Land in the Egibi archive].

— (1990), "Note on BSA 4, pp. 127 and 150-1 and Neo-Babylonian Agriculture. III. Cultivation," *Bulletin on Sumerian Agriculture* 5 (Cambridge): 218-265.

Evers, S. M. (1993), "George Smith and the Egibi Tablets," *Iraq* 55:107-117.

George, A. R. (1985-86), "The Topography of Babylon Reconsidered," *Sumer* 44:7-24.

— (1992), "Babylonian Topographical Texts," *Orientalia Lovaniensia Analecta* 40 (Leuven).

Joannès, F. (1990), "Cadastre et titre de propriété en Babylonie achéménide," *NABU* 1990/10

Jursa, M. (1995), "Die Landwirtschaft in Sippar in neubabylonischer Zeit," *AfO* Beiheft 25 (Wien).

Krecher, J. (1970), *Das Geschäftshaus Egibi in Babylon in neubabylonischer und achämenidischer Zeit.* Habilitationsschrift [unpublished] (Münster/W.).

Lanz, H. (1976), *Die neubabylonischen ḫarrānu-Geschäftsunternehmen*, Münchner Universitätsschriften. Beiträge zur rechtswissenschaftlichen Grundlagenforschung, 18 (Berlin):148-165 [Das Haus Egibi].

Liverani, M. (1996), "Reconstructing the Rural Landscape of the Ancient Near East," *JESHO* 39:1-41.

Martirosjan, A. (1977), "Arendnye operacii v delovom dome Ègibi v 543-522 gg. do n. è," *Akad. Nauk Arm SSR 1997/7* (Erevan):84-91.

Müller, G. G. W. (1995/96), "Die Teuerung in Babylon im 6. Jh.v.Chr.," *AfO* 42/43, 163-175.

Nemet-Nejat, K. R. (1982), *Neo-Babylonian Field Plans* (Roma).

Reade, J. E. (1986), "Introduction," in E. Leichty, *Catalogue of the Babylonian Tablets in the British Museum*, 6, (London):xiv-xvi.

Roth, M.T. (1991), "The Dowries of the Women of the Itti-Marduk-balāṭu Family," *JAOS* 111/1:19-37.

Ungnad, A. (1941-44), "Das Haus Egibi," *AfO* 14:57-64.

Weingort, S. (1939), *Das Haus Egibi* (Berlin).

Wunsch, C. (1995-96), "Die Frauen der Familie Egibi," *AfO* 42/43:33-63.

13

The Biblical "Town" as Reality and Typology: Evaluating Biblical References to Towns and Their Functions

Baruch A. Levine
New York University

Genesis 4:16-26 presents an ideological assessment of the components of civilization in capsule form. We read that after his fratricidal murder was exposed, Cain, Adam's surviving son, left God's presence and betook himself to the land of Nod, East of Eden. There, his wife bore him a son named Enoch. Cain then built a town, Hebrew *'îr*, and named it after his son, Enoch. This is the Bible's way of enunciating the dynastic principle associated with the early political development of towns. Enoch was slated to rule the town, succeeding his father, Cain. There may even be economic significance in the fact that the first town was constructed outside the horticultural/agricultural "garden," an innuendo that has not been missed in modern scholarship

We read further of Enoch's descendants, to whom are attributed the proverbial occupations — metallurgy, musical instruments, pastoral pursuits, and tent dwelling. Then we are told that Adam had another son named Seth, a replacement for the slain Abel, and that Seth in turn had a son named Enosh, which in Hebrew means "man, human being." The text goes on to state: "It was then that the invocation of Yahweh's name commenced" (Gen 4:26). This refers, of course, to the origin of religion, a feature of civilization that could hardly be attributed to a descendant of Cain! The traditional resolution of this incongruity was to have Adam sire another son, untainted by criminality.

A second primeval genealogy, presented in Genesis, chapter 5, presumably introduces another person named Enoch, who, we are told, never died in the normal way, for God took him away. I suspect that this report actually represents the genealogical rehabilitation of the former Enoch, son of Cain. As such it serves to reinforce the awareness that towns and civilization, state and economy, have the potential for violence and oppression, a theme encountered time and again in biblical literature.

The import of the above "myths of origin" is that towns have genealogies as do families and peoples, gods and kings. In Genesis, chapter 10, we read of Nimrod, who began to assemble his kingdom in Babylon, and in Uruk and Akkad, and that he built Nineveh and Calah, and some other towns we cannot as easily identify. This reflects the heroic strain in the biblical view of urban centers: their attribution to individuals of notable prowess, like Nimrod the "hero," in Hebrew, *gibbôr*. Some of these heroes, themselves, bear the names of towns and lands, as was true of Nimrod/Nimrud, himself.

It is, however, in the story of the so-called Tower of Babel that we encounter a major ideological pronouncement on the potentialities of urbanization (Genesis, chapter 11). After leaving the fertile plain of Eden, humankind, then of one language and governed by common laws (for that may be what the Hebrew *ûdebārîm 'aḥādîm*, literally: "of the same words" truly means) found a valley, and set about baking bricks for the construction of "a town with a tower" (*'îr ûmigdāl*), a way of indicating a fortified town. The apprehension expressed by humankind in this narrative is that without a fortified town they would not be able to remain together; that they would be dispersed. The apprehension attributed to the deity in the biblical narrative is that the tower, a sort of ziggurat reaching to heaven, would enable humankind to overthrow God, a recognizable mythological theme. In more clearly political terms, the human urge to aggregate in fortified towns implies that in reverse, the way a conqueror, or ruler can reduce the power of nations and other groups is to disperse their urban populations, to destroy their fortified towns, and thereby prevent regrouping. This is nothing short of an ideological statement on the policy of deportation so widespread in the ancient Near East at various times. In an indirect, and somewhat underhanded way, the biblical author is confirming the function of the town as an aggressive power base.

Here ends the primeval history (Genesis 1-11), except for a routine, priestly genealogy. We have, in effect, a blatantly etiological collection of narratives, beginning with creation, whose agenda and tone prompt a consideration of the conception of the town in biblical literature. The fact that the primeval history, so-called, comes at the beginning of the Bible does not signify that this is the earliest tradition. Its position does suggest, however, that the primeval history, itself comprised of several literary strata, expresses crystallized viewpoints, or representative ones, perhaps, regarding the town as an entity. These viewpoints are charged with apprehension and are suggestively negative in their messages.

Pursuing the method I employed in my contribution to the first volume of proceedings, I propose here to attempt an evaluation of some of what the Hebrew Bible has to say on the subject of towns, with an emphasis on their economic functions. This is part of an effort to fathom the biblical authors' attitudes toward urbanism and to assess the degree of their realism. I am at the beginning of my investigations and remain in great need of external evidence in order to place the biblical record, with all its diversity, into identifiable historical contexts.

Biblical terms for "town" and their implications

The most characteristic Hebrew word for "town" is *ʿîr* (plural *ʿārîm*), which evidences no identifiable etymoloy. A frequent synonym is Hebrew *qiryāh* and variant forms, like *qeret*, as in Phoenician-Punic *Qrthdšt* = "Carthage," meaning something like "Newtown." These terms may derive from a West-Semitic root *q-r-h*, "to cover with a roof, with beams," and may possibly be cognate with Hebrew and West-Semitic *qîr*, "wall."[1] More will be said about these terms further on. Understandably, the connotations of Hebrew *ʿîr* range widely, which further complicates our understanding. The same is true, of course, in many languages, ancient and modern, as we would expect of terminology describing structures, complexes, and delimited areas whose form and extent, as well as political, economic, and social character were subject to continuous change.

From *The Oxford English Dictionary* one learns that classical terms for cities or towns usually express one of two themes: either they connote, in the first instance, the community or citizenry inhabiting the city, which is the case with Latin *civitas*, from which comes English "city;" or, like Latin *urbs*, they connote the place, or constructed complex, within which the citizenry resides, the physical plant. Of course, semantic predications go in both directions (as the connotations attendant upon the Greek term *polis* indicate), but Hebrew *ʿîr* decidedly belongs with Latin *urbs* and genuinely corresponds to the adjective "urban" as we use it in English. The same would be true of Hebrew *qiryāh*. It is for this reason that both of these terms will be translated "town," rather than "city," precisely because English "town" derives from Old English *tuun/tûn*, Old Saxon and Middle Low German *tûn*, Celtic *dun*, with cognates in Danish and Dutch, all connoting a range of physical locales and structures, including "fence, castle, camp, enclosed place, country house or manor, estate," and the like.[2] I know of no biblical Hebrew term that etymologically corresponds to English "city," with its social matrix, unless we consider derivatives of the *y-š-b,* "to dwell, reside," such as the early and rare term *sebet* and the more frequent *môšāb,* "settlement," (plural *môšābôt*), "settlements," which connote "town" in the priestly literature and its offshoots, especially in Chronicles. Note the compound term *'îr môšāb,* "urban settlement."[3]

It is true, of course, that the term *bâit,* "house, household," attaches itself to toponyms and as such assumes the functional sense of "manor, town, city," and in this extended meaning would identify a town in initially material terms as the domicile of a family or clan, royal or otherwise. Thus, in Amos 7:13, *miqdāš melek 'îr mamlākāh* is best translated "royal temple and 'family seat' of the kingdom," synonymous with *'îr hammelûkāh/hammamlākāh,* "royal town, capital" in 2 Sam 12:26 and 1 Sam 27:5, respectively. In fact, it might be useful at this point to survey biblical Hebrew usage associated with *'îr* and *qiryāh* to learn what we can about the construction and design of towns, with an eye to understanding their functions. It emerges that biblical usage is generally realistic, and for the most part, may be correlated with archaeological evidence from material culture.

Some years ago, Professor Benjamin Mazar opened an archaeological conference in Jerusalem by stating that Num 13:17-20, Moses's charge to the spies dispatched to recconnnoitre Canaan, was a remarkable biblical passage because, in fact, it summarized the archaeological agenda. It reads as follows:

> Observe the land: What is its condition? And the people inhabiting it: are they strong or feeble, few or numerous? And what of the land they inhabit: is it bountiful or lacking? And what of the towns where they dwell: are they built as unwalled settlements or as fortified towns?

This excerpt supplies two significant terms of reference: the rare term *maḥanîm,* "unwalled settlements," and the frequent *mibṣārîm,* "fortified towns." The latter, in varying forms, is the most frequent specification of Hebrew *'îr,* whereas the most frequent verb associated with *'îr* is the verb *b-n-h,* "to build," often nuanced as "to fortify," by building a city wall and/or a watch-tower.[4] This recalls the plan of primeval humankind expressed in Genesis 11. In Ezek 40:2 we encounter the characterization *kemibneh 'îr,* "like the construction of a town," describing what the prophet saw in his vision atop a mountain, with reference to the temple quarter of the rebuilt Jerusalem. This, in turn, points to a prominent, virtually universal feature of terms for "town" or "city," namely, that they may be understood to designate quarters or precincts within the larger town, much like the French *ville* and *cité*, respectively. This flexibility of usage will prove to be significant in the ensuing discussion.

Similar in meaning to Hebrew *maḥanîm*, "unwalled settlements," are forms such as *perāzôn, perāzôt,* and *perāzî*, all of which connote the opposite of fortified towns, which is to say, open, unwalled settlements. Thus, 1 Sam 6:18: *mē ʿîr mibṣār weʾad koper happerāzî*, "from fortified town to open village," introducing the frequent term *koper/kepār*, "village."[5]

A full review of biblical Hebrew usage relevant to the term *ʿîr* would carry us in several directions. In general, it can be said that there is sufficient textual evidence to reconstruct the physical plan of a biblical town, with its gates and towers and access roads, Hebrew *mesillôt* (Jud 20:30-32, 45; 2 Chron 9:11), though hardly enough evidence to speak of economic functions in detail. We may, however, take note of a few special cases in biblical literature that refer to economic and administrative functions. As an example, it is recorded that Solomon constructed *ʿārê hārekeb*, "the towns for chariotry" (1 Kings 9:19, 10:26), where weaponry was stored.

Mentioned alongside such towns are *ʿārê miskenôt*, a term that is more difficult to translate, but that clearly refers to towns designated as storage depots. It is best translated "towns for storage." This function emerges from usage in 2 Chron 32:28, a source from the Achaemenid period, where we read of "storage depots *(miskenôt)* for the grain crop and wine." (cf. 2 Chron 16:4). It was this very type of installation that the Israelites were conscripted to build for Pharaoh (Exod 1:11), and in 2 Chron 17:12 we find an interesting entry: *birāniyyôt weʿārê miskenôt*, "fortresses and towns for storage." Hebrew *birāniyyôt* is cognate with Hebrew/Aramaic *bîrāh birtāʾ*, and Akkadian *birtu*, "fortress," in context "capitol," hence "capital."[6]

Etymologically, the term *ʿārê miskenôt* is yet more revealing. It apparently derives from the noun *sôkēn*, which represents a Hebrew cognate of Akkadian *šaknu*, late biblical Hebrew/Aramaic *segān*, "governor, magistrate, superintendent," a term that flourishes in the Persian period and long thereafter.[7] Allowing for the wide semantic range of this term, which moves from the political to the administrative and managerial context, one could say that towns classified as such operated as administrative centers under the control of certain officials, where goods were stored and redistributed. As will be explained in considerable detail, this very designation could apply to Shiloh of the Middle Bronze III and early Iron Age, as well as to other Canaanite, then Israelite towns. Like so many languages, ancient and modern, biblical Hebrew has a category of "large town" (*'îr gedôlāh*), applied to Nineveh, Calah, Jerusalem, and Gibeon (Gen 10:12, Jos 10:2, Jer 22:8, Jonah 1:2-3, 2:4), in contrast to a small town with few inhabitants (Koh 9:14).

On Hebrew *qiryāh*, and related *qeret*, the following observations may be offered: a motif associated with this terminology is urban tumult, expressed by the verb *h-m-h*, "to throng, be tumultuous, which suggests population density."[8] The verb *k-n-n*, "to set on foundations, to establish," is occasionally employed to describe the founding and/or fortifying of a town (Num 21:28, Hab 2:12). Fortification is also suggested by the description *qiryat 'ōz*, "fortress, bastion" (Prov 10:15, 18:1). We also find that the contrast indicated by *'îr-śādeh*, "town-country," is also expressed by *qiryāh-śādeh* in Micah 4:10. According to Lament 2:11, a *qiryāh* has *reḥôbôt*, "plazas, open avenues."

The biblical *qiryāh* is occasionally described as being lofty or as having high urban structures within it (Deut 2:36, Isa 26:5, Prov 9:3), and it has *še'ārîm*, "gates." (Prov 8:3, Job 29:7). Especially relevant is Isa 25:2-3: "For you (God) have turned a town (*'îr*) into a stone heap, a fortified town (*qiryāh beṣûrāh*) into a ruin; the citadel of foreigners from having been a town. . . . Therefore, a fierce people must honor you; the *qiryāh* of fierce nations must fear you." Finally, there is the characterization of Mount Zion as *qiryat melek rab*, "the capital of the great King," a symbolic reference to the God of Israel"(Ps 48:3).

Of etymological significance is the terminology of Neh 2:8 (cf. Neh 3:6, 2 Chron 34:110). The verse in question speaks of a letter to one in charge of orchards ordering him to supply timber "for roofing (*leqārôt*) the gatehouses of the temple fortress (*'et ša 'ārê habbîrāh 'ašer labbâit*), and for the town wall, and the house where I shall reside." This is a virtual proof — text for the terms *qiryāh, qeret* — showing their derivation from a verb meaning "to roof over [with beams]." Usage of the Aramaism *bîrāh*, "fortress, capitol," (see above) is also significant (cf. Neh 7:2, 1 Chron 29:1, 19). The overall reference is, of course, to the rebuilt Jerusalem.

Although I am not presently able to present a comprehensive treatment of Nehemiah's memoires as a source of information about Judean urbanization in the Achaemenid period, it would be interesting to pursue evidence from the book of Nehemiah a bit further. We find in chapter 3 of that book rather detailed descriptions of what we would today call "urban renewal," more precisely, the rebuilding of the outer walls of Jerusalem, which complements data elsewhere provided on the restoration of the Temple and other parts of the city. Some study has been made of the layout of the city of Jerusalem as described in Nehemiah 3, but what is impressive in the present context is the technical terminology available from this single chapter and what we may learn from it about the officialdom and craftsmen residing within Jerusalem's walls.

I have touched upon this matter elsewhere, but only tangentially. (Levine 1993). I argued that the verb Hiphil, (*heḥezîq*) "to take hold of," used so frequently in Nehemiah, chapter 3, did not connote the actual repairing or construction involved in fortifying Jerusalem, but rather what Akkadian *ṣabātu* means in similar contexts, especially the comparable D- and S-stems, *ṣubbutu* and *šuṣbūtu*, namely, to assume or give control over property for purposes of renewal or as feudal holdings. This becomes significant in the present discussion because it would seem that priests, various local and provincial officials, estate managers, and landowning families from the population centers of Judea were assigned and assumed responsibility for constructing specific sections of the city wall and the gate houses.

Nehemiah, chapter 3, enumerates the following groups of craftsmen who were quartered together, usually in a common building: (1) metal workers — *ṣôrepîm*; (2) perfumers — *raqqāḥîm*; (3) small merchants — *rôkelîm*; and (4) professional soldiers — *gibbôrîm*. Then, there were the priests (*kôhanîm*), Levites (*leviyyîm*), and temple servitors (*netînîm*); special mention is made of the residence of the High Priest, Eliashib. Repeatedly, we read of officials entitled *śar ḥaṣî pelek, śar pelek*, "magistrate of half the district; magistrate of the district."[9] Thus, we read of two persons, each identified as magistrate of half of the district of Jerusalem (Neh 3:9, 12). Similarly, there were two heads of the two half districts of Beth-Zur and Qe'ilah (= Keilah), sites considerably to the south of Jerusalem, north of Hebron. The following locales are designated *pelek*: Beth Hakkerem, just to the south of Jerusalem, and Mizpeh, considerably to the north of Jerusalem.[10] Notwithstanding an inconsistency or two, these designations are employed precisely.

What emerges is a description of Jerusalem as a provincial capital, laid out to accommodate its priesthood, its bureaucracy, and its craftsmen. Officials of outlying towns or districts, as well as prominent landowners from the province of Judea maintained residences or headquarters in the capital. These are registered as "men of X-location." Listed locations of origin include Jericho, near the Dead Sea; Gibeon, not far north of Jerusalem; Tekoa, considerably to the south of Jerusalem just north-east of Beth-Zur; and Zanoah, south-west of Jerusalem.[11] Were these the *ḥôrîm*, "aristocrats," mentioned alongside the *segānîm* (Neh 3:16, 4:8, 13, 5:7, 7:5), who may have been landowners and estate managers rather than government officials? In terms of geographical distribution, districts and places of origin listed reach all the way from Mizpeh in the north to Beth-Zur in the south of Judea.

It is unclear from the biblical text who empowered the various officials listed above, whether the Persian authorities or the Jewish leadership, officials like Nehemiah, a Persian Pehah of Judea, who was at the same time a Jew and leader of his people. There is a reference in Neh 3:7 to two men from Gibeon who were somehow associated with the Persian Pehah of 'Abar Naharah. The wording is enigmatic: "pertaining to/belonging to the 'throne' (*kisse*') of the Pehah of 'Eber Hannahar." For the most part, however, it would appear that reference is to the Jewish priesthood and to the internal Jewish administration, serving, in this case, under Nehemiah. As has been noted elsewhere, Nehemiah 5 depicts a confrontation between Nehemiah and other Jewish leaders, and there was, of course, the major conflict between the Judeans and the powerful Jews of Samaria.

There is much more to be learned from Nehemiah 3 about the physical layout of Jerusalem toward the end of the fifth century BCE under Persian rule, and about its economy as well. My purpose here was merely to show that one could initiate a discussion of the urban economy of Achaemenid Jerusalem from the biblical text. It would become apparent early on that without external evidence, proper answers cannot be found to the many questions raised by the biblical text itself.

Against the background of the above review of descriptive terminology, I will explore two models of urbanization in biblical Israel, moving back in time. I will begin in the most recent phase, relatively speaking, by examining the biblical towns of asylum, a model of urbanization that highlights the relationship between temple and town. Although we possess no direct archaeological evidence pertaining to towns of asylum, no town in which an inscription has been found designating it as such, there is reason to regard these biblically projected towns as realistic entities. We will then proceed to discuss biblical Shiloh, a short-lived but fascinating cult-center in the Ephraimite hills, which has been excavated rather extensively in recent years. We have the final report of Israel Finkelstein (1993) and his associates, which deals in considerable detail with economic and political issues. In the case of Shiloh, it is possible to correlate the biblical record with the archaeological history of the site quite persuasively. Comparison of Shiloh with Bethel, another excavated site, will prove to be informative.

Towns of asylum

The standard Hebrew designation for "town of asylum" is *'îr miqlāṭ* (plural, *'ārê miqlāṭ*). It combines the term *'îr* with the verb *q-l-ṭ,* which is virtually restricted to the context of asylum and yields a clear sense from later usage. It means "to draw in, take in, absorb"[12] and suggests that the notion of asylum meant, in fact, that zones had been designated where one would be accepted, or allowed entry under prescribed circumstances, and there protected. The relevance of investigating "towns of asylum" in a general discussion of urbanization lies in the fact that such asylum zones were located at what were or, in most cases, had been cult-centers, with their temples, or less elaborate installations, and that these towns represent the institutionalization of the almost universal notion of "sanctuary." Once inside a temple, or holding onto an altar, or once gaining access to some similarly sanctified environment, a person may not normally be apprehended, put to death, or otherwise punished. One is under the protection of the patron deity. Such towns may thus shed light on at least one of the functions of urban centers. In general, some biblical towns owe, if not their initial formation, their growth and continuity to cultic functions, to the fact that temples and other forms of cult sites had been located within them and had defined their status to a great extent at various periods. Essentially, asylum makes sense only in sacred space.

Most scholarship dealing with the biblical towns of asylum has focused on legal and social issues relating to homicide, as well as questions of dating the biblical evidence. Perhaps the most informative of these studies is by Alexander Rofé (1986) who carefully traces biblical statements in literary-historical sequence. Rofé is on the mark in assigning the Deuteronomic, Deuteronomistic, and priestly prescriptions governing the towns of asylum to schools of authors who accepted the Deuteronomic doctrine of cult centralization, and in regarding them as relatively late. As Rofé explains, and as will be shown here, the reference to the right of asylum in the Book of the Covenant (more precisely Exod 21:12-13) harks back to a time before the doctrine of cult centralization had been promulgated and when all then legitimate cult-sites could absorb fugitive homicides. The need to establish fixed towns of asylum is first indicated in core-Deuteronomy (more precisely Deut 19:1-10) and is to be explained as an expected consequence of the very doctrine of cult centralization. With only one legitimate cult-site in operation (at least officially so), alternative zones of asylum of a noncultic status became necessary to protect manslayers in what Rofé regards as a praiseworthy effort to pursue justice.

But, Rofé limits himself almost entirely to the legal and social aspects of the right of asylum, against the background of the blood feud. Here, a modest attempt will be made to discuss towns of asylum as functioning entities, venturing some speculations as to how the operation of a system of asylum zones may have affected the towns in which they were located and how they reflected the local histories of the relevant towns, themselves.

Several narratives illustrate the right of asylum, as well as the limitations of that right and infringements upon it. Solomon gave orders to seize both his fraternal rival Adonijah and David's powerful general Joab, and put them to death even though each of them, fleeing for his life, had seized the horns of the temple altar (1 Kings 1:50-51, 2:28, and following). These narratives clearly indicate where the right of asylum originates, highlighting its essentially cultic matrix: it is a form of divine protection. Nob, designated *'îr hakkôhanîm*, "town of the priests" (in 1 Sam, chapters 21 and 22), may have been a veritable town of asylum. It is mentioned in Neh 11:31 as a Benjamite town, alongside Anathoth, which was Jeremiah's home town. Of Jeremiah it is said that he was "from the priests who are in Anathoth" (Jer 1:1). In fact, although the Samuel narrative does not say so explicitly, David may have sought refuge in Nob while fleeing from Saul precisely because it was a sanctuary town. While there, he was indeed protected. Nonetheless, when it became known to Saul that Ahimelek, the chief-priest of Nob, had given aid and comfort to David, he ordered him and all of his priests slain. In Neh 6:10-11 of a much later period, we read that Nehemiah was advised by a prophet named Shemayah to seek refuge in the Jerusalem temple from those who were coming to kill him. It is questionable, however, whether this has anything to do with asylum, and it is more likely that the temple was a secure place when the doors were bolted. Nehemiah resisted this advice because it would have made him look fearful, arousing scorn against him.

The cultic matrix is evident in some biblical legal statements pertaining to towns of asylum, and to chronicles that refer to their establishment, or their designation in this role. These legal sources can be summarized quite simply and even sequenced in chronological order, at least relatively so. The earliest statements of law occur in Exod 21:12-13 in the context of homicide, as part of what is known as *The Book of the Covenant*, a collection of laws that may well go back to the ninth century BCE and most likely represents a Northern Israelite document.

For one who kills another without premeditation God will provide a "place," Hebrew *māqôm*, to which he may "flee," expressed by the Hebrew verb *n-w-s*, which turns out to be the operative verb in virtually all biblical laws of asylum, and even in the narrative of Joab's flight (1 Kings 2:28). Hebrew *māqôm* is synonymous with *'îr* in Deut 21:19, and in Ruth 4:10, *'îr* is paralleled by "the gate of his *māqôm*." The statement of Exod 21:12-13 is immediately followed by one governing premeditated murder, which prescribes the following disposition, in contrast: "From My very altar must you apprehend him to face death." There is no town, or *māqôm*, for the outright murderer.

By our reckoning, the next relevant statement of law is in Deut 19:1-13, part of core-Deuteronomy, which may be dated to the mid-eighth century BCE and which even more probably represents a Northern Israelite document. Here we read of the designation, or "setting apart" (the Hebrew verb *hibdîl*), of towns within the land granted by God where the homicide may "flee." The total area of the country is to be divided into three districts, and in each, a town is to be designated for this purpose. The law then proceeds to enumerate projected circumstances under which a homicide would qualify for asylum and concludes with an addendum to the effect that if the land is enlarged, three more towns are to be added to meet the growing needs. The actual term *'îr miqlāṭ* does not appear in this statement of law and might well be the invention of later priestly writers who have given us the rather elaborate statement of law on this subject found in Numbers 35. The term *'îr* does occur repeatedly, however.

But, we're getting ahead of the story. Chronologically, the next statement comes in the Deuteronomistic introduction to the book of Deuteronomy, most likely a composition of the mid- to late seventh century BCE originating in Judah. Deut 4:41-43 reports that Moses separated (Hebrew *hibdîl*) three towns in Transjordan to which a homicide might "flee." The list of the towns, which are named, appears schematic, with one town located in the north-Moabite Mishor (Betser), within the territory of the Israelite tribe of Reuben, the second at Ramoth in Gilead of the Gadites, and the third in Golan-Bashan of the Manasssites.

To summarize up to this point, we can say that whereas *The Book of the Covenant* suggests a cultic basis for the towns of refuge, the two traditions of Deuteronomy are formulated in an administrative mode, either with general legal emphasis, or more specifically, as a strategy for dealing with the blood feud. This is a striking tendency, and most probably reflects Deuteronomy's adherence to the doctrine of cult centralization, as has been suggested above. Whereas in earlier times there were sanctuaries operating throughout the land, as is inferred by Exodus 21, the subsequent restriction to one central temple would have impeded access to most fleeing homicides. Hence, the need for regional zones of asylum, for which no cultic status is adduced. Conceivably, the actuality that the earlier, regional cult-centers may have survived was suppressed by the authors of the Deuteronomic school so as to deny legitimacy to any other than the central temple. By indirection, the avoidance of cultic references in Deuteronomy endorses the originally cultic basis of asylum.

This brings us to the priestly law of homicide in Numbers 35, which I would date to the Achaemenid period. It is here that a different nexus of cult and asylum is introduced. No legitimate temples stood in the designated towns of asylum, but their administration is given to the Levites, for whom this constituted a reassignment, we could say. Furthermore, the death of the High Priest would occasion an amnesty, as will be noted in due course. Num 35:1-8 prescribe the establishment of Levitical towns, forty-eight in all, including the six towns of asylum specified further on in Num 35:9-34, three on either side of the Jordan. The administration of the towns of asylum is assigned to the Levites. In highly schematic fashion, and through a blending of the earlier statements, a plan for the Levitical towns is laid out, and this would apply as well to the towns of asylum. The towns are to be walled and square, with open areas outside the walls in four directions. The Hebrew term for such open areas is *migrāš*, which we render "town plot," a term occurring as well in Lev 25:32-34 and spun off in the Joshua traditions and in Chronicles. It also figures in the plans for the rebuilt Jerusalem preserved in Ezekiel, chapters 45 and 48. Actually, the provisions of Num 35:1-8 are, in this regard, based on the earlier priestly law presented in Leviticus 25. The term *migrāš* would seem to derive from a verb meaning "to drive, corral," thereby suggesting a pastoral origin, but such delimited areas were also used for domestic farming as garden plots adjacent to the towns, as the composite term *śedēh migrāš 'îr*, "the field of the town plot," indicates. More will be said on this subject in due course.

Numbers 35, in effect, combines the provisions of earlier statements to produce an elaborate law governing the towns of asylum, where one who found refuge could remain, protected from harm by blood avengers, until the death of the incumbent chief priest of Israel, at which time an amnesty would be proclaimed, and he could leave.

Important elaborations are to be found in Joshua 20, also from the Achaemenid period, by my reckoning. The procedures governing the granting of asylum are spelled out in anticipation of the records of the Levitical towns in Joshua 21, and of a statement of policy toward Transjordan that comes in Joshua 22. The fleeing homicide was to make a declaration at the town gate before the elders, who would then "gather him into the town and provide him with a residence," expressed by the Hebrew verb '-s-p, a more frequent verb synonymous in this context with q-l-ṭ. Upon the death of the High Priest, the homicide was allowed to return to his home town with impunity and there await trial.

What is most interesting is that Joshua 20, while repeating the three Transjordanian towns mentioned in Deuteronomy 4, adds the names of three Cisjordanian towns of asylum: Kedesh in Galilee, Shechem in the Ephraimite hills, and Hebron in the Judean hills. Now, there were many towns named Kedesh, Kadesh, or the like, and their names belie the presence of a cult-site within them at some point in time. As for Shechem and Qiryat-Arba', that is, Hebron, they certainly had temples located in them in certain periods. Finally, in a late list of towns of asylum preserved in 1 Chron 6:42-45, most likely from the fourth century BCE we read that the towns of asylum, thirteen in number, were granted to the descendants of Aaron. Included are Hebron and Anathoth, and also Debhir and Beth-Shemesh, whose very names testify to the presence of a temple at some early period. Clearly, the later, most likely Achaemenid traditions, in Numbers, Joshua, and the evidently Achaemenid writings of Chronicles, in contrast with the preceding Deuteronomic traditions, support, in varying degrees, the hypothesis that towns of asylum were located at cult centers and that initially they had drawn their legal sanction from that reality. Jos 20:9 attests a unique term 'ārê hammô 'ādāh, "assembly towns," which may refer to religious assemblages, not necessarily held in or around temples.

Biblicists have called attention to the fact that the designation of towns of asylum in Transjordan collides with attitudes stated elsewhere in biblical literature toward the Transjordanian Israelite settlements, and as well, with doctrines denying the sanctity of Transjordan, an area often considered to lie outside the Promised Land. It would take us far afield to attempt an analysis of the differing biblical traditions related to this issue, but some comment can be offered on the Transjordanian question with an eye to the actual character and function of the towns of asylum.

Clearly, the Deuteronomist, represented by Deuteronomy, chapter 4, discussed above, was very concerned with the status of the Transjordanian Israelite settlements in central Transjordan, primarily, in the land of Gilead. These were identified in the tribal scheme as the territories of Reuben, Gad, and a clan affiliated with Manasseh. The Deuteronomist took his cue from the JE historiography of Numbers, chapters 21-25, 32, where this theme is highlighted. What is presented as a chronicle of the Israelite advance through Transjordan is, underneath it all, a way of relating to the fact that a sizable Israelite community inhabited Transjordan at least as early as the first expansions eastward under the United Monarchy, or soon thereafter, during the Omriad period, in the early ninth century BCE. It is even possible that Transjordan had been settled by Israelites in the initial stages of that process, in the late twelvth or early eleventh centuries. That is what the JE writers of Numbers would have us believe, and this conclusion may even be suggested by the Moabite stela of Mesha, who, in the mid-ninth century BCE, speaks of Gadites inhabiting the north-Moabite Mishor "from before memory," Moabite-Hebrew *m'lm/mē 'ôlām*. Historically, it is more likely that the Israelites, like the Arameans after them, would have come down from the North instead of moving up from the South. Those Israelite communities endured and surely prospered at various periods. The expedition of Shishak c. 925 BCE left permanent damage to parts of Gilead, and eventually Tiglatpileser III depopulated much of that area in the late seventh century (734-721 BCE), as he had done to the population of northern Israel. Tiglatpileser III did not bring a permanent end to Israelite/Jewish settlement in Transjordan, however, because Jewish settlements persisted there and grew in extent during the Persian and Hellenistic periods, as we know.

In general terms, the question of relationships with and attitudes toward the Transjordanian community appears to have been of much greater concern in certain quarters than we had imagined. Now, Numbers 35, of priestly authorship, takes its cue from the JE historiography and from the Deuteronomist, and accordingly provides for Transjordan the same institutions of asylum as for the land of Israel, proper. This is understandable in the Book of Numbers, since interest in the Transjordanian Israelite community is so intense, and the preserved early traditions, such as are imbedded in Numbers 32, directed attention to that region. In contrast, core-Deuteronomy and Joshua 20-22 provide for towns of asylum only within the land, proper. In fact we find in Joshua 22 a rigorous denunciation of the Transjordanian-Israelite community.

I cannot, at the present time, account for all of these differences in policy, which must surely reflect real, historical situations. All I can say is that it is more realistic to provide for the needs of the Transjordanian community, which existed, after all, whereas doctrinaire exclusion of that community, where we find such attitudes, should be regarded as less realistic and more ideological and tendentious. Such exclusion should be attributed to specific policies that withheld recognition from this actual part of Israelite/Jewish society. I find no difficulty in discovering concern for Transjordan among biblical writers of the Achaemenid period, because Jews lived there in large numbers.

At this point, I would like to backtrack, in order to resume discussion of the plan of the towns of asylum outlined in Joshua 20, and of the Levitical towns, so-called, in Num 35:1-8 and Joshua 21. Attention is also drawn to 1 Chronicles 6, which provides the most specific information we possess on this subject. We must also consider the plan for the rebuilt Jerusalem in Ezekiel, chapters 45 and 48. It emerges that there is a complex of biblical traditions in which the extramural *migrāš* is prominent. The term *migrāš* was introduced by the priestly writers and their successors in the Achaemenid period, as I see it. My reasons for suggesting this provenience will be clarified as we proceed.

We begin with Lev 25:29-33. After setting down the law governing arable land, the text makes an exception: urban dwellings may be permanently alienated if not redeemed the first year after their sale, whereas arable land could be redeemed indefinitely. The terminology is complex, yet instructive. We read of *bêt môšāb 'îr ḥômāh*, "a dwelling in a walled town," and of another type of house referred to as *bātê haḥaṣērîm*, "houses located in unwalled areas." The form *ḥaṣērîm* is elsewhere known only in late biblical sources. In Isa 42:11 reference is to the dwelling of the semi-nomadic Kedarites. More directly relevant are references to the haserim in the environs of towns, which we find in late portions of Joshua, such as Joshua, chapter 15, perhaps dating from the time of Josiah in the late seventh century or later, and in other parts of Joshua (Jos 13:23, 28, 16:9, 19:8, 21: 21:12). We re-encounter similar references in Nehemiah (11:25, 30, 12) and in 1 Chronicles (4:33, 6:42, 9:22, 25). This permanent feature of towns in the Achaemenid period interacts with references to the *migrāš*, as we shall see presently.

According to Leviticus, chapter 25, houses located in such open areas outside the town shared the status of arable land. In a related matter, there is provision for the *migrāš*-property of the Levitical towns. They constitute the permanent *'aḥuzzāh*, "acquired estate," of the Levites and may never be alienated, which means that these open areas could never be pledged as security for debt. The point established by this law is that the Levitical town owned the open areas collectively, a fact indicated by the wording of the law. One who acquires an urban dwelling in a Levitical town buys it from the Levites and loses possession of it on the Jubilee, and one may never acquire a Levitical town plot, to start with.

Lev 25:29-33 may be elucidated by 1 Chron 6:35-45, already referred to above. After listing the descendants of Aaron, the text goes on to tell us where they resided:

> And these are their settlements (*môšābôt*), by their circular enclosures (*ṭîrôt*) within their borders. . . . They were granted Hebron in the territory of Judah, together with its town plots (*migrāšîm*) all around it. But the field [= arable land] adjacent to the town and its unwalled settlements (*ḥaṣērîm*) they granted to Caleb, son of Jephunneh.

And so, the distinction made in Leviticus 25 between the status of the *migrāšîm* and that of the *ḥaṣērîm* correlates precisely with what 1 Chron 6 states in clearly differentiating between what is owned collectively by the priests, on the one hand, and what went to the tribal leader, Caleb, on the other.

Num 35:1-8 is the next step. The forty-eight Levitical towns, to include the six towns of asylum, were all to have open areas outside their walls, in all four directions, and their precise dimensions are given in a schematic way. There is reference only to cattle and other livestock and similar property, not to gardening, however. I wonder whether this isn't explicable in terms of the projected *mis en scène* in Numbers and even in Chronicles, where the text is presumably describing the Israelites when they first entered the land and were engaged in pastoral pursuits. In reality, terms such as *migrāš, ḥaṣērîm,* and *ṭîrôt* progress in their connotations from pastoral to agricultural settings and for the most part were introduced in the exilic and postexilic periods.

It seems that the complex *ʿîr-migrāš* is almost consistently limited to Levitical towns and towns of asylum. This is not where the term originated, of course. In 1 Chron 5:16 we read of "all the *migrāšîm* of Sharon," in a context unrelated to Levitical towns. In other words, the phenomenon of the *migrāš* was more general, but for a complex of reasons, the priestly writers and their successors found in it a category that suited the economic and legal status of cult-based towns. Whoever gave us Ezekiel, chapters 45 and 48 utilized this model for the rebuilt Jerusalem, with the Temple at its center, and with *migrāšîm* all around. The biblical *migrāš* may be compared to Akkadian *tawwertum/tamirtu*, "surrounding area, surrounding field," designating arable areas in the environs of towns.[13]

Knowing what we do of the welfare function of temples, it is possible that *ʿîr*, in the composite term *ʿîr miqlāṭ*, originally referred more precisely to a quarter of a town than to the town in its entirety. Thus, in 2 Kings 10:25, *'îr bêt habba'al* is best translated: "the quarter of the Baal temple, "located within the town of Samaria. This became clear to me in my study of the Temple Scroll, a document edited by Yigael Yadin, where the term (*'îr hammiqdāš*), which I then translated "Temple City," occurred prominently, referring to the temple quarter of Jerusalem. That document is now dated to the early-to-mid second century BCE. Yadin had concluded that the prescriptions of that sectarian scroll applied to all of Jerusalem, and I challenged his view on the grounds that he had misunderstood the sense of Hebrew *'îr* in context (Levine 1979).

It is likely that fugitives claiming asylum were lodged in a special quarter of town. In effect, forced residence in the town of asylum constituted a form of detention, and detainees would undoubtedly have received rations from the temple or its successor institution. Conceivably, they would have been put to work. There is no evidence as to how long it would take to bring such fugitives to trial, if indeed that was to occur in reality. I suspect that towns of asylum served a penal function, after all. It is generally thought that incarceration was not a penal practice in biblical Israel, but I no longer think the matter is so simple. Detention and penal incarceration cannot be completely disassociated from each other. It is likely that in reality the towns of asylum served as virtual prisons, and that the experience of the homicide resembled that of the indentured servant forced to live on the estate of his creditor and constrained from returning to his own family for a period of years. The indentured "slave" worked on the farm, whereas the fugitive worked in town! In fact, it is likely that not only targeted homicides bided their time in towns of asylum, but those evading taxation and conscription, the homeless, and others.

In the Achaemenid period, the cultic realities had changed in the areas of Jewish settlement. In Judea there were apparently no rivals to the temple of Jerusalem, but in Shechem-Gerizim, in Ephraim, the so-called Samaritan temple stood, a fact that might induce us to take the naming of Shechem as an asylum town in Joshua 20 seriously. In Transjordan there may have been cult sites, as well. But, even if earlier temples no longer functioned in the cultic way, the towns in which they stood might have retained their role as towns of asylum, allowing for some shifting in institutional functions. It may be pure speculation, but quite possibly the Nethinim of whom we read in Ezra-Nehemiah, and who corresponded so singularly to the *širkūtu* of the Neo-Babylonian documents, had some function associated with the asylum quarters, as the Levites surely had. (Levine 1963)

There are those who date the laws governing towns of asylum to an early period or who consider admittedly late references to them to be merely residual memories. The argument is that once a central judicial network is in operation, such legal practices were no longer required. This is simply not true. In tribal or clannish societies, the blood feud persists, and the legal distinctions between premeditated murder and other forms of homicide are seldom as clearly perceived as we think. There is also the consideration that there was more to this biblical institution than merely its judicial aspect, as has been emphasized here. One is left wondering whether a town benefited from being a place of asylum, or whether such was a drain on the local economy. I think probably the former.

The welfare function of ancient temples (and of more recent ones) provides the context for further investigation of the biblical towns of asylum. This conclusion is merely reinforced by their association, in certain biblical traditions, with towns where priests and Levites clustered and points to the economic roles of temples. This is the direction in which I plan to take the inquiry further, searching all the while for external models applicable to the towns of asylum, preferably from the Achaemenid period.

The case of Shiloh: the interaction of economy, administration, and cult

The recent archaeological excavations at biblical Shiloh, conducted between 1981-1984 and published in a final report by Israel Finkelstein and his associates in 1993, offer an unusual opportunity to undertake a controlled comparison of the biblical and the archaeological evidence.[14]

I begin with the biblical record. We are introduced to Shiloh in Jud 21:19 and following. Without going into a review of the sequence of events that occasioned reference to this town, we learn from the biblical passage that an annual pilgrimage festival, Hebrew *ḥag*, was to take place at Shiloh. There then follows what is perhaps the most precise location given anywhere in the Bible for a particular site: Shiloh is "northward of Bethel, to the east of the road that runs northward from Bethel toward Shechem, and south of Lebonah." The implications of this description will become evident when we review the archaeological evidence, because location and natural environment provide the key to the role of Shiloh. Shiloh stood atop a hill more than 700 m above sea level, with surrounding hills rising about 800 m, at the northern end of a fertile valley. A permanent large water supply came from 'Ein Seilun, about 900 m to its northeast. Shiloh's high position vis-à-vis the surrounding area added to its security.

It was undoubtedly the same sort of annual pilgrimage festival referred to in Judges that prompted a certain Elkanah from the Ephraimite hills to make a trip to Shiloh, where his barren wife, Hannah, vowed to dedicate her to-be-born son, who was to bear the name of Samuel, to temple service. This we read in 1 Samuel 1-3, the most informative source about Shiloh as a regional cult-center. Evading all sorts of narrative concerns and limiting ourselves to information about Shiloh's functions as a cult center, we can state the following: the fact that the sanctuary at Shiloh is designated *bêt YHWH*, literally: "House of Yahweh," a term otherwise reserved for the Jerusalem temple, at least makes it likely that a permanent temple building stood at Shiloh (1 Sam 2:24). It was customary to pronounce vows when on a pilgrimage and to accompany such activity with sacrificial offerings. The occasion of a pilgrimage afforded private access to cult-sites and to the services of their priests. An elaborate cult, served by a clan priesthood, was active at Shiloh, and the Ark, a type of numinous icon carried into battle, was housed there. As a temple, Shiloh was the locus of theophany, as expressed in the story about the voices little Samuel heard during the night. The nexus of prophecy and cult, reflected in the personality of the cult prophet, Samuel, is also brought out in the narratives about Shiloh. In effect, priesthoods, even if clan based, often co-opted new members into their ranks in the very way indicated by the present story and in other ways as well.

The remaining biblical references to Shiloh are less significant for the present discussion and have only suggestive historical importance. They will be taken up when we survey the archaeological evidence, since there are indications that after a period of abandonment following its destruction by the Philistines in the eleventh century BCE, Shiloh had an a modest afterlife as a cult center.

Were we to speculate on the character of Shiloh and its economic and political functions solely on the basis of the biblical evidence and by drawing on corollary biblical evidence of other cult centers, we might not become at all aware of the initial reasons for the town's existence. Biblical concerns are pretty much restricted to the cultic and the prophetic, with special attention to the military role of the Ark and the ideology of the wars of conquest. In all fairness, however, the biblical record does not present an inaccurate picture, as far as it goes, and in fact correlates well with modern discovery. In fact, the mention of vineyards in the festival narrative of Judges 21 is exceedingly realistic, as we shall see.

Enter the archaeological evidence. The map shows that Shiloh lies between Bethel and Shechem near the South-North road from Jerusalem to Shechem, confirming with only minor modifications the biblical pinpointing of its location. Danish expeditions excavated Shiloh (Seilun) at various times, but their efforts led to less than comprehensive results. The renewed excavations under Israel Finkelstein were able to delineate several principal periods during which Shiloh was operative. The principal early period of massive construction is represented by Stratum VII, covering from approximately 1650-1550 BCE, or late MB III. Only ceramic remains were discovered earlier than this phase. There is then a lull during the Late Bronze Age, represented by stratum VI, when, however, large quantities of cult objects were deposited at the site. We then encounter the massive construction of Iron Age I (1150-1050 BCE), Stratum V. This is, of course, the period that concerns us most, because it corresponds to the period of reference in biblical literature. Shiloh enjoyed a continuous, though limited history into the Byzantine period.

The summary to follow is based on the final excavation report. A composite of pre-Israelite Shiloh emerges as we survey discoveries in the principal areas of excavation in Stratum VII, or late MB III. Moving from East to West, the MB III fortification wall has been uncovered from Area D to the northeast, through areas M, K, H, and F, and then southward in the Western sector through area C to area J. There was also a glacis, whose primary purpose was to reinforce the fortification wall. Though no remains of MB III internal construction were discovered in some of the areas surrounded by the wall, a row of cellars was found in the northern sector running from area F in the west to area M in the east. Information about what lay inside the fortification wall is limited to the northern sector because the southern sector and the summit of the mound were too damaged by later construction. There is no evidence of residential dwellings in this northern sector, though such may have stood in the southern sector. The upshot of these findings is that in late MB III, or stratum VII, a wall encompassed an area of approximately 1.7 hectares, possibly giving up an advantage of standing at the extremity of the northern terrace of the mound, which might have facilitated better defense.

Finkelstein is of the view that a cult site stood at MB III Shiloh. Many cult objects — cult stands, votive bowls, and bull-shaped zoomorphic vessels — were discovered in the storeroom adjacent to the wall in area F, as well as metal objects. There is also the fact that in Late Bronze Age I there was cultic activity at Shiloh, even though the site was uninhabited. Large dumps of cultic debris date to that period, which clearly suggests that worshipers continued to visit the site even while it was un-inhabited, because of its earlier importance. This situation was replayed in Iron Age II. Finkelstein supposes that the MB III temple stood on or near the summit of the mound, which was located nearer the northern slope. Such was the case at contemporary Shechem and Bethel. The cultic debris of LB I was found on the northeastern slope, and earthen fills were directed to the summit. There is, however, no evidence of residential dwellings at MB III Shiloh. Finkelstein compares Shiloh with the con-temporary remains from nearby Shechem and Bethel, and also from Hebron in the Judean hills. There are many similarities in size, layout, and function that link these MB III towns in a network of sorts.

What unites these towns is their location in mountainous regions. Finkelstein contrasts their functions not only with lowland sites, which were generally larger and included residential areas, but with Samaria, for instance, in the northern highlands. Based on these observable differ-ences, Finkelstein arrives at some important conclusions about the formation and functioning of MB III Shiloh. The walls of lowland towns were essentially for fortification, since these towns were inhabited by siz-able populations. In highland towns like Shiloh, the outer wall served as revetment and was placed most advantageously for that purpose. Finkelstein uses the term "highland stronghold." If the MB lowland sites were city-states, how are we to classify the different character of towns like Shiloh, Bethel, Shechem, and more distant Hebron in sociopolitical terms?

Finkelstein attempts to estimate the manpower requisite for the con-struction of such highland strongholds and concludes that only a leader who held sway over a fairly extensive area, a regional "headman" or chief-tain, could have amassed the necessary workforce, estimated at about 3,000 men, to accomplish such construction within a reasonable period of time. Furthermore, it would appear that no more than several dozen persons were present continuously within the small, walled area of the town, most likely officials and priests. Finally, since only eight other sat-ellite villages are located within a radius of 5 km of Shiloh, manpower would have had to be assembled from a much wider radius.

Finkelstein proposes that there were two networks of highland strong-holds in the late MB III period: in the North, Shechem was first among towns, exercising some hegemony over Shiloh and Bethel, and in the central mountain range, Jerusalem, holding the same position with re-spect to Hebron. At each highland stronghold, a chief of sorts held sway, and he administered the storage facilities of his town, represented at Shiloh by the row of cellars inside of the northern wall. As this hill country became populated and horticulture flourished, the lowland areas desired the produce of the vineyards and orchards of Shiloh and its environs, and an administrative structure would have come into being to control such domestic trade or exchange. Without deciding between Alt's differentiation of the lowland city-states and the highland territorial centers, and the views of Kempinsky and Naʻaman, who attribute a higher state of political development to the highland strongholds than Alt or Finkelstein, as discussed by Finklestein in his report, it is fair to conclude that the reason for Shiloh's early existence was primarily economic, leading to the establishment of storage and redistribution centers. In a word, Shiloh was the seat of a chiefdom, with the title of city-state better reserved for Shechem, to its north.

Lawrence Stager has been studying what he refers to as "port power" in the Levantine coastal societies of the Early Bonze Age, and his insights bear on our understanding of how Shiloh and other highland centers of the Middle Bronze Age operated as redistribution centers, extending their range. Briefly stated, it can be proposed that exchange and redistribution flourished in Canaan of the Middle Bronze Age IIA (c. 2000-1550 BCE) not only between the coastal lowlands and the interior mountain regions, but with the added input of ports, where imported wares and materials were shipped far inland. In the other direction, the produce of the highlands, which included timber, wine, oil, and resin, was in great demand, and was shipped down not only to the coastal lowlands, but also on to the ports for export.[15]

Moving now to the Late Bronze Age, or Stratum VI, approximately 1550-1350 BCE, we encounter a sizable dump in area D, associated with a cult place, as the ceramic and other evidence indicates. Finkelstein summarizes the transition from MB to LB at Shiloh in considerable detail. At the end of MB, the fortified towns were destroyed and villages abandoned, bringing an end to the large population increase and to the construction projects of MB II and III. All that remained at Shiloh was a cult place, with all economic and productive administration eliminated. This deterioration may have resulted, in part, from Egyptian activity, but also from internal factors unknown to us.

Finkelstein explains that there was a pattern of isolated cult centers, like Deir ʻAlla in the Jordan Valley at the end of the LB age, which served a nomadic population. In other words, once a site, for reasons more practical than not, had become a cult center and a place of pilgrimage, it might remain in that function even after other functions earlier associated with it had ceased. Nevertheless, indications are that when the Iron Age I settlers, whom the biblical record would classify as Israelites, arrived at Shiloh, the site had been abandoned for about two centuries.

Once again it is probable that the new population was attracted to the site of Shiloh by virtue of the same factors that account for its earlier history. Stratum V is highlighted by the pillared buildings found in area C. These are most reliably dated to the second half of the 12th and early 11th centuries BCE. This means that the period of Shiloh's prominence was limited to about fifty years, as the site was destroyed by the Philistines at about the middle of the 11th century. This is supported by the ceramic evidence. Because excavations could not be conducted in the southern sector, we can only speculate that the Iron Age sanctuary stood pretty much where the MB III building had. Most likely, cultic buildings covered most of the area of Stratum V, raising the question as to the extent of other activities at Iron Age I Shiloh.

Finkelstein shares the view of earlier scholars that a stone sanctuary stood at Iron Age I Shiloh, and I strongly agree. The architectural remains elsewhere on the site are representative of early Israelite construction. If Shiloh was not the only Israelite cult center in the Ephraimite hill country of early Iron Age, it was nonetheless singular in its structural indications of public cultic activity. It was a temenos. This is further reinforced by the results of the archaeological surveys in the area, which reveal a great density of villages in the surrounding area, 26 within a radius of 5-6 km, more than in any other part of southern Samaria. What is more, it was Shiloh that promoted settlement in the surrounding area.

Much more could be said about the results of excavation and surveying, but I would rather turn my attention at this point to certain issues that interest me and concern the subject of this conference. The first observation to be made is that Israelite Shiloh had a prehistory that determined its subsequent selection by the Israelites. Initially, MB III Shiloh was selected because of its favorable location and natural and topographical environment, and represented a highland stronghold suitable for regional administration, storage, and distribution of horticultural products, as well as pastoral pursuits. The lowland communities brought agricultural products to Shiloh and received horticultural products from Shiloh, which was not, after all, a real town in the social sense; it was not a community.

We may now venture some concluding observations. There is a cyclic aspect to the archaeological history of Shiloh. As already noted, during the lull of the LB age, large amounts of votive objects were deposited at the site even though it was not in operation. Then, the Israelites came, and there was economic development and significant cultic activity, as well, for a brief period. Soon Shiloh was again destroyed. There followed a period of abandonment, but some activity was resumed at Shiloh in late Iron Age II, during the seventh and possibly eighth century. Buildings were built on the terrace to the north of the mound at the end of the Iron Age, but there is not adequate evidence to determine the extent of activity there. Shiloh was definitely in decline compared with the general increase in settlement in southern Samaria. When Jeremiah taunted his listeners (Jeremiah, chapter 7, 26:6) that what had happened to Shiloh would happen to Jerusalem and its temple, his listeners knew whereof he spoke: Shiloh would never rise again, although some cultic activity may have persisted there, as is suggested by the strange incident recounted in Jeremiah 41 about eighty men who came from Shechem, Shiloh, and Samaria to offer incense at the temple in Jerusalem.

What interests me most about the history of Shiloh is that it illustrates the virtual permanence of the sanctity that attaches to cult sites. The iconoclasm commanded by Deuteronomy 12:2-3, aside from the fact that it represents later, eighth century BCE northern Israelite ideology, actually does not require the abandonment of pre-Israelite pagan cult sites, nor probably the razing of cultic edifices. After a general dictum about destroying the *meqômôt*, "cult sites," where the nations worshipped, the text goes on to specify what this meant: "You shall smash their altars, and break down their cultic stelae, and their 'asherah-posts shall you burn in fire, and the statues of their gods shall you cut down, and you shall annihilate their name from that site." The specifications do not include the buildings, necessarily, and certainly not the ground.

The question has been debated extensively, but to me it is obvious that sacred ground remained sacred, and that early Israelites repaired to previously operating cult sites like Shiloh and Bethel, and undoubtedly Shechem and Hebron and other sites. Of course, the same economic and administrative factors that had initially determined site selection continued to apply, but prior site-sanctity also figured significantly. What is important is that previous idolatrous activity did not deter Israelites from rebuilding older sites; nothing in their religious outlook kept them away from such sites as Bethel, a notable example of the very cyclic process of which we are speaking. Sanctity of space was not religion-specific.

The *locus classicus* is Jacob's experience at Bethel recounted in Genesis 28, a *hieros logos* of that major, northern Israelite cult center, where in the mid-eighth century the prophet Amos spoke. The tale is told as if

Jacob merely happened upon the *māqôm*, "cult site," for that is what this Hebrew term means in certain contexts and probably what it connotes here, not simply "place." In other words, if read carefully, even the biblical version implies that Jacob was aware that the site had been sacred, but was probably unaware initially that Yahweh, his clan deity, was present there.

Admittedly, some ambiguity remains in the narrative, but certain implications seem clear enough. That the author perceived the site to be in ruins when the incident occurred is suggested by relating that Jacob gathered stones to serve as a makeshift shelter. When Jacob awakens, he is overcome with the awareness that Yahweh is present at the cult site, and that he was at the site of a temple, *bêt 'elôhîm*, a gate to heaven. To be precise, he exclaims as follows: "'In fact, Yahweh is present at this cult site, but I had not known.' He experienced fear, and said: 'How awesome is this cult site. This is none other than a divine temple, and this is the gate to heaven.'" In other words, Jacob knew the site was cultic, but did not realize that his own God was present there until his dream informed him of this.

Jacob proceeds to erect a cultic stela, a *maṣṣēbāh*, which he consecrates by anointing it with oil, and he names the site *bêt 'Ēl*, thereby alluding to his participation in the El cult. Again referring to Elohim instead of Yahweh, Jacob vows a tithe to the temple to be built there, if Elohim protects him and restores him to his home, proclaiming that henceforth Yahweh shall be his Elohim.

Can we synthesize this tale, charged as it is with religious perceptions, with the archaeological history of Bethel? The pre-Israelite background of Bethel differed somewhat from that of Shiloh, though both had an extensive pre-Israelite history as cult centers. According to Albright and Kelso, who published their final report in 1968, Bethel, in contrast to Shiloh, which had been uninhabited for two centuries before the Israelites arrived, was indeed occupied during the Late Bronze Age, more extensively in the earlier phase, prior to the thirteenth century, BCE.[16] This came after an extensive urban, cultic history during the Middle Bronze Age, at a site whose history reaches back to c. 3200 BCE. And yet, excavations show a major conflagration at the end of the Late Bronze Age, as well as what Albright and Kelso call "a cultural break" between LB II and Iron I evidenced in masonry, ceramics, and architecture. Although I sense that Albright and Kelso may have attributed too much historicity to the Joshua traditions, it is remarkable to what an extent the account in Jud 1:22-26, telling of the Josephite conquest of Bethel, dovetails with Genesis 28. Whereas the former is more historical in its focus, telling of the conquest of the town by an Israelite tribe, the Genesis account is more religious in its concern with the legitimacy of the cult of Bethel. It is quite possible that the author of Genesis 28 was projecting the pre-Israelite phase after the LB II destruction, when the site lay in ruins, attempting to explain the Israelite rebuilding of the site in cultic perspective by attributing the origin of the major northern Israelite temple at Bethel to one of the Patriarchs.

Quite clearly, Bethel had been one of the major, preexistent cult sites in Canaan, where altars with blood on them have been found and which lay in ruins when the Israelites arrived on the scene. It was, if our reading of the Bethel etiology is correct, a site recognized for its sanctity. It was consequently rebuilt for the same practical reasons that account for its long history as a major town, primarily its location on major roadways, and was concurrently appropriated as an Israelite cult center. I could say more about the El toponymic and the early development of Yahwism as reflected in Genesis 28, but that would carry us far afield.

Here it is relevant to suggest that this is what happened historically in the case of Shiloh, as we now know. In fact, there was a chain of early Israelite cult centers located at sites where MB towns, and in the case of Bethel, an LB town had stood. These had been destroyed and were rebuilt by the Israelites. These sites include Shechem, Bethel, Shiloh, and Hebron (Tel Rumeidah), and probably others.

The subsequent histories of the various sites differed, of course. We are told that the Ark moved to Jerusalem after a Judean named David established that town as his capital, and when the Jerusalem temple was built. Soon after, Judah and Israel again went their separate ways. As Ps 78 puts it: Yahweh became enraged at the religious aberrations of northern Israel, their bamot and idols, and abandoned the sanctuary of Shiloh in favor of Jerusalem, choosing Judah and the House of David, and manifesting his presence on Mt. Zion, which he loves. In sharp contrast, Bethel enjoyed a period of growth and prominence in Iron Age II and was destroyed only ca. 724 BCE by the Assyrians. Near the end of the Assyrian period, after remaining unoccupied, the shrine was apparently put into service again, for whom it is not clear, perhaps for the foreigners settled there. It was the necropolis located at Bethel that Josiah, king of Judah, destroyed after annexing it in 622 BCE (2 Kings 23:15- 20).

Conclusions

I would question whether any biblical towns owed their origin to temples, or to some sacred significance originally attached to them, although if we had more information we might find priestly towns with such a history. Even in such instances, we would have to ask why temples were built where they were. Unless we are speaking of far-off peak shrines or distant desert retreats, most temples and smaller cult installations were located where human activity thrived, not the reverse. It occurs to me that Shiloh, before its actual, pre-Israelite history became known, was thought by some to have been selected for other than practical reasons, because it does not lie directly on a main road, like Bethel or Shechem. Now it turns out that it first served as a mountain stronghold and redistribution center governed by a headman, or petty ruler, to whom a network of villages was subservient. For such purposes, it was well situated. The cultic significance of Shiloh derived from its practical significance, but once this sanctification took hold, it survived the practical fortunes of the site in the LB age. It is estimated that cultic functions may have actually predominated in the early Israelite period, and thereafter. The case of Shiloh cautions us against positing a unified theory of the formation of cities, and suggests that there are many interacting factors to be considered. Ultimately, only the archaeological history of a site can tell us how the city was founded. What is most telling about Shiloh is that it was not a city, in the sense of being a community.

From investigating the subject of towns of asylum we learn that the presence of a temple could secondarily determine the character of a town, and make it appropriate for specific functions that would not have accrued to it had no sacred institution been associated with it at a fairly early stage. This nexus is recast in the later alignment of the towns of asylum with the priestly and Levitical towns, which were distributed accessibly in various regions of the country. In a word, local priests, Levites and other cultic functionaries were assigned new tasks.

The city has a future in the biblical plan for a better world society. Nineveh repented, in Jonah's parable if not in reality, and was consequently spared. Isaiah informed the citizens of Jerusalem c. 701 BCE what it would take for that temple city truly to become the City of God, a phase of urban perfection to which we have not yet arrived as the second millennium of the present era draws to a close.

DISCUSSION

Dandamayev: Michael suggested that temples preceded towns. I was wondering if this would be a universal model. Now from this paper I see with satisfaction that there will be other models also. This model is convincing to me. I quite agree with you that sacred grounds remain sacred. The population can be depopulated or removed completely but the area will remain sacred to the people that come there. The newcomers might be completely different ethnically or culturally and introduce other cults, but the same spaces will remain sacred to them.

Speaking about the idea of sanctuary or a place of refuge, it was not unique to the Israelites but also existed among other nations. For instance, in the Northern Caucasus if somebody committed a murder and then managed to escape to another place, the population of the latter had to support and protect him. The last case I know of was in 1913 in Daghestan.

Stager: I was interested in the way you approach these cites in which you have a new religious movement or institution replacing or superseding what was there before, and making the claim that they could use the same basic structure that was there and simply change the appurtenances for new symbols. I think that is a much better explanation of some of these sites than the notion that these earlier Israelites always set up their cult sites outside of the city so as to avoid the old Canaanite sites or the even more preposterous notion that they razed these temple sites and put up a tent to represent the tabernacle of a prior period.

Unfortunately, with Shiloh we don't have the temple. However, there is a temple sequence in the vicinity of Shiloh that supports your hypothesis dramatically — it is the reuse of the Canaanite fortress temple of El-Berith at Shechem, and its conversion to an Israelite temple during the 12th-11th centuries BCE as reflected in Judges 9. My mentor G. Ernest Wright thought the great Fortress Temple (No. 1) ceased to be used in the Middle Bronze Age. Unfortunately the floor levels that related to the temple architecture had been severed by the earlier Austro-German expedition. Wright linked the Late Bronze and Iron Age I floor levels to two flimsy walls, which I have demonstrated belong not to the biblical Temple of El-Berith but to an Iron Age II four-room building that has nothing to do with sacred architecture. By eliminating this as the Temple of El-Berith it then is obvious that building must be linked to the old Canaanite temple, which in the 12th-11th centuries became an "Israelite" temple; same site, same building, but different cult.

Levine: This is extremely interesting because it would be evidence for the fact that there was nothing wrong with reusing the building. It is interesting that in later tradition, not relating to this specifically but as a general category, re-use enhanced the sanctity of a place. If you take a place of somebody else's religion and make it yours (and you see this all through out the Near East), I happen to think that there is something transcendental about this. It is amazing to me how people squirm to get away from it.

By the way, I tried to piece together the El issue in the second volume of the Anchor Bible Commentary on Numbers that is nearing completion. In that story El has not been synthesized with Yahweh, but I have adopted the idea of a regional pantheon. El, El-Yahweh, these are all acceptable to a certain point even to the 9th century, and some of these stories, like that of Gideon, are showing how the Ba'al cult gets thrown out for totally Marxist reasons. The Ba'al cult was a real threat, so it is no good. It wasn't that Ba'al was a bad guy. He was the same good guy that El was, only younger. There is no aspect of one being better than the other. Ba'al was thrown out because he was a threat. That's all. El was eventually synthesized, but this a presynthesis period. El is not just an epithet. It means El. In that respect I think Albright, Cross, and everybody were on the right track, although they carried it too far, that the patriarchs worshipped El. They worshipped El, Yahweh, and goodness knows who else, because this was that phase where this was a friendly region. Yahweh is so to speak now a member of the club, and El thinks he's fine, and all these neighboring gods welcome Yahweh. That is what we see happening.

Renger: You brought up the matter of asylum, and Dandamayev points out that there are ways of granting asylum for an individual person in the next village. Perhaps it is not necessary to have the institutionalized cities of asylum. You describe Siloh as a structure with walls and without a living community. Could these be centers of refuge for villages around, which Finkelstein thought were established secondarily around these things? I am reminded of what David Oates described for the third millennium in the Gezire. There were walled towns with no real settlements inside, and these were centers of refuge. Do you think that could be possible?

Levine: Yes, it definitely could be possible for Shiloh. To go back to the towns of asylum: what worked in Russia wouldn't necessarily have worked elsewhere. It probably wouldn't work in many places in the Near East today.

I can think of several stories in the Bible whose real purpose is to denounce the granting of asylum by people in the next village, town, or tribe in the intertribal confederation. There are the stories of retaliation in Judges and in Samuel. There was retribution for people who sheltered criminals, because there was some kind of covenantal pact either within the tribe or within the confederation of tribes. The internecine Benjaminite war was triggered by a situation of that sort, or the curse against the Jobesh-Gilhaad — if you don't come, we wipe you out.

One gets the impression that there was some kind of networking going on, and this would not work. You might go to another tribe, or someone not bound to you, but you couldn't go just to the next town.

People who argue for merely having a central judiciary or whatever are arguing for the nomadic romance of a sparse population and no system of judges, but that is ridiculous. So I think this is a fairly late phenomenon. You have to understand that the right of asylum is at sanctuaries and means seizing the altar. My assumption is that you pick several well-placed sites and give them some sort of support (rations or whatever) and put them symbolically under the protection of a temple or what had been a temple in that place.

NOTES

1. On usage of the verb *q-r-h*, "to cover with a roof, with beams," see Neh 2:8, 3: 6, 1 Chron 3:7, 2 Chron 34:11. Also note the noun *qôrāh*, "beam," in 2 Kings 6:2,5, Song of Songs 1:17). On Hebrew *qîr* as a town wall, see Num 35:4, Jos 2:5.

2. On English "city," see *The Oxford English Dictionary*, 2nd Edition, Oxford: Clarendon Press, 1989, Volume III, 252-254; on English "town," see *ibid*. Volume XVIII, 319-322.

3. The term *šebet*, "settlement," occurs in Num 21:15 in an old poetic excerpt, where *lešebet 'Ār* is best translated "toward the settlement of Ar." (Cf. 2 Sam 23:8, an enigmatic passage, where *bešebet Tahkemônî* probably means: "in the settlement of Tahkemoni/Hakmoni," namely, of a person by that name [Cf. 1 Chron 11:11, 27:32]. The more common term *môšāb*, in the sense of "settlement," occurs in Num 24:21, whereas the feminized plural *môšābôt*, "settlements," is frequent in Leviticus, chapter 23, and in Ezekiel, chapter 6. On the composite term *'îr môšāb*, "urban settlement," see 2 Kings 2:19, Ezek 48:15, Pss 107: 4,7, 36.

4. Given forms include singular *'îr mibṣār*, "fortified town" (2 Kings 3:19, 10:2, Jer 1:18), and plural forms of the same. Especially note 2 Kings 17:9; 18:8: *mimmigdal nôṣerîm 'ad 'îr mibṣār*, "from guard tower to fortified town." Also frequent is the plural *'ārîm beṣûrôt*, "fortified towns" (Num 13:28, 2 Sam 20:6). Especially note Deut 3:5, "All of these were fortified towns (*'ārîm beṣûrôt*), with a high wall, double gates and bar."

5. On form of the root *p-r-z*, connoting settling in unwalled areas, see Deut 3:5, Jud 5:7, 11, Ezek 38:11, Zech 2:8, Esther 9:19.

6. On the Hebraized form *bîrāh*, "fortress, capitol," hence "capital," see late sources in Esther and in Dan 1:1, Neh 1:1, 2:8, 7:2, 1 Chron 29:1,19. The determined Aramaic form *birtā'* occurs in Ezra 6:2 and frequently in the Aramaic of the Achaemenid period and thereafter. See Hoftijzer and Jongeling (1995), Part One, 155-156, s.v. *byrh*. In Akkadian, the cognate *birtu* is attested from Old Babylonian down through Neo-Babylonian, and entered Aramaic from Akkadian. See *CAD B*, 261-263, s.v. *birtu* A.

7. The title *sôkēn*, a West-Semitic realization of Akkadian *šaknu*, occurs only once in the Hebrew Bible, in a late passage in Isa 22:15:"Betake yourself to this [certain] chancellor (*sôkēn*); to Shebna who is in charge of the palace." In the alternative West-Semitic realization *segān*, known in Hebrew and in Aramaic, this title occurs in contexts suggesting official status, in some cases associated with the royal establishment. Cf. Jer 51: 23, where plural *segānîm* occurs alongside Pehah's, or Persian provincial governors. (Also cf. Ezek

23:6, 12, 23.) On Akkadian *šaknu* and its various meanings see *CAD S* I, 180-192. On Aramaic *segān,* frequently attested in the Aramaic of the Achaemenid period and thereafter, see Hoftijzer and Jongeling (1995), Part Two, 777-778. For usage in post-biblical Jewish sources, including the Mishnah, see Levy (1964), III, 475-476, s.v. *segen,* and ibid. 476, s.v. *segān, signā'.*

8. On the Hebrew verb *h-m-h,* "to throng, be in tumult," and the derivative noun *hāmôn,* "throng, tumult," in association with towns, see 1 Kings 1:41, Isa 22:2, Isa 5: 14, 32:14.

9. Cognates of Hebrew *pelek,* "district," possibly occur in Phoenician (Hoftijzer and Jongeling 1995, Part Two, 915-916, s.v. plk -1), but surely in Akkadian (*Ahw* 863, s.v. *pilku* I) and in later Jewish Aramaic. See Levy (1964), IV, 52-53, s.v. *pelāk, pilkā',* "district."

10. The reader is referred to a recent atlas, Aharoni and Avi Yonah (1993), 129, map no. 170, for these locales during the Achaemenid period, in what became the province of Yehud.

11. Refer to the atlas and map cited in Note 10, just above.

12. s.v. *qālat/qelāt, qelîtāh, qiltā',* "to absorb; absorption; one detained."

13. On Akkadian *tamirtu* see *CAD A* I, 380-381, s.v. *ālu,* 1, 4, b "surroundings (of the city)."

14. See I. Finkelstein (1993), especially: "The History and Archaeology of Shiloh from the Middle Bronze Age II to Iron Age II," 371-393.

15. By verbal communication from Lawrence Stager at this colloquium.

16. See W. F. Albright, and J. L. Kelso (1968), especially: "The History of Bethel," 45-53.

BIBLIOGRAPHY

Aharoni, Y., and M. Avi-Yonah (1993), *The Macmillan Bible Atlas*, 3rd Edition, with A. F. Rainey, Z. Safrai (Macmillan Publishing Company, New York; Carta, Jerusalem).

AHw Akkadisches Handwörterbuch, by Wolfram von Soden (Otto Harrassowitz, Weisbaden).

Albright, W.A., Kelso, J. (1968), *The Excavation of Bethel, The Annual of the American Schools of Oriental Research*, Vol. 39 (American Schools of Oriental Research, Cambridge, MA).

CAD The Assyrian Dictionary (University of Chicago).

Finkelstein, I. (1993), *Shiloh: The Archaeology of a Biblical Site*, with Sh. Bunimovitz, Z. Edelman, *et al. Monograph Series of the Institute of Archaeology* 10 (Tel Aviv University, Ramat Aviv).

Hoftijzer, J. A., and K. Jongeling (1995), *Dictionary of the North-West Semitic Inscriptions*, 2 Parts (E.J.Brill, Leiden).

Levine, B. A. (1963), "The Nêtinîm," *Journal of Biblical Literature* 82:207-212.

— (1979), "The Temple Scroll: Aspects of its Historical Provenance and Literary Character," *Bulletin, American Schools of Oriental Research* 232:4-25.

— (1993), "On the Semantics of Land Tenure in Biblical Literature: The Term *'aḥuzzāh*," in M.Cohen, *et al* (eds.), *The Tablet and the Scroll (Near Eastern Studies in Honor of William W. Hallo)* (CDL Press, Bethesda, MD):134-39.

Levy, J. (1964), *Wörterbuch über die Talmudim und Midraschim*, 4 volumes (Wissenschaftliche Buchgesellschaft, Darmstadt).

Oxford English Dictionary, 2nd Edition 1989 (Clarendon Press, Oxford), 20 volumes.

Rofé, A. (1986), "The History of the Cities of Refuge in Biblical Law," *Scripta Hierosolymitana*, Volume 31: *Studies in Bible*, ed. S. Japhet (Hebrew University-Magnes Press, Jerusalem):205- 239.

B. LEVINE

PART IV

METHODOLOGY DISCUSSION AND SUMMARY

14

Methodology Discussion

Hudson: This afternoon I hope we may address some of the problems that remain unresolved about how real estate prices emerged in the earliest cities. What were the practices that came to be woven together over the course of many centuries, ultimately to transform rules for alienating land into the creation of a veritable real estate market?

More specifically, did a point in time arrive in the ancient Near East when the sale of gardens, orchards, and townhouses (and finally, subsistence crop land) can reasonably be called market phenomena? If so, how important did such sales become relative to inheritance, foreclosure, public allocation to soldiers or veterans, and other forms of land transfer in the periods with which your papers deal?

Your papers have made it clear that assyriologists have good reason to be wary of using modern economic terminology such as "market price." If such categories are unsuitable to analyze Mesopotamian urban relations, I would like to ask whether we may agree that *some* kind of economic principles were at work. The open question is whether there was an *archaic* economic vantage point. Even if we reach a negative consensus that there were few discernible "market" relationships at work in the Bronze Age Near East, we still would be obliged to explain what forces *did* shape urbanization and control over urban real estate and the surrounding cropland. Can we therefore create less anachronistic concepts while still retaining an economic point of view?

The oral discussion has shown how misleading the portmanteau term "market" can be. When most economists use the word, all they mean really is sale at a price. A market sale in the modern sense of the term would occur at an economically *rational* price. But many Mesopotamian land alienations did not meet this condition. There were no price-clearing markets at standardized prices set by supply and demand. Sales were occasional and often were made under conditions of duress or to relatives and other non-arms-length acquirers.

You have taken care to emphasize the broad array of dynamics that led to the transfer of landed properties. By the 7th and 6th centuries BC these forces led to a concentration of real estate holdings, from the Near East to the Greek cities. To what extent was this an economic phenomenon, as distinct from one of crude military seizure? Searching back in time for antecedents, why did properties held by some important individuals get larger from c. 2000 BC onward in Mesopotamia, while many cultivators lost their lands? Just as important, why did many large landholding families appear to lose control over their lands after a few generations, as the documents seem to imply? Did palace rulers act to counter a rival economic power from emerging?

The traditional reason for transferring land always has been the death of its holder. For the fortunate children, inheritance is truly "the old fashioned way" to acquire real estate, even in today's market economies. Mesopotamian alienations of the land to outsiders appear as exceptions to the customary inheritance rule — exceptions that took thousands of years to become formalized into "market" sales. Nuzi's "adoptions" of creditors or other buyers as a means of alienating cropland reflects how strong was the need to couch such transfers in terms of the traditional institutions of inherited tenure rights.

Many land transfers to or from the palace probably were coercive, as the Bible tells us in the case of Naboth's vineyard. At the very least, they were a transfer between unequals. This should give pause to calling sales to the palace in the third millennium (*e.g.,* as attested by the Stele of Manishtushu) entirely voluntary market transactions. Conversely, there are royal gifts *to* individuals. Stone (1987 [see p. 226 for full reference]) and Charpin (1986 [see p. 223 for full reference]) cite the case of the Nippur temple at the end of the third millennium, from which time we see the temple's prebend lands run more or less as the personal property of an Amorite chieftain's family.

In discussing the most appropriate terminology for these early transfers of landed property, the neutral term *alienations* recognizes that much real estate was forfeited to creditors. The first step was for them to take the land's crop. This was not yet an alienation of the land itself, but it was almost the equivalent, for to take the usufruct was to take the land's economic value.

Labor was needed to harvest the crop, and in the first instance it was supplied by the debtor and his family members. This labor originally was of greater concern to the creditor than title to the land itself, given the scarcity of early labor for hire.

What remained to be achieved before a land market could emerge was to create the formalities of transferring title to the land as such (rather than just to its crop), to make these transfers irreversible (that is, not subject to redemption or to royal Clean Slates), and to let the new holders use the land as they wished. Rather than leaving the former holder and his family physically on the land, new owners came to exercise their rights of possession by hiring labor or farming the land with slaves to grow capital-intensive cash crops such as dates (or in the west, olives) rather than barley. The essence of "the market," when it emerged, was thus to shift rights over the land's use away from cultivators to absentee owners.

The forfeiture of land for debt arrears obviously was economic, but such forced sales were not exactly "market" transactions. Such credit relations long preceded the emergence of a land market, but helped bring such a market into being. Distress sales of land to outsiders may be viewed as abbreviating the process of running into debt and subsequently forfeiting one's land-tenure rights. Creditors appear to have preferred to see sales to third parties, reimbursing themselves out of the sales proceeds.

What is striking is the traditional resistance to "market transactions" in land. In the Old Babylonian period, real estate debts and forfeitures were limited to merely temporary duration, so that land-tenure patterns returned to normal after a time. Personal debt was only permitted to interrupt customary land-tenure patterns temporarily (although to be sure, a generation might pass between Clean Slates).

The discussion of how land sales developed thus becomes an exercise in tracing how scattered and marginal sales under extraordinary conditions became increasingly important over the course of time and how prices came to reflect a roughly standardized level.

What is striking is that outright sale of land seems to have represented a relatively infrequent mode of land transfer. Some sales obviously were made under conditions of duress, e.g., pledging one's crop or land rights in times of drought, crop failure, or military attack. It seems to have been well understood that such properties were relinquished for less than the holder would have sold them voluntarily under normal conditions. In fact, under truly normal conditions, holders would not have relinquished their land at all, for it was a basic need to provide their food.

This is not to deny that some properties do seem to have been sold voluntarily by families whose size shrank, perhaps as a result of military conflicts or disease. A number of you have cited examples suggesting that what were sold most readily were relatively small parcels that were bought by relatives or neighbors. Such sales appear to be responses to repeated subdivisions among heirs from one generation to the next, creating uneconomically small microfundia. Apart from such sales, most voluntary land transfers seem to have been contracted among relatives. This is far from the arm's-length transactions that characterize modern real estate markets.

With these long dynamics in mind, we may specify the varied institutional elements that came together in time to form "the marketplace" for land. Formal contracts, witnesses, third-party sureties, and foreclosure procedures all were put in place long before a land market emerged as such.

These structural elements contained numerous nonmarket procedures, such as customary rules to reverse land transfers. The perceived problem with land alienations was that they resulted from economic distress. Such transfers were reversed in order to restore the (presumably) preexisting balance.

When such alienations became irreversible — and "modern" — they left absentee appropriators in possession of the land. One effect was to pry the crop usufruct away from the palace, despite fact that many foreclosers were royal officials who advanced the money that cultivators needed to make payments to the palace. For this reason, royal power had little interest in seeing subsistence real estate become a freely marketable asset, for it involved a loss of liberty for cultivators who depended on their tenure for their means of self-support.

Most sales and forfeitures accordingly were deemed distortions of the normal order. Southern Mesopotamia dealt with such transfers by establishing customary rights of former holders and their relatives to repurchase lands that had been lost, and by royal *andurarum* and *misharum* edicts restoring lands to their traditional holders. These safety valves limited the workings of "market forces." For a market sale to occur, the land would have had to be irreversibly transferable.

Real estate sales occurred most readily in the case of improved urban townhouses, vegetable gardens, and orchards. Not being part of the community's stock of self-support subsistence land, such properties, in which private capital had been invested, could be sold without depriving their holders of their basic means of livelihood. If there was a market for real estate, it thus seems to have developed primarily in the cities.

So we are brought back to the irony that I suggested at the beginning of our conference and to which Prof. Levine has just returned in his discussion of cities and temples of refuge: most urban areas consisted largely of public temples, storehouses, other public buildings, and open spaces that were not owned by private families for their own benefit. Yet it was in the vicinity of these public, often sacred buildings that private houses and other real estate became freest from the customary restrictions that limited the alienability of rural subsistence land.

One question that naturally occurs to an economist is the extent to which the prices paid for urban properties reflect the cost of capital improvements — that is, of building the house or planting the trees in the orchard and waiting for them to mature — as compared to the raw land price.

It also would help to know whether there are documented cases of buyers purchasing urban gardens or orchards in order to build houses on them. This must have occurred, as in the modern world. Were such transfers so isolated that their prices were scattered, reflecting the seller's urgent needs as compared to the buyer's power at a given moment of time? Can one find a price *pattern* to such transfers by neo-Babylonian times? If so, this would imply some degree of market mentality.

In sum, there certainly was transfer of the land at a price. But in many cases properties must have been alienated at distress prices, mainly through debt foreclosure, or sold to the king at what may have been a forced price. An economic analysis of land and townhouse transfers would segregate each type of real estate alienation in its own appropriate category.

I think that the most important finding of this colloquium has been that land sales seem to have been among the latest of all to develop "market relationships." Before the land could be sold free of communal overrides (such as redemption rights by relatives and others) and free of royal Clean Slates, we find barley and other commodities being freely bought and sold, rent rates becoming fairly standardized (usually at a third of the crop by the end of the third millennium), and prebend rents being freely bought and sold in the Old Babylonian period. Interest rates were standardized for commercial silver loans, and there was a more or less customary barley-interest rate of a third of the crop (sometimes rising to 50 percent or more).

Land transfers thus were slow to become "market" transactions, precisely because the land was the most deeply embedded of all social institutions, being the ultimate source of livelihood for most families. Prof. Zaccagnini has just reminded me that when families fell into distress, the last thing they sold was their homestead. First they sold their children (daughters first, then sons), then their livestock, and then their own labor as bondsmen. Only as a last resort did they part with the fields that provided their basic means of support. (Prof. Stager has pointed out how the burials of family members beneath the floors of homes in his region worked to reinforce the inalienability of these properties.)

The issue before us is thus the extent to which we can discern an economic dimension, as compared to preeconomic, communalistic, or religious (sacred) dimensions. To what extent were various aspects of urbanization deliberately kept noneconomic, including through such sanctions as redemption rights and royal edicts to counter the economic forces threatening to polarize society. "Wisdom literature" and religion (culminating in the Bible) reinforced the ethic of reversing expropriations of the community's citizens from their customary means of self-support on the land. (As late as the time of Solon, the prohibition of foreign land ownership in Athens precluded alien bankers from foreclosing on loans and thereby expropriating Athenian citizens from their ancestral homesteads.) What appears in one sense to be an economic dynamic thus was just as much a political one.

Prof. Lamberg-Karlovsky has pointed to what appears to be a conscious decision *not* to adopt certain social practices such as writing and account-keeping. Might a decision have been made to avoid a commercialization of land tenure? After all, our own century — indeed, this very week — has seen Russia's parliament reject the idea of a land market. Did a similar rejection occur in antiquity? Certainly the second millennium witnessed an ebb and flow of royal power in Babylonia vis-à-vis that of local officials and grandees over the issue of who ultimately held authority over the land's usufruct and, in time, formal ownership of the land.

The ultimate question is how "the market" ended up becoming the dominant shaping force of modern urbanized economies. This brings us back to the fundamental issue before this colloquium: How did real estate alienations — and ultimately, markets — first come into being, and what problems were caused along the way?

The question is much like asking how a tadpole turned into a frog. How did real estate markets evolve out of the preexisting set of institutions governing land tenure — evolve in a way that ultimately became something quite different?

Can we say that the market was inevitable? Was it inevitable that cities would become shaped primarily by market forces and indeed, real estate speculation? By the same token, is it possible that a time will come when society may decide to reject "the market" as the major force shaping cities? We already have seen this occurring in Soviet Russia and other formerly communist countries. Is there a nonmarket manner of organizing real estate in the modern world? Or have markets always been inevitable?

Renger: First, you talk about Sumer. I think it may be anachronistic to lump together several thousand years of Mesopotamian history that underwent quite a substantial and systematic structural change. To come to grips with what occurred, we must pay more attention to each distinct period — prehistory prior to written records, the third millennium, the late third millennium, early second millennium, and subsequent periods. By paying attention to how Babylonia proper differed from the area of rainfed agriculture in Assyria, we may be able to discern different traits in terms of land tenure, urbanization, and so on.

The danger of your economic approach is that rather than looking for antecedents of modern urban real estate markets, you seem to be looking for their outright replica in antiquity. I think this approach is wrong. We should try to look at ancient societies in a different way than we look at modern economies. It is a question whether it is appropriate to use analytical methods and tools that were developed to describe modern market economies to analyze societies quite different from ours. Nobody is challenging an anthropologist who analyzes an indigenous New Guinea community in sociological terms that do not apply modern theories of class stratification and the like. But economists lump it all together. I think this is our basic difference. I hope we may it follow up in our subsequent discussion.

Hudson: I agree fully with what you are saying. I tried to make it clear that the purpose of convening this conference is precisely to deal with different institutional structures and to explain how they came to be transformed over time. Your papers describe the dynamics at work in the particular periods in which you specialize. Given the vastness of the overall study of ancient Mesopotamia, we have selected just one important dimension of these dynamics. What I am trying to find out is how these differences pertain to the economic character of urbanization, especially with regard to the transfer of real estate. I want to know how your periods differed from one another? How was real estate transferred and at what prices? How did the property that was transferred acquire its value? Then, we can ask what changes occurred over time and from one region to another.

I agree that when economists talk today, their categories refer to phenomena that have become decontextualized. I want to restore a historical sense of context by focusing on your particular periods and then ask how we got from one point to the next.

Renger: That is exactly the point.

Levine: It is sometimes referred to on the synchronic level as "patternism" versus "individualism." This is a basic contrast in methodology, and it influences the subject matter being dealt with.

Van De Mieroop: I think one of the important difficulties we face is the limited evidence available to us. You can ask questions based on your ideas of economic structures and on contemporary ideas of how economies work, but we have to work with a data base that doesn't necessarily provide answers to these questions. We cannot give a simple answer before we see what in fact are the data and how little you can get from our information about the questions that you are asking.

Hudson: I think this is going to come up in most cases. My point is that now that many of you have reached pretty much the limit of documentation for your particular areas, it is necessary to fill in the blanks — the areas for which data are *not* available. I agree that this task is too time-bound to be left to economists. But if you do not fill in the blanks, you will have economists imposing their theories willy-nilly. I would rather hear what you can infer or hypothesize based on the evidence with which you are familiar, sketchy as it may be.

Levine: But the limited nature of the evidence will determine our answers.

Hudson: I know that the documentary and archaeological record is limited. My question is whether we can pick up the scattered threads and come up with a plausible scenario about what is most likely to have occurred?

Van De Mieroop: I am not saying that our data is limited so much in amount as it is in scope. What the documentation meant to the ancient Mesopotamians is very different than what this documentation means to us. The role it played was different.

Hudson: Can you be specific?

Van De Mieroop: If you talk about real estate prices, do you talk about the size of the holdings, or about the value of the land underneath the houses? These are crucial dimensions for our interpretation with which their documentation was not concerned, however.

Hudson: By the way, it hasn't arisen in Russia today either. But we know that it is important. Is there any basis for making plausible inferences.

Renger: There you have a point. It concerns how different societies can have different conceptions of what is economically important. It might have been difficult to explain to the Russians or to ancient societies that a piece of urban land has more value than, say, a seat and meal in a restaurant. So with your Russian examples we get a glimpse of how different value systems can be in different societies even in our day.

Hudson: I feel this conference will have made progress if we could establish that there in fact was not any modern real estate market in antiquity, and that land did not have a meaningful value. If true, that in itself would be a negative finding well worth establishing. We then could proceed to pinpoint just when and where in history land and real estate *did* come to have prices and be bought and sold under what could be called market conditions.

Wunsch: There is something else that we also cannot trace in our records at all: dependency relationships. Social systems can be viewed as webs of power, and this doesn't depend only on economics. Although it is even more difficult to trace dependency and power relationships in our texts, it is necessary to bear in mind that an economy consists not of only exchange of goods and property at given prices, but is something much more. We would need to know these undocumented relationships among individuals in order to draw a clear picture of ancient Mesopotamia's urban or urban/rural relations.

Levine: This is the old question of the suitability of theoretical models that are not constrained by the evidence at hand. Would it be better to generate a model from the evidence alone — that is, to stop where the evidence stops and to try to generate a model from what we have, sparse as it may be? If we do that, we will have to leave out a lot.

Alternatively, would it be preferable to set up an ideal model and specify all its different slots and categories, and then say which elements have to be left blank?

In my own field, and in the humanities generally, we have been overwhelmed by theoretical models that plunge ahead without being constrained by time or space or context. It is done all the time, without consideration of time or synchronic or diachronic factors or the limits of the empirical evidence available.

Which is better? Or do we need both? Are they too different to really compare? We obviously learn something from theoretical models. Would we be better sticking to the old system of using the evidence we have?

Hudson: If I don't ask these questions I will worry that you may have had evidence that simply hasn't gotten into the record in a systematic way. After all, this is the case in our own time. There are many land-value statistics produced, but despite the empirical statistical importance of land value, they play virtually no role in modern economic theory. So this theory not only does not describe ancient Mesopotamia, it does not well describe our own epoch either. My concerns in asking you to review the available data thus is not an idle one.

I will be satisfied if you are able to demonstrate that the data (or lack thereof) indicate that there wasn't really a market, because then I can look for its development later on. I want to find out where, when and how an urban and rural real estate market developed. If I end up ruling out all of your periods, then so be it.

Zaccagnini: What do you mean by "market"?

Hudson: Landed property changing hands at a price — and, I should add, a price that has a more or less consistent pattern. I want to see when these transfers became irreversible and how social overrides such as redemption rights, Clean Slates, and other constraints came to be dropped (if they indeed were ever in place to begin with).

Zaccagnini: This is not enough to define a market. Real estate transactions in which landed property is transferred against a "price" do not per se imply the existence of a real estate market in the modern sense. This is a technical question, but it is an essential one in my opinion, because in ancient Mesopotamia and adjacent regions land was owned, mortgaged, inherited, leased, alienated (and purchased) by private people, family and village communities, city and temple institutions, etc., in accordance with different juridical, institutional and procedural patterns. Of course land had a value — or if you want, a "price" — which however was not exclusively, or even primarily, determined by sheer economic factors and even less by market dynamics.

It is my belief that, in the millennial course of ancient Near Eastern history, a series of social, moral, and possibly also religious factors very often had a fundamental impact on the "neutral" and impersonal economic dimension — especially if this derives from our modern schemes — of the regime of land property and land transfer mechanisms. The immense wealth of data retrieved from ancient Near Eastern archives need to be placed in their specific historical frameworks before any sound attempt towards their economic evaluation can be undertaken. The same would hold true if we were to deal with modern Rome, its surrounding Campagna Romana, or whatever else. Therefore I totally agree with what Prof. Renger said, as an introduction to the present discussion.

Tideman: I want to give my version of what Michael is trying to express. One can imagine the allocation of land being determined by fights, by everyone getting together and deciding who should have what, by the king saying "You get this, and you get that." But at some point in time you get to a situation where the person who is acknowledged to be within the community (the person who has exclusive use of the land or who decides who lives there or whatever) is able to generate a change in which someone else instead is the person who has exclusive use of the land or who has a claim on its income.

When is the first time we see what a modern lawyer would call consideration for a re-identification of someone else as the person who has exclusive use of the land? At what point in time in each of your societies does this phenomenon emerge? I think that is what Michael is asking all of you to focus your attention on. What we want to understand is where the individual possessor is able to transfer possession to someone else for some kind of consideration.

Hudson: One of the most frequent forms of land transfer I find in Mesopotamia by Old Babylonian times occurs through forfeiture for debt. This certainly isn't a market transaction as such. But it was an *economic* transaction, and it helped pave the way for the emergence of market structures. I want to trace the long evolutionary developments that ended up creating such a structure.

Records refer to land being transferred "at the full price." They say that if the land *was* transferred at the full price, then it does not revert to the *status quo ante* after Clean Slates. Perhaps I should have phrased my question about markets in terms of the ways in which land tenure and the crop usufruct was used. And what was meant by "full price"?

Prof. Zaccagnini mentions the Campagna Romana. That is a perfect example. Arnold Toynbee focuses on this transaction in his book on *Hannibal's Legacy.* At the end of the Punic Wars the wealthiest Roman families had contributed money and jewelry to the war effort in what appeared to be a show of patriotism. Then, after Rome had won the war, these families said, "Now we want to be repaid. We want all this money back."

What did Rome do? The treasury was bare, having been drained to pay for the war. The government (controlled by the wealthy senators, to be sure) said that it had one asset that it could use in payment: the Campagna. It gave this land to the richest families, and that became the single most fatal factor leading to economic polarization in the second century BC.

So here we have a transfer. But like those occurring in Russia today, it occurred at a giveaway price. I want to find out how land was transferred increasingly with reference to some uniformity of price? To what extent was land transferred by royal decree? Was there an increasing degree of *economic* criteria for interpersonal transfers? At what point did cultivators recognize that they were going to lose their land for debt arrears, and decide to sell it at something like "the full price" so as perhaps to keep something over the debt balance before the latter grew to exceed the land's value? What I want to find is a morphology of how economic factors rose or fell relative to phenomena such as debt foreclosure, royal appropriation, and other supramarket (or submarket) factors. What is the role of "economic" factors relative to noneconomic or nonmarket factors?

Steinkeller: I want to return to what you said about exclusive personal possession of the land. We know that this really doesn't begin before late antiquity. Earlier we had always a hierarchy of prices, to be sure. That is a very recent and modern concept and is not what I deal with in my paper.

Levine: When we first started this project, Michael and I decided that rather than having economists talk about what they didn't know from some theoretical point of view, we would bring together people who were not necessarily economists but were interested in exploring the economic aspects of material they knew very well. I think that the major interest of the people here who are specialists in the ancient world is to understand it as broadly and deeply as possible. But certainly one cannot neglect the economic aspects; that is our agenda here. What we would like to create is some meeting of the minds.

My caveat is that I was brought up very traditionally. Either you know what you are talking about or you don't. Specific knowledge of the cultures that are being discussed, their literature, their institutions, their archeology, and so forth is a prerequisite for any attempt to speak authoritatively. In terms of learning, interpretation, and analysis, how do we get to the point where we can talk to each other with a common vocabulary?

There has to be a certain amount of learning on our part about what economists do, the theories and models they work with, and what they mean when they talk about these things. There also has to be a great effort made on your part, Michael, to familiarize yourself and absorb valid reports and analyses of the material we are discussing. Until we get to that point there is bound to be some sort of tension, because it often appears to us that you are talking in broad generalities over wide expanses of time and space, and gliding over significant differences that actually are the meat of what we do.

We are very focused in what we want to know. We spend our whole lives studying archives, and here you come along and tell us so and so. Suppose I say, well, now let's talk about the age of Pericles. I wouldn't talk about Solon until I had studied Greek and really understood where he was coming from. When he had an enactment giving women the right to inherit, as in Numbers, I had to look at that because someone said that Solon did it. I realized there was a whole other world, and I looked for some authority who was going to tell me, because I couldn't spend the rest of my life studying Greek. So I have to rely on authorities.

We had the impression that you were relying on us to give you a vantage view point on this world that we are devoting our lives to. We have to look to you for your insights as to what makes the world go round and what you see as continuous and universal. That is where we are right now. We are trying to initiate a dialog as to how to relate to the past. What is the value of the past?

You don't have to sell me on the past. I couldn't live without it. I love it. My only answer to why I do what I do is because I love it. I don't need any practical justifications. The world can be very happy and solve its economic problems not knowing anything about what we are talking about. Now you want to attach a certain relevance to what we are doing, which makes me happy because you won't call me an antiquarian. Some of the questions asked are of the kind that if you studied one year with any of us, the question wouldn't be asked or wouldn't be formulated that way. Here I am and I'm being asked a question. I'd say well, sign up for the doctoral program and maybe in five years you will understand how to answer that question. And you could say the same thing to us. You could berate us for talking about economics and say that we don't know the first thing about what makes the world go round? So let's learn about each other.

Tideman: For me, what characterizes economics is the presumption that people are basically out for themselves. This is something that I don't believe is exactly true, but it is a simplifying assumption that permits us to understand a lot. The difference between an economic world and a noneconomic world is that the latter is something like an ideal family where everybody does what they are supposed to do and nobody ever worries about whether they get anything back for what they do. An economic world is a world where people do something only because it is in their own interest. If they do something for somebody else, it is because it is part of an exchange. They get something back.

Reciprocity is something in between. You do somebody a favor in the expectation that you will get something back someday, in some fashion, but just how and how much is not specified. Like Michael, though knowing even less of your period, I too impose my general framework on what I hear. I see a growing trend as we progress through time. The world is more and more economic. There are more and more elements of exchange, of people giving up something for something specified. I recognize that there also are many other elements involved. It would be interesting to know the details for each place and time.

One of the characteristics of some areas of exchange is what economists call the thinness of markets. This means that there are relatively few transactions, and as a consequence, prices can fluctuate widely in a relatively short interval of time. An example of a thin market might be the market for classic Ford Thunderbirds from 1954-1964. The small number of people who are interested, and the fact that they are so scattered, makes it possible for prices to vary wildly from one transaction to the next. One of the thoughts that I have as I look at these ancient land transactions is that while there are a lot of things that might explain the wide variation in land prices, one of the factors may be simply the thinness of markets.

Harrison: The big economic question concerns what is happening to the distribution of land and its yield. Who gets it and where does it go? If you follow the flow of rent, after you have paid off the cultivator (and you can't avoid that), after you have paid the people who administrator the state (today, by paying taxes), rent is the remaining revenue available for investment in the culture, broadly defined. What happens to that usufruct?

That was the question posed at the beginning of this colloquium. If we can't answer it, it is not because you don't want to, but quite honestly because you don't know the answers from the available documentation.

Who paid for the maintenance of the canal? Did the landowners whose sites were closest to the canal release or hand over the full surplus to invest in the infrastructure (in this case the canal)? Or, unlike the case with the temples or the family structures way back when the surplus was shared so that everybody was taken care of, by Neo-Babylonian times a stage was reached when part of that surplus is being siphoned off. Is it going into the pockets of the landowner or the state?

Cultural monuments originally were financed out of that rent surplus. But at some point, individuals began to keep that surplus. I am not saying that there has got to be one day in BC when that happens. But the story of civilization to me is the disposition of that surplus income. So in that case it is not so much the land-tenure system that is important, or even as Michael put it, the question of land prices. What we ultimately are talking about, and what really matters when you get to the core of what is going on in the dynamics of history, is who is getting that value?

Economically, the value is always there, in premarket times as well. The value of the land always existed. It may have been formally shared by egalitarian communities and there may have been a price, even though there was no market.

At some point in time, that surplus started to go into someone's private pockets. That is what we need to identify because now we have a dislocation of the most severe kind. I would beg that when you reanalyze history you find that it is this dislocation that results in a ripple effect on many other phenomena. So what we want to know is in these early cases we have the first kinds of land reallocation, why was land being reallocated in the temple economy, in the pre-market economy as some of you call it. Was it because the temple was being efficient that they had to shift land around? Or were individuals jockeying around for power by obtaining more of the land, because in doing so they could keep a larger surplus? Were there external influences, as Michael argues, external princes coming along and squeezing the peasants who have to pay the tax, fall into debt, and end up losing their land?

Whatever the explanations (and there may be many), we need to know in order to understand the economy of the temple, and come back to the question of what was happening to that surplus. If individuals were losing the land because of external influences, why was the temple not able to protect those individual members of the community in some way?

The next point I would like to make concerns the varied motives for buying land. Were owners looking to make a profit? I was told that if you bought land, you could keep a third or even half of the crop yield. I also am told about the pursuit of status. Of course, rental income enabled one to increase his status. In any event, the status and power motives flourish even in today's market economies.

There certainly are severe imperfections in what we call the land market today. Rental leases were fixed in your period, and we have rent controls today. I also hear about distortions such as high prices for kin. We heard the story this morning about the Egibi family selling off smaller plots farther away and buying small plots closer to where they were located. They would have been willing to pay a location premium.

The dissimilarity between your period and the modern world is that in your societies, everybody who is a member of the community had the right of access to land. It was a definition of citizenship. But this no longer is the case today. You can only obtain land if you have the money to buy it.

One fundamental change, I suspect, is the attitude to land. Land was sacred once upon a time and was treated with a reverence and shared. We derived our right because of our membership in a community where the land was special. It then lost that sacred character, and it became a commercial asset. When did that happen? I believe that if you can identify those points in time, then you have something very interesting to say about the commercial activities going on at that time.

The distribution of income, and specifically of the surplus income, shows us the character of society at large. Territorial domination had a vertical redistribution in which people at the bottom are being impoverished. Was it that the king had an agenda to acquire that surplus? They didn't have to conquer the territory to do so. I think it is a mistake to think strictly in terms of land tenure being the crucial thing. What is misleading the people of Russia today is their belief that they must have private possession and ownership of land. That is not what's really important. The question is who gets that surplus income. By focusing on this phenomenon of surplus income, you can start to analyze society on a deeper basis. So I think that using the concept of "market" may be misleading. The fact is that many terms are misleading even to modern economists. The word "profit" distorts reality by being conflated with rent and interest to mean simply the surplus squeezed out. Economists thus also have to rethink or refine many of their concepts. Neoclassical economics has so transformed the terminology that if you want to analyze, say, land relations in today's economies, you are crippled by not having access to the concept of rent as a distinct category of income.

You therefore can enrich our own understanding of what is going on today by clarifying what was going on in your particular periods. But it would help if you were asking questions such as how much taxation was taken, where it came from and where it went, for this is at the core of a long historic dynamic.

Lamberg-Karlovsky: I can't help feeling that what you are saying is, in a way, what we are doing, but we are not thinking of it in your terms. The contrasts and comparisons that you have drawn between the Bronze Age and modern worlds show a superficial similarity. Both epochs have gods. Both have temples. They both have priests, and they both have cosmologies. But that doesn't mean that the religions are the same.

What strikes me here is that you want to say that homologous structures are analogous, and they are not. The worlds we are talking about are different societies with different cultural manifestations. The categories of analysis may be the same, but that doesn't mean that our world is the same as that of the Old Babylonian period. They are profoundly different. What you want to do is to find that somehow these categories and only these categories that modern economists deal with today are valid for understanding the past and operated in an identical manner.

I think that the bank, its presence or absence as a social institution, is indeed profoundly significant. Its absence in the Mesopotamian world structures that economy in a different way from our modern world with its credit relationships. Credit at a distance matters, as we all know with our plastic cards. How functionally did credit at a distance operate in that world where transportation communication was vastly different? I think that in terms of setting these categories, you are preaching to the converted. They are in fact our categories. They are the things that individuals here have talked about. But you want to make that ancient world a capitalist world in which rent is terribly significant. Michael, in addressing the nature of the ancient economy, was more right than wrong when he said it is mixed. What you want to do is to force individuals here to your conclusions about how that ancient world operated.

Harrison: What I want to know is where were the surplus resources that enriched those societies. Where did they come from? If they originally were social in character, when did they start to become privatized? Of course, you are right that there are two different worlds, but the method that we have inherited came from somewhere in the past. That is what we are asking: where did it come from? That is a legitimate question which people like you are going to have to answer at some point, because it originated in your period.

Lamberg-Karlovsky: Let's say that some of them are primordial: land ownership. In the United States, the American Indians have been regarded as not owning land. The white settlers who came to this country dispossessed them of land, rationalizing this by the notion that the native populations did not have concepts of private land ownership. But, we know now from early ethnographic reports that tribal groups such as the Blackfoot and Dakota did indeed own territories. The possession of one group's specific territory was distinguished from territories owned by other groups.

What happened was a reduction of territoriality by a fissioning of groups. First, a tribe "owns" a large territory. The tribe fissions into lineages, which claim parts of that territory. The lineage fissions into clans, etc.

We know that hunters and gathers owned the rights to territories. They possessed private property in the context of their material goods. We decontextualize the past in order to create a model of an ancient communal organization, an egalitarian society that simply did not exist.

Harrison: You are quite right. But there was a qualitative difference between the land-tenure system that you are referring to, which you can trace through to the Early Dynastic period in Mesopotamia, and what we have today. The private ownership of land goes back to then, as you suggest, and then continues back even further. But I believe that the earliest systems must have had some form of sharing or allocating access to the territorial homeland that produced the surplus.

Lamberg-Karlovsky: There is a sharing of territory in the modern nation state. The modern nation state claims the legal right to territoriality in much the same way in which a tribal group claimed the legal right to the territoriality of their day.

Harrison: The surplus of the territories then was distributed in a different way than it is now. Now it is the product of the private land owner.

Van De Mieroop: Somehow you see the ancient Near East as at the root of our western culture and civilization. Why should that be the case? Why in fact should we believe in the existence of a contemporary ideology at some distant point in time, for instance, the Marxist ideology of communal ownership at some distant time? I admit that this has been encouraged by many scholars in our field, hypothetically leading to a more primitive capitalist economy and then leading to a fully developed economy in the western mold. I think it is not correct to think this way. If you want to look at the system that exists in contemporary England, go look at the earliest economic systems that existed there and explain the economic system in 1066 on the basis of what it became. Do not go back to Sumer. When we scholars of Sumer and Babylon look at our economic systems, we also should not postulate some primitive democracy or whatever. We should look at them in terms of their own merits, yet analyze them with concepts and ideas that we can get from later economic history. We have to be very careful in comparative studies not to let the comparisons dominate our analysis.

We do understand the idea of a surplus. We know it comes from somewhere and that it is used for something, but if we are going to analyze it, let us analyze it in its own terms.

Hudson: Could your point be inverted? Can one ask when a given period's economic characteristics disappear? To what extent did they survive, and how did these institutions permutate and survive into our modern world? We know that they became decontextualized and, in the process, transformed. You are absolutely right in saying that your period was structurally different. But can we trace, like a tadpole turning into a frog, some process of transformation even if this involves quantum leaps rather than being continuous?

Van De Mieroop: I don't think that is a valid question. Why should there be a relationship with antiquity?

Lamberg-Karlovsky: But it is a valid aspect in the context of evolutionary process. Things do change. It is a reasonable question to ask what causes that change.

Hudson: What I am asking really is whether we can write an economic history. I assume that nobody here holds the extreme position that it is impossible to write an economic history because every economy is run on different principles and institutions.

Levine: You can't write a linear economic history leading from all parts of the world to one place and one area.

Hudson: But you can invert that idea and trace today's institutions back in time to see how certain thematic tendencies emerged out of practices that once were very different. That is what I tried to do in showing how the urban buildings, temples and palaces, homes, and land in these sites began as public gathering places many thousands of years ago and ended up in today's world being privatized. I want to emphasize how even today America has gone one way, England went another way (it doesn't even use the terms "real estate" or "realtors" because of the character of English ground rent, which is counted as "personalty" rather than "realty"), and Russia and other countries went another way and may now go yet a new way.

Zaccagnini: Just for the sake of discussion, are we entitled to make a distinction between modern and ancient (including "archaic," "primitive," or whatever) economies? If so, where are we to place, and how are we to interpret the ancient Near Eastern evidence?

Could we also be reminded that there is another well-known, yet to all appearances almost entirely forgotten concept — the mode of production — that has never been alluded to in our conference. When we speak about the time when the ancients ceased to be ancient and started to become quasi- or semi-modern, discovering the advantage of rent or of other related economic practices, we should always be aware that what we are dealing with is only a particular aspect of a wider scenery, which I insist in defining as a mode of production. By resorting to this concept, and bearing in mind the specific and distinctive features of the various historical scenarios with which we are confronted, we can perhaps attain a reasonable degree of comprehension of the economic set-ups, which include land ownership, the various forms of land tenure, and one relevant segment of the exchange economy, namely, the transfer of real estate property. On the other hand, all this is part of more complex structural and dynamic networks that include institutional, juridical, and social factors. Thus, whenever we discuss "land ownership," "land tenure," "land sale or rent," we should always take into consideration the overall, or predominant, pattern of the ownership of the means of production — land in the first place — and the distinctive features of the organization and exploitation of the labor force. This can significantly diverge from time to time and from region to region.

Hudson: If I understand what you are saying, each of you is dealing with your period as a self-contained system, while we economists are looking for common denominators and almost universal building blocks that strip away the time-bound institutional context.

Zaccagnini: To a great extent, that's how it is. My impression derives from recent participation to conferences and reading collected essays whose aim was, in any case, an attempt towards a confrontation between ancient Near Eastern historians and modern economists. These are dialogues of the deaf. As a rule, each of us orientalists tends to concentrate on the philological elaboration (and a preliminary historical appreciation) of given data sets, but very seldom makes use of appropriate (if any at all) theoretical paradigms, which could allow us to better focus our inquiries.

On the other hand, a recurrent feature of the analytical approach exhibited by nonorientalists is an unconstrained tendency to ignore or deconstruct the historical identity of the various ancient Near Eastern sets of evidence and use some bits of them in support of fairly rigid paradigms. While acknowledging the full legitimacy — and the need — of resorting to adequate analytical tools in the study of ancient economies, I cannot accept the predominant tendency to telescope and squash some 2,500 years of ancient Near Eastern documentation, also in respect to (additional) comparative analysis with the Greek and Roman world, to say nothing of the Middle Ages.

Renger: Regarding your remark about dialogues of the deaf, I have tried to train myself by reading a certain number of books by economists. But your question about a continuation of what we have in Mesopotamian antiquity has a rather simple answer. That civilization was ended by a conquest. There was a forceful end put to it. That certainly should explain why these things did not find their continuation in the classical Greek and Roman world.

As to the question about the surplus, of course we think about it. I try to take the third millennium as an example, but this also is by and large true for later periods of Mesopotamian history. As long as you have self-sustaining institutional households that produce what they consume and consume what they produce, whatever is not eaten immediately is turned to a prestigious, ostentatious use. This is why they had the temples and made Nebuchadnezzar's splendid palace. This is ostentatious consumption. It is there to be admired, without any feeling that it should be put to an economic use.

I also want to make a remark that occurred when Marc was speaking. Economy and market are not the same. The economy is a way of allocating scarce resources and trying to survive. There are several ways to do this. Reciprocity, redistribution, and market exchange are different ways of acquiring what one needs to eat, to clothe oneself and to house oneself. I think that the economy is much wider than the market, but we tend today to conceive economies as being market economies. This is a relatively modern concept. My point is that economic analysis is very much a matter of definition. We should be clear about meanings.

Mr. Harrison mentioned with regard to the neoclassical economists that they misunderstand the term "rent." To make a final remark about modes of production, the Marxian understanding of it derives from the way in which the means of production are owned. They consisted largely of land throughout most of premodern period. It is also now land and machinery and tools and other things. But of course there is another way to describe different types of economies, in terms of reciprocity, redistribution, and market exchange. Someone like Frederick Pryor dwells on systems of exchange and distribution up into the modern world, where we also have our own social security systems. This is a system of redistribution and often of egalitarian redistribution. You can look at modern social security systems in these ways. We have different ways of labeling different types of economic structures, and I think this could be a fruitful way for us to explore different avenues, and to analyze and describe economic situations with regard to their social embeddedness.

Hudson: I am glad you mentioned the forceful end of the period, because each of you in discussing your period start at the beginning and stop at the end. But in between these periods are the so-called dark ages. These are the periods in which everything is up for grabs. At these times you find a free-for-all, and each time the earlier period's social integument gets weaker. If you collect these dark ages into a curve, you find a trend. Over the space of 5,000 years, you have much less of a social integument. Today it seems to be being stripped away. Throughout history one sees breakdowns of social linkages and a stripping away of protective social structures toward an individualism — and hence to the economics that characterizes today's world. If we look at economics as such — and as Prof. Tideman has pointed out, it is self-centered — then we are taking the perspective of a world that has stripped away much of what you have talked about. A metaphor for what Carlo mentioned would be one of those Baroque painting with a huge tree in the foreground and a little city in the background. We are looking from this foreshortened perspective.

Van De Mieroop: I think we are talking about different scales. You are talking about 5,000 years, and Carlo is saying maybe you should just look at 20 years. I agree with Carlo, and I can't agree with you that we should work on a 5,000-year time span and say that over this period we can see an increasing decline.

Hudson: If you connect all of the different ages together you can find that the rises and falls indeed make broad trend-curves. Let me give you an example. Prof. Renger mentioned social security as being egalitarian.

It is not going to be any more. In the United States they are proposing to invest social security proceeds in the stock market. The investment brokers have learned from General Pinochet's Chile that they can use the workers' pension savings and social security to bid up the stock market, create a financial bubble, and get rich off the capital gains. Instead of an egalitarian social security system, this will make stock-market investors richer, until one day there are more retirees and the stock market collapses, forcing yet a new system. So I indeed can see how the entire institutional system may change every generation or so. But instead of focusing on these ongoing transformations up close, I take a step back and look at the broad movement.

Stager: I was just wondering if in your search for these things, the market and so forth, if you haven't really been studying the wrong communities. Basically we have been talking about agrarian kingdoms. There are also coastal kingdoms, such as the Phoenicians established along a narrow strip of land now in Lebanon. These coastal kingdoms relate to various hinterlands through exchange networks rather than controlling production. c. 750 BCE the Phoenicians colonized coastal areas throughout the Mediterranean and gained great profits by exercising "port power." These traders had knowledge and information which no one else had. They knew rough price differentials, for example silver from Spain, what this precious metal (then a form of premonetary currency) would bring back home in Phoenicia. This was, I suppose, an early form of "venture capitalism." Surely they are operating for profit; however, this enterprise is not related to questions of land tenure or to privatization of property.

Hudson: In Sumerian literature one finds all these dialogues between the plow and other tools as to which is best. I feel as if we are in one of these Sumerian dialogues.

Renger: When I was in Chicago twenty-five years ago, someone in the history department developed the concept of a trade empire. He was talking about Turkey's trade empire and merchants who lived solely by the differentials between goods here and there. You could quote Mari as something like that in the ancient Near East, and also you have Phoenician trading towns like Tyre and Sidon. Probably we have something similar in southeast Asia in the Malabars in the 16th or 17th century. This is completely divested from land-tenure systems.

Hudson: That was the point I tried to make in my paper on archaic urban sites as neutral zones.

I am bewildered about one thing. While you have been giving papers, I have been thinking this is just what I want. You are telling me exactly what I need to know to trace how modern economic institutions evolved out of quite different but related ancestors. I feel that I have gotten something. Are you telling me that I haven't gotten anything out of this collapse?

Levine: No, we are telling you that you should try to get something else.

(Much laughter.)

Levine: We should probably come to an end now. We have had three wonderful days. A few of us are going to be talking about our future plans. Marc wrote a review of our initial privatization volume for the Journal of the American Oriental Society before he joined us, so we can claim objectivity on this matter. We want to keep going. Before we part, we want to say we are grateful to all of those difficult, tenacious economists who provided the money to have this conference.

(Applause.)

Levine: And we are grateful to Muhammed for hosting our colloquium.

(Applause.)

15

Summary Review:
From Open Lands to Private Ownership

Michael Hudson

When Baruch Levine and I began to ask for papers to be presented at this colloquium, we believed that the long sweep of civilization's urban dynamic could best be understood by examining how land-use patterns shaped cities *before* real estate markets evolved. We decided to start at the very beginning, deep in the Ice Age. For after all, every social system builds on what already exists. New adaptations of social institutions find the path of least resistance to lie in following past roads.

In the case of urbanization, the path started with temporary gathering places. By the time populations settled down on a year-round basis and built temples and walls, houses and workshops, they already had developed a long legacy of customs governing how to come together. Some of these institutions evolved out of the social need to exchange food, crafts, and other basic materials and also to contract marriages linking clans, to provide various forms of mutual support, and to resolve disputes.

The formalities that shaped seasonal gathering spots for such activities came to be elaborated in an increasingly permanent context. By the time the early cities of southern Mesopotamia were established, the defining physical and social areas consisted of temples, gates, open plazas, streets, and quays. These sites were centers of economic activity, but were not themselves for sale as privately owned property. It would take thousands of years for urban and rural land, houses, and other properties to become "real estate" under the control of particular owners and their families. It would take longer yet for the land to become an object of commercial investment (to say nothing of so modern a phenomenon as price speculation).

In the beginning, Alexander Marshack points out, the organizing principle had to be time. Hunter-gatherers, who normally were widely dispersed, needed a common means of reckoning just when to come to designated areas. Such gatherings were as much temporal as geographic events. Marshack therefore emphasizes the role played by conceptual and occasional notational calendars in timing the festivals that were the raison d'être of the most archaic gathering places.

Ease of access to such sites was important. He points out that the major Upper Paleolithic gathering spots, such as Les Eyzies' caves, were situated on riverine locations. The elaborate art that survives from these seasonal gathering sites appears to be of a ceremonial character, attesting to the complexity of the rituals being performed tens of thousands of years before the urban civilizations of Mesopotamia and Egypt.

It was more or less natural for compact sites in which far-flung groups of people had to congregate on mutually planned occasions to be structured, by analogy, as spatial calendars. While animals migrated back and forth across the fields and forests to mate, moult, and give birth in rhythms that marked the pulse of the archaic year, the sun and moon swept back and forth between their northern and southern solstice points on the eastern and western horizons. Marshack's review paves the way for examining the calendrical cosmology and physical plan of complex societies from preurban to early urban. Indeed, many Mesopotamian cities, and especially their temples, were conceived as scale models of the year. The four quarters of such cities corresponded to the year's seasons, and the four or twelve city gates symbolized the year's seasons or months. Such calendrical analogies integrated space and time, creating a cosmology that reflected the ritualistic role played by early cities.

Marshack also shows that the first written notations were calendars. They were associated with "urbanization" in the sense of scheduling when group members would come together. Professor Lamberg-Karlovsky finds that subsequent notation — the transition from commercial tokens and bullae to written cuneiform tablets for record-keeping — was essential to the economic planning of southern Mesopotamia's city-temples and palaces. However, he warns against calling any structure from southern Mesopotamia's Ubaid Period (fifth- to fourth-millennia-BC) a "temple" simply because it contains writing, storerooms, or is large in size. Writing also was used for private trade and investment, property transfers, and contracts.

Rather than speaking of material technology evolving in and of itself on the basis of inherent patterns, most participants in this colloquium emphasize that there were various ways to apply most technologies and hence to urbanize. These ways were sufficiently flexible that each region created its own distinctive system. Lamberg-Karlovsky, for instance, points to the striking fact that although northern Mesopotamia used tokens, bullae, and seals for thousands of years, it seems to have deliberately *not* adopted the written tablets that mark the great phase change in southern Mesopotamia from the Uruk period onward.

With writing and account-keeping came weights, measures, and standardization, and this also shaped early urbanization. Politically, the ideology of Mesopotamian cities was to create an evenly measured and "straight" cosmology of economic and social relations. Sumerian and Babylonian iconography represents rulers characteristically holding the measuring stick and coiled measuring rope to lay out temple precincts. This defining royal task is illustrated on Gudea's statues F and B in Lagash at the end of the third millennium. Such orientation aimed at grounding cities and their rule symbolically in the eternal regularities of natural order, as reflected in the celestial movements of the heavens.

Size appears not to have played much role in early urban forms. Prof. Goelet points out that the Egyptian language had no word to distinguish large from small urban settlements, just as in Mesopotamia the word *uru* might mean a village or a large city. What was critical was the quality of "city-ness," a quality best found in the sanctified areas — sanctified by being ritually measured out and oriented, as reflected in the Egyptian city symbol ⊗ (widely discussed by urban cosmologists, *e.g.*, Wheatley 1971 [see p. 163 for full reference]). Significantly, orientation to the four cardinal directions was most pronounced for public buildings, especially the temples and related sacred monuments. Indeed, it was the temples above all that possessed the paradigmatic urban characteristics described by Childe a half-century ago (1950 [see p. 160 for full reference]).

At first glance a discussion of the cosmology of ancient urban sites might seem to have little to do with things as mundane as land use, and townhouse prices. But in archaic times the social and economic *kosmoi* had not yet become separated. The common objective was to create order, to make rules for people to come together in ways that were perceived to be grounded in nature and therefore mutually acceptable.

The path of least resistance was to make interpersonal relations symmetrical. It appears that when alien groups dealt with each other (at least in ways other than using brute military force), these arms-length relationships were best handled by a strictly formalized equity in treating one another. Indeed, such symmetry seems to be a natural human principle.

This is not to say that Mesopotamian societies were egalitarian. Rather, they needed to supply their members with certain basic needs. The need for food was ensured by allocating subsistence landholdings and protecting security of tenure by permitting such lands to be lost temporarily, not permanently.

In the commercial sphere, the principle of equity is exemplified by common prices, at least for transactions with the large public institutions. The fact that standardized prices are to be found most clearly in Mesopotamia's temples and palaces was inherent in their internal account-keeping and planning needs, which also called for sacred oversight of uniform weights and measures. Temples also oversaw the sanctity of contracts, including property transfers. All these were standardized and made subject to strict formalities. One result was to make cities places of lawful rule, in contrast to the often wild countryside and mountains.

Although it was natural for public institutions to play a central social role, Elizabeth Stone points out that this role was not geographically central. Unlike the case with medieval European cities, southern Mesopotamia's temples and palaces were located near the outer walls rather than in the center. This does not seem to be a by-product of urban sprawl as cities growing in one direction around these public buildings, for it characterizes newly built cities as well.

What might be the explanation for this evidently deliberate characteristic of Mesopotamian cities? Were they located near the commercial gate, reflecting their role in external exchange? Did their positioning signify control over the surrounding rural land from which city dwellers derived their means of support?

With regard to private houses within these cities, Professor Stone found prices rising and falling in keeping with urban prosperity. However, she did not find patterns of site values based on favorable location related to their proximity to the temples or palaces, or to the city gates or centers. Evidently the idea of rent-of-location was slow to develop and is even more difficult to trace in the records. For the Old Babylonian period, when property prices begin to appear in the documentary record, there may be no evidence for years at a time for prices or rents. Even where such records are found, no clear pattern of site values emerges.

We thus may ask, if the urban economy was not oriented in terms of land values, then what *was* the guiding organizational principle? How "economic" was it?

Professor Buccellati's excavations at Urkesh suggest that neighborhoods were based on kin groupings, as in the countryside. Furthermore, many "homesteaders" earned their livelihood within the cities. Hence, an urban property deemed necessary for one's livelihood on a par with urban land — presumably for full-time craftsmen, for instance — might be included in the Clean Slate proclamations. But in general, townhouses, gardens, and orchards were exempt from rules governing their redemption by their former owners. These properties generally were more freely alienable than was rural subsistence land, which was long maintained inalienable as the source of livelihood for most families.

Yet the public structures that were the defining characteristic of archaic Near Eastern cities lay outside of the market process. It took thousands of years for privately owned houses and other buildings to emerge as the defining force shaping the organization of cities. (In this transformation of public urban space into personally owned real estate, the present volume represents a logical continuation of our 1994 colloquium on privatization.) There was a long symbiosis between public and private, partly because a major role of townhouses related to the interaction between their owners and the temples and palaces as administrators, officials, and "merchants" involved in the exchange of commodities and other economic functions that interfaced with these large institutions.

Things changed as southern Mesopotamia became more ethnically and socially heterogeneous. Professor Kosyreva finds that land sales after about 2000 BC were made primarily among people with Semitic names. She infers that this reflects the distinctively private rather than communal land-tenure practices that Professor Steinkeller finds in the north.

These observations reflect the extent to which regional differences influenced the way in which urban and rural land transfers became economic. Practices least embedded in communalist traditions (and hence, most open to "market forces") are found in the geographic periphery to southern Mesopotamia. The diffusion of economic practices is seen to play a role in both directions.

Inasmuch as subsistence land provided the basic means of self-support for most families, it could not be sold or otherwise alienated. But, urban townhouses were not necessary for this role. Society could afford more leeway for the transfer of these properties. Given their more or less free alienability, the question naturally arises as to how their prices were determined.

There seems no trace of an early intention to increase real estate values, to say nothing of anything as modern as real estate developers hoping to see temples or other public structures built near their own sites so as to increase the value of their property.

A basic question to be asked is the extent to which housing and land prices or rentals were standardized. If so, what factors determined their pricing? Secondly, if we are looking for the point at which a real estate "market" may have emerged, it is necessary to ask whether urban property sales were only occasional and scattered. Did the prices at which they were transferred reflect internal family relations or the relative power between sellers and buyers at a given moment of time, often under distress conditions? Neither of these conditions would meet the modern definition of market sales, which must be open to all buyers.

We may hypothesize that as land came to be bequeathed, bought, sold, and sometimes forfeited, a general idea of value was reflected in its prices. Sales prices would have reflected commercial criteria based on the rental income that the property might yield, or its use-value to its owner-occupant, or perhaps its resale value. What does the archaeology of urbanization and the philological analysis of texts and archives have to say about how urban (and rural) land acquires value and begins its long historical price appreciation?

By describing settlement patterns and land use in each major region (while taking care to distinguish rural subsistence land from commercial gardens and townhouses), this colloquium might be called "The Prehistory of Real Estate." The periods under discussion are still a long way from seeing real estate be commercialized to anywhere near the degree found in modern times, as Professor Renger and others at this colloquium have emphasized throughout the oral discussion.

What makes this inquiry so important is that today, urban real estate represents the largest category of asset values for nearly all economies — much more valuable than all the farmland, oil wells and mines, plants and factories, machinery and equipment together for America, Europe, and Japan.

Of course, inasmuch as land's economic role predates its free alienability, it is clear that we cannot *begin* with the market, but can only end up there. On the other hand, we may ask how prices could have been assigned to real estate for sale (or forfeiture) to new owners without some calculation of its rental value or yield. But what was the logic at work? Did the same principles apply to all acquirers symmetrically — to heirs and other relatives, the royal palace and local grandees, neighbors, outside "arm's length" buyers, and foreclosing creditors?

What acted in place of a price-making real estate market was the public character of early urban land. Temple and palace property remained noncommercial (although it certainly was an economic and commercial center), creating land-use patterns long before a commercial market for urban real estate developed. But the "spillover" effect (or what economists call "externalities") that public buildings and parks have on improving the value of surrounding real estate in today's world has not been found by this colloquium's members. It seems that there was no particular advantage to being located near a temple, the city gates, or in the center of

Babylonian cities. If the key to understanding the value of real estate in modern times is "location, location, location," this principle took some time to emerge; it was not primordial. Or at least the locational principle of neighborhood real estate was not yet commercial but reflected family or clan ties or professional associations. High- and low-status families are found living virtually next door to each other, seemingly without regard for the neighborhood's income or wealth levels. All that can be said is that land and townhouse prices appear to rise and fall with the economic fortunes of their communities.

What happened socially as land became valuable in the city and countryside? At what point in history did urban property become more valuable than rural land? This dynamic appears to have gained momentum only after the end of the epoch discussed by this colloquium's papers. Dealing with the neo-Babylonian period, Professor Dandamayev finds that prices for rural lands and townhouses were higher than those of the Old Babylonian epoch, despite the fact reported by Herodotus that the land was burdened with tribute to the Persians.

Professor Stone points out that urban land in Nippur did grow more expensive as the city's prosperity increased. But, who got the gain? It would have been anachronistic for the government to have raised property taxes to reflect this increase in value. Did the entire gain then remain with the private owners?

Even in classical antiquity (after about the 7th century BC) it is difficult to find the classical relationship between land values and yields. The problem lies in determining how the land's yield was perceived at the time. Modern economists would calculate the yield net of the tax levy or other payments owed to the public authority as a civic obligation for holding land. But Professor Dandamayev reports that neo-Babylonian archives say nothing of what these taxes and fees were, or how they affected real estate values. We know only of levies that appear at the royal level, where they were viewed as obligations of subservience, probably having little relation to the calculation of net property yields and values. Nor do resale values appear to have been integrated into this world view. It took the modern epoch for real estate promotion to flower. The archaeologist and assyriologist certainly would not expect to find anything so modern as owners of "underutilized" vegetable gardens (probably the closest ancient approximation to modern urban parking lots) holding these while waiting for property values to appreciate.

Throughout all antiquity, to be sure, land was a prestige asset. Rather than being the key to generating wealth, such land — and urban property — absorbed income and wealth earned elsewhere, especially in commerce and usury.

The real estate clause "sold at the full price"

Land alienations were held not to be valid unless "the full price" was paid. A modern economist would be tempted to infer that this indicates the existence of a fairly well-understood market, but that ancient societies recognized that strapped cultivators would only sell their lands ("lose their homestead") under conditions of extreme economic distress. This view would suggest that land sales were only valid if sold "at the full price," so as to save distressed sellers from being taken advantage of. However, the members of this colloquium find this not to be the case. The words do not seem to represent what they would in today's market economies. Transferring land "at the full price" appears to mean simply that all proper formalities were obeyed and properly witnessed by all the affected relatives and neighbors of the seller. In Sumerian times a formal meal with some exchange of presents would have been held to attest to the legitimacy of the land transfer. The meaning of "price" in the phrase "full price" thus appears to mean "condition of transfer." In archaic times the conditions of land transfer were much more far-reaching than merely paying a sum of money.

Dr. Wunsch and Prof. Van De Mieroop have explained why "normal" market values would not be reflected in the surviving documentation in any event. Mesopotamian contracts were not agreements drawn up by buyers and sellers prior to the land sale to stipulate the terms on which the transfer was to be made. Rather, they were designed to legally confirm that the transfer *had* taken place and that it had been properly witnessed and duly formalized. At the time of such transfers, earlier sale documents were turned over to the acquirers, so that the former owners would have no basis for asserting claims to the property. (Ammisaduqa's Edict stipulated that when he proclaimed *misharum*, all creditors who had obtained claims to the cultivator's labor and bondage, crop and/or land were to break their tablets and return the lands they had taken.)

The symposium members have emphasized the limitations of archaic documentation. As Dr. Wunsch explains, the record is inherently unlikely to show the course of prices, because real estate contracts did not play the role in the ancient Near East that they do in today's world. When real estate was transferred, all prior documentation was destroyed. And unlike modern contracts, those of the ancient Near East did not specify the terms on which the buyer and seller agreed to transfer the land. Rather, the role of real estate records was to preclude reversals of the land transfer by prior holders asserting their claim to ownership. To protect the new owner, the documents cite witnesses and state that the proper ceremonial acts have been performed. As further protection, all prior tablets were destroyed, so that there would be no basis for asserting redemption rights. (The Edict of Ammisaduqa tells us that when Babylonian rulers proclaimed *misharum*, the tablets transferring land to the creditors were to be broken, so that the rural land could be restored to its traditional holder free and clear of any residual claims.) We thus would not expect to find archives in which the prices of given pieces of property were traced conveniently over time for us. The closest we have is the Egibi archive, which promises to become a classic case study of real estate wealth in the neo-Babylonian period.

Nowhere in antiquity do we find speculators borrowing money to buy land and make a killing, or even to make a capital gain. To borrow was rather the first step towards losing one's property. Money-lending and real estate were antithetical, not symbiotic as they have become in today's world. The modern urban phenomenon is largely a byproduct of mortgage lenders recycling the economy's savings into loans for residential housing and commercial buildings. This makes the economic dynamics of modern real-estate markets basically different from those of ancient urbanization.

As mentioned above, urban real estate in today's world represents the economy's major asset. What tends to be overlooked is that mortgages represent about 70 percent of the commercial lending (and hence, debt) in modern economies. Most of this mortgage debt is attached to urban real estate. But in antiquity scarcely any real estate was bought on credit, although a delayed final payment might be owed, as noted by Professor Van De Mieroop and Dr. Wunsch elsewhere in this volume.

In sum, rural subsistence land seems to have begun by being embedded as a customary asset to which each member of the community had access. But it gradually became alienable and increasingly expensive — and hence an increasingly precarious basic need. But this is relatively late, from about the 7th century BC onward.

Trade in land (to say nothing of speculation) certainly is not primordial. It is quite modern, as is the practice of buying real estate on credit. These practices show how thoroughly our world has inverted the archaic state of affairs. These transformations will be elaborated in our 1998 colloquium on the dynamics of debt — and debt cancellations — in the ancient Near East.

BIBLIOGRAPHIC SHORT TITLES

AÄ *Ägyptologische Abhandlungen*

ABAW *Bayrische Akademie der Wissenschaften* (Abhandlungen)

AfO *Archiv für Orientforschung*

AHw *Akkadisches Handwörterbuch*, Wolfram Von Soden (Otto Harrassowitx, Wiesbaden)

AJSL *American Journal of Semitic Languages*

AM *Ancient Mesopotamia: Socio-Economic History. A Collection of Studies by Soviet Scholars*, I. M. Diakonoff, ed.

ANET *Ancient Near Eastern Texts*, Pritchard, ed.

AoF *Altorientalische Forschungen*

ArOr *Archiv Orientalni*

AnOr *Analecta Orientalia*

ASE *Archaeological Survey of Egypt*

ASJ *Acta Sumerologica*, Japan

AV *Archäologische Veröffentlichungen* (Deutsches Archäologisches Institut, Abteilung)

BdE *Bibliothèque d'Étude, Institut Français d'Archéologie Orientale*

BES *Bulletin of the Egyptological Seminar*

BiAe *Bibliotheca Aegyptica*

BIFAO *Bulletin de l'Institut Français d'Archéologie Orientale*

BiOr *Bibliotheca Orientalis*

BSA   *Bulletin on Sumerian Agriculture*

BSAK   *Beiträge, Studien zur Altägyptischen Kultur*

CA   *Current Anthropology.*

CAD   *The Assyrian Dictionary,* A. Leo Oppenheim et al., (Oriental
           Institute, Chicago 1956)

CAJ   *Cambridge Archaeological Journal*

CdE   *Chronique d'Égypte*

CDME   *Concise Dictionary of Middle Egyptian,* R.O. Faulkner (Oxford
           1962)

Center and Periphery
           Center and Periphery in the Ancient World, Michael Rowlands,
           Mogens Larsen, and Kristian Kristiansen, eds. (Cambridge
           1987)

City Inv
           *City Invincible: A Symposium on Urbanization and Cultural De-
           velopment in the Ancient Near East, Dec. 4-7, 1958,* Carl H.
           Kraeling and Robert M. Adams, eds. (Chicago 1960)

Circulation of Goods
           *Circulation of Goods in Non-Palatial Context in the Ancient Near
           East,* Alfonso Archi, ed. (= *Incunabula Graeca,* LXXII, Rome
           1984)

DLE   *A Dictionary of Late Egyptian,* L. H. Lesko and B. S. Lesko,
           eds., (Berkeley 1982-1990) five vols.

EA   *Early Antiquity,* I. M. Diakonoff, ed. (Chicago 1991)

Gesellschaftsklassen
           *Gesellschaftsklassen im Alten Zweistromland und in den
           angrenzenden Gebieten,* D. O. Edzard, ed. (Munich) (= ABAW
           75)

GM   Göttinger Miszellen

GOF   Göttinger Orientforschung

HUCA   Hebrew Union College Annual

JAA   Journal of Anthropological Archaeology

JAOS   Journal of the American Oriental Society

JARCE   Journal of the American Research Center in Egypt

JBL   Journal of Biblical Literature

JCS   Journal of Cuneiform Studies

JEA   Journal of Egyptian Archaeology

JEH   Journal of Economic History

JEOL   Jaarbericht van het Vooraziatisch-Egyptisch Genootschap "Ex
            Oriente Lux" (Leiden)

JESHO   Journal of the Economic and Social History of the Orient

JFA   Journal of Field Arhaeology

JNES   Journal of Near Eastern Studies

KRI   Ramesside Inscriptions, Kitchen, K. A. (Oxford 1968-1988) seven
            vols.

LÄ   Lexikon der Ägyptologie

MIFAO   Mémoires publiés par les membres de l'Institut Français
            d'Archéologie Orientale du Caire (Cairo)

NABU   Notes Assyriologiques Brèves et Utilaires

OA   Oriens Antiquus

OBO   Orbis Biblicus et Orientalis

OED   *Oxford English Dictionary*

OLA   *Orientalia Lovaniensia Analecta*

Or   *Orientalia*

Privatization
        Privatization in the Ancient Near East and Classical Antiquity,
        Hudson and Levine, eds. (Cambridge, MA 1996)

RA   *Revue d'Assyriologie et d'Archaeologie Orientale*

RAI   *Rencontre Assyriologique Internationale*

RdE   *Revue d'Égyptologie*

REA   *Research in Economic Anthropology: An Annual Compilation of
        Research*, George Dalton, ed.

RHist   *Revue Historique*

RIDA   *Revue Internationale des Droits de l'Antiquite*

RlA   *Reallexikon der Assyriologie*

RSO   *Rivista degli Studi Orientali*

SAK   *Studien zur Altägyptischen Kultur*

SAOC   *Studies in Ancient Oriental Civilization*

SARI   *Sumerian and Akkadian Royal Inscriptions,* Vol. I: *Presargonic
        Inscriptions,* Jerrold S. Cooper, ed. (New Haven 1986)

SciAm   *Scientific American*

SJAW   *Social Justice in the Ancient World,* Morris Silver, ed. (City Col-
        lege of New York, March 10-12, 1993). Oral papers

UF   *Ugarit Forshungen*

UGAÄ   *Untersuchungen zur Geschichte und Altertumskunde Ägyptens*

Urk. IV   *Urkunden der 18. Dynastie,* K. Sethe and W. Helck, (Berlin and Leipzig 1914-1961)

Wb.   *Wörterbuch der ägyptischen Sprache,* A. Erman and H. Grapow, eds. (Leipzig and Berlin 1928-1953) 5 vols.

Wirtschaft und Gesellschaft
         Wirtschaft und Gesellschaft im alten Vorderasien, J. Hermatta and G. Komoroczy, eds. (Budapest 1974)

WVDOG *Wissenschaftliche Veröffentlichungen der Deutschen Orient-Gesellschaft*

WZKM   *Weiner Zeitschrift für die Kunde des Morgeniandes*

ZA   *Zeitschrift für Assyriologie*